CONSUMER BEHAVIOUR

Sara Miller McCune founded SAGE Publishing in 1965 to support the dissemination of usable knowledge and educate a global community. SAGE publishes more than 1000 journals and over 800 new books each year, spanning a wide range of subject areas. Our growing selection of library products includes archives, data, case studies and video. SAGE remains majority owned by our founder and after her lifetime will become owned by a charitable trust that secures the company's continued independence.

Los Angeles | London | New Delhi | Singapore | Washington DC | Melbourne

5th EDITION

ZUBIN SETHNA

CONSUMER BEHAVIOUR

Los Angeles | London | New Delhi
Singapore | Washington DC | Melbourne

Los Angeles | London | New Delhi
Singapore | Washington DC | Melbourne

SAGE Publications Ltd
1 Oliver's Yard
55 City Road
London EC1Y 1SP

SAGE Publications Inc.
2455 Teller Road
Thousand Oaks, California 91320

SAGE Publications India Pvt Ltd
B 1/I 1 Mohan Cooperative Industrial Area
Mathura Road
New Delhi 110 044

SAGE Publications Asia-Pacific Pte Ltd
3 Church Street
#10-04 Samsung Hub
Singapore 049483

Editor: Matthew Waters
Editorial assistant: Charlotte Hanson
Production editor: Nicola Marshall
Copyeditor: Tom Bedford
Proofreader: Jane Fricker
Indexer: Silvia Benvenuto
Marketing manager: Lucia Sweet
Cover design: Francis Kenney
Typeset by: C&M Digitals (P) Ltd, Chennai, India
Printed in the UK

© Zubin Sethna 2023

Apart from any fair dealing for the purposes of research, private study, or criticism or review, as permitted under the Copyright, Designs and Patents Act, 1988, this publication may not be reproduced, stored or transmitted in any form, or by any means, without the prior permission in writing of the publisher, or in the case of reprographic reproduction, in accordance with the terms of licences issued by the Copyright Licensing Agency. Enquiries concerning reproduction outside those terms should be sent to the publisher.

Library of Congress Control Number: 2022946944

British Library Cataloguing in Publication data

A catalogue record for this book is available from the British Library

ISBN 978-1-5297-5406-3
ISBN 978-1-5297-5405-6 (pbk)

At SAGE we take sustainability seriously. Most of our products are printed in the UK using responsibly sourced papers and boards. When we print overseas we ensure sustainable papers are used as measured by the PREPS grading system. We undertake an annual audit to monitor our sustainability.

TABLE OF CONTENTS

List of Figures   x
List of Tables   xiv
About the Author   xvi
Preface to the Fifth Edition   xviii
Using This Book   xxii
Endorsements   xxv

PART ONE   CONSUMER BEHAVIOUR IN CONTEXT   1

1. Understanding Consumer Behaviour 5
2. Decisions, Behaviours and Interactions 41
3. Consumption in B2C vs. B2B 91
4. Consumer Technology and Innovation 125

PART TWO   CONSUMERS AS INDIVIDUALS (THE PSYCHOLOGICAL ISSUES)   173

5. Drive, Motivation and Hedonism 177
6. The Self and Personality 219
7. Perception 255
8. Learning and Knowledge 299
9. Attitude Formation and Change 341

PART THREE   CONSUMERS AS SOCIAL ACTORS (THE SOCIOLOGICAL ISSUES)   377

10. Reference Groups 381
11. Age, Gender and Familial Roles 417
12. Culture and Social Mobility 461
13. Ethical Consumption 501
14. Sustainable Consumption 541

Index   575

LECTURERS

There is a wealth of online content and resources, including PowerPoint slides, and a teaching guide to support your teaching (in class or via your VLE) and your students' learning.

Visit https://study.sagepub.com/sethna5e to set up or use your instructor login to access.

CONTENTS

LIST OF FIGURES.................................... X

LIST OF TABLES XIV

ABOUT THE AUTHOR XVI

PREFACE TO THE FIFTH EDITION .. XVIII

USING THIS BOOK.......................... XXII

ENDORSEMENTS XXV

PART ONE
CONSUMER BEHAVIOUR IN CONTEXT

1

UNDERSTANDING CONSUMER BEHAVIOUR

Introduction 5
Defining consumer behaviour 6
Consumer behaviour in context.................. 12
Consumer behaviour and the marketing mix: A brief insight..................... 13
Consumers, relationship marketing and marketing planning............................. 13
Antecedents of consumer behaviour............................... 18
Psychology.. 19
Sociology.. 22
Anthropology.. 23
Economics.. 24
Neuroscience... 26
Summary.. 27
More online.. 32
References... 32

2

DECISIONS, BEHAVIOURS AND INTERACTIONS

Introduction 41
Decision-making using goals 42
Decision-making models........................... 45
Interrupts 50
Risk and uncertainty 52
Pre-purchase activities 54
The search effort 55
Factors affecting the external search for information 56
Making the choice 60
Categorisation of decision rules................. 61
Involvement 63
Dimensions of involvement....................... 67
Involvement with brands 68
Increasing involvement levels 70
Loyalty in buyer behaviour 70
Unsought goods.. 72
Summary.. 74
More online.. 79
References... 79

3

CONSUMPTION IN B2C VS. B2B

Introduction 91
The decision-making unit 92

Influences on buyers 98
Classifying business customers 103
Business and commercial
organisations 103
Reseller organisations 104
Government organisations 106
Institutional organisations 107
Buyers' techniques 108
The Buygrid framework 110
Value analysis 112
Evaluating supplier capability 114
Evaluating supplier performance 114
Summary 116
More online 119
References 120

4

CONSUMER TECHNOLOGY AND INNOVATION

Introduction 125
Artificial intelligence (AI) replaces
human interactions 127
Metaverse 129
Machine learning 129
Robotics and unmanned aerial
vehicles (UAVs)/drones 130
Virtual reality (VR) and
augmented reality (AR) 132
The Internet of Things (IoT) 133
Mobile technologies 133
Big data and analytics 134
Platforms and blockchains 135
Innovation 137
Adoption of innovation 142
Categories of innovation adopters 145
Innovative products 152
Marketing approaches to
new product launches 154
Resistance to innovation 155
Summary 158
More online 162
References 162

PART TWO CONSUMERS AS INDIVIDUALS (THE PSYCHOLOGICAL ISSUES)

5

DRIVE, MOTIVATION AND HEDONISM

Introduction 177
Drive 178
Motivation 181
Classifying needs 182
Motivational factors 190
Individual factors 192
Motivational conflict 194
Goals 196
Heuristics 199
Hedonism 201
Understanding motivation 205
Research into motivation 206
Summary 207
More online 211
References 211

6

THE SELF AND PERSONALITY

Introduction 219
Self-concept 219
Personality 230
Approaches to studying personality 231
Type approach 233
Traits and factors 236
Psychographics 238
Summary 241
More online 244
References 245

7

PERCEPTION

Introduction 255
Elements of perception 256
Creating a world-view 258
How we process data in our head 262
Culture and perception 264
Environmental influences............................267
Perception and store atmospherics............267
Perception and consumers'
characteristics and behaviour 274
Combining factors 275
Subliminal perception 279
Colour.. 281
Passing off, brandalism and subvertising.... 284
Summary 284
More online.. 289
References.. 289

8

LEARNING AND KNOWLEDGE

Introduction 299
Defining learning 300
Studying learning 301
The need for knowledge 318
Sources of consumer knowledge 330
Summary..331
More online.. 334
References.. 334

9

ATTITUDE FORMATION AND CHANGE

Introduction 341
Defining attitude.. 342
Dimensions of attitude 344
Attitude formation 347
Attitude measurement 349

Functions of attitudes..................................350
Attitude and behaviour 352
The duality of private vs.
public attitudes 356
Attitude vs. situation 356
Attitude towards adverts vs.
attitude towards the brand.........................357
General vs. specific attitudes 358
Changing attitudes......................................359
Cognitive dissonance.................................. 364
Summary... 366
More online.. 369
References.. 369

PART THREE
CONSUMERS AS SOCIAL ACTORS (THE SOCIOLOGICAL ISSUES)

10

REFERENCE GROUPS

Introduction 381
Formation of reference groups 382
Influence of reference groups 387
Modelling 394
Mechanisms of personal influence
and word of mouth...................................... 394
The emergence of word of mouse 402
Summary... 405
More online.. 409
References.. 409

11

AGE, GENDER AND FAMILIAL ROLES

Introduction 417
How old are you? (Cohorts and
subcultures developed using age)................418

Defining families 422
Influence of children on
buying decisions 426
Changing nature of the family 435
Gender roles 438
Other functions of the family 442
Roles in family consumption 444
Summary 447
More online 451
References 451

12

CULTURE AND SOCIAL MOBILITY

Introduction 461
Culture 462
Subcultures 473
Social mobility (aka class) 482
Summary 486
More online 491
References 492

13

ETHICAL CONSUMPTION

Introduction 501
Definitions and categories 503
Ethics and the person 510
Ethics and the public 517

Disposal and recycling 518
Summary 525
More online 532
References 532

14

SUSTAINABLE CONSUMPTION

Introduction 541
Definitions 543
A short look back on recent history 546
Principles of sustainable consumption 548
Consumption 558
Summary 562
More online 566
References 566

INDEX 575

LIST OF FIGURES

Figure 1.1	Consumer behaviour dynamics	11
Figure 1.2	Businesses and relationship marketing	15
Figure 1.3	Antecedents of studying consumer behaviour	19
Figure 1.4	Contributions from psychology	20
Figure 1.5	Contributions from sociology	22
Figure 1.6	Elastic demand curve	26
Figure 2.1	Drivers for end goals	44
Figure 2.2	Developing goals	45
Figure 2.3	The decision-making process	47
Figure 2.4	Actual and desired states	48
Figure 2.5	Programmed and non-programmed problem-solving	50
Figure 2.6	Temporary effects of an interrupt	51
Figure 2.7	Reducing risk	53
Figure 2.8	Information searching	55
Figure 2.9	Limits on the information search	57
Figure 2.10	Factors affecting the external search for information	58
Figure 2.11	An example of a decision-making process for a holiday purchase	62
Figure 2.12	Howard–Sheth model	63
Figure 2.13	Involvement continuum	64
Figure 2.14	Categories of involvement	65
Figure 2.15	Dimensions of involvement	69
Figure 2.16	Categorising consumers	70
Figure 2.17	Increasing involvement	71
Figure 2.18	Reasons for postponing purchase of unsought goods	73
Figure 3.1	Relationships in the DMU	96
Figure 3.2	Environmental influences on buyer behaviour	100
Figure 3.3	Organisational influences on buyer behaviour	102
Figure 3.4	Types of purchase	105
Figure 3.5	Tiers of government and their typical purchases	106
Figure 3.6	Factors in institutional marketing	107
Figure 3.7	Trade-offs in type of buying situation	110
Figure 3.8	The Buygrid framework	111

LIST OF FIGURES

Figure 4.1	The influence of social media	138
Figure 4.2	The product life cycle	139
Figure 4.3	Product dropped shortly after introduction	140
Figure 4.4	Effects of marketing activities on the product life cycle	140
Figure 4.5	Failed product	140
Figure 4.6	Models of the adoption and diffusion process	143
Figure 4.7	Classification of innovators	146
Figure 4.8	Variables that affect innovativeness	147
Figure 4.9	Dissonance reduction strategies	150
Figure 4.10	Communication variables associated with innovativeness	152
Figure 4.11	Degrees of innovation	153
Figure 5.1	Creating a drive	178
Figure 5.2	Dimensions of motives	181
Figure 5.3	Zuckerman's Hierarchy of Stimulation	185
Figure 5.4	Maslow's Hierarchy of Needs	186
Figure 5.5	The values and lifestyles (VALS) model	189
Figure 5.6	Dual-factor theory	192
Figure 5.7	Emphases on power, affiliation and achievement	193
Figure 5.8	Motivation conflict	195
Figure 5.9	A hierarchical model of consumer goals	197
Figure 5.10	A model of goal-determination processes	198
Figure 5.11	Hedonism vs. utilitarianism	202
Figure 6.1	The person as artwork	221
Figure 6.2	Relationship between components of self-concept	227
Figure 6.3	Self-monitoring	228
Figure 6.4	The id, the ego and the superego	232
Figure 6.5	Cartoon projective technique	233
Figure 6.6	Reisman's typologies	234
Figure 6.7	Myers–Briggs Type Indicator	235
Figure 7.1	Selectivity and synthesis	257
Figure 7.2	Information processing types	263
Figure 7.3	Influences on perceptual mapping	264
Figure 7.4	Elements in the environment	267
Figure 7.5	Perception and store atmospherics	268
Figure 7.6	Adapted Mehrabian–Russell model	271
Figure 7.7	The functional environment	272

LIST OF FIGURES

Figure 7.8	Perceptual responses	275
Figure 7.9	Linear additive model	276
Figure 7.10	Linear averaging model	277
Figure 7.11	The configural model	277
Figure 7.12	Subliminal advertising	280
Figure 7.13	Colour in marketing	283
Figure 8.1	Learning	301
Figure 8.2	Classical conditioning	302
Figure 8.3	Ordering of stimuli	303
Figure 8.4	Operant conditioning	310
Figure 8.5	Cognitive learning	310
Figure 8.6	Factors in cognitive learning	311
Figure 8.7	Five elements of cognitive learning	317
Figure 8.8	Reasoning and cognitive learning	317
Figure 8.9	Knowledge and risk	318
Figure 8.10	Categorising knowledge	320
Figure 8.11	Product expert knowledge	322
Figure 8.12	Brand association	323
Figure 8.13	Relative price information	324
Figure 8.14	Advantages of having purchase knowledge	326
Figure 8.15	Consumption knowledge	327
Figure 9.1	Dimensions of attitude	345
Figure 9.2	Starting points for attitude formation	346
Figure 9.3	Attitude formation	348
Figure 9.4	Strength of attitudes	350
Figure 9.5	Functions of attitudes	351
Figure 9.6	The theory of reasoned action	353
Figure 9.7	The theory of planned behaviour	354
Figure 9.8	The cycle of attitude and behaviour	355
Figure 9.9	Effect of situation on attitude	357
Figure 9.10	Changing beliefs	360
Figure 9.11	Consistent vs. inconsistent attitude	361
Figure 9.12	Peripheral and direct routes to attitude change	362
Figure 9.13	Cognitive dissonance	364
Figure 9.14	Post-purchase dissonance	365
Figure 10.1	An individual and his reference groups	388
Figure 10.2	Modifying behaviour through groups	390

Figure 10.3	Mechanisms for controlling behaviour	391
Figure 10.4	Factors in modelling	394
Figure 10.5	Mechanisms of personal influence	396
Figure 10.6	Multistage interaction model	397
Figure 10.7	Forces driving influentials	399
Figure 11.1	Defining characteristics of families	422
Figure 11.2	Determinants of decision-making style in families	425
Figure 11.3	Children's stages of development as consumers	429
Figure 11.4	Children's persuasion tactics	430
Figure 11.5	Effects of falling birth rate	436
Figure 11.6	Drivers for gender role change	439
Figure 11.7	Estimated size of the global LGBT community	441
Figure 11.8	Other functions of the family	443
Figure 11.9	Family roles and decisions	445
Figure 11.10	Communication pattern and children's influence	447
Figure 12.1	The social environment	462
Figure 12.2	Elements of culture	463
Figure 12.3	Dimensions of culture	467
Figure 12.4	High-context vs. low-context cultures	469
Figure 12.5	Culture and subculture	474
Figure 12.6	Stages in acculturation	481
Figure 12.7	Studying social class	484
Figure 13.1	Variables determining environmental preferences and practices	507
Figure 13.2	The ethical consumer's choices	514
Figure 13.3	Ethical consumerism and its constituent areas of interest	515
Figure 13.4	Disposal options	519
Figure 13.5	Good Thoughts, Good Words and Good Deeds	526
Figure 14.1	The 'triple bottom line' represented as three overlapping sectors	548
Figure 14.2	Nested diagram of sustainability	548
Figure 14.3	The fourth pillar of sustainability	549

LIST OF TABLES

Table 1.1	The seven Ps from a consumer behaviourist lens	13
Table 1.2	Transactional marketing vs. relationship marketing	15
Table 2.1	Examples of purchase end goals	44
Table 2.2	Goal and interrupt strengths	51
Table 2.3	Categorising consumers according to involvement	69
Table 2.4	Decision-making model for unsought goods	73
Table 3.1	Classification summary of buying organisations	103
Table 3.2	Assessing suppliers	114
Table 3.3	Evaluation approaches	115
Table 4.1	Attributes necessary for adoption	143
Table 5.1	Classification of consumer motives	182
Table 5.2	Using modelling for positive reinforcement	194
Table 5.3	Examples of heuristics	200
Table 6.1	Components of self-concept	226
Table 6.2	Relevance of self-image	226
Table 6.3	16 personality factor (PF) trait analysis	237
Table 6.4	Lifestyle types	238
Table 7.1	Conventions about perception	256
Table 7.2	Colour perceptions	281
Table 8.1	Extinction	304
Table 8.2	Learning from experience	312
Table 8.3	Managing the learning process	314
Table 9.1	Attitudinal metrics	343
Table 9.2	Dimensions of attitude	345
Table 9.3	Example of a belief set	348
Table 9.4	Functions of attitudes	351
Table 10.1	Effects of reference groups on consumer choice	390
Table 10.2	Determinants of reference group influence	393
Table 10.3	Word of mouth	401

LIST OF TABLES

Table 11.1	Conflict resolution in families	427
Table 11.2	Tactics used by children to influence their parents	431
Table 11.3	The family life cycle	436
Table 11.4	Roles in family decision-making	445
Table 11.5	How children perceive themselves to have influenced the purchase of different products	446
Table 12.1	Ethnic groups and religion in the UK	476
Table 12.2	Acculturation framework for ethnic entrepreneurs	479
Table 12.3	UK socio-economic groupings (JICNARS)	482
Table 12.4	The Socio-Economic Classification System	483
Table 13.1	Early categories of ethical consumers	509
Table 13.2	National Consumer Council's 'UK Green Consumers'	509
Table 13.3	The guilt checklist of ethical consumption	511
Table 14.1	Highlights of water, energy and food consumption	542
Table 14.2	Definitions of greenwashing	554
Table 14.3	The Greenwashing Index Scoring Criteria	557

ABOUT THE AUTHOR

Professor (Dr) Zubin Sethna is a born and bred Londoner – Wimbledon in fact – and this is from where he remembers his earliest lesson in consumer behaviour. Year after year he would watch the crowds gather in neat queues to buy tickets to watch the tennis; all in the heat of summer. So one year, as an 11-year-old, he decided to sell ice-cold cans of a famous cola drink to the waiting crowds. And whilst John McEnroe was shouting the now infamous words 'you cannot be serious' on Centre Court, Zubin was thinking the very same thing when, much to his surprise, captive individuals in the crowd were willing to spend £3 a can to quench their thirst!

As an avid proponent of 'practice what you preach', Zubin has successfully launched six businesses (one of which won a National Award). As Managing Consultant at Baresman Consulting (www.baresman.com), he has integrated marketing/consumer behavioural strategy with management consultancy and training for numerous organisations both in the UK and internationally, and across a variety of industry sectors (including Healthcare, Professional Services, Music, Travel, Manufacturing, Retail, IT, Education and 'Cottage' industries). Zubin and his partner, Navaz, have also been running a very successful Kumon Education Centre in North West London for the past 17 years, helping nearly 300 children to excel in maths and English – and ultimately achieve their dreams.

Zubin is also a seasoned academic and a published author. His research interests lie at the interface of entrepreneurship, marketing and ethnicity (in fact, his PhD thesis examined the entrepreneurial marketing activities of the Zarathustrian entrepreneur). He is a Visiting Professor of Entrepreneurship and Marketing at ATLAS SkillTech University (India) and has conducted various lecture tours around India and China as well. In addition, he has delivered online academic courses for universities in France, Spain, Italy and Dubai.

Zubin's day job (!) is as a Professor of Entrepreneurial Marketing and Consumer Behaviour, and he regularly delivers keynote addresses to conferences and for corporate clients around the world. His administrative duties are as a Director of Content – responsible for managing an undergraduate and postgraduate portfolio totalling nearly 1500 students, as well as leading the PhD programme at Regent's.

Between 2016 and 2022, Zubin had the privilege of being the Editor-in-Chief of the internationally respected *Journal of Research in Marketing and Entrepreneurship* – where he's still an Associate Editor – and is also a reviewer for a variety of leading marketing and business journals, including the *Journal of Business Research, European Journal of Marketing, Journal of Marketing Management* and *Journal of Strategic Marketing*. Zubin also co-leads the Academy of Marketing's Special Interest Group on 'Entrepreneurial and Small Business Marketing' together with his colleague Professor Rosalind Jones, as well as having a place on the Advisory Board of the Global Research Conference on Marketing and Entrepreneurship (www.marketing-entrepreneurship.org/).

He still occasionally finds time to get out on his Specialized Roubaix, although it's usually more a Tour de Barnet than a Tour de France! Most recently, Zubin has been infatuated with riding around on his Boosted Board – an electric longboard skateboard – and has consequently acquired the nickname 'Professor Boosted'; a name which his three children, Mahya, Kai and Kaus, are thoroughly embarrassed about!

PREFACE TO THE FIFTH EDITION

We can safely say that the past three years since the fourth edition of this book came out (2019) will remain memorable for some years to come. Having just started to grapple with the effects of Brexit in the UK we were thrown into turmoil (like we've never experienced) with the onset, spread and grip of the global pandemic known as Covid-19. Whilst this has primarily been a health crisis, we know that the ramifications have led to both social and economic crises. So when I say that it will remain memorable for some years, what I actually mean is that its severe and far-reaching repercussions are, and will continue to be, felt across the world.

Industries were devastated. With businesses being closed (some indefinitely, and some permanently), millions of people lost their jobs (in fact the equivalent of nearly 255 million full-time jobs were lost) as a direct result of the pandemic. Many of those (young people and women) worked in the informal economy. We have already seen that economic recovery is a) unstable, and b) uneven, meaning that this will automatically lead to greater inequality in the years to come. Women also represent the majority of workers in sectors such as accommodation, food services, health and social care. They've had to assume additional responsibilities at home.

Schools, colleges and universities closed, causing disruption and irreparable damage to almost half of the world's students, who were affected by a loss of education. Given the societal damage that Covid-19 has caused, some say that there is a real potential that millions of girls in some countries may not have gone back to school, which has then put them at risk of adolescent pregnancy, child marriage and violence.

In amongst all of this doom-and-gloom, surprisingly there is some positive news. In 2020 whilst the world was in lockdown – meaning we were confined to our homes for a significant period of time – the global energy-related CO_2 emissions actually fell by 5.8%. This was the largest ever decline in global CO_2 emissions in history.

Other areas of society which have been affected include our notion of, perspectives on, and ability to trust. We learnt that physical spaces, surfaces and other people could not be trusted as they could all be a source of infection. Thus our emotional ability to trust others came down to our own judgement on other people's competence to act with integrity and care about others, whether it be a physical setting or online through the contact tracing app. (Remember the strap line *'Stay home, Protect the NHS, Save lives'*?) Add to that debates on why it was OK to spend 10 minutes in close proximity to get groceries but not OK to spend 2 hours in a cinema... or why one should wear a mask even when going for a walk in the fresh air, and we can see that prejudice and unconscious bias now have a vehicle with which to wreak havoc – as indeed we saw with the exclusion and beratement of some minority groups, leading to civil disobedience.

Sadly, we've all lost something during the pandemic. Whether it's income, financial security, freedom, identity or the extremely harsh scenario of having lost a loved one.

PREFACE TO THE FIFTH EDITION

We know that these psychological effects can lead to depression, anxiety and anger. The only way that we will see this through is by sharing both the burden which we face and the spaces which we occupy. Given the scarcity of goods, resources, currency, many of us are having to make do with what we have. So there's been a shift in our psyche from consumption to production.

However, this said, we still live in a world in which consumers are greatly influenced by the 'haves' and 'have-nots'; by those who have the ability to spend (and *oh boy* have they been spending post-Covid!) and those who are just starting to gear up to demand products and services in the near future. Thus, all of us consume, even those who lead a relatively monastic existence: this is what makes the study of consumer behaviour so interesting and delves into the heart of the marketing concept. From the earliest utterings of religious prophets such as Zarathustra, who lived in the 6th century BCE, to political prophets in the 21st century, we know that without customers there is no business, and since everything is ultimately driven by the consumers, their needs and wants become paramount. However, over the past 15 years we have seen many changes in consumer behaviour which have been driven, predominantly, by changes in geodemographics and technology. Innovation has been followed by disruptive innovation, and many products and brands have swiftly found themselves being launched into globalised consumer markets. We've seen these changes (both macro- and micro-environmental) highlighted in academic research as well as commercial research, and we've taken the opportunity to talk about the effects of these on consumer behaviour. The newcomers in this space are undoubtedly technology-driven: the increasing dominance of all things mobile related (not least of all, mobile marketing), social media platforms, etc. and on the flip side we have cyber-attackers, who are also continuously finding ways to illegally and unknowingly engage the consumer through a variety of media. Changes of this nature are likely to continue as we hurtle towards 2025. This raises many questions: Are we prepared and able to face all the challenges that may come our way? Do we continue to understand who the customers are, and why they behave in the way that they do? Do we know where they are and where they are heading? Do we understand what they are saying? How much homage do we pay to ethical and sustainable consumption?

The huge success of the first four editions of *Consumer Behaviour* is largely due not just to the contemporary nature of the material, but to a relaxed yet informative writing style which I know both students and educators value and love! With the fifth edition, I've ensured that the text, theoretical depth and the practical examples of both 'consumer behaviour in action' and 'brand experiences' all remain very accessible to the reader. My approach with this edition of *Consumer Behaviour* has been to continue to take a truly international perspective on the subject. Our case studies incorporate examples from a variety of geographic locations (UK, Europe, USA, UAE and India) as well as from a number of different industry sectors (fashion, automotive, technology, politics, travel transport and leisure, food retailing, social media/social enterprise and the emergency services). This has also meant that academic disciplines other than marketing have also made tremendous contributions – psychology, sociology, anthropology, economics and neuroscience form the scientific base on which consumer behaviour stands as an academic subject. I have tried, in this book, to provide a concise and fairly comprehensive overview of the main aspects of consumer behaviour, but inevitably there are omissions, so at the end of each chapter I have offered some further reading on aspects that you may find particularly insightful.

Core textbooks like this one cannot just be the creation of a couple of people. In particular I would like to thank Matthew Waters, Charlotte Hanson and Nicola Marshall at SAGE. This fifth edition would not have seen the light of day without their dedication, support, understanding and patience in our post-Covid world! My family, the communities within which I live and my life experience have all provided a consistently rich source of examples – many of which have been used here. Perhaps most importantly, my undergraduate and postgraduate students should be thanked for making me think: some by asking awkward questions, some by submitting thought-provoking coursework, some by making me laugh, and some by needing a deeper explanation than I was really ready to provide. I'm humbled to learn that it changed your life, Karlotta. A special shout-out goes to my four current PhD students (John, Cathy, Julia and Abbie) to whom I act as a *'Zubervisor'* (thanks John!). Finally, I'd like to thank my friend and fellow academic, Emeritus Professor Jim Blythe, who started me on this journey. *Pip Pip...*

Zubin Sethna

North London

USING THIS BOOK

LEARNING OBJECTIVES

Highlight everything you should know or understand by the end of each chapter.

GLOSSARY TERMS

To help you spot the important terms you will need for revision purposes, each new concept appears in coloured text and is defined in the margin.

SUMMARY

Covers all the essential information from each chapter and puts it in the context of consumer behaviour as a whole.

BRAND EXPERIENCES

Examples of how existing brands operate to help you see the relevance of each aspect of consumer behaviour.

CRITICAL REFLECTION

Designed to develop your critical thinking and employability skills. They are short challenges from the workplace.

CONSUMER BEHAVIOUR IN ACTION

Additional examples to highlight what actually goes on in the real world.

KEY POINTS

Recap the key topics for review at the end of each chapter.

HOW TO IMPRESS YOUR EXAMINER

The authors' own advice for standing out from the crowd and proving you know your stuff!

REVIEW QUESTIONS

Help test your understanding of what you have just read.

CASE STUDY AND QUESTIONS

Offer a detailed look at real-life examples and help you apply your knowledge by working through the questions.

FURTHER READING

Suggested titles for further reading to enhance your background knowledge.

ENDORSEMENTS

In my journey of building a consumer brand from scratch, many of my 'do or die' decisions have been made by putting my consumers at the forefront. Professor Zubin Sethna has produced the most comprehensive work on consumer behaviour that I have ever seen, by far. It covers consumer behaviour from all angles including an understanding of psychological and sociological issues. Throughout, the book is superbly illustrated with diagrams and consumer behaviour is brought to life by several real-world case studies, all enabling the reader to obtain a complete and thorough understanding of the subject. It is a must-read for students and practitioners alike!
Lord Karan Bilimoria of Chelsea, CBE DL, Founder and Chairman of Cobra Beer

Whether we like it or not, artificial intelligence is here to stay and the speed at which its applications are adopted by the consumer will only continue to rise. Lifestyle considerations, spending shifts, motivational movements and value adjustments, to name but a few, are all part of the behavioural impact which differ from generation to generation and across the gender spectrum. Zubin Sethna has very eloquently captured the nuances of consumer behaviour by identifying key theories and strategies which take a consumer-centric approach and will undoubtedly help organisations and individuals minimise risk and benefit from the commercial opportunities.
Stuart Sherman, Founder and CEO, IMC, Toronto

The fifth edition of this bestselling book on *Consumer Behaviour* is up to date with material for a post-Brexit and post-Covid consumerist world. It is full of relevant examples from a regional, national and global perspective. As with previous editions, Zubin's writing style is academic yet current, relevant and easy to read. The book is packed with sections on 'critical reflection', 'consumer behaviour in action' and 'brand experiences' all of which help to really bring the conceptual academic frameworks to life and from a practice-based perspective. Of notable significance are the chapters on both ethical and sustainable consumption. This text continues to be a must-have for students studying consumer behaviour.
Dr Jaideep Prabhu, Professor of Marketing, Jawaharlal Nehru Professor of Indian Business and Enterprise, Director of the Centre for India & Global Business (CIGB), Cambridge Judge Business School, University of Cambridge

A must-read for students who would like to explore consumer behaviours from a psychological and marketing perspective. Every edition so far has made important updates and kept this book on the top of my reading list for UG and PG students. The secret of the book is to have a neat structure and to keep its digestible format, unlike many of its overloaded competitors.
Dr Jan Breitsohl, Senior Lecturer in Marketing, Adam Smith Business School, University of Glasgow

Over the last 15 years our societies have been rocked by game-changing events. Back in 2008 we saw the start of the *global financial crisis*, and although the environment within which business is conducted may have changed, ultimately, all business still depends on someone buying something. We buy things in order to meet our physical and emotional needs; business exists to create wealth, and to distribute it in ways that enable people to create relatively worthwhile lives for themselves. Of course, the *'how'* we buy things has also dramatically changed as a result of the global pandemic we have come to know as Covid-19. As a side note for readers here, whilst there may well be times when I refer to the impact that the pandemic has had on our lives, I certainly do not want to turn it into the sole focus – there are many other impacts which collectively shape our consumer behaviour!

If businesses are to succeed in creating wealth, they need to understand what it is that people need and want, and to ensure that it is available in the right place, at the right time and at a price consumers are willing to pay. This is the very foundation of all marketing – even businesses that sell only to other businesses rely, ultimately, on consumers buying products.

Apart from the obvious importance of understanding how people buy and consume, consumer behaviour is inherently interesting because it is about people (and we are *all* consumers, of course). Part One of this book looks at the basics of understanding consumer behaviour (Chapter 1). Chapter 2 then examines the deeper processes that consumers engage with when making decisions and, of course, this would not be complete without investigating the interaction that consumers have with brands. Chapter 3 takes a look at the differences between consumption patterns exhibited by individuals in B2C (business-to-consumer) and B2B (business-to-business) markets. At this point, Chapter 4, the final chapter in Part One, then takes a look at one of the most important areas, currently, for marketers – consumer technology and innovation. Companies are constantly striving to bring to market new products in order to stay ahead of the competition, but at the same time, innovation means taking a risk. Understanding how people relate to, and are impacted by, new products is an essential component of any company's new product strategy. In the 21st century, service industries have become far more important than manufacturing industries on almost every measure. Both technology and continued innovation have a big part to play in this transition; thus the potential impact that both have on consumers is a key issue that marketers must understand. These introductory chapters set the scene for the more detailed chapters that follow.

PART ONE CONSUMER BEHAVIOUR IN CONTEXT

Chapter 1 Understanding Consumer Behaviour
Chapter 2 Decisions, Behaviours and Interactions
Chapter 3 Consumption in B2C vs. B2B
Chapter 4 Consumer Technology and Innovation

PART TWO CONSUMERS AS INDIVIDUALS (THE PSYCHOLOGICAL ISSUES)

Chapter 5 Drive, Motivation and Hedonism
Chapter 6 The Self and Personality
Chapter 7 Perception
Chapter 8 Learning and Knowledge
Chapter 9 Attitude Formation and Change

PART THREE CONSUMERS AS SOCIAL ACTORS (THE SOCIOLOGICAL ISSUES)

Chapter 10 Reference Groups
Chapter 11 Age, Gender and Familial Roles
Chapter 12 Culture and Social Mobility
Chapter 13 Ethical Consumption
Chapter 14 Sustainable Consumption

CHAPTER 1

UNDERSTANDING CONSUMER BEHAVIOUR

LEARNING OBJECTIVES

After reading this chapter you should be able to:
- Explain how the study of consumer behaviour has evolved.
- Show how consumer behaviour relates to marketing decision-making.
- Explain why relationships are harder to establish in business-to-consumer situations than in business-to-business situations.
- Describe the scope and nature of psychology and sociology.
- Describe the scope and nature of anthropology.
- Describe the relationship of economics with the study of consumer behaviour.
- Explain the role of exchange in improving people's welfare.
- Explain how the terms 'luxury' and 'necessity' relate to consumer behaviour.

CHAPTER CONTENTS

Introduction
Defining consumer behaviour
Consumer behaviour in context
Consumer behaviour and the marketing mix: A brief insight
Consumers, relationship marketing and marketing planning
Antecedents of consumer behaviour
Psychology
Sociology
Anthropology
Economics
Neuroscience
Summary
Key points
How to impress your examiner
Review questions
Case study: Consumer behaviour in Britain: Past and present
Further reading
References

More online: https://study.sagepub.com/sethna5e

INTRODUCTION

Every day we buy things. We exchange our money for goods and services, for our own use and for the use of our families; occasionally we make impulse purchases (Djafarova and Bowes, 2021; Fenton-O'Creevy et al., 2018), but mostly we choose things we think will meet our needs on a day-to-day basis, and we intermittently make buying decisions that will affect our lives for years to come (Coary and Poor, 2016). At the same time, we make decisions about disposing of worn-out or used-up possessions. All these decisions and exchanges have implications for ourselves, our families, our friends, the environment, the businesses we buy from, the employees of those businesses, and so on.

Customer
Someone who makes the decision to buy a product

The key concept of marketing is customer centrality: we cannot ignore customer decision-making. Understanding the processes involved in making those decisions is central to establishing policy both from a micro (internal) perspective and also a macro (external) perspective.

Consumer behaviour and industrial buyer behaviour have been studied by marketers since long before marketing became an academic subject. The academic subjects that preceded marketing include economics (the study of supply and demand), sociology (the study of group behaviour), psychology (the study of thought processes), neurology (the study of brain function) and anthropology (the study of what makes us human). Each of these disciplines has looked at the problem from a different angle, and each will be discussed in greater detail throughout the book.

DEFINING CONSUMER BEHAVIOUR

All of us are consumers: all of us behave in a particular way. This does not mean that all of our behaviour can be defined as consumer behaviour, of course. Specific consumer behaviour has been defined as follows:

Consumer behaviour is the activities people undertake when obtaining, consuming and disposing of products and services. (Blackwell et al., 2001)

Consumer
Someone who uses, consumes and/or enjoys the benefit of a product/service

Products
A bundle of benefits

App
Software designed to fulfil a particular purpose; an application, usually downloaded by a user onto a mobile device

This definition is widely used, but it still leaves some questions to answer. First, what do we mean by 'obtaining'? This presumably includes all the activities that lead up to making a purchase, including searching for information about products and services, and evaluating the alternatives. 'Obtaining' may not involve an actual purchase, but most consumer behaviour researchers and writers ignore this angle: a child who promises to keep their room tidy in exchange for payment towards a new gaming app is clearly obtaining a product, but this is not usually regarded as part of a study of consumer behaviour. Likewise, presumably for ethical reasons, theft was usually ignored as an aspect of consumer behaviour up until recently (Dootson et al., 2018). However, as innovation transforms the way in which consumers receive their goods, a new academic light shines on theft (Hasford et al., 2022; Hicks et al., 2022) and these types of studies have now started to form as a core constituent of studies in consumer behaviour.

CRITICAL REFLECTION

Dootson et al. (2018) talk about 'deviant consumer behaviour' as having serious negative effects on organisations, employees and other customers. It is true that research to date has largely focused on understanding why consumers engage in deviant behaviours, but less focus has been placed on exploring how to deter them. So where does the ethical/moral line lie when grocery shopping? Is it, for instance, acceptable to pick and eat a grape, while walking around the supermarket, in the name of 'sampling'? Or would you deem it acceptable to keep quiet if the checkout person charged you a lower price for an item which you knew to have a much higher one? In this continuing era of austerity in many countries around the world, and when a lot of people face severe financial hardship to the point where 'food bank usage in the UK reaches the highest rate on record' (Bulman, 2018), would you turn a blind eye to someone stealing a carton of milk? This is in an environment where 'participation in non-standard or low-income work such as zero-hour contracts, involuntary part-time work and self-employment is increasingly a feature of the labour market but where working women still have to resort to food bank use in times of financial hardship' (Beatty et al., 2021). Of course, these questions are not new to us; in the 6th century BCE, a philosopher in Ancient Greece called Anarcharsis said, 'the market is a place set apart where men may deceive one and other'. Thus, *trust* becomes of paramount importance; trust between people and in organisations is the key. Let's take, for example, the self-checkout in grocery stores. As of the second quarter (Q2) of 2018, 95% of American consumers had encountered at least one form of self-service retail and 49% used them on a weekly basis at the supermarket (pymnts.com, 2018), however in 2021 a survey noted that 67% of shoppers had experienced a failure at the self-checkout lane (Editions CNN, 2022). In a study by a team at Voucher Codes Pro, a sales coupon website, 2532 shoppers were quizzed about their supermarket habits. The study found that close to a quarter had committed theft at a self-checkout machine at least once. (A figure from the same report suggested that the total cost of items stolen through self-checkout machines in 2017 came in at more than £3.2 billion, up from £1.6 billion in 2014 [Moshakis, 2018]). Some steal by accident, the study found, perhaps on account of a scanning error – honest mistakes. But many perpetrators know exactly what they are doing (see for instance work by Amasiatu and Shah, 2019, who investigate fraud in e-retailing). Research from the National Association for Shoplifting Prevention in the USA showed that there are approximately 27 million shoplifters (or 1 in 11 people) in the USA. And all of this is in spite of various measures being taken to deter the would-be thief – including more visible security guards, anti-theft packaging and CCTV surveillance cameras with video analytical software to monitor customer behaviour. This enables the retailer to make assumptions about, for instance, why someone lingers in a particular area for longer than is 'normal' in a supermarket!

Is the overall environment making it easier to steal? In 2016, criminologists (Beck and Hopkins, 2016) at the University of Leicester published a paper that reported on the impact of recent developments in mobile-scanning technology. The study was led by Adrian Beck, an Emeritus Professor of Criminology, who has spent more than 25 years researching losses in the retail industry. In the report, he (together with his colleague Dr Matt Hopkins) had suggested that retailers who rely on self-scanning technology inadvertently create environments that encourage theft. In the self-checkout aisle, for example, human interaction is often pared back to a minimum, which reduces the perception of risk on the part of a potential perpetrator. 'It's about the degree of opportunity it provides people who wouldn't normally do something deviant', explains Beck. 'It presents them with opportunities they wouldn't normally have.' The retailers have certainly made it easier to steal their products, but from a manufacturer's viewpoint, shoplifting can only be a good thing. If the product is attractive to shoplifters, more of it will leave the retailer's premises, and since the retailer has already paid the manufacturer for the goods, the manufacturer doesn't care whether

© iStock.com/stnazkul

the goods are bought or stolen from the retailer! Of course that's not to say that manufacturers are actively encouraging pilfering; it's just that retailers and e-tailers are partly trusting us to 'do the right thing'. What is for sure is that technology has a big part to play. Social media and the various platforms and forums that exist make it easier to dispose of stolen items. Websites such as YouTube have numerous videos showing people how to steal, some from seemingly experienced criminals divulging the 'tricks of the trade'. Other forums provide a platform for unhappy employees to expose organisational secrets. You could assume that a sure way of dealing with such behaviour is to toughen up on aspects of punishment. But with resources being stretched every which way, some interesting decisions are being made on how to tackle this situation: the police department in Dallas, Texas is questioning the cost–benefit of operations that try to capture a teenager who has stolen something worth $20 and will actually refuse to prosecute anyone who steals something for less than $50. I'll let you decide what message this sends out to the public…

Other issues in physically 'obtaining' a product might include *where* people buy the product (offline or online), the different ways in which people *pay* for the products (cash, credit card, bank loan, payday loan, hire purchase, interest-free credit, and so forth), *who* the product is for (themselves or a gift), *how* the new owner gets the purchases home, and how all of these decisions are affected by branding, and by social elements such as influence and peer pressure. Of course, there is also the issue of *what* is being bought. So for instance, some supermarkets are being scammed by shoppers who are passing expensive avocados off as cheap carrots at self-service checkouts! Emmeline Taylor, a Senior Lecturer in Criminology at the University of London, had become aware of the trend in Australia but has now seen it happening in the UK as well. Carrots are one of the cheapest vegetables in supermarkets, leading to some customers purposely selecting the 'carrots' option when weighing avocados on the electronic tills, thereby reducing the cost of their shopping. There are rumours that this type of 'product switching' is becoming so common that some shoppers in the UK are not aware it is a crime as it has become a way of 'gamifying' an otherwise mundane routine (Wheaton, 2018).

Consuming refers to the ways in which people use the products they have, whether bought or acquired. This includes where the product is consumed, when (in terms of on what occasions the product might be used) and how the product is used. In some cases people use products in ways that were not intended by the manufacturer: this is called re-invention. For example, a biologist might buy a turkey-basting syringe to use for taking water samples from a river, a gardener might buy a china serving dish to use as a plant pot, and a cleaner may use vinegar in a spray bottle to remove limescale. Consumption is necessary for our health and well-being: obviously some consumption is not good for us (overconsumption of alcohol, drug abuse or even using a mobile device while driving – which is not just 'not good' for us but illegal in many countries), but most of our consumption is essential for living and relating to other people (Frey, 2018; Nie et al., 2022; Richins, 2001; Scott, 2018).

Disposal of products when they are worn out or no longer needed has become a 'hot topic' in recent years due to environmentalism and a keen interest in sustainability issues (Genç and Di Benedetto, 2018; Radtke et al., 2022). Increases in environmental problems require companies to be more aware towards the environment and take precautions regarding the problems. As a result, companies have started to embrace the concept of a green supply chain, which includes environmental issues rather than the concept of a supply chain that is based on financial performance and profitability (Hilal, 2022; Sezen and Çankaya, 2018). Disposal includes the disposal of packaging – whether it is recycled, burned or goes into landfill, packaging represents a major problem for the 21st century. Given that landfill sites around the world are filling up fast, turning non-recyclable material into recyclable is something that many consumers are thinking about (and learning about through the innovative techniques of virtual reality – Esmaeili and Thwaites, 2021) and something that a company called TerraCycle (www.terracycle.com) has excelled at. Knowing how people dispose of products can be crucial to marketing them. For example, in some less industrialised countries empty metal cans are used to make oil lamps, ashtrays, drinking vessels and so forth. Changing the design or size of the can may well affect sales. Likewise, a system for trading in used or worn-out items can be a major boost for sales of new items: second-hand car trading is based entirely on this principle. Most recently, there have been some limited projects using plastic waste to make roads! In fact, it was whilst Toby McCartney was on a trip to India that he witnessed people melting down plastic they found on local landfill sites to repair potholes. While the method he witnessed on that trip wasn't particularly environmentally practical, McCartney left with the idea of using waste plastic to replace and reinforce the roads in the UK and beyond. And his company MacRebur was born (www.macrebur.com). It's aiming to challenge three major world issues: repurposing millions of tonnes of waste plastic, saving millions in the cost of road repairs and strengthening our existing roads. However, the jury is still out as far as the efficacy of such a strategy is concerned (Conlon, 2022) given that there are several environmental and social considerations to paving with plastic that are overlooked, such as where the inherent chemicals in the plastics end up.

Disposal
Divestment of a product when it is worn out or used up

CONSUMER BEHAVIOUR IN ACTION: A SYSTEM FOR TRADING-IN

The car industry has a dilemma, every year, about how to arouse the market for new cars. But did you know that trading in old cars for new ones was reputedly invented by General Motors dealers in the 1930s as a way of stimulating the market for new

(Continued)

cars? Trade-in also solved the problem of what to do with a car once it was a few years old and perhaps not looking as new as it once had. The second-hand cars that were traded in could be sold to people who could not afford a new car, and so the number of people who were driving could be increased dramatically. And there is a marked difference in the figures too. So, for instance, in 2021, whilst new cars sold (in year to date) totalled just over 1.65 million (SMMT, 2022a), in the same period UK used car transactions grew 11.5% with over 7.5 million units changing hands (SMMT, 2022b).

In 1995 Mrs Katherine Freund of Portland, Oregon, had an idea for extending the trade-in concept and at the same time improving road safety. Her son was run over by an elderly driver in 1988 (the son recovered fully) and it occurred to Katherine that there were many elderly people on the road who really shouldn't be driving, but who felt that they had little choice in a world (and especially in a country) dominated by cars. So Katherine instituted a scheme whereby senior citizen drivers could trade in their cars in exchange for rides. The elderly people are credited with rides, but the cars are operated by volunteers supplemented by a few paid drivers, and the scheme is self-financing. The rides are very much cheaper than using taxis so the credit in the scheme lasts a long time, and the service runs 24 hours a day, 7 days a week. One of the main advantages of the scheme is that it allows elderly people to remain part of the community and continue to do everything they used to do when they were still driving. The other advantage is that the roads are much safer – the over-75 age group has more accidents than any other group except teenagers.

This novel peer-to-peer approach to trade-in has created an entirely new opportunity for older drivers: at the same time, it maintains their mobility and makes life safer for others. As a way of disposing of no-longer-needed cars it is second to none!

Although the traditional model of using buses and trains is one of the best ways of moving people in high-density areas, the digital environment (technology and the internet) plays a strong part in such examples of transportation. IT and global positioning systems, together with data from online networks, provide us with information (using various global positioning systems) on when and where vehicles (public and private) and people are located and therefore create efficient transportation opportunities. Private for-profit organisations such as Uber and Zipcar are taking full advantage of such revolutions in transportation by offering an alternative model to the traditional shared community mobility model of mass transportation using buses and trains. Then there are of course the waterways. In London, the River Thames plays a vital role in keeping London moving. For instance, whilst constructing the Thames Tideway Tunnel (a 25 km super sewer being constructed to tackle the problem of sewage pollution in the River Thames), approximately 35,000 tonnes of material excavated during the works was removed from site by barge in line with Tideway's commitment to remove as much material as possible by river. Similarly, all reinforcement cages for the walls have been delivered to site by barge.

UNDERSTANDING CONSUMER BEHAVIOUR

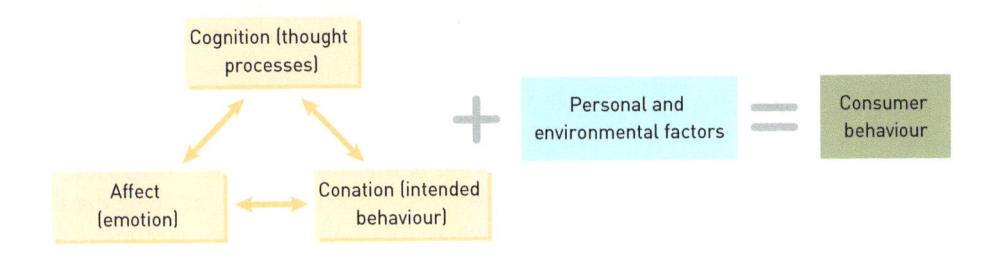

FIGURE 1.1 Consumer behaviour dynamics

Another definition of consumer behaviour runs as follows:

The dynamic interaction of affect and cognition, behaviour, and environmental events by which human beings conduct the exchange aspects of their lives. (Bennett, 1995)

This almost 30-year-old definition still has the advantage that it regards consumer behaviour as dynamic, and emphasises the interaction of many different elements in determining consumer behaviour. (Recently corroborated by Papista et al., 2018.)

The general model of consumer behaviour presented in Figure 1.1 shows that basic attitudes (formed of thought, emotion and intended behaviour) together with personal and environmental factors result in the creation of actual behaviour. Marketers are able to influence this process at several points – they can influence thought processes by providing relevant information at the right time, they can influence emotion by using appealing communication and imagery, and they can provide suitable environmental stimuli (for example, user-friendly websites or inviting shops) to stimulate purchases. Marketers can even encourage greater consumption of the product – good marketing does not start at the point of sale nor does it end there!

Academic researchers may well consider consumer behaviour as the field of study that concentrates on consumption activities. In the past the study of consumer behaviour has mainly focused on why people buy. More recently, the focus has moved to include looking at consumption behaviour – in other words, how and why people consume.

Studying consumer behaviour is an interesting study not just for marketers, but even for non-marketers, because we are all consumers. Ultimately, consumers hold all the power in the business world – as Sam Walton, founder of WalMart, famously said:

There is only one boss – the customer. And he can fire everyone in the company, from the chairman on down, simply by spending his money somewhere else.

Walton always regarded himself as an agent for his customers, finding them the best value for money: this simple philosophy moved WalMart from one small store in Arkansas to being the world's largest 'bricks and morter' retailer within Walton's lifetime.

CONSUMER BEHAVIOUR IN CONTEXT

The fundamental basis for marketing thinking is that the customer (or consumer) should be at the centre of everything the firm does. While there may be some dissent about whether the marketing concept always applies, for marketers, customers are the key concern. This means that an understanding of how and why people make purchasing decisions is crucial to formulating a marketing plan.

In the first instance, purchasing behaviour relates strongly to how the market is segmented. The whole purpose of **segmentation** is to determine which potential buyers are most likely to behave favourably towards our organisation and its products and services: most segmentation methods bear at least some relationship to consumer behaviour issues.

Geographic segmentation breaks the market down according to the location in which the potential customers live. Where someone chooses to live, or is forced to live, is either an example of decision-making or dictates decision-making. Someone living in a cold climate is compelled to buy warm clothing, heating equipment, insulation products for the home, and so forth.

Psychographic segmentation and behavioural segmentation clearly relate very directly to consumer characteristics and behaviour. Psychographic segmentation is based on people's thought processes and attitudes – clearly the starting points for behaviour.

Behavioural segmentation is based on what people do – what hobbies they have, what foods they eat, how they travel, work and spend their spare time.

Demographic segmentation is based on consumers' wealth, age, gender and education levels (among other things), each of which relates directly to purchasing decisions. There is more on psychological factors involved with 'consumers as individuals' in Chapters 5 to 8, and more on attitude in Chapter 9.

Over a decade ago the idea of 'co-creation' was first proposed (Vargo and Lusch, 2004). The idea was that consumers are not simply users of value (and, by extension, destroyers of value as they use up products), but should instead be considered as co-creators of value (Vargo and Lusch, 2004). The thinking is that goods and services only have value when they are used – an electric drill has no value if it simply stays on the retailer's shelf, but it does create value when someone buys it and uses it. This perspective, known as **service-dominant logic** (S-DL), supposes that in fact all products are service products, since consumers are not buying a drill, nor are they buying holes, but are in fact buying a hole-drilling service for which they will provide some of the effort and therefore create some of the value. S-DL has a strong appeal – after all, someone who needs to drill a hole could (presumably) hire someone to come and drill the hole for them or could buy (or hire) a drill and do it themselves. The value created is much the same in each case, but the relative contributions by the consumer and the supplier are very different.

Segmentation
The act of dividing up a market into groups of people with similar needs

Geographic segmentation
Dividing a market into smaller groups based on location

Psychographic segmentation
Dividing a market according to the psychological profiles of potential customers

Behavioural segmentation
Dividing up a potential market according to the behaviour of its members

Demographic segmentation
Dividing up a market according to people's age, income and social standing

Service-dominant logic
The view that all value is co-created by the consumer and the supplier, and thus that all value can be considered as a service

UNDERSTANDING CONSUMER BEHAVIOUR

There are a great many conceptual implications involved in service-dominant logic, and academics continue to debate the practical implications for organisations (Gummesson et al., 2018; Haverila et al., 2022; Hietanen et al., 2018; Lindsey Hall et al., 2022; Nowicki et al., 2018). Nor have there been many topics in marketing which have met with such immediate popularity and critique as Vargo and Lusch's S-DL (Hietanen et al., 2018). However, there is certainly research supporting the idea that modern consumers are not prepared simply to accept what manufacturers provide for them, but instead seek to re-invent, add value and communicate new ideas to each other entirely independently of producers (Hewer and Brownlie, 2010; Kolyperas and Sparks, 2018).

CONSUMER BEHAVIOUR AND THE MARKETING MIX: A BRIEF INSIGHT

Marketing management has previously been considered to consist of *controlling* elements of the marketing mix (first developed by Booms and Bitner, 1981). Although the marketing mix has been widely criticised by academics because it tends to imply things being done *to* consumers rather than things being done *for* consumers, it is still widely taught and accepted because it offers a relatively simple way to understand what marketers do. Putting each element of the mix into a separate 'silo' is one way of simplifying the real world, but looked at from the consumer's viewpoint the distinctions between the elements may not be valid at all. For example, price is regarded as a cost from the consumer's viewpoint but might also be regarded as a promotion – a money-off special offer could be regarded as a major incentive to buy now rather than postpone the purchase. In other words, the seven Ps model may be fine for the marketers to understand but may not be appropriate from the consumer's viewpoint. Therefore Table 1.1 shows how consumer behaviour relates to the seven Ps model of the marketing mix.

Marketing mix
The combination of activities which creates an overall approach to the market

CONSUMERS, RELATIONSHIP MARKETING AND MARKETING PLANNING

Relationship marketing seeks to establish long-term relationships with customers rather than focusing on the single transaction. The differences between relationship marketing and transactional marketing are shown in Table 1.2.

Relationship marketing
Marketing in such a way as to generate a long-term partnership with customers

Transactional marketing
Marketing in which the marketer focuses on an individual sale, not on the long-term relationship with customers

TABLE 1.1 The seven Ps from a consumer behaviourist lens

Product	The bundle of benefits consumers acquire is the basis of their decision-making. Deciding which benefits are essential, which are desirable, which do not matter, and which are actually not benefits at all but drawbacks is the starting point for all rational decisions
Price	The cost of a product goes beyond the price tag in most cases. If the product is complex, there will be a learning cost attached to figuring out how to use it; if the product is dangerous, there may be a cost attached to consequent injury. If the product is visible to others, there may be an embarrassment cost. Some products require more effort to use – an electric can opener is easier to use than a hand-operated one, but costs more money. In some cases, these extra costs may exceed the price tag – consumers will take account of them, and will weigh them in the decision, but producers will only be able to obtain the price on the tag

(Continued)

TABLE 1.1 (Continued)

Place	Convenient locations for making purchases are essential; in fact it would not be too much to say that the easier marketers make it for consumers to find the product, the more product will be sold – this is partly why some brands pay a lot of money for their products to be displayed prominently in numerous retail outlets. Like price, the location can affect the decision in ways that do not benefit the producer – equally, producers can sometimes charge a premium for delivering location benefits. Corner shops (convenience stores) used to be a good example: although they are invariably more expensive than supermarkets, being within easy reach of home offers a clear advantage that is worth paying for. However, this level of advantage has not gone unnoticed by the big retailers who have, over the past few years, utilised their price advantage and muscled in on this turf by opening their smaller, local stores, for example 'Sainsbury's Local', 'Tesco Express', 'Little Waitrose'
Promotion	Promotion is not something that is done to consumers, it is something they consume. People surf the web, buy magazines, watch TV shows, go to the cinema and ride on public transport. Although they do not usually do these things in order to be exposed to advertisements, when bombarded with advertising, they usually pay at least some attention to them and frequently they enjoy the experience. Furthermore, people often use media such as classified advertisements and directories (offline and online) in an active search for information about goods they might like to buy
People	Business is not about money; it is about people. The people who run businesses and deal with the public need to understand how other people react in purchasing situations. In some cases, the product is the person: people, consumers, become loyal to the same hairdresser, the same doctor, the same restaurant chef. Unsurprisingly, the people who work with the customers – who are customer-facing – tend to be the most customer-orientated. Proximity to the customer is a more important factor in this than are the attitude and behaviour of senior management (Hui and Subramony, 2008). In other words, senior management may or may not be customer-orientated, but the very nature of working with customers will in itself tend to focus people on customer need
Process	The way in which services are delivered affects the context within which people buy as well as their propensity to buy. For example, a meal out might be a 10-minute lunch stop at a fast-food outlet, or it might be a prolonged, eight-course dinner for two in a Michelin-starred restaurant. The process is completely different in each case, and so is the price: in the first case, the consumer may only go through a limited problem-solving process; in the second case, the process may well be longer because the need to get it right is greater. This is called involvement (see definition on p.18)
Physical evidence	Physical aspects of the service encounter often relate to the pleasure one feels from receiving the service rather than the practical aspects. The surroundings and ambience of a restaurant, the food itself and the quality of the menus all affect people's perception of the 'whole' service

B2B
Business-to-business

B2C
Business-to-consumer

Establishing a relationship in a business-to-business (B2B) context turns out to be a great deal easier than establishing a relationship in a business-to-consumer (B2C) context (see Chapter 3 for more on organisational buyer behaviour). The reasons for this may include the following:

1. Businesses change their needs less often than do consumers.
2. There are fewer suppliers and customers in B2B markets.
3. B2B transactions almost always involve the personal relationships that seek engagement from the organisation, its salespeople and the buyers, whereas B2C relationships are often impersonal, since people often buy goods online or in self-service stores.
4. The possibilities for mutual advantage in establishing relationships are often much greater in a B2B context.

Relationship marketing is firmly rooted in the basic idea that it is cheaper to retain an existing customer than to recruit a new one. Prior research (conventional wisdom) advocates a positive, linear association between relationship investments and relationship performance. Jayanti (2021) examines consumer evaluations of institutional context as a moderator for the trust–loyalty relationship. Luu et al. (2018) have challenged the aforementioned conventional wisdom and advance the extant literature by investigating the potential curvilinear effects of suppliers' different relationship marketing programmes (i.e. social, financial and structural). But whilst there is still a certain appeal to this idea of 'relationship investments and relationship performance', acquiring new customers is a difficult business, whereas keeping someone on board should only be a matter of making sure their needs are continuously met and perhaps occasionally exceeded. In consumer markets, this is a great deal harder than it sounds. As shown in Figure 1.2, consumer needs change relatively rapidly: the needs of someone aged 18 are likely to change dramatically by the time they are 25, and again by age 40. Likewise, a couple who have just had a baby together will find that their needs are perhaps not as urgent as their baby's, quite apart from the probable change in their spending pattern which will bring its own financial needs and requirements. Second, there is a great deal more choice as regards suppliers in consumer markets, leading to a great many more ways to spend one's money. People can easily be tempted away from their existing supplier and towards a new supplier. Third, with greater choice provided by the internet and so many tempting offers around, suppliers need to ask themselves the crucial question – 'What is the incentive for my consumers to remain loyal to me?' Providing an extra-nice service is just not enough.

TABLE 1.2 Transactional marketing vs. relationship marketing

Transactional marketing	Relationship marketing
Focus on single sale	Focus on customer retention
Orientation on product features	Orientation on product benefits
Short timescale	Long timescale
Little emphasis on customer service	High emphasis on customer service
Limited customer commitment	High customer commitment
Moderate customer contact	High customer contact
Quality is the concern of the production department	Quality is the concern of all

Source: Christopher et al. (1991).

Macro-environmental factors *Micro-environmental factors*

- Needs change slowly
- Transactions involve personal contact between buyers and salespeople
- Fewer suppliers and customers
- Greater possibilities for mutual benefit

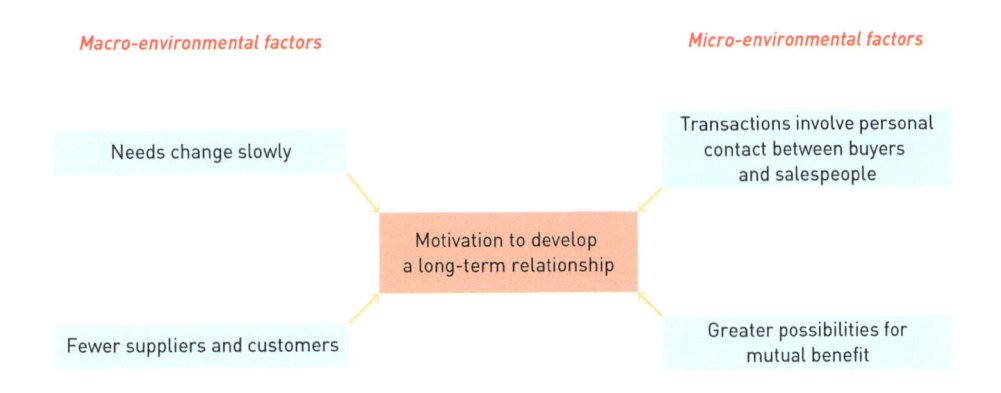

Motivation to develop a long-term relationship

FIGURE 1.2 Businesses and relationship marketing

People generally have become much more aware of marketing and marketers (Adams et al., 2018; Arora and Kumar, 2018; Genoveva, 2022). There is now a much greater understanding of the marketing techniques used to influence the buyer's decision-making process (Kanwal et al., 2022; Kemp et al., 2018), and consequently a greater distrust of marketers (Jones and Taylor, 2018). This distrust is also visible in B2B markets (Schmitz et al., 2022). There is evidence that this alienation of consumers is linked to the use of new technology – the internet allows consumers to take control of the exchange process in a way that has been impossible in the past, and thus they are able to take over some of the role of marketers in managing exchange (Huang et al., 2021; Mady, 2011; Mittendorf, 2018).

Relationship marketing has become closely associated with direct marketing, simply because the best way to establish a relationship with a customer is to have direct dealings (Kim and Kumar, 2018; Minguez and Javier Sese, 2022). Unfortunately, direct marketing has also become associated with other forms of marketing communication – unsolicited direct mail and direct telephone marketing, both of which are extremely unpopular with the public in general; this is probably another reason why relationship marketing is less successful with consumers than with industrial buyers.

Understanding how people create and maintain relationships in their personal lives is obviously useful when considering how people create and maintain business relationships. Businesses are not about profits: they are about people, which goes some way towards explaining the explosion and impact of social enterprise (Arora et al., 2021).

CRITICAL REFLECTION

If businesses are about people, why is it that companies consistently report their successes and failures in financial terms? Why not report on how pleased our customers are with the experience, or on how loyal they are? Why not report on how many customers recommended us to their friends?

Or would it be too difficult to do these things? How do we know whether people are recommending us anyway? The market researchers should be able to find out. Actually it's just a different perspective on 'reporting' the numbers. But while it's obviously easier just to count up the money coming in, just a little more use of data analytics could help us to identify how the numbers translate into customers. For example, the UK Customer Satisfaction Index helps organisations to 'benchmark customer satisfaction results with industry peers and best-in-class companies' (www.instituteofcustomerservice.com/research-insight/ukcsi/). What this means for marketers is that they can link their company's market strength and financial performance with the various drivers of satisfaction and loyalty, and report on what businesses are actually about – people!

Marketing planning is the process of defining activities that will support business goals and establishing a timeline for when that work will be completed.

Marketing planning has often been considered in terms of managing the product/service portfolio, developing new offerings, launching products, managing the product life cycle, and so forth. This involves planning communications that explain the features and benefits of an organisation's offerings and seek to persuade consumers to buy from them. It involves deciding which channels of distribution should be used and what price will provide the organisation with a good return on its investment.

This way of looking at marketing suffers from a serious flaw in that it is not customer-centric; it is very firm-centric. Suppose we were to act in a completely customer-centred manner. We would then be seeking to manage the customer portfolio, considering which customers (or groups of customers) we can serve profitably and which we cannot. We would consider which marketing communications would appeal most to the groups we want to keep, and which would be off-putting to the groups we want to lose. We might consider the customer's life cycle rather than the product's life cycle, and consider price in terms of what consumers will think is fair. For example, Denmark's largest bank, Danske Bank, has an interesting way of being customer-centric. They have really understood what appeals to today's banking customers and have developed a variety of product and service offerings to meet their needs. Danske Bank has used innovative digital solutions to ensure that their marketing planning takes account of the things that matter to their customers. They provide a graphic, real-time overview of their customers' spend using a variety of formats – e-banking, tablet and mobile banking. The importance of the smartphone is taken into account with apps such as MobilePay and MPesa (Bounfour, 2018), which enable business customers to receive payments from their customers via smartphone. One of the biggest gripes that banking customers have today, especially business customers, is that their bank managers are inaccessible and therefore it's difficult to develop a relationship. So Danske Bank's 'online meeting' tools enable customers to 'meet' their bank representatives at a time and place that suits both the customer and the bank. In addition to that, Danske Bank is also making strides as an environmentally friendly organisation and was recently awarded the Environmental Leadership award at the 2021 Responsible Business Awards.

CRITICAL REFLECTION

Can we really let consumers run the business? After all, if we ask people what they are willing to pay for a product, they are likely to pitch the price as low as they think they can get away with. The same applies to services – many people want a lot of value but are only prepared to pay a little for it!

Not to mention the competitive nature of the race. As one organisation offers one level of service, everyone else must, at the very least, match it, if not exceed it. Does this mean that before long we get to a point where we are grovelling to the customers?

For example, in France one would never argue with the chef. If one likes one's steak well done, the waiter will suggest the idea to the chef, but after muttering something about 'Les sales anglais!' the chef will produce a steak which looks as if it needs a bandage. Contrast this with America, where the customer tells the chef exactly what to put in and leave out of the food: 'No salt, hold the mayo, just a little tabasco', and so forth. No doubt the American chef is much more customer-centred, but aren't we, as the customers, paying for his expertise? What's the point of going to a restaurant

(Continued)

where we have a trained chef with years of experience, and then second-guessing the guy? Should restaurants move to providing bespoke, 'customized menus' (Lu and Chi, 2018; Park and Kang, 2022) for their customers? Can the customer be trusted to know what is best for them? After all, doctors and lawyers don't expect people to know what is best for their health or legal well-being. So where is customer-centrality really located? In France, or in America?

Marketing strategies should therefore not only seek to influence consumers, but they should also be influenced by them. Marketing planning for a consumer-led future means putting consumer behaviour at the centre of the firm's thinking. In the world that we live in today, it is the consumer who holds the power: there is evidence that people consider their spending power to be a form of voting, a way of expressing approval for what the supplier is offering (Anker et al., 2021; Shaw et al., 2006). Indeed, work by Anker et al. (2021) explores consumer dominance in social marketing by investigating the active and primary role in a range of mainstream marketing processes such as branding, product development and sales. We've seen this around the world with how people (through an increased literacy education and the production of capital) influence the political world (Luke, 2018). People are aware that they have choice: at first, when choice became widespread, people might have found this confusing and daunting, but as time has gone on people have found it empowering, and they do not hesitate to use their power (Davies and Elliott, 2006; Kirschen and Strbac, 2018). This newfound power in the hands of consumers is what has been referred to as 'consumers-to-business' (C2B) (Malik and Raheja, 2018; Pollák et al., 2022; Shankar et al., 2022; Urban et al., 2000).

For example, consumer research might show that a specific group of our customers is more profitable than another simply because they are more loyal. This means that we do not need to recruit new customers to replace those who drop out, which is substantially cheaper. We might therefore seek a) to ensure that we continue to retain these customers, and b) try to find more like them. Their loyalty comes from their purchase behaviour – their propensity to repeat purchases on a regular basis – which in itself may be a function of their personalities and the degree of their involvement with the products/services.

ANTECEDENTS OF CONSUMER BEHAVIOUR

It is really important for you, my reader, to understand that the study of consumer behaviour is, like marketing itself, a combination of other disciplines. As a study,

---

C2B
Consumers-to-business

Loyalty
The degree to which an individual will repeat purchase of a product

Involvement
The degree to which an individual is attracted to, and defined by, a product, service or brand

it draws its basic theories and research approaches from sociology, psychology, anthropology, economics and neuroscience. Academics aim to develop a body of specifically consumer-based research, but the influence of the other disciplines will always be at the forefront of the theory that develops, as shown in Figure 1.3.

All of these areas will be discussed in much greater detail throughout the book, but a quick overview of the basic contributions of each discipline should be helpful in understanding how consumer behaviour has developed as an academic study.

PSYCHOLOGY

Psychology is the study of mental processes. Psychologists study the ways people think, which is of course basic to understanding how people think about the products and services they buy. This includes learning about products/services, developing an overall perception of those items (as well as their associated brands) and fitting it into one's overall perception of the world, and the basic drives that encourage people to seek solutions for their needs.

Psychology
The scientific study of the human mind and its functions, including behaviour

Each of the contributions made by psychologists (as shown in Figure 1.4) will be covered in more detail in Part Two of this book, but for the time being here is a brief overview of the main issues.

DRIVE AND MOTIVATION

Drives are the basic forces that make us want to do things (see Chapter 5). A drive is created when the desired state of the individual is different from the actual state: the greater the difference, the stronger the drive. A drive that has a definite target becomes a **motivation**. Part of the marketer's job is to encourage drives to develop by encouraging shifts in the desired state (it is pretty much impossible to develop shifts in the actual state). The other part of the marketer's job is to direct drives towards a specific target. For example, a marketer might encourage a shift in the desired state by saying 'Isn't it about time you bought yourself a more luxurious but eco-friendly car?' and follow this by asking 'Why not treat yourself (and the planet!) to a new Tesla Model S?'

Drive
The basic force of motivation, which arises when the individual's actual state diverges from the desired state

Motivation
The internal force which encourages people to act in specific ways

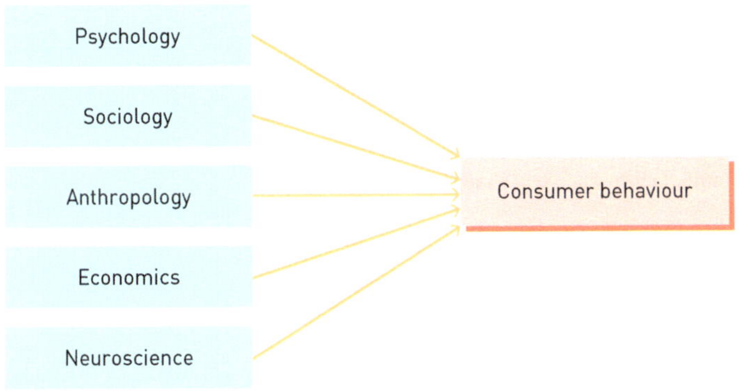

FIGURE 1.3 Antecedents of studying consumer behaviour

GOALS AND INCENTIVES

Goals
Specific targets towards which consumption behaviour is directed

Incentives
Reasons for action

A **goal** is the rational element of motivation (see Chapter 5). Motives are largely emotional: goals are the rationalisation of a motivation. For example, someone might decide that they really want to learn to fly an unmanned aerial vehicle (UAV, also known as a 'drone') – a largely emotional motivation at the moment, based on reading technology magazines or on an unspecified emotion. The goals that derive from this might be concerned with finding an appropriate CAA-registered flying school, saving up the money to pay for lessons, and/or freeing up the time to learn to fly it. The **incentive** for achieving these various goals is the satisfaction of the need (and also the fact that drones are finding their way into all aspects of our lives! [Bauer et al., 2021; Kumar, 2018; Royo-Vela and Black, 2020]).

PERSONALITY AND SELF-CONCEPT

Personality
Those factors which make up the individual's mental processes

Self-concept
The belief one has about oneself

Personality is a combination of the various traits that determine who we are (see Chapter 6). The type of person we are dictates what we like and what we dislike, our preferred ways of dealing with our consumption problems, our preferred lifestyles and so forth. **Self-concept** is about how we see ourselves – this includes how we see ourselves in terms of consumption patterns, branding and other consumption-based aspects. For example, we each have preferred brands, which we feel reflect and express our own personalities. Some of us are Mercedes drivers, for some of us it's Ford; some of us wear Converse footwear while others prefer Nike; and of course, there is the perennial argument about which football team should be in the Premier League. What we buy and wear (and who we support) expresses who we are.

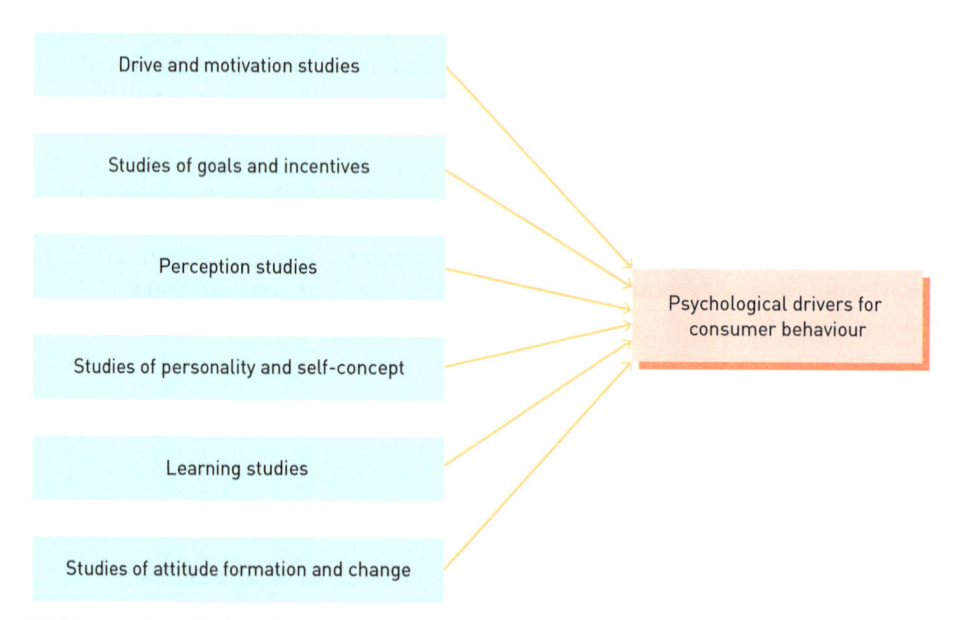

FIGURE 1.4 Contributions from psychology

- Drive and motivation studies
- Studies of goals and incentives
- Perception studies
- Studies of personality and self-concept
- Learning studies
- Studies of attitude formation and change

→ Psychological drivers for consumer behaviour

PERCEPTION

Perception
The process of creating a mental 'map' of reality

Perception is about the way we make sense of the world (see Chapter 7). Each of us has a particular view of the world, a perceptual map, which enables us to make sense of what is happening around us. We assemble this map by taking in information through our senses and using it to develop an understanding of how the world works and where different things fit into it. Psychologists study the ways in which people sometimes filter out unnecessary information, or conversely group information together into useable 'chunks' and arrange the information to create the perceptual map. Marketers are interested in these processes in order to ensure that their brand is mapped into the most effective place in the consumers' perceptions.

The word perception is often used to mean 'untrue' but in fact this is not the case. The only truth we have is what we hold in our minds, so a person's perceptual map *is* the truth for that person. Even though we each have different perceptual maps, they are near enough to each other for us to be able to communicate and cooperate.

LEARNING

Learning is the behavioural changes that result from experience (see Chapter 8) and you won't be surprised to learn that this is not a new concept. One of the earliest references to this can be found in the *Nichomachean Ethics* in around 350 BCE, where it is reported that Aristotle wrote, 'for the things we have to learn before we can do them, we learn by doing them'. This has been referred to as 'experiential learning' and defined as 'learning through reflection on doing' (Felicia, 2011; Stein, 2018). In turn, how we learn is critical to marketing communications, because marketers want people to remember the messages and act upon them in ways that are favourable to the organisation.

Learning
Changes in behaviour that are a result of experience

ATTITUDE FORMATION AND CHANGE

Attitudes consist of knowledge, feelings and proposed behaviour (see Chapter 9). An attitude is a tendency to behave in a consistent manner towards a given stimulus: in other words, people tend to react the same way every time towards something about which they have an attitude. For marketers, understanding how attitudes are formed and how they can be changed is useful in creating appropriate attitudes towards brands, products and services. Sometimes attitudes need to be demolished and rebuilt if the brand is to continue successfully. An example of this is the negative attitudes held about the car marque Skoda from the Czech Republic. Since the early 1970s the brand was suffering from a steady decline in attitudes towards its image, largely due to poor workmanship and outdated design. The Volkswagen Group took over in the early 1990s and Skoda became a part of their family of brands. However, the negative image was difficult to change and every time the word Skoda was mentioned in conversation, it would be a subject for humour. Volkswagen naturally considered changing the brand name, but research conducted among the UK public found that the name had a 100% brand recall. Whether this was positive or negative recall was not the point – very few brands enjoy a 100% brand recall. Skoda decided that it wasn't the name, but the attitudes of the people that needed to change. With the launch of their new car, the Fabia, they instigated a campaign that tackled this attitude head on by challenging consumers to sit up, take notice and be impressed by what they saw. So, the central message in their marketing communications revolved around 'It's so good that you won't believe it's a Skoda'. This triggered a positive change in sales, considerations, image and above all attitude.

Attitudes
A propensity to respond in a consistent manner to a given stimulus or object

Psychology is not the only behavioural science, however. It is mainly concerned with the individual, but human beings are herd animals: we operate in groups. In prehistoric times, being part of a group meant the difference between surviving and not surviving: even today, people who do not fit in with one or more groups usually lead unhappy lives, and there is medical evidence to suggest that they do not live as long as other people either (Kail and Cavanaugh, 2018). The behaviour of people in groups is the province of sociology.

SOCIOLOGY

Group behaviour is crucial to human beings, and therefore is crucial to understanding what motivates people to buy specific brands. Buying the wrong brand can be embarrassing: we are all aware of how, in our early teens, we have to have the right label on clothing, engage with the right apps, use the right terminology/language, see the right films and stream the right music from Spotify to fit in with the desired group. Adolescent rebellion is actually just a drive to join a group of other like-minded individuals. The contributions from sociology are shown in Figure 1.5 and described below: the following topics will be covered in much greater detail in Part Three of the book when we examine consumers as social actors.

REFERENCE GROUPS

People identify groups they would like to join, and also groups they would prefer not to be associated with (see Chapter 10). Almost all such groups involve some type of consumption: clothing to wear, things to use in the group activities, or shared consumption of group-owned items. Most of us define ourselves at least in part by the groups we belong to, whether it is our work group, our group of friends, our family group, our religious group or our group hobbies.

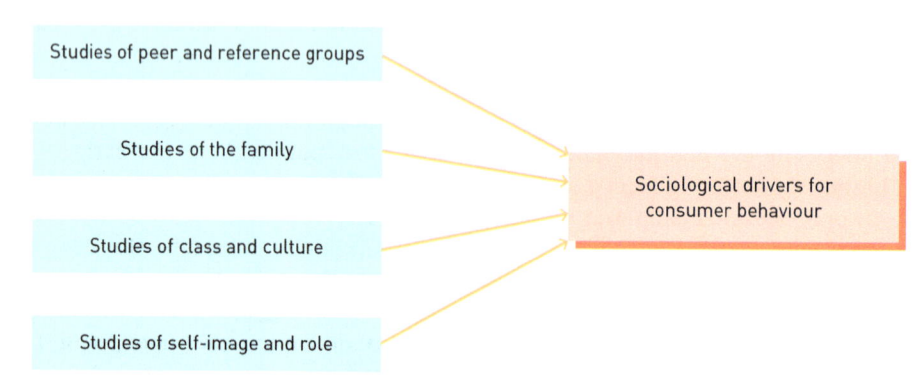

FIGURE 1.5 Contributions from sociology

Family
A group of people who exhibit shared consumption and who are bound by ties of genetic relationship or adoption

FAMILY

The **family** is probably the most important reference group because it exerts the most influence on us (see Chapter 11). Families share consumption of many things (food, housing, energy, thinking, beliefs, etc.) and our early upbringing greatly influences our behaviour in later years.

CULTURE AND SOCIAL MOBILITY

Culture is the set of beliefs and behaviours that distinguishes one large group of people from another, and it includes such issues as religious beliefs, language, customs, class distinctions and accepted norms of behaviour. For marketers, culture is one of the driving forces of behaviour, including consumption behaviour (and we investigate this in more detail in Chapter 12), but perhaps more importantly it is a minefield in which communications and brands can cause offence to people from other cultural backgrounds. In particular, religious beliefs can create problems for marketers since people are often inflexible about religious taboos or restrictions.

Culture
The set of beliefs, behaviour, customs and attitudes that are common to a large group of people

SELF-IMAGE AND ROLE

The images we form of ourselves are almost entirely derived from feedback from other people (see Chapter 6). This feedback is derived in turn from the images we project as part of our role in life, both offline and online. In fact, we each perform many roles in our dealings with others: as friends, work colleagues, children, fathers, mothers, professionals and so forth. We judge ourselves as being good at each of these roles by the feedback of the people we deal with every day. So, this begs a question of the current, digitally savvy population – is the only way one can know if one has good friends by the likes one gets on a recently posted selfie?

Role
The place one has within a group

Likes
An online widget for expressing positive feeling towards a visual or a statement that someone has uploaded

People often define themselves, at least in part, by the products they consume (Kanungo et al., 2022; Tangsupwattana and Liu, 2018). Possessions become an extension of the individual – an extended self – and thus project who the person is to others (Hanley et al., 2022; Mittal, 2006). Indeed, many acts of consumption are tribal and role-supporting, even when they do not define the self (Miliopoulou, 2021; Ryan et al., 2006).

Selfie
A photograph that one has taken of oneself with a smartphone or webcam and shared via social media

ANTHROPOLOGY

Anthropology is a wide-ranging academic discipline, covering everything that makes us human. Anthropology is all about the study of people (human beings) as a whole, from the past and present; and from small, isolated homogeneous cultures to large social networks. Of course, the journey of human evolution that has taken place over the past two millennia is an extremely complex one and thus anthropology draws its knowledge from a number of related spheres – socio-cultural, physical and biological sciences, as well as the humanities. The relationship to consumer behaviour thus, accordingly, comes from a variety of anthropological perspectives. First and foremost are the socio-cultural aspects of anthropology. Meaning is derived from how people live and therefore what they consume. Closer scrutiny of the similarities and differences in gender, race, nationality and class all provide further clues as to the 'meaning of life' for various consumers. These data help organisations to provide consumers with products and services related to a variety of sectors, including health, education, environment, agriculture and social change. Second, it is the biological and cultural processes which together shape growth, development and behaviour; behaviour that has led humans to adapt to the diverse environments within which they live, work and consume. Cognitive anthropology has been used to study the problem-solving behaviour of green consumers (Auriffeille, 2021; Wagner-Tsukamoto and Tadajewski, 2006). Interestingly, a natural extension of anthropology is now being examined by some UK universities in the form of 'digital anthropology': proposed theoretically as a method by Boellstorff (2012), it is the study of collective lives online or using digital channels (Miller and Horst, 2012; Miller and Wang, 2021).

ECONOMICS

Economics is the study of demand. Economists study demand in the individual transaction, at the level of the firm and its customers (*micro-economics*), and also the overall level of demand in the economy (*macro-economics*). Although micro-economics appears at first sight to explain consumer behaviour, in fact, it only really explains *rational* behaviour. Economists consider such concepts as utility, value for money and **economic choice**, not such nebulous ideas as whether one's friends will admire one's new outfit through social media likes.

Economics has provided consumer behaviour theorists with a number of useful concepts that help to explain the rational side of consumer behaviour, and it's worth highlighting a couple of them here in this introduction as their relationship to consumer behaviour is quite insightful.

THE ECONOMIC CHOICE

This simply means that someone cannot spend money on something if he or she has already spent the money somewhere else. So consumers have a choice: a choice of what to spend their money on. This implies that all companies are competing with all other companies for the consumer's money: people have only a certain amount of money they can spend or commit to borrowing. Of course, economic choice is somewhat blurred by the wide availability of credit. People can be persuaded to borrow the money to buy whatever they want, which means that factors other than money may come into the equation. The theory of *choice* still holds true, though, if we consider the economic choice of how we spend our time, or how we use other resources such as our cars or our homes. The theory really talks about use of limited resources in aiming to satisfy one's needs.

Marketers have certainly taken on board the concept of the economic choice, broadening out the spectrum of competitors to include anyone who aims to satisfy similar needs in consumers. Take, for example, cinema owners. They recognise a wide range of other entertainment places as competitors (live theatre, casinos, online films/gaming and bowling alleys, among others) and in recent years have developed *entertainment complexes* where a variety of leisure activities can take place under one roof. This is not just an example of a deeper understanding of who the competition is; it is also an example of how an organisation can help people make the best use of limited leisure time. With time as the constraining variable, such complexes can make best use of economic choice theory. Bringing this argument to more recent times, we know that in a post-Covid world, cinemas are now also suffering and are on the verge of demise (Kelner, 2022; Major, 2022).

Economics
The study of demand

Economic choice
The choice made when one is unable to afford to buy both alternatives

ELASTICITY OF DEMAND

We have already established that demand is a model of consumer behaviour. It attempts to identify the factors that influence the choices that are made by consumers. In neoclassical micro-economics, the objective of the consumer is to maximise the utility that can be derived given their preferences, income, the prices of related goods and the price of the good for which the demand function is derived. So, the next natural step in this economic theory is to ask 'How far can an organisation stretch its price point before the demand for that product or service snaps?' Although a rise in prices generally means a reduction in demand (there are some exceptions – most notably fuel and energy), there is a question about the degree to which demand is affected by price. In some cases, a rise in price appears to make very little difference to demand (*inelastic demand*) – salt is the example usually given for this, because it is extremely cheap (and therefore a tiny percentage of a person's income), has no real substitutes and is purchased quite infrequently, so even a doubling of the price would probably go unnoticed. Other products fall into this category: a rise in the cost of water bills doesn't mean that people will disconnect their water supply, and if a commuter relies on a particular train route to get to work, a rise in the fare will usually only result in a very small decrease in demand, as the alternative modes of transport may be very limited. The opposite of these scenarios is where the price directly affects demands (*elastic demand*). Some fast-moving consumer goods (FMCG) seem to be dramatically affected by even small changes in price: this usually happens if there is a close substitute available, for example if the price of beef rose relative to the price of lamb. In these circumstances, price calculations need to be carried out extremely carefully as a mistake could result in a dramatic loss of business.

FMCG
Fast-moving consumer goods, also known as consumer packaged goods (CPG), are products that are sold quickly and at a relatively low cost

There are elasticities other than price. For example, income elasticity of demand tells us that some products are affected by increases in the individual's spending money. In some cases, this will produce an increase in demand – as people become richer, they are likely to buy more clothes and more entertainment products, for example; or as people become more environmentally conscious, there may be an increase in the number of electric vehicles being sold. In other cases, the demand for an individual product might reduce as people become wealthier: a higher income might lead someone to buy a more luxurious brand of automobile, say a Mercedes, rather than a Ford. In some cases, a general rise in income reduces demand fairly dramatically, and the humble bread is an example. As people become richer, there is a tendency to buy less bread and eat more meat and vegetables instead. In recent years, rising standards of living in emerging economies such as China and India have led to steep rises in the cost of many foods, globally, as people in those countries are able to afford more meat and vegetables, and thus do not rely as much on cheap, staple foods such as rice and bread.

Figure 1.6 shows an elastic demand curve. Here the demand for the product is affected greatly by the price – even a small increase in price has a fairly profound effect on the demand for the product.

FIGURE 1.6 Elastic demand curve

Elasticity
The degree to which demand is affected by other factors, for example price changes

One point that arises from the elasticity concept is that there is no product that has a completely inelastic demand curve. In other words, there is no product that has a demand curve that is entirely unaffected by price. This means that there is no product that is an absolute necessity of life – if this were the case, the producer could charge anything at all for the product and people would have no choice but to pay, since the alternative would be death. This is an important issue for marketers, because it shows us that there is no theoretical basis for considering some products as necessities and other products as luxuries. The difference exists only in the minds of consumers. To some people, a car would be a luxury; to others it is a necessity. Likewise, water might be considered as a necessity of life, yet some people rarely (if ever) drink just plain water: they drink tea, beer, fruit juice, cola or any one of many different products containing water, all of which are substitutes for the plain and simple tap water.

NEUROSCIENCE

Neuroscience is the study of the ways in which the human brain works. A sub-branch of the discipline, neuro-economics, is the fusion of neuroscience and economics. This field of study analyses the relationship between the internal organisation of the brain and an individual's behaviour (Chavaglia et al., 2015). In other words, it seeks to explain an individual's economic behaviour in terms of the part played by the physiological makeup of the brain in individual decision-making, the social interaction that an individual has (online and offline), and then finally on other external factors like the market within which the individual makes the resulting economic decisions.

Neuroscience
The study of the ways in which the human brain works

Adaptation
The process by which goals are influenced by contextual issues

Neuroscientists, and especially evolutionary neuroscientists, see the brain as the result of a long series of evolutionary adaptations leading to a set of domain-specific computational systems. These systems have evolved to solve recurring problems – originally these problems were characterised by survival problems (finding food, evading predators, cooperating with tribe members and so forth) and reproduction problems (finding a suitable mate, protection and feeding of children and so forth). These problem-solving systems act to adapt behaviour in order to improve the individual's chances of surviving, prospering and reproducing (Garcia and Saad, 2008). In the modern world, the same systems are applied to apparently new problems – career progression, financial management, learning to operate a smartphone and many other tasks that did not exist when our ancestors evolved on the African savannah.

Evolution is, in general, a very slow process, and in the case of human beings it has been further hindered by our dominance of the environment: people are less likely to make fatal mistakes and thus remove themselves from the gene pool.

If neuro-economics can successfully map brain activity onto economic behaviour (Dennison et al., 2022), then neuroscientists hope to explain consumer behaviour in terms of evolutionary and survival factors. As yet the discipline is in its infancy, but neuroscientists have already identified some of the mechanisms by which people are affected by packaging (Stoll et al., 2008), and have also identified a dedicated response to celebrity-based advertising (Gakhal and Senior, 2008). Work on neuro-economics has also recently been extended to looking at the irrationality of the voter during political elections (Chavaglia et al., 2015) and our understanding of human responses to climate change (Sawe and Chawla, 2021).

SUMMARY

Consumer decision-making is therefore not isolated from all other human behaviour. People try to behave in ways that enable them to enjoy their lives, to relate to their friends and families, and to contribute to society at large. In almost all cases this behaviour is likely to involve consumption of products and services produced by other people: this is the province of consumer behaviour.

Consumer behaviour studies derive from many different academic disciplines, as well as from direct studies by marketing academics. As a field of study, it has an appeal to most of us because it is, after all, about people. For marketing practitioners, understanding the ways in which people make decisions about their purchasing behaviour is clearly of crucial importance in planning almost every aspect of managing the exchange process.

KEY POINTS

- The study of consumer behaviour is largely derived from other disciplines.
- Consumer behaviour is at the centre of all marketing decision-making.
- Relationships are harder to establish in business-to-consumer situations than in business-to-business situations.
- Psychology is about internal thought processes; sociology is about behaviour within groups.
- Neuroscience is the study of the ways in which the human brain works; anthropology is the study of what makes us human.
- Economics is the study of demand.
- Exchange always makes both parties better off.
- 'Luxury' and 'necessity' are subjective terms: they have no objective reality.

HOW TO IMPRESS YOUR EXAMINER

Relate your answers to the real world. Use examples – this shows that you understand the theory and can put it into a business context. While you are reading the book, try to think of examples of your own – everybody else will know the examples from the book, the examiner included!

REVIEW QUESTIONS

1. Given that we have established that demand is a model of consumer behaviour, how might marketers use this knowledge to affect consumer choices?
2. Would you expect salt to have an inelastic demand curve, or an elastic demand curve? Why?
3. If a product has an inelastic demand curve, what does that imply for marketers?
4. If a product has an elastic demand curve, what are the implications for marketers?
5. How might group behaviour affect purchasing behaviour?
6. Why does exchange always make both parties better off?
7. What is the importance of the concept of perception to marketers?
8. Why is learning important to marketers?
9. Why are customers more important to a firm than, say, employees?

CASE STUDY: CONSUMER BEHAVIOUR IN BRITAIN: PAST AND PRESENT

Back in 2016 the UK voted to leave the European Union! After a relationship that was started back in 1972 by the then Prime Minister Edward Heath, in 2016 51% of voters opted to leave... also known as **Brexit**. But this relationship had been about more than just trade to satisfy consumer demand and the eventual unshackling of bureaucratic chains leading to a free trade policy. Whether it's 'free' trade or a contractual trade agreement, what we know is that trade itself is an important tool with which countries and the world have always functioned in order to satisfy the consumerist needs that their populations have. Let's go back in history. Even in prehistoric times people traded with each other. In the English Lake District a stone axe factory was discovered in the 1930s: the factory, dating from around 4000 BC, produced axes for trade. The axes were sold throughout the UK and Ireland, and some were found as far away as the south of France.

By Phoenician times, trade had increased dramatically. Around 700 BC, Phoenician traders plied the Mediterranean in sophisticated merchant ships, exchanging

Brexit

Merges the words Britain and exit, and is used to signify Britain's exit from the EU sandalwood, cedar, pine, fine linen, wine, salt and dried figs for raw materials such as ivory, papyrus, silk, amber, ostrich eggs and metals. It was the Phoenicians who introduced wine into Egypt, and some successful Phoenician merchants had as many as 50 ships. Naturally, they guarded their trade routes jealously, so they had a military navy to protect their merchant vessels. Phoenician traders also engaged in cross-trade, buying spices and silk from the Far East from Arab caravans and selling them on into Greece and Spain. Some scholars say that the Phoenicians ventured out of the Mediterranean to Britain and even the Americas in search of new trade opportunities. But by far the greatest empire was that developed and conquered by the Persians, from a humble start in what we now know as Southern Iran. From the 6th century BCE onwards, the Persians dominated the neighbouring lands from as far east as the Himalayas to the shores of the Aegean Sea and Egypt. They had a very welcoming attitude towards new ideas and practices, and were very willing to adapt their own. In fact, Herodotus once wrote, 'The Persians are greatly inclined to adopt foreign customs.' Of course, such a vast empire would need a very slick administrative system, and indeed the Persians had designed one together with a road network that spanned more than 1600 miles. Nevertheless, the swiftness of their operations meant that they were able to transmit messages across this range (Human Rights Watch, 2014). This was also largely due to the fact that the people in charge were highly educated, and meticulously detailed with their recording of data – which we would today refer to as 'big data' – administrative details, payments to workers, information on quality of products, quantity of goods being bought and sold, maintenance and repair schedules, and strategic planning.

In Roman times, the demand for exotic animals for the Coliseum shows meant that traders had to capture and ship wild animals from Africa. Giraffes, hippos, rhinoceroses and lions were all rounded up and shipped across the Mediterranean. The trade grew so much that it led to the extinction of the Libyan lion. (The Romans' environmental record was poor at best – they also created the Sahara Desert by over-farming.)

By the 16th century trade was becoming worldwide. Better ships (mainly being built in India by Persian migrants called Parsees), better navigation and the need to find new markets led to a rapid expansion of exploration – the Far East and the Americas became accessible to European ships in search of precious metals, jewels, spices and exotic foods such as tea, coffee, potatoes and tomatoes. Trade within Europe became taxed and regulated, leading to widespread smuggling: governments sought to protect their own industries and farmers by imposing heavy taxes on imports, but even this could not prevent trade. In India, the Parsee merchants became a valuable 'conduit' between Britain and the Far East, along the Silk Route. In Britain, wine and brandy were smuggled in from France, while cotton and wool were smuggled into France from Britain. This two-way trade had to exist since there was no way of converting French money into British money, except as gold.

During the late 18th and early 19th century, Britain had a near-monopoly on industrial, mass-produced goods. British factories could produce far more than the domestic market could consume, so the surplus was exported. Since factory-produced goods were vastly cheaper than their hand-made equivalents, there were large profits to be made from international trade. In this case, Britain built an empire on the basis of trading manufactured goods for raw materials. As other European countries industrialised, further tariff barriers were erected, restricting trade;

(Continued)

after the First World War, these barriers became extremely onerous, to the point where trade became almost impossible and industry stagnated throughout Europe. The Second World War changed things again, catastrophically; when the war was over, France and Germany agreed the first of the trade agreements which would eventually result in the creation of the European Union.

Currently, trade between the member states of the EU is without barriers (apart from a very few exceptions). Virtually anything that can be sold in one member state can be sold in any other, and there is free movement of people and capital as well.

Following the invocation of 'Article 50 of the Lisbon Treaty' (the formal legal process of withdrawal), there has been much political, social and economic unrest both in the UK and in mainland Europe. It centres partly on Britain's place in the world's largest market becoming a little unsteady. Sterling (the British currency) fell sharply initially but has recovered, trading markets like the FTSE have reacted with steep fluctuations, racial tensions have increased in various communities up and down the country, and the leading political parties have many internal splits. In the spirit of preserving both the integrity of the EU and the interests of the remaining countries, Brussels has understandably already sidelined Britain. 'Economies of scale' may no longer apply as Britain will have to negotiate many bilateral trade deals with individual countries. Part of the problem is that prior to the referendum, no one had set out any guiding principles for negotiations with the rest of the EU, and the UK continues to struggle with developing an outline framework for what these guiding principles should or will look like.

whole_world_land_oceans_12000.jpg licensed with PD-US Gov-NASA

The bottom line is that both the collegiality with our EU neighbours and the subsequent trade in Europe has made us wealthy, not just financially but in the broadest sense of the word. However, the referendum has also given all of us a lot more to think about. After nearly four millennia of trading with our closest neighbours, our lives may have been richer and we have greater wealth (all through consumer choices and trade), but Britain's future and indeed the future of the EU are now uncertain and insecure.

No sooner had the UK got to grips with the impact of Brexit than we collectively faced the surprise global pandemic of the coronavirus disease (Covid-19): an infectious disease caused by the SARS-CoV-2 virus. This effectively brought the entire world to a standstill with many countries going into '**lockdown**' mode in order to prevent further spread of the virus. The Office for National Statistics (ONS, 2022) in the UK reported that around three in ten adults (29%) across Great Britain reported always or often maintaining social distancing when meeting up with people outside their household. Homeworking in the UK more than doubled during the pandemic. In February 2022, more than three-quarters (77%) of those who worked from home at some point

Lockdown
A restriction policy for people, community or a country to stay where they are, usually due to specific risks (such as Covid-19) that could possibly harm people if they move and interact freely

said it improved their work–life balance, while around half reported they had fewer distractions (53%). This is coupled with the fact that during lockdown the percentage of people reporting very high levels of happiness had risen considerably compared to pre-pandemic levels. As we try and resume some normality back into our lives we find that there is a marked impact on society. People are spending more time on keeping fit and less time travelling compared with pre-pandemic levels. Online shopping had been growing in recent years, but the pandemic appears to have accelerated the trend with large increases in the online sales seen during the periods of national restrictions. And even with a short decline early in 2022, we're still seeing that online spending is accounting for almost 27% of all official retail sales.

CASE STUDY QUESTIONS

1. What sociological changes have come about due to trade in Europe?
2. How does trade affect anthropological questions?
3. How did price competition help the rise of the British Empire?
4. Why is trade so important in the European Union?
5. Britain has faced an economic 'double-whammy' with Brexit followed closely by the Covid-19 pandemic. In your opinion, how will these impact society and the resulting consumer behaviour?

FURTHER READING

What Can We Know about the Cost of Brexit So Far: A Policy Briefing, written by John Springford (www.cer.org.uk/publications/archive/policy-brief/2022/cost-brexit-so-far). One of many articles written to try to make sense of the trajectory that the UK is taking post-Brexit.

Beyond COVID-19: The New Consumer Behaviour is Sticking in the Tissue Industry, written by McKinsey & Company (www.mckinsey.com/industries/paper-forest-products-and-packaging/our-insights/beyond-covid-19-the-new-consumer-behavior-is-sticking-in-the-tissue-industry). You can listen to this on SoundCloud too!

Economics, by Richard Lipsey and Alec Chrystal (Oxford: Oxford University Press, 2011), is a comprehensive text covering all aspects of economics. It is written in a clear, straightforward style and covers the ground well.

The Silk Roads: A New History of the World, by Peter Frankopan (London: Bloomsbury Publishing, 2015), is a book that delves deep into history, religion, economics, international affairs, and investigates the root of some of the societal situations that we find ourselves in today. The author concludes by saying that 'Western fashion houses like Prada, Burberry and Louis Vuitton are building huge stores and seeing spectacular sales figures across the Persian Gulf, Russia, China and the Far East (so that with delicious irony, fine fabrics and silks are being sold back to the place where silk and fine fabrics originated).'

(Continued)

Anthropology: The Basics, by Peter Metcalf (Abingdon: Routledge, 2005), is a fascinating introduction to the subject. There are plenty of examples, some of which you can try yourself, and some excellent in-depth looks at cultural issues.

Sociology, by Anthony Giddens (Cambridge: Polity Press, 2009), is now in its 6th edition. The latest version includes a chapter on war and terrorism, and it is jargon-free and comprehensive.

Games People Play: The Psychology of Human Relationships, by Eric Berne (Harmondsworth: Penguin Books, 2010), is a humorous way of looking at the ways in which people relate to each other. Berne describes the various interactions in terms of games, with winners and losers and rules. This is not a serious textbook, but it is a fun read and it offers some entertaining insights into human interaction.

Freakonomics: A Rogue Economist Explores the Hidden Side of Everything, by Steven D. Levitt and Stephen J. Dubner (Ontario: Harper Perennial, 2005), is another popular-science book. It's very much a light read, and the academic rigour is definitely questionable – but what the authors are looking to do is to shake up some traditional thinking, and examine some economic behaviour from a different angle (for example, they show that New York drug dealers would earn more working in minimum-wage jobs). Not to be taken too seriously, but good fun nonetheless.

MORE ONLINE

For additional materials that support this chapter and your learning, please visit:

https://study.sagepub.com/sethna5e

REFERENCES

Adams, A., Agbenorhevi, J.K., Alemawor, F., Lutterodt, H.E. and Sampson, G.O. (2018) Assessment of the consumers' awareness and marketing prospects of organic fruits and vegetables in Techiman, Ghana. *Journal of Food Security*, 6 (2): 55–66.

Amasiatu, C.V. and Shah, M.H. (2019) The management of first party fraud in e-tailing: A qualitative study. *International Journal of Retail & Distribution Management*, 47 (4): 433–52.

Anker, T.B., Gordon, R. and Zainuddin, N. (2021) Consumer-dominant social marketing: A definition and explication. *European Journal of Marketing*, 56 (1): 159–83.

Arora, M. and Kumar, A. (2018) Consumer awareness towards brand equity. *Asian Journal of Management*, 5 (8): 100.

Arora, P., Kumar, H., Mathur, C.A.S. and Roy, N. (2021) Social entrepreneurship – crafting new business model: Case study on Narayana Hrudayalaya and Gramin bank. *Ilkogretim Online*, 20 (5): 3125–30.

Auriffeille, D.M. (2021) 'Before she was born, I ate cheerios and beer for dinner': A qualitative examination of green parenting in Lowcountry South Carolina. *Humanity & Society*, 45 (4): 439–70.

Bauer, J., Moormann, D., Strametz, R. and Groneberg, D.A. (2021) Development of unmanned aerial vehicle (UAV) networks delivering early defibrillation for out-of-hospital cardiac arrests (OHCA) in areas lacking timely access to emergency medical services (EMS) in Germany: A comparative economic study. *BMJ Open*, *11* (1): e043791.

Beatty, C., Bennett, C. and Hawkins, A. (2021) Managing precarity: Food bank use by low-income women workers in a changing welfare regime. *Social Policy & Administration*, *55* (5): 981–1000.

Beck, A. and Hopkins, M. (2016) Managing the frontiers of retail innovation. https://losspreventionmedia.com/managing-the-frontiers-of-retail-innovation/ (accessed 20 November 2022)

Bennett, P.D. (1995) *Dictionary of Marketing Terms*. Chicago, IL: American Marketing Association.

Blackwell, R.D., Miniard, P.W. and Engel, J.F. (2001) *Consumer Behaviour*, 9th edn. Mason, OH: Southwestern.

Boellstorff, T. (2012) Rethinking digital anthropology. In H.A. Horst and D. Miller (eds), *Digital Anthropology*. Oxford: Berg Publishers. pp. 39–60.

Booms, B.H. and Bitner, M.J. (1981) Marketing strategies and organisational structures for service firms. In J.H. Donnelly and W.R. George (eds), *Marketing of Services*. Chicago, IL: American Marketing Association. pp. 47–52.

Bounfour, A. (2018) Africa: The next frontier for intellectual capital? *Journal of Intellectual Capital*, *19* (3): 474–9.

Bulman, M. (2018) Food bank use in UK reaches highest rate on record as benefits fail to cover basic costs. *Independent*, 24 April. www.independent.co.uk/news/uk/home-news/food-bank-uk-benefits-trussell-trust-cost-of-living-highest-rate-a8317001.html (accessed 12 July 2018).

Chavaglia, J.N., Filipe, J.A., Ferreira, M.A.M. and Caleiro, A. (2015) Neuroeconomics: Decisions in extreme situations. *EC Business Management*, *1* (1): 14–21.

Christopher, M., Ballantyne, D. and Payne, A. (1991) *Relationship Marketing*. Oxford: Butterworth–Heinemann.

Coary, S. and Poor, M. (2016) How consumer-generated images shape important consumption outcomes in the food domain. *Journal of Consumer Marketing*, *33* (1): 1–8.

Conlon, K. (2022) Plastic roads: Not all they're paved up to be. *International Journal of Sustainable Development & World Ecology*, *29* (1): 80–3.

Davies, A. and Elliott, R. (2006) The evolution of the empowered consumer. *European Journal of Marketing*, *40* (9/10): 1106–21.

Dennison, J.B., Sazhin, D. and Smith, D.V. (2022) Decision neuroscience and neuroeconomics: Recent progress and ongoing challenges. *WIREs Cognitive Science*, *13* (3): e1589.

Djafarova, E. and Bowes, T. (2021) 'Instagram made me buy it': Generation Z impulse purchases in fashion industry. *Journal of Retailing and Consumer Services*, *59*: 102345.

Dootson, P., Johnston, K.A., Lings, I. and Beatson, A.T. (2018) Tactics to deter deviant consumer behavior: A research agenda. *Journal of Consumer Marketing, 35* (6): 577–87. https://doi.org/10.1108/JCM-10-2015-1575

Editions CNN (2022) Nobody likes self-checkout: Here's why it's everywhere. https://edition.cnn.com/2022/07/09/business/self-checkout-retail/index.html (accessed 11 July 2022).

Esmaeili, H. and Thwaites, H. (2021) Addressing environmental awareness through immersive VR experiences, gamification and hypothetical scenario development. *Virtual Creativity, 11* (2): 223–36.

Felicia, P. (2011) *Handbook of Research on Improving Learning and Motivation*. Hershey, PA: IGI Global.

Fenton-O'Creevy, M., Dibb, S. and Furnham, A. (2018) Antecedents and consequences of chronic impulsive buying: Can impulsive buying be understood as dysfunctional self-regulation? *Psychology & Marketing, 35* (3): 175–88.

Frey, B.S. (2018) Happiness and television viewing. In *Economics of Happiness*. SpringerBriefs in Economics. Cham: Springer Nature. pp. 51–4.

Gakhal, B. and Senior, C. (2008) Examining the influence of fame in the presence of beauty: An electrodermal neuromarketing study. *Journal of Consumer Behaviour, 7* (4/5): 331–41.

Garcia, J.R. and Saad, G. (2008) Evolutionary neuromarketing: Darwinizing the neuroimaging paradigm for consumer behaviour. *Journal of Consumer Behaviour, 7* (4/5): 397–414.

Genç, E. and Di Benedetto, C.A. (2018) Sustainable new product development. In P.N. Golder and D. Mitra (eds), *Handbook of Research on New Product Development*. Cheltenham: Edward Elgar. pp. 227–49.

Genoveva, G. (2022) Tiktok platform opportunity: How does it influence SMEs brand awareness among Generation Z? *Sriwijaya International Journal of Dynamic Economics and Business, 5* (3): 273–82.

Gummesson, E., Doyle, G., Storlazzi, A., Annarumma, C., Favretto, G., Tommasetti, A. and Vesci, M. (2018) Health myths and service-dominant logic. In P. Adinolfi and E. Borgonovi (eds), *The Myths of Health Care*. Cham: Springer Nature. pp. 231–51.

Hanley, A.W., Bettmann, J.E. and Baker, A.K. (2022) The self-extension dimensional assessment: An instrument development study. *Psychology of Consciousness: Theory, Research, and Practice*. https://doi.org/10.1037/cns0000329

Hasford, J., Kidwell, B., Hardesty, D.M. and Farmer, A. (2022) Your cheatin' heart: How emotional intelligence and selfishness impact the incidence of consumer fraud. *Journal of Consumer Research, 49* (1): 112–31.

Haverila, K., Haverila, M. and McLaughlin, C. (2022) Development of a brand community engagement model: A service-dominant logic perspective. *Journal of Consumer Marketing, 39* (2): 166–79.

Hewer, P. and Brownlie, D. (2010) On market forces and adjustments: Acknowledging customer creativity through the aesthetics of debadging. *Journal of Marketing Management, 26* (5/6): 428–40.

Hicks, M., Stickle, B. and Harms, J. (2022) Assessing the fear of package theft. *American Journal of Criminal Justice*, 47 (3): 399–420.

Hietanen, J., Andéhn, M. and Bradshaw, A. (2018) Against the implicit politics of service-dominant logic. *Marketing Theory*, 18 (1): 101–19.

Hilal, F. (2022) The effect of green supply chain management practices and competitive advantage on financial performance. *International Journal of Business*, 27 (1): 1–13.

Huang, Y., Chen, Y. and Tan, C.H. (2021) Regulating new digital market and its effects on the incumbent market: Investigation of online peer-to-peer short-term rental. *Information & Management*, 58 (8): 103544.

Hui, L. and Subramony, M. (2008) Employee customer orientation in manufacturing organisations: Joint influences of customer proximity and the senior leadership team. *Journal of Applied Psychology*, 93 (2): 317–28.

Human Rights Watch (2014) *World Report*. www.hrw.org/world-report/2014 (accessed 24 October 2015).

Jayanti, R.K. (2021) An institutional theory perspective on retailer loyalty. *Journal of Relationship Marketing*, 20 (2): 156–76.

Jones, M.A. and Taylor, V.A. (2018) Marketer requests for positive post-purchase satisfaction evaluations: Consumer depth interview findings. *Journal of Retailing and Consumer Services*, 41: 218–26.

Kail, R.V. and Cavanaugh, J.C. (2018) *Human Development: A Life-Span View*. Boston, MA: Cengage Learning.

Kanungo, R.P., Gupta, S., Patel, P., Prikshat, V. and Liu, R. (2022) Digital consumption and socio-normative vulnerability. *Technological Forecasting & Social Change*, 182: 121808.

Kanwal, M., Burki, U., Ali, R. and Dahlstrom, R. (2022) Systematic review of gender differences and similarities in online consumers' shopping behavior. *Journal of Consumer Marketing*, 39 (1): 29–43.

Kelner, S. (2022) The demise of Cineworld suggests that the magic of the movies has gone forever. https://inews.co.uk/opinion/the-demise-of-cineworld-suggests-the-magic-of-the-movies-has-gone-forever-1811226 (accessed 25 August 2022).

Kemp, E.A., Borders, A.L., Anaza, N.A. and Johnston, W.J. (2018) The heart in organizational buying: Marketers' understanding of emotions and decision-making of buyers. *Journal of Business & Industrial Marketing*, 33 (1): 19–28.

Kim, K.H. and Kumar, V. (2018) The relative influence of economic and relational direct marketing communications on buying behavior in business-to-business markets. *Journal of Marketing Research*, 55 (1): 48–68.

Kirschen, D.S. and Strbac, G. (2018) *Fundamentals of Power System Economics*. Chichester: John Wiley & Sons.

Kolyperas, D. and Sparks, L. (2018) Exploring value co-creation in Fan Fests: The role of fans. *Journal of Strategic Marketing*, 26 (1): 71–84.

Kumar, V. (2018) Transformative marketing: The next 20 years. *Journal of Marketing*, 82 (4): 1–12.

Lindsey Hall, K.K., Qi, J. (Miracle), Richey, J.R.G. and Patil, R.K. (2022) Collaboration, feedback, and performance: Supply chain insights from service-dominant logic. *Journal of Business Research, 146*: 385–97.

Lu, L. and Chi, C.G.Q. (2018) Examining diners' decision-making of local food purchase: The role of menu stimuli and involvement. *International Journal of Hospitality Management, 69*: 113–23.

Luke, A. (2018) Genres of power: Literacy education and the production of capital. In *Critical Literacy, Schooling, and Social Justice*. Abingdon: Routledge. pp. 161–85.

Luu, N., Ngo, L.V. and Cadeaux, J. (2018) Value synergy and value asymmetry in relationship marketing programs. *Industrial Marketing Management, 68*: 165–76.

Mady, T.T. (2011) Sentiment toward marketing: Should we care about consumer alienation and readiness to use technology? *Journal of Consumer Behaviour, 10* (4): 192–204.

Major, A. (2022) Not streaming near you: FilmStruck's failure and the demise of the cinema-specific model. *Popular Communication, 20* (1): 60–76.

Malik, S. and Raheja, K. (2018) E-commerce: Emerging internet technologies and technological innovation in the business world. In M.S. Kirthy and R. Jabez (eds), *New Trends in Business Management*, Vol. 88. Hyderabad: Zenon Academic Publishing. pp. 88–97.

Miliopoulou, G.-Z. (2021) Brand communities, fans or publics? How social media interests and brand management practices define the rules of engagement. *European Journal of Marketing, 55* (12): 3129–61.

Miller, D. and Horst, H.A. (2012) *The Digital and the Human: A Prospectus for Digital Anthropology*. In H.A. Horst and D. Miller (eds), *Digital Anthropology*. Oxford: Berg Publishers. pp. 3–35.

Miller, D. and Wang, X. (2021) Introduction: Smartphone-based visual normativity: Approaches from digital anthropology and communication studies. *Global Media & China, 6* (3): 251–8.

Minguez, A. and Javier Sese, F. (2022) Why do you want a relationship, anyway? Consent to receive marketing communications and donors' willingness to engage with nonprofits. *Journal of Business Research, 148*: 356–67.

Mittal, B. (2006) I, me, and mine: How products become consumers' extended selves. *Journal of Consumer Behaviour, 5*: 550–62.

Mittendorf, C. (2018) Trust and distrust in two-sided markets: An example in the sharing economy. In *Proceedings of the 51st Hawaii International Conference on System Sciences*. Hilton Waikoloa Village, Hawaii, USA, January 3–6.

Moshakis, A. (2018) Nation of shoplifters: The rise of supermarket self-checkout scams. *The Observer*, Crime. www.theguardian.com/global/2018/may/20/nation-of-shoplifters-supermarket-self-checkout (accessed 12 June 2018).

Nie, X., Yang, Z., Zhang, Y. and Janakiraman, N. (2022) How does global–local identity affect consumer preference for access-based consumption? Investigating the mediating role of consumption openness. *Journal of Marketing Research (JMR), 59* (3): 555–77.

Nowicki, D., Sauser, B., Randall, W. and Lusch, R. (2018) Service-dominant logic and performance-based contracting: A systems thinking perspective. *Service Science*, *10* (1): 12–24.

ONS (Office for National Statistics) (2022) Impact of coronavirus (COVID-19) on lifestyle. www.ons.gov.uk/peoplepopulationandcommunity/healthandsocialcare/conditionsanddiseases/articles/coronaviruscovid19latestinsights/lifestyle. (accessed 10 June 2022).

Papista, E., Chrysochou, P., Krystallis, A. and Dimitriadis, S. (2018) Types of value and cost in consumer–green brands relationship and loyalty behaviour. *Journal of Consumer Behaviour*, *17* (1): e101–13.

Park, S. and Kang, J. (2022) More is not always better: Determinants of choice overload and satisfaction with customization in fast casual restaurants. *Journal of Hospitality Marketing & Management*, *31* (2): 205–25.

Pollák, F., Markovič, P., Vavrek, R. and Konečny, M. (2022) Return to the new normal: Empirical analysis of changes in e-consumer behavior during the COVID-19 pandemic. *Behavioral Sciences*, *12*: 85.

pymnts.com (2018) New data: Consumers' (shifting) expectations from self-service retail. www.pymnts.com/self-service-retail/2018/diebold-nixdorf-cashierless-customer-service/ (accessed 12 July 2018).

Radtke, M.L., Ordovás de Almeida, S. and Espartel, L.B. (2022) What brought me here? Different consumer journeys for practices of sustainable disposal through takeback programmes. *Sustainability*, *14*: 5003.

Richins, M. (2001) Consumer behaviour as a social science. *Advances in Consumer Research*, *28*: 1–5.

Royo-Vela, M. and Black, M. (2020) Drone images versus terrain images in advertisements: Images' verticality effects and the mediating role of mental simulation on attitude towards the advertisement. *Journal of Marketing Communications*, *26* (1): 21–39. https://doi.org/10.1080/13527266.2018.1425896

Ryan, C., McLoughlin, D. and Keating, A. (2006) Tribespotting: A semiotic analysis of the role of consumption in the tribes of *Trainspotting*. *Journal of Consumer Behaviour*, *5* (September–October): 431–41.

Sawe, N. and Chawla, K. (2021) Environmental neuroeconomics: How neuroscience can inform our understanding of human responses to climate change. *Current Opinion in Behavioral Sciences*, *42*: 147–54.

Schmitz, C., Lee, Y.-C., Isenberg, L. and Lilien, G.L. (2022) Managing ad hoc sales encounters in B2B markets. *Industrial Marketing Management*, *105*: 33–47.

Scott, M.L. (2018) What factors influence over-consumption and how can marketers use this information to improve customers' well-being? In R.P. Hill, C.M. Lamberton and J. Swartz (eds), *Mapping Out Marketing: Navigation Lessons from the Ivory Trenches*. Abingdon: Routledge. pp. 130–32.

Sezen, B. and Çankaya, S.Y. (2018) Green supply chain management theory and practices. In *Operations and Service Management: Concepts, Methodologies, Tools, and Applications*. Hershey, PA: IGI Global. pp. 118–41.

Shankar, V., Grewal, D., Sunder, S., Fossen, B., Peters, K. and Agarwal, A. (2022) Digital marketing communication in global marketplaces: A review of extant research, future directions, and potential approaches. *International Journal of Research in Marketing*, *39* (2): 541–65.

Shaw, D., Newholme, T. and Dickinson, R. (2006) Consumption as voting: An exploration of consumer empowerment. *European Journal of Marketing*, *40* (9/10): 1049–67.

SMMT (2022a) December and full year 2021 car sales. https://media.smmt.co.uk/december-2021-new-car-registrations/ (accessed 15 July 2022).

SMMT (2022b) Used car sales Q4 2022. www.smmt.co.uk/category/vehicle-data/used-car-sales-data/#:~:text=Used%20car%20sales%3A%20Q4%202021,up%20119.2%25%20with%2040%2C228%20transactions. (accessed 15 July 2022).

Stein, M. (2018) Theories of experiential learning and the unconscious. In *Experiential Learning in Organizations*. Abingdon: Routledge. pp. 19–36.

Stoll, M., Baecke, S. and Kenning, P. (2008) What they see is what they get? An fMRI-study on neural correlates of attractive packaging. *Journal of Consumer Behaviour*, *7* (4/5): 342–59.

Tangsupwattana, W. and Liu, X. (2018) Effect of emotional experience on symbolic consumption in Generation Y consumers. *Marketing Intelligence & Planning*, *36* (5): 514–27.

Urban, G.L., Sultan, F. and Qualls, W.J. (2000) Placing trust at the center of your internet strategy. *MIT Sloan Management Review*, *42* (1): 39–48.

Vargo, S.L. and Lusch, R.F. (2004) Evolving to a new dominant logic for marketing. *Journal of Marketing*, *68* (January): 1–17.

Wagner-Tsukamoto, S. and Tadajewski, M. (2006) Cognitive anthropology and the problem-solving behaviour of green consumers. *Journal of Consumer Behaviour*, *5* (May–June): 235–44.

Wheaton, O. (2018) People stealing avocados from supermarket self-service checkouts by pretending they're carrots. *Independent*, 26 May. www.independent.co.uk/news/uk/home-news/avocados-carrots-self-service-scam-supermarkets-checkout-stealing-a8370621.html (accessed 30 May 2018).

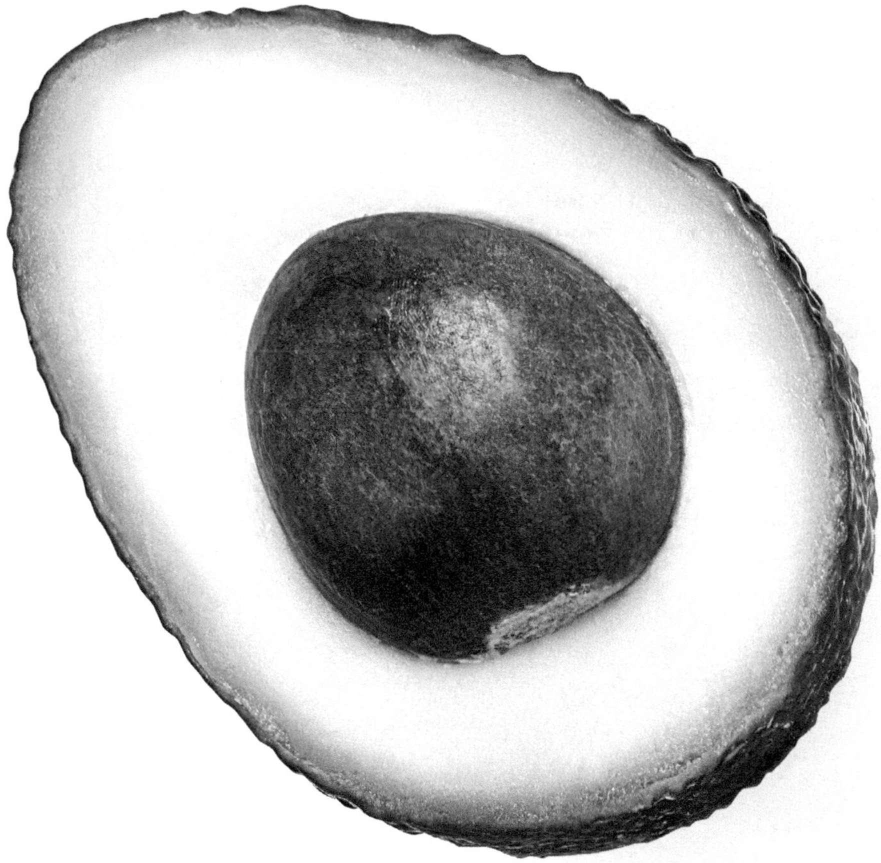

PART ONE CONSUMER BEHAVIOUR IN CONTEXT

Chapter 1 Understanding Consumer Behaviour
Chapter 2 Decisions, Behaviours and Interactions
Chapter 3 Consumption in B2C vs. B2B
Chapter 4 Consumer Technology and Innovation

PART TWO CONSUMERS AS INDIVIDUALS (THE PSYCHOLOGICAL ISSUES)

Chapter 5 Drive, Motivation and Hedonism
Chapter 6 The Self and Personality
Chapter 7 Perception
Chapter 8 Learning and Knowledge
Chapter 9 Attitude Formation and Change

PART THREE CONSUMERS AS SOCIAL ACTORS (THE SOCIOLOGICAL ISSUES)

Chapter 10 Reference Groups
Chapter 11 Age, Gender and Familial Roles
Chapter 12 Culture and Social Mobility
Chapter 13 Ethical Consumption
Chapter 14 Sustainable Consumption

CHAPTER 2

DECISIONS, BEHAVIOURS AND INTERACTIONS

LEARNING OBJECTIVES

After reading this chapter you should be able to:

- Describe the role of goals in decision-making.
- Explain the importance of being included in the 'consideration set'.
- Explain some of the limiting factors on information searches.
- Explain how decision rules are established and used.
- Explain the relationship between involvement and information processing.
- Show how involvement relates to end goals and values.
- Describe how dimensions of involvement can be used to segment markets.
- Explain what is meant by unsought goods.
- Describe the significance of loyalty and branding in buyer behaviour.

CHAPTER CONTENTS

Introduction
Decision-making using goals
Decision-making models
Interrupts
Risk and uncertainty
Pre-purchase activities
The search effort
Factors affecting the external search for information
Making the choice
Categorisation of decision rules
Involvement
Dimensions of involvement
Involvement with brands
Increasing involvement levels
Loyalty in buyer behaviour
Unsought goods
Summary
Key points
How to impress your examiner
Review questions
Case study: Celebrating International and Emirati Women's Day
Further reading
References

More online: https://study.sagepub.com/sethna5e

INTRODUCTION

Each day millions of consumers make numerous decisions. In fact, various internet sources estimate that an adult makes about 35,000 remotely conscious decisions each day (Sahakian and Labuzetta, 2013)! These range from sizeable purchases such as buying a house to relatively inconsequential decisions such as when buying shoe polish to complex decisions about which coffee to order in the local coffee shop (and remembering not to order a 'tall' oatmilk latte with an extra shot in Costa)! And as the number of choices has increased exponentially, so has the number of decisions consumers have to make. Oh and the list does not end there, and it's somewhat cyclical. We have choices about what to eat, what to wear, what to purchase, what we believe, what jobs and career choices we'll pursue, how we vote, who we spend our time with, who and how we will date, is marriage an option, what we say and how we say it, whether or not we should have children, what we will name our children, who will our children spend their time with, what will they eat, etc. So, this chapter is concerned with the ways consumers approach making purchase decisions and what their goals and motivations are. The methods used depend on whether the product is novel or tried and tested; whether the purchase is routine or out of the ordinary; whether the product is a new one, or a repeat of a previous purchase.

Any plan of action carries with it a degree of risk, but the lower the risk to consumers, the more likely they are to buy the product and the less likely they are to complain afterwards. If consumers are familiar with the brand, the perceived risk is reduced, and so the chapter also looks at branding as a way of reducing risk for the consumer.

DECISION-MAKING USING GOALS

Sometimes goals will conflict. In these circumstances, the strongly active goal will inhibit competing goals until the stronger goal has been achieved, at which point the weaker or less active goal will re-emerge (Brendl et al., 2002). For instance, in recent years and since their launch in 2015, we have seen many organisations and individual entrepreneurs trying to balance the need for achieving the **United Nation's Sustainable Development Goals** whilst battling with the three main challenges of instability, implementation and governance. We'll talk more about these in Chapter 14.

Table 2.1 gives some purchase end goals and motivations, with examples. In practice, marketers have little influence over consumers' main goals, since these often derive from basic values. Marketers can try to influence the less abstract end goals, such as the desired functional or psychosocial consequences, through promotional strategies. For example, although it may be difficult to persuade someone that he or she ought to dress well in order to impress other people, we can much more easily influence those who already believe in dressing to impress, perhaps encouraging them to shop at a specific retailer or buy specific clothing brands. Thus these factors act as drivers for end goals, as shown in Figure 2.1.

UN Sustainable Development Goals (SDGs)

A collection of 17 interlinked global goals designed to be a 'shared blueprint for peace and prosperity for people and the planet, now and into the future', and intended to be achieved by 2030

BRAND EXPERIENCES: AMAZON IS 'RELENTLESS'

Since its inception, Amazon.com has evolved over the past almost 40 years. What started out as predominantly an American online bookstore has now grown significantly into a multinational technology company which focuses on e-commerce, cloud computing, digital streaming and artificial intelligence. Numerous commentators have referred to it as 'one of the most influential economic and cultural forces in the world' and it is one of the world's most valuable brands. And Amazon continues to astound us with their numbers. They also tend to keep their numbers to themselves so it can be tricky to find relevant stats, and given the pace at which Amazon grows, it's not always easy to get accurate stats either. So, before we start looking in detail at consumer decision-making (and the whys and wherefores), let's take a brief moment to be amazed by numbers from Amazon as compiled below (as of the last reported period):

- Amazon customer statistics show the e-commerce giant receives 2.2 billion unique US visitors a month.
- There were over 2 million third-party seller businesses on Amazon in 2021.
- Amazon has 1.2 million employees in 2022 and hired 270,000 new employees in the second half of 2021 to cater to its one-day and same-day delivery pledges. It has also taken the number one position on *LinkedIn's Top Employer* ranking.
- Amazon's retail sales will reach roughly $729 billion by Q4 of 2022 and is the second company ever to hit the $1 trillion market capitalisation club!
- During the holiday rush, some Amazon warehouses ship over 1 million items a day.
- In 2022, 40% of e-commerce sales will come from Amazon. Or put that another way, for every $5 that shoppers will spend on digital platforms, $2 will go to Amazon.
- Amazon customer statistics show Prime has over 200 million customers worldwide.
- Employees can bring their best friends to work and as a result, Amazonians at the Seattle headquarters share workspace with 6000 dogs every day!
- 100,000 robots 'work' in Amazon warehouses worldwide to pick items and enhance the efficiency of human workers.
- Amazon Prime Air (a drone-based delivery system which has already made successful demo deliveries in the UK and US) will deliver orders within 30 minutes of their placements.
- Jeff Bezos almost called his company 'Relentless'. But others didn't think much of it. Jeff, however, liked this name enough to purchase a domain name. Now, when you type relentless.com, the site redirects you to Amazon.com.

Source: Adapted partially from https://techjury.net/blog/amazon-statistics/#gref.

Optimising satisfaction to achieve such end goals is common with websites competing for business, as the following examples show:

- www.9point5woodworks.com – With a new attitude to bespoke woodwork for the design conscious, this website works with new designs/techniques as well as more established woodwork techniques to develop interesting new furniture and wooden learning resources.
- www.ministryofsupply.com – Many companies make clothes that are appropriate for the office, but Ministry of Supply relies on more than just comfortable materials and good design; they also use science. The startup founders enlisted the help of MIT and NASA scientists to create 'the world's first performance dress shirt'.

Consumers' relevant knowledge about the product category (or, if you prefer, the problem category) is obviously important in problem-solving (Crosby and Taylor, 1981), so inexperienced purchasers are likely to take a knowledgeable friend with them when they go to make a major purchase, such as an electric vehicle. Sometimes relevant knowledge is brought forward from the individual's memory, and some knowledge is acquired during the purchasing process (Biehal and Chakravarty, 1983). Any brands that have simply been remembered are part of the **evoked set** and for regular purchases or familiar product categories these may be the only brands that are considered. The result of the information search process is to create

Evoked set
The group of brands a consumer can remember spontaneously

Consideration set

The group of brands that a consumer believes will meet his or her need, and that are therefore seriously being considered for purchase

choice alternatives, which are further refined into a **consideration set**. The consideration set is the group of products that will be actively considered.

In Figure 2.2, the many brands in the evoked set, and the even more numerous brands that might be brought to the individual's attention, are filtered and refined to create the consideration set, which may only comprise a few brands. The individual will then usually select one or possibly two brands to feed into the goal hierarchy as being the desirable brands for solving the need problem.

TABLE 2.1 Examples of purchase end goals

Dominant end goal	Basic purchase motivation	Examples
Optimise satisfaction	Seek maximum positive consequences	Buy dinner at the best restaurant in town rather than risking a cheap diner
Prevention	Avoid potential unpleasant consequences	Buy weatherproofing for a house so as to maintain the good appearance of the house, and protect its value
Resolve conflict	See satisfactory balance of positive and negative consequences	Buy a moderately expensive car of very good quality so as to avoid high maintenance costs and unreliability, while still keeping within a reasonable expenditure
Escape	Reduce or escape from current aversive circumstances	Buy an anti-dandruff shampoo, in order to prevent future bouts of dandruff and embarrassment
Maintenance (satisfy)	Maintain satisfaction of a basic need with minimal effort	Buy bread at a local shop. This satisfies the need for bread without having to go to the out-of-town hypermarket where you do your main weekly shopping

Source: Christopher et al. (1991). Reproduced with permission.

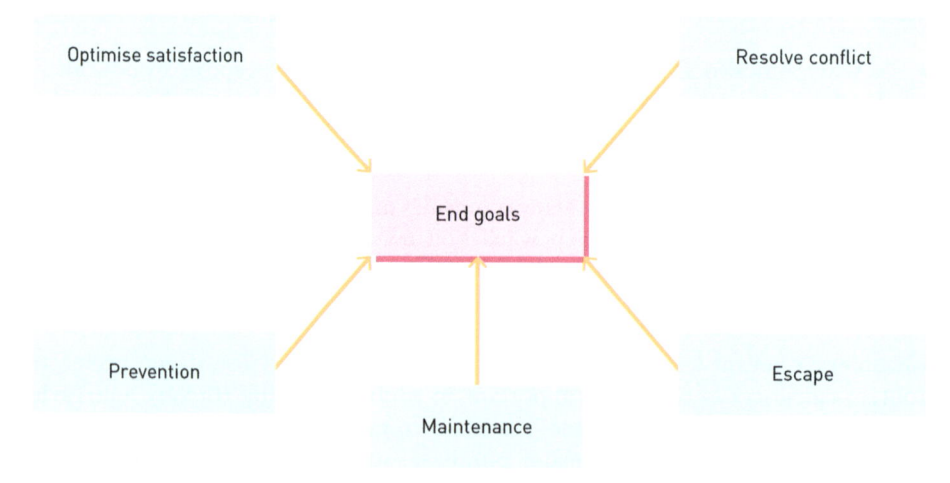

FIGURE 2.1 Drivers for end goals

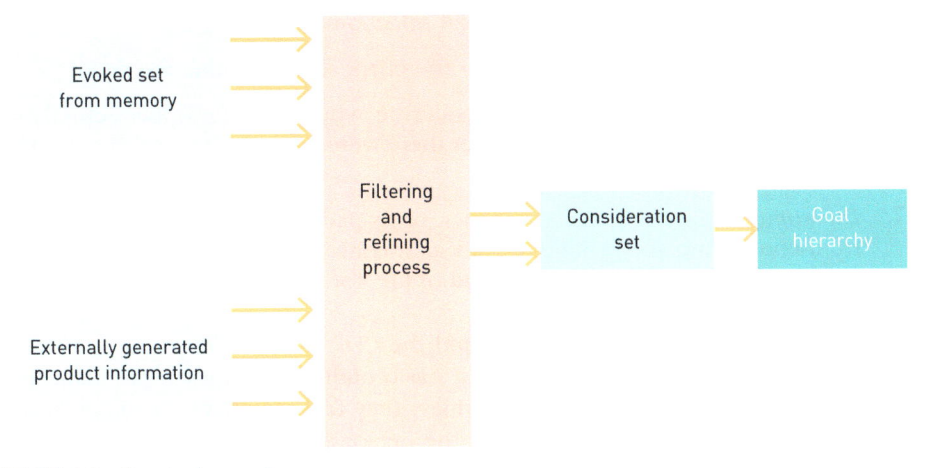

FIGURE 2.2 Developing goals

DECISION-MAKING MODELS

Decision-making models are often complex and involve many stages. The John Dewey model (Dewey, 1910), outlined more than 100 years ago, gives the following five stages:

1. A difficulty is felt (need identification).
2. The difficulty is located and defined.
3. Possible solutions are suggested.
4. Consequences are considered.
5. A solution is accepted.

This model of decision-making is probably excessively rational, and is certainly far more complex than most purchase situations warrant. Life is simply too busy to spend much time agonising over which brand of biscuit to buy.

Later, Engel, Kollat and Blackwell developed the EKB model of consumer behaviour, which became the CDP (consumer decision process) model (see Figure 2.3), and which follows seven stages (Blackwell et al., 2005). These are:

1. *Need recognition.* The individual recognises that something is missing from his or her life.
2. *Search for information.* This information search may be internal (remembering facts about products, or recalling experiences with them as a result of services) or external (reading about possible products, surfing the internet or visiting shops, etc.).
3. *Pre-purchase evaluation of alternatives.* The individual considers which of the possible alternatives might be best for fulfilling the need.

4. *Purchase.* The act of making the final selection and paying for it.
5. *Consumption.* Using the product for the purpose of fulfilling the need.
6. *Post-consumption evaluation.* Considering whether the product actually satisfied the need or not and whether there were any problems arising from its purchase and consumption.
7. *Divestment.* Disposing of the product, or its packaging, or any residue left from consuming the product (either as a conscientious consumer or as a result of legislation, for instance 'end of life' for vehicles).

The similarity between Dewey's model and the CDP model is obvious, and similar criticisms apply, but both models offer a basic outline of how people make consumption decisions. People do not buy unless they feel they have a need. A need is felt when there is a divergence between the person's actual state and their desired state. The degree of difference between the two states is what determines the level of motivation the person feels to do something about the problem, and this will in turn depend on a number of external factors.

There are two possible reasons for a divergence between the desired and the actual states: one is that the actual state changes, the other is that the desired state changes. In practice, it is rare for the actual states and the desired states to be the same, since this would imply that the consumer is perfectly happy and has everything that he or she could possibly want, which is rarely the case in an imperfect world.

Causes of shift of the actual state might be taken from the following list (Onkvisit and Shaw, 1994):

Assortment depletion
The reduction in one's overall quantity of possessions

- *Assortment depletion.* Consumption, spoilage or wear and tear on the stock of goods or products within the individual's assortment.
- *Income change.* This can be upwards, through a salary increase or windfall, or downwards through, for example, redundancy.

Causes of shifts in the desired state are often more to do with marketing activities. This is because new information may change the individual's aspirations. If the individual sees a better car, hears a better digital radio or otherwise becomes aware of a better solution to the problem, there is likely to be a shift in the desired state. From a marketing viewpoint, this approach is most effective when consumers are already dissatisfied with their present and potentially outdated products.

Psychology of complication
The tendency for people to make their lives more complex, and therefore more interesting

Changing desire is often brought on by a change in actual state; for example, a windfall (or even a pandemic!) might prompt an individual to start up an enterprise or a social enterprise that they have always dreamed of. The relationship between these factors is shown in Figure 2.4.

Psychology of simplification
The tendency for people to make their lives less complex and therefore less stressful

The psychology of complication says that people complicate their lives deliberately by seeking new products, even though they are fairly satisfied with the old one. The **psychology of complication** is the opposite of the **psychology of simplification**, which says that consumers try to simplify their lives by making repeat purchases of a familiar brand (Hoyer and Ridgway, 1984). It is probable that both these mechanisms act on people at different times.

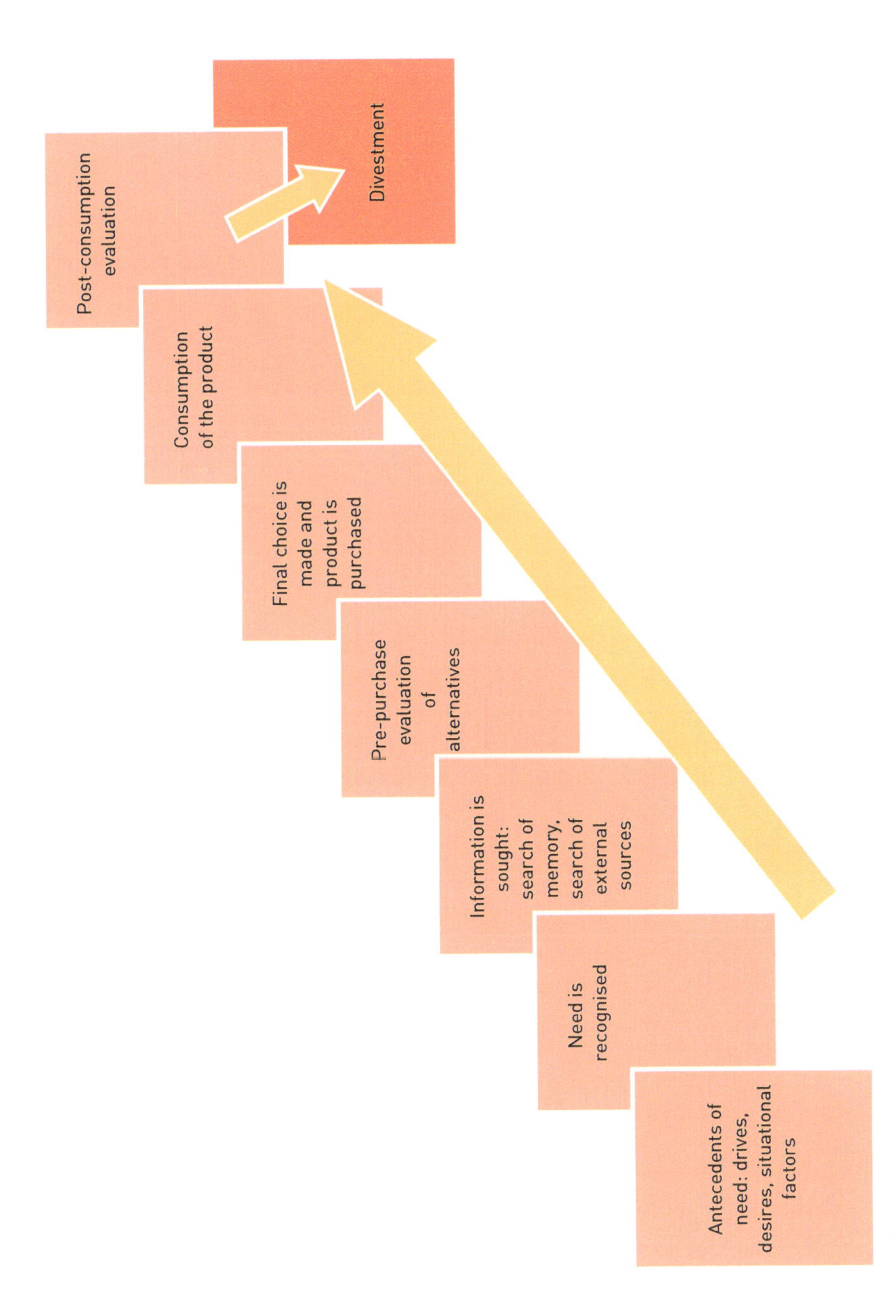

FIGURE 2.3 The decision-making process

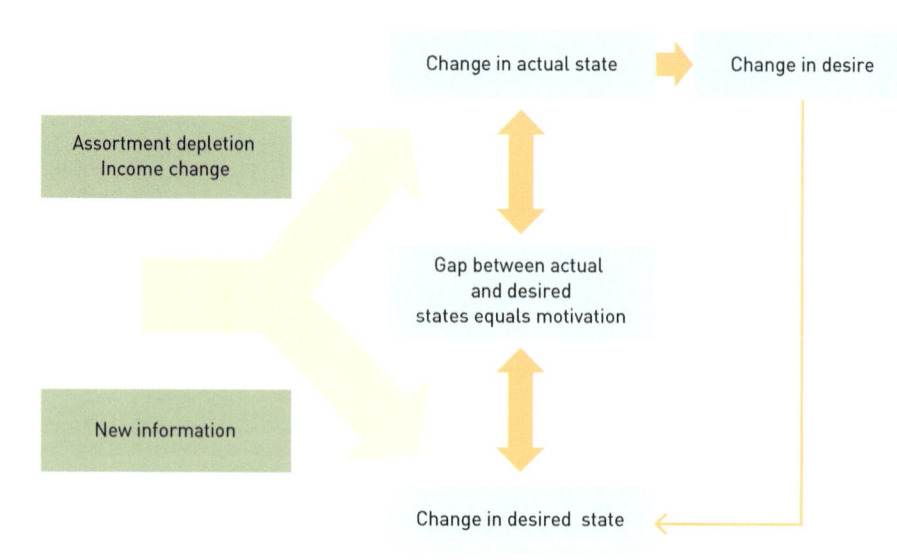

FIGURE 2.4 Actual and desired states

Consumer-dominant logic of marketing

The logic which captures consumers' active and primary role in a range of mainstream marketing processes such as branding, product development and sales

CRITICAL REFLECTION

Marketers are often accused of creating needs; indeed, marketing academics often define marketing as 'satisfying the wants and needs of customers' (Kotler et al., 2013) as a result of meeting the needs of the marketplace by designing products and services and then communicating them (Elliot et al., 2010). This view has somewhat evolved now with the emergent '**consumer-dominant logic of marketing**' (Anker et al., 2021). However, there is still a view that somehow marketers can persuade people to want things for which they actually have no use – and of course marketers hotly deny this. This of course raises ethical issues (Nantel and Weeks, 1996; and for more information on this hot topic see Chapter 13 later in this book). For example, how truthful is the advertising that is used to communicate a message (Nelson et al., 2021)? Does it distort reality? Does it create artificial needs (Takala and Uusitalo, 1996)?

In practice, of course, marketers have very little influence over the actual state of consumers, but do they have influence over the desired state of consumers? Emphatically yes – otherwise all that advertising is just going to waste. For instance, a number of commentators over the past 20 years (Aljefree and Alhothali, 2022; Cornil et al., 2022; Harper, 2006; Herédia et al., 2017; Watson et al., 2021) have noted that marketers are blamed for the obesity epidemic in children around the world. The intimation was that it is marketers who have negotiated for schools to install vending machines serving unhealthy soft drinks in order to entice children to be desirous of fizzy drinks, and who have utilised fast-food marketing strategies in their campaigns. So is it all right to seek to change people's desired state (Folkvord et al., 2022)? Is it ethical? Or are we simply continuing the process that all people indulge in – advising each other about ways to make our lives more enjoyable and comfortable?

Since people often make decisions on the basis of immediate gain and emotion, neurological factors often contribute to our understanding of how and why people buy (Chew, 2022; Foxall, 2008).

Assortment adjustment is the act of entering the market to replenish or exchange the assortment of products the consumer owns. Assortment adjustment can be *programmed* (habitual) or *non-programmed* (new purchases) (see Figure 2.5). Non-programmed assortment adjustment divides into three categories. *Impulse purchases* are not based on a plan, and usually just happen as the result of a sudden confrontation with a stimulus – for example, in-store promotions might trigger an impulse purchase. People often buy as a result of lowered stimulation levels; in other words, bored shoppers might buy as a result of a stimulating promotion in-store (Garrido-Morgado et al., 2021; Sharma et al., 2010).

Assortment adjustment can take the form of either **assortment replenishment**, that is, replacing worn-out or consumed products, or **assortment extension**, adding to the range of products owned. Assortment replenishment will usually require very little information searching or risk, since the product is already known. Assortment extension is more likely to lead to an extensive problem-solving pattern.

Impulse buying has been further subdivided into four categories (Hawkins, 1962): *pure impulse*, based on the novelty of a product; *reminder impulse*, which relates to a product that has been left off the shopping list; *suggestion impulse*, which is about products that fulfil a previously unfelt need; and *planned impulse*, which occurs when the customer has gone out to buy a specific type of product but is prepared to be swayed by special offers.

For example, someone may set out to the supermarket to buy the week's groceries, plus something for lunch today. On the way round, he sees a jar of almond-stuffed olives and decides to buy some to try (pure impulse). Next he notices the green lasagne, which reminds him he's out of pasta (reminder impulse), and also on the shelf near it a recipe book for pasta (suggestion impulse). Finally, he notices that some Chinese Century Eggs are on special offer and decides to buy some for lunch (planned impulse). This type of scenario is familiar to most people who shop in supermarkets, and indeed supermarkets will often capitalise on this in the way the shelves are stocked and in the way the store is laid out.

The other two types of non-programmed decision-making involve either limited decision-making or extended decision-making. Of the two, limited decision-making is probably the most common.

Limited decision-making takes place when the customer is already familiar with the product class and merely wants to update his or her information or fill in a few gaps revealed by the internal search. This is typical behaviour for someone who is replacing a car; since this is usually an infrequent activity, consumers often find it necessary to check out what new models are available and renew acquaintance with the price levels being charged (especially when resources are limited too [Bhui et al., 2021]), even though (as a driver) the consumer will have considerable knowledge of what a car is and what it can be expected to do.

Assortment adjustment
The process of substituting some possessions for others in order to improve one's overall position

Assortment replenishment
Replacing possessions that have been worn out or used up

Assortment extension
Increasing one's overall quantity of possessions

Limited decision-making also tends to occur when the consumer is not completely satisfied with the existing product and seeks a better alternative. Here the individual is only looking for something that overcomes the perceived problem with the existing product. A trigger for this might be a change of context: someone who moves home will have their usual routines disrupted and may be open to changing his or her purchasing behaviour across a spectrum of goods (Neal et al., 2008). We quite often see this with individuals making investment choices and who are deciding where to invest their hard-earned money and where past performance does not guarantee future results (Weiss-Cohen et al., 2022).

Extended decision-making occurs when the consumer is unfamiliar with the product class, form and brand. For example, the majority of us are still unaware of consumer drones and the current state of the art in remote-controlled aircraft. This is a new class of product and an interested consumer would have to undertake a fairly extensive information search before committing to a particular model. Extended decision-making is caused by unfamiliarity; consumers who know little about the product category, brands and so forth will tend to shop around more.

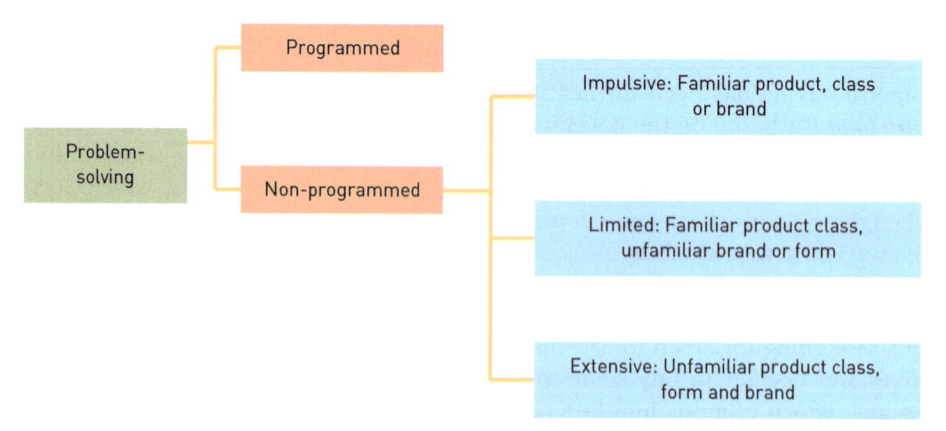

FIGURE 2.5 Programmed and non-programmed problem-solving

Source: Onkvisit and Shaw (1994). Used by kind permission.

INTERRUPTS

Interrupt
Something that diverts an individual away from a goal, usually temporarily

Sometimes the buying process cannot be followed exactly because events occur that force the individual to rethink the situation. These events are called **interrupts**, and they fall into four categories:

1. *Unexpected information that is inconsistent with established beliefs.* For example, if the shop that the consumer had expected to buy from has changed hands or closed, the individual has to look for a new supplier.

2. *Prominent environmental stimuli.* An in-store display might offer an alternative to the original purchase (perhaps by offering a large price discount on a similar product). This may divert the consumer away from his or her usual brand choice, or at the very least cause the consumer to consider switching.

3. *Affective states.* Hunger, boredom or tiredness during a shopping trip might lead to a change in goal. This may be a change away from looking for a new jacket, and towards looking for the coffee shop.
4. *Conflicts.* These are the motivational conflicts (further discussed in Chapter 5). If an individual is confronted with an approach–approach conflict, or an approach–avoidance conflict, there will be a temporary cessation of goal attainment while new goals are formulated and the conflict is resolved.

The effect of interrupts will depend on how consumers interpret the interrupting event. On the one hand, the interrupt may activate new end goals (as when the shopping trip turns into a search for a cup of coffee). On the other hand, a choice heuristic might be activated – for example, if the unexpected information is a friend recommending a brand, this may activate a heuristic about acting on friends' recommendations. Sometimes the interrupt is severe enough that the individual shelves the problem-solving behaviour indefinitely (for example, if the unexpected information is that the person has lost his or her job, the buying of a new jacket might be postponed indefinitely; or if a prominent environmental stimulus such as a substantial governmental tax increase on diesel fuel is levied, one might think twice about buying a diesel vehicle and consider switching to an electric vehicle) (see Figure 2.6).

Heuristic
A decision-making rule; sometimes also seen as a shortcut rule (see Chapter 5 for further detail)

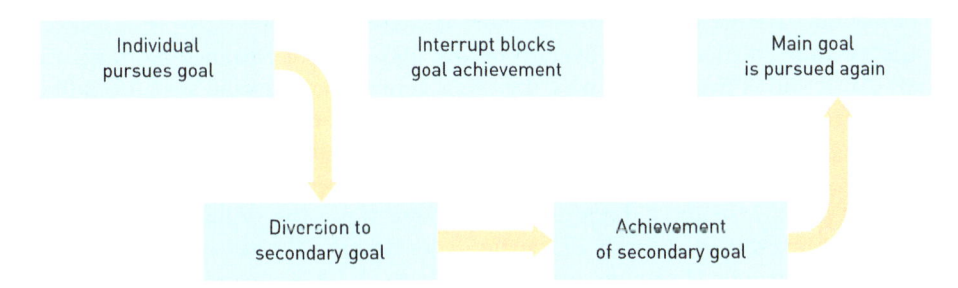

FIGURE 2.6 Temporary effects of an interrupt

TABLE 2.2 Goal and interrupt strengths

	Strong goal	**Weak goal**
Strong interrupt	Powerful stress set up in the individual	Goal will be ignored or abandoned, and a secondary goal will be established
Weak interrupt	Goal will continue to be pursued	Goal may be interrupted or abandoned, or interrupt may be ignored

The strength of the interrupt is also important (see Table 2.2). If the goal is a strong one, and the interrupt weak, the individual is unlikely to be diverted. A weak goal and a strong interrupt will clearly result in a break in the problem-solving behaviour (for example, the intention to check the prices online for a possible purchase of a holiday following a windfall is unlikely to take precedence over a desperate need to go to pay an outstanding utility bill). A weak goal and a weak interrupt may or may not result in a divergence from the planned behaviour, and a strong interrupt and a strong goal are likely to lead to considerable stress on the individual.

In most cases people tend to resume an interrupted task fairly quickly. Even though a marketer might be able to distract somebody away from their shopping to have a cup of coffee or a snack, the shopping task will be resumed fairly quickly afterwards.

RISK AND UNCERTAINTY

Inexperienced buyers have, by definition, less knowledge of the product category they are trying to buy into. Any action by a consumer could produce unpredictable consequences, some of which might be unpleasant. These consequences form the perceived risk of the transaction. Financial risk is present since the consumer could lose money; for houses, cars and other major purchases the risk is great because the commitment is long term. Because the risk is reduced as knowledge increases, greater perceived risk will tend to lead to greater information search efforts, and the benefits of such a search will be correspondingly greater. If the consumer feels certain about the decision already, there will be correspondingly less benefit in carrying out a search for information. Between individuals, a further factor is the degree to which the individual is risk-averse – clearly some people are quite happy to take risks in life, whereas others are more cautious. This can be a crucial factor in some marketing situations: for example, financial advisers in Britain are required by law to assess the individual's degree of risk-aversion before making recommendations for investments or borrowing. People tend to become more risk-averse as they grow older, since it would be more difficult to recover from any loss (see for instance work by Kim et al., 2022, which investigates how the older generation's income structure affects equity purchases). In recent years, there have been several scandals concerning the mis-selling of financial products (Armour et al., 2017; Barr, 2022; Gilad, 2015; Singh and Dipika, 2018), in particular high-risk high-return products sold to people who are in fact risk-averse and did not realise that there was a risk of losing part (or even all) of their investment. A study of female dentists found that as age increased, the risk-averse behaviour of women declined (McGrath and Rossomando, 2015), perhaps due to dentists wanting (or probably 'needing') to keep up to date with technological advancements, in order to remain competitive.

The fear of losing face with friends and associates is the major component of social risk, especially when trying to avert a negative outcome (Khan and Mohsin, 2017; Levkovski and Popovski, 2022). It is determined in part by product visibility; consumers who buy an inappropriate car can risk ridicule from their family, friends and colleagues, and might therefore carry out a more extended information search to ensure that the car will not provoke this reaction.

Perceived cost is the extent to which the consumer has to commit resources to the search. People will frequently cut the search down simply because it is taking too much time, money or effort. This is because the potential loss of making a wrong purchase decision is seen as being less than the cost of making a full search.

Risk reduction strategies are shown in Figure 2.7. The main tactic for reducing risk is to increase one's knowledge about the product category. A prospective commercial drone purchaser is likely to seek a great deal of advice from a great many sources and is likely to have the aircraft thoroughly inspected by a qualified and experienced UAV engineer. If the risk is still perceived to be high, the consumer will simply not make the purchase. This is why most retailers offer money-back guarantees or no-quibble return policies: such guarantees reduce risk for the consumer, so making the purchase more likely. Since most purchases work out reasonably well, products seldom need to be returned.

People often spend considerable time looking both online and offline, increasing their knowledge of the product categories before buying and in order to reduce risk of making the wrong decision. It used to be the case that the need to inspect products personally as a way of reducing risk had been identified as a barrier to internet purchase (Dailey, 2003). On the other hand, some aspects of internet purchase appear to reduce people's aversion to risk: especially as *returns* are so easy to process. In a pre-pandemic world, sales made by e-tailers (internet companies such as Amazon.com, Asos and Made.com), which do not have any physical stores, surpassed online sales of store-based UK retailers (£21.8 billion vs. £21.5 billion) for the first time in 2015, according to a Mintel report. However, according to Rigby (2022) general retail sales have recently been falling (both online and offline) as the post-pandemic cost of living crisis has hit demand.

People will frequently choose the middle-ranked or mid-priced brand as a compromise between buying the worst alternative on the one hand, and risking spending too much by buying the 'best' brand on the other. In a two-choice situation, a brand's chances of being bought are helped if a third brand is available that places it in the middle range (Sheng et al., 2003). This implies that a company in second place to a major brand should consider introducing a third, cheaper, brand into the market in order to boost sales of its existing brand. This begs the question about the extent to which brand salience influences brand choice intention of new customers (Ngo et al., 2022), and it's something we revisit in Chapter 9 when we look at how attitudes are formed.

Other tactics for reducing risk might include seeking help from a competent friend, or taking out insurance against the risk, or hedging the risk by setting aside resources (typically money) to cover against anything going wrong.

Mood can have an effect on risk-taking behaviour: people tend to buy more lottery tickets if the weather is bad, but whether this is a way of making life more exciting in dull weather or whether it is a way of cheering oneself up with the prospect of a big win is debatable (Bruyneel et al., 2006; Fu et al., 2021).

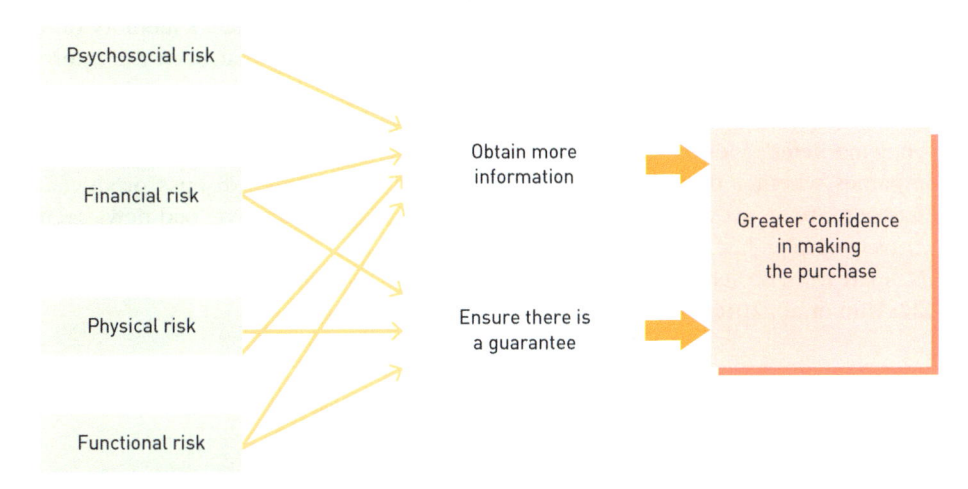

FIGURE 2.7 Reducing risk

PRE-PURCHASE ACTIVITIES

Having recognised the need, the consumer will undertake a series of pre-purchase activities.

The information search comes from two sources: an internal search (from memory) and an external search (from outside sources). In both cases most of the information originates from seller-based sources, and is therefore readily available and low-cost. If the internal information search is insufficient, that is to say the individual does not have enough knowledge of the product category to be able to make a choice, an external search will be undertaken.

Sources of information might be marketer dominated (advertising, blogs, vlogs, brochures, product placements in films and TV shows, websites, salespeople, retail displays, Twitter campaigns and so forth) or non-marketer dominated (friends, family, influential journalists, opinion leaders, consumer organisations, government and industry reports, news stories and so forth) (Figure 2.8). Word of mouth/mouse (Sethna et al., 2013) communications are generally more powerful than any marketer-generated communications, for the following reasons:

- Word of mouth/mouse is interactive, because it involves a discussion between two or more parties (online or offline). This forces those involved to think about the communication.
- It allows for feedback and confirmation of the message in a way that one-way communications like advertising do not.
- Because the source is a friend/family member, or indeed a trusted peer review, who has no profit motive (unlike the marketer), the communication is more credible.

'Peer review' is now an important consideration for many companies. These people, known as **influencers**, often discuss products and services: they like to talk about their own recent purchases, to advise people about purchases and even to discuss recent controversial marketing communications. And so the debate about what is more important – **word of mouse** or word of influencer – is brought to the fore (Jamil and Qayyum, 2022). It should be noted that non-marketer-generated sources are themselves influenced by marketers, and also much of the consumer's memory of the product comes from marketer-generated communications, so that even the internal search is affected by marketers.

From a marketer's viewpoint, the problem is that people will talk about products and companies whether the firm likes it or not and may very well discuss products in negative terms. A great deal of word of mouth therefore is negative; bad news seems to travel twice as fast as good news, and there is very little marketers can do about this, apart from be seen to be responsive in some shape or form (Colmekcioglu et al., 2022; Kim et al., 2016; Yin et al., 2016).

Sometimes an individual will set out with the belief that he or she has sufficient internal information to make the purchase, but is then presented with new information

Influencer
A person with the ability to influence potential buyers of a product or service by promoting or recommending the items on social media

Word of Mouse
people passing along messages about a company or product (or anything else) through digital forums

at the point of purchase. In other cases, people experience 'choice paralysis' brought on by having too wide a range of possible products to choose from: a consumer 'overchoice' (Manolică et al., 2021; Shankar et al., 2006). Because choosing involves a degree of emotional effort as well as cognitive effort (people often become stressed when faced with a choice between expensive options) the individual may well make a hasty choice (Baumeister, 2004). In other words, if the individual is finding it hard to choose, he or she might cut the decision-making process short by just grabbing the nearest product, simply to end the stress of trying to reach a decision. Most recently we have seen this in Shah et al.'s (2021) paper which reflects on the factors that may have caused the hasty adoption of 5G smart learning technology in order to maintain 'normal operations' in the education sector.

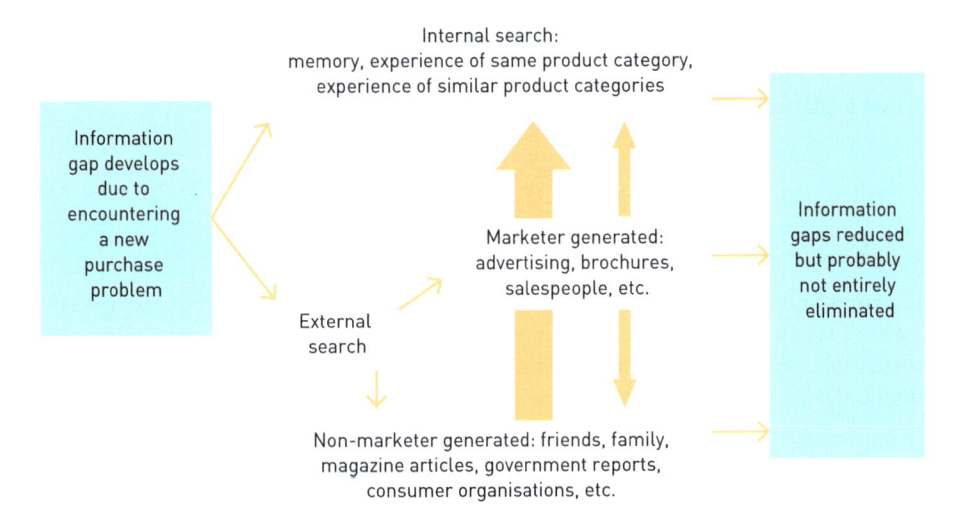

FIGURE 2.8 Information searching

THE SEARCH EFFORT

It is common for people with limited information to base their decisions on price, simply because they lack the necessary understanding to make a judgement based on other features of the product.

Search efforts are not very extensive under most circumstances, even for major purchases such as houses, because of the amount of time and effort that has to be expended. Usually consumers will continue to search until they find something that is adequate to meet their need, and will then not look any further – with comparison websites carving out a niche for themselves. A Financial Conduct Authority (FCA, 2014) report stated that most customers use the option of short-listing uppermost quotes on price comparison websites before making decisions.

Information searches such as those carried out on the internet and price comparison websites can be time-consuming, but as users become more adept, and as website design improves, searching is becoming much more rapid, as is the measurement of the user interaction (Jansen et al., 2022). It is likely that people will become more price sensitive as the ease of searching becomes greater – the cost of searching is low in terms of both money and time, so it becomes easier to shop around for bargains (Campo and Breugelmans, 2015; Melis et al., 2015). Limits on the search are shown in Figure 2.9.

In some cases, consumers will visit websites that carry complaints about companies, for example www.aspokesmansaid.com. This is a public platform that leverages the power of social media to force a response to a consumer complaint about a company. Online product recommendation agents gather information from consumers, then search the web to find products that match the consumer's needs; there is evidence to show that these agents should offer more than one solution for the consumer to choose from, which of course dilutes the advantage to some extent (Aggarwal and Vaidyanathan, 2003). Apart from specialist recommenders like aspokesmansaid.com, there are of course other popular examples such as Twitter and Facebook, which both provide a platform for consumer complaints.

FACTORS AFFECTING THE EXTERNAL SEARCH FOR INFORMATION

The extent and nature of the external search for information will depend on a range of factors connected with the consumer's situation, the value and availability of the information, the nature of the decision being contemplated and the nature of the individual. Figure 2.10 illustrates how these factors interrelate.

The type of problem-solving adopted will depend on the task at hand. A programmed decision pattern will lead almost immediately to purchase; these are the regular, always-buy-the-same-brand-type decisions. Non-programmed decisions may still lead immediately to a purchase by impulse, but this type of decision pattern will more likely lead to limited or extensive information search patterns.

The perceived value of the information is important (He et al., 2022; Magsayo, 2021) in terms of how extensive the information search will be. In other words, the extent of the external search depends on how valuable the information is. If there is plenty of information in the 'internal files' within the consumer's mind, the extent of external information seeking will be correspondingly less: consumers who are highly familiar with the product will search less than those who are only moderately familiar with it (Bettman and Park, 1980).

The relevance of this information is also a factor; if it's a long time since the last purchase, the stored information may not be relevant any longer. New alternatives may have developed or the product may have improved. If the individual was satisfied with the last product (which may by now have been consumed or has worn out) the internal information will probably be regarded as relevant, and the search will be less extensive or non-existent (Kiel and Layton, 1981).

DECISIONS, BEHAVIOURS AND INTERACTIONS

Time is a cost relating to search. It is sometimes measured in opportunity cost, or in terms of what the person could be doing instead of spending time searching. For example, highly paid people may value their time highly because they can earn more money at a desk than they save by shopping around, so they are prepared to spend money in order to save time. Poorer consumers may be more prepared to spend time shopping around in order to save money (Matli and Ngoepe, 2021; Urbany, 1986).

Many costs used to be the *out-of-pocket expenses* of searching. So, clearly a consumer who wanted to buy organic virgin olive oil might compare different brands in Waitrose but is unlikely to drive to Sainsbury's to compare prices, and would certainly not fly to Italy even though some olive oil would almost certainly be cheaper there from the source. Of course, with the internet awash with product comparison websites galore, such searches now take a matter of milliseconds, and cost virtually nothing.

The psychological costs of the information search include frustration, trawling through websites, latency, avoiding pop-ups, retargeted online advertising, driving to visit different shops, talking to shop assistants and generally giving a lot of thinking time to the search. Often people become overwhelmed with the quantity of information available, and will be unable to reach a decision because of information overload.

Latency
The delay before a transfer of data begins following a 'search' instruction, for its transfer, on a website

Sometimes the reverse happens and the consumer actually enjoys the shopping experience as entertainment. Ongoing search is different from external search in that consumers go to look for product information to augment stored product knowledge, often just for the fun of it. This can be a more important motivator than a genuine need to buy something (Bloch et al., 1986). Getting the balance right across the omnichannel continuum is a tricky one (Neslin, 2022).

Situational factors will also affect the product information search. The search will be limited, for example, if there is an urgent need for the product. If one's car has broken down on a motorway, one is unlikely to phone around for the cheapest breakdown service. Other variables might include product scarcity, or lack of available credit.

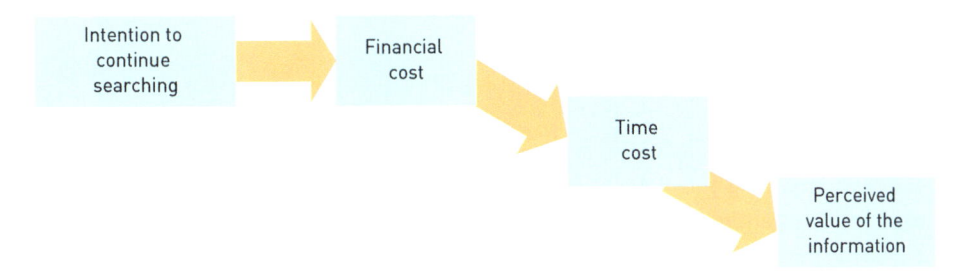

Intention to continue searching → Financial cost → Time cost → Perceived value of the information

FIGURE 2.9 Limits on the information search

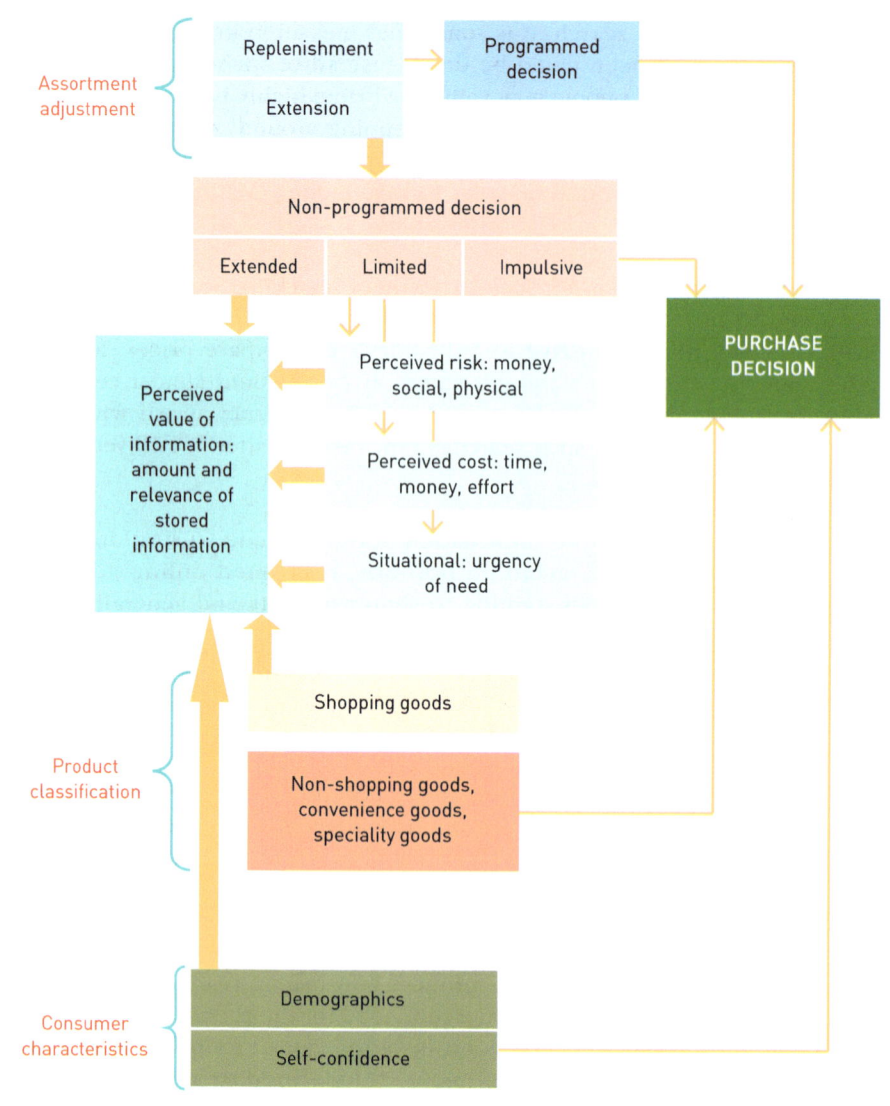

FIGURE 2.10 Factors affecting the external search for information

CRITICAL REFLECTION

Do we enjoy shopping? In fact, most of us do at one time or another – we go to the shops when we are on holiday, we wander round high streets trying on clothes or we wander round antiques markets looking at the antiquities. Browsing in bookshops, exploring new technologies, trying out new electronic equipment, even cruising the aisles of the newly sprouting organic supermarkets all provide entertainment for some people.

So where does that leave internet shopping? Can consumers enjoy the same tangible thrill while accessing the internet either from a laptop or a mobile device? How can we try on the dress, or test drive the wheels convincingly, when they are only on a screen? Well, our friends in South Korea have a solution. Back in 2011 they created the first successful augmented reality supermarket chains in subways. Called E-Marts, these virtual stores and 'connected shelves' sell their goods via glowing pictures on subway platforms. Shoppers waiting for a train can simply look at the walls to view potential groceries, scan the respective QR codes with their smartphone, and then have their groceries delivered by the time they reach their homes. But if you add sensors on smart shelves (Microsoft technology developed this for its Kinect gaming tool) you can track the age and gender of passing shoppers so that offers can be instantly displayed to match the assumed needs, wants and desires of that demographic!

And as we're *talking tech* here, let's have a look at some even more recent developments... very soon we'll see storefront windows becoming interactive and revolutionising the architecture of high streets. Displaying goods will simply become a thing of the past when these screens will enable shoppers to see entire catalogues, forthcoming offers and new ranges by tapping their fingers on the glass – even when the shop is closed.

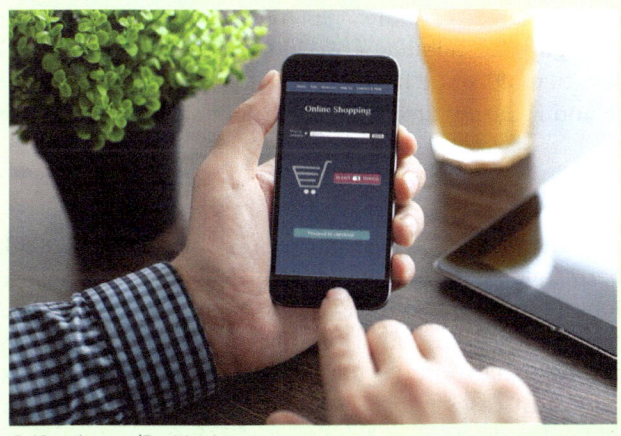

© iStock.com/Prykhodov

Did you think that holograms were only something in *Star Wars* films? Well very soon we'll see holograms in changing rooms which will enable shoppers to try on clothes without the need to get undressed using radio-frequency identification technology (having had their body image pre-scanned in 3D).

You may have encountered speed dating, but nothing has really prepared the shopping market for 'speed shopping'. For those people who still need to physically walk around a supermarket, can you picture a world where you walk into the supermarket, having input your shopping list on a mobile app, which will then link to in-store beacons (technology that can pinpoint your location in store) and within seconds you'll be sent a map of the store and the order in which you can pick up your desired goods in as short a time as possible, knowing where the queues are, which aisles are congested and whether any products are close to selling out?

And finally, if that's not personalisation enough, what about personalised pricing? What if stores got rid of public pricing altogether on their products, but used vast in-store data mines that will gather all they can about an individual – where they shop, what they buy, their income and brand loyalty, and then use that profile and purchase history to give the customer a better deal? Safeway supermarket has been running a programme in the USA called 'Just For U', which is an app-based promotion to create individually tailored pricing, making shopping a more meaningful experience.

In terms of product classification, shopping goods are those for which a new solution has to be formulated every time. Non-shopping goods are those for which the person already has a complete preference and specification, and therefore is able to buy the same brand almost all the time (Botha et al., 2020; Bucklin, 1963). For example, tomato ketchup is usually a non-shopping product, whereas a 55" curved OLED TV is a shopping product.

Consumer characteristics are those features of the consumer that affect the information search. Demographics affect the search in that outshoppers (people who shop outside the area in which they live) have higher incomes, and are mobile. This factor may be product-specific, since outshopping most frequently occurs when buying groceries at an out-of-town shopping centre or buying consumer durables. Outshopping can also occur in the form of a shopping trip to a major city, or even a day trip to another country to take advantage of lower prices there – think medical tourism (Zhong et al., 2021).

People feel varying levels of pain in paying for things. Spendthrifts feel relatively little pain in making purchases, whereas careful savers (tightwads) feel a great deal of pain in making purchases. Tightwads outnumber spendthrifts by a ratio of 3 to 2, so it is important for marketers to understand how and why the pain of paying varies across the population (Khan and Hemsley-Brown, 2021; Rick et al., 2008).

MAKING THE CHOICE

Having gone through the procedures of collecting information, whether by a lengthy search or by simply remembering all the necessary facts, people make a choice based on the collected information. The first procedure is to establish a consideration set, which is the group of products from which the final choice is to be made. Option framing means creating a base model for the decision, then adding or subtracting options from it: in most cases people will limit the number of options under consideration, and will tend to delete more than they add (Biswas, 2009; Mayer et al., 2022).

Consumers construct the consideration set from the knowledge obtained in the information search. They will often use cut-offs, or restrictions on the minimum or maximum acceptable values. Typically consumers will have a clear idea of the price range they are willing to pay, for example, and any product priced outside this zone will not be included. Incidentally, this price range may have a minimum as well as a maximum; price is often used as a surrogate for judging quality. Again, marketers need to know what the consumer's cut-off point is on given specifications; this can be determined by market research.

Signals are important to consumers when judging product quality. A signal could be a brand name, a guarantee and even the retailer the product is bought from. Because it is common for consumers to equate quality with high price, a useful tactic for low-priced manufacturers is to undermine this perception in as many ways as possible. The use of price as a quality signal is somewhat reduced when other signals are present. For example, if the consumer is easily able to judge the quality by inspecting the product, the relationship may not apply.

DECISIONS, BEHAVIOURS AND INTERACTIONS

Finally, consumers will often select a decision rule or heuristic. Consumers develop these rules over a period of time; for example, a rule might be always to buy the best quality one is able to afford at the time. Some consumers have rules about brand names, or shops they know and trust, or people whose preferences they will always respect.

Figure 2.11 shows an example of a decision-making process for a holiday purchase. The consumer begins with a choice of five different holidays, which form the consideration set. The relevant information about each holiday has been included, and now the decision rules need to be applied. First of all, the consumer decides that a long flight would be difficult with children so he or she sets a limit of 3 hours. This cuts out Greece and Florida. Then there is a cut-off on cost (not to go above £2500). This cut-off has no relevance, since none of the remaining holidays cost above £2500, but the consumer also uses price as a signal by which to judge quality, and cuts out the tent in France because it is too cheap. The remaining decision rule is that there must be something for the children to do, and this leaves only the apartment in Spain as the final choice.

Sometimes the consumer will find that applying all the decision rules cuts out all of the alternatives, so that a revision of the rules needs to take place. This can result in establishing a hierarchy of rules according to their relative importance (Bettman, 1979). There is also an effect caused by simply thinking about the product group – people often judge the desirability of the options on the basis of their ability to consider the options in advance. In other words, being able to think through and understand the implications of owning a product tends to make the product more desirable (Leising et al., 2021; Morewedge et al., 2010).

CATEGORISATION OF DECISION RULES

Non-compensatory decision rules are absolute; if a product does not meet the decision rule for one attribute, this cannot be compensated for by its strength in other areas. In the holiday example in Figure 2.11, despite the fact that the Florida location is near to Disneyland, and is therefore a very strong candidate as far as entertaining the children is concerned, the cost and the flight time rule it out. In the lexicographic

> **Non-compensatory decision rule**
> A heuristic that cannot be offset by other factors

Atlantico Apts, Majorca. S/C, ten mins from beach, discos and clubs. £1800

Las Olas Apts, Spain. S/C, near beach, pool, children's activities. £2400

Green Cay, Florida. Hotel, near beach, pool, Disneyland 10 miles. £3300

Hotel Dionysos, Greece. B/B, beach five mins, children's activities. £1900

Camp du Midi, France. Luxury tent, children's activities, lake beach. £1500

Cut-off one: flight time less than 3 hours

Cut-off two: price below £2500 Signal: price above £1500 to ensure quality

Decision rule: there must be something for small children to do

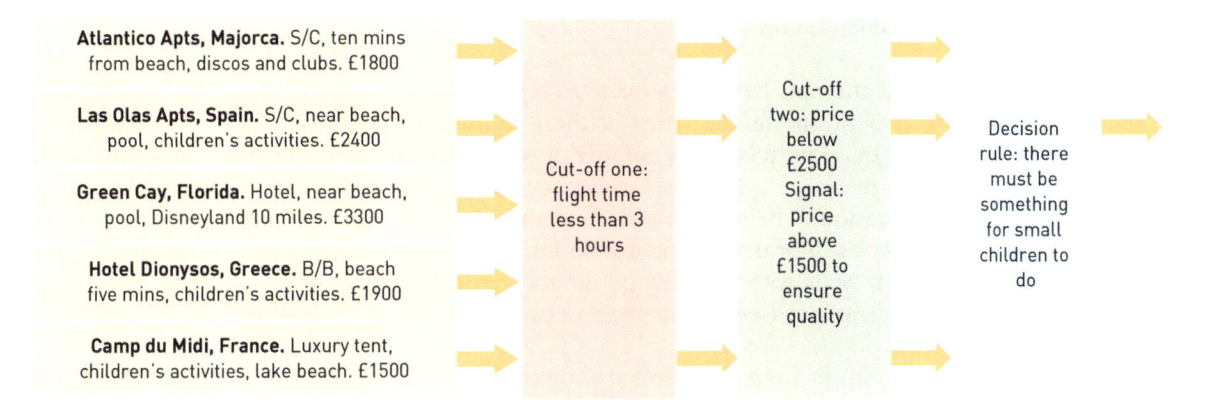

FIGURE 2.11 An example of a decision-making process for a holiday purchase

approach the consumer establishes a hierarchy of attributes, comparing products first against the most important attribute, then against the second most important, and so forth. Decisions can be made by elimination of aspects whereby the product is examined against other brands according to attributes, but then each attribute is checked against a cut-off.

Conjunctive rule

A heuristic by which brands are compared to all cut-offs until only a few surviving brands remain

The **conjunctive rule** is the last of the non-compensatory rules. Here each brand is compared in turn against all the cut-offs; only those brands that survive this winnowing-out will be compared with each other.

Compensatory decision rules allow for trade-offs, so that a weakness in one area can be compensated for in another. The simple additive rule involves a straight tally of the product's positive aspects, and a comparison of this tally with the tally for other products. The product with the most positive attributes will be the one chosen. A variation of this is the weighted additive approach, which gives greater weight to some attributes than to others. In each case, though, the products do not necessarily have to have all the attributes in common (or, indeed, any of them).

Phased decision strategies may involve using rules in a sequence. For example, the consumer may use a non-compensatory cut-off to eliminate products from the consideration set, then use a weighted additive rule to decide between the remaining products.

Two more special categories of decision rule exist. First, the consumer may need to create a constructive decision rule. This means establishing a rule from scratch when faced with a new situation. If the rule thus created works effectively, the consumer will store it in memory until the next time the situation is encountered, and 'recycle' the rule then. Second, affect referral is the process whereby consumers retrieve a 'standard' attitude from memory. For example, a consumer may strongly disapprove of a company's business practices (ZMEScience, 2015), which may prevent the inclusion of its products in the consideration set.

If consumers are using a weighted additive rule, it would be useful to know which attributes are given the greatest weightings. If they are using a conjunctive rule with cut-offs at known levels, the product can be designed to fall within the cut-offs. To become part of the consideration set it must pass the cut-offs and signals employed in the decision process.

Several attempts have been made to bring the factors in consumer decision-making together in one model. Most of these models are complex, since there are many factors that interrelate in a number of ways; an example is the Howard–Sheth model shown in Figure 2.12. This is a somewhat simplified version; the original requires one diagram to be superimposed on another. In the diagram the solid arrows show the flow of information; the dotted lines show the feedback effects. Essentially, the diagram deals with the way the inputs are dealt with by perception (see Chapter 7) and by learning (see Chapter 8) and eventually become outputs.

Following on from the purchase, there will be an evaluation of both the product itself and the decision process. The learning process will feed back into the internal search, and new heuristics will be developed.

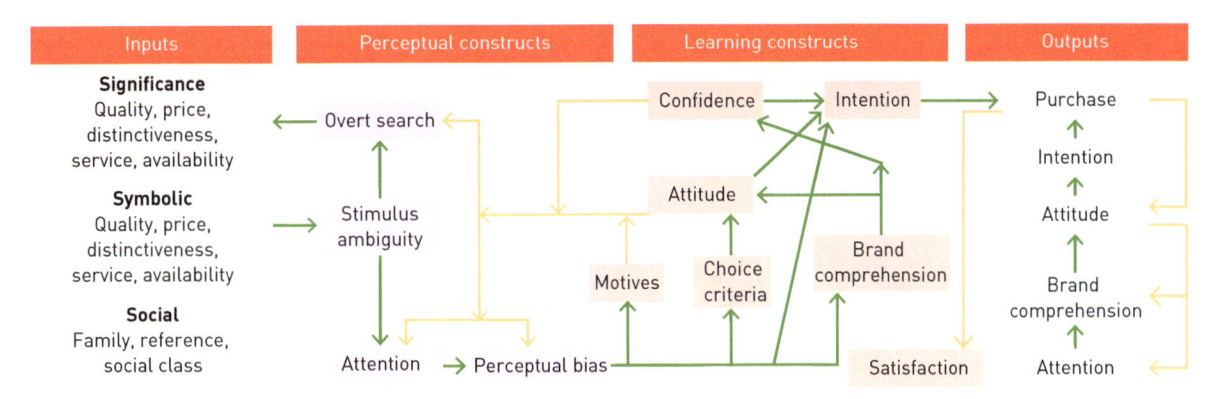

FIGURE 2.12 Howard–Sheth model
Source: Adapted from Howard and Sheth (1969).

INVOLVEMENT

Involvement is the perceived relevance of the object based on the person's inherent needs, values and interests (Zaichowsky, 1985). It is about the degree to which the individual feels attached to the product or brand, and the loyalty felt towards it. Involvement has both cognitive and affective elements: it acts on both the mind and the emotions.

BRAND EXPERIENCES: MY EMOTIONAL ATTACHMENTS

Do we really become that emotionally attached to products? Surely we are not so shallow that the most important thing in our lives is a brand of cereal? Well perhaps it is when you've three tired and grumpy children sitting at the breakfast table! People are often in the habit of saying 'I really love my car!', but isn't that just a figure of speech? Saying that we like something a lot is not the same as saying we love it, and saying that we think a product is the best available does not mean that we cannot live effectively without it.

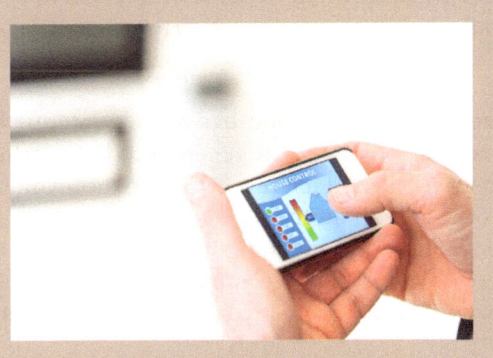

© iStock.com/GregorBister

Well, let's take some products that we're familiar with and add some emotion into the equation…

- iPhone – 'My phone can do anything' (hhhmmm, it may be true, I can remotely shut my curtains from a 1000 miles away, and using Hive – a British Gas app – my home heating system recognises when I am 3 miles from home and automatically switches the heating on in winter!).
- Bose noise-reducing headphones – 'increases my very personal space' (absolutely, if you put some blinkers on too, you'd be in a world of your own!).

(Continued)

> You get the picture… In the course of a long life, we fall in love with many people and products – but are we so blinded by our love of particular products that we cannot be aware, at all, ever, of the possibility of change? (When it comes to people, that's a different textbook!)

| Inertia | Willingness to listen | Interest in anything about the product | Active search for information | Total commitment |

Regular routine purchases of generic products ⟷ Identification with a brand to the point of obsession

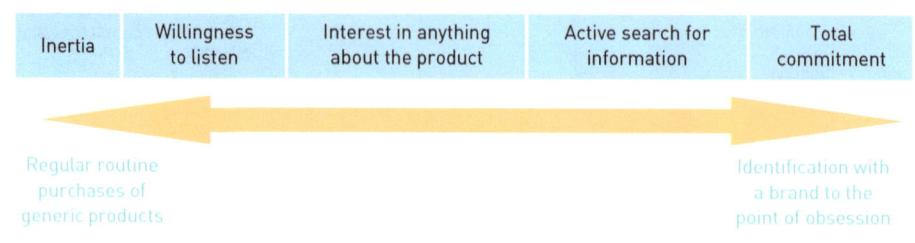

FIGURE 2.13 Involvement continuum

Involvement is sometimes seen as the motivation to process information (Mitchell, 1979). At a low level of involvement, individuals only engage in simple processing of information; at high levels of involvement, people will link incoming information to their pre-existing knowledge system, in a process called elaboration (Otker, 1990). The degree of involvement will lie somewhere on a continuum from complete **inertia** through to high involvement where we might expect to find an intensity of feeling that borders on the religious. At the extreme, we would expect to find people who worship celebrities, or are fanatical about religious beliefs or who have a brand tattooed onto their skin (Harley-Davidson owners have been known to do this). Such *extreme* people have often become involved with cult product offerings such as Star Trek memorabilia, Vans shoes or the Volkswagen Beetle. There is of course a dark side to all of this, and it rears its ugly head when extreme overvalued beliefs are rigidly held and which are the motive behind most acts of terrorism and mass shootings (Rahman, 2018).

Figure 2.13 shows the continuum in action. Someone who has no real interest in the product category and makes only routine purchases of generic products (or no purchases at all) exhibits inertia. Someone with a mild interest in the product exhibits a willingness to listen to explanations or advice about the product. Someone who is involved at a medium level would take an interest in anything he or she happens to see concerning the product, and someone who is highly committed would actively seek out information. Finally, someone who is totally committed to the brand identifies with it to the point of obsession.

Figure 2.14 summarises categories of involvement. Involvement is not always confined to products. People can experience message–response involvement or advertising involvement in which they become eager to process information obtained from advertising (Batra and Ray, 1983). In some cases, the messages are passive (as in the case of TV advertising), whereas in other cases messages involve more effort on the part of the observer (for example print advertisements) and some marketing communications permit a great deal of interaction (web-based advertising).

Inertia

Making decisions out of habit rather than from any conscious loyalty

DECISIONS, BEHAVIOURS AND INTERACTIONS

```
Product involvement        Message–response involvement
            ↘                    ↙
              Types of involvement
            ↗                    ↖
Purchase situation              Ego involvement
involvement
```

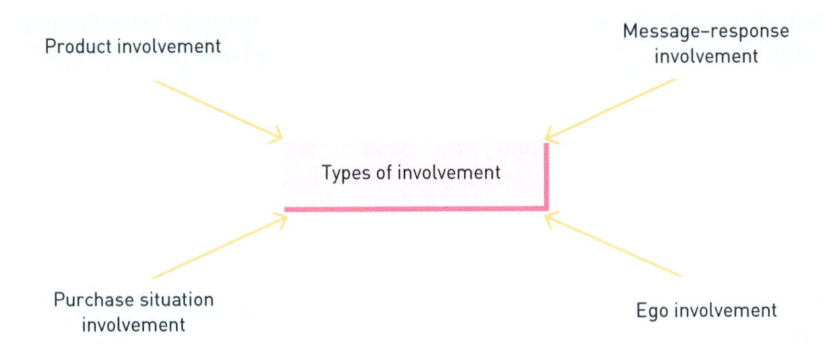

FIGURE 2.14 Categories of involvement

Purchase situation involvement is about the different contexts in which purchase takes place. For example, if one were buying a gift for a new partner, one might be extremely involved in the purchase since there is a high social risk involved if a mistake is made. If, on the other hand, the gift-buying is almost obligatory (e.g. buying a birthday gift for a relative one has little liking for and rarely sees), the involvement level will be considerably lower.

Ego involvement is about the importance of the product to the individual's self-concept. Making a mistake in purchase could lead to a high social risk – the individual's self-concept might be damaged, to embarrassing effect. For example, a committed vegan would be horrified to find that a supposedly vegan product contained animal fat. In some cases, the product purchase is linked to a 'tribe': such communities are supported by social networking sites, celebrity affiliations and self-generated communications (Hamilton and Hewer, 2010; Mock et al., 2022).

High product involvement is driven by the degree to which the individual feels that the product's attributes are linked to end goals or values. Lower levels of involvement occur if the attributes only link to function, and very low levels of involvement occur if the product attributes are irrelevant to consequences.

In other words, high-involvement products are those that figure strongly in the individual's lifestyle. They involve decisions that are important to get right, preferably first time. In most cases these products are ones the consumer knows a lot about, and about which he or she has strong opinions. This means that high-involvement consumers are hard to persuade: they will not easily be swayed by advertising, or even by persuasive sales pitches. For example, a website developer might favour specific software, but if the software is unavailable he or she is unlikely to be persuaded by a salesperson that a different application is just as good. The discrepant information is ignored or disparaged, so the source of the information (the salesperson) will lose esteem in the eyes of the developer.

Levels of involvement are influenced by two sources: personal sources and situational sources. Personal sources (also called **intrinsic self-relevance**) are derived from the means–end knowledge stored in the individual's memory, and are influenced both by the person and by the product. People who believe that the attributes of the product link to important end goals are likely to be more heavily involved with

Intrinsic self-relevance

Sources of involvement derived from means–end knowledge stored in the individual's memory the product because the importance of the end goal means that it is more important to be right first time. Even products such as snacks can have personal involvement issues – pre-teen girls have been shown to have very specific requirements for snacks, based on what friends find acceptable (Dibley and Baker, 2001). Involvement does not necessarily depend on the outcome being positive; sometimes involvement might be greater if the possible outcomes are negative (Doyle et al., 2021), since the consumer will take care to choose products that will avoid negative outcomes.

CONSUMER BEHAVIOUR IN ACTION: NFT IN THE ART WORLD AND BEYOND

In the previous edition of this book, we examined the artist Hormazd Narielwalla and the way in which he used his bespoke Savile Row tailoring patterns to create artworks exploring the body in abstract form (www.narielwalla.com). We continue the theme of art but discuss some of the current trends in the art world. Non-fungible tokens (NFTs) exploded onto the art scene back in 2019 when a piece of work by a digital artist known as Beeple was sold for $69 million at a Christie's online auction. Since then we have seen a plethora of galleries and artists trying to capture a piece of this seemingly lucrative market. So what exactly is it? An NFT is a piece of artwork stamped with a unique string of code and stored on a virtual ledger called a blockchain. Then once the marketing machine starts up and campaigns go viral, generating some consumer confidence with some pandemic ennui thrown in for good measure, what you see is an absolute explosion of interest in the NFT market which ultimately drives up the price of digital artworks very quickly and very steeply.

But in the background what we don't hear about in the popular press is the fact that NFTs have a ginormous environmental footprint. The creation of an average NFT is estimated at being over 200 kilograms of planet-warming carbon. In fact, by some estimations 300 items of digital art (100 each of three art pieces) could burn through the same amount of electricity that an average European would otherwise use in two decades or the equivalent of driving 500 miles in a typical American gasoline-powered car. Would you be happy to 'roll 500 miles'?! That's a lot of juice for a jolly! Part of the issue is that the foundational technology, blockchain, produces enormous greenhouse emissions. There is a complex process that must be undergone. Let me try and explain. An artist uploads a piece of art and starts a process known as mining (or 'mint it'). This involves complex puzzles which need A LOT of computing power which in turn needs A LOT of energy. Ethereum, which seems to be the platform of choice for NFTs, began by using a consensus mechanism that involved proof-of-work (PoW). This allowed the nodes of the Ethereum network to agree on the state of all information recorded on the Ethereum blockchain and prevented certain kinds of economic attacks. However, Ethereum switched off proof-of-work in 2022 and started using proof-of-stake instead. If an artist wanted to add an asset (their artwork) to the blockchain's master ledger, miners were required to compete with each other to solve a cryptographic puzzle. So essentially their computers were required to rapidly generate numbers in a frenzied race of trial and error. Miners were making in excess of more than 170 quintillion attempts a second to produce new blocks, according to the trading platform Blockchain.com. (A quintillion is 1 followed by 18 zeros.) I'll just let that sink in for a while. The miner who arrived at the right answer first was the winner and got her or his asset added to the blockchain.

> Proof-of-stake (PoS) underlies Ethereum's consensus mechanism. Ethereum switched on its proof-of-stake mechanism in 2022 because it is more secure, crucially less energy-intensive, and better for implementing new scaling solutions compared to the previous proof-of-work architecture.
>
> Many smaller artists have seen NFTs as an opportunity to glean more exposure for their work and in the process receive further recognition and ultimately perhaps some lucrative sales. Or at least that's what the hype over digital tokens would have us believe. In reality, the initial investment it takes seems to be prohibitive for many smaller artists. What we've seen are some of the big firms taking a punt at developing a niche for themselves. Here are a handful of examples which you may want to, pardon-the-pun, *mine* further:
>
> In order to try and mitigate counterfeit shoes, Nike has patented shoes as NFTs. Consumers are able to create digital sneakers called CryptoKicks 'the block-chain compatible sneakers'. Whenever a Nike enthusiast buys a genuine pair of shoes, a digital representation with a cryptographic token will accommodate the ownership details.
>
> The American Brewing company Anheuser-Busch hosted a #NFTBeerFest event for Budweiser NFT holders. Those who purchased either a Budweiser Heritage Can or Royalty Collection NFT then had access to free beer, tours, giveaways and entertainment at the occasion. So we can see that these NFTs also help brands with community building and providing more exclusive content to a select group of their fans.
>
> Gucci, the Italian fashion brand, has taken a slightly different approach with the launch of Vault – an all-new online store. They have launched several sets of NFT collections which complement and compliment the brand's 100-year-old heritage.

DIMENSIONS OF INVOLVEMENT

It is possible to use these dimensions of involvement (see Figure 2.15) to segment the market for a given product. For example, for some people an Apple Watch might have a strong sign value, while for others it has a strong pleasure value: the approach to each of these groups would be different in terms of marketing communication. There are, of course, other factors at play here too – a high status sign can give pleasure to an individual, not to mention the possible hedonistic and functional values that could also be derived from owning such products.

Laurent and Kapferer (1985), whose seminal paper initially showcased this five-factor model for assessing the dimensions of involvement, described the factors as follows, together with references to recent studies on each area:

1. The personal interest a person has in the product category, its personal meaning or importance. For example, people often become very involved in art galleries or orchestras (Gurel and Nielsen, 2018; Kolbe, 2022).
2. The perceived importance of the potential negative consequences associated with a poor choice of product (risk importance) (Lin et al., 2018; Shi et al., 2022).
3. The probability of making a bad purchase (Bhandari and Rodgers, 2018).
4. The pleasure value of the product category (Hassenzahl, 2018; Uklańska, 2021).
5. The sign value of the product category (how closely it relates to the self) (Bhatt et al., 2018; Worm and Stine-Morrow, 2021).

Chocolate scores high in terms of pleasure, but low on sign value (unless of course you are talking about something like Rococo Chocolates!) and risk value. The evidence is, therefore, that different products may be high involvement for different reasons.

INVOLVEMENT WITH BRANDS

People often develop relationships with brands. Typical examples might be favourite cars, perfumes, clothes, cigarettes, coffee and so forth. Research by Brann Consulting showed that people are more likely to think of their brand of coffee as a friend than they are to think of their bank this way: banks are acquaintances at best, enemies at worst. This may seem surprising considering that banks are composed of people, whereas coffee is inanimate, but it is perhaps due to the fact that coffee is consumed at home or with friends whereas bank services are often regarded as an unpleasant necessity.

The relationships that the individual has with both the brand and the product are very closely intertwined. Drivers often develop affectionate relationships with their cars, personalising them with stickers and accessories, and not infrequently giving them a name. Drivers even talk to their cars (sometimes in less than flattering terms), and with cars nowadays, let's not be surprised if the cars talk back! And recently a lot of us have been talking to our voice-activated personal assistant, Siri! But how many of us would switch loyalties and employ the services of either Alexa (from Amazon Echo) or Google Assistant? Involvement also has an influence on decision-making styles (Bauer et al., 2006). Even when the products themselves might be considered to have few differences, people are prepared to pay more for the branded product and retailers are prepared to make the differentiation between own-brand and branded products (Uzelac et al., 2022; Valdés de la Fuente and Elexpuru, 2022). Research in the USA showed that people would pay more for branded pork than for unbranded pork (Ubilava et al., 2011).

Involvement can also be considered in terms of attachment theory, specifically avoidance and anxiety factors. Avoidance factors are those that make people shun relationships due to a fear of intimacy, while anxiety factors are those that make people fear loss, anxiety or rejection. People who are low or high on both dimensions report high satisfaction with brands, whereas people who are high on one dimension and low on the other report low satisfaction rates (Thompson and Johnson, 2002). This means that people with a fear of becoming dependent and a fear of loss will be less likely to form relationships with brands and will therefore have no problems with them, whereas people who have no fear of becoming dependent and also no fear of loss will have many favourite brands. There are age and gender differences in brand relationship formation (Boisvert and Ashill, 2022; Murillo, 2022): when considering the two propositions 'I understand the brand' and 'The brand understands me', women use both dimensions to judge their closeness to the brand, whereas men judge only by their own actions towards the brand (Kauppinen-Räisänen et al., 2018; Monga, 2002).

For any given product category, people can be classified according to their level of involvement, as shown in Table 2.3. The relationship between these factors is shown in Figure 2.16. Even when the product has other products associated with it, the involvement may apply only to one of the products: for example, someone might be staunchly loyal to a brand of gin (say Hendrick's) without caring much which brand of tonic water (Fentiman's, Canada Dry or Schweppes) goes in with it. While it is true that some people may be heavily involved in several brands, there is no evidence that high involvement in one brand will lead to high involvement in another brand from a different product category.

Involvement does not always equate with price. A high-involvement product is not necessarily a high-priced one, nor is a low-involvement product always a cheap one. Beer drinkers can be heavily committed to their brand of beer, costing only a few pounds a pint, whereas other people might not care what make of car they drive as long as it gets them from point A to B. High involvement always has a strong affective component, and this does not necessarily mean a high cost commitment – people also fall in love with cheap (or rather, *more cost-effective*) products.

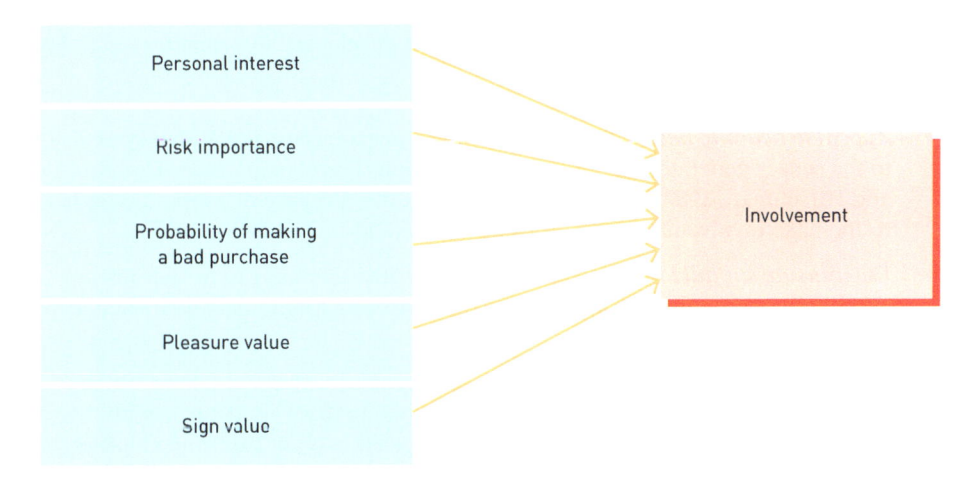

FIGURE 2.15 Dimensions of involvement

TABLE 2.3 Categorising consumers according to involvement

Brand loyalists	These are people who buy what they think is the 'best' brand in the category. This is because they tend to have strong views about the relevance of the brand to their daily lives – the brand itself has personally relevant consequences for them, and they are highly involved with it
Routine brand buyers	These people have a favourite brand, but don't necessarily feel involved with it at a personal level. Typically, they will buy the same brand on a regular basis, but would not have a big problem in buying a substitute brand if their usual brand were unavailable. In other words, they have a low level of involvement with the brand
Information seekers	These people feel strongly about the product category, but do not identify one brand as superior. They have positive means–end information about the category, and spend time and effort choosing the final brand within the category, but have low involvement in the actual brand
Brand switchers	These people do not have a strong view about the brands on offer, and will choose whichever happens to be the most convenient at the time of purchase. They have low involvement with the brand, even if they have high involvement with the product category

Source: Adapted from Peter and Olson (1994).

| Brand switchers | Information seekers | Routine brand buyers | Brand loyalists |

Low involvement ←——————————————→ High involvement

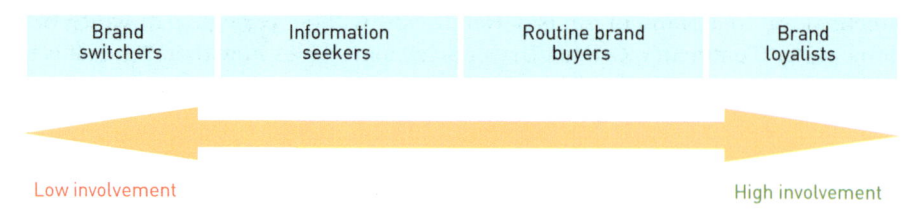

FIGURE 2.16 Categorising consumers

INCREASING INVOLVEMENT LEVELS

From a marketer's viewpoint, increasing consumers' involvement levels is clearly a priority. Marketers will try to increase consumer involvement with the products whenever it is possible to do so, since this will make communications easier and loyalty levels higher. As Figure 2.17 summarises, there are various fundamental techniques available to marketers for encouraging consumers to process relevant information, as follows (Stewart and Furse, 1984):

- *Appeal to hedonic needs.* Any form of marketing communication that appeals to the senses generates higher levels of attention (Haase et al., 2020; Holbrook and Hirschman, 1982). There is evidence that the pleasure of shopping tends to increase involvement with clothing (Michaelidou and Dibb, 2006).

- *Use unusual stimuli to attract attention.* Using 5D technology to further involve the participant and inculcate a real experience, including elements such as rainwater, aroma and smoke.

- *Use celebrity endorsement.* The viewer's involvement with the celebrity is likely to transfer to the product (Auerbach, 2021), although there are dangers with this approach both when looking at 'meaning transfer' (Tian et al., 2022) and ultimately the consumer response to negative celebrity publicity (Wang and Kim, 2019).

- *Use prominent stimuli*, such as fast action or loud music or in humorous places. This will help to capture the viewer's attention using environmental stimuli originating from sight, sound and sociability (Chan and Lowe, 2021; Hungenberg et al., 2020).

- *Develop an ongoing relationship with consumers.* This can often be done by using a well-designed interactive website to generate involvement or online brand communities (OBCs) (Carlson et al., 2021).

Ultimately, of course, consumers develop their own ideas about involvement, and will only become involved in products that appeal to their innermost selves. Marketers can only facilitate a process that would have happened (at least to some extent) in any case.

LOYALTY IN BUYER BEHAVIOUR

Involvement with a brand should, in the vast majority of cases, lead to feelings of loyalty. In recent years, marketers have taken the view that it is better to generate loyalty and therefore retain customers than it is to keep recruiting new customers. This view has been expressed most clearly by Ehrenberg, who proposed the 'leaky

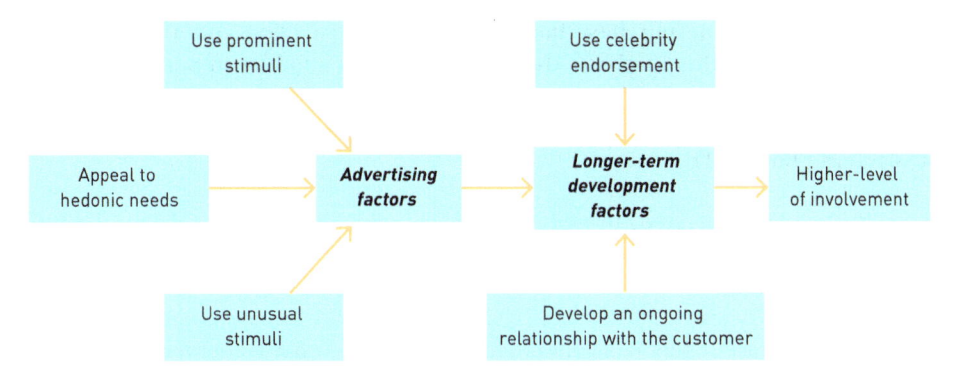

FIGURE 2.17 Increasing involvement

bucket' theory. In the past, most companies have operated on a 'leaky bucket' basis, seeking to refill the bucket with new customers while ignoring the ones leaking away. According to seminal research by Gupta et al. (2004), a 1% improvement in customer retention will lead to a 5% improvement in the firm's value. In other words, customer retention is five times as effective as cutting costs, especially as a 1% improvement in customer acquisition cost only generates a 1% increase in firm value. Ehrenberg (2000) noted that loyalty differs far less between brands in a category than does the number of buyers for each brand. Recent work by Dawes et al. (2015) has succinctly encapsulated some of the areas used to measure behavioural loyalty towards brands:

- Repeat-purchase rate (Colombo et al., 2000; Fader and Schmittlein, 1993).
- Tenure (length of time a buyer remains a buyer) (East et al., 2001; Reichheld and Teal, 1996).
- Share of category requirements (Bhattacharya et al., 1996; Jung et al., 2010; Pare and Dawes, 2011).
- Repertoire size (Banelis et al., 2013; Uncles and Ehrenberg, 1990).
- Purchase frequency (Morrison, 1966; Sharp and Sharp, 1997).
- Proportion of buyers who are solely loyal (Raj, 1985).

Satisfaction is not necessarily enough to generate loyalty, however. East et al. (2006) found no evidence that satisfaction breeds loyalty, but have found evidence that satisfaction leads to personal recommendations and therefore to recruitment of new customers. In fact, in many ways people are not loyal, and their loyalty cannot be bought: only a small percentage of loyalty card holders actually are loyal (Allaway et al., 2006; Khan et al., 2020), because most people carry several cards (Meyer-Waarden and Benavent, 2006; Pesonen et al., 2019). Loyalty to the store tends to be higher in the case of online suppliers, which may be a function of trust (Buttner and Goritz, 2008; Ruiz-Molina et al., 2021). Trust lends itself to purchase incidence, meaning that heavy buyers of a category buy more brands, and are consequently less loyal to any particular brand (Banelis et al., 2013). There are also those who make only one-off purchases and should therefore not count as 100% loyal (Uncles and Lee, 2006).

The importance of the purchase has an effect on satisfaction and also on loyalty: the more important the purchase, the more disastrous a failure in performance will be and the greater the effect on satisfaction and loyalty. Perhaps surprisingly, if the purchase importance is low, perceived performance has a stronger influence on satisfaction (Tam, 2011).

If loyalty can be generated, though, it does increase profitability (Helgesen, 2006; Lin and Bowman, 2022). It also has the effect of reducing the evaluation of brand extensions – people tend to assume that the extension will be as good as the original brand (Hem and Iversen, 2003; Peña, 2022). When a brand grows, therefore, it is the change in penetration which is generally larger than the change in loyalty (Baldinger et al., 2002; Dawes, 2009; Socha, 2022).

UNSOUGHT GOODS

Unsought goods
Products that are bought as a result of coercion rather than through desire

So far, we have looked at consumer behaviour when seeking out goods to meet a specific, recognised need. While most products fall into the category of being sought out as a way of meeting a need, there is a category of **unsought goods** that consumers do not look for.

Unsought goods are those goods for which consumers will recognise a need, but which they nevertheless tend to avoid buying. Examples are life insurance, wills and funeral plans (usually because people prefer not to contemplate their own death), and some home improvements (because major capital expenditures can always be postponed).

The possible reasons for not seeking out the products, summarised in Figure 2.18, are as follows:

- People do not like to think about the reasons for needing the products. Because people do not like to think about old age and death, they prefer not to think about pensions and insurance.

- Given the vast number of stories in the press (for instance the Payment Protection Insurance [PPI] scandal or the 'Diesel Emissions Test Scandal'), the consumer has come to perhaps mistrust marketers of such products.

- The products are expensive or require a long-term commitment, and people do not like to risk making a mistake.

- There is no urgency about seeking a solution. Retirement may be a long way off, or the roof may last another year or two.

- The consumer may not see any immediate benefit. In the case of life insurance, the insured person never benefits directly since the policy only pays out on proof-of-death.

- Some unsought goods are new on the market, so the level of knowledge about them is low and the individual automatically rejects any marketing approach because the benefits are not obvious. Trust in both the product and the brand needs to be established first before information can be transferred.

DECISIONS, BEHAVIOURS AND INTERACTIONS

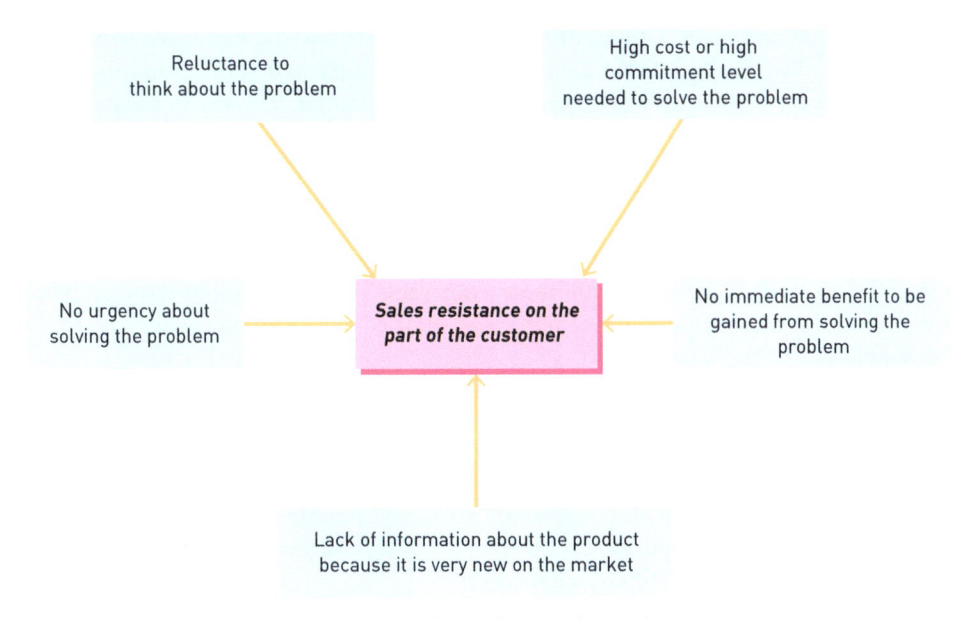

FIGURE 2.18 Reasons for postponing purchase of unsought goods

Reasons feeding into **Sales resistance on the part of the customer**:
- Reluctance to think about the problem
- High cost or high commitment level needed to solve the problem
- No urgency about solving the problem
- No immediate benefit to be gained from solving the problem
- Lack of information about the product because it is very new on the market

TABLE 2.4 Decision-making model for unsought goods

Stage	Techniques for management
Need recognition	Sales representatives activate the need by asking questions about the individual's current circumstances – for example, a representative from a breakdown insurer (AA or RAC) selling 'peace of mind' to those who recognise that they may have to call upon such services at some stage soon due to the age/condition of their motor vehicle
Information search	The sales representative performs a lengthy presentation, explaining the product's features and benefits. Questions and objections are dealt with as they arise
Evaluation of alternatives	The salesperson 'no-sells' competitors by pointing out ways in which the competitors' products are inferior. This is of course quite culture- and country-specific; for instance, such practices would not be deemed professional or be tolerated in the UK
Choice decision	The salesperson closes the sale by using a phrase or technique that elicits a yes or no decision
Post-purchase evaluation	The company may follow up on the sale by sending comments forms, the salesperson may call back to elicit feedback, or a sales manager might call back. In the case of buyer's remorse, there will be a return visit by the salesperson or by a sales manager

Marketers can overcome these problems with a series of tactics, but the main one is to use salespeople to explain the benefits of the product and close the sale. These salespeople usually have to overcome an initial resistance to the idea of spending time listening to a presentation, since the consumer of unsought goods is not engaged in an information search and is therefore unlikely to want to spend time and resources on a sales presentation. The salesperson will therefore need to employ a tactical device to gain the customer's attention for long enough to activate the need for the product. Table 2.4 shows how a salesperson can contribute to each stage of decision-making for this type of purchase. Admittedly, not all companies use the high-pressure selling techniques illustrated in Table 2.4. Some organisations will seek to highlight the positive aspects of their own service and will draw attention to some of the negatives that are avoided.

The selling techniques used for unsought goods have attracted a great deal of adverse publicity, but it is worth bearing in mind that the vast majority of double-glazing owners are perfectly happy with the product, as are the vast majority of timeshare owners. Generally speaking, while some vulnerable people are often targeted, most people are not naive enough to commit large sums of money to products they do not want and do not see a need for.

SUMMARY

This chapter has been about consumer decision-making processes. The processes often happen largely below the conscious level, and people often fall in love with a product without having much real knowledge of it, but the processes nevertheless occur, even if only at the subconscious level.

Decision-making flows from both needs and attitudes (something we'll look more at in Chapter 9). People need to be able to justify their decisions, both in terms of cost and of the usefulness of the products/services they buy; marketers need to be able to influence the decision by influencing attitudes, cost and utility as well as understanding the mental processes people go through both before and after making purchases.

KEY POINTS

- Needs become activated when there is a divergence between the actual and the desired states.
- Any information search is likely to be limited, since there is a cost attached as well as a risk reduction aspect.
- Heuristics are decision rules intended to reduce cognitive effort and risk.
- Interrupts usually only delay problem-solving behaviour, but the delay depends on the strength of the interrupt and the strength of the goal.
- The type of problem-solving undertaken will depend in part on whether the consumer is replenishing the assortment or extending it.
- The consideration set doesn't include every possible solution.
- Most decisions involve decision rules, either pre-programmed or invented on the spot.
- Involvement is the motivation to process information.
- High involvement is linked to end goals and values.
- Dimensions of involvement can be used to segment markets.
- Word of mouth is a strong factor in high-tech purchases.
- Unsought goods are those for which people recognise a need, but still avoid buying.

HOW TO IMPRESS YOUR EXAMINER

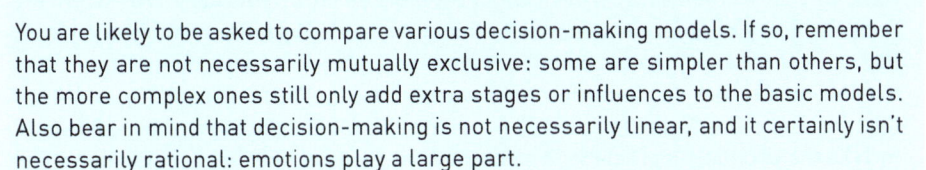

You are likely to be asked to compare various decision-making models. If so, remember that they are not necessarily mutually exclusive: some are simpler than others, but the more complex ones still only add extra stages or influences to the basic models. Also bear in mind that decision-making is not necessarily linear, and it certainly isn't necessarily rational: emotions play a large part.

Candidates sometimes forget that goals go in hierarchies, both in terms of which goals are more important than others and in terms of which **sub-goals** need to be achieved if the main goal is to come to fruition. In Chapter 5, we'll investigate Huffman's Model which will help you avoid this error. A further common error is to forget the role of heuristics in enabling people both to set goals and to achieve them – so make it a rule never to forget about heuristics!

Sub-goal
A target that forms part of a greater aim, and needs to be achieved before the main goal can be achieved

REVIEW QUESTIONS

1. What type of information search would you expect someone to undertake when buying a new type of television?
2. How might a marketer seek to make an interrupt more effective?
3. How might a compensatory decision rule operate when buying an expensive item such as a new car?
4. What factors cause people to become involved in products or brands?
5. How might a marketer increase involvement?
6. How can marketers reconcile the sale of unsought goods with the marketing concept?
7. What causes a product to move from being an unsought good to being a sought good?
8. Why might someone become involved with a brand, rather than with the benefits of the product itself?

CASE STUDY: CELEBRATING INTERNATIONAL AND EMIRATI WOMEN'S DAY

As an educator, author, entrepreneur, husband and father, it seems evident to me that we should have a day dedicated to celebrating women's achievements. But 30 mins browsing the WWW and it is also evident that perhaps not everyone feels the same as I do.

(Continued)

No it's not about feminists wanting to man-hate. In fact, celebrations such as International Women's Day (which was first marked on 28 February 1909 when the Socialist Party of America coined it National Women's Day) aim to achieve equality and so are actually open for people from across the gender spectrum. Other titles in reference to the day include Civil Awareness Day, Anti-Sexism Day and Anti-Discrimination Day (Proudfoot, 2022). From the early 1900s the day shifted to 8 March. In 1975 the UN made it official and so we had our modern International Women's Day as we know it now. The message in 2022 is quite clear: a) to celebrate the social, economic, cultural and political achievements of women, and b) to mark a call to action for accelerating gender parity.

There are, of course, women who are treated by men as equals, where conscious decisions have been made by men to interact and behave in a particular way. But in celebrating women, we're not talking about individuals but women everywhere. And we're doing this because there are still some startling facts (Togetherband, 2022) that send a chill down my spine each time I read them.

There are more than 250 million women alive today who were married before their 15th birthday, many against their will. Or to put it another way, that's 28 girls a minute being forced to marry against their will. This is a worldwide problem driven by deep-rooted patriarchal beliefs that girls only have value in roles as traditional housewives and homemakers, therefore it is not worth investing time and money into education or a life beyond marriage. The pandemic has exacerbated the issue: according to UN Women (Azcona et al., 2021), 10 million more girls are at risk of becoming child brides by 2030 as a direct result of Covid-19.

According to the World Health Organization (WHO, 2021), it is estimated that one in three women will experience some kind of physical or sexual abuse in her lifetime. As a result of national lockdowns, cases of domestic abuse skyrocketed in what the UN called the 'shadow pandemic'. Calls to domestic violence helplines increased during the pandemic by 40% in Malaysia, 50% in China and Somalia and a huge 79% in Colombia.

The Global Gender Gap Report 2021 (WEF, 2021) found that at our current rate, it will take another 135.6 years to achieve equality between men and women globally. Like many points here, the gender gap has only been worsened by the pandemic, with women facing higher redundancy rates and greater job instability as a result of economic shock. Reports suggest that 5% of all employed women lost their jobs, compared with 3.9% of employed men. Data from LinkedIn also showed a decline of women's hiring into leadership roles, creating a reversal of 1 to 2 years of progress across multiple industries.

In the United States, there are fewer women in leadership positions than there are men named John. Yes, you read that correctly: there are more men called John than women holding leadership roles. According to the 2018 Women in the Workplace report (McKinsey and Company, 2018), only 38% of management positions are held by women. And for those that do break the glass ceiling, they are twice as likely as men to be mistaken for junior employees. Despite everything that went on through 2020, some good news was that about 8% of Fortune 500 companies had female CEOs – an all-time high, but still far from the 50% we should be seeing.

The character of The Joker has won the same number of Oscars as the whole of womankind ever has for 'Directing'. In fact, in the 93-year history of the Academy Awards, just eight women have been nominated in the Best Director category. Ever. Until Chloé Zhao's win in 2021 for *Nomadland*, the only winner was Kathryn Bigelow in

2010 for the film *The Hurt Locker*. The character of The Joker, on the other hand, has earned an Oscar for both Heath Ledger (Best Supporting Actor, 2009) and Joaquin Phoenix (Best Actor, 2020).

There are 181 million girls and young women not in education, employment or training. We all know that when we educate girls, we enrich both individuals and communities – in every sense of the word too, from better employment prospects to better healthcare, educating young girls is essential. When girls miss out on education this increases the risk of forced marriage, trafficking and poverty. According to UN Women (Azcona et al., 2021), half of all refugee girls enrolled in secondary school before the pandemic will not return to school, and in sub-Saharan Africa, up to 1 million girls may drop out of school due to pregnancy during the Covid-19 crisis. There's still a long way to go, but we can celebrate that two-thirds of developing countries have now achieved gender equality in primary education.

Seventy-two countries don't allow women to open a bank account. Research from the World Bank shows that only 65% of women have bank accounts in comparison to 72% of men. Some countries are putting in serious work to try and close this gender gap, such as India, where current statistics show 83% of men have a bank account compared to 77% of women – a gap that has narrowed to 6% from 20% in 2014. Yet there are some countries where the situation is worse. Saudi Arabia is among the countries that bar women from opening a bank account or obtaining credit without permission from a guardian, while others require a woman to be married before she can access financial services.

According to a 2019 study by the Mental Health Foundation (mentalhealth.org.uk., 2019), 10% of women have felt so bad about their appearance that they have self-harmed. In a similar survey, King's University (Tennessee, USA) found that 87% of women compare their body to images they consume on social and traditional media, and 50% of those compare them unfavourably. Campaigns such as 'Be Real' are working to combat body image issues by encouraging people to take a pledge to champion body positivity.

Women make up 70% of the health workforce but hold fewer leadership positions than men in the sector. The coronavirus pandemic has truly shown us all how much we rely on the essential workers who run our health services. Globally women make up the majority of the workforce in this sector but are underrepresented in leadership and also paid less than their male counterparts. What's worse is that much of the early **PPE** was sized to fit men, leaving women on the frontline unnecessarily exposed to the virus.

With the rise in homeschooling as a result of lockdowns, women have ended up bearing the brunt of the increased domestic workload. Whether that means teaching children, managing the household, cooking or cleaning, women took on three times more work around the house and unpaid care compared to men even before the pandemic. Since then, data from 16 countries have shown that women with children at home spent 31 hours per week on childcare during Covid-19 – up from 26 hours previously.

Women face higher poverty rates than men – particularly if they are from a non-white background. It isn't a surprise that women face higher poverty rates than men – wage inequality, unpaid labour, unemployment, the gender education gap all play a part in this. According to an American Progress report, 12.9% of women in the US were living in poverty in 2018, with the highest rates found amongst Native Americans, Native Alaskans, Black women and those from a Hispanic background.

(Continued)

PPE – personal protective equipment

Components of PPE include gloves, gowns, shoe and head covers, masks and respirators as well as other face and eye protection

Under an umbrella of facts such as these, it is heart-warming to learn that back in 2015, Her Highness Sheikha Fatima bint Mubarak, lovingly known as The Mother of the Nation, launched Emirati Women's Day. Her Highness Sheikha Fatima is the wife of the UAE's Founder, the late His Highness Sheikh Zayed bin Sultan Al Nahyan. She is the Chairwoman of the General Women's Union, Supreme Chairwoman of the Family Development Foundation and President of the Supreme Council for Motherhood and Childhood. In 2017, UN Women honoured Sheikha Fatima for her endeavours toward gender equality and empowerment in the UAE. Emirati women have made their nation proud with their remarkable achievements in arts, business, science and almost every other field. They have worked tirelessly to help make the UAE the epitome of progress and prosperity. Emirati Women's Day on 28 August is celebrated yearly to commemorate women's power and their role in developing the nation. The day honours the creation of UAE's General Women's Union on 28 August 1975. The special day highlights the contributions of Emirati women and applauds their dedication, strength and achievements that have helped to shape the nation. The theme of the seventh Emirati Women's Day was 'Inspiring Reality... Sustainable Future' and focused on local Emirati women's ambitions. It also recognised that Emirati women have secured key roles throughout the country. This has only become possible due to the stern laws and regulations safeguarding women's rights. Some of the key achievements have included Aisha al-Mansoori becoming the UAE's first female Emirati captain on Etihad Airways and Dr Mona Khashwani from Sharjah's al-Qassimi Women and Children's Hospital who became the UAE's first Emirati physician to perform robotic surgery using the advanced Da Vinci system.

There is hope yet that we can keep the conversation going and make decisions which alter our behaviours and influence our interactions to further gender equality.

CASE STUDY QUESTIONS

1. How does deciding to educate women and girls help to save lives?
2. In what ways will empowering women to work help economies to grow?
3. Why and how do legal protections improve when governments focus on behaviours which foster gender equality?
4. When women interact with and are active in peace negotiations, conflict is less likely to occur. Why do you think that is?
5. Why do you think the Emirati women are forging ahead in this space, in such leaps and bounds?

FURTHER READING

For an indication of some of the surrogates people use when deciding on whether to buy a new product, see Roger Bennett and Helen Gabriel (2000) Charity affiliation as a determinant of product purchase decisions, *Journal of Brand and Product Marketing*, 9 (4/5): 255–68. It turns out that people's perception of the value-for-money aspects of products sold by charities affects their view of other products that may be entirely unrelated to the first products.

For a much deeper account of loyalty programmes and involvement, take a look at Wan Jou-Wen's book *The Effect of the Reward Programme Scheme: The Effect of Timing of Reward, Business Longevity and Involvement on Consumers' Perception and Behavioural Intention Toward the Reward Programme* (Saarbrücken: VDM Verlag, 2009). The title is almost as long as the book, but it does offer a very deep (and academic) insight into the interrelationship between loyalty programmes, involvement and timing.

Many models of consumer behaviour seem to assume that people think about what they are doing when making decisions. Gerd Gigerenzer disagrees – and his book *Gut Feelings: Short Cuts to Better Decision Making* (Harmondsworth: Penguin, 2008) outlines the idea that we make our best decisions based on gut instinct rather than conscious thought. This is a book for people who enjoy some controversy!

Involvement, and especially involvement in luxury brands, is alive and well and lives in Japan. *The Cult of the Luxury Brand: Inside Asia's Love Affair with Luxury*, by Radha Chadha and Paul Husband (London: Nicholas Brealey International, 2006), tells the whole story of how Asian countries have discovered consumerism – and gone for it in a big way.

An aspect of decision-making which is often ignored is the decision to say 'enough is enough'. John Naish's book *Enough: Breaking Free from the World of Excess* (London: Hodder Paperbacks, 2009) offers as its main premise the idea that human beings are hard-wired to grab as much as they can of anything they like, when in fact there is a point at which further acquisitions simply become tiresome. It's an interesting read for those who have doubts about the consumerist society in which we live.

Jonathan Fields' *Uncertainty: Turning Fear and Doubt into Fuel for Brilliance* (New York: Portfolio Hardcover, 2011) is a self-help book. The author talks about ways of reducing the fear that arises from uncertainty – and he certainly experienced the downside of uncertainty, having opened a new business in Manhattan the day before the 9/11 terrorist attacks.

MORE ONLINE

For additional materials that support this chapter and your learning, please visit:

https://study.sagepub.com/sethna5e

REFERENCES

Aggarwal, P. and Vaidyanathan, R. (2003) Eliciting online customers' preferences: Conjoint vs. self-explicated and attribute-level measurement. *Journal of Marketing Management*, 19 (1/2): 157.

Aljefree, N.M. and Alhothali, G.T. (2022) Exposure to food marketing via social media and obesity among university students in Saudi Arabia. *International Journal of Environmental Research and Public Health*, 19 (10): 5851.

Allaway, A.W., Gooner, R.M., Berkowitz, D. and Davis, L. (2006) Deriving and exploring behaviour segments within a retail loyalty card programme. *European Journal of Marketing*, 40 (11/12): 1317–39.

Anker, T.B., Gordon, R. and Zainuddin, N. (2021) Consumer-dominant social marketing: A definition and explication. *European Journal of Marketing*, 56 (1): 159–83.

Armour, J., Mayer, C. and Polo, A. (2017) Regulatory sanctions and reputational damage in financial markets. *Journal of Financial and Quantitative Analysis*, *52* (4): 1429–48.

Auerbach, M.P. (2021) Person marketing: Using celebrities to endorse products. Online: *Salem Press Encyclopedia*. Great Neck Publishing: Research Starters.

Azcona, G., Min, Y., Bhatt, A., Brauchle, J., Fillo, G.F., Page, H. and Zhang, Y. (2021) Progress on the Sustainable Development Goals: The gender snapshot 2021. UNWomen, United Nations Statistics Division. www.unwomen.org/en/digital-library/publications/2021/09/progress-on-the-sustainable-development-goals-the-gender-snapshot-2021 (accessed 28 May 2022).

Baldinger, A.L., Blair, E. and Echambadi, R. (2002) Why brands grow. *Journal of Advertising Research*, *1*: 7–14.

Banelis, M., Riebe, E. and Rungie, C.M. (2013) Empirical evidence of repertoire size. *Australasian Marketing Journal*, *21*: 59–65.

Barr, L. (2022) FCA faces legal threat in rate scandal. *Mail on Sunday*, 16 January, p. 128.

Batra, R. and Ray, M.L. (1983) Operationalising involvement as depth and quality of cognitive responses. In A. Tybout and R. Bagozzi (eds), *Advances in Consumer Research*. Ann Arbor, MI: Association for Consumer Research. pp. 309–13.

Bauer, H.H., Sauer, N.E. and Becker, C. (2006) Investigating the relationship between product involvement and consumer decision-making styles. *Journal of Consumer Behaviour*, *5* (July–August): 342–54.

Baumeister, R.F. (2004) Self-regulation, conscious choice, and consumer decisions. *Advances in Consumer Research*, *31* (1): 48–9.

Bettman, J.R. (1979) *An Information Processing Theory of Consumer Choice*. Reading, MA: Addison–Wesley.

Bettman, J.R. and Park, C.W. (1980) Effects of prior knowledge and experience and phase of choice processes on consumer decision processes: A protocol analysis. *Journal of Consumer Research*, *7* (August): 234–48.

Bhandari, M. and Rodgers, S. (2018) What does the brand say? Effects of brand feedback to negative eWOM on brand trust and purchase intentions. *International Journal of Advertising*, *37* (1): 125–41.

Bhatt, S., Lee, J., Deutsch, J., Ayaz, H., Fulton, B. and Suri, R. (2018) From food waste to value-added surplus products (VASP): Consumer acceptance of a novel food product category. *Journal of Consumer Behaviour*, *17* (1): 57–63.

Bhattacharya, C.B., Fader, P.S., Lodish, L.M. and Desarbo, W.S. (1996) The relationship between the marketing mix and share of category requirements. *Marketing Letters*, *7* (1): 5–18.

Bhui, R., Lai, L. and Gershman, S.J. (2021) Resource-rational decision making. *Current Opinion in Behavioral Sciences*, *41*: 15–21.

Biehal, G. and Chakravarty, D. (1983) Information accessibility as a moderator of consumer choice. *Journal of Consumer Research*, *10* (June): 1–14.

Biswas, D. (2009) The effects of option framing on consumer choices: Making decisions in rational versus experiential processing modes. *Journal of Consumer Behaviour*, 8 (5): 284–99.

Blackwell, R.D., Miniard, P.W. and Engel, J.F. (2005) *Consumer Behaviour*, 10th edn. Mason, OH: Thomson Southwest.

Bloch, P.H., Sherrell, D.L. and Ridgway, N.M. (1986) Consumer search: An extended framework. *Journal of Consumer Research*, 13 (June): 111–26.

Boisvert, J. and Ashill, N.J. (2022) The impact of gender on the evaluation of vertical line extensions of luxury brands: A cross-national study. *Journal of Product & Brand Management*, 31 (3): 484–95.

Botha, E., Creaven, G. and Mandy, J. (2020) Conveniently healthy: The impact of health endorsements on brand trust, brand loyalty and brand equity in fast moving consumer goods convenience versus shopping goods. *South African Journal of Business Management*, 51 (1): 1–9.

Brendl, M., Markman, A. and Irwin, J.R. (2002) Suppression and activation of competing goals. *Advances in Consumer Research*, 29: 5–7.

Bruyneel, S., DeWitte, S., Franses, P.H., DeKimpe, M. and Arnik G. (2006) Why consumers buy lottery tickets when the sun goes down on them: The depleted nature of weather-induced bad moods. *Advances in Consumer Research*, 33: 46–50.

Bucklin, L.P. (1963) Retail strategy and the classification of consumer goods. *Journal of Marketing*, 27 (January): 50–5.

Buttner, O.B. and Goritz, A.S. (2008) Perceived trustworthiness of online shops. *Journal of Consumer Behaviour*, 7 (1): 35–60.

Campo, K. and Breugelmans, E. (2015) Buying groceries in brick and click stores: Category allocation decisions and the moderating effect of online buying experience. *Journal of Interactive Marketing*, 31: 63–78.

Carlson, J., Rahman, S.M., Rahman, M.M., Wyllie, J. and Voola, R. (2021) Engaging Gen Y customers in online brand communities: A cross-national assessment. *International Journal of Information Management*, 56: 102252.

Chan, F.F.Y. and Lowe, B. (2021) Placing products in humorous scenes: Its impact on brand perceptions. *European Journal of Marketing*, 55 (3): 649–70.

Chew, M. M.-T. (2022) Reinterpreting how and why people consume counterfeit fashion products: A sociological challenge to the pro-business paradigm. *Fashion Theory: The Journal of Dress, Body & Culture*, 26 (2): 237–61.

Christopher, M., Ballantyne, D. and Payne, A. (1991) *Relationship Marketing*. Oxford: Butterworth–Heinemann.

Colmekcioglu, N., Marvi, R., Foroudi, P. and Okumus, F. (2022) Generation, susceptibility, and response regarding negativity: An in-depth analysis on negative online reviews. *Journal of Business Research*, 153: 235–50.

Colombo, R., Ehrenberg, A. and Sabavala, D. (2000) Diversity in analyzing brand-switching tables: The car challenge. *Canadian Journal of Marketing Research*, 19: 23–36.

Cornil, Y., Plassmann, H., Aron, W.J., Poitou, B.C., Clément, K., Chabert, M. and Chandon, P. (2022) Obesity and responsiveness to food marketing before and after bariatric surgery. *Journal of Consumer Psychology, 32* (1): 57–68.

Crosby, L.A. and Taylor, J.R. (1981) Effects of consumer information and education in cognition and choice. *Journal of Consumer Research, 8* (June): 43–56.

Dailey, L. (2003) Understanding consumers' need to personally inspect products prior to purchase. *Advances in Consumer Research, 30*: 146–7.

Dawes, J. (2009) You need more customers: The key is how many you have, not how much they buy. *Marketing Research*, Summer: 30–1.

Dawes, J., Meyer-Waarden, L. and Driesener, C. (2015) Has brand loyalty declined? A longitudinal analysis of repeat purchase behaviour in the UK and USA. *Journal of Business Research, 68*: 425–32.

Dewey, J. (1910) *How We Think*. Boston, MA: DC Heath & Co.

Dibley, A. and Baker, S. (2001) Uncovering the links between brand choice and personal values among young British and Spanish girls. *Journal of Consumer Behaviour, 1* (1): 77–93.

Doyle, C., Douglas, E. and O'Reilly, G. (2021) The outcomes of sexting for children and adolescents: A systematic review of the literature. *Journal of Adolescence, 92*: 86–113.

East, R., Hammond, K. and Gendall, P. (2006) Fact and fallacy in retention marketing. *Journal of Marketing Management, 22* (1/2): 5–23.

East, R., Lomax, W. and Narain, R. (2001) Customer tenure, recommendation and switching. *Journal of Consumer Satisfaction, Dissatisfaction and Complaining Behaviour, 14*: 46–54.

Ehrenberg, A. (1988) Repeat-buying: Facts, theory and applications, 2nd ed, London: Edward Arnold; New York: Oxford University Press. Reproduced in the *Journal of Empirical Generalisations in Marketing Science, 5*: 392–770 (www.empgens.com).

Elliot, G., Rundle-Thiele, S. and Waller, D. (2010) *Marketing*. Milton, QLD: John Wiley and Sons.

Fader, P.S. and Schmittlein, D.C. (1993) Excess behavioral loyalty for high-share brands deviations from the Dirichlet model for repeat purchasing. *Journal of Marketing Research, 30* (4): 478–93.

FCA (Financial Conduct Authority) (2014) Price comparison website: Consumer market research report. www.fca.org.uk/static/documents/research/price-comparison-website-consumer-research.pdf (accessed 22 September 2015).

Folkvord, F., Naderer, B., Coates, A. and Boyland, E. (2022) Promoting fruit and vegetable consumption for childhood obesity prevention. *Nutrients, 14* (1): 157.

Foxall, G.R. (2008) Reward, emotion and consumer choice: From neuroeconomics to neurophilosophy. *Journal of Consumer Behaviour, 7* (4/5): 368–96.

Fu, H.-N., Monson, E. and Otto, R. (2021) The relationship between unexpected outcomes and lottery gambling rates in a large Canadian metropolitan area. *Critical Gambling Studies, 2* (1): 55–67.

Garrido-Morgado, Á., González-Benito, Ó., Martos-Partal, M. and Campo, K. (2021) Which products are more responsive to in-store displays: Utilitarian or hedonic? *Journal of Retailing*, 97 (3): 477–91.

Gilad, S. (2015) Political pressures, organizational identity, and attention to tasks: Illustrations from pre-crisis financial regulation. *Public Administration*, 93 (3): 593–608.

Gupta, S., Lehmann, D.R. and Stuart, J.A. (2004) Valuing customers. *Journal of Market Research*, 41 (1): 7–18.

Gurel, E. and Nielsen, A. (2018) Exploring the visitors' perceptions and experiences of museums. In M. Kozak and N. Kozak (eds), *Tourist Behavior*. Tourism, Hospitality & Event Management Series. Cham: Springer Nature. pp. 141–55.

Haase, J., Wiedmann, K.-P. and Bettels, J. (2020) Sensory imagery in advertising: How the senses affect perceived product design and consumer attitude. *Journal of Marketing Communications*, 26 (5): 475–87.

Hamilton, K.L. and Hewer, P.A. (2010) Tribal mattering spaces: Social networking sites, celebrity affiliations and tribal innovations. *Journal of Marketing Management*, 26 (3/4): 271–89.

Harper, M.G. (2006) Childhood obesity strategies for prevention. *Family Community Health*, 29 (4): 288–98.

Hassenzahl, M. (2018) The thing and I: Understanding the relationship between user and product. In M. Blythe and A. Monk (eds), *Funology 2*. Human–Computer Interaction Series. Cham: Springer Nature. pp. 31–42.

Hawkins, S. (1962) The significance of impulse buying today. *Journal of Marketing*, 26 (April): 59–62.

He, L., Hsin-han Shen, C. and Shiu, C.-Y. (2022) Is fair value information fairly priced? Evidence from IPOs in global capital markets. *Journal of Banking and Finance*, 135: 106368.

Helgesen, O. (2006) Are loyal customers profitable? Customer satisfaction, customer (action) loyalty and customer profitability at the individual level. *Journal of Marketing Management*, 22 (3/4): 245–66.

Hem, L. and Iversen, N.M. (2003) Transfer of brand equity in brand extensions: The importance of brand loyalty. *Advances in Consumer Research*, 30: 72–9.

Herédia, A.M., Hipólito, J., Nunes, O., Ribeiro, L., Moura, T. and Laneiro, T. (2017) Fast-food marketing strategies and their impact on childhood obesity. *Journal of Spatial and Organizational Dynamics*, 3: 296–315.

Holbrook, M.B. and Hirschman, E.C. (1982) The experiential aspects of consumption: Consumer fantasies, feelings and fun. *Journal of Consumer Research*, 9 (September): 132–40.

Howard, J.A. and Sheth, J.N. (1969) *The Theory of Buyer Behaviour*. New York: John Wiley.

Hoyer, W.D. and Ridgway, N.M. (1984) Variety seeking as an explanation for exploratory purchase behaviour: A theoretical model. *Advances in Consumer Research*, 11: 114–19.

Hungenberg, E., Slavich, M., Bailey, A. and Sawyer, T. (2020) Examining minor league baseball spectator nostalgia: A neuroscience perspective. *Sport Management Review*, *23*(5): 824–37.

Jamil, R.A. and Qayyum, A. (2022) Word of mouse vs word of influencer? An experimental investigation into the consumers' preferred source of online information. *Management Research Review*, *45* (2): 173–97.

Jansen, B.J., Jung, S.-G. and Salminen, J. (2022) Measuring user interactions with websites: A comparison of two industry standard analytics approaches using data of 86 websites. *PLoS One*, *17* (5): e0268212.

Jung, S., Gruca, T. and Lopo, R. (2010) Excess loyalty in CPG markets: A comprehensive examination. *Journal of Empirical Generalisations in Marketing Science*, *13* (1): 1–13.

Kauppinen-Räisänen, H., Björk, P., Lönnström, A. and Jauffret, M.N. (2018) How consumers' need for uniqueness, self-monitoring, and social identity affects their choices when luxury brands visually shout versus whisper. *Journal of Business Research*, *84*: 72–81.

Khan, I., Fatma, M., Shamim, A., Joshi, Y. and Rahman, Z. (2020) Gender, loyalty card membership, age, and critical incident recovery: Do they moderate experience-loyalty relationship? *International Journal of Hospitality Management*, *89*: 102408.

Khan, J. and Hemsley-Brown, J. (2021) Student satisfaction: The role of expectations in mitigating the pain of paying fees. *Journal of Marketing for Higher Education*, 1–23. https://doi.org/10.1080/08841241.2021.1973646

Khan, S.N. and Mohsin, M. (2017) The power of emotional value: Exploring the effects of values on green product consumer choice behavior. *Journal of Cleaner Production*, *150*: 65–74.

Kiel, G.C. and Layton, R.A. (1981) Dimensions of consumer information seeking behaviour. *Journal of Marketing Research*, *18* (May): 233–9.

Kim, S.J., Wang, R.J.H., Maslowska, E. and Malthouse, E.C. (2016) Understanding a fury in your words: The effects of posting and viewing electronic negative word-of-mouth on purchase behaviors. *Computers in Human Behavior*, *54*: 511–21.

Kim, S.-W., Kim, Y.-M., Jansen, D.W. and Yanxin, L. (2022) Does the elderly's private pension ownership intensify aggregate equity demand? Empirical evidence in the US. *Investment Analysts Journal*, *51* (2): 83–93.

Kolbe, K. (2022) Unequal entanglements: How arts practitioners reflect on the impact of intensifying economic inequality. *Cultural Trends*, *31* (3): 257–72.

Kotler, P., Burton, S., Deans, K., Brown, L. and Armstrong, G. (2013) *Marketing*, 9th edn. Harlow: Pearson Publishing.

Laurent, G. and Kapferer, J. (1985) Measuring consumer involvement profiles. *Journal of Marketing Research*, *22* (February): 41–53.

Leising, D., Vogel, D., Waller, V. and Zimmermann, J. (2021) Correlations between person-descriptive items are predictable from the product of their mid-point-centered social desirability values. *European Journal of Personality*, *35* (5): 667–89.

Levkovski, S. and Popovski, V. (2022) Social capital and subjective well-being at youth in social risk. *Economic Development / Ekonomiski Razvoj*, 24 (1): 149–62.

Lin, C. and Bowman, D. (2022) The impact of introducing a customer loyalty program on category sales and profitability. *Journal of Retailing and Consumer Services*, 64: 102769.

Lin, X., Featherman, M., Brooks, S.L. and Hajli, N. (2019) Exploring gender differences in online consumer purchase decision making: An online product presentation perspective. *Information Systems Frontiers*, Springer, 21(5), pp. 1187–1201, October.

Magsayo, R.T. (2021) Intention to continue using mobile learning: The effects of perceived values and role of locus of control. *The International Journal of Information and Learning Technology*, 38 (5): 493–517.

Manolică, A., Guță, A.-S., Roman, T. and Dragăn, L.M. (2021) Is consumer overchoice a reason for decision paralysis? *Sustainability*, 13: 5920.

Matli, W. and Ngoepe, M. (2021) Extending information poverty theory to better understand the digital access and inequalities among young people who are not in education, employment or training in South Africa. *Higher Education, Skills and Work-Based Learning*, 12 (3): 419–36.

Mayer, V.F., Santos, G.E. de O. and Marques, O.R.B. (2022) Option framing for upselling tourism services: Does cognitive availability prevent irrational choices? *Tourism Economics*, 28 (2): 476–94.

McGrath, J.J. and Rossomando, E.F. (2015) Risk-averse purchasing behavior of female dentists and innovation in dental practice. *Dental Hypotheses*, 6 (2): 53–9.

McKinsey and Company (2018) Women in the workplace. https://womenintheworkplace.com/2018#! (accessed 19 August 2020).

Melis, K., Campo, K., Breugelmans, E. and Lamey, L. (2015) The impact of the multi-channel retail mix on online store choice: Does online experience matter? *Journal of Retailing*, 91 (2): 272–88.

mentalhealth.org.uk (2019) *Body Image Report*. www.mentalhealth.org.uk/explore-mental-health/articles/body-image-report-executive-summary (accessed 20 October 2022).

Meyer-Waarden, L. and Benavent, C. (2006) The impact of loyalty programmes on repeat purchase behaviour. *Journal of Marketing Management*, 22 (1/2): 61–88.

Michaelidou, N. and Dibb, S. (2006) Product involvement: An application in clothing. *Journal of Consumer Behaviour*, 5 (September–October): 442–53.

Mitchell, A. (1979) Involvement: A potentially important mediator of consumer behaviour. In W.L. Wilkie (ed.), *Advances in Consumer Research*, Vol. 6. Provo, UT: Association for Consumer Research. pp. 191–6.

Mock, S.E., Misener, K. and Havitz, M.E. (2022) A league of their own? A longitudinal study of ego involvement and participation behaviors in LGBT-focused community sport. *Leisure Sciences*, 44 (6): 750–67.

Monga, A.B. (2002) Brand as a relationship partner: Gender differences in perspectives. *Advances in Consumer Research*, 29 (1): 36–41.

Morewedge, C. K., Gray, K., and Wegner, D. M. (2010) *Perish the forethought: Premeditation engenders misperceptions of personal control*. In R. Hassan, K. Ochsner, & Y. Trope (Eds.), *Self-control in Brain, Mind, and Society* (pp. 260–278). New York: Oxford University Press.

Morrison, D.G. (1966) Interpurchase time and brand loyalty. *Journal of Marketing Research*, *3* (August): 289–91.

Murillo, E. (2022) Enhancing brand understanding through brand training: A conditional process analysis of recent hires at an airline. *Revista Brasileira de Gestão de Negócios*, *24* (2): 312–31.

Nantel, J. and Weeks, W.A. (1996) Marketing ethics: Is there more to it than the utilitarian approach? *European Journal of Marketing*, *30* (5): 9–16.

Neal, D., Wood, W. and Pascoe, A.M. (2008) Triggers of real-world habits: implications for consumer behavior. In A. Y. Lee and D. Soman (eds), *Advances in Consumer Research, Volume 35*, Duluth, MN : Association for Consumer Research, pp. 125–28.

Nelson, M.R., Ham, C.D. and Haley, E. (2021) What do we know about political advertising? Not much! Political persuasion knowledge and advertising skepticism in the United States. *Journal of Current Issues & Research in Advertising*, *42* (4): 329–53.

Neslin, S.A. (2022) The omnichannel continuum: Integrating online and offline channels along the customer journey. *Journal of Retailing*, *98* (1): 111–32.

Ngo, L.V., Gregory, G., Miller, R. and Lu, L. (2022) Understanding the role of brand salience in brand choice decisions in the charity sector. *Australasian Marketing Journal*, *30* (3): 258–70.

Onkvisit, S. and Shaw, J.J. (1994) *Consumer Behaviour, Strategy and Analysis*. New York: Macmillan.

Otker, T. (1990) The highly involved consumer: A marketing myth? *Marketing and Research Today*, February: 30–6.

Pare, V. and Dawes, J. (2011) The persistence of excess brand loyalty over multiple years. *Marketing Letters*, *21* (2): 163–75.

Peña, M.B.P. (2022) Moderating effect of the extension fit and involvement in the relationship between the parent heritage brand attitude and extension loyalty. Application to the monumental complex of the Alhambra and the Generalife. *Management Letters/Cuadernos de Gestión*, *22* (1): 21–33.

Pesonen, J., Komppula, R. and Murphy, J. (2019) Plastic loyalty – Investigating loyalty card programs for a Finnish hotel chain. *Tourism Management*, *73*: 115–22.

Peter, J.P. and Olson, J.C. (1994) *Understanding Consumer Behaviour*. Burr Ridge, IL: Irwin.

Proudfoot, J. (2022) To all the people who question why I celebrate International Women's Day. *Marieclaire*. www.marieclaire.co.uk/opinion/why-i-celebrate-international-womens-day-688616 (accessed 17 May 2022).

Rahman, T. (2018) Extreme overvalued beliefs: How violent extremist beliefs become 'normalized'. *Behavioral Sciences*, *8* (1): 10.

Raj, S.P. (1985) Striking a balance between brand 'popularity' and brand loyalty. *Journal of Marketing*, 49 (Winter): 53–9.

Reichheld, F.F. and Teal, T. (1996) *The Loyalty Effect: The Hidden Force Behind Growth, Profits, and Lasting Value*. Boston, MA: Harvard Business School Press.

Rick, S., Knutson, B., Wimmer, E., Prelec, D. and Loewenstein, G. (2008) Neural predictors of purchases. *Advances in Consumer Research*, 35: 129–32.

Rigby, C. (2022) Retail sales fall online and offline in May as the 'post-pandemic spending bubble bursts': BRC/Barclaycard. https://internetretailing.net/industry/retail-sales-fall-online-and-offline-in-may-as-the-post-pandemic-spending-bubble-bursts-brcbarclaycard-24895/ (accessed 10 June 2022).

Ruiz-Molina, M.E., Gómez-Borja, M.-Á. and Mollá-Descals, A. (2021) Can offline–online congruence explain online loyalty in electronic commerce? *International Journal of Retail & Distribution Management*, 49 (9): 1271–94.

Sahakian, B.J. and Labuzetta, J.N. (2013) *Bad Moves: How Decision Making Goes Wrong, and the Ethics of Smart Drugs*. Oxford: Oxford University Press.

Sethna, Z., Jones, R. and Harrigan, P. (2013) *Entrepreneurial Marketing: Global Perspectives*. Bingley: Emerald Publishing.

Shah, S.K., Tang, Z., Sharif, S.M.F. and Tanveer, A. (2021) An empirical study of Chinese students' behavioral intentions to adopt 5G for smart-learning in Covid-19. *Smart Learning Environments*, 8 (1): 1–17.

Shankar, A., Cherrier, H. and Canniford, R. (2006) Consumer empowerment: A Foucauldian interpretation. *European Journal of Marketing*, 40 (9/10): 1013–30.

Sharma, P., Sivakumaran, B. and Marshall, R. (2010) Exploring impulse buying and variety seeking by retail shoppers: Towards a common conceptual framework. *Journal of Marketing Management*, 26 (5/6): 473–94.

Sharp, B. and Sharp, A. (1997) Loyalty programs and their impact on repeat-purchase loyalty patterns. *International Journal of Research in Marketing*, 14 (5): 473–86.

Sheng, S., Parker, A.M. and Nakamoto, K. (2003) Decision uncertainty, expected loss minimisation, and the compromise effect. *Advances in Consumer Behaviour*, 30: 47.

Shi, Z., Liu, X. and Srinivasan, K. (2022) Hype news diffusion and risk of misinformation: The Oz effect in health care. *Journal of Marketing Research*, 59 (2): 327–52.

Singh, S. and Dipika, M. (2018) Mis-selling of financial products: A review. *NOLEGEIN Journal of Financial Planning and Management*, 1 (2): 1–11.

Socha, M. (2022) Gucci casts a shadow on Kering in Q1: The Italian brand's exposure to China held sales growth to 13.4 percent in the period. *WWD: Women's Wear Daily*, 21 April, pp. 1–19.

Stewart, D.W. and Furse, D.H. (1984) Analysis of executional factors in advertising performance. *Journal of Advertising Research*, 24: 23–6.

Takala, T. and Uusitalo, O. (1996) An alternative view of relationship marketing: A framework for ethical analysis. *European Journal of Marketing*, 30 (2): 45–60.

Tam, J.L.M. (2011) The moderating effect of purchase importance in customer satisfaction process: An empirical investigation. *Journal of Consumer Behaviour, 10* (4): 205–15.

Thompson, M. and Johnson, A.R. (2002) Investigating the role of attachment dimensions as predictors of satisfaction in consumer–brand relationships. *Advances in Consumer Research, 29*: 42.

Tian, S., Tao, W., Hong, C. and Tsai, W.-H.S. (2022) Meaning transfer in celebrity endorsement and co-branding: Meaning valence, association type, and brand awareness. *International Journal of Advertising, 41* (6): 1017–37.

Togetherband (2022) 11 reasons why we need International Women's Day. https://togetherband.org/blogs/news/why-we-need-international-women-s-day (accessed 10 April 2022).

Ubilava, D., Foster, K.A., Lusk, J.L. and Nilsson, T. (2011) Differences in consumer preferences when facing branded versus non-branded choices. *Journal of Consumer Behaviour, 10* (2): 61–70.

Uklańska, K. (2021) Woman and pleasure: The attitude of Polish female students to pleasure, based on empirical studies from 2020. *Seminare, 42* (4): 93–108.

Uncles, M.D. and Ehrenberg, A.S.C. (1990) Brand choice among older consumers. *Journal of Advertising Research*, August/September: 19–22.

Uncles, M.D. and Lee, D. (2006) Brand purchasing by older consumers: An investigation using the Juster scale and the Dirichlet model. *Marketing Letters, 17* (1): 17–29.

Urbany, J.E. (1986) An experimental investigation of the economics of information. *Journal of Consumer Research, 13* (September): 257–71.

Uzelac, O., Dukić-Mijatović, M. and Lukinović, M. (2022) The role of branding agricultural products in better market valorization. *Ekonomika Poljoprivrede, 69* (2): 613–25.

Valdés de la Fuente, I. and Elexpuru, G.E. (2022) Is it rational for a large-retailer to sell an own-brand product similar to the branded product of a large manufacturer? A vertical product differentiation model. *Desarrollo y Sociedad, 90*. https://doi.org/10.13043/DYS.90.3

Wang, S. and Kim, K.-J. (2019) Consumer response to negative celebrity publicity: The effects of moral reasoning strategies and fan identification. *Journal of Product and Brand Management, 29* (1): 114–23.

Watson, W.L., Sarich, P., Hughes, C. and Dessaix, A. (2021) Monitoring changes in community support for policies on obesity prevention. *Australian and New Zealand Journal of Public Health, 45* (5): 482–90.

WEF (World Economic Forum) (2021) The global gender gap report 2021. www.weforum.org/reports/global-gender-gap-report-2021/digest (accessed 18 February 2022).

Weiss-Cohen, L., Newall, P.W.S. and Ayton, P. (2022) Persistence is futile: Chasing of past performance in repeated investment choices. *Journal of Experimental Psychology: Applied, 28* (2): 341–59.

WHO (World Health Organization) (2021) Devastatingly pervasive: 1 in 3 women globally experience violence. www.who.int/news/item/09-03-2021-devastatingly-pervasive-1-in-3-women-globally-experience-violence (accessed 17 July 2021).

Worm, T. and Stine-Morrow, E.A.L. (2021) May the flow be with you: Age differences in the influence of social motives and context on the experience of activity engagement. *Journal of Adult Development, 28* (4): 265–75.

Yin, D., Mitra, S. and Zhang, H. (2016) Research note – When do consumers value positive vs. negative reviews? An empirical investigation of confirmation bias in online word of mouth. *Information Systems Research, 27* (1): 131–44.

Zaichowsky, J.L. (1985) Measuring the involvement construct in marketing. *Journal of Consumer Research, 12* (December): 341–52.

Zhong, L., Deng, B., Morrison, A.M., Coca-Stefaniak, J.A. and Yang, L. (2021) Medical, health and wellness tourism research – A review of the literature (1970–2020) and research agenda. *International Journal of Environmental Research and Public Health, 18* (20): 10875.

ZMEScience (2015) Why Nestle is one of the most hated companies in the world. www.zmescience.com/science/nestle-company-pollution-children/ (accessed 22 September 2015).

PART ONE CONSUMER BEHAVIOUR IN CONTEXT

Chapter 1   Understanding Consumer Behaviour
Chapter 2   Decisions, Behaviours and Interactions
Chapter 3   Consumption in B2C vs. B2B
Chapter 4   Consumer Technology and Innovation

PART TWO CONSUMERS AS INDIVIDUALS (THE PSYCHOLOGICAL ISSUES)

Chapter 5   Drive, Motivation and Hedonism
Chapter 6   The Self and Personality
Chapter 7   Perception
Chapter 8   Learning and Knowledge
Chapter 9   Attitude Formation and Change

PART THREE CONSUMERS AS SOCIAL ACTORS (THE SOCIOLOGICAL ISSUES)

Chapter 10   Reference Groups
Chapter 11   Age, Gender and Familial Roles
Chapter 12   Culture and Social Mobility
Chapter 13   Ethical Consumption
Chapter 14   Sustainable Consumption

CHAPTER 3

CONSUMPTION IN B2C VS. B2B

LEARNING OBJECTIVES

After reading this chapter you should be able to:
- Describe and explain the main pressures that influence industrial buyers.
- Explain the role of the decision-making unit.
- Explain the role of customers in driving the reseller market.
- Describe approaches to government markets.
- Explain how to approach institutional markets.
- Show how industrial markets can be divided.
- Describe the different types of buying situation, and the factors that are involved for making buying decisions within those situations.
- Understand the role of team selling in industrial markets.

CHAPTER CONTENTS

Introduction
The decision-making unit
Influences on buyers
Classifying business customers
Business and commercial organisations
Reseller organisations
Government organisations
Institutional organisations
Buyers' techniques
The Buygrid framework
Value analysis
Evaluating supplier capability
Evaluating supplier performance
Summary
Key points
How to impress your examiner
Review questions
Case study: The Electric Car Scheme
Further reading
References

More online: https://study.sagepub.com/sethna5e

INTRODUCTION

Organisational buyers, also known as business-to-business (B2B) are often supposed to be more rational and less emotional than when they are buying items for consumption by their friends and family. However, it would be wrong to assume that organisational buying is always entirely rational: those responsible for making buying decisions within organisations are still human beings, and do not leave their emotions at the door when they come to work; so it seems unrealistic to suppose that they do not have some emotional or irrational input in their decision-making. Organisational buyers often struggle with the effective management of B2B services (Enyinda et al., 2021;

B2B
Business-to-business. Where there is an exchange of products, services or information between businesses

B2C
Business-to-consumer. Business organisations that sell directly to consumers for their own use

Hawkins et al., 2015; Rodriguez et al., 2018), especially when it comes to the paradoxes firms face when managing demand and supply activities (Gölgeci et al., 2019).

Businesses, government departments, charities and other organisational purchasers actually represent the bulk of marketing activities, yet much of the attention in marketing is focused on business-to-consumer (B2C) developed markets rather than on B2B markets. The reasons for this are obscure but may have much to do with the fact that we are all consumers and can therefore relate more easily to consumer marketing issues. However, there is some evidence to suggest that the process of marketing communications is the same in both (Reklaitis and Pileliene, 2019). Silva et al. (2020) investigated how companies evaluate the return-on-investment of social media marketing (SMM) programmes in both B2B and B2C firms. The results showed that there were some differences between B2B and B2C companies regarding SMM evaluation and investment but in general marketing managers for both types of firms use simple metrics to evaluate their SMM programmes. Interestingly, the results from a comparative analyses study by Reijonen et al. (2013) (and a similar study by Rudawska, 2019) found that a notable difference exists between emerging and developed markets, as our propensity for buying branded goods and our general brand orientation contribute to growth in the latter.

This chapter looks at the ways organisational buyers make decisions, and also at some of the influences those buyers are subject to. It should be noted here that the divide between B2B and B2C becomes somewhat fuzzy when using these terms in an online/internet context. The exchange here is referred to as e-business and the subsequent 'exchange' is also known as e-commerce. There are many examples of firms that serve both sectors. Samsung, Daewoo and Hyundai, for example, are more generally known for their B2C products such as mobile phones and kitchen appliances, but are also players with substantial influence in the B2B sector as three of the leading shipbuilders in the world. In fact, in 2021 Samsung Heavy Industries built the world's largest container ship in South Korea. The *Ever Ace* is a giant container ship measuring 1300 ft (400 m) – that's longer than four football pitches. It is capable of holding 23,992 containers and it's a far cry from the humble Samsung mobile phone.

THE DECISION-MAKING UNIT

Decision-making unit (DMU)
A group of people who influence, control or carry out purchasing activities

It is rare for an organisational purchasing decision to be made by only one person. Even in a small organisation it is likely that several people would have some input into the buying process at some stage or another. It is because of this that the decision-making process often becomes formalised, with specific parts of the process being carried out by members of the decision-making unit (DMU), so that roles and responsibilities are shared and quite often based on behavioural issues that affect managerial price-setting processes (Behera et al., 2022; Iyer et al., 2015; Pandey and Mookerjee, 2018; Prajogo et al., 2018). The advent and significant use of both big data and artificial intelligence in B2B decision-making is prevalent in the academic literature as well (Farrokhi et al., 2020; Troisi et al., 2020).

The DMU, also called the **buying centre**, often cannot be identified on the company organisation chart because it varies in make-up from one buying situation to another. Individuals may participate for only a brief time, for a specific buying decision, or alternatively may be part of the team right through the process from beginning to end.

Among the early proponents of the DMU, Webster and Wind (1972) developed a model which is still quite relevant today and is generally thought to contain the following categories of member:

- **Initiators**. These are the individuals who first recognise the problem.
- **Gatekeepers**. These individuals control the flow of knowledge, either by being proactive in collecting information or by filtering it. They could be junior staff members who are perhaps given the task to research potential suppliers of a particular component, or a receptionist or personal assistant who sees his or her role as being to prevent salespeople from 'wasting' the decision-makers' time.
- **Buyers**. These individuals are given the task of making the actual purchase. Often this is merely a case of completing the administrative tasks necessary for buying, but it is likely to involve finding suitable suppliers and negotiating the final deal. Buyers usually work to a specific brief, and may have very little autonomy, even though they may be the only contact a supplier's salespeople have at the purchasing organisation.
- **Deciders**. These are the people who make the final decisions, and may be senior managers or specialists. They may never meet any representatives of the supplying companies. Deciders generally rely on advice from other members of the DMU, so they are influenced strongly by gatekeepers.
- **Users**. These are people who will be using the products that are being purchased: they may be engineers or technicians, or even the maintenance staff who use cleaning products. Their opinions may well be sought by the deciders, and in many cases the users are also the initiators.
- **Influentials**. These people have direct contact with the deciders, and are often asked for advice. They are trusted advisers, but from the supplying company's viewpoint they are extremely difficult to identify. Influentials may be employees of the purchasing firm (for example, engineers, information systems managers or research managers) or they may be consultants (for example, architects, health and safety consultants or business advisers such as lawyers and accountants). An influential might even be the decider's best friend, tennis partner or favourite uncle.

The relationships are summarised in Figure 3.1.

These categories are not, of course, mutually exclusive. A user might also be an influential, or a gatekeeper might also be an initiator. The categories were originally developed to explain purchasing within families – which may be an example of the apparent similarities between B2B marketing and consumer marketing.

Buying centre
See Decision-making unit

Initiators
The members of a decision-making unit who first identify a need

Gatekeepers
People who control the flow of information to a decision-making unit

Buyers
Those with the responsibility of making the actual purchase of a product, often (in the industrial context) working to a specific brief

Deciders
Members of a decision-making unit who have responsibility for making a final purchase decision

Users
Those members of a buying group who will actually make use of a product (not necessarily consumers)

Influentials
People who are respected for their opinions and lifestyles, and who therefore inform purchase behaviour

Members of the DMU are, of course, human beings so they are affected both by rational and emotional motivations (VanBergen and Lurie, 2022). Buyers are affected by their like or dislike for the suppliers' sales representatives, and often buyers have their own work agendas, for example seeking a promotion, or feeling threatened in terms of job security, or even conducting a vendetta with a colleague. Any of these influences might affect the buyers' behaviour, but all of them would be difficult or impossible for a supplier's salesperson to identify correctly and act upon.

Members of a DMU are likely to be more risk-averse than consumers because they have more to lose in the event of a wrong decision: for a consumer the main risk is financial, but even that is limited since most retailers will replace or refund goods purchased in error. For industrial purchasers a serious mistake can result in major negative consequences for the business as well as embarrassment in front of colleagues, loss of possible promotion, or even losing one's job if the mistake is big enough. The professional persona of the industrial buyer is liable to be compromised by purchasing errors, which in turn means that the buyer will feel a loss of self-esteem.

CONSUMER BEHAVIOUR IN ACTION: BAD B2B DECISIONS

Retrospect is of course a wonderful thing. Some ideas seem amazing at the time and then fall flat. Then there are others which you wouldn't want to touch with a barge pole (at the time) but which turn out to be amazing. Over the years there have been some almighty calamities when it comes to bad decisions. Back in 1981, Amblin Productions called Mars Confectionery to offer them a proposition. They wanted to use Mars' M&M's in their film as a way of promoting the film on their packaging. Mars absolutely refused and so the company went elsewhere and used Reese's Pieces instead. The film in question was *ET*, which eventually grossed nearly $800 million. As an upshot of this, Reese's Pieces saw a 65% jump in sales months after *ET* was released! Those contributions played a massive role in allowing the Hershey Company to grow from strength to strength. Over three decades later, much of their success can still be attributed to this particular product placement. Let's stick with the movie industry to examine another mammoth 'bad decision'. Back in 2000, Netflix Inc. co-founder Reed Hastings asked the video retailer Blockbuster executives to publicise it in their stores. Netflix proposed that they would help Blockbuster to sell their brand online too. This essentially equated to Blockbuster being offered Netflix for a mere $50 million. Yes you've guessed it... Blockbuster was quick to say no and bring this particular potential movie trailer to an abrupt end. Bad move. Less than 10 years after, Blockbuster went bankrupt mainly due to the popularity of Netflix. Nowadays, Netflix has over 220 million subscribers worldwide and boasts content assets worth over $46 billion. Blockbuster clearly didn't want to 'Netflix and chill'. And in a final example we turn to total insensitivity. Two days after the World Trade Center suffered from the atrocious 9/11 terrorist attacks, a company called Quantum Tech issued the following press release (they were mindful enough to retract it within five minutes of issuing it – record time in the pre-Twitter era, but nonetheless the damage was done...): 'The collapse of the World Trade Center destroyed more than lives. It also took computers and the vital data stored on them. But at least one company – Morgan Stanley – was able to function the very next day. Why? They used an off-site remote backup facility that stored their data safely, far from the catastrophe.'

Depending on the purchasing situation, the relative power of each member of the DMU will be different. This makes it hard to know what each member's influence will be on any specific decision, within environments that are increasingly more complex and competitive (Besharov and Smith, 2014; Pomirleanu et al., 2022) and especially when corresponding to six B2B climate dimensions: human resources, service, interpersonal relationships, coordination, environmental and exploration. A forerunner to this work, Ronchetto et al. (1989) identified the following characteristics of individuals who will probably exert the most influence in a DMU:

- Important in the corporate and departmental hierarchy.
- Close to the organisational boundary.
- Central to the workflow.
- Active in cross-departmental communications.
- Directly linked to senior management.

Fairly obviously, buyers within organisations (industrial buyers) are most important in repetitive purchases while the members of the C Suite (i.e. CEO, managing director and other senior management) will only become involved in buying decisions that are unique, expensive or potentially expose the organisation to significant risk. It is because industrial buyers are likely to suffer from risk more than would be the case for consumers, that they use a variety of risk-reducing tactics and conduct their due diligence (Hawes and Barnhouse, 1987; Lattuch and Ruppert, 2021). Some of these include:

- Visit the premises of the potential supplier to observe its viability.
- Talk to existing customers of the supplier about their experience with the supplier.
- Multi-source the order (buy the same component or materials from several suppliers) to ensure a backup source of supply.
- Insert penalty clauses in the supplier's contract.
- Ask colleagues about the potential supplier.
- In choosing a supplier, favour firms that your company has done business with in the past.
- Confirm that senior management are in favour of using the supplier.
- Limit the search for, and ultimate choice of, a potential supplier to well-known firms only.
- Obtain the opinion of a majority of your colleagues as to whether the chosen supplier is satisfactory.

Of course, all of these have various personal characteristics attributed to them. Following on from this work, Veres (2012) and recently also Micić and Krstić-Ranđić (2022) explored the importance that was attributed to the individual competences, such as:

- Professional (financial, human resources, innovation, technological, project management, intellectual capital, knowledge management).
- Trustworthiness (experience, credibility, financial, ethics, authority).

- Communication (skill, willingness, language).
- Relational (network, relationship management, competence framework).
- Delegational (responsibility, powers, recognition of limits of competence, extension of competence, employee development).

So let's turn our attention to how some of these issues manifest when it comes to B2B and B2C consumption.

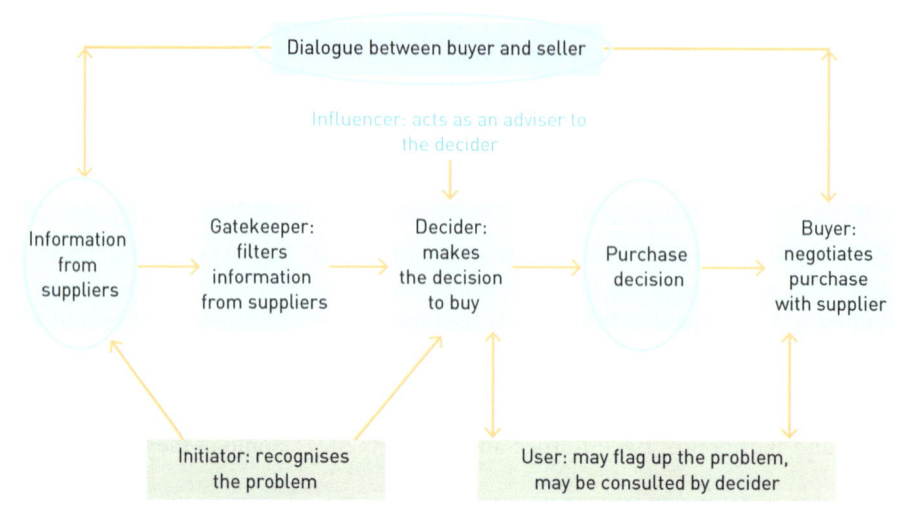

FIGURE 3.1 Relationships in the DMU

BRAND EXPERIENCE: WHY MICROSOFT IS VALUED BY ALL

In 2021, Microsoft once again surpassed Apple to take the top spot as the most valuable publicly traded company in the world. In contrast to many other companies, Facebook for instance, Microsoft ensures that its number one priority is to focus on customers and not revenue. Of course, if one delves into the history, it's not always been that way, but we can see today that firms who have an excessive focus on revenue and profit are certainly not doing as well, while Microsoft is dominating with its strategy. A large part of their success seems to stem from their strategy on diversity and inclusion (D&I). Firms that do not aggressively promote D&I underperform because minorities are not being fully utilised, know they are being underpaid, and underperform. When firms have to engage in this narrative, they usually force out their head of HR who talks about the programmes they have in place to deal with the problem (!). But we know that the real measure of whether a firm has nailed its D&I strategy is when the employees' become ambassadors for the brand. Minority employees at Microsoft speak in glowing terms about Microsoft's D&I efforts. They speak about how they are well treated, are asked for their opinions and answered in real time. They speak about how they are fairly treated regarding income and benefits and how they feel they are an equal part of Microsoft's employee family. Microsoft's Chief Product Officer, Panos Panay (the closest thing Microsoft has to Steve Jobs), has previously spoken about how one of the key designers for Windows and Surface is disabled and provides critical usability insights into product development, making Microsoft's products more inclusive. This achievement highlights that, unlike several other Big Tech firms (Apple, Amazon, Facebook and Google have all had serious problems with employee revolts), the employees at Microsoft, particularly minorities, appreciate that the effort is effective. This goes a long way to building the infrastructure that is ultimately going to enable a healthy and lucrative B2B ecosystem.

Many of the other leading tech companies (Apple, Amazon, Facebook and Google) all have a heavy focus on revenue and profit. This was the case at Microsoft too during most of Steve Ballmer's time as CEO. The company did really well financially but along the way it was obvious to see that they had lost focus on what was (or should have been) important. They were involved in some very poorly considered acquisitions and acquisition attempts (Yahoo and Nokia) but over the past 15 years they have pivoted toward strategically focusing on B2B as well as B2C needs, satisfaction and loyalty – and this has held them in good stead.

What happens when a company stops focusing primarily on revenue and profit and shifts its focus to the people that buy and use its products? Consistent, substantial improvement in financial performance. Microsoft is fortunate that the people who buy and use its products are the same, be they institutional buyers or direct customers. This user/customer connection is in sharp contrast to Facebook and Google, whose revenue comes from advertisers. The people who use those platforms become the product, not the customers.

Microsoft and Bill Gates are famous for their internet pivot and driving .NET across the company. Most companies are siloed to a high degree, making standard components and frameworks impossible to implement across the business. Microsoft does not appear to suffer from that problem, and this was on display at Microsoft Ignite 2021 (an annual conference for developers and IT professionals hosted by Microsoft) as the company unveiled its collaboration and communication products. Microsoft uses its products internally, so it benefits both its customers and its employees when the company develops something with a competitive advantage. When companies provide services, they often conflict with automation efforts that get blocked because they risk revenues. Microsoft's structure limits these conflicts substantially. During Ignite, the company presented market-leading levels of automation working towards a time when a business manager, without any coding help from IT or a third party, could write their code using natural language processing and Microsoft's increasingly capable artificial intelligence. Microsoft appears better able, and willing, to integrate common frameworks and capabilities across its efforts and push for advancements customers want, even if those advancements reduce service revenue opportunities.

Historically, the tech industry has been defined by companies that focused excessively on profit and revenue, setting the tone for the technology sector. That resulted in a growing divide between what institutional customers want and what tech companies deliver. Microsoft has uniquely shifted focus to emphasise customer needs even if that shift lessens service revenues. Ironically, this has resulted in stronger financial performance. Perhaps Microsoft acts as an example at the top, so that hopefully more companies will transition from mining customers for money to finding new ways to solve customer problems. Rather than locking customers into an ecosystem which equally locks new customers out, Microsoft creates interoperability and migration bridges that allow customers to move about more easily and trusts that these customers will move toward a vendor that cares for them – and away from vendors that do not. The ability or desire to focus on what customers want over revenue, profit and competitive responses has proven elusive for most companies. Microsoft has demonstrated that this focus is not only possible but has substantial financial benefits.

INFLUENCES ON BUYERS

Buyers are affected by individual, personal factors as well as environmental and organisational factors. On a personal level they are subject to many of the same influences on the buying decision that consumers have: the desire to play a role, for example, may cause a buyer to be difficult to negotiate with as he or she tries to drive a hard bargain. The desire for respect and liking may cause a buyer to want to give the order to a salesperson who is exceptionally pleasant or helpful, and to deny the order to a salesperson who is regarded as being unpleasant or pushy. Much of the early work done by Loudon and Della Bitta (1993) on this subject is still valid today. Their contention was that business buyers are likely to be affected by some or all of the following environmental influences which are summarised in Figure 3.2:

- *Physical influences.* The location of the purchasing firm relative to its suppliers may be decisive, since many firms prefer to source supplies locally. This is especially true in global markets, where a purchasing company may wish to support local suppliers, or may prefer to deal with people from the same cultural background. In many cases, buyers seem reluctant to source from outside their own national boundaries, even when cost and quality considerations mean that the foreign supplier would be better.

- *Technological influences.* The level of technological development available among local suppliers will affect what the buyer is able to obtain, but the technology of the buyer and the seller must also be compatible. International technical standards remain very different for most products, which means that cross-border sourcing can be complex. Despite efforts within the European Union to harmonise technical standards, Europe still does not have standardised electrical fittings, plumbing fittings or even computer keyboards. For this reason, European firms often find it easy to trade with former colonies thousands of miles away simply because the technical standards are identical.

- *Economic influences.* These divide into the macro-economic environment (which is concerned with the level of demand in the economy, and with the current taxation regime within the buyer's country) and the micro-economic environment, which is about the firm's current financial health. Obviously, the state of the company finances dictates buyers' budgets for good or ill. Macro-economic conditions can affect buyers' ability to buy goods as well as the firm's need for raw materials: if demand is low, demand for raw materials will also be low. On a more subtle level, the macro-economic climate affects the buyer's confidence in the same way as it affects consumer confidence. For example, a widespread belief that the national economy is booming will encourage buyers to commit to major investments in stock, equipment and machinery. In a global context, the fact that countries enter and leave recessions at different times will affect the timing of marketing efforts on the part of vendors. Of course, the converse is true as well. Countries that are in economic trouble send ripples across to other nations, who may then believe that hard times are coming their way too.

- *Political influences.* Governments frequently pass laws to regulate businesses, particularly in international trade. Trade sanctions, trade barriers (both tariff and non-tariff), and preferred-nation status all affect the ways in which buyers are permitted or encouraged to buy. In some cases, governments

- *Legal influences.* Laws may lay down specific technical standards that affect buyer decisions. Buyers may be compelled to incorporate safety features into products or may be subject to legal restrictions in buying some raw materials. Often, suppliers can obtain competitive advantage by anticipating changes in the law (Teixeira et al., 2021). For example, in May 2007 a scandal regarding food additives broke when a Chinese company supplied animal feed containing melamine, a compound used in the manufacture of plastics. American pet food manufacturers incorporated the feed in their products, causing thousands of pets to die from kidney failure and other diseases. In fact, adding melamine to food products was banned in China only a few weeks after the supply had been made.

- *Ethical influences.* In general, buyers are expected to act at all times for the benefit of the organisation, not for personal gain. This means that, in most cultures, buyers are not allowed to accept gifts and/or bribes, for example. However, in some cultures the act of giving gifts/money or some other inducement in order to dishonestly persuade someone to act in one's favour – bribery – is built into normal business life, which leaves the vendor with a major ethical problem – refusing to give a bribe is likely to lose the business, but giving a bribe is probably unethical or illegal in the company's home country. The Organisation for Economic Co-operation and Development (OECD) Anti-Bribery Convention has now been widely adopted, so most companies would be breaking the law if they were to offer or accept bribes. For instance, in the UK, the Bribery Act 2010 makes it an offence if a commercial organisation fails to prevent persons associated with them from bribing another person on their behalf. So, as a general rule, buyers are likely to be highly suspicious of doing business with a salesperson who appears to be acting unethically – after all, if the salesperson is prepared to break the law and cheat his or her employer, he or she might be even more prepared to cheat the buyer. (More on ethics in Chapter 13.)

- *Cultural influences.* When dealing internationally, cultural influences come to the forefront: in the UK it may be customary to offer a visitor a cup of tea or coffee, whereas in India it is customary to offer a glass of water first and foremost, and in China it's food! (Dim Sum originated as a way for Chinese businessmen to offer their visitors a symbolic meal, as a way of establishing rapport.) There is evidence that national culture is less important than it once was, however; other barriers to international trade, such as language (Kitenge and Lahiri, 2022), political issues (van Ommeren et al., 2021), geographic distance (Yue et al., 2022) and even time zone differences (Oberhofer et al., 2021) are often more important (Pressey and Selassie, 2003). Within the national culture is the corporate culture, sometimes defined as 'the way we do things round here'. Corporate culture encompasses the strategic vision of the organisation, its ethical stance and its attitudes towards suppliers, among other things. In addition, many businesspeople act in accordance with their professional culture. Each of these will affect the way business is done.

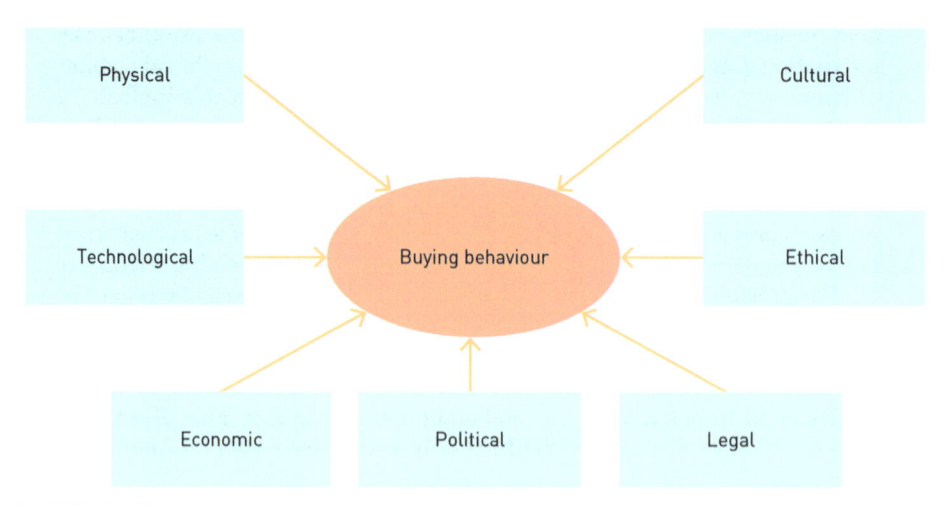

FIGURE 3.2 Environmental influences on buyer behaviour

Kapitan et al. (2018) have devised a 30-item scale measure of B2B sustainability positioning using a quantitative sample of buyers. Items investigated include sustainability credibility, environmental impact, stakeholders, resource efficiency and holistic philosophy. (You can read more on Ethical Consumption in Chapter 13 and Sustainable Consumption in Chapter 14.)

Organisational factors derive from corporate culture, as well as from strategic decisions made by senior management within the firm. Organisational policies, procedures, structure, systems of rewards, authority, status and communication systems will all affect the ways buyers relate to salespeople. Figure 3.3 shows the main categories of organisational influence on buyers' behaviour.

CONSUMER BEHAVIOUR IN ACTION: WSUP.COM

WSUP (Water and Sanitation for the Urban Poor) was the brainchild of Jeremy Pelczer, former CEO of Thames Water, and the late Richard Sandbrook, co-founder of Friends of the Earth. In 2003, Thames Water, as a result of their international operations, recognised that water utilities were not always best placed to meet the needs of the urban poor in the developing world nor did these contracts always best meet their commercial requirements. Richard, Jeremy and others realised that there was a need to address this by bringing together the skills of the private sector, governments and NGOs. A meeting of approximately 60 organisations was called to discuss this concept and to identify which would join Thames Water to develop the vision into reality. In 2005, seven organisations agreed to create WSUP as a non-profit company, limited by guarantee, registered in England and Wales, with each of these organisations becoming a Member and providing a Board Director. (Additionally, WSUP has four non-Executive Directors.) The Department for International Development helped to guide the concept and was one of the first funders to support the initiative. WSUP evolved to working in six core countries in order to identify and test the most effective ways of delivering water and sanitation services to the urban poor. As WSUP grew, they set up teams in each country which are led by a Country Programme Manager reporting to a UK based Programme

> Director. This setup has enabled much better local implementation and connectivity with the in-country institutions mandated to deliver these services, and as a result a much better basis for effective sector change. Improved water and sanitation services underpin almost every other developmental goal. Water, sanitation and hygiene play an essential role in many other critical areas of development, including building resilience to climate change, improving school attendance and reducing inequality. WSUP works under the following themes as part of its core commitment to meeting Sustainable Development Goals 6, 11 and 13 – clean water and sanitation, sustainable cities and communities and climate action, respectively. As cities grow rapidly, the need for improved water and sanitation services is increasing sharply. But there simply isn't the capacity within many service providers to provide these services, particularly to low-income customers. They might lack adequate sources of investment, suffer from high water losses in their network and lack the experience needed to provide services that are suitable for residents living in informal settlements. High population density, poor hygiene conditions and weak national health infrastructure mean that disease outbreaks in low-income communities could be catastrophic. WSUP is providing urgent support to the most vulnerable communities through hygiene promotion, emergency water access and handwashing stations. Alongside these short-term measures WSUP is also focusing on the long-term availability of water supplies, particularly for the poorest in cities. This includes strengthening utilities and encouraging service providers to work with communities to improve water access. Extending services to marginalised communities is not just about building infrastructure or supporting service providers such as utilities or the private operators. There is also a need to improve policies and regulations, to create a stronger enabling environment for the provision of services. Ineffective regulation can disincentivise utilities to improve service delivery, and unclear or outdated policies can make it difficult for institutions to know what their responsibilities are. WSUP's work has focused on supporting regulators to drive change for the poorest residents, guiding city authorities on the development of equitable water, sanitation and hygiene (WASH) strategies, as well as pushing for the implementation of citywide approaches that can tackle the lack of safe sanitation. By engaging with regional and national governments and regulators, as well as international initiatives, WSUP is helping to overcome systemic barriers which prohibit equitable access to clean water, safe sanitation and hygiene.

Buying tasks differ greatly between firms but may also differ significantly within firms. For example, the buying task for a supermarket clearly differs from that for a manufacturing company, since the supermarket intends to sell the vast majority of its purchases unchanged, whereas the manufacturer is largely concerned with sourcing components and raw materials. The supermarket has other, internal variations in the buying task: buying canned goods will be totally different from buying fresh produce such as vegetables or fresh fish. Equally, the manufacturer will have a different approach when buying basic raw materials compared with buying components, and yet another set of approaches when buying lubricating oil or business services or new factory premises. The different purchasing tasks affect the buyer's thinking and negotiating approach, so firms will usually have separate buyers for each type of buying task.

The structure of the organisation falls into two categories: the formal structure is what shows on the organisation chart; the informal structure is the network of personal relationships that dictates staff behaviour in most cases. The formal organisation structure determines such issues as the degree of centralisation in purchasing decision-making, the degree to which buying decisions follow a formal procedure (i.e. how constrained by the rules the buyers are) and the degree of specialisation in buying for different purposes or different departments in the organisation.

The informal structure dictates such issues as rivalry between buyers, recognition by management, cooperation between buyers in maintaining each other's status in the eyes of the boss, and so forth. The maze of informal relationships can be extremely complex, especially for a salesperson observing it from the outside, and this complexity is likely to be crucial in the success or failure of key-account selling. In the global context, the informal structure is subject to many cultural influences – the Far Eastern concern with gaining or losing face, for example, can be a crucial factor in doing business. The informal structure is also the major factor in determining who will be the most important influentials in the decision-making unit; some colleagues' opinions may be regarded as more trustworthy than others, for example.

FIGURE 3.3 Organisational influences on buyer behaviour

The organisation's technology base also affects the buyer's level of control over purchasing. For example, computer-controlled stock purchasing, particularly in a just-in-time purchasing environment, can limit the buyer's ability to negotiate deals and in many cases removes the buyer from the process altogether. Models for inventory control and price forecasting are also widely used by buyers, so that in many cases the negotiating process is virtually automated with little room for manoeuvre on the part of the buyer. If this is the case, the selling organisation needs to go beyond the buyer to the other members of the DMU in order to change the rules or find creative ways round them. E-commerce in B2B marketing relies, for example, on some the following factors (Chen et al., 2022; Claycomb et al., 2005):

- Partner selection.
- Cooperative norms with customers and compatibility with existing systems.
- Lateral integration within the firm.
- Corporate reputation and technocratic specialisation.
- Decentralisation of information technology and the role of trust.

The characteristics of the people involved in the organisation will determine the organisational culture and therefore will influence the interpretation of the rules under which the purchasing department operates. At senior management level the character of the organisation is likely to be a function of the senior management, and in many cases the organisation's founder will have set his or her personality firmly on the organisation's culture. Off-White is clearly an offshoot of Virgil Abloh's personality, as Spanx is an offshoot of Sara Blakely's.

CLASSIFYING BUSINESS CUSTOMERS

A business customer is one who is buying on behalf of an organisation rather than buying for personal or family consumption. In everyday speech we usually talk about organisations as the purchasers of goods, but of course this is not the case: business customers, in practice, are human beings who buy on behalf of organisations.

Organisations might be classified according to the types of buying and end-use they have for the products. Table 3.1 shows a summary of the commonly accepted classifications, followed by a fuller explanation. It is important to understand the different buying and selling situations that arise here, and how these situations will affect the buyer behaviour (especially as in this B2B context the buyer is not typically the 'consumer').

TABLE 3.1   Classification summary of buying organisations

Type of organisation	Description
Business and commercial organisations	These organisations buy goods that are used to make other goods, and also those items that are consumed in the course of running the organisation's business. These organisations buy foundation goods and services (goods used to make other products), facilitating goods and services (those that help an organisation achieve its objectives) and entering goods and services (those that become part of another product)
Reseller organisations	Resellers buy goods in order to sell them on to other organisations or to final consumers. Typically, resellers will be wholesalers or retailers, but they may also be agents for services, for example travel agents or webmasters who act as facilitators for other firms
Governmental organisations	Governments buy everything from paperclips to submarines through their various departments. Because national and local government departments operate under specific rules that are often rigid, negotiations can be difficult to conduct: buyers are often severely constrained in what they can do. Contracts are often put out to tender, with the lowest bidder being awarded the contract
Institutional organisations	Institutional organisations include charities, educational establishments, hospitals and other organisations that do not fit into the business, reseller or government categories. These organisations may be in the market for almost any kind of product, but they are used to achieve institutional goals that probably do not include profit

BUSINESS AND COMMERCIAL ORGANISATIONS

Business and commercial organisations can be segmented as original-equipment manufacturers (OEMs), users and aftermarket customers. Original-equipment manufacturers buy foundation, entering and facilitating goods, including machinery and equipment used to make products, and products that are incorporated directly into the final product. For example, computer manufacturers may buy machine tools to make computer cases and also buy silicon chips from specialist producers: the chips are incorporated into the final product, but the same type of chip might be

OEM

Original-equipment manufacturer makes systems or components that are used in another company's end product incorporated in computers from several different OEMs. Apple's M1 Ultra, currently the world's most powerful chip for a personal computer, is an example.

For OEM buyers, the key issue will be the quality of the products or services. Such buyers are usually operating to fairly exact specifications laid down by their own production engineers and designers; it is unlikely that the supplying firm will be able to do very much to have the specification changed, except by approaching the designers during the design process. This means that introducing a new product to an OEM will be a lengthy process, since the supplying company will need to establish a long-term relationship with the customer in order to become involved at the design stage for new products.

User customers buy products that are used up within the organisation, either as components in their own equipment or to make the equipment perform properly, for example lubricating oils or cleaning products. These products are not resold, but may be bought in considerable quantities. Many of these user products are services – accountancy or legal services, cleaning services, and maintenance or building services are all contained within the firm and not resold.

Aftermarket customers are those involved in the maintaining, repairing and overhauling (MRO) of products after they have been sold. For example, central heating systems are likely to be maintained by independent contractors rather than the original manufacturers or installers. The reason for this is that maintenance requires an investment in expensive testing equipment and different training from that required for installation or manufacture. These contractors buy the components, supplies and services they need from the most convenient supplier.

MRO
A company that carries out maintenance, repair and overhaul

The classification split between OEM, users and aftermarket customers is only relevant to the supplier. OEMs can also be user customers for some suppliers. For example, a plastic moulding company may sell components to an OEM and plastic tools to a user as well as plastic replacement parts to an aftermarket organisation: in some cases these may even be the same organisation. Buying motivations for each type of purchase are clearly very different, and the supplying firm is likely to be dealing with different buyers for each category of product if the customer company is a large one. As shown in the example in Figure 3.4, the same suppliers sometimes provide goods or services for several firms in the supply chain. In some cases there will be considerable crossover between firms.

RESELLER ORGANISATIONS

The majority of manufactured goods are sold through reseller organisations such as retailers and wholesalers. Intermediaries provide useful services such as bulk breaking, assortment of goods and accumulation of associated product types: due to increased efficiencies resulting from these services, intermediaries tend to reduce overall prices for the final consumer. Cutting out the intermediaries usually reduces efficiency and tends to increase prices; if this were not so, the intermediaries would be unable to justify their existence and firms would simply bypass them.

Reseller organisations are driven almost entirely by their customers. The value chain consists of elements including trust, brand, price tolerance and word of mouth communications (Nikhashemi et al., 2021). This means that they will buy only those products they believe will sell easily; there is therefore a premium on employing buyers who have a clear understanding of customer needs. Unlike the OEM buyers, there is little need for resellers to understand the technical aspects of the products they buy – they merely need to feel confident that the ultimate consumers will want the products.

Reseller organisations carry out the following basic functions:

- Negotiation with suppliers.
- Promotional activities such as advertising, sales promotion, providing a sales-force, etc.
- Warehousing, storage and product handling.
- Transportation of local and (occasionally) long-distance shipments.
- Inventory control.
- Credit checking and credit control.
- Pricing and collection of price information, particularly about competitors.
- Collection of market information about consumers and competitors.

For manufacturers, this places a premium on establishing close, long-term relationships with resellers. Shared information, as part of an integrated channel management strategy (Zhang et al., 2022), becomes crucial to forward planning.

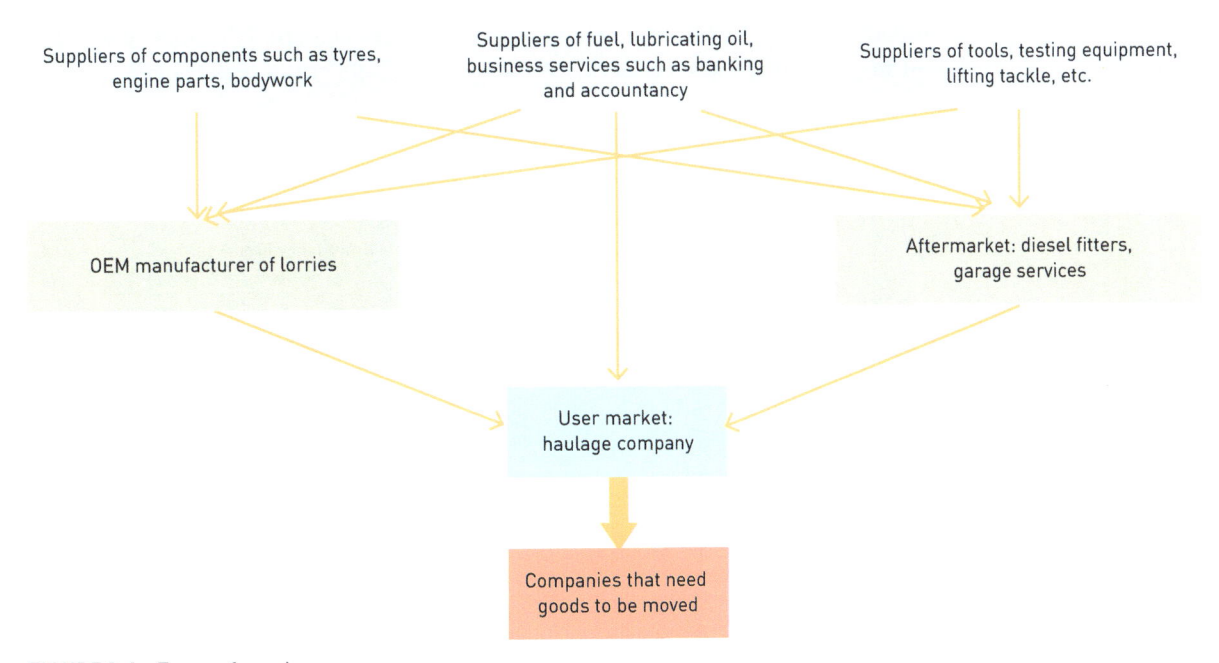

FIGURE 3.4 Types of purchase

GOVERNMENT ORGANISATIONS

Government and quasi-government organisations are major buyers of almost everything. In some markets the government is heavily involved in industry. For instance, all insurance in India used to be a government monopoly and the oil industry in Mexico is controlled by PEMEX, a quasi-government entity. China is the world's largest producer and exporter of consumer electronics products. Governments are thought to be the largest category of market in the world, if all levels of government are included in the equation. The structure of government varies from one country to another: for example, in Spain there is the national government based in Madrid, the regional governments (e.g. the Junta de Andalucia), the provincial governments (e.g. Provincia de Granada) and the local town halls (e.g. Ayuntamiento de Ugijar). Sometimes these local town halls group together to form an alliance that carries out mutually beneficial activities such as tourism marketing or funding a local swimming pool, but frequently they act independently of one another within the frameworks of their own jurisdictions. Figure 3.5 summarises the types of purchase that might be made by each of the tiers of government.

Because of the strict rules under which most government organisations operate, special measures are often needed to negotiate deals. In particular, government organisations almost always put contracts out for tender, so that firms are asked to bid for contracts. The UK government calls their system 'Contracts-Finder', which lets companies search for information about contracts worth over £10,000 with the government and its agencies. The contract is usually offered to the lowest bidder, unless there are overwhelming reasons to do otherwise. From a supplier's viewpoint, this is likely to be problematic since the lowest price is likely to be the least profitable price, so selling firms will often try to circumvent the process by ensuring that they become involved before the tender is finalised. In this way it may be possible to ensure that the tender is drawn up in a way that favours the proactive firm over its competitors (for example, by including features that competitors cannot offer), thus ensuring that competitors either do not bid at all or bid at too high a price.

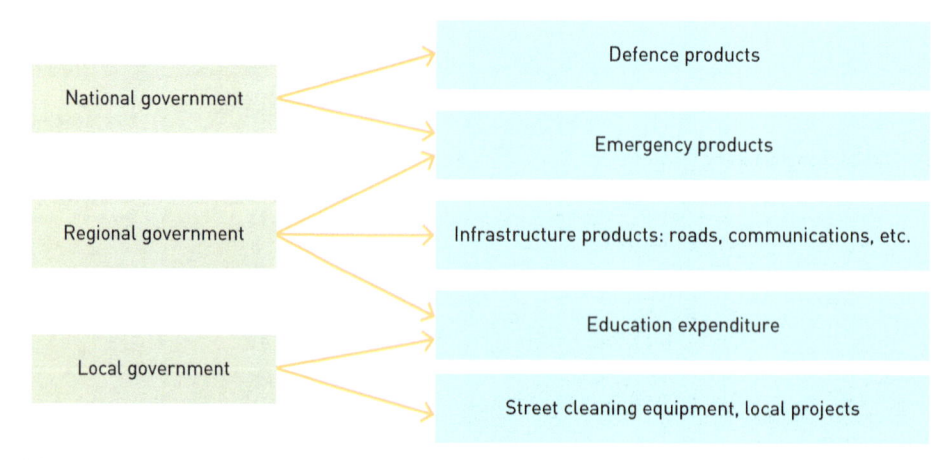

FIGURE 3.5 Tiers of government and their typical purchases

In some cases, governments need to purchase items that are not available to the general public or to other businesses. Military and defence hardware is an obvious example; clearly ordinary businesses are not allowed to buy submarines or nuclear bombs. On a more subtle level, there are many other examples of specialist markets.

So, goods such as handguns are not permitted for private organisations in the UK, but can be sold to the army or the police force; some types of computer software are only appropriate for use by the tax authorities; and academic research is paid for largely by the government in the UK.

From a marketing viewpoint, these specialist markets present an interesting challenge, since in some cases the products need to be tailored to a specific government or a specific government department. This may mean that there is considerable scope for negotiation, but since the contract will still have to go out to tender (under competitive and fair practice legislation and can be found easily through www.gov.uk/contracts-finder), the bidding company may find that it has spent a lot of time developing a specification for a contract that is then awarded to another firm.

In some circumstances governments may issue a 'cost-plus' contract, in which the organisation is given a specific task to carry out, and charges according to the cost of the contract plus an agreed profit margin. In the early days of space exploration this type of contract was common, since it was impossible to predict what the costs might be when dealing with an unknown set of circumstances. More recently these contracts have fallen into disrepute since they reward inefficiency and waste.

INSTITUTIONAL ORGANISATIONS

Institutions include charities, universities, hospital trusts and non-profit organisations of all types, schools and so forth. In some cases, these are government-owned but independent for the purposes of purchase and supply (for example, secondary schools); in other cases, they are totally independent (for example, registered charities). The traditional view of these organisations is that they are chronically under-funded and therefore do not represent a particularly wealthy market, but in practice the organisations actually have a very substantial aggregate spending power. Figure 3.6 summarises the factors that have to be taken into account in marketing to institutions.

The marketing organisation may need to be creative in helping the institution to raise the money to buy its products because budgets are almost always very tight. For example, a firm that produces commercial industrial drilling equipment may find that it has a substantial market at Oxfam, since Oxfam drills wells in many arid regions within developing countries. Oxfam relies on public generosity to raise the money to buy the equipment, so the manufacturer may find it necessary to part-fund or even manage a fundraising campaign in order to make the sale.

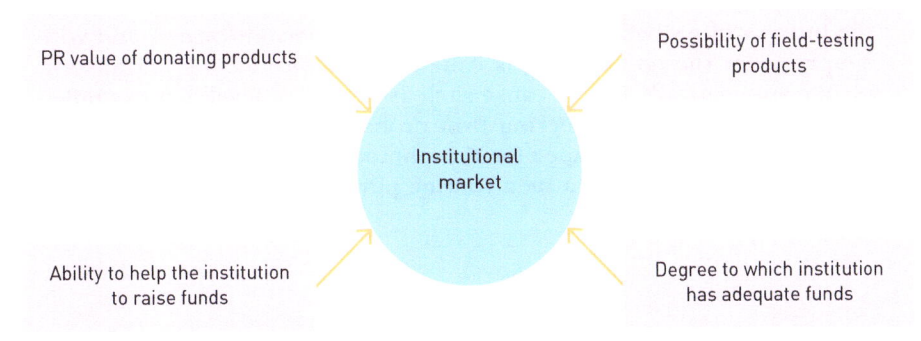

FIGURE 3.6 Factors in institutional marketing

CRITICAL REFLECTION

We are often told that marketing is about managing the exchange process, yet government departments and many institutions seem to lay down the ground rules from the start. Marketers have to play by the buyers' rules to be in the game at all – so how can they possibly be managing the process? Pushed from one set of constraints to the next, it would seem that the average marketer is just a pawn in the buyers' hands!

Yet maybe that is how it should be if customers are at the centre of everything we do. Not to mention that the management process itself could be construed as a clearing house for pressures rather than as a directive force – in a sense, no manager is actually in control, so why should marketers be any different?

Suppliers are often asked to contribute to charities, in cash or in products. This may not always be possible, since the supplier's only market might be the charities, but in some cases firms may find it worthwhile to supply free products to charities in order to gain PR value, or sometimes in order to open the door to lucrative deals with other organisations. For example, a charity working in a developing country might be prepared to field-test equipment that could then be sold to a government department in the same country.

BUYERS' TECHNIQUES

Buyers use a wide variety of techniques according to the buying situation they are faced with. Buying situations are generally divided into three types:

Straight rebuy

A situation in which a previous order is simply repeated in its entirety

1. **Straight rebuy.** Most organisational buying is routine: for example, a car manufacturer needs to buy much the same number of wheel nuts each month. A straight rebuy is a situation where the buyer is buying the same product in very much the same quantities from the same supplier. In these circumstances the buyer needs no new information, and does not need to engage in much negotiation either. Prudent buyers may occasionally look at other possible sources of components in order to ensure that no new technology is available or that other suppliers are not able to supply the same components more cheaply, but in general the order placement is automatic. In some cases the whole process is automated through an electronic data interchange link with a supplier, or there may be an automatic buying procedure facilitated through the internet without any human involvement. If the product is of minor importance, or represents a low commitment in terms of finance or risk, the buyer will probably not undertake any information search and will simply order the goods. This is called *causal purchasing*, because it results automatically from a cause such as low stock level. For example, a buyer for a large engineering firm probably spends very little time deciding on brands of paper for the photocopier. On the other hand, buying copper cable might be a routine purchase, but the buyer might

monitor the market for alternatives occasionally. Such buying is called *routine low-priority buying* because it has a lower priority than would be the case if an entirely new situation were being faced. The company is unlikely to get into serious trouble if it pays 10% more than it should for cable, for example.

2. **Modified rebuy**. In this situation, the buyer re-evaluates the habitual buying patterns of the firm with a view to changing them in some way. The quantities ordered, or the specification of the components, may be changed. Even the supplier may be changed. Sometimes these changes come about because the buyer has become aware of a better alternative than the one currently employed (perhaps through environmental scanning), or sometimes the changes come about because competing suppliers succeed in offering something new. Internal forces (increases or decreases in demand for components) might trigger a renegotiation with suppliers or a search for new suppliers. In such circumstances the buyer is faced with a limited problem-solving scenario in which he or she will need to carry out some negotiation with existing or new suppliers, and will probably need to seek out new information as well. The buyer may well require potential suppliers to bid against each other for the business: the drawback of this approach is that it often results in damaging a well-established relationship with existing suppliers.

3. **New task**. This type of buying situation comes about when the task is perceived as being entirely new. Past experience is therefore no guide, and present suppliers may not be able to help either. Thus the buyer is faced with a complex decision process. Judgemental new task situations are those in which the buyer must deal with technical complexities of the product, complex evaluation of alternatives and negotiating with new suppliers. Strategic new task situations are those in which the final decision is of strategic importance to the firm – for example, a bank looking for software for online banking will be investing (potentially) hundreds of thousands of pounds in retraining staff, and in transferring existing records, not to mention the risks of buying software that lacks the necessary security features or that fails under high demand. In these circumstances, long-range planning at director level drives the buying process, and the relationship with the suppliers is likely to be both long term and close.

Modified rebuy
A purchase that, although similar to previous purchases, has been changed in a minor way

New task
A type of purchase for which previous experience does not exist

From the viewpoint of the business marketer, the main chance of winning new customers will come in the new task situation. The risks for buyers involved in switching suppliers are often too great unless there is a very real and clear advantage in doing so; such an advantage is likely to be difficult to prove in practice. In the new task situation, potential suppliers may well find themselves screened out early in the process, and will then find it almost impossible to be reconsidered later.

The various trade-offs in the buying situation are shown in Figure 3.7.

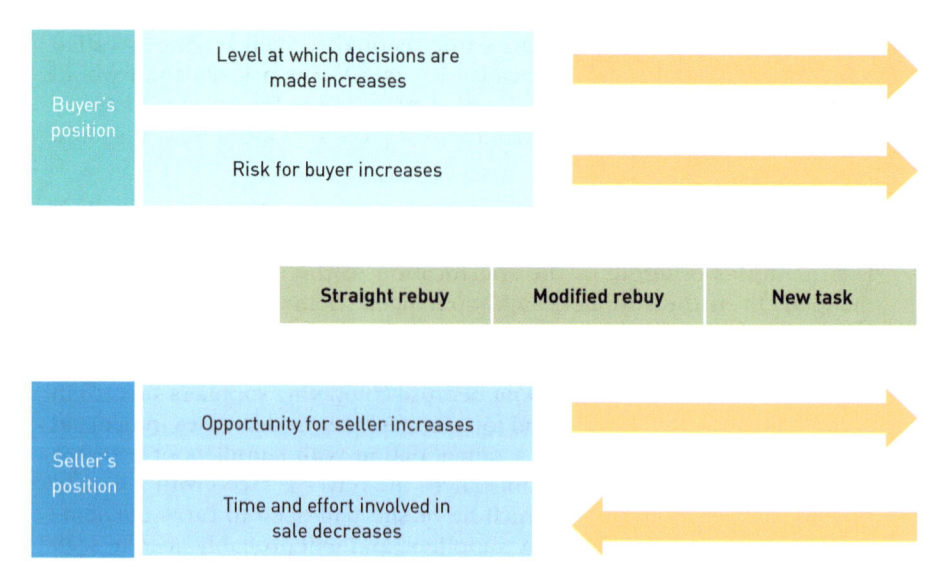

		Straight rebuy	Modified rebuy	New task
Buyer's position	Level at which decisions are made increases	→		
	Risk for buyer increases	→		
Seller's position	Opportunity for seller increases	→		
	Time and effort involved in sale decreases	←		

FIGURE 3.7 Trade-offs in type of buying situation

THE BUYGRID FRAMEWORK

Organisational buying can be seen as a series of decisions, each of which leads to a further problem about which a decision must be made (Cardozo, 1983; Iyer et al., 2015; Yang, 2018). From the viewpoint of the supplying firm, it would certainly be valuable to be able to diagnose problems by examining the sequence of decisions (Mojir and Sudhir, 2022). The difficulty here is that the decision sequence is probably not known to the marketer unless the firms involved already have a close relationship. If the sequence can be known, marketers can identify the stage at which the firm is currently making decisions and can tailor the approach accordingly.

The industrial buying process can be mapped against a grid, as shown in Figure 3.8. The most complex buying situations occur in the upper left portion of the framework and involve the largest number of decision-makers and buying influences. This is because new tasks require the greatest amount of effort in seeking information and formulating appropriate solutions, but also will require the greatest involvement of individuals at all levels of the organisation. The more people who are involved, the more complex the decision process because each individual will have a personal agenda.

However, the Buygrid framework is not without its criticism. Like most models it tends to over-simplify the case. As in consumer decision-making, the sequence may not be as clear-cut and events may take place in a different order in certain circumstances. For example, a buying firm may not be aware that it has a problem in a particular area until a supplier approaches the firm with a solution, thus cutting out several stages of the process: the firm may well recognise the need and the problem, but will probably not need to acquire proposals and select a supplier since the supplier is already offering a solution. Second, suppliers go to great lengths to differentiate themselves from competitors as effectively as they can, so that the buyer is unlikely to have any other potential suppliers of the exact product on offer. Third, the model assumes a rational approach to purchasing which is often simply not there. Finally, the boundaries between new task, modified rebuy and straight rebuy are by no means clear-cut.

	Buying situations		
Stage	New task	Modified rebuy	Straight rebuy
Anticipation or recognition of a problem (need) and a general solution			
Determination of characteristics and quantity of needed item			
Description of characteristics and quantity of needed item			
Search for and qualification of potential sources			
Acquisition and analysis of proposals			
Evaluation of proposals and selection of supplier(s)			
Selection of an order routine			
Performance feedback and evaluation			

FIGURE 3.8 The Buygrid framework
Source: Johnston and Lewin (1994).

Buyers are influenced by both rational and emotional considerations. The potential supplier needs to be aware of the personal agendas of each member of the decision-making unit. Even at a rational level, each member of the DMU will apply different criteria for judging which suppliers should be included and which excluded – also known as the supplier selection problem (SSP) (Hawkins et al., 2015; Kelly and Coaker, 1976): the finance director might emphasise low prices, whereas the chief designer might be concerned with product quality, and the production manager with reliable delivery. The buyer might be concerned with the relationship with the supplier's salespeople. And so strategic SSP becomes quite a significant issue, for instance, in renewable supply chain management. Selecting a strategic green supplier can not only discover the sustainable development of supply chains but also optimise the consumption rate of resources and decrease the negative environmental effects, which adopts a green development context (Masoomi et al., 2022). In many cases, brand equity is less important than issues of price and delivery (Bendixen et al., 2004; Mourad et al., 2011). At the personal and emotional level, office politics, rivalries, jockeying for promotion, liking or disliking the salesperson and many other factors will affect different members of the DMU in different ways.

In the case of key-account management, this problem of dealing with different members of the DMU is often overcome by taking a team approach to the sale. This is so that both the different **key-account manager** (KAM) frameworks and KAM performance drivers can be further understood (Herhausen et al., 2022). While the key-account manager handles the initial contact and the management of the process, other specialists are brought in to deal with financial and technical aspects. In this

Key-account manager
A salesperson who has the responsibility of dealing with the most important customers of a firm

way each member of the DMU is speaking to someone with whom he or she has a common language and a common understanding of the conceptual environment within which each specialty operates.

Managing the key-account networks means identifying the key network, developing a strategy for managing the individuals who operate within the network and developing methods at the operational level for managing those actors (Gupta et al., 2019; Ojasalo, 2004). The responsibility for managing the actors is often divided between the members of the selling team. The internal culture of the firm (and the external culture, in an international context) affects the nature of each of these network types.

According to Moller and Svahn (2004), there are three types of business networks (see below) and Knoke (2018) makes the case for business networks in the new political economy:

1. *Stable.* These are networks that are perhaps still growing, but they are following a predictable course.
2. *Established.* These networks are fixed and relatively unchanging, and the rules are known by the members.
3. *Emerging.* These networks are still growing and changing.

Work conducted by La Rocca et al. (2015) provides a powerful case for focusing on the role that interaction behaviours play in business relationships. In their model, there are two perspectives that could be examined: the socio-cognitive perspective and the practice-based approach to both markets and marketing. More recently, Gupta et al. (2019) have noted that cross-function ties in the within-seller network serve a complementary role, but only in relation to similar function ties in the buyer–seller network. In contrast, within-seller centralisation supports both network density and similar function ties in the buyer–seller network and, thus, emerges as a valuable KAM team characteristic. These findings suggest multiple ways for firms to align inter-firm and intra-firm KAM networks to improve account profitability.

VALUE ANALYSIS

Value analysis

The process of calculating the worth of a purchase in terms of the returns made from its use

Mindfulness

The quality or state of being conscious or aware of something

Value analysis is a method of evaluating components, raw materials and even manufacturing processes in order to determine ways of cutting costs or improving finished products. Value-in-use is defined as a product's economic value to the user relative to a specific alternative in a particular application (Kijewski and Yoon, 1990). Value-in-use is the price that would equate the overall costs and benefits of using one product rather than using another. Value can also be seen from the lens of interpretive experiences (Eck et al., 2022). Eck et al. examined environmental interpretation narratives and tested their influence on participants' **mindfulness** and the value of their interpretive experiences. Their results suggest that mindful interpretation can positively influence visitor interpretive experiences, which in turn provides value during and after their experience.

Proponents of a similar concept, Vargo and Lusch (2004) and Vargo et al. (2019) used their service-dominant logic (S-DL) framework to explain how competencies are used in achieving competitive advantage. Veres (2012) explains that in order for the firm to create competitive advantage (and thus to develop a 'value-creating problem-solving' strategy) it has to leverage the intangible assets of the company. Quite often, when organisations are under pressure to perform, the intangible assets suddenly manifest themselves in technology, products and/or management (Veres, 2012). How well the organisation has the ability and capability to 'learn' will determine the final competencies that it has. The final contribution that S-DL makes here is to do with the value-offer (something that is done by the supplier) and value-creation (something that is carried out by the buyer); a concept Vargo and Lusch (2004) call 'co-creation'.

For example, consider LED light bulbs. Even though these bulbs are between five and ten times as expensive to buy as compared to the old tungsten-filament bulbs, they last at least five times as long and use only 20% of the electricity. For a domestic consumer this represents a considerable saving, more than enough to cover the initial outlay for the bulbs, but for a business customer the saving is even greater, since the cost of paying someone to replace blown light bulbs is significant. The global LED lighting market is predicted to reach almost $160 billion by 2026 (Placek, 2019).

CRITICAL REFLECTION

Van Zeeland and Henseler (2018) have written about the behavioural response of the professional buyer to social cues from the vendor and how to measure it. And so it stands to reason that the methods of assessment shown in Table 3.2 all rely on some kind of judgement on the part of the buyer. Even the financial figures filed at the company record office require interpretation – and may even have been manipulated or 'massaged' to make the company look more financially viable than it actually is.

So why bother with what is, after all, a somewhat time-consuming exercise? Presumably a rogue supplier would have little difficulty in pulling the wool over the eyes of a buyer who probably lacks the engineering training to understand what is in front of him or her. In contrast, an honest supplier would probably provide pictures showing all the defects and imperfections that might well lose the contract. So should each attribute from Table 3.2 be examined in miniscule detail?

Some buyers do use the type of calculation seen in Table 3.2 to assess alternative solutions to existing problems. A capable salesperson will be prepared with the full arguments in favour of the new solution, including all the relevant factors that make the product more attractive. By contrast, astute purchasers will fully involve potential suppliers in the discussions and in the value analysis process.

TABLE 3.2 Assessing suppliers

Attribute	Assessment method
Technical capability	Visit the supplier to examine production equipment, inspect quality control procedures and meet the engineering staff
Managerial capability	Discuss systems for controlling processes, meet the managerial staff and become involved in planning and scheduling supplies
Financial stability	Due diligence. Check the accounts filed at Companies House or another public record office, run a credit check, examine annual reports if any
Capacity to deliver	Ascertain the status of other customers of the supplier – would any of these take priority? Assess the production capacity of the supplier, warehouse stocks of the product, reputation in the industry

EVALUATING SUPPLIER CAPABILITY

Purchasers also need to assess the capability of potential suppliers to continue to supply successfully. This is a combination of assessing financial stability, technical expertise, reliability, quality assurance processes and production capacity. In simple terms, the purchasing company is trying to ensure that the potential supplier will be in a position to keep the promises it makes. Business customers can gain competitive advantage from tracking the performance of suppliers because they are better able to manage the supply chain (Bharadwaj, 2004).

EVALUATING SUPPLIER PERFORMANCE

Even after the contract is awarded, the purchasing company will probably re-examine the supplier's performance periodically and analyse the relationship between quality management, performance appraisal and pay for performance (Bayo-Moriones and de la Torre, 2022). In some cases, suppliers have been known to relax and reduce their service level once the contract is awarded, and of course the circumstances of the buying organisation are likely to change over time. If the relationship with the supplier is to continue, then (like all other human relationships) it must adapt to changing circumstances. The basic evaluation methods are outlined in Table 3.3. All of these methods involve some degree of subjectivity, in other words each method requires buyers to make judgements about the supplier. Expressing the evaluations numerically makes the method appear more credible, but if the basic assumptions are incorrect, no amount of calculation will generate the right answer. Those involved in evaluation exercises of this nature should be aware that the evaluation exercise itself should be evaluated periodically, and the (usually subjective) criteria used by the various individuals involved need to be checked.

In fact, suppliers tend to adapt more often than do purchasers when there is an ongoing relationship (Brennan et al., 2003). This is due to the relative power each has (buyers being more powerful in most circumstances), and managerial preferences. Suppliers who are market-orientated tend to develop a greater customer intimacy, which may also drive suppliers to change (Tuominen et al., 2004). Buyers who are themselves market-orientated tend to become more loyal to their suppliers (Jose Sanzo et al., 2003). Having said that, suppliers do sometimes end unprofitable relationships; many B2B relationships are unprofitable, and often companies lack the skills to make relationships profitable, so they simply end them (Helm et al., 2006; Masso and Vahter, 2021) or buyers switch suppliers (Holma et al., 2021).

TABLE 3.3 Evaluation approaches

Approach	Explanation
Categorical plan	Each department having contact with the supplier is asked to provide a regular rating of suppliers against a list of salient performance factors. This method is extremely subjective, but is easy to administer
Weighted-point plan	Performance factors are graded according to their importance to the organisation: for example, delivery reliability might be more important for some organisations than for others. The supplier's total rating can be calculated and the supplier's offering can be adjusted if necessary to meet the purchasing organisation's needs
Cost-ratio plan	Here the buying organisation evaluates quality, delivery and service in terms of what each one costs. Good performance is assigned a negative score, i.e. the costs of purchase are reduced by good performance; poor performance is assigned a positive score, meaning that the costs are deemed to be greater when dealing with a poor performer
Fuzzy AHP (analytic hierarchy process) and goal programming	Fuzzy AHP and goal programming are combined to identify suitable suppliers and allocate orders in the supply chain. The mathematical models develop the goals of minimising periodic budget, minimising defect rate, maximising the total value of purchase and maximising demand. Whilst the results are subjected to sensitivity analysis, it will help a manufacturer in selecting a suitable supplier to allocate the order for maximising the profit, improving the quality of product, enhancing the supplier–buyer relationship, strengthening the supply chain, reducing the risk of purchasing decision and improving customer satisfaction

CRITICAL REFLECTION

Much of the emphasis in later chapters will be on the purchaser's evaluation of suppliers. But what about the other way round? A balanced view determines that customers are not always **plaster saints**.

Some are late payers, some impose unreasonable restrictions, some reject supplies for the flimsiest of reasons, and some are just plain unpleasant to deal with.

So should suppliers have their own systems for assessing purchasers? Should we just grovel at the feet of any organisation willing to buy our goods – or should we stand up and be counted? After all, without supplies no company can survive – so presumably we are equally important to one another.

Maybe this is really the purpose of segmenting our markets – and what is really meant by segmentation.

Plaster saint

A person who makes a show of being without moral faults or human weakness, especially in a hypocritical way

SUMMARY

Both buyers and sellers have a large number of influences on their decision-making. At the very least, buyers have their own personal agendas within the companies they work for; in the broader context, a wide range of political, environmental and technological issues will affect their decision-making. The end result is likely to be a combination of experience, careful calculation and gut feeling.

Although industrial buyers are often assumed to be much more rigorous in their buying, and less swayed by emotion, this is only partly true; consequently, they are as susceptible to good marketing as any other person, and can be influenced by good marketing communications and especially by good salespeople.

KEY POINTS

- Buyers are subject to many pressures other than the simple commercial ones; emotions, organisational influence, politics and internal structures are also important factors.
- The decision-making unit (DMU) or buying centre is the group of people who will make the buying decision. The roles and composition of DMUs vary widely.
- Business and commercial organisations are likely to be swayed most by past experience with a vendor, product characteristics and quality.
- Resellers are driven by their customers.
- Government markets are large, and almost always use a tendering system.
- Institutional markets may need special techniques to help them afford to buy the products.
- Markets can be divided into those buyers who buy products designed to make other products or who will incorporate the purchase into their own products (original-equipment manufacturers); those who consume the product in the course of running their businesses (user markets); and those who serve the aftermarket.
- A purchase may be a straight rebuy, a modified rebuy or a new task. These are given in order of increasing complexity, and do not have discrete boundaries.
- A team approach to buying usually dictates a team approach to selling.

HOW TO IMPRESS YOUR EXAMINER

Industrial buyer behaviour is not always included in consumer behaviour courses, and you should question 'why not?!' because there are parallels between the ways consumers meet their needs and the ways buyers make decisions. If you are asked about industrial buying behaviour, it is worth remembering that buyers are also human beings – they are as affected by emotion and 'gut feeling' as anyone else, but need to keep this in control in the working environment. Using parallels from family decision-making will show that you understand the issues.

REVIEW QUESTIONS

1. How would you expect a government department to go about buying a new cloud-based computer system?
2. How might internal politics affect a buyer's behaviour?
3. What factors might be prominent in the buying decision for cleaning materials?
4. What factors might a supplier take into account when evaluating a purchasing company?
5. How might the directors of a company go about setting standards for evaluating suppliers? What objective criteria are available?
6. What are the main problems with evaluating supplier performance?
7. How should a seller approach a government department?
8. What are the main differences between marketing to commercial organisations and marketing to charities?
9. How might a seller find out who the influentials are in the DMU?
10. How might a seller act to reduce the risk for the buyer?

CASE STUDY: THE ELECTRIC CAR SCHEME

With inflation rapidly increasing, latest figures indicate that there will be a big pay squeeze, with employers struggling to give pay rises in line with inflation. In a perfect storm for employees, the labour market continues to remain tight, making it imperative that employers retain their best employees. But what can employers do to keep talent when they aren't able to give bumper pay rises? Sometimes it is necessary to be creative with employee benefits, and one way to do that is by offering employees something aspirational, such as the chance to have an electric car.

Introducing an electric vehicle salary sacrifice scheme to an employees' benefits package is a great way of keeping the workforce happy, while not breaking the bank through pay rises. Such schemes have mutual benefits for both employers and employees, while at the same time promoting sustainability by encouraging employees to reduce their carbon footprint.

The Electric Car Scheme (ECS) started because for many companies the government tax incentives were hard to access. In April 2020 the government created a tax incentive to help employees choose electric cars, go green and save on income tax. Having looked at setting up a similar scheme for their own business at the time, they (now owners of ECS) came away really disappointed. So they decided to set up ECS: the only dedicated electric car salary sacrifice specialist in the UK.

There are many other schemes out there in the market but they expect the company to take all the risk. If employees go on parental or sick leave, the business would pay the early exit fee for returning the lease car. This can of course be a significant cost!

(Continued)

The lease deals that were being offered were very expensive. The best deals on the market were more than 25% cheaper than what other schemes were offering. This pretty much wiped out the tax benefit altogether! So whilst the government incentive was there, it wasn't accessible.

The Electric Car Scheme solves these problems. The employer should not take on the risk of paying for a car if an employee leaves, has a child or falls ill. ECS protects the business by taking on the risks. It works with a wide range of car lease companies to find the best value lease on the market for each car. Employees should then get the very best lease deals, as well as the full tax benefit, and they shouldn't be limited to one expensive supplier.

So how does it work in practice? Companies sign up to ECS to access their admin support and risk protection at no cost to the employer. Together, the scheme is launched to the employees through webinars, emails, on-site visits and more. There is, of course, a dedicated account manager who will support employees with car selection, delivery and other ongoing support. Employees are then able to drive a brand new electric car, funded by a reduction in their gross salary. Simple! The employer leases the vehicle, provides it as a benefit to the employee and recovers the cost through salary sacrifice. All at no cost to the company, and this means that employees are able to drive any brand-new electric vehicle at a 30–60% discount through salary sacrifice. Companies and employees are able to access any manufacturer, model and extras with ECS. ECS maximises employee savings by sourcing the best value lease on the market through its network of lease providers. ECS can add maintenance, servicing, MOT, breakdown cover and tyre replacements as an optional package. Employees benefit from peace of mind and further savings as this is included in their salary sacrifice. ECS provides fully comprehensive car insurance with GAP insurance included. This provides the employer (ECS's B2B client) with peace of mind that vehicles are covered. If employees are interested in installing a home charger, this can be included with the car – making the switch even easier. In many instances with other lease agreements out there in the market, early termination typically costs the employer or employee 50% of the remaining lease costs. ECS includes protection for employers and employees against early termination fees should the vehicle need to be returned early for a variety of reasons.

ECS provides automated monthly payroll reporting, supports yearly tax reporting and helps its clients remain HMRC compliant – all at both the employee and employer level. Companies can roll out the scheme without worrying about extra administrative burden. There are no setup costs, and the fee is equivalent to the employer's tax savings so the scheme can be rolled out at no cost to the business. And remember, a dedicated account manager will be on hand to help companies sign up, launch the scheme to employees and provide ongoing support.

CASE STUDY QUESTIONS

1. Why have governments introduced tax incentive schemes?
2. Why did ECS feel it needed to develop B2B relationships?
3. Why has ECS simplified the entire decision-making process?
4. How does ECS use its key account managers for the benefit of their clients?
5. What processes have ECS put into place to ensure that the administrative burden to clients is kept to a minimum?

FURTHER READING

The following is a small selection from the many available books/blogs on business-to-business marketing.

https://newnorth.com/insights/ – If you're looking to learn B2B marketing, this content can help. They cover pretty much everything – from tactics to theories (and even the occasional opinion piece on the state of the industry).

https://blog.hubspot.com/ – As you might expect from the company that literally invented the idea of inbound marketing, they do an extremely good job of a) creating a lot of content, and b) ensuring that all of their content is very valuable. If you're looking for general marketing advice, this is a worthwhile stop. No, they aren't specifically focused on B2B – they serve B2C firms, too. But they have a wealth of content dedicated to the B2B space.

www.markempa.com/blog/ – Markempa (formerly known as The B2B Lead blog) is run by Brian Carroll, who's a leading researcher in empathy-based marketing. As you may be able to tell from the blog's former title, yes, it is specifically focused on B2B. Brian has been running this publication since 2003, and it continues to hit the mark – not only is it insightful and helpful, but it's actually pretty funny, too.

The Reputation Playbook: A Winning Formula to Help CEOs Protect Corporate Reputation in the Digital Economy, by Jennifer Jenson (Petersfield: Harriman House, 2014). This book provides a detailed look at traditional B2B brands and organisations that understand the value of social media and the transparency the latter bring to us as customers. Some excellent examples and case studies are used.

To Sell Is Human, by Daniel H. Pink (New York: Riverhead Books, 2012). A detailed insight into what actually makes a sale, and what makes people want to buy.

There Is No B2B or B2C: It's Human to Human #H2H, by Bryan Kramer (San Jose, CA: Pure Matter, 2014). The author takes a perspective here that focuses on creating a dialogue that helps solve consumer needs, as opposed to separating marketing into B2B and B2C.

The B2B Executive Playbook: The Ultimate Weapon for Achieving Sustainable, Predictable and Profitable Growth, by Sean Geehan (Cincinnati, OH: Clerisy Press, 2011). A great text about how to target potential and current clients.

Thinking, Fast and Slow, by Daniel Kahneman (New York: Farrar, Straus and Giroux, 2011). Outlines two 'systems' and ways of thinking which enable readers to predict how others will think, make decisions and which strategies could be used to satisfy consumer needs.

MORE ONLINE

For additional materials that support this chapter and your learning, please visit:

https://study.sagepub.com/sethna5e

REFERENCES

Bayo-Moriones, A. and de la Torre, R. (2022) Analysing the relationship between QM, performance appraisal and pay for performance. *Total Quality Management & Business Excellence*, 33 (9/10): 1056–83.

Behera, R.K., Bala, P.K., Rana, N.P. and Kizgin, H. (2022) Cognitive computing based ethical principles for improving organisational reputation: A B2B digital marketing perspective. *Journal of Business Research*, 141: 685–701.

Bendixen, M., Bukasa, K.A. and Abratt, R.A. (2004) Brand equity in the business to business market. *Industrial Marketing Management*, 33 (5): 371–80.

Besharov, M.L. and Smith, W.K. (2014) Multiple institutional logics in organizations: Explaining their varied nature and implications. *Academy of Management Review*, 39 (3): 364–81.

Bharadwaj, N. (2004) Investigating the decision criteria used in electronic components procurement. *Industrial Marketing Management*, 33 (4): 317–23.

Brennan, R.D., Turnbull, P.W. and Wilson, D.T. (2003) Dyadic adaptation in business-to-business markets. *European Journal of Marketing*, 37 (11): 1636–65.

Cardozo, R.N. (1983) Modelling organisational buying as a sequence of decisions. *Industrial Marketing Management*, 12 (February): 75.

Chen, S., He, Q. and Xiao, H. (2022) A study on cross-border e-commerce partner selection in B2B mode. *Electronic Commerce Research*, 22 (2): 1–21.

Claycomb, C., Iyer, K. and Germain, R. (2005) Predicting the level of B2B e-commerce in industrial organisations. *Industrial Marketing Management*, 34 (3): 221–34.

Eck, T., Ellis, G. and Jiang, J. (2022) Effects of mindful interpretation strategies on interpretation value-during-use and interpretation value-after-use. *Journal of Outdoor Recreation and Tourism*, 39. https://doi.org/10.1016/j.jort.2022.100527

Enyinda, C.I., Enyinda, I.E., Mbah, C.H. and Ogbuehi, A.O. (2021) Managing marketing–sales–service relationship conflict in a B2B multinational firm. *Thunderbird International Business Review*, 63 (6): 719–33.

Farrokhi, A., Shirazi, F., Hajli, N. and Tajvidi, M. (2020) Using artificial intelligence to detect crisis related to events: Decision making in B2B by artificial intelligence. *Industrial Marketing Management*, 91: 257–73.

Gölgeci, I., Karakas, F. and Tatoglu, E. (2019) Understanding demand and supply paradoxes and their role in business-to-business firms. *Industrial Marketing Management*, 76: 169–80.

Gupta, A., Kumar, A., Grewal, R. and Lilien, G.L. (2019) Within-seller and buyer–seller network structures and key account profitability. *Journal of Marketing*, 83 (1): 108–32.

Hawes, J.M and Barnhouse, S.H. (1987) How purchasing agents handle personal risk. *Industrial Marketing Management*, 16 (November): 287–93.

Hawkins, T.G., Gravier, M.J., Berkowitz, D. and Muir, W.A. (2015) Improving services supply management in the defense sector: How the procurement process affects B2B service quality. *Journal of Purchasing and Supply Management*, 21 (2): 81–94.

Helm, S., Rolfes, L. and Gunther, B. (2006) Suppliers' willingness to end unprofitable customer relationships. *European Journal of Marketing*, 40 (3/4): 366–83.

Herhausen, D., Ivens, B., Spencer, R. and Weibel, M. (2022) Key account management configurations and their effectiveness: A quasi-replication and extension. *Industrial Marketing Management*, 101: 98–112.

Holma, A.-M., Bask, A., Laakso, A. and Andersson, D. (2021) Conceptualizing the supplier switching process: An example from public procurement. *Journal of Business & Industrial Marketing*, 37 (7): 1530–41.

Iyer, G.R., Hong Xiao, S., Sharma, A. and Nicholson, M. (2015) Behavioral issues in price setting in business-to-business marketing: A framework for analysis. *Industrial Marketing Management*, 47: 6–16.

Johnston, W.J. and Lewin, J.E. (1994) A review and integration of research on organizational buying behaviour. Marketing Science Institute, Working Paper Series, 94–111.

Jose Sanzo, M., Leticia Santos, M., Rodolfo, V. and Alvarez, L.I. (2003) The role of market orientation in business dyadic relationships: Testing an integrator model. *Journal of Marketing Management*, 19: 73–107.

Kapitan, S., Kennedy, A.-M. and Berth, N. (2018) Sustainably superior versus greenwasher: A scale measure of B2B sustainability positioning. *Industrial Marketing Management*, 76 (January): 84–97. https://doi.org/10.1016/j.indmarman.2018.08.003

Kelly, P. and Coaker, J.W. (1976) Can we generalise about choice criteria for industrial purchasing decisions? In K.L. Bernhardt (ed.), *Marketing 1776–1976 and Beyond*. Chicago, IL: American Marketing Association. pp. 330–3.

Kijewski, V. and Yoon, E. (1990) Market-based pricing: Beyond price–performance curves. *Industrial Marketing Management*, 19 (February): 11–19.

Kitenge, E. and Lahiri, S. (2022) Is the internet bringing down language-based barriers to international trade? *Review of International Economics*, 30 (2): 566–605.

Knoke, D. (2018) *Changing Organizations: Business Networks in the New Political Economy*. Abingdon: Routledge.

La Rocca, A., Snehota, I. and Trabattoni, C. (2015) Construction of meanings in business relationships and networks. *The IMP Journal*, 9 (2): 163–76.

Lattuch, F. and Ruppert, E. (2021) Human resources, organizational learning and due diligence: Avoiding the honeymoon hangover effect in mergers & acquisitions. *Development and Learning in Organizations: An International Journal*, 36 (3): 12–14.

Loudon, D.L. and Della Bitta, A.J. (1993) *Consumer Behaviour: Concepts and Application*. New York: McGraw-Hill.

Masoomi, B., Sahebi, I.G., Fathi, M., Yıldırım, F. and Ghorbani, S. (2022) Strategic supplier selection for renewable energy supply chain under green capabilities (fuzzy BWM-WASPAS-COPRAS approach). *Energy Strategy Reviews*, 40. https://doi.org/10.1016/j.esr.2022.100815

Masso, J. and Vahter, P. (2021) Joining and exiting the value chain of multinationals and the performance of suppliers: Evidence from inter-firm transaction data. University of Tartu – Faculty of Economics & Business Administration Working Paper Series, 136: 3–32.

Micić, I. and Krstić-Ranđić, J. (2022) Setting a competence framework to strengthen organizational strategic performance. *Ekonomija: Teorija i Praksa*, 15 (1): 61–77.

Mojir, N. and Sudhir, K. (2022) A structural model of organizational buying for business-to-business markets: Innovation adoption with share-of-wallet contracts. *Journal of Marketing Research*, 6 (1). https://doi.org/10.1177/00222437221084

Moller, K. and Svahn, S. (2004) Crossing East–West boundaries: Knowledge sharing in intercultural business networks. *Industrial Marketing Management*, 33 (3): 219–28.

Mourad, M., Ennew, C. and Kortam, W. (2011) Brand equity in higher education. *Marketing Intelligence & Planning*, 29 (4): 403–20.

Nikhashemi, S.R., Valaei, N., Rezaei, S. and Bressolles, G. (2021) The hidden chain of branded telecommunication services delivery: Value, trust, brand, price tolerance and word of mouth communication chain. *Journal of Relationship Marketing*, 20 (3): 204–40.

Oberhofer, H., Pfaffermayr, M. and Sellner, R. (2021) Revisiting time as a trade barrier: Evidence from a panel structural gravity model. *Review of International Economics*, 29 (5): 1382–417.

Ojasalo, J. (2004) Key network management. *Industrial Marketing Management*, 33 (3): 195–205.

Pandey, S.K. and Mookerjee, A. (2018) Assessing the role of emotions in B2B decision making: An exploratory study. *Journal of Indian Business Research*, 10 (2): 170–92.

Placek, M. (2019) LED lighting: Global market size 2020–2026. www.statista.com/statistics/753939/global-led-luminaire-market-size/ (accessed 10 February 2022).

Pomirleanu, N., Gustafson, B.M. and Townsend, J. (2022) Organizational climate in B2B: A systematic literature review and future research directions. *Industrial Marketing Management*, 105: 147–58.

Prajogo, D., Toy, J., Bhattacharya, A., Oke, A. and Cheng, T.C.E. (2018) The relationships between information management, process management and operational performance: Internal and external contexts. *International Journal of Production Economics*, 199: 95–103.

Pressey, A.D. and Selassie, H.G. (2003) Are cultural differences over-rated? Examining the influence of national culture on international buyer–seller relationships. *Journal of Consumer Behaviour*, 2 (4): 354–68.

Reijonen, H., Hirvonen, S., Nagy, G., Laukkanen, T. and Gabrielsson, M. (2013) The impact of entrepreneurial orientation on B2B branding and business growth in emerging markets. *Industrial Marketing Management*. doi: 10.1016/j.indmarman.2015.04.016

Reklaitis, K. and Pileliene, L. (2019) Principle differences between B2B and B2C marketing communication processes. *Management of Organizations: Systematic Research*, 81: 73–86.

Rodriguez, R., Svensson, G. and Román, S. (2018) Comparing the life-cycles of service sales between buyers and sellers in business relationships through a teleological lens. *International Journal of Business Excellence*, 15 (1): 95–113.

Ronchetto, J.R., Jr, Hutt, M.D. and Reingen, P.H. (1989) Embedded influence patterns in organizational buying systems. *Journal of Marketing*, 53 (4): 51–62.

Rudawska, E. (2019) Sustainable marketing strategy in food and drink industry: A comparative analysis of B2B and B2C SMEs operating in Europe. *Journal of Business & Industrial Marketing, 34* (4): 875–90.

Silva, S.C., Duarte, P.A.O. and Almeida, S.R. (2020) How companies evaluate the ROI of social media marketing programmes: Insights from B2B and B2C. *Journal of Business & Industrial Marketing, 35* (12): 2097–110.

Teixeira, F., Ferreira, J.J. and Veiga, P.M. (2021) Does law as resource bring a competitive advantage to companies? *Management Research: Journal of the Iberoamerican Academy of Management, 20* (3): 193–211.

Troisi, O., Maione, G., Grimaldi, M. and Loia, F. (2020) Growth hacking: Insights on data-driven decision-making from three firms. *Industrial Marketing Management, 90*: 538–57.

Tuominen, M., Rajala, A. and Moller, K. (2004) Market-driving versus market-driven: Divergent roles of market orientation in business relationships. *Industrial Marketing Management, 33* (3): 207–17.

van Ommeren, E., Poletti, A. and De Bièvre, D. (2021) The European Union and the political economy of enforcing international trade rules. *European Union Politics, 22* (3): 377–400.

van Zeeland, E. and Henseler, J. (2018) The behavioural response of the professional buyer on social cues from the vendor and how to measure it. *Journal of Business & Industrial Marketing, 33* (1): 72–83.

VanBergen, N. and Lurie, N.H. (2022) More rational or more emotional than others? Lay beliefs about decision-making strategies. *Journal of Consumer Psychology, 32* (2): 274–92.

Vargo, S.L. and Lusch, R.F. (2004) Evolving to a new dominant logic for marketing. *Journal of Marketing, 68* (January): 1–17.

Vargo, S.L., Lusch, R.F. and Koskela-Huotari, K. (2019) *The Sage Handbook of Service-Dominant Logic*. London: Sage.

Veres, Z. (2012) Uncertainty-reducing project-competences as organizational capabilities. *The IMP Journal, 6* (2): 154–66.

Webster, F.E. and Wind, Y. (1972) *Organisational Buying Behaviour*. Englewood Cliffs, NJ: Prentice-Hall.

Yang, J. (2018) *Personalized Campaign Recommendation and Buyer Targeting for B2B Marketing*. Doctoral dissertation, Rutgers University Graduate School, Newark.

Yue, C., Lai, Y., Khachatryan, H. and Hodges, A. (2022) Effect of geographic distance on domestic trade: A case of the US Green industry. *Agribusiness, 38* (1): 154–74.

Zhang, M., Lin Sun, Y.L. and Moustapha, F.A. (2022) Integrated store service quality measurement scale in omni-channel retailing. *International Journal of Retail & Distribution Management, 50* (7): 839–59.

PART ONE   CONSUMER BEHAVIOUR IN CONTEXT

Chapter 1   Understanding Consumer Behaviour
Chapter 2   Decisions, Behaviours and Interactions
Chapter 3   Consumption in B2C vs. B2B
Chapter 4   Consumer Technology and Innovation

PART TWO   CONSUMERS AS INDIVIDUALS (THE PSYCHOLOGICAL ISSUES)

Chapter 5   Drive, Motivation and Hedonism
Chapter 6   The Self and Personality
Chapter 7   Perception
Chapter 8   Learning and Knowledge
Chapter 9   Attitude Formation and Change

PART THREE   CONSUMERS AS SOCIAL ACTORS (THE SOCIOLOGICAL ISSUES)

Chapter 10   Reference Groups
Chapter 11   Age, Gender and Familial Roles
Chapter 12   Culture and Social Mobility
Chapter 13   Ethical Consumption
Chapter 14   Sustainable Consumption

CHAPTER 4

CONSUMER TECHNOLOGY AND INNOVATION

LEARNING OBJECTIVES

After reading this chapter you should be able to:

- Describe the current technological concepts and consumer technologies that exist and show how some of them are making an impact on the lives of consumers.
- Explain how the product life cycle drives innovation.
- Describe some of the characteristics of innovators.
- Show how innovators are not necessarily innovators under all circumstances.
- Describe different types of innovation.
- Explain the role of mavens in the adoption of innovation.
- Explain how resistance to innovation can happen, and formulate some ideas for dealing with this problem.

CHAPTER CONTENTS

Introduction
Artificial intelligence (AI) replaces human interactions
Metaverse
Machine learning
Robotics and unmanned aerial vehicles (UAVs)/drones
Virtual reality (VR) and augmented reality (AR)
The Internet of Things (IoT)
Mobile technologies
Big data and analytics
Platforms and blockchains
Innovation
The influence of 'product life cycle' in innovation
Adoption of innovation
Categories of innovation adopters
Innovative products
Marketing approaches to new product launches
Resistance to innovation
Summary
Key points
How to impress your examiner
Review questions
Case study: Gravity takes over
Further reading
References

More online: https://study.sagepub.com/sethna5e

INTRODUCTION

Consumer technology, or consumer tech, refers to any form of technology that is intended for use by consumers among the general public, as opposed to technology created for governmental, military or commercial use. Consumer tech comes in a variety of different forms and offers a wide range of technological capabilities, encompassing many of the most commonly seen items that we utilise daily. But before we get into showcasing some of the tech and technologies, let's dwell a little on the history. This will give us a sense of where we have come from and where we are heading.

The roots of consumer tech can be traced back to the 19th century, with inventions from the likes of David Edward Hughes, Heinrich Rudolph Hertz, Nikola Tesla, Jagadish Chanda Bose and several others facilitating the manipulation of electricity for widespread use throughout the world. In 1896, Guglielmo Marconi developed the first practical radio-wave communication system, allowing contact to be made with parties at a distance for the first time.

Marconi's utilisation of radio waves opened the door for consumer tech and allowed others to explore cutting-edge methods to improve the ways we interact with our world. Bose's experiments introduced the use of semiconductor junctions and extreme high frequencies, while John Ambrose Fleming and the combination of Robert von Lieben and Lee De Forest were able to pioneer the use of diodes and amplifier tubes in the 20th century's first decade. In 1927, Philo Farnsworth publicly demonstrated the first television, and by just 1947, William Shockley and Bell Labs invented the transistor – fundamentally altering the way signal is amplified and significantly reducing the size of electronic components. In 1959, transistors became small enough to be packaged in quantity within a single chip, known as an integrated circuit and laid the groundwork for the technological innovations that continue to be implemented today.

Much of the consumer tech we still interact with daily was invented during this period of innovation between the end of the 19th century and the mid-20th century, including computers (first developed between 1940 and 1945), transistor radios (introduced in 1954) and the microwave oven (1946).

The consumer tech industry benefits from a cycle of continuous growth, allowing prices of current and legacy generations of hardware and software to drop as technological capabilities improve and updated products are rolled out. This is driven by improvements in manufacturing efficiency, automation, varying labour costs and the constant improvement of semiconductor design, which the consumer tech/electronics industry heavily relies on. These improvements and the creation of products that are thousands of times more capable than predecessors enable form factors to shrink and prices to decrease – creating a technological revolution with the power to reshape our world. Computers were once an exclusive product and would require an entire room to store just a few megabytes. Semiconductor functionality essentially doubles every two years due to the shrinking size of physical components and the increase in the number of transistors that can fit on an integrated circuit chip, a principle known as **Moore's Law**. Today, more powerful computers exist in most of our pockets in the form of smartphones, capable of housing hundreds of gigabytes of data with unlimited amounts of cloud space available at all times.

Technology has evolved to better meet and fulfil the needs of people, and, as a result, people are now constantly interacting with consumer technology. Several categories and subcategories of customer technology exist, with plenty of overlap. As more products are introduced at conferences like the Consumer Electronics Show and others, these categories will inevitably expand. We see new, disruptive technologies and trends that are emerging and that are fundamentally changing not only how businesses and the global economy operates – the key questions are, how and why do consumers interact with it? Hopefully by the end of this chapter we'll be better informed about

Moore's Law

The number of transistors on a microchip doubles about every two years, while the cost of computers is halved evolutionary technologies and trends that provide us with opportunities or indeed threats; and this will of course help us to adapt, thrive and innovate. Let us now invite you to stop and take a snapshot of each emerging technology.

Our first stop looks at the opportunities that are available to us. There are a number of senior commentators (in fact 72% of global CEOs) who have rightly identified that the next 10 years will be more critical for their industry than the last 50 years (Forbes Insights, 2016) as companies invest in intangible assets such as databases (to handle big data), proprietary algorithms and expert workers, instead of the traditional physical assets like factories and inventory. This suggests that creative destruction is accelerating (Govindarajan and Srivastava, 2018; Siegel and Krishnan, 2020). However, there is no going away from the fact that by embracing the digital economy, companies could gain competitive differentiation (Siaw and Okorie, 2022; Weinstein, 2021). The field is wide open; only 5% of organisations feel that they have mastered digital to a point of differentiation from their competitors (Accenture Interactive, 2015) and only 9% of companies have access to real-time data for financial analysis and planning, whilst only 18% use predictive modelling to analyse big data (AFP Online, 2016).

ARTIFICIAL INTELLIGENCE (AI) REPLACES HUMAN INTERACTIONS

Some decades ago, artificial intelligence (AI) was confined to entertainment. People marvelled at the power this technology had, but today AI and machine learning is a hot topic. Many of our brand experiences already occur without any human interaction (Centric Digital, 2015), and the average person has more conversations with bots than with their spouse (Gartner, 2016)!

The use of conversational AI applications in text and voice has surged (Rizomyliotis et al., 2022; van Noordt and Misuraca, 2022). These include sophisticated virtual assistants and chatbots that have automated customer service and have taken it to another level. AI-powered machines work better, move faster and lift greater loads than humans. However, technology can't move forward without the help of humans. There is a need for engineers to develop and test AI systems for the technology to grow. Therefore humans and AI are not interchangeable, and one could assume that, therefore, AI can't exist without people. Some of the reasons that are quoted for why AI won't replace humans include:

- Lack of emotional intellect.
- AI can't show feelings.
- Humans build relationships.
- Can't do creative work.
- Can't find creative solutions.

Here's why that's absolutely *baloney*. Artificial intelligence technologies are revolutionising business operations and society as a whole (Pelau et al., 2021). The focus of successful stories is on the algorithms' progress and development. The BERT

Baloney
Foolish or deceptive talk; nonsense

transformer neural network, for example, is a new kind of algorithm intended to revolutionise natural language processing. At the same time, AI is moving into new areas such as concept design (Duan and Zhang, 2022), tiny technology (Alajlan and Ibrahim, 2022) and multimodal applications (Varga et al., 2021) – discoveries that will expand AI's range in various sectors. Artificial intelligence models are now capable of generating text, audio and images that are virtually indistinguishable from genuine data. AI has the potential to produce and evaluate art (Gangadharbatla, 2022), music, poetry, plays and even video games. We can anticipate more complicated and seemingly natural creative output from our increasingly inventive and capable electronic companions as new models like GPT-4 and Google's Brain redefine the limits of what's possible. So for instance, take 'machine vision' – a type of AI that enables machines to comprehend and interpret pictures and videos. Advances in machine learning, such as artificial neural networks, have enabled considerable progress in computer vision (Maier et al., 2022). AI machine learning algorithms are generally trained on images to identify and categorise items. This has a wide range of applications in many disciplines, including:

- autonomous vehicles
- healthcare
- farming
- manufacturing
- agriculture.

There have long been concerns that machines or robots would take human jobs and possibly eliminate some occupations. As businesses move through generating data and developing AI-literate cultures (Kumar, 2022) within their staff, we will increasingly interact with or alongside machines that employ smart and cognitive capabilities to help us improve our abilities. Many of us are already used to employing tools to assess which leads are worth pursuing and what value we may get from potential consumers in certain areas, such as marketing. We'll increasingly use technologies in the knowledge industries, such as law, to help us sift through the ever-growing amount of data available to discover the nuggets of information we need for a specific activity (Kohn, 2022). Smart tools and services are becoming available that can assist us in doing our tasks more efficiently, and by 2030, most people will find that they are a part of their everyday working life in just about every profession.

Cybercrime has been identified as a major threat to global prosperity by the World Economic Forum, which urged nations worldwide to work together to address it. We are becoming more vulnerable to cybercrimes as we rely more on machines. Because every device linked to the internet provides an attacker a gateway to exploit its flaws, we are becoming increasingly prone to cybercrimes. With connected devices growing increasingly sophisticated, identifying and repairing existing vulnerabilities is getting harder and harder. AI may assist in detecting suspicious activity by analysing network traffic patterns (Rawindaran et al., 2021).

And then of course there is the Metaverse!

METAVERSE

To help you get a sense of how vague and complex a term 'the metaverse' can be, here's an exercise: Mentally replace the phrase 'the metaverse' in a sentence with 'cyberspace'. Ninety per cent of the time, the meaning won't substantially change. That's because the term doesn't really refer to any one specific type of technology, but rather a broad (and often speculative) shift in how we interact with technology (Belk et al., 2022; Upadhyay and Khandelwal, 2022). And it's entirely possible that the term itself will eventually become just as antiquated, even as the specific technology it once described becomes commonplace.

Broadly speaking, what the technology companies refer to when they talk about 'the metaverse' can include virtual reality – characterised by persistent virtual worlds that continue to exist even when you're not playing – as well as augmented reality that combines aspects of the digital and physical worlds. However, it doesn't require that those spaces be exclusively accessed via VR or AR. Virtual worlds – such as aspects of Fortnite that can be accessed through PCs, game consoles and even phones – have started referring to themselves as 'the metaverse'. Many of the companies that have jumped on board the metaverse bandwagon also envision some sort of new digital economy, where users can create, buy and sell goods. Evidence of this comes from the Metaverse Fashion Week (https://metaversefashionweek.com/), which saw global brands including Hugo Boss stage virtual fashion shows, as well as virtual after-parties and other immersive experiences (such as live music performances). Hosted by metaverse platform Decentraland, virtual visitors were able to buy the digital wearables featured on the catwalk, as well as real-life designs and non-fungible tokens (NFTs). With more fashion brands expected to invest in the metaverse, and the likes of Gucci already releasing digital items, the virtual fashion week is a way for brands to test the water (and pique consumer interest in digital fashion).

> **Non-fungible tokens (NFTs)**
> A record on a blockchain which is associated with a particular digital or physical asset. The ownership of an NFT is recorded in the blockchain, and can be transferred by the owner

With the lines between online and physical worlds becoming increasingly blurred, we are likely to see more brands take a hybrid approach to experiential in future. In the more idealistic visions of the metaverse, it's interoperable, allowing you to take virtual items like clothes or cars from one platform to another, though this is harder than it sounds. While some advocates claim new technologies like NFTs can enable portable digital assets, we're not sure if this is quite true as bringing items from one video game or virtual world to another is an enormously complex task that no one company has yet solved.

MACHINE LEARNING

The impact of machine learning on our lives as consumers is destined to be huge. Artificial intelligence can predict where epidemics will happen. Artificial Intelligence in Medical Epidemiology developed a platform with 87% accuracy in predicting dengue fever outbreaks 3 months in advance, and they've been targeting other diseases such as Ebola and Zika (Deloitte Consulting, 2016). If you think that's fast, in initial tests a machine-learning algorithm created at Carnegie Mellon University was able to predict heart attacks 4 hours in advance with 80% accuracy (The Economist, 2016). There are applications of AI closer to home too.

> **Machine learning**
> A field of computer science that uses statistical techniques to give computer systems the ability to 'learn' with data, without being explicitly programmed

After watching just 600 hours of TV, an MIT deep-learning AI algorithm was able to predict future human interactions after two people met 60.5% as accurately as human subjects (MIT, 2016). Following on from this, and after watching 5000 hours of TV, Google's DeepMind AI was able to lip read 34% more accurately than a professional lip reader (Hodson, 2016). There are ways to augment our skills and expertise, with the majority of workers and consumers doing so by accessing intelligent personal assistants (IDC Research Inc., 2015). The very same personal assistants together with smart-bot instructors will, in the future (by 2030), be able to personalise lessons for each individual student, making the largest company on the internet, by far, an education-based company (Business Insider, 2016). This prediction came from Thomas Frey (a senior futurist at the DaVinci Institute) and his vision for 2030 includes an enhanced version of today's massive open online courses (MOOCs), the kind of instruction you may find with Khan Academy, Coursera or MIT OpenCourseWare. Only, the instructors won't be humans beamed through videos. They'll be bots, and they'll be smart enough to personalise each lesson plan to the child sitting in front of the screen.

At the other end of the spectrum, the impact of AI on the macro-environment and on governments, in particular, is immense. In the last two decades, 9.6% of the Earth's total wilderness areas has been lost, equalling an estimated 3.3 million square kilometres (Watson et al., 2016). Many Latin American governments are turning to AI to aid in their forest conservation efforts (Cool Green Science, 2016) by employing a program that uses real-time rainfall data to predict how green a given habitat should be and then matches that prediction up against images of the habitat from an Earth-monitoring satellite. Differences in greenness between what is predicted and what is observed, right down to the pixel, suggest habitat conversion by human activity.

One final point here is to do with business decisions. Making business decisions is a critical process, with many experts suggesting that a successful future of AI will only result if a partnership exists: humans define the problems to be tackled or questions to be asked (and importantly, have the final say on which is the best answer given the context of their business), whilst AI is used to analyse large volumes of data to provide a basis for the decision. There is a very clear example of why humans are critical to the decision-making process and will not be disappearing any time soon. Let's take the recent case of Uber. During a major terror attack in London in 2017, the company's AI pricing algorithm doubled ride prices. Of course, as one would expect, this resulted in a lot of bad publicity being generated and, worryingly, accusations of price gouging. The algorithm is better at setting prices in real time than humans, yes – but a human would have been more likely to realise that doubling prices during a tragedy is not ethical business practice.

ROBOTICS AND UNMANNED AERIAL VEHICLES (UAVS)/DRONES

Drones and robots are being used to navigate spaces people can't reach (Tsung et al., 2022). Some examples are a robot snake that can crawl through pipes and a robotic eel that can search out water pollution (Yang, X. et al., 2022). California-based startup Doxel has developed an artificial intelligence system that operates drones and robots to monitor every inch of a construction project and alert managers to potential problems. Doxel's deep learning algorithms can also measure the quality and progress of the work in real time, comparing it to the original budget and schedule. They are equipped with LIDAR and HD cameras to visually monitor an entire construction project, even in small, dark spaces that are difficult for humans to reach and see. The system then uses deep learning algorithms to measure the quality and progress of the work in real time, comparing it to the original budget and schedule. The system can process three-dimensional data and determine how much material has been installed correctly, and where the project is in danger of running over budget. Project managers can then use this information to make changes early in the project and boost productivity. Errors can be spotted and fixed immediately, before they lead to cost and time over-runs (Deloitte Consulting, 2018). Amazon uses more than 520,000 Kiva and Proteus (fully automated robots) in its global warehouses, which reduce operating expenses by approximately 20%. Bringing robots to its distribution centres that have not yet implemented them would save Amazon a further $2.5 billion (Bloomberg, 2016). This is of course rather fortuitous, as 79% of US consumers have indicated that they would select drones as a delivery option if it meant they could receive packages within an hour (Walker Sands, 2016). And it's not just packages that we're talking about delivering. In February 2018, Chinese technology firm Ehang released a video of its first passenger test flights almost a year after entering a drone taxi partnership with Dubai's Roads and Transport Authority. The agreement, signed in February 2017 at the World Government Summit, saw the RTA partner with Ehang trial the Ehang184 autonomous aerial vehicle. During the passenger tests the craft completed a 300 m vertical climb, carried 530 kg, flew a routed flight of 9.3 miles and achieved a high cruising speed of 130 km/h. It also carried a total of 40 different people, including Ehang's CEO, across both single- and dual-seater vehicles and took to the skies in weather conditions ranging from fog to gale force winds. The vehicle can carry a passenger up to 10 miles or for roughly 23 minutes of flight before needing to stop for an hour recharge, and a touch interface allows the passenger to select their destination and sit back in a cushioned seat with an air conditioner. With emerging new technologies, however, there are always going to be some ethical considerations that we as a society have to grapple with. The European Union is proposing new laws that require robots to be equipped with emergency 'kill switches' and to be programmed in accordance to science fiction writer Isaac Asimov's 'laws of robotics', stipulating that robots must never harm or 'kill' a human and always obey orders from their creator. Robots must protect their own existence – unless doing so would cause harm to a human (CNN News, 2017).

Back on the ground we're led to believe that self-driving vehicles have the potential to save millions of lives, given that 1.4 million people die and 50 million are injured each year in auto accidents, nearly 95% of which are caused by human error (togetherforsaferroads.org, 2022). And this statistic doesn't change too much even when analysing self-driven vehicles. A study conducted by Axios, which spans 2014 through 2018, found that when the self-driving cars were in autonomous mode and driving on their own, 38 incidents occurred while moving. In all but two of those cases, the accidents were caused by humans. Tesla Autopilot has now (at time of going to press) had 15 fatalities. tesladeaths.com provides an updated record of Tesla fatalities and Tesla accident deaths that have been reported (a total of 304 at time of going to press) and as much related crash data as possible (e.g. location of crash, names of deceased, etc.). This sheet also tallies each claimed and confirmed Tesla Autopilot crash, i.e. every instance of when Autopilot was activated during a Tesla crash that resulted in death. This is of course an immensely sad situation for all concerned, and there are many teething troubles to address. What's even more concerning is that because of the savings that are offered to businesses, self-driving trucks are expected to be more rapidly adopted than self-driving cars. They are already hauling iron ore in Australia, convoying across Europe and appearing on roadways across the globe (Solon, 2016).

VIRTUAL REALITY (VR) AND AUGMENTED REALITY (AR)

Augmented reality (AR) is an interactive experience of a real-world environment whereby the objects that reside in the real world are 'augmented' by computer-generated perceptual information, sometimes across multiple sensory modalities, including visual, auditory, haptic, somatosensory and olfactory. The overlaid sensory information can be constructive (i.e. additive to the natural environment) or destructive (i.e. masking of the natural environment) and is seamlessly interwoven with the physical world such that it is perceived as an immersive aspect of the real environment (Batat, 2021). Let's start with Pokémon Go – probably the most well-known game associated with augmented reality. It uses mobile device GPS to locate, capture, battle and train virtual creatures, called Pokémon, which appear as if they are in the player's real-world location. Within just 2 months, Pokémon Go was downloaded 500 million times globally. To date it has been downloaded more than a billion times, and the app has generated nearly $2 billion in revenue. There are 8 million daily active users and in 2018 there was an all-time high of 133 million monthly active users.

Gaming inevitably moves into becoming a part of our real lives, and there currently are 100 million consumers shopping using augmented reality (so the prediction by Gartner [2016] came true), with over 1 billion people worldwide who regularly use an AR/VR platform to access apps, content and data (IDC Research Inc., 2017).

> **Augmented reality**
> A technology that superimposes a computer-generated image on a user's view of the real world, thus providing a composite view

BRAND EXPERIENCES: GEO-TARGETED PRICING SERVICES

A new pricing solution developed by Darwin Pricing LLC called Geo-Pricing enables e-commerce businesses to personalise prices and promotions based on a customer's location. It is a new pricing service that generates geo-targeted prices and promotions. The service uses machine learning artificial intelligence to optimise the sales of e-commerce retailers. Darwin Pricing uses artificial neural networks to provide a real-time model of the varied prices in different locations.

Using machine learning algorithms, the service creates optimal prices and promotions for each customer, depending on their geographical location. This enables e-commerce retailers and brands to personalise their pricing for each customer, thereby generating more profit. Additionally, the real-time collection of data responds to any market changes, further boosting the accuracy of the pricing system. Through a number of strategies using the data provided by Darwin Pricing, businesses can boost their sales, for example by constructing sales campaigns based on competing local retailers in any city, and creating personalised discounts for customers about to exit without a purchase. Darwin Pricing also offers a customisable coupon box, compatible with smartphones and tablets. This feature can increase social media followers and sign-ups to newsletters. E-commerce businesses can install Darwin Pricing as a plug-in. The service is fully customisable so that each business can tailor it to their specific needs. Moreover, Darwin Pricing uses REST API, an API that uses HTTP requests to manage data.

Therefore, along with standard e-commerce platforms, any online store can incorporate it. Many plug-ins are already integrated in Darwin Pricing, for example Shopware, Shopify, Magento Commerce, osCommerce, Websphere Commerce, WordPress, PrestaShop, Hybris, 3dcart, Oracle Commerce and Demandware. If desired, other plug-ins are also integrable. We already have access to geo-spatial retail innovations such as a shopping app that alerts users when an item on their wish list is nearby. Another example is an app used by customers to alert stores about empty shelves. Darwin Pricing also enables businesses to increase profits. The service is unique because it uses geographical data and personalisation to create more equal wealth distribution. But from the consumers' perspective, how else can e-commerce retailers and brands improve their performance using AI?

Source: Adapted from Deloitte's 2018 Artificial Intelligence Innovation Report, which can be found at www.deloitte.com.

THE INTERNET OF THINGS (IOT)

The Internet of Things (IoT) is the network of physical devices, vehicles, home appliances and other items embedded with electronics, software, sensors, actuators and connectivity which enables these things to connect and exchange data, creating opportunities for more direct integration of the physical world into computer-based systems, resulting in efficiency improvements, economic benefits and reduced human exertions (Bouguettaya et al., 2021; Narayanan et al., 2022). This all sounds quite complex, so in reality, how will this affect (is this affecting!) our lives? Usage-based automobile insurance enabled by the IoT is estimated to grow by nearly 1200% by 2023. This insurance uses real-time information about a driver's actual driving to assess actuarial risk. Thanks to these sorts of cost savings and profits for businesses and increased revenues for the public sector, the IoT could be worth $19 trillion by 2025 (EY, 2015). Barcelona already uses the IoT to optimise urban systems and enhance citizen services. To date, it has saved $95 million annually from reduced water and electricity consumption, increased parking revenues by $50 million a year and generated 47,000 new jobs (Datasmart, 2016). A new report from Transforma Insights and 6GWorld has shown that IoT operations in 2030 will save more than eight times the energy they consume, amounting to net savings of 230 billion cubic metres of water and eliminating one gigaton of CO_2 emissions.

MOBILE TECHNOLOGIES

We as consumers are engaging with brands across an increasing number of touch points from websites and social media to in-store, mobile and tablets. Whichever channel is used to access products and services, consumers expect a customised and personalised experience that is optimised specifically for them. Flexibility and convenience have risen to new levels and all of this leads to improving the customer experience, but the increased customer expectation continues to be a challenge for businesses that have to manipulate enormous amounts of data in order to understand how to effectively engage each individual (Reynolds et al., 2018; Witayangkurn et al., 2022).

Mobile technology has and is having a huge influence on us, for instance in agriculture (Khan et al., 2022), banking (Geebren, 2022) and education (Tang et al., 2021). In particular though, its influence in retail cannot be ignored nor understated (Liang et al., 2021). As mobile connected consumers, the majority of purchases in retail now happen on mobiles (Luceri et al., 2022; Royal Mail, 2018). As consumer adoption of all things mobile increases, we are seeing the technology take a huge leap forward. Retail businesses are fast developing location-based apps to connect even more with their valued customers (Schrage et al., 2022) and, internally within the organisation, using mobile to enable staff with tablets to engage with products and customers on the shop floor. We have already been experiencing mobile usage in store for things like mobile payments, which can also be collected via tablets. The transition from 'mobile first' to 'mobile only' is beginning (Government Technology, 2022). Some societies are still on the curve, some are ahead. But further adoption by all demographics will increase the development of the sector. Retailers are still learning how to engage the connected consumer, but different strategies need to be introduced to create a wider reach. Millennials who understand 'mobile only' will help the industry develop even quicker (Bangamuarachchi et al., 2022). In 2022, three out of every four of China's e-commerce transactions are carried out on a mobile phone.

However, 2 billion individuals and 200 million small businesses in emerging economies lack access to basic financial services and credit. The broad adoption of mobile banking in developing nations could help create 95 million new jobs and increase GDP (gross domestic product) by $3.7 trillion by 2025 (Manyika et al., 2016; Cardasco et al., 2021).

5G
Term for the next-generation of mobile networks beyond the 4G LTE mobile networks of today. 5G will feature network speeds of 20 G/bps or higher and have a latency that is milliseconds

Once fully available, **5G** data speeds will be 1000 times faster than today. This revolutionary leap will enable ubiquitous connections across the Internet of Things, engagement across virtual environments with only millisecond latency, and whole new big data applications and services (RCR Wireless News, 2016).

BIG DATA AND ANALYTICS

Big data
Extremely large data sets that may be analysed computationally to reveal patterns, trends and associations, especially relating to human behaviour and interactions

The combination of **big data** and neural networks is helping to unlock the value of data businesses already have by revealing patterns that they can use to create and improve offerings or productivity (Elia et al., 2022), or to gain an advantage over the competition (Koksal, 2022; Petit and Teece, 2021). In-memory computing speeds are 1000 to 1 million times faster than the previous most advanced computing techniques, enabling big data analytics processing to be reduced from hours or days to real time (Angskun et al., 2022; Cavicchioli et al., 2022; Chatterjee et al., 2022; Research and Markets, 2017).

The release of machine learning and neural network model builders, such as Gluon and Google's TensorFlow, are also making it easier for software engineers to create and run deep learning systems without specialised training (Mohammad et al., 2022). This will make deep learning tools increasingly accessible to even small and medium-sized enterprises (Shi and Huang, 2022). Among executives, nearly 81% characterise their big data investments as successful, while only 1.6% deemed them failures.

In spite of the successes, executives see lingering cultural barriers hindering full adoption and value realisation (New Vantage Partners, 2017), which can ultimately have an impact on the global value chain (Rengarajan et al., 2022).

Big data are enabling us to collate information which ultimately aids with combating issues that face us as a whole society. For example, the International Labour Organization notes that in 2021 an estimated 50 million people are trapped in some form of modern slavery in 167 countries. They are bought and sold in public markets, forced to marry against their will and provide labour under the guise of 'marriage', forced to work inside clandestine factories on the promise of a salary that is often withheld, or on fishing boats where men and boys toil under threats of violence. They are forced to work on construction sites, in stores, on farms or in homes as maids. Labour extracted through force, coercion or threats produces some of the food we eat, the clothes we wear and the footballs we kick. The minerals that men, women and children have been made to extract from mines find their way into cosmetics, electronics and cars, among many other products (Global Slavery Index, 2018). Advanced analytics and big data are also enabling coordinated efforts to combat human trafficking networks and engage rapid responses when victims are located. While there is only limited information compiled globally on trafficking persons for the purpose of organ removal, it is possible to get some insight by looking at the broader statistics on organ transplants. However, the use of analytics and big data has provided an opportunity to better understand these networks and integrate resources to combat them. Google, Salesforce.com and Palantir have provided funding and expertise to develop a database and analytics platform that performs two major functions (Grothaus, 2013): a) it gathers and synthesises trafficking data and identifies patterns, and b) it enables a localised, coordinated response.

PLATFORMS AND BLOCKCHAINS

Blockchain has certainly captivated us, but very few of us actually understand what it is, or indeed what it means for us. Steven Johnson's article in *The New York Times* (2018) goes some way to explaining blockchain to the uninitiated. Johnson explains how by its very nature the blockchain has the potential to be truly disruptive – so disruptive that it's frequently likened to the internet in the mid- to late 90s – and on the verge of revolutionising the way we live and interact in a number of sectors; for example, food supply chains (Liu et al., 2022), creative industries (CIM, 2022), healthcare (Lu et al., 2021) and the public sector (Kassen, 2022). The framework on which Bitcoin and other cryptocurrencies were built isn't overseen by any one company or institution; rather it lives on a network of thousands of personal computers – a secure, distributed ledger, as it were. This is what is so significant about blockchain platforms: by creating a secure database across many different computers, this system removes the need for a bank or any other institution to exist at the centre overseeing and regulating the data.

> **Blockchain**
> A shared, immutable ledger that facilitates the process of recording transactions and tracking assets in a business network

Greater insight into buyer behaviour can be derived by using 'platforms' that provide real-time data gathering, forecasting and trend analysis. As many as 82% of executives questioned by Accenture (2016) believed platforms will be the glue that brings organisations together in the digital economy. The top 15 public platforms already have a market capitalisation of $2.6 trillion. There are a number of companies vying to develop platforms for predictive advertising, including Programmai, which uses AI to identify and target new prospects with ads based on what is already known about a company's existing customers or visitors. Their software can notify a business of how likely someone is to make a purchase, calculate future lifetime value, and automate ad bidding strategy decisions – allowing companies to focus ads on where they will have the biggest impact. A similar approach is taken by Indianapolis-based DemandJump (a customer acquisition platform that helps companies target customers with precision), which uses analytics to help marketers decide where to place ads in order to take advantage of up-to-the-minute trends. Their artificial intelligence marketing platform, dubbed TrafficCloud, collects data on page views, and can link customer activity across devices in order to present a detailed analysis of traffic between sources. The company's analytics can then pinpoint which sites have the greatest influence in a brand's competitive area, and which sites can help drive the highest number of customers to the brand. DemandJump's proprietary algorithms use machine learning, graph theory, algebraic topology and natural language processing to 'map each client's entire digital ecosystem' and show marketers exactly what to do next to maximise revenue growth and stay ahead of market changes.

The World Economic Forum has predicted that by 2027, blockchains could store as much as 10% of global GDP. One thing that most people in the space agree on is that it's not really a question of if, but rather when. The technology is somewhat foundational in nature and therefore it could be a while before we see its widespread adoption. Interestingly, however, Africa is leapfrogging the developed world's traditional banking systems through fast adoption of mobile- and internet-based technology, and is poised to take advantage of the disruptive opportunity that blockchains offer (Bithub Africa, 2018). Then there are economies such as India, where to combat corruption and tax evasion in its cash economy (only 2.6% of its citizens pay taxes), the Indian government devalued 80% of its currency in 3 hours (DNA, 2016). The solution here is seemingly to eliminate the need for credit cards, debit cards and ATMs in 3 years by switching to biometric payments.

Finally with blockchain (although we've only just begun), there's already quite a lot of excitement around the idea of 'smart contracts' – that is, any number of financial agreements that are set in motion automatically once the terms of a contract have been met. This could be virtually any kind of contract and executed without the help of a lawyer or accountant, which means greater speed and lower costs. Still, researchers have warned that smart contracts as they exist today have a wide variety of security vulnerabilities (Fiorentino and Bartolucci, 2021).

Cybersecurity
Protection of computer systems from theft of or damage to their hardware, software or electronic data, as well as from disruption or misdirection of the services they provide

Cybersecurity is a hot topic and we foresee that it will continue to be so over the next 10 years. A lack of data protection, side effects of a global pandemic and an increase in exploit sophistication have led to a huge increase in hacked and breached data from sources that are increasingly common in the workplace, such as mobile and IoT devices. On top of this, Covid-19 has ramped up remote workforces, creating opportunities for cyberattacks. Recent security research suggests most companies have poor cybersecurity practices in place, making them vulnerable to data loss. To successfully fight against malicious intent, it's imperative that companies make cybersecurity awareness, prevention and security best practices a part of their culture.

As many as 92% of companies have experienced commercial consequences as a result of a data breach (Gemalto, 2018). The rate at which companies are purchasing stand-alone cybersecurity insurance policies is going up year on year according to the Risk Management Society. The average cost of a data breach was $4.24 million in 2021, the highest average on record, and the average time to identify a breach in 2021 was 212 days. Personal data were involved in 45% of breaches in 2021 and identity theft rose 42% in 2020 compared to the year before. Some historic data breaches include:

- A 2021 LinkedIn data breach exposed the personal information of 700 million users or about 93% of all LinkedIn members.
- An attack on Microsoft in March 2021 affected more than 30,000 organisations in the US, including businesses and government agencies.
- Using a single password, hackers infiltrated the Colonial Pipeline Company in 2021 with a ransomware attack that caused fuel shortages across the US.
- Nearly 48 million people had their personal information stolen in a 2021 T-Mobile data breach.
- Personal data belonging to more than 100 million Android users were exposed in a 2021 data leak due to misconfigured cloud services.

INNOVATION

The word **innovation** itself is quite subjective. There are many synonyms that could be used to describe it: change, upheaval, transformation, alteration, revolution, renovation, variation, restyling, remodelling, reorganising and metamorphosis are among a few. In essence, what we are talking about is the translation of a new idea into a product or service or a new method/way of doing something which creates value for consumers (or for which consumers will pay money!). And there is of course an element of risk-taking. This is especially true because **revolutionary innovations** create new markets. Take, for example, the Benz Patent-Motorwagen, built and patented in 1886, which is widely regarded as the world's first automobile and which changed the face of transportation over the following 20 years. This was one of the first modern-era innovations. Other major innovations that have appeared since include telecommunications and its younger sibling the mobile telephone, analogue photography, computers and the World Wide Web. **Evolutionary innovations**, however, occur as a result of incremental advances in both technology and processes (for example, take Henry Ford's mass production vehicle, the Model-T, which within a short space of time destroyed many competitors in the fledgling automobile industry). There are many societal contexts within which innovation can be described. In the world of business, when organisations successfully innovate, they have deliberately applied their imagination, together with real data/information and a little initiative, in order to derive greater or different values from the available resources. Innovation is therefore said to be the lifeblood of successful companies. Firms that fail to innovate are thought to become moribund very quickly, and eventually to disappear altogether because competitors introduce new products that supersede the old ones.

However, this constant stream of innovation does create problems from a consumer behaviour viewpoint. Decision-making and information-gathering are both at their most complex when consumers are considering an innovative product. Thousands of

---

Innovation
The translation of a new idea into a product or service (or a new way of doing something) which creates value for consumers

Revolutionary innovation
These drastic, radical and momentous changes are sometimes also referred to as 'discontinuous innovations' as they are often disruptive and brand new, forcibly overthrowing the 'old'

Evolutionary innovation
Occurs as a result of incremental advances in both technology and processes

new products are launched onto the market every year, with varying success rates; the vast majority never recoup their development costs. (Estimates of new product success rates vary, largely due to the difficulty of defining what constitutes success.)

The influence that social media has on consumers today is undoubtedly a major factor in the decision-making process. Figure 4.1, an infographic by Leverage New Age Media, just shows the kind of power those social media platforms wield over the consumer.

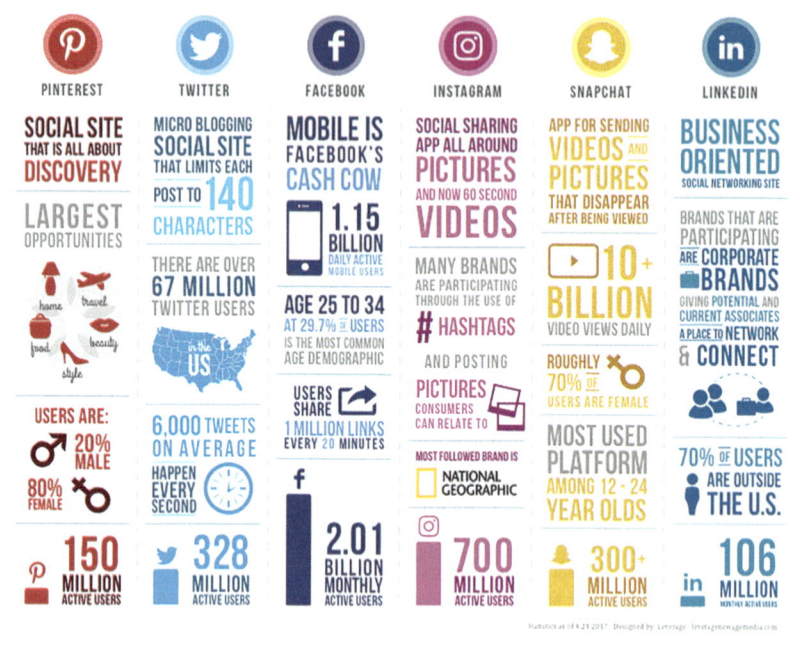

FIGURE 4.1   The influence of social media

©Leverage, LLC. Used with permission.

Source: https://leveragenewagemedia.com/.

THE INFLUENCE OF 'PRODUCT LIFE CYCLE' IN INNOVATION

Innovation means that products are constantly being superseded by newer, more effective products. For this reason firms seek to develop new products; those firms that fail to innovate will, eventually, only be producing products that are obsolete. However, the timescales for such cycles are continually shrinking. Either the route to market is shortening, or there are many more people on the road. Tuten and Solomon (2015) highlight some very interesting statistics about the reach of social media. They start by telling us that it took 38 years for the medium of radio to reach 50 million listeners. Television, however, took 13 years to reach 50 million viewers. And if you think that transition was short, think about the fact that the internet only took 4 years to reach 50 million people. Of course, the most impressive statistic is that Facebook added 100 million users to its platform in less than 9 months! So what exactly is the product life cycle?

CONSUMER TECHNOLOGY AND INNOVATION

The product life cycle illustrates the process of introduction, growth, maturity and obsolescence in products. Products tend to lose money when they are first introduced, because the amount of marketing support they need is not justified (in monetary profit terms) by the initial sales as the product tries to become established in the market. As the product moves into a growth phase, financial profits begin to come in, and when the product becomes well-established (i.e. mature) the profits are also at a peak. Eventually, the product will go into decline as competing products enter the market, or fashions change, or the market becomes saturated.

In fact, the situation is often much more complex than this, so the basic product life cycle (as shown in Figure 4.2) does not always describe what actually happens in practice. The product life cycle is a useful concept for explaining what happens to products, but it suffers from a number of weaknesses. First, the model is no use for making predictions, because there is no good way of knowing what the length of the maturity phase will be: for a fashion item, the maturity phase might only last a few months, whereas for a staple product such as bread (in all its various forms) the maturity phase has already lasted several thousand years and shows no sign of changing. Second, the model ignores the effects of marketing activities. If a product's sales are declining, marketers might decide to reposition the product in another market, or might run a major promotional campaign, or might decide to drop the product altogether and concentrate resources on another product in the portfolio. These alternatives are shown in Figures 4.3 and 4.4.

Third, the model does not account for those products that come back into fashion after a few years in the doldrums. Recent automotive examples include the Fiat 500, Mini Cooper and Volkswagen Beetle. Products such as the yo-yo seem to undergo revivals every 10–15 years.

FIGURE 4.2 The product life cycle

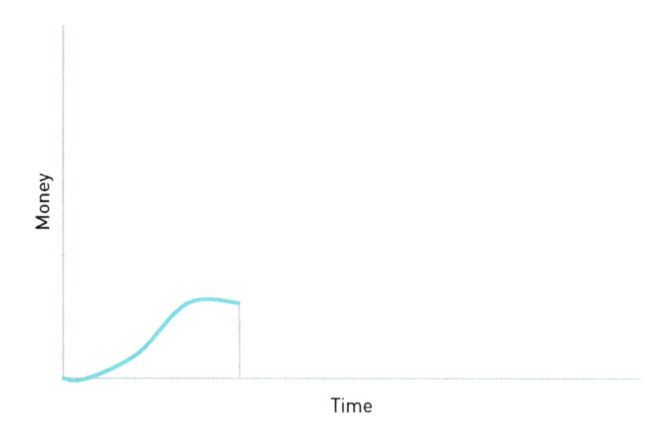

FIGURE 4.3 Product dropped shortly after introduction

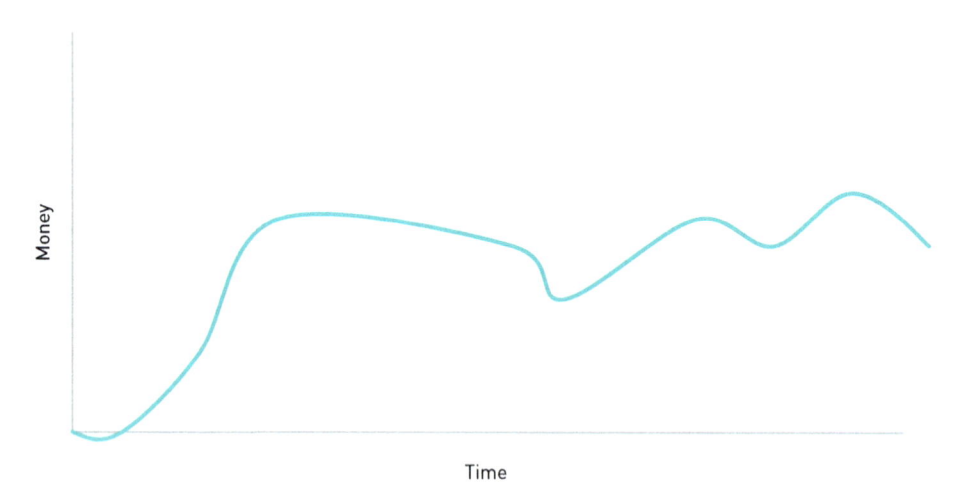

FIGURE 4.4 Effects of marketing activities on the product life cycle

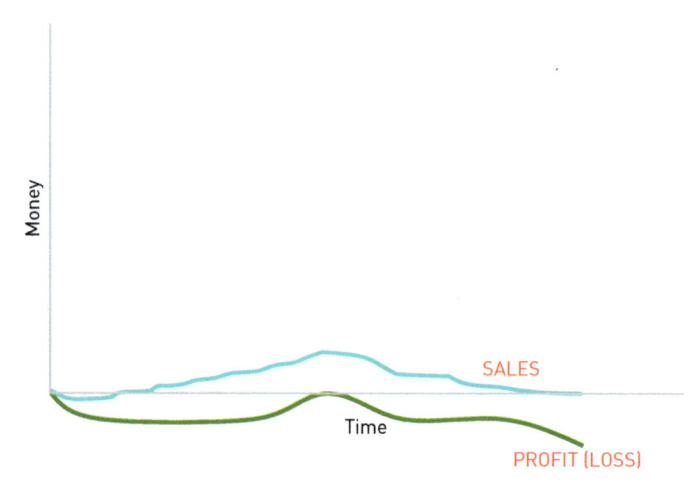

FIGURE 4.5 Failed product

CONSUMER TECHNOLOGY AND INNOVATION

Fourth, the model does not take account of the fact that the vast majority of new products fail. This would give a life cycle such as that shown in Figure 4.5, where the product never moves into profit. There are of course many examples of this in history as rarely does a successful entrepreneur triumph with their first idea. Indeed, for a detailed look at some monumental failures, one could go along to the Museum of Failed Innovation, set up by Dr Samuel West in Sweden. Initially, the bedrock principles for his doctoral research focused on 'how a playful work environment promotes creativity and an important part of playfulness is experimentation and being allowed to fail'. This prompted him to think about the fact that, if there are so many examples of failure everywhere, why are they swept under the carpet when there's so much to learn? So the museum showcases product failures such as a handheld Apple computer, a Kodak camera, a Betamax recorder and a forgotten flavour of Coca-Cola, and further ranks them using categories such as 'innovation, design, implementation and disruption'.

Finally, the product life cycle looks at only one product, whereas most marketing managers have to balance the demands of many different products, and decide which of them is likely to yield the best return on investment (or perhaps which one will take the company nearest to achieving its strategic objectives).

CRITICAL REFLECTION

It is not unusual for products to disappear almost as soon as they are launched: test marketing sometimes shows disappointing results, so the product is taken off the shelves. In recent times we have seen a number of technology products fail. Google Glass was one such product.

Google developed a pair of high-tech glasses that scanned your surroundings and beamed relevant information to your retina. But it needed a very large battery in order for the glasses to download and process the sheer amount of data. This made the design of the glasses very bulky and somewhat distracting from their original purpose. In another example, Amazon was left with $83 million worth of unsold Fire Phones, a product they launched to compete with iPhone/Android smartphones or other **smart products**. But given that the $199 device did not offer the consumer anything better (e.g. superior technology/features), it only took 4 weeks for the company to reduce the price to just 99 cents! One would have to question the consumer research that was done during the development phase of the product. Was there a need? Who would buy it and why?

There are also products that appear to be eminently sensible and yet do not find a market, possibly through a lack of professionalism on the part of the marketers. So should there be a marketer's life cycle instead? If the product doesn't perform, should we keep the product and fire the managers?

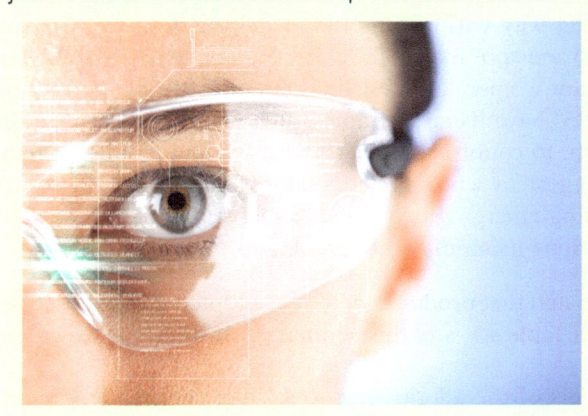

© iStock.com/eternalcreative

Smart product
A data processing object which has interactive functions and which combines the physical and software interfaces

The product life cycle can be explained in terms of consumer behaviour. In the introduction and growth stage, innovative consumers are adopting the product. In the maturity phase, more cautious consumers buy the product, until finally another product comes along which has more benefits or which does a better job, and people switch to the new product. The basic problem for marketers lies in knowing how long the maturity phase will last; the product life cycle does tell us, though, that all products eventually fade and die (or at least go into hibernation for some time before re-emerging), and marketers should therefore develop new products to replace the old ones as these products fall out of favour with consumers.

Although we can be reasonably sure that all old products will eventually fail, we cannot by any means be sure that a new product will succeed. The lack of a good predictive system for forecasting product success wastes resources since producers will spend time and effort making things that consumers do not want to buy. The ideal outcome for a producer is to develop products that become **culturally anchored** – that become part of modern life. Recent examples are the mobile telephone, cable television and the personal computer – none of which would have been part of the average household 30 years ago, but which now would be difficult to manage without. In practice such breakthroughs are hard to achieve. Nowadays, each of us interacts with other people using communications technology and that technology places us, the end user, at the centre of every digital experience. Understandably, with so much at stake for firms, there has been a great deal of research interest in innovation, with many researchers trying to determine what the critical factors are in new product success (Almeida et al., 2020; Cherubini et al., 2015; Navickaitė, 2022; Salmen, 2021; Tarhini et al., 2015; Urban et al., 2015).

> **Cultural anchoring**
> The process by which an innovation becomes part of everyday life

ADOPTION OF INNOVATION

The process of adoption of innovation is as much to do with communication throughout the population as with individual decision-making (Cordasco et al., 2021). Each individual will make decisions by the processes already outlined for existing products; the main difference is that there will be many fewer sources of information about an innovative product, since few people will have any experience of it as yet. But that's where the power of the internet, World Wide Web and social media help mitigate this problem, especially in developing economies. By using such innovation, mobile health has come a long way with things like 'tracking devices' (Grosová et al., 2022; Modena et al., 2018) and apps like MomConnect, a mobile phone test-based information service for pregnant women and new mothers in South Africa (Skinner et al., 2018). Barrett et al. (2015) have listed examples such as South Africa leading developments in mobile health, to countries in East Africa leading mobile financial services. This, they further suggest, 'is why large companies such as IBM, Cisco, GE, Siemens and Microsoft are using emerging economies as labs in which to develop, test, and scale service innovations using digital technologies'.

Everett M. Rogers (1983) postulated that products would be adopted if they possessed most of the attributes shown in Table 4.1, and the seminal work still rings true today.

There have been several models of the adoption process, most of which assume a somewhat complex process of assessing the new product. In the case of radically new products (those that will alter the user's lifestyle) this may well be so, but since most products that are classified as new are, in fact, adaptations of existing products, it might be safe to assume that consumers do not necessarily carry out a lengthy evaluation of the type assumed by most researchers. Five adoption models are shown in Figure 4.6.

AIDA model

Attention → Interest → Desire → Action

Adoption Process model

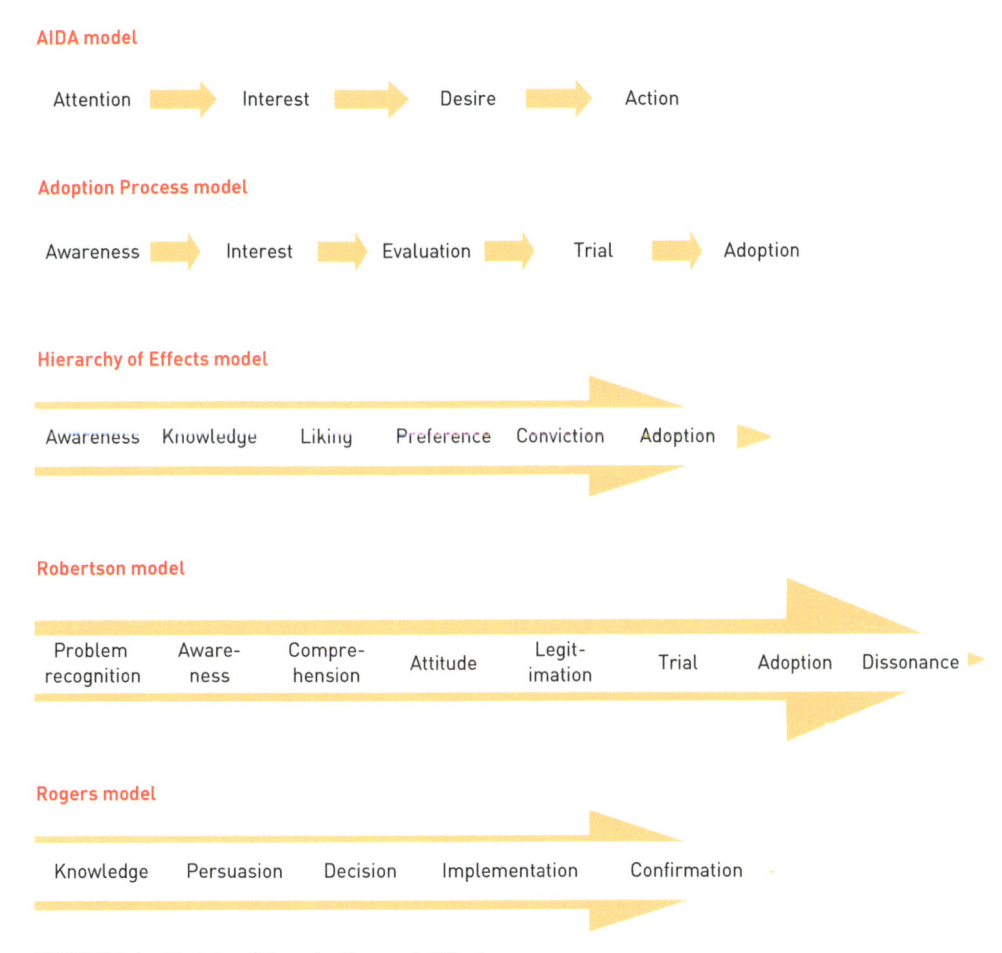

Awareness → Interest → Evaluation → Trial → Adoption

Hierarchy of Effects model

Awareness → Knowledge → Liking → Preference → Conviction → Adoption

Robertson model

Problem recognition → Awareness → Comprehension → Attitude → Legitimation → Trial → Adoption → Dissonance

Rogers model

Knowledge → Persuasion → Decision → Implementation → Confirmation

FIGURE 4.6 Models of the adoption and diffusion process

TABLE 4.1 Attributes necessary for adoption

Attribute	Explanation	Examples
Relative advantage	The product must have some advantage over the products already on the market. It must offer the consumer a better range of benefits than the existing solution, in other words	Before the Sony Walkman was launched, the only way to listen to stereo-quality music was to carry a 'ghetto-blaster' on your shoulder. The Walkman replaced this cumbersome and antisocial device within a few years – and iPods/phones have replaced the Walkman equally effectively, with wireless and Bluetooth providing the relative advantage now
Compatibility	The product must fit in with the consumer's lifestyle	Video on demand (e.g. Netflix, Amazon Prime, NowTV, Blinkbox, among others) has become extremely popular, allowing people to watch TV shows or movies at times that suit them, rather than the broadcaster

(Continued)

TABLE 4.1 (Continued)

Attribute	Explanation	Examples
Complexity	The product must not be too complex for the consumer to understand	Amazon's Kindle device was designed around the concept of being so simple to use that people would forget the device and simply enjoy reading the book. In other words, it was designed to be as easy to use and intuitive as a paper book. As technology has progressed, even the complexity of the screen makes it 'very easy on the eye' compared to reading a book
Trialability	Products that can be tried out and are easy to use are far more likely to succeed	Whenever a motor manufacturer launches a new vehicle people are invited to test drive it for a short period. The thrill of driving a new car with the alluring aroma of new leather is sometimes too much to resist adoption!
Observability	The more observable the product, the quicker the diffusion process. If other potential consumers are able to see the product in use, this is bound to raise interest in it	Part of the reason for Apple's worldwide success is that it can clearly be observed in use without even being seen; the iconic white ear buds show that the customer has an Apple product

Diffusion

Diffusion of innovation is a theory that seeks to explain how, why and at what rate new ideas and technology spread through cultures and are adopted by consumers/users

The AIDA model is probably among the oldest models in marketing. It is commonly quoted when considering promotions, but it applies equally well to adoption and diffusion of innovation. The model is somewhat too simplistic, however; it implies that the process is mechanical, without any conscious thought on the part of the individual who adopts the product. There is also the view that the model implies something being done *to* consumers (leading them through a process) rather than something that is done *for* them (meeting a need).

The Adoption Process model includes some thought on the part of the customer. In this case, becoming interested in the product leads to some serious evaluation before trial and adoption. This model portrays adoption as a sequence that the individual follows, using conscious thought and interaction with the product to come to the adoption decision.

The Hierarchy of Effects model suggests that each stage of the process leads the customer closer to the decision – as each stage is passed, the individual is further up the hierarchy and therefore becoming more committed. Obviously an individual might drop out of the model at any stage, and thus the sale will not happen, but the model implies that people must normally pass through each stage in the correct order if a sale is to result. This is a suspect proposition, since people are likely to skip stages or even buy the product on impulse without any real evaluation at all.

Robertson's (1967) model is by far the most complex, seeking to break down the process into more stages. Robertson shows how the attitude is formed rather than simply subsuming it into a category of 'liking'. This model provides more of an insight into the internal workings of the adopter's mind, rather than simply describing behaviour.

Rogers (1983) includes the concept of persuasion in his model. Persuasion does not necessarily come from outside, however – it may just as easily come from within the individual. Persuasion is clearly of interest to marketers, whether it is marketing-generated or whether it is produced socially via peer pressure (normative compliance). We have known for some years now that this intricate and rapidly developing phenomenon of persuasion has given rise to the development arena of experimental data of new behavioural, neurological models (Lindstrom, 2011). There are two perspectives that could be taken here. One, from a macro-perspective, is that persuasion theorists have investigated the goals, the process of persuasion and the centrality of attitude. Two, from a micro-perspective, is that they have derived a number of persuasion theories to explain behavioural influence. Building on Rogers' (1983) theories, a more up-to-date study by Petrosyan and Dimitriadis (2018) of traditional persuasive tools and techniques, along with the first-hand perspectives of persuasion trends, sheds further light on this macro- and micro-perspective.

The main feature that all these models have in common is that they imply that adoption of innovation is a linear process, following logical steps. This may or may not be true – individuals may follow a straight line, or they may be diverted by circumstances. The models also show that innovations take a period of time to be adopted, meaning that it also takes some time before a new product begins to show a return; this is implicit also in the shape of the product life cycle curve, where the introduction phase shows a slow start as consumers get used to the idea of the new and innovative product.

CATEGORIES OF INNOVATION ADOPTERS

A second focus in the research has been on the consumers most likely to buy new products – in other words, the **innovators**. The reason for this is that there is an assumption that innovation is diffused by word of mouth, or that innovators are likely to influence others to buy the products. This is implicit in the product life cycle, and in Rogers' observability criterion (Rogers, 1983). Consumers also have access to a new channel of communication called 'word of mouse'. With the internet creating opportunities for marketing in all sectors, it has also enabled companies of all sizes to have more direct contact with consumers and to place more emphasis on the recommendations of others, or user-generated content (Stokes and Nelson, 2013).

It is perfectly feasible to classify consumers in terms of their attitude to new products; the problem with identifying innovators is that they are not usually innovative in all their buying habits. That is to say, an innovator for state-of-the-art audio-visual equipment is not necessarily an innovator for breakfast cereals, and although there is some evidence that there may be a kind of super-innovator who likes virtually everything that is new, these people are difficult to find, and it is debatable whether they are likely to influence other buyers anyway.

Everett Rogers classified consumers as innovators (2.5% of the population), **early adopters** (13.5%), **early majority** (34%), **late majority** (34%) and **laggards** (16%) – see Figure 4.7. These classifications were originally devised from agricultural product adoptions, but have been widely accepted as applying to more general consumer products equally well. The percentages given are arbitrary; everybody is at some point along a continuum, and Rogers decided that those whose scores lay more than two standard deviations from the mean would be classed as innovators, those whose scores lay between one and two standard deviations would be early adopters, and

Innovators
A person who introduces new methods, ideas, or products

Early adopters
Those who, although not the first to buy a new product, do so very shortly after its introduction

Early majority
Those who adopt a new product after it has been on the market for a while, but before most people have adopted it

Late majority
People who only adopt a new product after most people have already done so

Laggards
People who are the last to adopt a new product

those whose scores lay within one standard deviation from the mean would be the early majority. Scores below the mean were classified in the same way: those within one standard deviation of the mean were classified as the late majority, and everyone else as laggards. This means that Rogers' classifications involve circular reasoning: people are innovators because they innovate, and laggards because they are slow to innovate. You should note also that the classification tells us nothing about the characteristics of the people involved.

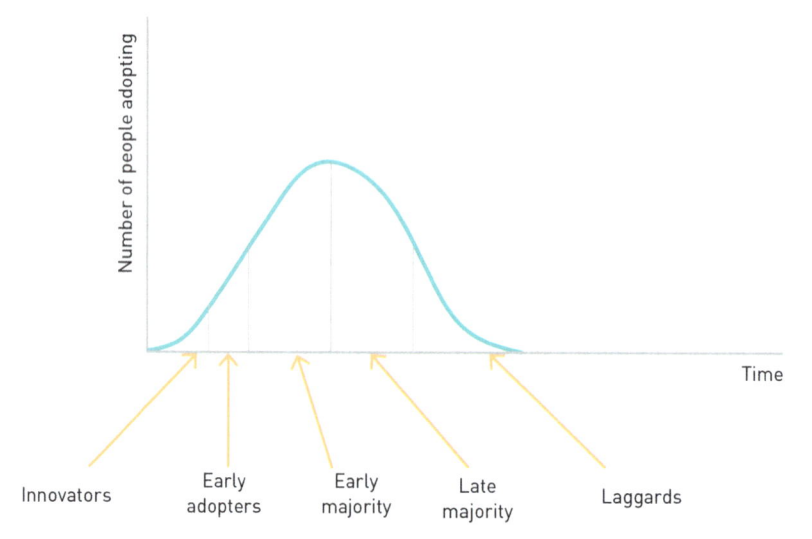

FIGURE 4.7 Classification of innovators

BRAND EXPERIENCES: AUTOMATIC NUMBER PLATE RECOGNITION

We've already seen that the level of interaction that consumers have online with each other and with other organisations is increasing exponentially. There are lots of digital channels that are available to us and that allow others to delve deep into our own lives. Organisations that understand this have already changed their products, services and the way in which they build their new applications so that they can tap into these 'points of access'. In doing so, organisations can supposedly create experiences that are not only interesting and engaging for consumers but, more importantly, are highly personalised for the individual, and therefore seek to build the consumer's trust.

Think about your own life just for one moment and ask yourself the question, is it all about me? My Twitter feed, my playlist, my pinboard, my blog, my Facebook friends, my new Jawbone Jambox speakers, customised online by me!

How do organisations take advantage of all of these customers' preferences and habits? How do they weave the daily experiences into a context that's relevant to the audience they are trying to target? And how important is it that during each '**moment of truth**' the customer is kept informed and delighted? Digital technologies can already enable organisations to imitate 'customer intimacy', the notion that the organisation knows their customer intimately. We see this manifesting itself online by the advertisements that quickly 'pop up' and which reflect your latest purchases. The systems are still not perfect: even after people make online purchases, pop-ups continue to promote similar products, which is somewhat irritating since there is clearly no longer a need for the product.

Moment of truth

The moment or instance of contact or interaction between a customer and an organisation that gives the customer an opportunity to form or change an impression about the organisation

CONSUMER TECHNOLOGY AND INNOVATION

> As consumers, we encounter a digital experience every way we turn, from the smart refrigerator in our kitchen to the adaptive security system in our home (which we can monitor from our smartphone). We can install a smart lighting system (Engineering.com, 2014; Lee et al., 2022) in our homes and offices which will react to environmental factors. When we sit in our car, it has already learned the driver's habits (Ask.cars.com, 2013; Yang, L. et al., 2022) and can fine tune the car's performance accordingly (let alone the automatic seat configuration depending on whether it's the owner or her husband who opens the car door). Finally let's not forget that Big Brother is always watching us in big cities with the digitalised 'Automatic Number Plate Recognition' systems, and that's even before we get to the car park, which has digital parking meters!

There are of course many benefits to having all this digital technology. Sports fans love the fact that stadiums which are accessible 'online' provide shorter lines and can offer a plethora of associated content which really engages the fan from a variety of perspectives. Event-goers also love being notified of flash sales (Bajarin, 2014) on nearby food and merchandise. The technology can therefore be a two-edged sword: on the one hand, creating a convenient world in which much of the thinking has been done for us, but on the other creating a world in which we become ruled by the machines that serve us.

Innovativeness is the degree to which a person tends to adopt innovations earlier than other people (Hong et al., 2021). It can be measured very simply using the Goldsmith–Hofacker Innovativeness Scale, which uses six questions to determine an individual's innovativeness in respect to a particular product category (Goldsmith and Hofacker, 1991). The Goldsmith–Hofacker scale is, in a sense, too simplistic because it merely asks what the individual's behaviour is, without finding out what it is about people that makes them innovators. In order to try to discover what it is that makes somebody an innovator, studies have been carried out into known innovators to find out what they have in common.

Innovativeness
The degree to which an individual or firm creates or adopts new products

Three main groups of variables have been identified thus far: socio-economic factors, personality factors and communication behaviour (see Figure 4.8). It should be noted, again, that all these studies are based on limited product categories, and are therefore not necessarily generally applicable.

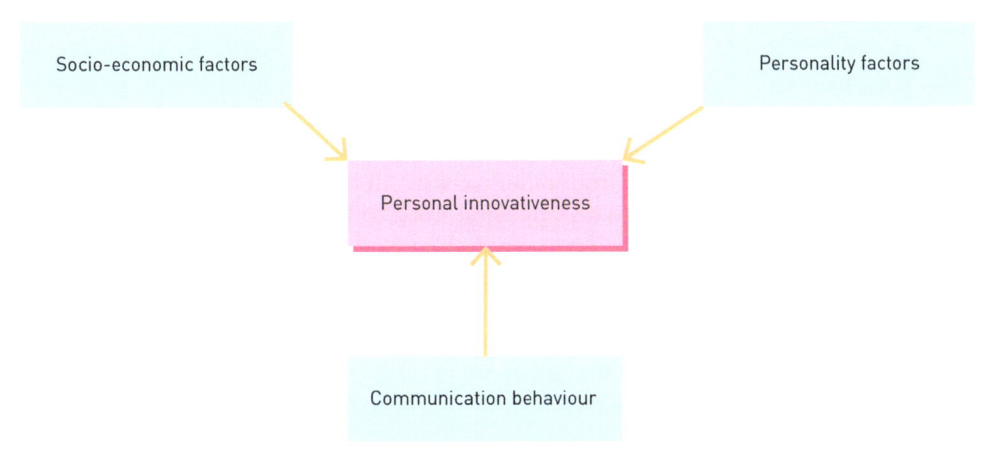

FIGURE 4.8 Variables that affect innovativeness

Socio-economic variables

Those factors that derive from an individual's class and income

Socio-economic variables that are positively related to innovativeness are as follows:

- education
- literacy
- higher social status
- upward social mobility
- larger-sized units
- commercial rather than subsistence orientation
- more favourable attitude towards credit
- more specialised operations.

Clearly, higher-income people are in a much better position to take the risk of buying new products. Those who are educated and literate are also more likely to hear about new products before other people do.

Personality and attitude variables associated with innovativeness are as follows:

- empathy
- ability to deal with abstractions
- rationality
- intelligence
- favourable attitude towards change
- ability to cope with uncertainty
- favourable attitude towards education
- favourable attitude towards science
- achievement motivation
- high aspirations.

There are some personality traits that militate against innovativeness, however:

- dogmatism
- fatalism.

One personality trait that appears to have a strong influence is the degree to which someone likes to be different from other people. All of us have a need to be assimilated into the group, and also an opposing need to be distinct from the group, in other words, an individual. Someone's position on that continuum will influence their attitude to innovation (Boeve-de Pauw et al., 2022; Jiang et al., 2021; Timmor and Katz-Navon, 2008).

M.J. Kirton (1986) showed that consumers can be classified as either adapters or innovators. The differences between the two are quite clear (Subotic et al., 2018).

Adapters tend to take existing solutions and adjust them as necessary to fit the current need problem; innovators tend to look for radical solutions. Kirton's Adaption–Innovation Index has proved to be a very reliable measure of innovativeness.

Cognitive innovators tend to be those who seek out new intellectual experiences, whereas **sensory innovators** are those who seek new sensory experiences. In both cases the innovators are seeking something new for its own sake; and there is ample research to indicate that novelty is an attractive feature of a product in its own right.

Cognitive dissonance is the psychological tension that results from holding two conflicting ideas at the same time. Which way do you go? The term came originally from work by Carl Festinger in the late 1950s, in which he experimented on people's motivation to lie. Festinger recruited students to perform a tedious task (specifically, putting pegs into holes, rotating the pegs a quarter-turn, then removing the pegs). He then told the students that he needed more recruits for the tests, and asked them to 'sell' their friends the idea of helping with the tests by telling them that the experiment was really interesting and good fun. He offered some students a dollar for telling this lie, and others $25 (a considerable sum in 1957). Interestingly, the ones who were only paid a dollar actually began to believe the lie themselves: Festinger's explanation for this was that they could not justify their statements on the basis that they were being paid to make them, therefore the statements had to be true (Festinger, 1957).

The mechanism by which dissonance arises is simple. When working through the goal hierarchy, the consumer will form a view of what it will be like to own the product, and will develop a perceptual map of the anticipated benefits. The perceptual map is a mental picture of what life will be like with the product included. The expectancy disconfirmation model (Oliver, 1980) says that satisfaction and/or dissatisfaction is the result of comparing pre-purchase expectations and post-purchase outcomes.

In the realm of consumer behaviour, post-purchase dissonance arises when the idea that a product was going to be a good purchase turns out to be wrong. The new information (that the product was not a good purchase) conflicts with the existing information, and the individual needs to resolve the dissonance. Pre-purchase expectations fall into three categories, as follows:

1. **Equitable performance**. This is a judgement regarding the performance one could reasonably expect given the cost and effort of obtaining the product (Woodruff et al., 1983).
2. **Ideal performance**. This is what the individual really hoped the product would do, if the world were a perfect place (Holbrook, 1984).
3. **Expected performance**. This is what the product probably will do (Leichty and Churchill, 1979).

The level of dissonance depends on the following factors:

- The degree of divergence between the expected outcome and the actual outcome.
- The importance of the discrepancy to the individual.

Cognitive innovators
Those who seek new intellectual experiences

Sensory innovators
Those who seek new sensory experiences

Cognitive dissonance
The perception of contradictory information, and the mental toll of it. Relevant items of information include a person's actions, feelings, ideas, beliefs, values, and things in the environment

Equitable performance
The level of product quality that the consumer would expect, given the price paid and the other circumstances of purchase and use

Ideal performance
The best possible outcome of buying a given product

Expected performance
The level of product quality that the individual anticipates

- The degree to which the discrepancy can be corrected.
- The cost of the purchase (in terms of time, money and risk).

For example, if someone buys an iPhone that turns out to have a scratch on the outer box, this is probably only a minor fault that does not affect the working of the equipment and is, in any case, easily corrected. (This is unless of course the phone is going to be a gift – in which case it would not be seen as a minor issue.) In many cases, however, the customer would simply accept the scratch without bothering to seek redress from the supplier: if the scratch is a small one, it probably is not worth the effort of taking the box back to the retailer for replacement, especially as the retailer might claim that the customer could have scratched the box while transporting it. Some studies have shown that only one-third of dissatisfied customers will complain or seek redress: the remainder will boycott the products in future or simply complain to others (Abdul-Talib and Mohd Adnan, 2017; Day, 1984; Sari et al., 2017). In the case of minor dissonance, or in cases where there is a high cost of complaint (for instance, returning goods to the duty-free shop at a foreign airport), the reluctance to complain is perfectly understandable.

Dissonance reduction is not always straightforward. Cognitive dissonance is a motivator to process information or to act, because the individual is driven to reduce dissonance wherever possible. Dissonance can occur at any point in the purchase cycle: when considering a major purchase, pre-purchase dissonance can easily affect the way decisions are arrived at, and in particular can easily delay the final purchase as the individual spends time reducing dissonance. Inevitably some doubt will remain, of course.

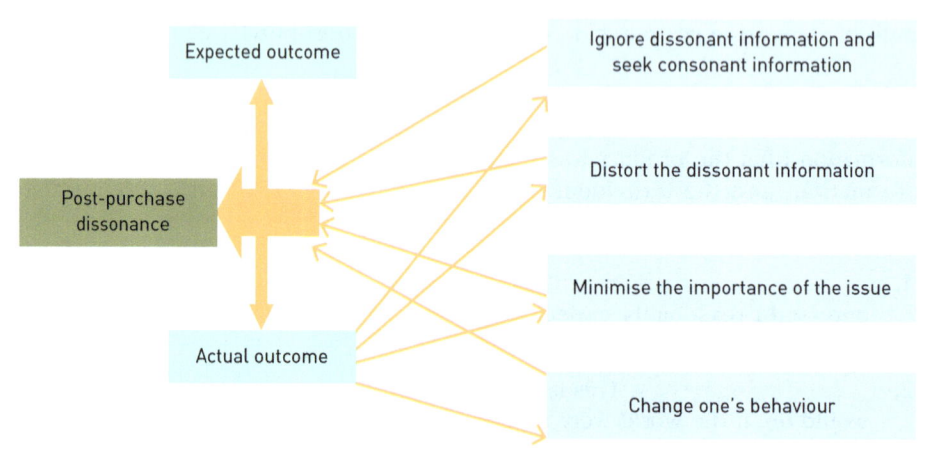

FIGURE 4.9 Dissonance reduction strategies

In Figure 4.9, the gap between the expected outcome and the actual outcome is what causes the post-purchase dissonance. The actual outcome is used as the benchmark for choosing which route to go down in reducing the dissonance, and the end result of the dissonance-reducing activity is fed back into the dissonance itself to cause the reduction.

From a marketer's point of view, it is important to reduce post-purchase dissonance. The evidence is that people will try to do so themselves, often by complaining about the product. If they do not win redress from the supplier, they will complain about the product to their friends and family. If people experience dissonance, there are four general approaches they take to minimise the problem. These are as follows:

1. *Ignore the dissonant information and look for positive (consonant) information about the product.* For example, a newly purchased car may be slower than expected, but on the plus side it is solidly built and reliable.
2. *Distort the dissonant information.* The car may be slow, but at least it's faster than taking a bus.
3. *Play down the importance of the issue.* The car is slow, but it goes from A to B eventually.
4. *Change one's behaviour.* Perhaps the consumer will sell the car, trade it in for something else or buy a bicycle.

Marketers are able to back up these general approaches. Some car manufacturers, aware that their cars are reliable rather than exciting, will make use of this in their advertising. For example, Volkswagen used the slogan 'If only everything in life was as reliable as a Volkswagen' for several years. This was ironic given the 2015 scandal in which they were caught using hidden software that would falsify the nitrogen oxide emission levels from thousands of their diesel vehicles worldwide. The battle for compensation still continues in 2023! In general, it is better to avoid the occurrence of post-purchase dissonance by ensuring that the purchaser has accurate information about the product and its performance; in other words, ensuring that the customer's perceptual map conforms as closely as possible to later experiences of using the product.

The last set of variables that affect innovativeness consists of those associated with communications, as can be seen in Figure 4.10.

Although innovators for one product group are not necessarily innovators for other groups, there are some correlations. For example, technophiles are people who like technology for its own sake, and who are prepared to take an interest in (and even buy) new audio-visual equipment, laptops/tablets and electronic gadgets, etc. (Kumar, 2022). On the other hand, technophobes have a loathing for such devices (McClure, 2018; Nimrod, 2021). In general, the level of involvement with the product category will go a long way towards explaining an individual's innovativeness: research has shown that people who are very environmentally aware are also likely to adopt new environment-friendly products. This is due to a favourable configuration of values, beliefs and norms (Jansson et al., 2011).

Feick and Price (1987) identified a group of influencers they called *market mavens* (see also Chapters 6 and 10). A market maven is someone who has an intense interest in, and a high level of knowledge about, a specific category of product. Mavens are able to provide price and availability information to others, as well as information about the products themselves: in effect, they act as an extension of the gatekeeper role in disseminating information about new products. The mavenic notion suggests

Technophiles
People who like new technology for its own sake

Technophobes
People who are fearful of new technology

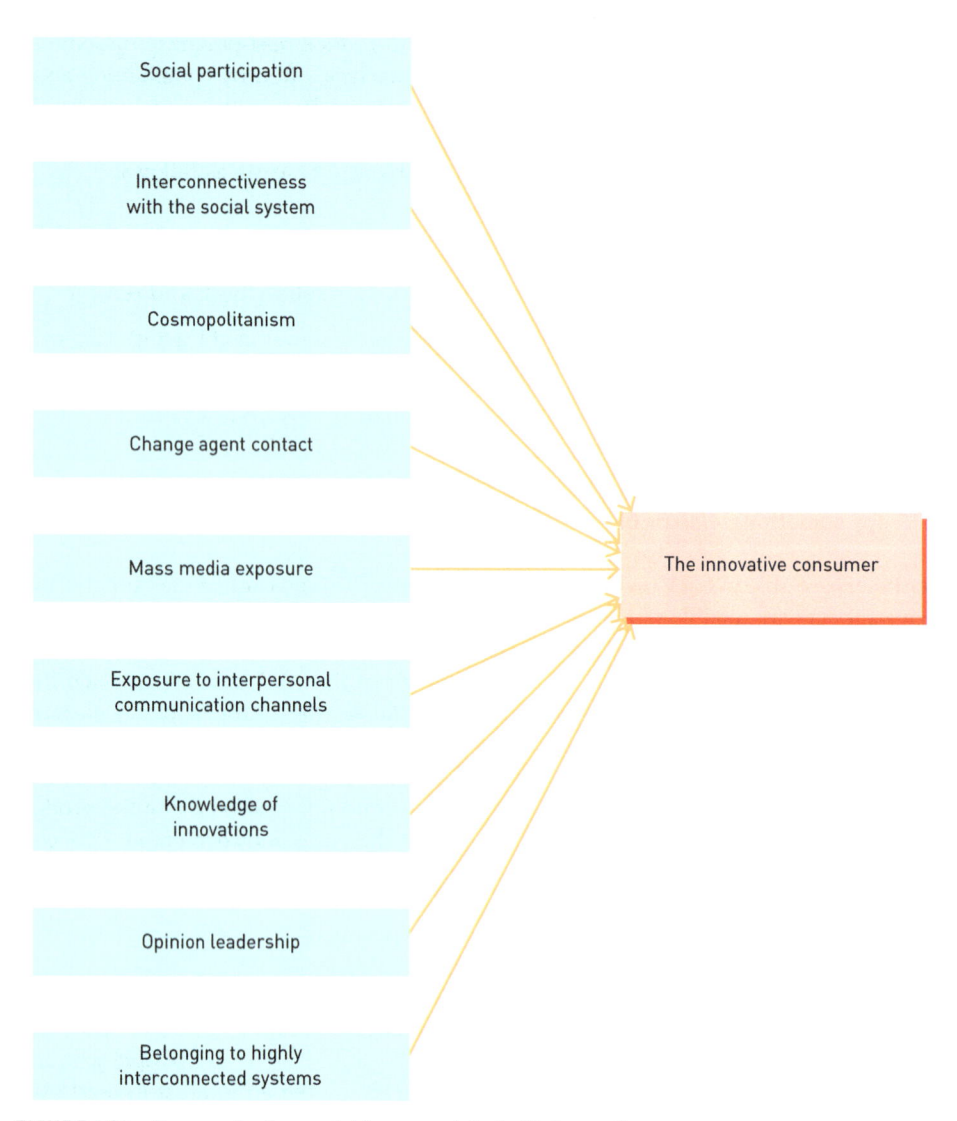

FIGURE 4.10 Communication variables associated with innovativeness

that mavens are usually motivated by the desire to share information, to show off their knowledge and to help others in reaching the right decisions (Walsh et al., 2004). Mavens are also sometimes known as *infomediaries*, particularly when they operate predominantly online: many forums, blogs and helpdesks are inhabited by such experts, who enjoy helping others with purchasing decisions.

INNOVATIVE PRODUCTS

From the viewpoint of a marketer, it would appear that there is a demand for newness *per se*. In other words, as a general rule people like new things and like to feel that the product they buy now is better than the one they bought previously. On the other hand, people are not necessarily prepared to take the risk of buying products that are radically different from their existing purchases.

CONSUMER TECHNOLOGY AND INNOVATION

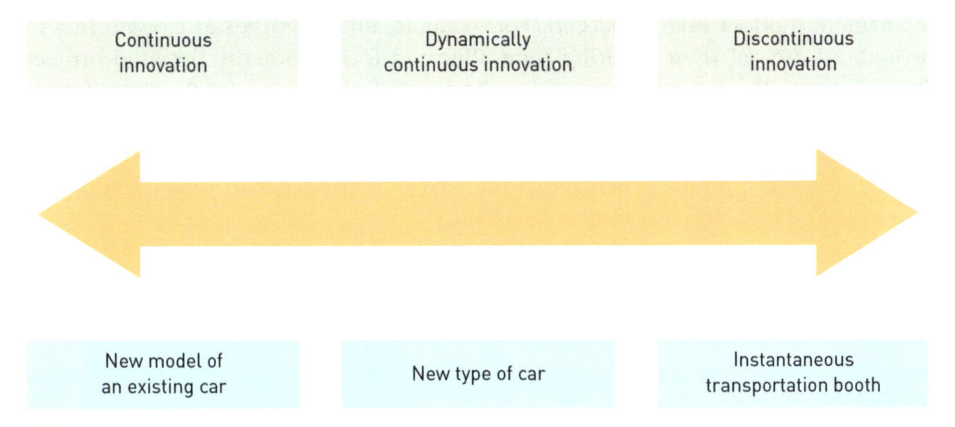

FIGURE 4.11 Degrees of innovation

In terms of the effect on the consumer's lifestyle (and consequently the risk to the consumer), innovations, from a theoretical perspective, may be classified (see Figure 4.11) under three headings (Herring and Roy, 2007; Robertson, 1967):

1. **Continuous innovation**: a relatively minor change in the product, for example the packaging or the styling.
2. **Dynamically continuous innovation**: changes that materially affect the core functioning of the product. An example might be a coupé version of a family saloon.
3. **Discontinuous innovation**: a product that is new to the world, and changes the lifestyles of those who adopt it. In recent years the Kindle electronic book and the iPhone have revolutionised people's approach to reading and to communications respectively.

For someone to take the risk of adopting a technologically advanced product (i.e. a discontinuous innovation) there must be a corresponding advantage. The technology acceptance model (Bagozzi and Warshaw, 1992; Davis, 1989) states that new technology adoption relies on two factors: ease of use and usefulness. If a product is too difficult to use in practice it will not be adopted readily, even if it is really useful; likewise, a product that is easy to use but fulfils no useful function will not be adopted. It is for this reason that both the Kindle and the iPhone were designed to be simple to use: both are intuitive in use, with little need for an instruction manual.

The technology acceptance model has been criticised on the grounds that it has limited heuristic value, and very little predictive value – in other words, it doesn't help much with decision-making or with predictions of the potential success of a new technology (Chuttur, 2009). Having said that, it is still widely used as an explanatory tool for understanding new product success (and failure) when considering discontinuous innovation (Cheng, 2019).

A study by Calentone and Cooper (1981) found that the most successful new products were, in fact, only incremental improvements on existing products, rather than radically new products; this study also emphasised the need for the product to have a marketing synergy rather than be simply a wonderful idea that only the engineering

---

Continuous innovation
A new product that follows closely on from a previous product and has a clear relationship to the previous product

Dynamically continuous innovation
The development of a new product that differs radically from its predecessors while still retaining some commonality

Discontinuous innovation
Developing a new product that relates only distantly, or does not relate at all, to previous products

department thought might succeed. For example, all employees at Google Inc. can have about 20% of their working time allocated to individually initiated projects. This promotes the notion of everyone (across different units, levels and divisions) having a responsibility towards digital innovation, and maximising creativity (Avital and Te'eni, 2009; Yoo et al., 2012). But of course this will only work when the culture in an organisation allows such individualised improvisation to capture successful outcomes and is tolerant of impending failures too!

Benchmarking is the process by which firms compare their activities with the best in the industry, and try to match the best practice of their competitors in each area. The aim is to become the best of the best. To this end, motor manufacturers buy their competitors' cars and strip them down to see how they are made and what their features are, then try to emulate the best of them in their own product offerings. This is called reverse engineering. Inevitably this will lead to more copying of competitors' products if the philosophy is applied to new product development.

MARKETING APPROACHES TO NEW PRODUCT LAUNCHES

Combining decision-making theory and diffusion theory, it is possible to come up with some broad recommendations for launching new products:

1. *Need recognition.* Marketers should activate needs by mentioning them in advertising. The advertising needs to make people aware of what's new, and how it will have a **relative advantage** over current competitors.
2. *Pre-purchase activities or search.* Information sources are strongly linked to marketing strategy; brochures, product information adverts, leaflets, PR activities and salespeople all contribute to the process. Marketers should ensure that there is an emphasis on the product's **compatibility** with the target market's lifestyles and aspirations.
3. *Evaluation and purchase decision.* Salespeople have a strong contribution to make to this part of the process; marketers must ensure a high quality of presentation of information materials, and the salesforce must be able to guide consumers through the **complexity** of the product.
4. *Act of purchase and consumption.* The product has to be right for the task, and fulfil the manufacturer's claims. Allowing the customer to try out the product is a good means of reducing the risk, so **trialability** is a key issue in this context.
5. *Post-purchase evaluation.* After-sales service has a strong role to play here, and ideally there should be some **observability** in the product if there is to be rapid diffusion of the product to the broader market.

Some new products have greater potential than others for consumer acceptance. Sometimes it is difficult to analyse exactly what it is that makes one new product more acceptable than another – if marketers knew this, there would be fewer failures of new products. There is, after all, no point in trying to market a product for which consumer acceptance will be limited.

One route around the acceptance problem is mass **customisation**. Here customers are able to design the product or service themselves from a range of possible options:

Benchmarking
Measuring the firm's performance against that of other firms across a wide range of factors

Relative advantage
The degree to which a new product is superior to the one it replaces, altering it in some way

Compatibility
The degree to which a new product matches the individual's existing lifestyle, attitudes and possessions

Complexity
The degree to which a new product requires extensive learning before it can be used effectively

Trialability
The degree to which a product can be tested before the customer needs to commit to its adoption

Observability
The degree to which the purchase of a new product can be seen by others

Customisation
Redesigning a product to make it fit a customer's needs more exactly

the application of this concept ranges from NikeID (where customers can design their own unique trainers) to a number of startups who are competing for a share of the 'on-demand services' market by offering platforms and apps to take advantage of the current trend towards providing instant solutions for daily and onerous tasks (take, for example, the case of Uber transportation which uses an app to link drivers with passengers). It is no surprise that leading the way currently is the evolution of 3D printing. The advantage is that customers are able to design something that meets their own needs very closely indeed, and do not have to accept (or pay for) features that are only present because most people want them. This level of need for digital design has found itself moving into all industry sectors – even clothing (with websites such as www.continuumfashion.com enabling female customers to 3D print their own bikinis from solid nylon). At first sight, it would seem that a driver for mass customisation would be that customers can save money by paying only for features they actually need, but in fact research shows that such customers are actually prepared to pay a substantial premium in order to design something to their own specification. This may be due to a better perceived fit, it may be due to perceived uniqueness of the product or it may be simply pride of authorship – the pleasure of knowing that one has created something unique. In addition, websites such as www.thingiverse.com enable individuals to upload their user-created digital designs, which are then licensed and shared so that they can be physically created using 3D printers, laser cutters or milling machines.

RESISTANCE TO INNOVATION

Resistance to innovation can come from several sources, as can facilitation of innovation. First, channels of communication might create a barrier: as we'll see in Chapter 11, communications received from respected family members and opinion leaders will be taken seriously and often acted upon, whereas communications from a member of a dissociative group will be ignored or will tend to militate against action. Poorly executed advertising and branding campaigns can create negative attitudes about the product, as can other poorly executed approaches such as insensitive salespeople, over-persuasive email shots or negative press coverage. On the other hand, some forms of communication have greatly aided the adoption of innovation – the internet has provided a wide variety of online blogs and forums that have enabled people to exchange information rapidly about new products. The net result is that those who are likely to adopt the product hear about it much faster than they might have done a few years ago. Of course this also means that the rate at which bad news travels will also increase. By far the most efficient and effective way of keeping the public informed when disaster strikes is by using mobile communications. Take, for instance, social media site Facebook's Safety Check button. It is a feature that can be activated by the company during either natural or human-made disasters to determine whether people in the affected geographical area are safe. So, for example, within hours of an earthquake in Nepal in May 2015, doctors working in the area were able to click one button on Facebook in order to inform their friends and family that they were OK and not in trouble (Medscape, 2015).

However, the social system can also create a barrier. The social system is the physical, cultural and social environment within which decisions are made: for marketers, it usually corresponds to the market segment (or target market). For example, there is a social system that functions in most jobs or professions: lawyers discuss cases,

Young Farmers societies organise social events, academics have conferences and students have Student Unions. Social systems might have traditional values, in which case innovation is likely to be stifled, or they may have modern values, in which case innovation is likely to be stimulated. The characteristics of social systems which were identified by Rogers and Shoemaker (1971) still ring true in today's societal makeup:

- A positive attitude towards change.
- An advanced technology and skilled labour force.
- A general respect for education and science.
- An emphasis on rational and ordered social relationships rather than on emotional ones.
- An outreach perspective, in which members of the system frequently interact with outsiders.
- A system in which members can easily see themselves in different roles.

Social systems can be of any size, up to and including entire countries. The prevailing social climate will be discussed in more detail in Chapter 10, but it clearly has relevance for innovation.

The chief technology officer, Mr Gopichand Katragadda, at Tata Sons Ltd (part of Tata Group of Companies) has spoken about technological trends that will affect the R&D budgets of major international organisations. Here are three key trends he lists:

1. *Digital assistants.* Let your smartphone do the work for you. Applications such as Siri (Apple) and Google Assistant have changed the way that we interact with our smartphone by giving it access and letting it take control of our data. Add a layer of an open-source computing platform such as Sirius (designed by the University of Michigan) to the smartphone and cloud computing, and digital assistants can provide a multitude of opportunities and applications in all sorts of sectors – especially combined with the power of 'wearables'.

2. *Aggregator apps.* With the rise of companies such as Uber, whose app and company are valued at $67 billion, aggregator apps which connect buyers and sellers are obviously doing something right. This digital technology uses Bluetooth to transmit and receive messages to and from various mobile devices. This, coupled with cloud messaging (a technology that pushes messages and updates to an individual smartphone), means that industry sectors such as transport, retail and social enterprise are set to be revolutionised. Can you see the possibilities?

3. *Commercial drones.* Also known as an unmanned aerial vehicle (UAV), but more commonly known as a drone, this is an aircraft without a human pilot on board: a flying robot. These devices have come a long way in the past few years. They are made of composite material structures and use nanotechnology batteries, which give them a battery life of up to 30 minutes. And when you combine this with artificial intelligence, chaos theory and cloud computing, the use for such devices is endless and is opening up myriad applications: film-making, industrial inspection, security firms, real estate, precision agriculture and medical facilities, to name a few. But how does this translate into a commercial application that could be marketed successfully?

Aggregator

A website or software that aggregates a specific type of information from multiple online sources (e.g. data, news, reviews, social networks, blogs, payments)

Well think about if drones could enable organisations to deliver products. Amazon is already talking about delivering small packages to customers via its Prime Air service. This future service will deliver packages up to five pounds in weight in 30 minutes or less using small drones. The drones will fly under 400 feet and the total weight will be less than 55 pounds. Amazon wants to take full advantage of sophisticated 'sense and avoid' technology to safely operate beyond the line of sight to distances of 10 miles or more. Can you envisage a day when we'll have UAV-based food delivery and your pizza is delivered via a drone? You may be surprised to learn that a company in California has already launched the 'Burrito Bomber', a UAV that uses GPS navigation to drop burritos by parachute! Commercial photography has an obvious stake herein enabling aerial shots of properties, concerts, etc., to be taken by the drone-savvy photographer. Of course security services could also use these images in conjunction with face recognition systems to identify 'wanted' people! And it doesn't just stop at identifying people – wildlife could be surveyed and documented using high-flying drones. We could of course also use the very same technology in search and rescue missions using solar-powered UAVs, which can reportedly stay airborne for 5 years – which then actually triggers a final thought… could these solar-powered drones act as movable wireless access points for remote parts of the world where the infrastructure prohibits such access? Interesting, right?

API
An 'application programming interface' is a software intermediary that allows two applications to talk to each other. An API is the messenger that delivers your request to the provider that you're requesting it from and then delivers the response back to you

BRAND EXPERIENCES: AI TO GAUGE ARGH!

Digital innovation has touched our life in many ways, but the jury is still out on whether we actually want innovation or are just looking for improvement. In a recent survey (Code Computerlove, 2018) it was found that 38% of consumers were 'looking for improvements over new innovations', and in addition that there should be better and more seamless integration between various devices. This, compared to the 17% who said that they were looking for 'something they haven't experienced before', suggests that improvements will provide a winning formula – for the time being at least. Generation Z is continually challenging brands to move beyond the concept of 'one size fits all'. Personalisation is a prerequisite. What's really exciting is the way in which digital innovation is changing how we as consumers interact with products and services. Take for example 'Immersive VR' (virtual reality), which is creating new inroads for companies to reach their audiences. Back in 2016, a couple of creative directors launched an exhibition called 'Disney and Dali: Architects of the Imagination'. Here, users can move around, go inside and engage with elements of one of the artist's early paintings. The result is a creation of a world where people are free to explore as they wish and, ultimately, provides a more engaged way to experience art.

Let's move on from Immersive VR to taking a quick look at AI and AR (artificial intelligence and augmented reality). Apple recently acquired 'Emotient': a startup that is using AI to read people's emotions by analysing facial expressions. A step too far, we hear you say? (...especially in light of General Data Protection Regulation in the UK and Europe). Well, the practical application of such AI is fascinating and could give brands an even deeper dataset to work with. Take, for example, The TasteFace app, which was built on Microsoft's Emotion **API** and which uses facial recognition to gauge people's reactions to **Marmite**, using an algorithm to convert these expressions into a sliding scale of love and hate!

Marmite
Marmite is a sticky, dark brown food paste with a distinctive, powerful flavour, which is extremely salty. This distinctive taste is reflected in the marketing slogan: 'Love it or hate it'. Such is its prominence in British popular culture that the product's name has entered British English as a metaphor for something that is an acquired taste or tends to polarise opinions

SUMMARY

In this chapter we have seen a chain of events unfold. Some individuals will have a revolutionary idea, for example the Wright brothers with their invention of an aeroplane. It was other individuals who made the evolutionary advances by implementing the innovation so that it could be used for commercial airlines, military purposes and also to deliver airmail. Adoption of new products is a somewhat hit-and-miss affair. Companies need to engage with some form of innovation regularly in order to avoid being left with an obsolete product portfolio, but on the other hand it is extremely difficult to predict consumers' responses to innovative products. Many firms therefore simply make minor incremental changes to their products rather than making radical innovations. It is our ability to innovate digital technologies which enables organisations to make such small changes in a cost-effective way.

Nevertheless, most people like some novelty in their lives, and many people like a lot of novelty. The words novelty and personalisation may be interchanged in this context, and a classic example of this 'in action' is www.moonpig.com, a company set up by Nick Jenkins in 2000 which sells personalised greeting cards online. Moonpig holds a 60% market share in the UK among online card specialists, underpinned by 89% brand awareness in June 2021. Its unique selling point has now evolved into its ability to personalise a range of products – from gift boxes, food gifts and wall art to T-shirts, alcoholic gifts and phone cases.

The problem for marketers lies in knowing which innovations and which new product categories will be acceptable and to which target market segments.

KEY POINTS

- The product life cycle shows that all products eventually become obsolete and must be replaced.
- Innovators for one product category are not necessarily innovators for any other product category.
- The most successful products are often *me-toos* or continuous innovations.
- Mavens have a high level of interest in specific product categories, and enjoy airing their knowledge.
- Innovation can be continuous, dynamically continuous or discontinuous.
- Resistance to innovation can come from many sources.

HOW TO IMPRESS YOUR EXAMINER

The world of consumer technology and innovation is changing at lightning speed. Make sure you're using examples that reflect what's going on now and also what's about to change the way we live forever!

REVIEW QUESTIONS

1. What is the most significant interaction that you, as a consumer, have had with technology?
2. From your consumer perspective, how can e-commerce retailers and brands improve their performance using AI?
3. How will the IoT affect your life?
4. What is the role of mavens in word of mouth communication?
5. What is the key difference between a dynamically continuous innovation and a discontinuous innovation?
6. Why is the product life cycle difficult to use as a predictor?
7. How might a marketer speed up the adoption process?
8. Why do most new products fail?
9. Why do most new tech products lose money at first?
10. What can marketers do to help overcome barriers to adoption?

CASE STUDY: GRAVITY TAKES OVER

Inventors like Richard Browning have been trying to build jetpacks for a century. Now they're here, what do we do with them?

The first time someone flies a jetpack, a curious thing happens: just as their body leaves the ground, their legs start to flail. Adrenaline floods into the bloodstream. The lumbrical muscles in the feet tighten, toes grasp desperately at the earth. It's as if the vestibular system can't quite believe what's happening. This isn't natural. Then suddenly, thrust exceeds weight, and – they're aloft. Millions of years of evolution are overcome in an instant, two dimensions become three. Latitude, longitude, altitude.

It's that moment, lift-off, that has given jetpacks an enduring appeal for over a century. Human beings have long dreamed of flying outside the confines of an aircraft, but without lift-off, existing means – parachutes, hang gliders, wing suits – are really elegant ways of extending a fall.

'It's indescribable, in an overwhelming, visceral kind of way', Richard Browning says. Browning, who is 41, brown-haired and bearded, with the lean physique of an endurance athlete, is the founder and CEO of the jetpack start-up Gravity Industries. (Its slogan: 'We build 1,000 horsepower jet suits'.) He is also the company's main designer and chief test pilot. Since launching Gravity in 2016, Browning has taken off thousands of times, performed live demonstrations in more than 30 countries, set a Guinness World Record (twice) and accrued more than 10 million YouTube views for his

(Continued)

exploits. But he still remembers his first lift-off: it was November 2016, on a farmyard a few minutes from his house in Salisbury.

As a child Browning would spend his holidays home from boarding school helping out in his father's workshop. Together they would build model gliders from balsa wood, then drive up to a nearby hilltop to launch them. 'Thanks to my father and my grandfather, I could probably describe how a jet engine works at the age of ten', he says.

The engine Browning bought was a micro gas turbine. Essentially jet engines in miniature, micro gas turbines work by compressing air at extremely high velocity, then burning it with fuel (usually kerosene) to generate thrust. Although far too small for civilian aircraft, the technology has advanced rapidly in recent years, largely thanks to amateur enthusiasts and a growing market for military training drones. 'The world of micro gas turbines had been entirely dominated by model aircraft people, so they'd accelerated in this kind of unbound way', Browning says. The chief draw is their size: an engine not much larger than a 2 litre Coke bottle and weighing only 1.9 kg can put out 22 kg of thrust. Join a few together, Browning theorised, and you'd have enough power to lift a person.

Browning fired up the engine as soon as it arrived. 'My god, the noise was unbelievable', he says. Encouraged, he built an aluminium arm housing, and repurposed the trigger from a power drill as a throttle. Soon he was standing in a country lane with what looked like a supercharged leaf blower on one arm, attached to a fuel tank in a mop bucket. 'It was a profound moment', he says. He worried that the torque from the engines would twist his arm off, but 'it was just a spongy push, like a firehose of water'.

Over the following months, Browning's jet suit became an obsession. Every night, he would wake up at 1 am, work for three or four hours on the suit in a spare bedroom, and then sleep on the train commute into London. One engine became two, then four, then six: two attached to each arm mount, and one strapped around each ankle. The fuel bladder he hid inside a rucksack, secured with a climbing harness. At first, he kept the idea mostly to himself. 'Nobody thought that it would work', he says. At weekends, Browning would drag his family out to the farmyard to test it. While his children played, Browning attempted to fly.

The early tests were a string of failures. Browning couldn't stay aloft, managing only a series of elongated bounds. He frequently fell, and when he tried using a safety harness he found himself being thrown around like a marionette. The engines were temperamental, and expensive. Every breakage required sending it back to the German manufacturer for refurbishment. 'It was just chaos', he says. 'A little pop and a flash and a bit of smoke, and something would have shorted. I was completely exhausted and thinking, what am I doing?' Still, with each failure, there was progress. 'I was driven by a slightly irrational excitement for the journey', he says. 'I kept thinking: this works.'

Then, one weekend in November 2016, it happened. After another brief Moon bounce, Browning held down the throttle trigger, leaned hard on his arm engines and – lift-off. There's footage of the moment: Browning, one leg flailing, flying across the courtyard, and landing slightly off balance. The flight lasted a little more than six seconds. But still, one thought crossed his mind as he beamed for the camera: 'I just flew! I just flew!'

The applications for such technology and innovation are endless. Go and take a look at their website first (https://gravity.co/). Then make your list of possibilities.

Source: Case adapted from Franklin-Wallis (2020).

CASE STUDY QUESTIONS

1. Why is it so important for 'man to fly'?
2. Who should bear the cost of these technological transformations?
3. What would be the driving force behind the adoption of such technological products?
4. Is this a quirky and temporary fad or have companies like this really got something here?
5. What other products/services could organisations complement their collection with?

FURTHER READING

Morris et al. (2013) Smart-home technologies to assist older people to live well at home, *Journal of Aging Science, 1* (1): 101, concludes that older adults were reported to readily accept smart-home technologies, especially if they benefited physical activity, independence and function and if privacy concerns were addressed. Given the modest number of objective analyses, there is a need for further scientific analysis of a range of smart-home technologies to promote community living. You can read the article at www.omicsonline.org/open-access/smart-home-technologies-to-assist-older-people-to-live-well-at-home-2329-8847.1000101.php?aid=12044.

The UK is set to become a world leader in the additive manufacturing (3D printing) sector by 2025, or post-Brexit! This is what the Additive Manufacturing UK National Strategy 2019–2025 says at least. You can find the full report online here: http://am-uk.org/project/additive-manufacturing-uk-national-strategy-2018-25/.

Gartner (2018) predicted that 3D printing will change business models and that 75% of aircraft will use 3D printed parts by 2021. A summary of this report makes for interesting reading and can be found online here: www.3ders.org/articles/20171213-gartner-predicts-2018-3d-printing-changes-business-models.html.

Reeves and Mendis (2015) have written a report (commissioned by the UK government's Intellectual Property Office), which addresses some of the key issues: *The Current Status and Impact of 3D Printing within the Industrial Sector: An Analysis of Six Case Studies.* The publication is available from the IPO website (www.gov.uk/IPO).

Innovations can easily disrupt industries, and sometimes even very large companies fall victim to someone else's innovation. *The Innovator's Dilemma: When New Products Cause Great Firms to Fail,* by Clayton Christensen (Boston, MA: Harvard Business School Press, 1997), shows how new ideas create big problems.

Following on from this book, Christensen co-authored another with Jeff Dyer and Hal Gregerson. This book, *The Innovator's DNA: Mastering the Five Skills of Disruptive Innovators* (Boston, MA: Harvard Business School Press, 2011), outlines the traits and behaviours that innovators exhibit – in particular those who come up with the radical ideas that disrupt business for their competitors.

(Continued)

Websites are notorious for disappearing, but this one is great fun provided it is still around when you buy this book: http://uk.businessinsider.com/biggest-product-flops-in-history-2016-12. Although it is mainly concerned with brand extensions, it does highlight some fairly appalling new product launches – and although we shouldn't gloat over someone else's failure, there are certainly lessons to be learned here.

The Art of Innovation: Success through Innovation the IDEO Way, by Tom Kelley (with Jonathan Littman) (London: Profile Books, 2001), describes techniques for becoming more innovative. It is written entirely from a practitioner's viewpoint: Kelley is the co-founder of an innovation and design company, and outlines how the firm brainstorms for ideas (including how not to manage a brainstorming session).

The Effect of Negative Ties on the Innovative Consumer's Creativity: An Empirical Study of New Service Idea Generation in a Social Networking Environment, by Phillippe Duverger (Cambridge: Proquest/UMI Dissertation Publishing, 2011), is a PhD thesis that explores the relationship between social networking and the empowerment of consumers as innovators for the firms they buy from. Although the thesis is very academic in style, and therefore hard going at times, the author offers some very good insights into ways in which consumer creativity can be fostered, and ways in which it can be damaged.

MORE ONLINE

For additional materials that support this chapter and your learning, please visit:

https://study.sagepub.com/sethna5e

REFERENCES

Abdul-Talib, A.N. and Mohd Adnan, M.M. (2017) Determinants of consumer's willingness to boycott surrogate products. *Journal of Islamic Marketing*, 8 (3): 345–60.

Accenture (2016) Technology vision. www.accenture.com/gb-en/insight-technology-trends-2016 (accessed 18 May 2017).

Accenture Interactive (2015) Digital transformation in the age of the customer. https://insuranceblog.accenture.com/wp-content/uploads/2017/05/Digital-Transformation-in-the-Age-of-the-Customer-POV.pdf (accessed 13 August 2017).

AFP Online (2016) Benchmarking survey. www.afponline.org/publications-data-tools/reports/survey-research-economic-data/2016FPAbenchmarkingSurvey/afp-fp-a-benchmarking-survey (accessed 31 July 2017).

Alajlan, N.N. and Ibrahim, D.M. (2022) TinyML: Enabling of inference deep learning models on ultra-low-power IoT edge devices for AI applications. *Micromachines*, 13: 851.

Almeida, O., Figueiredo, P.S., Estevão Beal, V. and Passos, F.U. (2020) Critical success factors of product development projects in the automotive industry. *Journal of Technology Management & Innovation*, 15 (2): 56–69.

Angskun, J., Tipprasert, S. and Angskun, T., (2022) Big data analytics on social networks for real-time depression detection. *Journal of Big Data*, 9 (1): 1–15.

Ask.cars.com (2013) What is an adaptive transmission? http://ask.cars.com/2013/09/what-is-an-adaptive-transmission.html (accessed 28 June 2015).

Avital, M. and Te'eni, D. (2009) From generative fit to generative capacity: Exploring an emerging dimension of information systems design and task performance. *Information Systems Journal*, 19 (4): 345–67.

Bagozzi, R.P. and Warshaw, P.R. (1992) Development and test of a theory of technological learning and usage. *Human Relations*, 45 (7): 660–86.

Bajarin, T. (2014) Meet Levi's Stadium, the most high-tech sports venue yet. *Time*, 18 August. http://time.com/3136272/levis-stadium-tech/ (accessed 26 January 2016).

Bangamuarachchi, W., Chamantha, A., Meegahapola, L., Ruiz-Correa, S., Perera, I. and Gatica-Perez, D. (2022) Sensing eating events in context: A smartphone-only approach. *IEEE Access*, 10: 61249–64.

Barrett, M., Davidson, E., Prabhu, J. and Vargo, S.L. (2015) Service innovation in the digital age: Key contributions and future directions. *MIS Quarterly*, 39 (1): 135–54.

Batat, W. (2021) How augmented reality (AR) is transforming the restaurant sector: Investigating the impact of 'Le Petit Chef' on customers' dining experiences. *Technological Forecasting & Social Change*, 172: 121013.

Belk, R., Humayun, M. and Brouard, M. (2022) Money, possessions, and ownership in the Metaverse: NFTs, cryptocurrencies, Web3 and Wild Markets. *Journal of Business Research*, 153: 198–205.

Bithub Africa (2018) *The African Blockchain Opportunity*, 1st edn. http://bithub.africa/booksale/ (accessed 1 August 2018).

Bloomberg (2016) How Amazon triggered a robot arms race. www.bloomberg.com/news/articles/2016-06-29/how-amazon-triggered-a-robot-arms-race (accessed 19 September 2016).

Boeve-de Pauw, J., Ardies, J., Hens, K., Wullemen, A., Van de Vyver, Y., Rydant, T., De Spiegeleer, L. and Verbraeken, H. (2022) Short and long term impact of a high-tech STEM intervention on pupils' attitudes towards technology. *International Journal of Technology & Design Education*, 32 (2): 825–43.

Bouguettaya, A., Sheng, Q.Z., Benatallah, B., Neiat, A.G., Mistry, S., Ghose, A., Nepal, S. and Yao, L. (2021) An Internet of Things service roadmap: A blueprint for leveraging the tremendous opportunities the IoT has to offer. *Communications of the ACM*, 64 (9): 86–95. https://doi.org/10.1145/3464960

Business Insider (2016) A top futurist predicts the largest internet company of 2030 will be an online school. www.scmp.com/tech/innovation/article/2057614/top-futurist-predicts-largest-internet-company-2030-will-be-online (accessed 18 January 2017).

Calentone, R.J. and Cooper, R.G. (1981) New product scenarios: Prospects for success. *American Journal of Marketing*, 45: 48–60.

Cavicchioli, R., Martoglia, R. and Verucchi, M. (2022) A novel real-time edge-cloud big data management and analytics framework for smart cities. *Journal of Universal Computer Science*, 28 (1): 3–26.

Centric Digital (2015) How omni-channel customer experiences drive brand transformation. https://centricdigital.com/blog/digital-transformation/how-omni-channel-experiences-drive-brand-transformation/ (accessed 13 July 2018).

Chatterjee, S., Chaudhuri, R. and Vrontis, D. (2022) Big data analytics in strategic sales performance: Mediating role of CRM capability and moderating role of leadership support. *EuroMed Journal of Business*, *17* (3): 295–311.

Cheng, E.W.L. (2019) Choosing between the theory of planned behavior (TPB) and the technology acceptance model (TAM). *Educational Technology Research & Development*, *67* (1): 21–37.

Cherubini, S., Iasevoli, G. and Michelini, L. (2015) Product-service systems in the electric car industry: Critical success factors in marketing. *Journal of Cleaner Production*, *97*: 40–9.

Chuttur, M.Y. (2009) Overview of the technology acceptance model: Origins, developments and future directions. *Sprouts: Working Papers on Information Systems*, *9* (37). www.globelegislators.org/pdfjs/test/pdfs/TAMReview.pdf (accessed 10 February 2015).

CIM (2022) What do blockchain technologies imply for digital creative industries? *Creativity & Innovation Management*, *30* (3): 585–95.

CNN News (2017) Europe calls for mandatory 'kill switches' on robots. https://money.cnn.com/2017/01/12/technology/robot-law-killer-switch-taxes/index.html (accessed 19 September 2017).

Code Computerlove (2018) Driving digital effectiveness with product thinking. www.codecomputerlove.com/blog/product-thinking-stats (accessed 11 July 2018).

Cool Green Science (2016) 10 innovations that are changing conservation. https://blog.nature.org/science/2016/06/02/10-innovations-changing-conservation/ (accessed 19 July 2016).

Cordasco, C., Gherhes, C., Brooks, C. and Vorley, T. (2021) An institutional taxonomy of adoption of innovation in the classic professions. *Technovation*, *107*: 102272.

Datasmart (2016) How smart city Barcelona brought the Internet of Things to life. https://datasmart.ash.harvard.edu/news/article/how-smart-city-barcelona-brought-the-internet-of-things-to-life-789 (accessed 10 March 2018).

Davis, F.D. (1989) Perceived usefulness, perceived ease of use, and user acceptance of information technology. *MIS Quarterly*, *13* (3): 319–40.

Day, R.L. (1984) Modeling choices among alternative responses to dissatisfaction. In T.C. Kinnear (ed.), *Advances in Consumer Research*, Vol. 11. Duluth, MN: Association for Consumer Research. pp. 496–9.

Deloitte Consulting (2016) *Artificial Intelligence Innovation Report*. www2.deloitte.com/content/dam/Deloitte/at/Documents/human-capital/artificial-intelligence-innovation-report.pdf (accessed 18 November 2017).

Deloitte Consulting (2018) *Artificial Intelligence Innovation Report*. www2.deloitte.com/content/dam/Deloitte/de/Documents/Innovation/Artificial-Intelligence-Innovation-Report-2018-Deloitte.pdf (accessed 10 September 2018).

DNA (2016) Demonetization: This is a new Indian sunrise. www.dnaindia.com/analysis/column-this-is-a-new-indian-sunrise-2273153 (accessed 15 November 2016).

Duan, Y. and Zhang, J. (2022) A novel AI-based visual stimuli generation approach for environment concept design. *Computational Intelligence and Neuroscience, 2022*: 8015492.

Economist, The (2016) Of prediction and policy. *The Economist*, 20 August. www.economist.com/finance-and-economics/2016/08/20/of-prediction-and-policy (accessed 21 August 2017).

Elia, G., Raguseo, E., Solazzo, G. and Pigni, F. (2022) Strategic business value from big data analytics: An empirical analysis of the mediating effects of value creation mechanisms. *Information & Management, 59* (8). https://doi.org/10.1016/j.im.2022.103701

Engineering.com (2014) Smart light bulb saves energy as it learns. 14 September. www.engineering.com/ElectronicsDesign/ElectronicsDesignArticles/ArticleID/8489/Smart-Light-Bulb-Saves-Energy-as-It-Learns.aspx (accessed 26 January 2016).

EY (2015) Cybersecurity and the Internet of Things. www.ey.com/Publication/vwLUAssets/EY-cybersecurity-and-the-internet-of-things/%24FILE/EY-cybersecurity-and-the-internet-of-things.pdf (accessed 21 August 2017).

Feick, L.F. and Price, L.L. (1987) The market maven: A diffuser of marketplace information. *Journal of Marketing, 51*: 83–97.

Festinger, L. (1957) *A Theory of Cognitive Dissonance*. Stanford, CA: Stanford University Press.

Fiorentino, S. and Bartolucci, S. (2021) Blockchain-based smart contracts as new governance tools for the sharing economy. *Cities, 117*: 103325.

Forbes Insights (2016) Now or never: 2016 global CEO outlook. www.forbes.com/forbesinsights/kpmg_ceo_global_2016/index.html (accessed 21 August 2017).

Franklin-Wallis, O. (2020) Inside Gravity's daring mission to make jetpacks a reality. *Wired Magazine*. www.wired.co.uk/article/gravity-jetpacks (accessed 18 June 2021).

Gangadharbatla, H. (2022) The role of AI attribution knowledge in the evaluation of artwork. *Empirical Studies of the Arts, 40* (2): 125–42.

Gartner (2016) Top strategic predictions for 2017 and beyond: Surviving the storm winds of digital disruption. www.gartner.com/doc/3471568/top-strategic-predictions-surviving-storm (accessed 18 February 2018).

Geebren, A. (2022) *Understanding Analytical Factors which Influence Trust and Satisfaction within Mobile Banking*. Unpublished Thesis.

gemalto (2018) 2017 data breach level index: Full year results are in… https://blog.gemalto.com/security/2018/04/13/data-breach-stats-for-2017-full-year-results-are-in/ (accessed 1 August 2018).

Global Slavery Index (2018) Global findings. www.globalslaveryindex.org/2018/findings/global-findings/ (accessed 1 September 2018).

Goldsmith, R.E. and Hofacker, C.F. (1991) Measuring consumer innovativeness. *Journal of the Academy of Marketing Science, 19* (3): 209–22.

Government Technology (2022) Moving from mobile-first to mobile-only. *Government Technology Online Magazine, 35* (5): 10. www.govtech.com/.

Govindarajan, V. and Srivastava, A. (2018) Reexamining dual-class stock. *Business Horizons, 61* (3): 461–6.

Grosová, S., Kutnohorská, O. and Botek, M. (2022) Determinants influencing the adoption of new information technology supporting healthy life style: The example of wearable self-tracking devices. *Quality Innovation Prosperity / Kvalita Inovácia Prosperita, 26* (1): 24–37.

Grothaus, M. (2013) How Google is fighting sex trafficking with big data. www.fastcompany.com/3009686/how-google-is-fighting-sex-trafficking-with-big-data (accessed 10 September 2018).

Herring, H. and Roy, R. (2007) Technological innovation, energy efficient design and the rebound effect. *Technovation, 27* (4): 194–203.

Hodson, H. (2016) Google's DeepMind AI can lip-read TV shows better than a pro. *New Scientist*, 21 November. www.newscientist.com/article/2113299-googles-deepmind-ai-can-lip-read-tv-shows-better-than-a-pro/ (accessed 21 November 2016).

Holbrook, M.P. (1984) Situation-specific ideal points and usage of multiple dissimilar brands. In J.N. Sheth (ed.), *Research and Marketing*, Vol. 7. Greenwich, CT: JAI Press. pp. 93–131.

Hong, W., Liu, R.-D., Ding, Y., Jiang, R., Sun, Y. and Jiang, S. (2021) A time-lagged study of two possible routes from personal innovativeness to life satisfaction in adolescents: Learning and social interaction on mobile phones. *Personality and Individual Differences, 182*: 111075.

IDC Research Inc. (2015) IDC FutureScape: Worldwide big data and analytics 2016 predictions. www.idc.com/getdoc.jsp?containerId=259835 (accessed 19 September 2016).

IDC Research Inc. (2017) IDC FutureScape: Worldwide IT industry 2017 predictions. www.idc.com/getdoc.jsp?containerId=US41883016 (accessed 9 August 2018).

Jansson, J., Marell, A. and Nordlund, A. (2011) Exploring consumer adoption of a high involvement eco-innovation using value-belief-norm theory. *Journal of Consumer Behaviour, 10* (1): 51–60.

Jiang, Y., Wang, X. and Yuen, K.F. (2021) Augmented reality shopping application usage: The influence of attitude, value, and characteristics of innovation. *Journal of Retailing and Consumer Services, 63*: 102720.

Johnson, S. (2018) Beyond the Bitcoin bubble. *The New York Times Magazine*, 16 January. www.nytimes.com/2018/01/16/magazine/beyond-the-bitcoin-bubble.html (accessed 18 July 2018).

Kassen, M. (2022) Blockchain and e-government innovation: Automation of public information processes. *Information Systems, 103*: 101862.

Khan, N., Ray, R.L., Zhang, S., Osabuohien, E. and Ihtisham, M. (2022) Influence of mobile phone and internet technology on income of rural farmers: Evidence from Khyber Pakhtunkhwa Province, Pakistan. *Technology in Society, 68*: 101866.

Kirton, M.J. (1986) Adapters and innovators: A theory of cognitive style. In K. Gronhaugh and M. Kauffman (eds), *Innovation: A Crossdisciplinary Perspective*. New York: John Wiley. pp. 65–85.

Kohn, M. (2022) Clearview AI, TikTok, and the collection of facial images in international law. *Chicago Journal of International Law*, 23 (1): 195–234.

Koksal, A. (2022) *The Application of Competition Law Tools to Big Data Related Market Power in the EU*. Unpublished Thesis, University of Exeter.

Kumar, R. (2022) *Reluctant Technophiles: India's Complicated Relationship with Technology*. London: Sage.

Lee, C.-T., Chen, L.-B., Chu, H.-M. and Hsieh, C.-J. (2022) Design and implementation of a leader-follower smart office lighting control system based on IoT technology. *IEEE Access*, 10: 28066–79.

Leichty, M. and Churchill, G.A. Jr (1979) Conceptual insights into consumer satisfaction and services. In N. Beck (ed.), *Educators' Conference Proceedings*. Chicago, IL: American Marketing Association. pp. 509–15.

Liang, Y., Lee, S.-H. and Workman, J.E. (2021) How do consumers perceive mobile self-checkout in fashion retail stores? *International Journal of Retail & Distribution Management*, 50 (6): 677–91.

Lindstrom, M. (2011) You love your iPhone: Literally. *New York Times*, 1 October, p. A21 (New York edition).

Liu, S., Hua, G., Kang, Y., Edwin Cheng, T.C. and Xu, Y. (2022) What value does blockchain bring to the imported fresh food supply chain? *Transportation Research Part E*, 165: 102859.

Lu, L., Liang, C., Gu, D., Ma, Y., Xie, Y. and Zhao, S. (2021) What advantages of blockchain affect its adoption in the elderly care industry? A study based on the technology–organisation–environment framework. *Technology in Society*, 67: 101786.

Luceri, B., Tammo Bijmolt, T.H.A., Bellini, S. and Aiolfi, S. (2022) What drives consumers to shop on mobile devices? Insights from a meta-analysis. *Journal of Retailing*, 98 (1): 178–96.

Maier, M., Blume, F., Bideau, P., Hellwich, O. and Abdel Rahman, R. (2022) Knowledge-augmented face perception: Prospects for the Bayesian brain-framework to align AI and human vision. *Consciousness and Cognition*, 101. https://doi.org/10.1016/j.concog.2022.103301

Manyika, J., Lund, S., Singer, M., White, O. and Berry, C. (2016) How digital finance could boost growth in emerging economies. McKinsey Global Institute. www.mckinsey.com/featured-insights/employment-and-growth/how-digital-finance-could-boost-growth-in-emerging-economies (accessed 6 April 2017).

McClure, P.K. (2018) 'You're fired', says the robot: The rise of automation in the workplace, technophobes, and fears of unemployment. *Social Science Computer Review*, 36 (2): 139–56.

Medscape (2015) The emerging role of social media in disasters. www.medscape.com/viewarticle/847183_3 (accessed 11 July 2015).

MIT (2016) Teaching machines to predict the future. http://news.mit.edu/2016/teaching-machines-to-predict-the-future-0621 (accessed 6 April 2017).

Modena, B.D., Bellahsen, O., Nikzad, N., Chieh, A., Parikh, N., Dufek, D.M., Ebner, G., Topol, E.J. and Steinhubl, S. (2018) Advanced and accurate mobile health tracking devices record new cardiac vital signs. *Hypertension, 72* (2): 1–21.

Mohammad, N., Muad, A.M., Ahmad, R. and Yusof, M.Y.P.M. (2022) Accuracy of advanced deep learning with tensorflow and keras for classifying teeth developmental stages in digital panoramic imaging. *BMC Medical Imaging, 22* (1): 1–13.

Narayanan, A., Korium, M.S., Melgarejo, D.C., Hussain, H.M., Sousa De Sena, A., Silva, P.E.G., Gutierrez-Rojas, D., Ullah, M., Nezhad, A.E., Rasti, M., Pournaras, E. and Nardelli, P.H.J. (2022) Collective intelligence using 5G: Concepts, applications, and challenges in sociotechnical environments. *IEEE Access, 10*: 70394–417. https://doi.org/10.1109/ACCESS.2022.3184035

Navickaitė, G. (2022) New product development and market launch in cosmetics industry. *Mokslas: Lietuvos Ateitis, 14.* https://doi.org/10.3846/mla.2022.15668

New Vantage Partners (2017) Big data executive survey 2017. http://newvantage.com/wp-content/uploads/2017/01/Big-Data-Executive-Survey-2017-Executive-Summary.pdf (accessed 22 December 2017).

Nimrod, G. (2021) Not good days for technophobes: Older internet users during the COVID-19 pandemic. *Educational Gerontology, 47* (4): 160–71.

Oliver, R.L. (1980) A cognitive model of the antecedents and consequences of satisfaction decisions. *Journal of Marketing Research, 17*: 460–9.

Pelau, C., Dabija, D.-C. and Ene, I. (2021) What makes an AI device human-like? The role of interaction quality, empathy and perceived psychological anthropomorphic characteristics in the acceptance of artificial intelligence in the service industry. *Computers in Human Behavior, 122*: 106855.

Petit, N. and Teece, D.J. (2021) Innovating big tech firms and competition policy: Favoring dynamic over static competition. *Industrial & Corporate Change, 30* (5): 1168–98.

Petrosyan, A. and Dimitriadis, N. (2018) Applying persuasion science in marketing communications: A comparison of marketing communications professionals in Armenia and Greece. In S.M. Riad Shams, D. Vrontis, Y. Weber and E. Tsoukatos (eds), *Business Models for Strategic Innovation: Cross Functional Perspectives.* Abingdon: Routledge. pp. 85–106.

Rawindaran, N., Jayal, A. and Prakash, E. (2021) Machine learning cybersecurity adoption in small and medium enterprises in developed countries. *Computers, 10*: 150.

RCR Wireless News (2016) 2017 Predictions: Behind the scenes with 5G – 2017 lays groundwork for telecom revolution. www.rcrwireless.com/20161220/opinion/2017-predictions-behind-the-scenes-with-5g-2017-lays-groundwork-for-telecom-revolution-tag10 (accessed 6 April 2017).

Rengarajan, S., Narayanamurthy, G., Moser, R. and Pereira, V. (2022) Data strategies for global value chains: Hybridization of small and big data in the aftermath of COVID-19. *Journal of Business Research, 144*: 776–87.

Research and Markets (2017) Global in-memory computing market – growth, trends and forecasts (2016–2021). www.researchandmarkets.com/research/6tdsq6/global_inmemory (accessed 6 December 2017).

Reynolds, R., Sutherland, R., Nathan, N., Janssen, L., Lecathelinais, C., Reilly, K., Walton, A. and Wolfenden, L. (2019) Feasibility and principal acceptability of school-based mobile communication applications to disseminate healthy lunchbox messages to parents. *Health Promotion Journal of Australia, 30* (1): 108–13.

Rizomyliotis, I., Kastanakis, M.N., Giovanis, A., Konstantoulaki, K. and Kostopoulos, I. (2022) 'How may I help you today?' The use of AI chatbots in small family businesses and the moderating role of customer affective commitment. *Journal of Business Research, 153*: 329–40.

Robertson, T.S. (1967) The process of innovation and the diffusion of innovation. *Journal of Marketing, 31* (1): 14–19.

Rogers, E.M. (1983) *Diffusion of Innovation*. New York: Free Press.

Rogers, E.M. and Shoemaker, F. (1971) *Communication of Innovation*. New York: Macmillan.

Royal Mail (2018) Online shoppers in the UK make 80% of their retail purchases online, up from 74%. www.royalmailgroup.com/online-shoppers-uk-make-80-their-retail-purchases-online-74 (accessed 31 July 2018).

Salmen, A. (2021) New product launch success: A literature review. *Acta Universitatis Agriculturae et Silviculturae Mendelianae Brunensis, 69* (1): 151–76.

Sari, D.K., Mizerski, D. and Liu, F. (2017) Boycotting foreign products: A study of Indonesian Muslim consumers. *Journal of Islamic Marketing, 8* (1): 16–34.

Schrage, R., Meißner, L., Schütte, R. and Kenning, P. (2022) Acceptance of in-store apps: Factors that influence the intention to adopt location-based retail apps – insights from Germany. *International Journal of Retail & Distribution Management, 50* (6): 760–77.

Shi, W. and Huang, Q. (2022) The blockchain technology applied in the development of real economy in Jiangsu under deep learning. *Computational Intelligence and Neuroscience, 2022*. https://doi.org/10.1155/2022/3088043

Siaw, C.A. and Okorie, C. (2022) Value co-creation on technology-enabled platforms for business model responsiveness and position enhancement in global value chains. *Strategic Change, 31* (1): 9–18.

Siegel, J. and Krishnan, S. (2020) Cultivating invisible impact with deep technology and creative destruction. *Journal of Innovation Management, 8* (3): 6–19.

Skinner, D., Delobelle, P., Pappin, M., Pieterse, D., Esterhuizen, T.M., Barron, P. and Dudley, L. (2018) User assessments and the use of information from MomConnect, a mobile phone text-based information service, by pregnant women and new mothers in South Africa. *BMJ Global Health, 3* (2): e000561.

Solon, O. (2016) Self-driving trucks: What's the future for America's 3.5 million truckers? *The Guardian*, Tech, 17 June. www.theguardian.com/technology/2016/jun/17/self-driving-trucks-impact-on-drivers-jobs-us (accessed 31 August 2018).

Stokes, D. and Nelson, C.H. (2013) Word of mouth to word of mouse. In Z. Sethna, R. Jones and P. Harrigan (eds), *Entrepreneurial Marketing: Global Perspectives*. Bingley: Emerald Publishing. pp. 243–58.

Subotic, M., Maric, M., Mitrovic, S. and Mesko, M. (2018) Differences between adaptors and innovators in the context of entrepreneurial potential dimensions. *Kybernetes*, 47 (7): 1363–77.

Tang, K.-Y., Hsiao, C.-H., Tu, Y.-F., Hwang, G.-J. and Wang, Y. (2021) Factors influencing university teachers' use of a mobile technology-enhanced teaching (MTT) platform. *Educational Technology Research & Development*, 69 (5): 2705–28.

Tarhini, A., Ammar, H. and Tarhini, T. (2015) Analysis of the critical success factors for enterprise resource planning implementation from stakeholders' perspectives: A systematic review. *International Business Research*, 8 (4): 25.

Timmor, Y. and Katz-Navon, T. (2008) Being the same and different: A model explaining new product adoption. *Journal of Consumer Behaviour*, 7 (3): 249–62.

togetherforsaferroads.org (2016) Will self-driving vehicles save lives? www.togetherforsaferroads.org/will-self-driving-vehicles-save-lives/ (accessed 19 September 2017).

Tsung, C.-K., Chang, F.-S. and Liu, X.-Y. (2022) On the construction of an edge-based remote sensing framework: The applications on automated guided vehicles and drones. *Electronics*, 11: 1034.

Tuten, T.L. and Solomon, M.R. (2015) *Social Media Marketing*, 2nd edn. London: Sage.

Upadhyay, A.K. and Khandelwal, K. (2022) Metaverse: The future of immersive training. *Strategic HR Review*, 21 (3): 83–6.

Urban, S., Bobek, S. and Polona, T. (2015) Critical factors within organizations influencing effective use of CRM solutions. In S. Chatterjee, N.P. Singh, D.P. Goyal and N. Gupta (eds), *Managing in Recovering Markets: Proceedings in Business and Economics*. New Delhi: Springer India. pp. 223–33.

van Noordt, C. and Misuraca, G. (2022) Artificial intelligence for the public sector: Results of landscaping the use of AI in government across the European Union. *Government Information Quarterly*, 39 (3): 101714.

Varga, G., Stoicu-Tivadar, L., Nicola, S., Amaricai, E., Suciu, O., Dobrescu, C. and Sirbu, E. (2021) Multimodal interaction and AI in rehabilitation of rheumatoid arthritis. *Applied Medical Informatics*, 43 (suppl. S1): 40.

Walker Sands (2016) Walker Sands future of retail 2016: Reinventing retail. www.walkersands.com/walker-sands-future-of-retail-2016-reinventing-retail/ (accessed 29 July 2017).

Walsh, G., Gwinner, K.P. and Swanson, S.R. (2004) What makes mavens tick? Exploring the motives of market mavens' initiation of information diffusion. *Journal of Consumer Marketing*, 21 (2): 109–22.

Watson, J.E., Shanahan, D.F., Di Marco, M., Allan, J., Laurance, W.F., Sanderson, E.W. and Venter, O. (2016) Catastrophic declines in wilderness areas undermine global environment targets. *Current Biology*, 26 (21): 2929–34.

Weinstein, A.T. (2021) Business models for the now economy. *Journal of Business Strategy*, *42* (6): 382–91.

Witayangkurn, A., Arai, A. and Shibasaki, R. (2022) Development of big data-analysis pipeline for mobile phone data with Mobipack and spatial enhancement. *ISPRS International Journal of Geo-Information*, *11*: 196.

Woodruff, R.B., Cadotte, E.R. and Jenkins, R.L. (1983) Modelling consumer satisfaction using experience-based norms. *Journal of Marketing Research*, *20*: 296–304.

Yang, L., Jiang, S., Zhang, F. and Zhao, M. (2022) Travel time estimation by learning driving habits and traffic conditions. *Journal of Advanced Transportation*, *2022*: 1308488.

Yang, X., Zheng, L., Lü, D., Wang, J., Wang, S., Su, H., Wang, Z. and Ren, L. (2022) The snake-inspired robots: A review. *Assembly Automation*, *42* (4): 567–83.

Yoo, Y., Boland, R.J. Jr, Lyytinen, K. and Majchrzak, A. (2012) Organizing for innovation in the digitized world. *Organization Science*, *23* (5): 1398–408.

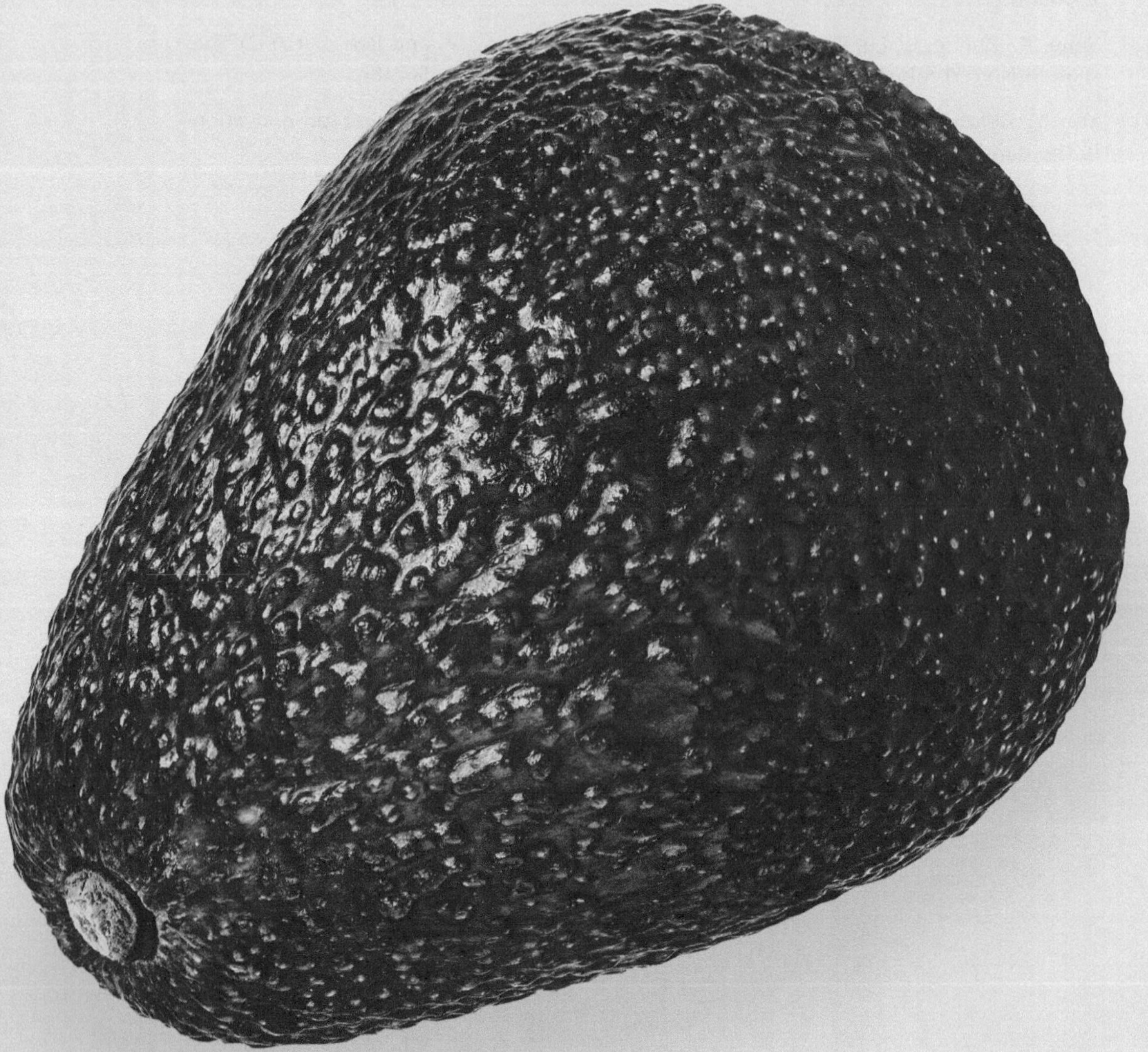

PART TWO

CONSUMERS AS INDIVIDUALS (THE PSYCHOLOGICAL ISSUES)

5	Drive, Motivation and Hedonism	177
6	The Self and Personality	219
7	Perception	255
8	Learning and Knowledge	299
9	Attitude Formation and Change	341

Psychology is the study of human thought processes. Psychologists have made a great many contributions to our understanding of how individual people make consumption decisions, not least in the areas of perception and learning.

Chapter 5 is about the basic urges that make individuals want to change their circumstances. Many of these urges centre around seeking pleasure, so marketers will usually try to make the buying and consuming processes as pleasurable as possible. This holds true even for such mundane, practical products as commercial vehicles and tools. Chapter 6 is specifically about the self and personality – what it is that makes us who we are. These differences between one person's mental make-up and that of another create the differences in choices and choice behaviour which drive marketing. For many people, marketing communication is mainly about establishing the brand in consumers' mental map, so an understanding of perception has a clear importance for them. Chapter 7 therefore looks at perception. For others, marketing's main aim should be to ensure that individual customers have a good experience of the products and come back to buy more – in which case the learning process becomes of great interest. This is the subject matter of Chapter 8. Finally in Part Two, Chapter 9 looks at the ways in which attitudes are formed and changed in individuals. Understanding how people develop their attitudes to brands, and how marketers might seek to change those attitudes, is an obvious area of interest. Equally important is understanding how people's attitudes towards one's brands might be changed by other forces (such as competitors). Maintaining a positive brand attitude is therefore equally important. Psychology always centres around the individual, and marketers would do well to remember that each of us is an individual, with our own particular traits, talents and failings. It is all too common for businessmen and women to refer to 'the consumer' as if all people were the same. Psychologists offer the antidote to this type of thinking.

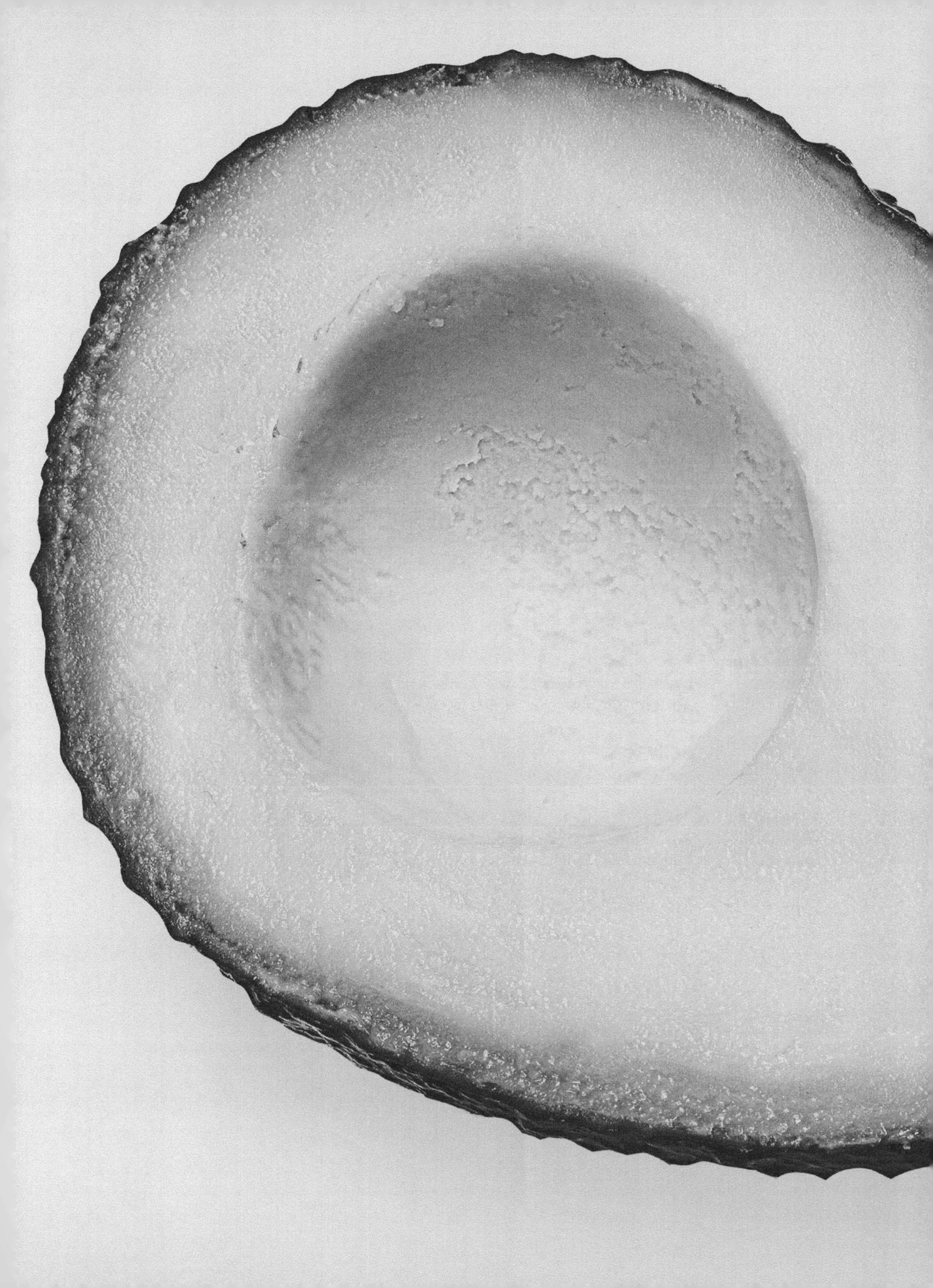

PART ONE CONSUMER BEHAVIOUR IN CONTEXT

Chapter 1 Understanding Consumer Behaviour
Chapter 2 Decisions, Behaviours and Interactions
Chapter 3 Consumption in B2C vs. B2B
Chapter 4 Consumer Technology and Innovation

PART TWO CONSUMERS AS INDIVIDUALS (THE PSYCHOLOGICAL ISSUES)

Chapter 5 Drive, Motivation and Hedonism
Chapter 6 The Self and Personality
Chapter 7 Perception
Chapter 8 Learning and Knowledge
Chapter 9 Attitude Formation and Change

PART THREE CONSUMERS AS SOCIAL ACTORS (THE SOCIOLOGICAL ISSUES)

Chapter 10 Reference Groups
Chapter 11 Age, Gender and Familial Roles
Chapter 12 Culture and Social Mobility
Chapter 13 Ethical Consumption
Chapter 14 Sustainable Consumption

CHAPTER 5

DRIVE, MOTIVATION AND HEDONISM

LEARNING OBJECTIVES

After reading this chapter you should be able to:

- Explain the role of the subconscious in motivation.
- Understand the difference between needs and wants.
- Explain how drives are generated.
- Explain the role of needs and wants in marketing.
- Explain the relationship between motivation and behaviour.
- Critique the concept of hierarchy of need.
- Explain how motivations change with changes in wealth.
- Explain the role of hedonism in purchasing behaviour.

CHAPTER CONTENTS

Introduction
Drive
Motivation
Classifying needs
Motivational factors
Individual factors
Motivational conflict
Goals
Heuristics
Hedonism
Understanding motivation
Research into motivation
Summary
Key points
How to impress your examiner
Review questions
Case study: Experiencing hedonism
Further reading
References

More online: https://study.sagepub.com/sethna5e

INTRODUCTION

Dissatisfaction is the beginning of all behaviour. If we were not dissatisfied, we would simply stick with what we have – there would be no need to change what we do. The gap between where we are now and where we want to be is what drives us to make changes in our lives, and of course this is what makes us change the products we own and the services we consume.

Understanding what motivates people has clear implications for marketers. If we know what drives people to buy particular products and services we are in a much better position to ensure that our products have the features and benefits that people want. If we understand how the pressure to buy develops, we can communicate better with people to show how we can meet their needs (before the need actually arises, in some cases). If we know how people rank their needs, we know when they are likely to be ready to buy our products. Of course, marketing practitioners do not yet have all the answers, so we are a long way from being able to predict consumption behaviour with anything like real accuracy.

Much of what drives us as individuals is the desire for pleasure (Davis and Papies, 2022; Liu, 2018). The activation of our in-built reward circuit triggers the projection of the neurotransmitter 'dopamine' to the nucleus accumbens, with the result that we encounter feelings of pleasure (Niehaus et al., 2009): the neuroscience of the customer experience (Zak, 2022). In the wealthier countries of the world, our basic survival needs have long been taken care of. We no longer simply eat to survive, for example: we eat more than enough simply for pleasure, so that few of us have ever experienced real hunger. The same applies to our housing, our clothing and so forth. We therefore look to satisfy our emotional, aesthetic needs – in other words, we look for things that are pleasurable or fun.

This chapter examines the forces that drive behaviour. Beginning with drive (the basis of all motivation), the chapter goes on to look at different studies of motivation, what role goals play in our lives and the role of hedonism (pleasure-seeking) in consumer behaviour.

DRIVE

Actual state
The condition in which the person happens to be at a given time

Desired state
The condition the individual would like to be in

Drive is the force that makes a person respond to a need. It is an internal stimulus caused by a gap between someone's **actual state** and their **desired state**. In other words, drive is created when the position someone is in at that moment differs from the position they would like to be in. A typical example would be someone becoming thirsty. The actual state is 'thirsty', the desired state is 'not thirsty', so a drive 'to get something to drink' is created.

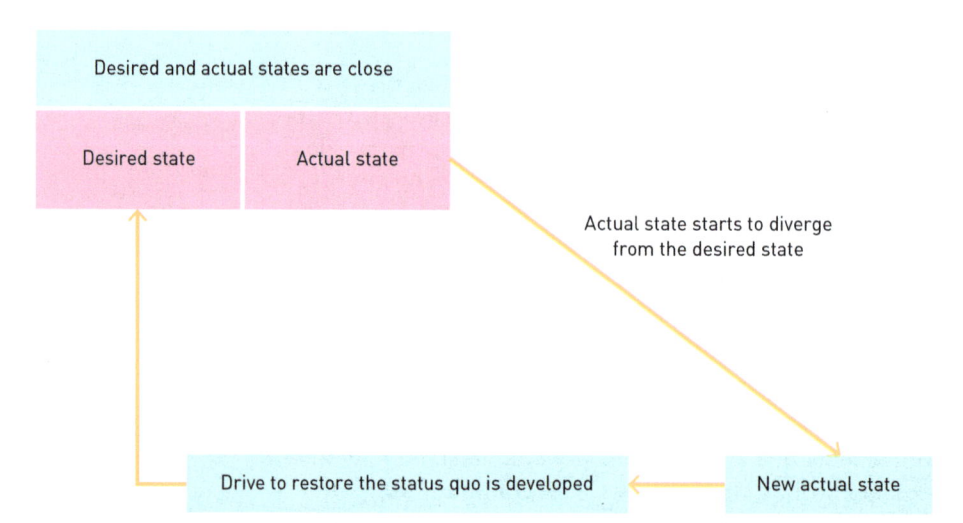

FIGURE 5.1 Creating a drive

As shown in Figure 5.1, the greater the gap between the actual state and the desired state, the greater the drive to do something about it. Once the gap between actual and desired states has closed, the drive disappears: our thirsty person, having had a drink, now no longer feels any pressure to look for a drink. The energy formerly devoted to finding something to drink can now be channelled elsewhere. In some cases, achieving the desired state may lead the individual to raise his or her sights and aim for something even better. For example, a relatively new driver who saves up for years to buy a high-specification BMW may finally buy the car, but immediately start saving for an even more expensive or perhaps more eco-friendly car (like a Tesla). These are what we sometimes refer to as goals, and we'll have a look at these in more depth a little later in this chapter.

Marketers cannot usually do very much about the actual state. We cannot make somebody thirsty, or hungry, or remove their possessions; what we can sometimes do is encourage people to revise their desired state, in other words encourage people to aspire to something new. Most of the effort marketers put into generating drives is directed at changing the desired state, in other words encouraging people to feel that they deserve something better than whatever they currently possess. Marketers can also remind people about their actual or desired states in order to encourage them to move a purchasing decision forward.

If the drive state is at a high level (i.e. the gap between the actual and desired states is large) the individual is more open to the idea of trying a new way of satisfying the need. This is fairly obvious: if a thirsty person finds that his or her favourite brand of soft drink is unavailable in the local shop, there are two choices available. Either the person can buy a different brand, or he or she can go to a different shop. If the person is not feeling especially thirsty, he or she might be prepared to make the trip to the next shop, but if the thirst is very strong the individual will be much more likely to buy a different brand. Most of us tend to overbuy (Parker et al., 2018) when food shopping if we are hungry because our drive level is high, for example.

If the drive state is at a low level, a reminder might stimulate the individual to take action. For example, when driving in Britain, it is common to see signs left by fast food vendors saying 'Teas, Coffees, Sandwiches, Burgers 500 Metres'. These signs are placed at the right distance from the vendor so that passing drivers have time to be reminded that they are getting hungry or thirsty before they pass the vendor.

The fast food vendor is unlikely to have analysed the psychology of drive, but will have found through trial and error that the sign needs to be approximately 500 metres away from the pop-up food stall/van in order to give drivers enough time to think, discuss with a passenger the possible need, and pull over safely. Reminding people that they may have a need is called *activating the need*. Although the motorist is not actively looking for a cup of coffee or a snack, the sign acts as a reminder that a cup of coffee is enjoyable, and helps to strengthen a low-intensity drive by moving the desired state further from the actual state. Motorists whose drive state is at zero (perhaps because they have just had lunch) will simply drive straight past.

CRITICAL REFLECTION

If one scours the web, there are a plethora of pages which showcase marketers telling us about how customer-orientated they are. To hear most of them talk, you would think they are engaged in some kind of charity work – meeting the customers' needs, listening to the customers, helping consumers achieve a lifestyle, and so forth.

Of course we know that they are trying to 'activate' a need.

The question is... is the need there?!? If it isn't, should we really be trying our best to put it there? Should we be messing around with people's drive states, trying to raise them and make them dissatisfied with life? In short, are we in the business of creating a need, then (just by chance) happening to have the solution to hand? Or is this what marketing cynics would call manipulation?

Over 20 years ago, Dame Zarine Kharas started a company called JustGiving and launched the UK's first online fundraising platform (www.justgiving.com) with a simple mission – 'to ensure no great cause goes unfunded'. It's the platform that helped Captain Tom Moore raise an awe inspiring £32.7 million and counting from over 1.5 million supporters at the peak of the coronavirus crisis. JustGiving is clearly a major player and has likely done more for online fundraising than any other organisation. It is a for-profit company owned by Blackbaud, Inc. It boasts 22 million users worldwide. It has all the benefits you'd expect from a big platform, including some great advice and resources to help charities raise more and get the most out of the platform. It has a 4.5 star 'excellent' rating on Trustpilot from 1650 reviews.

© iStock.com/Rawpixel Ltd

To date, the platform has helped people in 164 countries raise over $4 billion for good causes. If that's not creating a need 'to give', what is?

Optimum stimulation level (OSL)
The point at which a need has become strong, but before it has become unpleasantly so

Allowing the drive to become stronger can make the consumption experience more enjoyable. Delayed gratification (Flessert and Beran, 2018; Yanaoka et al., 2022) increases the pleasure of satisfying the need – although it is not always the case that this is worth the wait (Nowlis et al., 2003; Shimoni et al., 2022). Most of us enjoy a meal much more if we are really hungry, and even saving up for a special treat increases the pleasure when the goal is finally attained. Each of us has a level at which the drive provides a pleasant stimulus without being uncomfortable or threatening: this is called the **optimum stimulation level**, or OSL, and was first simultaneously published by both Hebb (1955) and by Leuba (1955) in the psychology literature as a seminal piece. If the drive goes above the OSL, the individual will seek to make an immediate adjustment by satisfying the need. If stimulation falls below the OSL, the individual is likely to allow the drive to strengthen before acting on it. In fact people often enjoy the anticipation more than they do the actual consumption (Chen et al., 2020; Raghunathan and Mukherji, 2003).

OSL is subjective, that is to say it varies from one individual to another. Research has shown that people with high OSLs like novelty and risk-taking, whereas those with low OSLs prefer the tried and tested. People with high OSLs also tend to be younger (Hahn and Popan, 2020; Raju, 1980).

Drive acts as the basic component for motivation: motivation is drive directed at a specific objective. If we consider drive as a general feeling that things are not as they should be, we can see that motivation is a drive that has crystallised into a definite decision to do something about the problem. Marketers are able to help people (or direct people) towards specific ways of satisfying the drive by giving them a specific solution which they might be motivated to adopt.

MOTIVATION

Motives can be classified according to the list shown in Table 5.1. Although it is difficult to separate out people's motivations for making a particular purchase, emotional and dormant motives often take precedence over rational and conscious motives.

Motives should be distinguished from instincts, which are automatic responses to external stimuli. A motive is simply a reason for carrying out a particular behaviour; instincts are pre-programmed responses that are inborn in the individual, and are involuntary. Although behaviour may result from an instinctive source (for example, ducking when a helicopter suddenly appears to fly out of a 3D cinema screen), virtually all consumer behaviour is non-instinctive, or **volitional**.

Volition
(or will) The cognitive process by which an individual decides on and commits to a particular course of action

Figure 5.2 shows the dimensions of motives. Motives can be classified across three dimensions, with the rational/conscious/primary ends relating to each other, as do the dormant/emotional/secondary ends. Any given motivation can be placed within the three-dimensional space represented by the diagram.

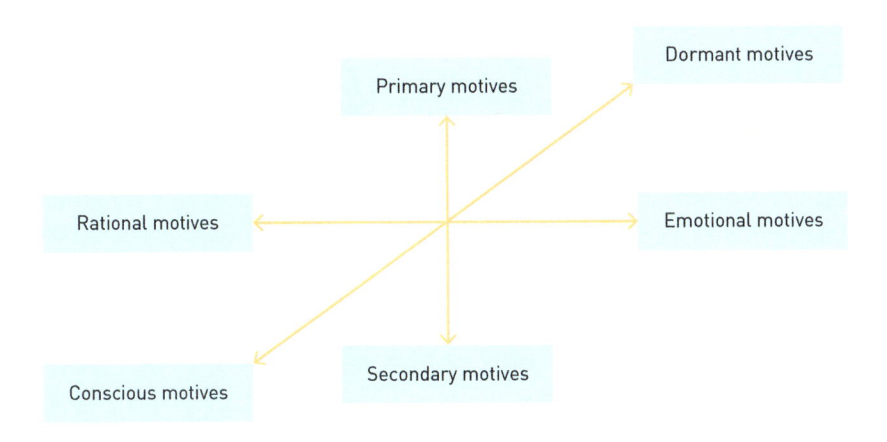

FIGURE 5.2 Dimensions of motives

Need
A perceived lack of something

Want
A specific satisfier for a need

CLASSIFYING NEEDS

There have been many psychological studies of motivation, and several that have focused on consumer behaviour issues. Needs are the basis of all motivation, so it may be worth remembering that needs are a perceived lack of something, whereas wants are specific satisfiers. In order for someone to recognise a need, the individual should not only be without something, but should also perceive this as something that would make life more pleasant or convenient. Unless the individual understands how the proposed product will make a positive difference to his or her lifestyle, the product will not be perceived as filling a need and the individual will not want it.

TABLE 5.1 Classification of consumer motives

Primary motives	The reasons that lead to the purchase of a product class. For example, an individual might look for a new (or newer) car to replace one that is becoming old, unreliable and perhaps too eco-unfriendly
Secondary motives	These are the reasons behind buying a particular brand. Our prospective car buyer might have reasons for buying a Volkswagen rather than a Mitsubishi, or a Tesla rather than a Mercedes
Rational motives	These motives are based on reasoning, or a logical assessment of the person's current situation. The car purchaser may need a car that will carry three children and a large amount of camping equipment, for example an SUV (sports utility vehicle), or one that is a hybrid (thus able to run on petrol and electricity and therefore save money)
Emotional motives	Motives having to do with feelings about the brand. Sometimes emotions get the better of us – our prospective car buyer may end up with a sports car, despite having three children and a tent to accommodate
Conscious motives	These are the motives of which we are aware. Because our car buyer knows they need a new car, this element of their motivation is conscious
Dormant motives	These motives operate below the conscious level. The car buyer's desire to buy a sports car may be linked to their approaching middle age, but they may not be aware of this!

CRITICAL REFLECTION

Humankind has provided us with many an example of 'perceiving a need'.

Take for example the Yamana tribe from Tierra del Fuego, which lies at the southernmost tip of South America. The region is buffeted by gales from the Antarctic, and is so far south that much of the land is covered in snow throughout the harsh winters. It is inhabited largely by penguins, and by a small number of hardy farmers who use the short summers to grow their crops, and then do whatever it takes to survive the winter.

The Yamana tribe inhabited this harsh country for thousands of years, but lacked something that most cold-country people discovered very early on: clothes. The Yamana never invented or discovered clothing, apart from tiny loincloths and a few strips of cloth worn for decorative purposes. They spent their days canoeing in the icy waters, hunting penguins (which formed a large part of their diet) and fishing. They had, however, discovered the ability to light a fire, so when the weather got really bad they would cluster round large bonfires to keep warm. It was the light of these fires that caused the early European explorers to call the country Land of Fire – Tierra del Fuego. There is some evidence that the Yamana underwent a biological adaptation to the conditions. European explorers (including Captain Cook) reported that Yamana tribespeople would often be sweating in conditions which the Europeans found cold even when fully dressed in winter clothing. For thousands of years the Yamana had felt no need whatsoever for clothes. Standing around their fires and cooking penguins in the winter, they had perfectly comfortable and happy conditions for living: although this may seem strange to us, their early contacts with Europeans must have seemed even stranger to them. Once the concept of clothing was explained, they suddenly recognised the need for it, and when the last pure-blooded Yamana died in the late 1990s they were certainly fully clothed and indistinguishable from any other Argentinians. Their traditional way of life, however, represented an extreme example of not recognising something as a need until a solution is presented.

There have been many attempts on the part of psychologists to develop lists of needs. It is worth looking at one of the earliest of such lists which was developed by Murray (1938), who listed 20 separate need categories. The list included categories such as: succourance, nurturance, sentience, deference, abasement, defendence, infavoidance, harmavoidance, achievement, counteraction, dominance, aggression, affiliation, autonomy, order, rejection, sex, understanding, exhibition and play. Murray developed this list from his extensive clinical experience rather than from a programme of organised research, so much of the evidence for the list is anecdotal. This said, virtually all these needs have consumer behaviour and thus marketing implications. The need for rejection is used by brand owners when they exhort consumers to reject own-label products, and the need for nurturance is emphasised in advertisements for cold cures and soup. The need for sentience is met by documentary cable stations such as the Discovery Channel and the History Channel. Murray's list is long, and by no means definitive, and some needs on the list conflict with each other, for example dominance and deference.

BRAND EXPERIENCES: VOIP SUPERPOWERS

Nextiva is a unique brand that oozes personality, despite being in one of the most boring and unsexiest industries out there – VoIP. VoIP is an acronym for 'voice over internet protocol' and is a technology that allows you to make and receive phone calls and video calls over the internet instead of landlines.

Most people consider VoIP the alternative to the local telephone company. If you have an internet connection, you can call anyone without the need for a traditional, local phone service or physical copper wires. All you need is high-speed internet and a VoIP service provider to handle the calls.

According to Future Market Insights (2022), the global mobile VoIP market size was worth $127 billion in 2022 and is expected to reach an eye-watering $255 billion by 2032.

There you go – now that I have your attention…

(Continued)

Nextiva does a cool job branding themselves as a commercial phone system with superpowers. Based out of sunny Scottsdale, Arizona, they've made an interesting use of branded hashtags, #AmazingService and #TeamNextiva, as a branding element. Nextiva also emphasises their positive company culture all over their landing pages as social proof. This is backed by their recognition from Glassdoor, being named one of the Top 100 Tech Companies to Work For in 2020. Other statistics include over a billion calls on their network, 100,000+ happy customers and 1000+ global employees. Nextiva also invests significantly into YouTube, often supporting industry recognition and achievements with brand videos to complement their marketing efforts.

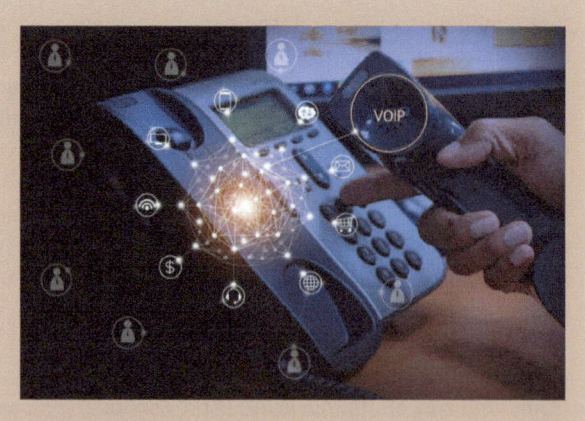

© iStock.com/EduLeite

It is because human beings are complex creatures with strong social bonds and we tend to have a broader range of needs than animals that we also have many needs that go beyond mere survival. Some commentators divide needs into primary needs, which are concerned with biological functions and survival, and secondary needs, which are concerned with everything else. In some cases, researchers have concentrated heavily on the idea that most needs are biologically determined. Internal genetic stimuli are driven by homeostasis, which is the tendency for any living entity to try to maintain a state of equilibrium: in the natural world, change is death. The drives that maintain homeostasis are involuntary, as is the behaviour that results from it. If one becomes too hot, for example, one begins sweating, and if one becomes too cold one develops goosepimples and may even begin shivering. A sudden shock will result in adrenaline entering the bloodstream, which may be exciting (a positive outcome, which is often generated by white-knuckle rides at theme parks) or may be merely frightening (a negative outcome, which may be generated by a near-accident or a threatening situation such as a street robbery).

Hunger and thirst are obviously biologically generated, but most eating and drinking happens as a result of social or aesthetic demands. Socially motivated eating might include dinner parties, meeting friends for a meal, business lunches and picnics. Curiosity is often supposed to be socially generated, and there is certainly evidence that exploration of the world has a connection with particular countries and cultures, but we also know that some curiosity is biological. Most carnivorous animals display an innate tendency to explore and investigate their environment: cats, dogs and humans all display this behaviour, and bears in zoos are generally happier if their food is hidden from them so that they have to explore and find it.

The best-known biological motivator is, of course, sex (Riley et al., 2018). Marketers have used sexual imagery in advertising throughout its history (Bailey et al., 2021), and at various times there have been advertisements that have over-stepped the boundaries of good taste and have been attacked or withdrawn. There is certainly evidence that Valentine's day gift-giving (Givi, 2021; Yang and Urminsky, 2018) is also associated with power relationships between the genders (Cruz Passos et al., 2020; Rugimbana et al., 2003).

Thrill-seeking

Experience-seeking

Risk decreases – the quiet life

Stimulation increases – the thrill-a-minute life

Disinhibition

Boredom

FIGURE 5.3 Zuckerman's Hierarchy of Stimulation

The arousal theory of motivation (Zuckerman, 2000) proposes that people need to be aroused if they are to become motivated (see Figure 5.3). People seek to maintain an optimum level of arousal: too little and they become bored, too much and they become stressed. Zuckerman developed a 'hierarchy' of stimulation, as follows:

1. *Thrill-seeking.* Through extreme sports, or adventure travel – the highest level of arousal.
2. *Experience-seeking.* Through travel, walking, the arts, books – the second highest level.
3. **Disinhibition** (removing the internal inhibitors that control behaviour). Social stimulation, parties, drinking alcohol, etc.
4. *Boredom.* The need to change things around, perhaps to buy new products, try new things, etc.

At the lowest end of the hierarchy – boredom – the individual has a risk-free but also stimulation-free existence: at the highest level – thrill-seeking – the individual has an exciting but dangerous life. Most people establish a balance between the quiet life and the stimulating life, at some point on the continuum which is specific to them.

The best-known motivation theory is probably Maslow's Hierarchy of Needs (Maslow, 1954) (see Figure 5.4), which sought to show that people are motivated to fulfil different needs in a specific order, beginning with survival needs (as the most pressing needs to satisfy) and ending with **self-actualisation** needs (the need to fulfil a long-held ambition, or to act independently of the pressures and opinions of other people, or to act for action's sake). The reasoning behind the model is that needs cannot always be met all at once. Sometimes one need must be fulfilled at the expense of another, creating motivational conflict.

Disinhibition
Removal of the internal inhibitors that constrain behaviour

Self-actualisation
The need to become the ideal self

At the lowest level of the hierarchy – *survival needs* – marketers offer houses, clothes and food. However, in most cases these are not sold as survival items – more commonly the marketing communications emphasise other aspects of the products such as their location, style and flavour. Relatively few products are offered purely on the basis of survival, and most of these are in the category of safety equipment for sports such as those that involve either air or water.

```
                    Self-
                 actualisation

                Aesthetic needs

                Cognitive needs

                 Esteem needs

                Belonging needs

                Security needs

                Survival needs
```

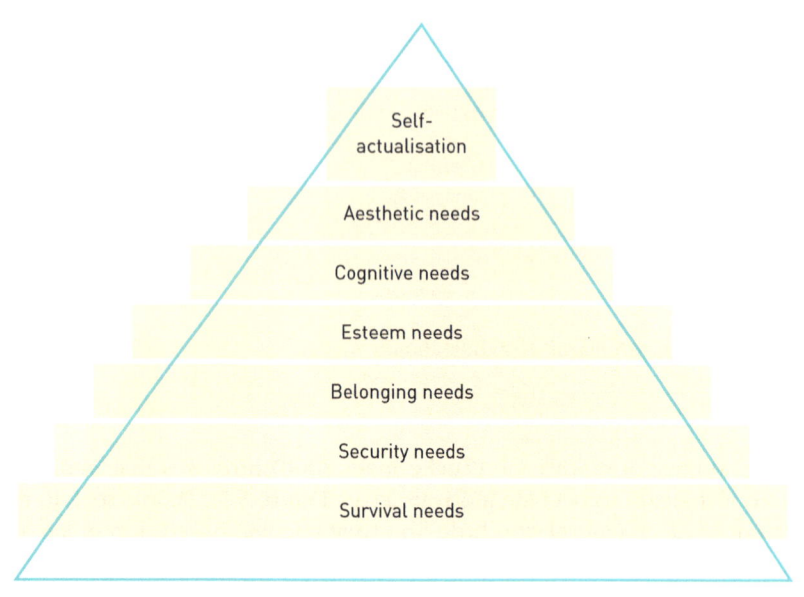

FIGURE 5.4   Maslow's Hierarchy of Needs

At the security level, people buy products such as insurance policies, savings plans, burglar alarms and car breakdown memberships. In recent years, we have developed new safety needs: we need to secure our computers and our data against fraudsters and malicious viruses, and we need to be careful about our personal information on social networking sites. This has led to the development of whole new industries, developing software to combat such dangers. People also spend money safeguarding their health, hence the huge sales of products designed to help people lose weight or give up smoking. The popularity of such products in the period immediately following the New Year celebrations indicates the degree to which people believe they should safeguard their health.

At the belonging level, we know attitudes towards 'belonging' have been changing over the past 60 years since Maslow first introduced his hierarchy. Social identity used to be measured using markers such as social class, religion, geographic location, income, etc., but as society has progressed and the standard of living has risen in most parts of the world (as compared to 60 years previously) people now belong to many offline and online groups and communities. People can thus align themselves to a wide variety of brands and lifestyles, which then enables them to indulge in buying a wide range of products: fashion clothing, club memberships, sports equipment and so forth. In order to be accepted as a member of a professional concierge service (www.innerplace.co.uk) that offers privileged access to the finest nightlife and entertainment in London, members not only need to pay their membership fees, they also need to know about the right venue – the service is aimed at 'like-minded urban socialites, who are well dressed, well heeled, well behaved and who know what they want'. Belonging needs are therefore of considerable interest to marketers.

Esteem needs include anything that someone buys as a status symbol. Products that make a statement about oneself include technological gadgetry, fashion, cars, expensive hobbies such as sailing, and exclusive sports such as polo. Almost any product might have an esteem value in the right quarters, and there are even circumstances in which a lack of consumption generates esteem – backpackers may have more respect for someone who has managed to cross Asia for less money than anyone else, for example. Esteem needs may also play a part in seemingly altruistic behaviour – people who buy *The Big Issue* (the UK magazine devoted to helping homeless people) do so not so much for the actual magazine content, but because there is a dimension of helping others in the purchase (Hetherington, 2018; Hibbert et al., 2005). This may be coupled to the fact that the magazine is a visible purchase helping a tangible individual, whereas with a contribution to a charity the individual beneficiary is usually not seen.

Aesthetic needs can be met in many ways. In the main, such needs are traditionally associated with the arts: paintings, sculptures, books, theatre, film and music being the main ways aesthetic needs have been met. However, a hiking holiday in an area of outstanding natural beauty is also a way of meeting aesthetic needs, as is a microlight aircraft or a yacht.

At the self-actualisation level, needs might be fulfilled in a great many ways. This is all about a person's ability to realise their own personal potential and growth, self-fulfilment in life and peak experiences (Maslow, 1943). In the 21st century – as part of the consumerist world that we live in – in some cases self-actualisation needs are met by actually reducing consumption, for example if the individual decides that a 'green' lifestyle should be adopted (Rusciano et al., 2018). Someone who has worked in a city for many years might, for example, buy a smallholding in the country and grow his or her own food, use solar power for electricity and run a wood-burning stove for heat. In other cases, it may be about pushing oneself to the absolute limit of physical and mental endurance – the peak experiences. Self-actualisation might include the concept of freedom: the ability to make choices as a consumer is an expression of freedom, and is derived in part from having the necessary wealth to buy whatever one wants or needs, and in part from a lack of legal restrictions on purchases (Mick and Humphreys, 2008). Of course it could also be said that although famous artists such as Van Gogh lived a life of poverty, they had arguably reached a point of self-actualisation through their creative work.

CRITICAL REFLECTION

Humans are born with a fear of falling, yet we often go to theme parks and fun fairs, and some of us indulge in 'extreme sports' such as cave diving, ice climbing, cliff jumping and bungee jumping. Falling off a bridge with lengths of elastic round your

(Continued)

> ankles is certainly thrilling, in that it gives you a huge adrenaline rush. But if we like to be thrilled by such things, why isn't it fun if someone pushes (forces) you into a situation?
>
> Of course the context and the situation have a lot to do with your reaction. If your friend playfully pushes you into a swimming pool, the normal response would be to laugh – but if a complete stranger did it, you'd probably not find it funny at all.
>
> So where do we draw the line? How do we decide what is fun, and what is frightening? When do we stop being frightened and 'enjoy' the thrill of jumping off a tower with a bungee strapped to our body? Why do we put our lives in danger (threatening our survival needs), whether it be giving up our well-paid jobs in favour of devoting our time and energy to a social enterprise or jumping off a cliff for a thrill – just for esteem or self-actualisation needs?

Maslow's hierarchy has been widely criticised for being too simplistic, and for ignoring the many exceptions that can easily be seen in everyday life. For example, an artist starving in a garret is clearly placing aesthetic or self-actualisation needs ahead of survival needs, and someone who gives up a good career in order to work with poor people in developing countries is giving up security in favour of esteem or self-actualisation needs. Such anomalies are commonplace. Another criticism of the hierarchy is that it is largely irrelevant to the vast majority of people in the wealthy countries of Europe and North America because they already have their survival and security needs taken care of, and indeed many of them are operating at the self-actualisation level already (Blythe and Hassenzahl, 2018; McNulty, 1985).

A further criticism is that an individual may move to different parts of the hierarchy even within a single day: for example, being primarily concerned with esteem needs during the working day, with aesthetic needs when enjoying an evening meal at a good restaurant, and with belonging needs when meeting friends for a drink afterwards.

One final criticism here comes from McLeod (2007), who highlighted that Maslow had tested the self-actualisation level with a sample of 18 white male subjects whom he believed displayed the characteristic qualities. This would cause considerable bias in the data sample, testing and collection.

These criticisms notwithstanding, Maslow's model is widely taught and widely referred to: there is little doubt that the needs themselves exist and can be categorised in this way, but whether they truly operate as a hierarchy is open to question. There may be evidence that the hierarchy operates for large groups of people, so that there will be a prevailing social paradigm in which some needs are brought to the forefront. Research by McNulty (1985) showed that an increasing number of people in the UK were operating at the self-actualisation level, presumably as a result of rising living standards. In the intervening 30 years or so, it would appear to the casual observer that this trend has not reversed, and has (if anything) accelerated. A five-year (2005–2010) longitudinal survey was conducted by Tay and Diener (2011), who tested Maslow's theory by analysing the data of 60,865 participants from 123 countries, representing every major region of the world. Their results showed that the existence of universal human needs regardless of cultural differences is very much a fact. However, the results also showed that ordering of the needs within the hierarchy was not necessarily correct in the way that was being displayed by the respondents of the survey. A variation of Maslow's hierarchy has been the VALS (values, attitudes and lifestyles) model (Mitchell, 1983), which describes nine different lifestyles and segments consumers accordingly, as shown in Figure 5.5.

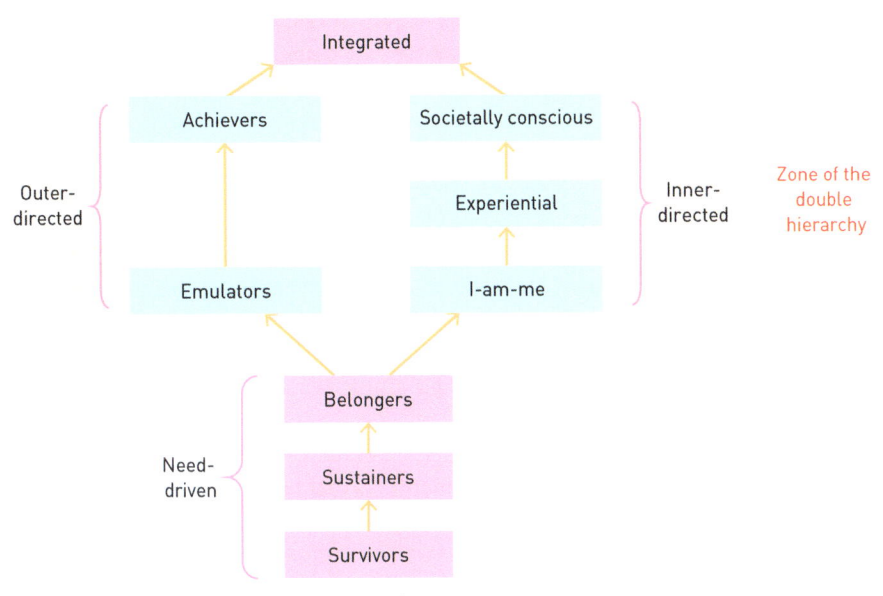

FIGURE 5.5 The values and lifestyles (VALS) model

The model by Arnold Mitchell was developed using data from a sample of over 1600 Americans and their partners who were asked about their primary motivation (the horizontal dimension) and the resources available to them (the vertical dimension). Here, we see segmentation based on the degree to which people innovatively use their resources such as previous education, income, self-confidence and leadership skills. They were also asked about how much they were driven by their knowledge, principles, ideals, achievements and their desire for social and physical activities. The model supposes that people at the lower levels (which correspond with Maslow's survival and security needs) are controlled by their basic needs for food, shelter and a measure of security. After these very basic needs have been met, there is a divergence: some people become inner-directed (driven by internal motives) while others become outer-directed (motivated by the opinions of others). Inner-directed people may become selfish and uncaring of other people's well-being, they may become interested in new experiences or they may fulfil a burning ambition to change the world for the better despite opposition. Outer-directed people may seek to copy other people whom they regard as successful, or may seek to impress other people by achieving or by conspicuous consumption. Finally, Mitchell postulates that people may adopt an integrated position, where concern and respect for others are combined with knowledge of their own needs and desires.

Mitchell's model has been used for market segmentation purposes, and the lifestyle types have been identified both in the USA and in Europe. As wealth increases, more people operate at the higher levels: we might reasonably expect that, as countries become wealthier, levels of consumption increase but so do levels of social concern, and levels of crime increase as more people become inner-directed.

CRITICAL REFLECTION

'I'm old enough and ugly enough not to care what other people think of me or say about me' is a statement often made by some older people in response to others' motivations and attitudes towards their purchases. Mitchell's categorisations are all very well for segmentation, but what happens when we are dealing with people at the self-actualisation level? By definition, these people might do *anything*! They are professional individualists.

Also, how clear are the boundaries? To say that someone is outer-directed means that they care about the opinions of other people – but do they care about the opinions of everyone else, or just a few people? Are they attracted to or repelled by the opinions of the other people in question? Then of course there is the significant question of how different family structures affect the categorisations. Do different family structures hold differing knowledge, principles and ideals? How does their desire (or lack of it) for social and physical activities mould their attitudes towards being either inner- or outer-directed?

Finally, if someone acts rebelliously, is this because they don't care what other people think – or because they care very deeply? Is that feeling age-dependent? Being a rebel is a statement made to impress other people, is it not?

The basic issue here is that people consistently refuse to be categorised!

MOTIVATIONAL FACTORS

An alternative approach to considering motivation was that advanced by Herzberg (1966). Herzberg was a medical researcher who developed the idea that some factors in life are motivational, while others are simply expected as a matter of course: the absence of these factors would be demotivating, but more of the same would not be motivational. Herzberg called the first group of factors motivators, and the second group **hygiene factors** (he was a medical researcher, remember). The hygiene factors needed to be present in order to prevent the 'disease' of demotivation. Herzberg's findings were considered revolutionary at the time of their publication because he claimed that salary is not a motivator – people expect a fair rate of pay for the work they are expected to do, so it is a hygiene factor, and only affects motivation if it is seen to be unfair in some way. For marketers, Herzberg's work is interesting in that it explains product **differentiation**. For example, anyone buying a car expects that it will have wheels, an engine, an enclosed space to sit in and space for luggage. Nowadays, people would expect it to have air conditioning, digital radio and USB connections as standard as well. These are hygiene factors, the basic core product features that any car would have. Lack of any of these would demotivate the customer. To generate motivation to buy, though, the vehicle manufacturer would need to add features as motivators: a WiFi-hub, smarter upholstery, alloy wheels, parking sensors, etc.

Hygiene factors
Those aspects of a product which consumers would expect as a basic feature of any product in the category

Differentiation
Providing a product with features that distinguish it from competing products

CONSUMER BEHAVIOUR IN ACTION: FLYING CARS

Let's start with a question. If you were designing a car for a major motor manufacturer, what would be the standard *must haves* and what would you put on the *optional extras list*? How would you differentiate your product to motivate customers to buy?

It's worth noting, perhaps, how far we've actually driven (*pardon the pun*) in the automobile space. The history of the automobile has been one of continuous adaptation, additional features and added inducements to buy. The basic need is for transportation: ever since the first human being jumped on the back of a horse we have wanted to travel further, faster and more comfortably, and although the earliest cars were less reliable (and sometimes slower) than horses, they at least had the convenience of starting fairly quickly (without the need for saddling and bridling) and of going pretty much where the driver wanted them to go rather than setting off into a field with the other horses.

Starting with Daimler and Benz's first practical automobile in 1885, manufacturers have added optional extras on a regular basis ever since. For example, in 1890 Canadian Thomas Ahearn invented the car heater. In 1901 disc brakes were added (invented by Lanchester). In 1911 Charles Kettering invented the starter motor, which eliminated the need for hand cranking the engine to start it (Kettering also invented Freon, the gas that has been identified as a major cause of holes in the ozone layer). In 1929 Paul Galvin invented the car radio, although it had to be bought as an optional extra: car manufacturers did not fit radios as standard until the 1970s. Galvin called his new radio the Motorola. Daimler introduced electric windows in 1948, and in 1966 British engineers developed electronic fuel injection. Not all the inventors were men, incidentally. Mary Anderson invented windscreen wipers (hand-operated at first), and Helen Blair Bartlett, a geologist, invented alumina ceramic insulators for sparkplugs in 1930.

Why all this innovation? Simple. Any car manufacturer could meet the basic hygiene factor of transportation. In order to motivate people to buy a specific model, manufacturers had to add extras, making the car more comfortable, safer, more reliable or more fun than the competitors' vehicles.

But have our requirements changed? Do we all crave state-of-the-art satellite navigation, radar-controlled cruise control, intelligent braking systems with ceramic brake pads and nitrogen-filled tyres? Do we in the 21st century now yearn for the flying car? Every so often someone will go back to basics and produce a car with 'no frills' for a low price, but the optional extras soon cease to be optional because price is not a good motivator – it is a hygiene factor!

Oh and by the way, in March 2022, AeroMobil did in fact announce the world's first four-seater flying car; more than a supercar and a light aircraft combined, it is a new species of vehicle which will start deliveries in 2024. AeroMobil's vehicles are the culmination of leading-edge automotive and aerospace design and engineering, advanced materials, luxury features and sophisticated styling. AeroMobil's vehicles are supercars that fly, light aircraft you can drive, transforming between modes in less than three minutes. These exceptional vehicles are the result of over ten years of research and development by an outstanding team of engineers and designers. Their pedigree includes luxury and supercar makers BMW, Aston Martin, McLaren, Mercedes Benz and Ferrari, and aerospace leaders Lockheed Martin, Rolls-Royce, Airbus and Diamond Aircraft, among others.

As a way of categorising needs, Herzberg's theory is undoubtedly useful, but part of the problem in applying the theory is that people have differing views on what should be a hygiene factor. Once again, it is difficult to make generalisations about people because we all have different priorities. (Herzberg's theories have also been applied to personnel management, but that is outside the scope of this book.)

In Figure 5.6, the motivation line rises as the individual recognises that the hygiene factors are improving, but this is really a reduction in demotivation. Motivation as such does not start until the motivators begin to arrive, but even so there is no sharp rise until the motivators go beyond expectations. At this point, further increases in hygiene factors have no real effect.

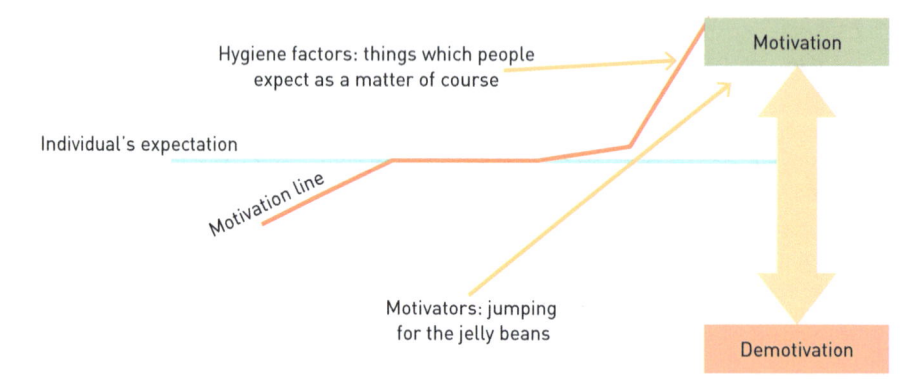

FIGURE 5.6 Dual-factor theory

INDIVIDUAL FACTORS

A third approach to analysing motivation is Vroom's Expectancy Theory (Vroom, 1999). Vroom suggested that motivation is the result of rational calculations made by individuals, taking into account the value of the reward itself, the expected likelihood of being able to obtain the reward and the effort needed to achieve the reward. The trade-offs between these factors are the subject of the calculation, and if the reward is not adequate compared to the effort needed to win it, the individual will simply not bother to try for it. Equally, if the likelihood of gaining the reward is perceived as being small, the individual will not be motivated to try. Vroom's theory has much to offer – it is more comprehensive in its approach than other theories, and it takes much greater account of individual differences than do either Maslow's or Herzberg's models. As we have seen already, individuals may believe that aesthetic needs are more important than survival needs, and (in terms of Herzberg) individuals may have different ideas of what constitute motivators and hygiene factors. Recently, however, Vroom's theory has been modified to include a fourth dimension (in addition to the existing three of Expectancy, Instrumentality and Valence has been added Social Context [Lloyd and Mertens, 2018]).

David McClelland suggested that people have three categories (Figure 5.7) of social need in terms of motivation: *achievement* (the need to excel at something), *affiliation* (the need to be part of a group) and *power* (the ability to control outcomes).

Different people place different levels of emphasis on these needs, but people who are achievers need constant feedback and praise, people who have a high need for affiliation will tend to want to fit in with their immediate social group, and people who seek power will try to dominate those around them (McClelland, 1955). McClelland's work has mainly been used in human resources management, but there are implications for consumer behaviour as well: a person with a high need for affiliation will buy things that make them popular and respected, a person with a high need for power will want to be in control of spending and so forth.

FIGURE 5.7 Emphases on power, affiliation and achievement

An aspect of motivation that is not considered in either of the above models is the idea of pain avoidance. Although needs are the basis of all motivation, there is a difference between the need to avoid bad consequences and the need to acquire a benefit. In most cases, someone who wishes to obtain a positive benefit from a purchase has only one way to obtain the benefits, whereas there are many ways to avoid a negative outcome. This was demonstrated by Skinner in his famous **experiments** with rats, in which rats were taught to push buttons in complex sequences in order to obtain food and avoid electric shocks; the rats became very inventive in the ways they avoided the shocks, but were unable to find any other way to obtain food (Skinner, 1953). Human beings are, of course, not rats: we are probably better able to understand the longer-term consequences of our behaviour than a rat would be (although some of us don't always take heed!), so we may be more susceptible to pain-avoidance messages. On the other hand, we may be even more inventive in avoiding the pain.

Experiment
A controlled activity in which a given stimulus is offered to respondents in order to discover their reactions

For example, **cautionary tale** advertising in which the negative consequences of an action are shown may result in someone behaving in the desired manner, or it may (and perhaps is more likely to) result in the individual avoiding the advertisement. This may be part of the reason why government campaigns against smoking or drinking often fail – shocking people by telling them about the diseases their habit might cause simply results in people not reading the warnings, unless of course the government passes legislation against such practices, thus making it illegal (e.g. the UK Parliament approved regulations to make smoking in cars carrying children illegal in 2015, and failure to comply can result in a £50 fixed penalty notice).

Cautionary tale
A story intended to illustrate the possible negative outcomes of a particular course of action

One way in which marketers can use pain avoidance in motivating consumers is by **modelling** (we talk more about this in Chapter 10). This is a process whereby people are shown the negative consequences of a given action through an actor who demonstrates the behaviour and suffers the consequences. For example, an advertisement might show a commuter who has been prosecuted for fare dodging, complete with a detailed account of the consequences of the action ('It was the embarrassment of having to stand up in court and admit fiddling a £5 fare. And I lost my job, because I now have a criminal conviction'). Another example might be a housewife who 'can't shift those greasy stains'. In each case the consumer is invited to see the potential negative consequences of fiddling the fare, or using the

Modelling
The act of demonstrating by example behaviour that the marketer would like the target audience to imitate

wrong washing powder. Modelling can also be used for positive reinforcement, of course (see Table 5.2), for example the advertisement about the regular man on the street who saved a fortune in car insurance payments by using the online portal 'moneysupermarket.com'.

Models should be as similar as possible to the target audience in order to promote the maximum amount of 'affiliation', but at the same time need to be seen as attractive; this may appear to be a contradiction in some cases, but models show us ourselves as we wish we were, rather than as we actually are.

For human beings, and especially human beings living in the developed and wealthier countries of the world, most physical needs have been met long ago. We are therefore driven much more by social, aesthetic or psychological needs than by physical needs. This manifests itself most clearly in our eating habits. We eat for pleasure (the flavour and texture of the food), for social purposes (going for a meal with friends, sharing a snack, going to a dinner party) and even as a means of self-expression (cooking a special meal for friends or family). These needs sometimes override our need to live a healthy lifestyle: we become obese or develop hardening of the arteries, bad teeth and many other diseases caused by eating the wrong things. This is especially the case in some developing economies where childhood obesity is reaching epidemic proportions (Khan et al., 2022; Lin et al., 2022; Midha et al., 2012), as well as in developed economies such as America (Santos et al., 2022; Taylor, 2018).

TABLE 5.2 Using modelling for positive reinforcement

Modelling employed	Desired response
Instructor, expert, salesperson using the product (in an advertisement or at the point of purchase)	Use product in the correct, technically competent way
Models in advertisements asking questions at the point of purchase (whether that is online, e-mobile or in-store)	Ask questions at the point of purchase that highlight product advantages
Models in advertisements receiving positive reinforcement or punishment for performing undesired behaviours	Extinction or decrease of undesired behaviours
Individual (or group) similar to the target audience using the product in a novel, enjoyable way	Use the product in new ways

Source: Adapted from Nord and Peter (1980). Reprinted with permission from *Journal of Marketing*, published by the American Marketing Association.

MOTIVATIONAL CONFLICT

When *needs* conflict, motivational conflict occurs. This can take one of three basic forms:

1. *Approach–approach conflict*. This happens when the individual is faced with two or more desirable alternatives. For example, the person might have been invited to a friend's weekend-away party when his or her football team is playing in the final, 300 miles away. Approach–approach conflicts are common, since most people have limited financial resources and often have to choose between spending money on one item, or spending it on a different item.

2. *Avoidance–avoidance conflict.* This occurs when the individual is faced with two or more equally unappealing choices. For example, someone might be faced with the choice of either buying new shoes to replace an old, comfortable pair, or continuing to wear the old pair despite the fact they are now letting in water and coming apart at the seams.

3. *Approach–avoidance conflict.* This occurs when the course of action has both positive and negative consequences. For example, some drugs have dangerous side effects. Most purchases have an element of approach–avoidance conflict since they involve spending money or giving up something else: many purchases of new products involve a **switching cost**, that is, the effort and sometimes cash expenditure involved in moving from the old product to the new one.

Switching costs
All the costs associated with changing from one particular product or service to another

The relationship between these motivational conflicts is shown in Figure 5.8.

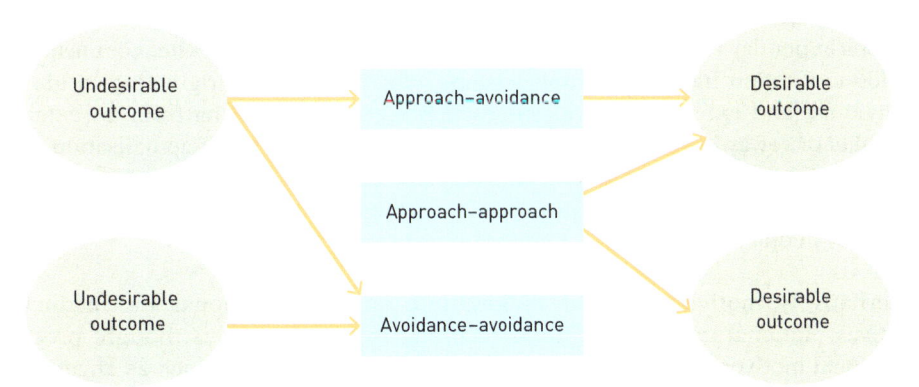

FIGURE 5.8 Motivation conflict

In many cases, the situation is far more complex than a simple dichotomy. This is because we are usually faced with several possible courses of action, each of which has both positive and negative consequences. If the motivational conflict is to be resolved, the individual needs to prioritise his or her needs. This is largely a matter for the individual concerned: even though Maslow tried to produce a general model for this, we have already seen that the model is far from perfect.

The intensity of the motivation is sometimes strong enough to override all other considerations, whereas at other times it may be much weaker. Sometimes motivational intensity is high due to a high level of drive (a 13-year-old who is being teased at school for wearing the wrong brand of trainers will be highly motivated to obtain the right and more acceptable brand, for example), and sometimes motivational intensity is high due to personal involvement with the product category. Involvement means that the individual places a high importance on having exactly the right product; for example, a pilot would place great importance on obtaining exactly the right spares, fuel and oil for the aircraft, since this affects the safety of the plane (and, of course, the pilot). Similarly, a musician might be very concerned to obtain the right instrument; an academic would be concerned to use the correct and most relevant resources (Delves Broughton, 2017), etc. Having to put some effort into the consumption experience will often increase the satisfaction the consumer has with the product – this is obviously the case with sports equipment, but may even be the case for such mundane items as self-assembly furniture (Wadhwa and Trudel, 2010). Each of us has at least some products with which we are highly involved.

From the viewpoint of marketing, generating involvement is clearly crucial to establishing loyal customers. The greater the involvement, the greater the degree to which consumers make an effort to satisfy the need, and the greater the propensity to remain loyal in future. In some cases, firms are able to run loyalty programmes to keep customers involved: supermarket loyalty cards and airline frequent flyer programmes are the usual examples. In other cases involvement is generated by the way the products are promoted, or by celebrity endorsement.

Motivations can be divided into positive and negative. People may act to obtain a reward, or may act to avoid an unwanted outcome. For example, someone may buy aspirin in order to treat a headache (obtain a positive outcome) or to take one half of an aspirin per day to prevent a heart attack (negative motivation). Other commentators divide motivation into internal motivations, which are those originating inside the individual, and external motivations, which are those resulting from an external stimulus or reward. An internal motivation may arise from a self-actualisation need (such as the desire to learn a new language), whereas an external motivation might arise from social needs or physical needs (such as a need to be accepted by a new group of people, or to move to a larger house).

Alternatively, motives might be divided into rational, emotional and instinctive motives. Rational motives are those resulting from a conscious thought process; emotional motives are those resulting from an irrational source such as anger, love, pride, jealousy and so forth. Instinctive motives arise from deeper drives, and may result in obsessive behaviour; in most cases, though, instinctive motives simply drive the occasional impulse purchase.

GOALS

As we have seen so far in this chapter, behaviour is driven by needs. Needs develop drives, and drives are focused into motivation, but motivation achieves nothing unless it is backed up by action. The process of converting a motivation into concrete action is one of developing goals. A goal is a concrete objective, one that dictates a specific plan of action, and one that carries with it its own decision-making, risks and rewards.

Any plan of action carries with it a degree of risk. Individuals will usually try to reduce the risks to an acceptable level, sometimes by developing rules of behaviour which have proved to be successful in the past. This type of decision-making is important to marketers because it enables practitioners to put risk-reducing measures in place. The lower the risk to consumers, the more likely they are to buy the product and the less likely they are to complain afterwards.

A goal is an external object towards which a motive is directed (Onkvisit and Shaw, 1994). Goals differ from drives in that the goal is external, and pulls the person in a given direction, whereas a drive is internal and pushes the individual. In this way the goal acts as an incentive to take a course of action (or refrain from taking a course of action, as the case may be). Having goals improves task performance: people are more risk-seeking when they have a specific, challenging goal (Larrick et al., 2001). If someone has a drive that needs to be addressed there may be several possible goals that would satisfy the drive. For example, if an individual feels the need for entertainment, this may lead to a drive to find something to do, which in turn causes the person to set some goals that would lead to some kind of entertainment. In these circumstances several possible alternatives exist, and marketers clearly need to remember that consumers have a choice.

Huffman et al. (2000) produced two models showing how goals relate and how they are determined. Figure 5.9 shows the first of these.

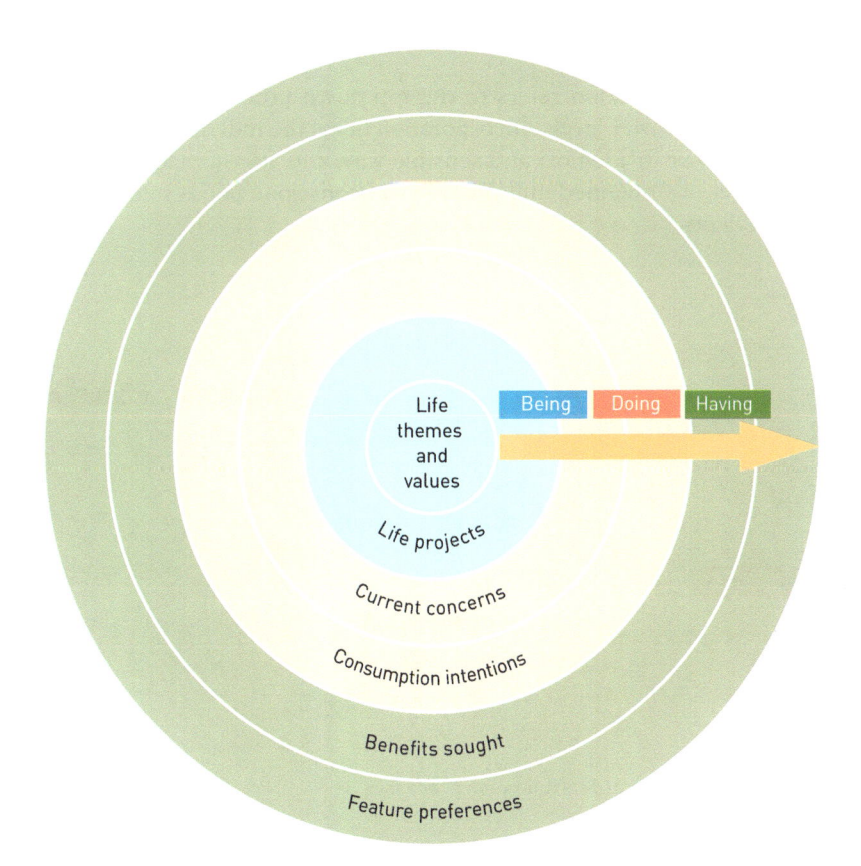

FIGURE 5.9   A hierarchical model of consumer goals

In Figure 5.9, the individual's goals begin with life themes and values. These are concerned with the kind of person we want to be, or the kind of person we are, and are unlikely to change significantly in the course of our lives. At the doing level we have immediate concerns, which lead to consumption intentions. Finally, at the having level, we would be concerned with specific benefits from products, which in turn leads to a search for specific features in the products we consume. For example, an individual might have a life theme of being a world traveller. This might translate into a life project to visit every continent in the world. In the process, current concerns (such as earning a living in a profession that allows plenty of time off for travel) might provide a set of goals: the consumption intention might be to have at least one long-haul trip each year. Finally, the individual would be looking for specific benefits from each trip (the possibility to learn about the local culture, for example), which would require specific features when planning each trip. This model shows a clear sequence from the general needs of the individual through to the final purchase goals for each individual product (in this case, each trip). There are likely to be many products and many sub-goals involved in leading a life that is dedicated to travel; the same would apply to someone whose life is based around being surrounded by artworks, or around having a large family, or sustaining a highly pressurised working career. The model shows the sequence of events that occurs, and also the relationship between the goals, but it does not illustrate the actual processes involved. These are shown in Figure 5.10.

In Figure 5.10, incorporation refers to the top-down process whereby higher-level goals shape goals at lower levels. Incorporation helps the individual to ensure that all the goals fit together in a logical and sensible way, and also it enables the individual to translate a set of ill-defined and possibly subconscious needs into a coherent set of choice problems.

FIGURE 5.10 A model of goal-determination processes

Abstraction

The process whereby lower-level goals help to determine what the higher-level goals must be if there is to be overall goal consistency

Abstraction refers to the bottom-up process whereby lower-level goals help to determine what the higher-level goals must be if there is to be consistency between the various goals.

Adaptation is the process by which goals are influenced by contextual issues such as the cultural and social environment, current concerns and consumption intentions. Contextual factors appear to operate in two ways: first, the context may activate a pre-existing set of sub-goals in the individual's memory. Different contexts generate different goals, for example one's goals when planning a visit to one's parents are very different from one's goals when planning a friend's stag night (also known as 'bachelor party'). Second, the context may influence the individual's thinking on what is actually possible. If someone does not believe, for example, that there is any chance whatsoever of being promoted at work, then he or she might not bother to apply for a promotional opportunity. In the case of *being*-level goals, someone might decide that their circumstances prevent them from ever becoming a particular type of person. At the *having* level, someone might decide that, much as they would enjoy driving a Tesla Model S, this is unlikely to happen because of financial constraints. Research shows that people with low incomes tend to set very stringent goals prior to their decision-making processes, and thus do not achieve their goals as often – consequently, they often feel less successful in life and do not enjoy the consumption experiences they do achieve (Scott and Nowlis, 2010).

HEURISTICS

Another way of simplifying the decision-making process is to establish rules for buying. These are called heuristics, and they consist of simple '*if... then*' decision-making rules, which can be established before any goals are set and the search procedure begins. Heuristics are also subject to alteration in the light of new knowledge, so sometimes they are established as the search procedure continues. Heuristics can be divided into three groups, as follows:

1. *Search heuristics*. These are rules for finding out information. For example, someone might establish a rule to the effect that they will always ask advice from a particular friend when making a major purchase.
2. *Evaluation heuristics*. These are rules for judging products. For example, someone might have a rule that they never buy products made in a country where child labour is widely used.
3. *Choice heuristics*. These are procedures for comparing evaluations of alternatives. For example, someone might have a rule of never buying the cheapest (or never buying the most expensive). In fact, most people do tend to go for the middle-priced product when offered a choice of three products at different price levels.

Some examples of these heuristics are given in Table 5.3 and can be applied equally well to both offline and online behaviours.

Kahneman and Tversky (1979) went so far as to suggest that people go through a fairly complex process of using heuristics to assess (and probably reduce) risk; for instance in understanding overeating (O'Connor and Kenny, 2022). Kahneman and Tversky (1979) proposed that people will identify possible outcomes and group ones that are seen as being essentially identical: those outcomes that would realise a more favourable result would be considered as gains, while those that would realise a less favourable outcome would be considered as losses. Following on from this, the individual would assess the likelihood of each outcome actually happening, and would be able to calculate which course of action to take in order to balance risk and reward. Kahneman and Tversky took the view that people would vary in their attitude towards risk-taking: some would be risk-averse, and would take the options they considered to be least likely to cause loss, whereas others who are happier to take risks might prefer an option that would lead to the greatest gain. The theory is called *Prospect Theory*, because it purports to explain how people weigh up the prospects of their decisions.

Downside risk is, of course, part of the equation. This might be calculated as the value of the potential loss, calculated against the likelihood of it happening. Someone who buys a Euro Lottery scratch card for £2 is well aware that the chances of winning anything are slight, and the chance of winning the €110 million jackpot is negligible, but the loss is limited to £2 so the risk is worth taking. Someone buying a second-hand car for £15,000 from a total stranger is taking a much greater risk: on the one hand, there might be a saving of £2000 over buying from a dealer, but on the other hand there might be a loss of £15,000. Someone who is a risk-taker might reason that the loss is unlikely to be the whole value of the car, but would probably be restricted to a few hundred for repairing something that the buyer has concealed. People use heuristics for this. Gan (2018) used Prospect Theory to conclude that managers are more inclined to risk-avoidance decision-making in the risk gain situation, while managers are more inclined to risk-seeking decision-making in the risk loss situation, which shows that managers' decision-making behaviour, risk preference and reward-risk models are obviously affected by situation factors (Zervoudi, 2018). Although Kahneman and Tversky (1979) offer a fairly complex formula to explain the calculation process, in fact people rarely calculate the odds. Normally, we use heuristics to simplify the process – the risk-averse don't often buy lottery tickets, and they buy their cars from dealers, and not from private sellers.

TABLE 5.3 Examples of heuristics

Search heuristics	Examples
Store selection	If you are buying meat, always go to the butcher across the street
Source credibility	If a magazine accepts advertising from products it tests and reports on, the tests may be biased in favour of the advertiser
Evaluation heuristics	**Examples**
Key criteria	If comparing processed foods, examine the sugar content
Negative criteria	If a salient consequence is negative (for example, high sugar content) give this choice criterion extra weight in the integration process
Significant differences	If the alternative is similar on a salient consequence (for example, all the alternatives are low sugar) ignore that choice criterion
Choice heuristics for familiar, frequently purchased products	**If choosing among familiar products...**
Works best	Choose the product that you think works best – the one that provides the best level of performance on the most relevant functional consequences
Affect referral	Choose the alternative you like best (in other words, select the alternative with the most favourable attitude)
Bought last	Select the alternative you bought last time (assuming it proved satisfactory)
Important person	Choose the alternative that an 'important person' such as a spouse, friend or child likes

Search heuristics	Examples
Price-based rule	Buy the least expensive alternative, or perhaps the most expensive alternative, depending on your beliefs about the relationship between price and quality
Promotion rule	Choose the alternative for which you have a special-offer coupon, or that you can buy at a reduced price (due to a sale or special offer)
Choice heuristics for new, unfamiliar products	**If choosing among unfamiliar products...**
Wait and see	Do not buy a new product until someone you know has used it for a while and recommends it. In the case of electronic products, wait until the next year or year after its introduction, when the price is likely to have reduced considerably
Expert consultant	Find an expert or more knowledgeable person, have them evaluate the alternatives in terms of your goals, then buy the alternative that the expert suggests

So heuristics are used to simplify decision-making. They may be stored in memory, or constructed on the spot based on information received, but in either case they allow the individual to reach rapid decisions without over-stretching their cognitive capacity (or brainpower). In the extreme, the use of heuristics leads to habitual behaviour. For example, someone might go to the same restaurant every Friday evening and sit at the same table each time and order the same dish. Routinised choice behaviour (Närvänen et al., 2020; Pillsbury, 2018) such as this is comforting and relaxing since it does not involve any decision-making at all. In fact, most people find it uncomfortable if their pleasurable routines cannot be carried out for whatever reason.

HEDONISM

Hedonism is the cult of pleasure (Inglis, 2021). In consumer behaviour, it refers to the pleasurable aspects of consumption: the flavour of food rather than its nutritional value, the comfort of a car rather than its performance, the appearance of clothing rather than its ability to keep out the cold (Holbrook and Hirschmann, 1982). Hedonic purchases are sometimes about a need for being cheered up, and can be triggered by feeling unhappy as well as by a normal day-to-day desire for comfort and pleasure (Wang et al., 2022). There is even evidence that a near-death experience can encourage greater pleasure-seeking behaviour (Sameer et al., 2021), as well as encouraging people to change their lifestyles (perhaps by dieting, or sometimes by stopping a diet) (Shiv et al., 2004). Recent research has investigated the characteristics of emerging hedonistic consumers in China (Chen et al., 2015; Li et al., 2018). They showed that hedonistic consumption value is positively associated with fashion orientation (the trends that society believe to be true among a wider population) (Emmanuel-Stephen and Gbadamosi, 2022), responsiveness to commercial stimuli (e.g. belief in advertisements), brand consciousness (an awareness about the existence and meaning of brands), a preference for foreign brands (Chen et al., 2015; Li et al., 2018) and a newfound relationship with the sharing economy (Christodoulides et al., 2021).

Marketers put a great deal of effort into designing products that not only work well, but also give pleasure to their owners. This is an important way to differentiate the

Hedonism
The cult of pleasure

product from those of competitors, and for some products hedonic content is virtually the entire product: fashion wear, cosmetics, holiday activities and many service sectors such as food and travel rely heavily on hedonism to sell their products.

When, for example, one thinks of hedonism, the last thing one would think of is the light commercial vehicle, or a van. At first sight, a vehicle for delivering groceries, building materials and furniture has to be as utilitarian as it gets – and for 60 or 70 years that was what manufacturers thought as well. Then in 1965 the industry was revolutionised by the Ford Transit. The Transit handled like a car, had comfortable seats, was relatively quiet and had good heating and ventilation systems. It was easy to load and a real pleasure to drive. Within a few years Ford had captured 30% of the UK light van market. The Transit became known as the People's Van: it was owned by small businesses, by budding rock bands, by hippies who slept in the back, by builders, by couriers and even by private citizens. Camper van versions, minibus versions, open truck versions and high-roof versions were all produced by Ford for the burgeoning market. The comfort and ease of handling made it ideal for drivers who were non-professionals, that is, drivers who delivered goods as part of their normal business rather than drivers who delivered for a living. Even delivery companies switched to Transits as they found that their drivers performed better when they were comfortable and not tired out by wrestling with heavy steering, or trying to coax some power out of a commercial engine. Drivers of the Transit van have been given a loving accolade and are now commonly referred to as the 'white van man'. Transits were fast and manoeuvrable. The police quickly adopted Transits as well, to use as transport for prisoners, as dog-carrying vehicles, or as scene-of-crime vehicles. Throughout its 50-year life the Transit has been the market leader. It still retains its core values: it is the People's Van because it is designed for people, not for companies. The Transit, more than any other van before it, caters to people's hedonic needs.

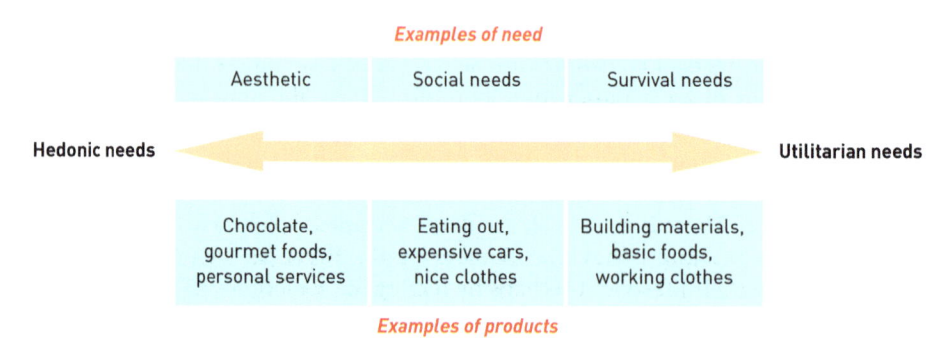

Examples of need

	Aesthetic	Social needs	Survival needs	
Hedonic needs	←			→ **Utilitarian needs**
	Chocolate, gourmet foods, personal services	Eating out, expensive cars, nice clothes	Building materials, basic foods, working clothes	

Examples of products

FIGURE 5.11 Hedonism vs. utilitarianism

Utilitarianism
The cult of practicality

Hedonism is sometimes regarded as the opposite of utilitarianism, which is the cult of practicality. In marketing, most products have utilitarian aspects, and some are almost entirely utilitarian: most business-to-business products are utilitarian (there is little hedonic value in a bag of cement, although what a builder builds with it might be extremely hedonic). The relationship between hedonism, utilitarianism, needs and products is shown in Figure 5.11. Utilitarian consumer products might include cleaning products, energy (electricity and gas), basic foods and most municipal services such as street cleaning and sewage removal.

In most cases, products have both hedonic and utilitarian features. Even a basic, cheap car has comfortable seats, a radio, a heater and so forth. This is because such comforts have become regarded as hygiene factors by most people (see above). This means that manufacturers are in a constant race to add even more hedonic features to differentiate their products and in order to stay ahead of the competition. Adding utilitarian features to hedonic products tends to generate negative feelings about the product, however. This may be because the 'pure pleasure' aspect is no longer pure – whereas adding hedonic features to a utilitarian product tends to lead to positive feelings about the product (Saldanha and Williams, 2008).

CRITICAL REFLECTION

Is it realistic for manufacturers and retailers to make a distinction between a consumer's hedonic needs and utilitarian needs? After all, what is a pleasure to some people is a necessity to others. For example, take sport: for many people, going to the gym is a fun thing to do, a real pleasure, whereas for others it is simply sweaty activity that they don't have to do. But supposing somebody had been told by the doctor to exercise more or risk heart failure? Such a person might take up a gym membership as the 'least worst' alternative, in other words exercise rather than die, but in fact hate every minute of it.

© iStock.com/ferrantraite

Equally, for a lot of people driving a car is a necessity, purely a means of getting from one place to another conveniently. For others, it might be a real delight – and certainly car manufacturers plug the hedonic aspects of driving far more than they talk about the utilitarian aspects.

Take, for example, BMW with their famous tagline 'The Ultimate Driving Machine', which has been with them since the 1970s. Then as part of their sponsorship of the 2010 Vancouver Winter Olympic Games, they launched a campaign called 'Joy'. Their Vice President of Marketing, Dan Creed, noted that the Joy campaign was specifically moulded in order to attract more women to the brand. The notion of 'joy' would 'warm the brand up and make it approachable' (Henry, 2012). Their recent advertisements have made a point of saying, 'We don't make sports cars. We don't make SUVs. We don't make hybrids. We don't make luxury sedans. We only make one thing. The Ultimate Driving Machine': an approach that reflects more hedonism than utilitarianism. Maybe the old saying about one person's meat being another person's poison (i.e. things liked or enjoyed by one person may be distasteful to another) has some truth in it! What other examples/scenarios can you conjure up which show either hedonic or utilitarian needs?

Hedonism also includes experiential needs (see for example Bronner and de Hoog, 2018; Bruwer and Rueger-Muck, 2018; Heath and Nixon, 2021). People need to have stimulating experiences: we have this in common with most other mammals, especially carnivorous ones. The need to learn by trying new things, the need to have something new to think about, and the need for excitement all stem from the need for new experiences. Experiential needs are met by playing sport (especially *extreme* or dangerous sports), by travel and by taking up new hobbies. Often such activities are in conflict with utilitarian and functional needs – there is really no utilitarian value in bungee jumping or driving from London to Mumbai in a Tata-made Land Rover Range Rover, but both fulfil an experiential need for someone. A number of commentators have suggested that competitive advantage can be gained by marketers if they concentrate on the consumers' experience of owning the product, and by a greater understanding of customer-perceived value (Fehrenbach and Herrando, 2021; Liu and Sun, 2015; Lu and Yi, 2022; McAlexander et al., 2002; Slater, 2000).

Hedonism also accounts for the utopian marketplace. This is the place where people dream (Galmstrup, 2015; Manuel and Manuel, 1979). Utopia and utopian concepts, which form the divide between what people actually need (Galmstrup, 2015; Stock, 2022) and what they dream of (Prince and Neumark, 2022), have been deconstructed as follows (Maclaran et al., 1999):

- *Sensory no-place.* This brings feelings of a world apart from the consumer experience.
- *Creating playspace.* This provides the open-ended playful nature of the utopian text contained within it.
- *Performing art.* This evokes the active life of people in the creation of utopian meanings.

Our dreams and fantasies do not, of course, always turn into reality, and in many cases people prefer to keep a fantasy as just that – remaining within Utopia. This does not prevent marketers from feeding the fantasies – custom car magazines frequently have average readerships aged below the minimum age to have a driving licence, for example.

Interestingly, people sometimes use guilt as a way of controlling their own behaviour. For example, someone who is trying to lose weight might deliberately make themselves feel guilty for eating a chocolate bar, in an attempt to avoid the behaviour in future (Dai et al., 2008), or indeed publicise their recent 'sin' on a Facebook support group! In some cases, people might use 'virtuous' behaviour (such as having salad for lunch rather than sausages and chips) as a guilt-reduction strategy for enjoying a chocolate bar later (Khan et al., 2009). It has even been found that simply having a healthy choice available may lead some people to choose the less healthy (but more attractive) alternative (Wilcox et al., 2010). This is less likely to happen if the individuals use a rejection strategy in decision-making, that is to say they operate by rejecting alternatives until there is only the healthy option left (Machin and Park, 2010). Resisting temptation may lead to an angry (or at least irritated/frustrated) mood afterwards – researchers Gal and Liu (2010) found that people who resisted the temptation of a chocolate bar were more likely to choose to see an anger-related film afterwards. In general, hedonic needs account for a large proportion of consumer spending. Over the past two decades, we've seen a trend towards service industries (as opposed to manufacturing industries) that are largely fuelled by hedonic needs, as people travel more, eat out more and enjoy the plethora of services that are provided for us as consumers. Hedonism is a major component in consumerism, which is the cult of consumption: people derive great pleasure from shopping, buying and consuming.

The concept of the consumer society has been around for some time now, and refers to the way in which most human activity in the developed world centres on consumption. We define ourselves by what we consume rather than by what we produce, we spend a large amount of our time consuming things or surfing the internet in order to learn about things to consume (which is itself a form of consumption) and it is impossible for us to have a social life without at the same time being a consumer. Consider the multitude of social media platforms (for example, Twitter, Facebook, LinkedIn, Xing, Snapchat, Instagram, YouTube and MeetUp, amongst many others), each feeding our innate curiosity and thirst for knowledge, information, ideas and incentives – which collectively enable us to consume even more.

All of this consumption activity is hedonic because it helps us to feel secure in who we are and what we do: it enables us to enjoy our lives more.

UNDERSTANDING MOTIVATION

One of the difficulties with understanding consumer motivation is that people are often unable to explain what has driven them to a specific action. In some cases this is because the motivation operates below the subconscious level, and in other cases it is because the person is not willing to admit to a particular motivation. This is easily observable in everyday life: people often lie about their reasons for taking, or not taking, a particular action since it would involve admitting to something they would prefer to keep to themselves. For example, someone may turn down an invitation to a friend's birthday party on the grounds of being unwell, when in fact the individual is afraid of seeing an ex-husband and his new wife, who may also be at the party. This might be embarrassing to admit to. In some cases, people are motivated by some need that is illegal or immoral, so would be extremely unlikely to admit to being motivated by the need. Equally, someone might be genuinely unaware, at a conscious level, of their real motivation – a reluctance to go to a concert might be a fear of crowds, but the individual might believe that actually he or she is too tired to go and would prefer a quiet night in.

In general, people are not so much rational as rationalising. A middle-aged man who is thinking about buying a sports car might actually want it because he wants to recapture his lost youth, but might rationalise the decision by talking about the car's fuel economy and good looks. 'I need a decent car to impress my clients' (thus invoking feelings of *esteem*) is a common rationalisation.

In the 1950s and early 1960s there was considerable interest in motivational research. Motivational researchers thought that they had discovered underlying reasons for consumer behaviour, and many of their propositions were seized on by marketers. Unfortunately, some of the propositions were so peculiar they could not reasonably be used – the idea that housewives were symbolically washing away their sins when they did the laundry, or were symbolically giving birth when they baked a cake were among the less credible ideas of the motivational researchers.

A further complication is that any given action is likely to be the result of several different motivations, some of which may even conflict with each other. Some actions are the result of a decision to take the 'least worst' alternative, or may be rationalised in some way in order to maintain an attitude. Sometimes people make wrong decisions, and rationalise their motives afterwards rather than admit their mistake.

Overall, then, it is difficult to penetrate the layers of motivations to find the nugget of true motivation within.

RESEARCH INTO MOTIVATION

Identifying consumer motivation is clearly far from simple. Finding out the true motivation for someone's behaviour is similar to finding out a hidden attitude (see Chapter 9). Researchers have started to uncover what lies behind the filter (especially online) and to decipher the motivations for using augmented reality face filters on social media and their effect on well-being (Javornik et al., 2022). Projective techniques in which respondents are asked to explain the motivation of a fictitious third party will often draw out the individual's real reason for behaving in a specific way: the respondent might be asked to fill in speech bubbles in a cartoon, or be asked what the 'typical' person might think, and so forth. This method was used to research children's motivations for smoking, an activity which (clearly) they would not want to discuss openly (Brucks et al., 2010).

A classic study carried out in the 1950s sought to establish the reasons for poor sales of instant coffee. Housewives were shown two shopping lists that were identical except that one list had instant coffee on it, while the other list had ground coffee. The respondents were asked to describe the type of housewife who would have drawn up each list: the instant coffee list was seen to belong to a woman who is lazy, badly organised and not a good housewife (Haire, 1950). The days of a housewife making instant coffee seem like a far cry given our current fascination with the Nespresso brand and its associated pods, and the fact that every Nespresso drinker knows only too well (and is further motivated by) the company's dedication to its sustainability programme (i.e. looking after its value chain and the recyclable pods). The CEO of Nestlé Nespresso SA, Jean-Marc Duvoisin, was quoted by Kanani (2014) as saying:

> *Sustainability is a business imperative for us, as we depend on a natural resource to deliver quality and consistency to consumers. Only 1–2% of the worldwide coffee crop meets our strict quality and aroma requirements. We believe that the best way to protect our supply of these rare coffees is to ensure the protection of the environment where our coffee is grown, as more sustainable farming increases the ability to produce consistent quality far into the future, and to provide a more sustainable and equitable outcome for farmers.*

SUMMARY

This chapter has considered the forces that encourage people to buy. Needs are the basic generators of drive, and consequently of motivation, so it might be true to say that need is the basis of virtually all behaviour. Drives develop when there is a gap between where we are and where we want to be – motivation develops when we can see a possible solution (or solutions) to the need problem. Some motivation relates to our physical, utilitarian needs, but as human beings we also have powerful social, aesthetic and pleasure needs, so much of our buying behaviour relates to drive, motivation and hedonism.

KEY POINTS

- Many motives are irrational or unconscious.
- Need is a perceived lack; want is a specific satisfier.
- Drive is caused by the gap between actual and desired states.
- Most marketing is about activating needs and directing wants.
- Motivation is complex, and cannot always be inferred from behaviour.
- Needs can be ranked, but there is considerable overlap.
- As wealth increases, motivations change.
- Many purchases are motivated at least in part by hedonic needs.

HOW TO IMPRESS YOUR EXAMINER

You are very likely to be asked a question about motivation. Having a clear understanding not only of the models, but also of their weaknesses, will help you to gain extra marks – for example, most motivation models derive from personnel management studies rather than consumer behaviour studies, so something is likely to have been lost in translation. Second, consider whether the models really stack up in practice – is Maslow's hierarchy really a hierarchy? Are people really not motivated by money, as Herzberg suggests? Third, the models usually operate on a 'one size fits all' basis, which clearly does not fit well with reality or indeed with augmented reality! People are different from each other, and have different motivations.

REVIEW QUESTIONS

1. Why do some people have higher OSLs than others?
2. What is the difference between primary and secondary motivations?
3. What are the main difficulties in categorising needs?

(Continued)

4. What are the main criticisms of Maslow's Hierarchy of Needs?
5. Why is punishment a poorer motivator than reward?
6. What is the purpose of modelling?
7. What is meant by approach–approach conflict?
8. Why is hedonism an important factor for marketers?
9. How might marketers find out which factors are regarded as hygiene factors in a product, and which are motivators?
10. In which areas of marketing would Vroom's Expectancy Theory have most relevance?

CASE STUDY: EXPERIENCING HEDONISM

The world is slowly starting to reopen, but perhaps social distancing shopping malls are here to stay, and physical retail will still face few takers.

Luxury brands, meanwhile, can leverage technology to connect with their customers.

The coronavirus pandemic has changed the landscape of the world and introduced us to lockdowns, disrupting supply chains and bringing new rules of consumption across the globe. Some reports estimate a total loss of $9 trillion due to the pandemic. The luxury industry is among the sectors worst hit by Covid-19. According to an article by Bain & Company (2020), the global luxury market shrunk by 15 to 35% in 2020. Luxury brands such as Burberry have shut down more than one-third of their physical stores; Kering, the owner of Gucci, has closed half of its stores in China since the outbreak intensified in 2020.

Did the challenges for luxury brands end as lockdowns softened, and social distancing norms were relaxed? The short answer is no.

Luxury brands thrive on hedonistic experience, and over the years, our interactions with brand managers have revealed that in-store experiences are a significant part of the value proposition. However, due to lockdowns and social distancing, consumers are unlikely to return to physical stores soon. According to McKinsey, consumers are expected to shop less frequently in physical stores for all items except groceries.

One critical component of any hedonistic consumption, including luxury, is emotional arousal. While all senses are capable of creating such arousals, sometimes sensory experiences can be replaced by narratives. Phrases like 'soft as silk' or 'smooth as butter' are essential to arouse consumer emotions and may replace the need for touching a product. Not only touch: the effect of smell can also be simulated. Perfume brands often express their product by attributing the fragrance to already known smells such as the 'Aroma of sandalwood' or the 'Scent of a red rose', all of which may facilitate emotional arousal. Similarly, research shows that even touching a product in a tablet or a smartphone can create the sensory experience of touch. Perception of tactile evaluations is enough to create a sense of ownership and product evaluation. These interactions necessitate the creation of web-based applications that are touch-based. Most luxury brands, however, have shied away from engaging customers in the digital environment. Going forward, this, however, may not be an option. Thus, creating arousals via digital means is the way forward.

Brands can deploy virtual showrooms too. One such example is Lenskart – it allows consumers to try various models of spectacles and sunglasses by placing them on their 3D scanned face. Similarly, a luxury condom brand, Unique Pull, has set up an interactive video where the brand showcases its 'Pull Strip' feature. This helps ensure the quality and uniqueness of a brand. By deploying virtual showrooms, brands may be able to compensate for a lack of physical experience. It is also feasible to create personalised solutions, which most luxury customers will appreciate.

Luxury branding is all about exclusivity. Augmented reality (AR) fits well with the luxury marketing narrative. AR devices such as Microsoft HoloLens create at-home experiences in collaboration with luxury brands. Remy Martin has launched a global mixed reality experience using Microsoft HoloLens, revealing the origin and processes involved in making the Cognac. By the use of this technology, the customer feels more connected to the brand. According to research conducted with a US-based luxury watch and jewellery e-commerce retailer, customers who received physical catalogues and emails had a higher response rate than those who received only emails. Physical catalogues mailed to existing customers will continue their engagement with the brand. With restrictions like social distancing and heightened awareness of personal hygiene in place, the catalogues may serve as an effective marketing tool. A common saying in football is what you do off the pitch is as vital as what you do on the pitch. Similarly, luxury brands must embrace that customers need to be engaged even when they are not purchasing. One way is by introducing unique and viral challenges.

Apart from creating hedonistic experiences, two important principles also aid luxury brands to not lose connection with their customers. First, highlighting the social activities that the brand engaged in during the pandemic may help it achieve high status in the minds of customers. Kering donated $1 million to Hubei Red Cross Foundation and Dolce & Gabbana funded a research project to study the immune system responses to the virus, for example. Second, following the huge economic losses from the pandemic across the globe, brands should not attempt to increase prices to make up their losses. They should slowly move to keep their customer base. This is a long-term, slow-paced strategy, but with potential to make up for losses over time.

© iStock.com / Tom Merton

One thing that evolution has taught us is that any species needs to adapt to survive. For luxury brands, adaptation is inevitable. Thankfully, we already have the tools and techniques that we can use to create new experiences for luxury consumers in a post-pandemic world.

Source: Adapted from Akella and Borah (2020). More data and insights from Forbes India can be found at www.forbesindia.com.

(Continued)

CASE STUDY QUESTIONS

1. Will the lack of a physical presence in some circumstances act negatively when customer motivation is concerned?
2. Did the challenges for luxury brands end as lockdowns softened, and social distancing norms were relaxed?
3. How important are emotional arousals to the luxury market?
4. Can augmented reality truly bring exclusivity to a luxury brand? Can you cite any examples?
5. Recouping the financial losses that have been suffered through the pandemic is obviously an issue for many companies; but at what cost?

FURTHER READING

Classical Motivation Theories: Similarities and Differences between Them, by Stephanie Hoffman, is that rare thing: a commercially published undergraduate dissertation. Stephanie is German, and the thesis is published by GRIN Verlag GmbH (Norderstedt, 2006). It provides a very useful and thoughtful set of comparisons between several classical motivation theorists (some of which have not been included in this chapter, for various reasons). Incidentally, the thesis got a B+.

For a psychologist's viewpoint on expectancy models, V. Henning, T. Hennig-Thurau and S. Feiereisen (2012) Giving the expectancy-value model a heart, *Psychology and Marketing*, 29 (10): 765–81, gives an interesting insight into motivation.

A lot of the time, our attitude towards hedonic behaviour is actually learnt from our family socialisation. Thus communication from within such environments can prove to be an important factor, especially for adolescent children. An excellent article by Hollmann et al. (2015) highlights the motivational antecedents and consequences of the mother–adolescent communication – a fascinating insight into the communication between parents and their children: J. Hollmann, J. Gorges, J. and E. Wild (2016) Motivational antecedents and consequences of the mother–adolescent communication, *Journal of Child and Family Studies*, 25, 767–80.

Christmas is, of course, a time for hedonic behaviour. For a useful overview of how people create meaning for their hedonic consumption, take a look at: C. Tynan and S. McKechnie (2009) Hedonic meaning through Christmas consumption: A review and model, *Journal of Customer Behaviour*, 8 (3): 237–55.

Caroline Tynan and Sally McKechnie also collaborated on a paper about the co-creation of value in hedonic consumption. This takes a somewhat non-traditional view of hedonism. The paper is: C. Tynan, S. McKechnie and C. Chhuon (2010) Co-creating value for luxury brands, *Journal of Business Research*, 63 (11): 1156–263.

There is, of course, a downside to hedonic consumption. Not everything that feels good is good for us – and this applies especially to alcohol. Students are famous for enjoying a drink – but maybe this next paper will provide some food for thought! E.N. Banister and M. Piacentini (2006) Binge drinking – do they mean us? Living life to the full in students' own words, *Advances in Consumer Research*, 33: 390–8.

MORE ONLINE

For additional materials that support this chapter and your learning, please visit:
https://study.sagepub.com/sethna5e

REFERENCES

Akella, L.Y. and Borah, S.B. (2020) How luxury brands can create hedonistic experiences, virtually. Forbes India. www.forbesindia.com/blog/coronavirus/how-luxury-brands-can-create-hedonistic-experiences-virtually/ (accessed 19 August 2022).

Bailey, R.L., Liu, J. and Wang, T. (2021) Primary biological motivators in food advertisements: Energy density and sexual appeals compete for appetitive motivational activation. *Communication Research*, *48* (3): 379–400.

Bain & Company (2020) Covid-19 crisis pushes luxury to sharpest fall ever but catalyses industry's ability to transform. Press Release. www.bain.com/about/media-center/press-releases/2020/covid_19_crisis_pushes_luxury_to_sharpest_fall_ever_but_catalyses_industrys_ability_to_transform/ (accessed 18 March 2021).

Blythe, M. and Hassenzahl, M. (2018) The semantics of fun: Differentiating enjoyable experiences. In M. Blythe and A. Monk (eds), *Funology 2*. Human–Computer Interaction Series. Cham: Springer Nature. pp. 375–87.

Bronner, F. and de Hoog, R. (2018) Conspicuous consumption and the rising importance of experiential purchases. *International Journal of Market Research*, *60* (1): 88–103.

Brucks, M., Connell, P.M. and Freeman, D. (2010) Children's ascribed motivations for smoking elicited by projective questioning. *Advances in Consumer Research*, *37*: 139–40.

Bruwer, J. and Rueger-Muck, E. (2018) Wine tourism and hedonic experience: A motivation-based experiential view. *Tourism and Hospitality Research*. https://doi.org/10.1177/1467358418781444

Chen, H.-J., Wong, S.W., Bilgihan, A. and Okumus, F. (2020) Capsule hotels: Offering experiential value or perceived as risky by tourists? An optimum stimulation level model. *International Journal of Hospitality Management*, *86*: 102434.

Chen, Z.X., Wang, C., Chan, A.K.K. and Zheng, Z.C. (2015) The characteristics of emerging hedonistic consumers in China: An empirical investigation. In A.K. Manrai and H.L. Meadow (eds), *Global Perspectives in Marketing for the 21st Century: Proceedings of the 1999 World Marketing Congress, Developments in Marketing Science*. London: Springer International. p. 63.

Christodoulides, G., Athwal, N., Boukis, A. and Semaan, R.W. (2021) New forms of luxury consumption in the sharing economy. *Journal of Business Research*, *137*: 89–99.

Cruz Passos, S., Silva Leite, R. and de Rezende Pinto, M. (2020) Personal values and gift giving act: A proposed connection. *Estudios Gerenciales*, *36* (155): 218–28.

Dai, X., Wertenbroch, K. and Brendl, M. (2008) Strategic motivation maintenance: The case of guilt-seeking. *Advances in Consumer Research*, *35*: 138–41.

Davis, T. and Papies, E.K. (2022) Pleasure vs. identity: More eating simulation language in meat posts than plant-based posts on social media #foodtalk. *Appetite*, *175*: 106024.

Delves Broughton, P. (2017). The business school tradition feels like an outdated Grand Tour. *Financial Times*, 7 October, p. 9.

Emmanuel-Stephen, C.M. and Gbadamosi, A. (2022) Hedonism and luxury fashion consumption among Black African women in the UK: An empirical study. *Journal of Fashion Marketing & Management, 26* (1): 126–40.

Fehrenbach, D. and Herrando, C. (2021) The effect of customer-perceived value when paying for a product with personal data: A real-life experimental study. *Journal of Business Research, 137*: 222–32.

Flessert, M. and Beran, M.J. (2018) Delayed gratification. In J. Vonk and T.K. Shackelford (eds), *Encyclopedia of Animal Cognition and Behavior*. Cham: Springer International. pp. 1–7.

Future Market Insights (2022) VOIP services market outlook (2022–2032) Report. www.futuremarketinsights.com/reports/global-voip-services-market (accessed on 27 October 2022).

Gal, D. and Liu, W. (2010) What movie would you watch with your salad? The implicit emotional consequences of exerting self-control. *Advances in Consumer Research, 37*: 122–5.

Galmstrup, A.M. (2015) Sites of globalization: New cities; reflecting on the dialectics between designer and client. In R. Saliba (ed.), *Urban Design in the Arab World: Reconceptualizing Boundaries*. Farnham: Ashgate Publishing. pp. 167–76.

Gan, T. (2018) Brain mechanism of economic management risk decision based on Kahneman's Prospect Theory. *NeuroQuantology, 16* (5): 401–6.

Givi, J. (2021) When a gift exchange isn't an exchange: Why gift-givers underestimate how uncomfortable recipients feel receiving a gift without reciprocating. *Advances in Consumer Research, 49*: 157.

Hahn, A. and Popan, E.M. (2020) Sensation seeking (thrill seeking). *Salem Press Encyclopedia*. 2pp.

Haire, M. (1950) Projective techniques in marketing research. *Journal of Marketing, 14*: 649–56.

Heath, T. and Nixon, E. (2021) Immersive imaginative hedonism: Daydreaming as experiential 'consumption'. *Marketing Theory, 21* (3): 351–70.

Hebb, D.O. (1955) Drives and the CNS (Conceptual Nervous System). *Psychological Review, 62*: 243–54.

Henry, J. (2012) BMW: Still the ultimate driving machine, not that it ever wasn't. *Forbes*, 31 May. www.forbes.com/sites/jimhenry/2012/05/31/bmw-still-the-ultimate-driving-machine-not-that-it-ever-wasnt/ (accessed 26 July 2015).

Herzberg, F. (1966) *Work and the Nature of Man*. London: Collins.

Hetherington, A. (2018) Ed's letter. *Big Issue Australia, 566*: 4.

Hibbert, S.A., Hogg, G. and Quinn, T. (2005) Social entrepreneurship: Understanding consumer motives for buying *The Big Issue*. *Journal of Consumer Behaviour, 4* (3): 159–72.

Holbrook, M.P. and Hirschmann, E.C. (1982) The experiential aspects of consumption: Consumer fantasies, feelings and fun. *Journal of Consumer Research, 9* (September): 132–40.

Huffman, C., Atneshwar, S. and Mick, D.G. (2000) Consumer goal structures and goal-determining processes: An integrative framework. In S. Ratneshwar, D.G. Mick and C. Huffman (eds), *The Why of Consumption*. London: Routledge. pp. 9–35.

Inglis, K. (2021) The universal pure pleasure machine: Suicide or Nirvana? *Philosophical Psychology*, *34* (8): 1077–96.

Javornik, A., Marder, B., Barhorst, J.B., McLean, G., Rogers, Y., Marshall, P. and Warlop, L. (2022) 'What lies behind the filter?' Uncovering the motivations for using augmented reality (AR) face filters on social media and their effect on well-being. *Computers in Human Behavior*, *128*: 107126.

Kahneman, D. and Tversky, A. (1979) Prospect Theory: An analysis of decision under risk. *Econometrica*, *47* (2): 263–92.

Kanani, R. (2014) CEO interview: Inside Nespresso's 2020 sustainability strategy. http://news.trust.org//item/20141217011005-2qaye (accessed 26 July 2015).

Khan, A., Khan, S. and Burton, N. (2022) Insufficient physical activity and high sedentary behaviour are associated with loneliness in adolescents with overweight/obesity: Evidence from 23 low- and middle-income countries. *Pediatric Obesity*, *17* (2): 1–4.

Khan, U., Dhar, R. and Fishbach, A. (2009) Guilt as motivation: The role of guilt in choice justification. *Advances in Consumer Research*, *36*: 27–8.

Larrick, R.P., Heath, C. and Wu, G. (2001) Goal-induced risk taking in strategy choice. In a symposium on goals and decision-making organised by Nathan Novemsky. In S.M. Broniarczyk and K. Nakamoto (eds), *NA - Advances in Consumer Research*, Vol.29. Valdosta, GA: Association for Consumer Research. pp. 5–7.

Leuba, C. (1955) Toward some integration of learning theories: The concept of optimum stimulation. *Psychological Reports*, *1*: 27–33.

Li, E.P.H., Li, F., Lam, M., Liu, W.S. and Zhao, X. (2018) Global fashion brands and the construction of 'Modern Girl' archetypes in the emerging Chinese market. *Fashion, Style & Popular Culture*, *5* (2): 201–20.

Lin, L., Chen, W., Sun, W., Chen, M., Li, J., Shen, J. and Guo, V.Y. (2022) Associations between adverse childhood experiences and obesity in a developing country: A cross-sectional study among middle-aged and older Chinese adults. *International Journal of Environmental Research and Public Health*, *19* (11): 6796.

Liu, S. (2018) What drives us? Chasing reward in a dopaminergic society. *Columbia Undergraduate Science Journal*, *11*. doi: 10.7916/CUSJ.V11I0.5654

Liu, Y. and Sun, Q. (2015) A comparative study of competitive brand based on customer-perceived value: Evidences from IAT. *Open Journal of Social Sciences*, *3*: 275–82.

Lloyd, R. and Mertens, D. (2018) Expecting more out of Expectancy Theory: History urges inclusion of the social context. *International Management Review*, *14* (1): 28–43.

Lu, M. and Yi, B. (2022) Homestay customers' perceived value mediates the influence of customer participation and host–customer interaction on customer satisfaction. *Social Behavior & Personality: An International Journal*, *50* (4): 1–11.

Machin, J. and Park, Y.W. (2010) Rejection is good for your health: The influence of decision strategy on food and drink choices. *Advances in Consumer Research*, *37*: 73–6.

Manuel, F.E. and Manuel, F.P. (1979) *Utopian Thought in the Western World*. Oxford: Blackwell.

Maslow, A.H. (1943) A theory of human motivation. *Psychological Review*, *50* (4): 370–96.

Maslow, A.H. (1954) *Motivation and Personality*. New York: Harper and Row.

McAlexander, J.H., Schouten, J.W. and Koenig, H.F. (2002) Building brand community. *Journal of Marketing*, *66* (1): 38–55.

McClelland, D.C. (1955) *Studies in Motivation*. New York: Appleton.

Maclaran, P., Brown, S., and Stevens, L. (1999) The Utopian Imagination: Spatial Play in a Festival Marketplace, in European *Advances in Consumer Research*, Vol 4, eds. Bernard Dubois, Tina M. Lowrey, and L. J. Shrum, Marc Vanhuele, Provo, UT : *Association for Consumer Research*, Pages: 304–09.

McLeod, S.A. (2007) Maslow's Hierarchy of Needs. www.simplypsychology.org/maslow.html (accessed 29 July 2015).

McNulty, W.K. (1985) UK social change through a wide-angle lens. *Futures*, August.

Mick, D.G. and Humphreys, A. (2008) Consumer freedom from consumer culture theory perspectives. *Advances in Consumer Research*, *35*: 18–19.

Midha, T., Nath, B., Kumari, R., Rao, Y.K. and Pandey, U. (2012) Childhood obesity in India: A meta-analysis. *Indian Journal of Pediatrics*, *79* (7): 945–8.

Mitchell, A. (1983) *The Nine American Lifestyles*. New York: Macmillan.

Murray, H.A. (1938) *An Exploration in Personality: A Clinical Experimental Study of Fifty Men of College Age*. London: Oxford University Press.

Närvänen, E., Kuusela, H., Paavola, H. and Sirola, N. (2020) A meaning-based framework for customer loyalty. *International Journal of Retail & Distribution Management*, *48* (8): 825–43.

Niehaus, J.L., Cruz-Bermúdez, N.D. and Kauer, J.A. (2009) Plasticity of addiction: A mesolimbic dopamine short-circuit? *American Journal on Addictions*, *18* (4): 259–71.

Nord, W.R. and Peter, J.P. (1980) A behaviour modification perspective on marketing. *Journal of Marketing*, *44* (Spring): 36–47.

Nowlis, S.M., McCabe, D.B. and Mandel, N. (2003) The effect of a forced delay after choice on consumption enjoyment. *Advances in Consumer Research*, *30*: 502–10.

O'Connor, R.M. and Kenny, P.J. (2022) Utility of 'substance use disorder' as a heuristic for understanding overeating and obesity. *Progress in Neuro-Psychopharmacology & Biological Psychiatry*, *118*: 1–10.

Onkvisit, S. and Shaw, J.J. (1994) *Consumer Behaviour: Strategy and Analysis*. New York: Macmillan.

Parker, J.R., Umashankar, N. and Schleicher, M.G. (2018) How and why the collaborative consumption of food leads to overpurchasing, overconsumption, and waste. *Journal of Public Policy & Marketing*. https://doi.org/10.1509/jppm.17.121

Pillsbury, R. (2018) *No Foreign Food: The American Diet in Time and Place*. Abingdon: Routledge.

Prince, R. and Neumark, T. (2022) Curious utopias: Dreaming big again in the twenty-first century? *Social Anthropology/Anthropologie Sociale*, *30* (2): 1–15.

Raghunathan, R. and Mukherji, A. (2003) Is hope to enjoy more enjoyed than hope enjoyed? *Advances in Consumer Research*, *30*: 85–6.

Raju, P.S. (1980) Optimum stimulation level: Its relationship to personality, demographics and exploratory behaviour. *Journal of Consumer Research*, *7* (3): 272–82.

Riley, A.L., Hempel, B.J. and Clasen, M.M. (2018) Sex as a biological variable: Drug use and abuse. *Physiology & Behavior*, *187*: 79–96.

Rugimbana, R., Donahay, B., Neal, C. and Polonsky, M.J. (2003) The role of social power relations in gift giving on St. Valentine's Day. *Journal of Consumer Behaviour*, *3* (1): 63–73.

Rusciano, V., Civero, G. and Scarpato, D. (2018) Urban gardens in the city of Naples: An empirical analysis. *Calitatea*, *19* (S1): 436–42.

Saldanha, N. and Williams, P. (2008) Mixed indulgences: When removing sin may backfire. *Advances in Consumer Research*, *35*: 138–41.

Sameer, Y.M., Elmassah, S., Mertzanis, C. and El-Maghraby, L. (2021) Are happier nations more responsible? Examining the link between happiness and sustainability. *Social Indicators Research*, *158* (1): 267–95.

Santos, M., Burton, E.T., Cadieux, A., Gaffka, B., Shaffer, L., Cook, J.L. and Tucker, J.M. (2022) Adverse childhood experiences, health behaviors, and associations with obesity among youth in the United States. *Behavioral Medicine*. https://doi.org/10.1080/08964289.2022.2077294

Scott, M. and Nowlis, S. (2010) The effect of goal-setting on consumption and consumer well-being. *Advances in Consumer Research*, *37*: 122–5.

Shimoni, E., Berger, A. and Eyal, T. (2022) Your pride is my goal: How the exposure to others' positive emotional experience influences preschoolers' delay of gratification. *Journal of Experimental Child Psychology*, *217*: 105356.

Shiv, B., Ferraro, R. and Bettman, J.R. (2004) Let us eat and drink for tomorrow we shall die: Mortality salience and hedonic choice. *Advances in Consumer Research*, *31*: 118–21.

Skinner, B.F. (1953) *Science and Human Behaviour*. New York: Macmillan.

Slater, N. (2000) The positive effect of a market orientation on business profitability: A balanced replication. *Journal of Business Research*, *48*: 69–73.

Stock, P.V. (2022) Food utopias, (mature) care, and hope. *International Journal of Sociology of Agriculture & Food*, *27* (2): 89–107.

Tay, L. and Diener, E. (2011) Needs and subjective well-being around the world. *Journal of Personality and Social Psychology*, *101* (2): 354–65.

Taylor, M.M. (2018) The obesity epidemic: Individual accountability and the social determinants of health. In *The Obesity Epidemic*. Cham: Palgrave Pivot. pp. 21–38.

Vroom, V.H. (1999) *Management and Motivation*. Harmondsworth: Penguin Business.

Wadhwa, M. and Trudel, R. (2010) The fruit of labour effect. *Advances in Consumer Research*, *37*: 77–80.

Wang, B., Xie, F., Kandampully, J. and Wang, J. (2022) Increase hedonic products purchase intention through livestreaming: The mediating effects of mental imagery quality and customer trust. *Journal of Retailing and Consumer Services*, *69*: 103109.

Wilcox, K., Vallen, B., Block, L.G. and Fitzsimons, G. (2010) Vicarious goal fulfilment: When the mere presence of a healthy option leads to an ironically indulgent decision. *Advances in Consumer Research*, *37*: 73–4.

Yanaoka, K., Michaelson, L.E., Guild, R.M., Dostart, G., Yonehiro, J., Saito, S. and Munakata, Y. (2022) Cultures crossing: The power of habit in delaying gratification. *Psychological Science*, *33* (7): 1172–81.

Yang, A.X. and Urminsky, O. (2018) The smile-seeking hypothesis: How immediate affective reactions motivate and reward gift giving. *Psychological Science*. https://doi.org/10.1177/0956797618761373

Zak, P.J. (2022) The neuroscience of customer experience. *MIT Sloan Management Review*, *63* (4): 1–6.

Zervoudi, E.K. (2018) Value functions for Prospect Theory investors: An empirical evaluation for US style portfolios. *Journal of Behavioral Finance*, *19* (3): 319–33.

Zuckerman, M. (2000) Are you a risk-taker? *Psychology Today*, November/December: 54–87.

PART ONE CONSUMER BEHAVIOUR IN CONTEXT

- Chapter 1 Understanding Consumer Behaviour
- Chapter 2 Decisions, Behaviours and Interactions
- Chapter 3 Consumption in B2C vs. B2B
- Chapter 4 Consumer Technology and Innovation

PART TWO CONSUMERS AS INDIVIDUALS (THE PSYCHOLOGICAL ISSUES)

- Chapter 5 Drive, Motivation and Hedonism
- Chapter 6 The Self and Personality
- Chapter 7 Perception
- Chapter 8 Learning and Knowledge
- Chapter 9 Attitude Formation and Change

PART THREE CONSUMERS AS SOCIAL ACTORS (THE SOCIOLOGICAL ISSUES)

- Chapter 10 Reference Groups
- Chapter 11 Age, Gender and Familial Roles
- Chapter 12 Culture and Social Mobility
- Chapter 13 Ethical Consumption
- Chapter 14 Sustainable Consumption

CHAPTER 6

THE SELF AND PERSONALITY

LEARNING OBJECTIVES

After reading this chapter you should be able to:

- Explain the role and purpose of self-concept.
- Describe the derivation of self-concept.
- Explain the mechanisms of inner and outer direction.
- Explain the reasons for an increase in inner-directedness.
- Explain self-monitoring.
- Describe the various ways in which personality is studied.
- Define personality.

CHAPTER CONTENTS

Introduction
Self-concept
Personality
Approaches to studying personality
Type approach
Traits and factors
Psychographics
Summary
Key points
How to impress your examiner
Review questions
Case study: Dove Self-Esteem Project
Further reading
References

More online: https://study.sagepub.com/sethna5e

INTRODUCTION

This chapter is about some of the factors that make up the individual person – the self. As we've already seen from the early chapters in this book, people are complex. Our individual mental make-up affects how we respond to communications, what and how we buy, and thus how we plan for our future lives. Put all of this together and you start to understand the 'personality' behind the individual self. From a marketing viewpoint, understanding the self and his or her personality is useful in segmenting markets and also in planning marketing communications.

SELF-CONCEPT

Of all the personality concepts which have been applied to marketing, self-concept has probably provided the most consistent results and the greatest promise of application to the needs of business firms.
(Foxall, 1980)

Self-concept is the person's ideas and feelings about him or herself. Baumeister (1999) adds the words *'including the person's attributes and who and what the self is'*. It has an important role to play in understanding consumer behaviour, since people will buy products that contribute to the self-concept. For example, a woman who thinks of herself as 'chic' will often choose clothes to enhance that image; or a man who thinks of himself as a 'do-it-yourself (DIY) handyman' will equip himself with the most sophisticated power tools.

Essentially, people project a role and this is confirmed (or denied) by other people. An example here could be new gender roles and their implications for families and societies (Bharti et al., 2022; Oláh et al., 2018). In order for the role to be confirmed, the person will try to develop all the exterior accoutrements appropriate to the role. In this sense, the person becomes a work of art (Figure 6.1), a sensory stimulus to other people, which is intended to generate affective and appropriate responses. The person may well use all five senses to generate the affective response: sight (by dressing appropriately, wearing make-up, etc.), hearing (by speaking with the right accent, or using the voice well), smell (by wearing perfume or deodorant), touch (by looking after the skin, perhaps by wearing clothes that feel good) and even taste (by using flavoured lipstick, mouthwashes). Zickfeld and Schubert (2018) argue that tearful individuals might be perceived as warm because they are perceived as feeling moved and touched; a notion that has also been investigated under the guise of 'cheater detection' – prerequisite for the evolution of social cooperation by the individual (Okubo and Ishikawa, 2019).

Some of these sensory stimuli will, of course, only be available to the individual's closest friends but most people at some time or another will consciously set out to create a work of art of themselves in order to 'make a good impression' on somebody, whether that be employer, family member, friend or lover. The extent to which people do this depends on the following factors:

1. The degree of importance attached to impressing the other person (or people).
2. The degree to which the individual anticipates that the 'target audience' can be impressed.
3. The cost in time and money of creating the desired image.

Clearly, though, the fact that people do create these works of art has led to the invention of whole industries to cater for the need – the cosmetics industry and fashion industry, to name but two. The forces involved can be very strong indeed; even in Nazi concentration camps people were prepared to trade food for clothing and cosmetics, thus placing their survival at risk for the purpose of maintaining their dignity (Klein, 2003). In some cases, fashion items also represent personality determinants and even rite-of-passage symbols (Belkin and Sheptak, 2018; Reeves, 2018). Research by Russell Belk showed that shoes can represent a **rite of passage** (a girl's first high heels, for example) and that people often define themselves by their footwear (brands of trainer, for example) (Belk, 2003).

Rite of passage
An event or action which marks a change in an individual's life circumstance

THE SELF AND PERSONALITY

Sight: Make-up, clothing, hairdressing, weight (too fat or too thin), tattoos, and even plastic surgery

Sound: Accent, voice modulation, 'script'

Smell: Deodorants, perfumes

Touch: Skin conditioners, depilation

Taste: Flavoured lipsticks, mouthwashes

→ The individual as work of art

FIGURE 6.1   The person as artwork

BRAND EXPERIENCES: ARE CHILDREN JUST 'SMALL ADULTS'?

My kids longed to have a debit card of their own; somewhere to put all that pocket money they were getting (not!). But seriously, apparently children in the UK get an average of £4.99 a week in pocket money (a drop from £7.71 in 2019!), and luckily for society, there are some children who want to learn good money-management habits. There's of course the issue that we live in an increasingly cashless society: we pay via PayPal, ApplePay or using our Chip'n'Pin most of the time. Enter goHenry – a digital banking solution for families that aim to make kids smarter at managing money by offering 8–18-year-olds a pre-paid Visa debit card and app with unique parental controls. Parents pay pocket money on to the goHenry card from their bank account. They can set spending limits and decide where and how the card can be used, for example whether it can be used for online purchases. They can also keep an eye on how their child is spending the cash. Children can earn more from their parents for completing tasks, while savings goals can be set for things they want to buy.

Most high street banks offer some kind of children's bank account, but the main difference between their products and goHenry is in the depth of parental controls. With goHenry, this includes:

Instant notifications. Every time your child uses the card, you get a notification on your own app.

Custom cards. goHenry offers a special custom card where you can get the name of your child on the front of the card, for example, goMahya or goKai or goKaus.

Spending limits. You can decide that your kid isn't allowed to spend more than £10 a week and the card won't work beyond that.

(Continued)

Rewards in return for completed tasks. You can set up the app so that money is paid into the child's account only if they have cleaned their room, done their homework or walked the dog.

Control over where the card is used. You can block both online purchases and ATM withdrawals.

Transactions from age-restricted stores are automatically blocked. goHenry won't allow the card to be used at betting shops, pubs, off licences, pornography websites and so on. However, don't forget that alcohol, for example, can be bought at regular grocery stores and goHenry won't be able to automatically block age-related transactions from shops that also sell other kinds of products.

Here's what's in it for the children:

Financial independence. They'll have a 'real' spending account, just like mum and dad!

Personalised cards. The standard card is included in the monthly fee, but for £4.99 your child gets to choose from a set of colours and designs.

Learning experience. Children will learn budgeting from a young age, so they'll be more likely to turn into financially responsible adults (that's the theory).

Alex Zivoder (CEO at goHenry) suggests that money management is a vital life skill, and the more parents support their kids to know how to manage money, the better. All of which reinforces the child's self-concept as a responsible individual. On Trustpilot, goHenry received an average mark of 4.2 out of 5, and a rating of Great, from over 6800 reviews. Users praised the customised kid's card, app functionality and ability to teach children good money habits, although there was some criticism of goHenry's fees.

CRITICAL REFLECTION

Re-inventing ourselves is a common event. Many people look back on their lives through pictures of themselves over the decades and the re-inventions they've been through. Think media images of Freddie Mercury or David Bowie through the ages. We change our hairstyle or colour, or our clothes, and effectively become someone slightly different. But are we justified in considering this to be a work of art? Art is supposed to make people rethink the world around them – does this really happen when someone gets a haircut?

Or perhaps the person-as-artwork (Figure 6.1) idea only applies at the extremes, where someone undergoes radical cosmetic (plastic) surgery or an extreme tattoo on a place on the body which is visible most of the time (for instance, tattoos on the face or head).

© iStock.com/iconogenic

Also, who is the artist here? The individual consumer, or the cosmetic surgeon, hairdresser, beautician or tattoo artist who carries out the work? What are the psychological effects on the individual of such re-invention? In some cases, such re-invention is of course necessary in order for the individual to feel 'normal' – for instance, after gender reassignment surgery, or perhaps reconstructive surgery after a mastectomy.

Self-concept is a learned construct. Children tend to look for role models to imitate; these may not always be the same people, and the child may try several different role models before settling on one that is (or feels) appropriate. Children can be crushed by a denial of the role being projected, for example if people laugh while the child is copying the behaviour of a favourite auntie or uncle. During the teenage years a further refinement occurs as the individual tries to develop an adult role, and again the role models may shift, typically away from family members towards a hero (pop star or sporting personality) or sometimes to an individual within a **peer group** (a school friend, for example). It is not uncommon for the role model to be an adult who is a few years older.

Peer group
Those people who are near to being one's equals

Self-esteem is the positive view of the self (Consiglio and van Osselaer, 2022). People with high self-esteem (Orth and Robins, 2022) have a natural expectation that they will be successful at what they aim to achieve. This belief feeds a propensity to take more risks (Harrington and Overall, 2021) and, furthermore, these people are very comfortable being the centre of attention. The opposite is true for those with low self-esteem who believe that they are doomed to fail (Schwinger et al., 2022). And thus they will do whatever it takes to avoid such embarrassing situations (Patrick and Xu, 2018).

CONSUMER BEHAVIOUR IN ACTION: WINNING MILLENNIALS

The Great Resignation. These three words have increasingly become part of boardroom conversations and media buzz in the last year or so, with employees quitting organisations in large numbers. Among those giving companies their two weeks' notice were Generation Zs (Gen Zs) and Millennials, a significant portion of the global workforce. What prompted this exodus? What do they care about that their employers were not paying attention to? What will drive their loyalty?

The Deloitte Global 2022 Gen Z and Millennial Survey was fielded between November 2021 and January 2022 to find answers to these questions and more. The survey – which covered 14,808 Gen Zs and 8412 Millennials across 46 countries – provides valuable insights into their views about work and the world around them. Survey responses indicate that Gen Zs and Millennials are deeply concerned about the state of the world. They are worried about climate change, wealth inequality, geopolitical conflicts and more, and they are resolved to drive change. But they are also struggling with the challenges of their everyday lives, from financial anxiety, to a lack of work/life balance, to consistently high stress levels. They want businesses and governments to do more to help.

(Continued)

Gen Zs and Millennials are concerned about managing their finances. Consider this: 29% of Gen Zs and 36% of Millennials selected cost of living (e.g. housing, transport, bills, etc.) as their greatest concern. Only around half of Gen Zs (47%) and Millennials (55%) feel they can comfortably pay their living expenses each month, and more than a quarter of Gen Zs (26%) and Millennials (31%) are not confident they will be able to retire comfortably. Potentially to alleviate these financial concerns, as many as 43% of Gen Zs and 33% of Millennials have a second part- or full-time paying job in addition to their primary job.

One might imagine this financial anxiety among Gen Zs and Millennials would prompt them to stay at their jobs. But the survey findings tell a different story: While loyalty is up from last year's survey, four in ten Gen Zs and nearly a quarter of Millennials would still like to leave their jobs within 2 years, and roughly a third would do so without another job lined up. The top reasons? Pay, feeling the workplace is detrimental to their mental health, and burnout.

Stress and burnout levels among Gen Zs and Millennials are high and present a significant retention issue for employers: 46% of Gen Zs and 45% of Millennials feel burned out due to the intensity and demands of their working environments. Similarly, 44% of Gen Zs and 43% of Millennials say many people have recently left their organisation due to high workload pressure. Employers may not yet be doing enough to address this challenge. The survey shows that, despite organisations focusing more on mental health in the workplace over the past 2 years, many Gen Zs and Millennials don't feel this is resulting in any meaningful impact on employees.

© iStock.com / Prostock-Studio

Source: Adapted from Parmelee (2022). Courtesy of Deloitte Insights.

Self includes gender, and there are many studies on how the individual's perception of gender affects purchasing behaviour (Baker et al., 2015; Bartikowski and Walsh, 2015; Lin et al., 2018; Oakley, 2015; Schmitt and Rasolofoarison, 2015), and spanning many country perspectives (Bashir et al., 2018 [Africa]; Laureti and Benedetti, 2018 [Italy]; Qasim et al., 2018 [Jordan]; Vicente-Molina et al., 2018 [Spain]). People typically form a view on the gender-appropriateness of brands: there is evidence that men are more concerned about this than women, being less prepared to adopt a brand extension that they perceive as coming from a 'feminine' brand (Jung and Lee, 2006). Ulrich and Tiisier-Desbordes (2018) made four points to do with gender and brand.

1. That men with 'resistant' masculinities are strongly attached to choosing masculine brands; others with more hybrid masculinities are more open to feminine brands and do not care about brand gender.
2. The importance of brand gender salience: men with more traditional masculinities interpret brands through the prism of gender first and over-interpret gendered cues in brand execution.
3. Feminine brands are considered as threats for men with traditional masculinities.
4. Brand extensions to the opposite sex are criticised by men with more traditional masculinities but appreciated by men with hybrid masculinities, independently of sexual orientation.

Men also tend to define masculinity in part through advertisements they see (although they may interpret what masculinity means in different ways) (Connor et al., 2021). Extensions from a 'male' brand are much more likely to be adopted (Essa Al Lily, 2022; Tuncay, 2006).

Self-concept has four attributes, as follows:

1. It is learned, not innate.
2. It is stable and consistent. Self-perception may change; self-concept does not. This accounts for brand loyalty, since self-concept involves an opinion about which products will 'fit the image'.
3. It is purposeful; in other words, there is a reason and a purpose behind it. Essentially, self-concept is there to protect and enhance a person's ego. It is therefore advisable not to attack a person's beliefs directly; people often become angry or at least defensive when this happens.
4. It is unique to the individual, and promotes individualism.

Self-concept breaks down into different components, or dimensions (Walker, 1992). These are shown in Table 6.1.

One other, which was not identified by Walker in Table 6.1, is the **extended self**. There are many objects, items, possessions that we might consider to be an extension of our self. And the spectrum is wide: from personal possessions to national monuments – there are a variety of items we use to denote our individual largesse.

Extended self
Items which consumers use as an extension of themselves to define their roles in society

There is some overlap, but the differences are quite marked between the dimensions. Each dimension has some relevance for marketers, and the implications are as shown in Table 6.2.

For marketers, the differences are useful. The ideal self predicts attempts at upward mobility: purchases of training courses, self-improvement classes, upmarket products, cosmetic surgery, etc. Looking-glass self is relevant for other-directed people.

TABLE 6.1 Components of self-concept

Component	Explanation
Real self	This is the actual, objective self, as others see us. There is a problem with this definition, since other people never know the whole story. This means that the 'real' self may be something other than the face shown to the world
Self-image	This is the subjective self, as we see ourselves. Self-image is likely to differ radically from the real self, but to an extent this is modified over time because of feedback from others. We modify our self-image in the light of the reactions of others
Looking-glass self	The social self, or the way we think other people see us. This does not always coincide with the way people actually see us, since we are not able to read minds. Feedback from others will be constrained by politeness or by a desire to project a self-image on the part of the respondent, so we are not always aware of what other people really think we are like
Ideal self	How we wish we were; this connects to the self-actualisation need that Maslow identified. This self is often the one that provokes the most extravagant spending, as the individual tries to make up the gap between self-image and ideal self
Possible selves	These are the selves we might become, or the selves we wish we could become

TABLE 6.2 Relevance of self-image

Dimension	Relevance to marketers	Examples
Real self	As the face that is shown to the world, this is the one that people most wish to influence	Conspicuous consumption of cars, houses, etc. Cosmetics, fashion and hairdressing
Self-image	Useful in two ways; first, the negative aspects of self-image influence the ideal self, and second, the positive aspects influence purchases that reinforce the self-image	Somebody whose self-image is 'cool' will not want to jeopardise that, and will buy appropriate products to match that image. Somebody whose self-image is poor will want to correct discrepancies
Ideal self	The aspect that leads to the greatest purchases of self-improvement products	Correspondence courses, cosmetics, cosmetic surgery, musical instruments and any number of other products that lead to self-development
Looking-glass self	The way we think others see us; this influences us in making changes to those views, or reinforcing views that are perceived as positive	A man who thinks his friends see him as being staid or boring might be prompted to buy something cool and trendy (perhaps a convertible sports car) in order to correct the image. Conversely, somebody more outer-directed might deliberately buy a car to fit in with the image he thinks he has with his friends; perhaps to buy an electric hybrid vehicle because his friends see him as an eco-friendly, down-to-earth person
Possible selves	The selves we might become, or the selves we wish to become, are not necessarily the same. We may fear what we might become (for example, being afraid of becoming overweight, or of contracting a serious disease, or of becoming an alcoholic)	In some cases marketers have a role in helping people to formulate and fulfil their dreams – education and training courses are an example. In other cases marketing techniques are used to enable people to avoid becoming what they fear being: social marketing campaigns encourage people to eat healthily, take exercise, cut down on smoking and over-eating, and control their alcohol intake

THE SELF AND PERSONALITY

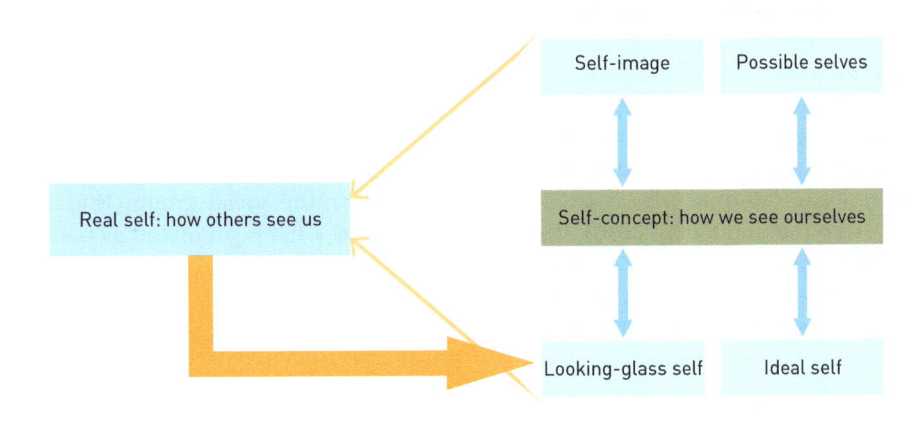

FIGURE 6.2 Relationship between components of self-concept

In Figure 6.2, self-concept is generated partly by internal factors such as looking-glass self, ideal self and self-image, but these are modified (particularly through looking-glass self) by the real self. This is because those around us give us feedback on how we are coming across, either by showing approval of what we do or by showing disapproval. These forces are so powerful that they even extend to online identities: researchers have found that similar-looking avatars tend to congregate together in virtual reality (Green et al., 2020, 2021; Lin et al., 2022), and are less friendly and welcoming than are groups of different-looking avatars. This therefore plays a role in web design, influencing both 2D and 3D designs (see for example Visinescu et al., 2015). Even owning the right set of virtual possessions is important in cyberspace (Bartoli et al., 2022; Wood et al., 2009).

In recent years, the concept of the **market maven** has developed (Goldring et al., 2022). Market mavens are people who define themselves as knowledgeable about the market for a particular product type: the word 'maven' derives from a Yiddish word for 'wise'. Such people enjoy sharing their knowledge with others, and enjoy the self-concept of being an expert; this improves their self-confidence as well (Clark et al., 2008; Kiani and Laroche, 2019). Obviously mavens are important to marketers (especially those in high-tech industries) (Khan et al., 2022), since they influence purchase decisions of others very strongly. Mavens differ from opinion leaders: opinion leaders tend to have high levels of emotional involvement with product categories, while mavens have a more intellectual, knowledge-based stance. Mavens also show a higher need for variety in their lives than do opinion leaders – in other words, they may well switch brands if they discover information that means the new brand is better (Stokburger-Sauer and Hoyer, 2009). Vloggers and YouTubers are increasingly seen as market mavens, but some would argue that they've gone a step too far by becoming social media sellouts (Farzin et al., 2020; Schwemmer and Ziewiecki, 2018).

Market maven
Someone who is a self-appointed expert about a particular product category or market

Self can also be categorised as actual self, ideal self and worst self (Banister and Hogg, 2003). This is a simpler model, but it includes the concept of the worst self – the self we are ashamed of. For marketers, products can be promoted as being good for avoiding the worst self, or can be promoted as being good for appeasing the worst self.

Self-image is relevant to what we think we deserve – what is the 'right' product for us. Teenagers use music consumption as a way of building social capital, creating boundaries and defining who is excluded or included in the social group (Nuttall, 2009; Westerlund and Partti, 2018). People are swayed by what is promoted as being 'just right for people like you' – children can be told they are having 'the special children's meal'; students can be swayed by a 'special student discount'; elderly people by the special 'senior citizen's service'. Sometimes this type of promotion can backfire – there may be fears about the quality of the service or product, for instance, and (especially in the case of older people) the self-image of the person might differ from the image the marketer has of this particular group. This is why advertising aimed at elderly people often uses actors in their 50s and 60s rather than actors in their 70s or 80s. A related but side issue is that people tend to relate more strongly to brands that contain letters from their own names: this is probably a subconscious association with the brand (Brendl et al., 2003).

Real self is not known to the consumer, although it is one of the greatest motivators in consumer behaviour. In the words of the Scottish poet Robert Burns, 'To see ourselves as others see us' is not in our gift – and this may be just as well. Achieving the ideal self is very much about getting appropriate applause and critical acclaim, so that we know whether we are getting it right; but perhaps more importantly there is the element of learning the lines and getting the production right in terms of costume, make-up and script. People therefore modify their behaviour according to the feedback obtained; this is called **self-monitoring** (Snyder, 1974), and self-monitoring theory has been used in many domains: education (Meltzer, 2018), digital health (Lund and Kappelgaard, 2018) and eating pathology (Schaefer et al., 2018).

Self-monitoring

The regulatory mechanism that controls behaviour, without outside intercession

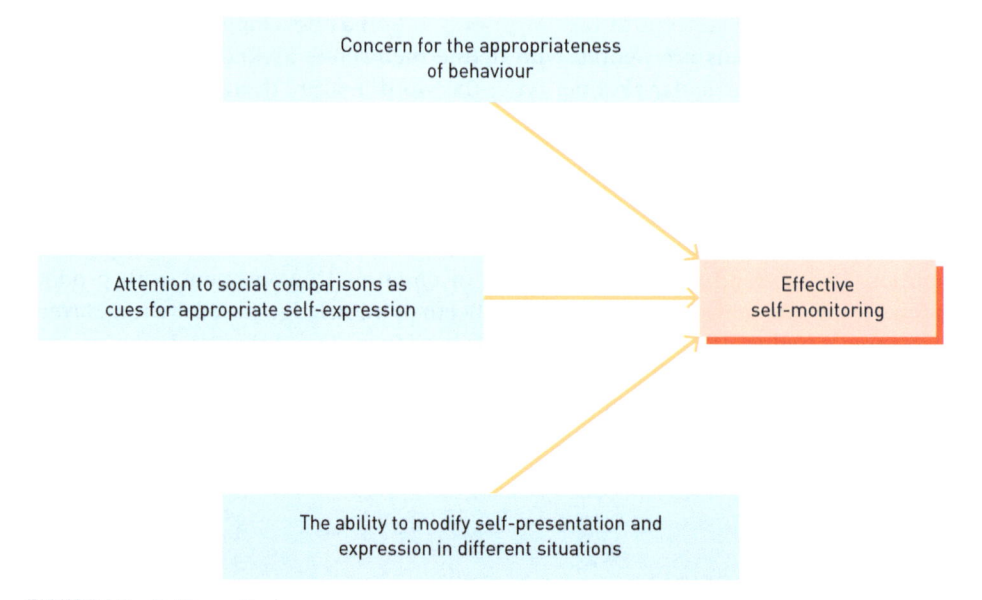

FIGURE 6.3 Self-monitoring

As shown in Figure 6.3, self-monitoring has three forms of expression: concern for the appropriateness of behaviour, attention to social comparison as cues for appropriate self-expression, and the ability to modify self-presentation and expression across situations (Nantel and Strahle, 1986). Another example is people's attitude to credit, especially in these times after the global economic recession: people with strong self-monitoring mechanisms, and people with low price-consciousness, are less likely to rely on credit cards than are people with low self-control or high price sensitivity (Kim and Son, 2021; Mokhtar et al., 2015; Perry, 2001; Wang et al., 2015). Such self-monitoring mechanisms only have a limited amount of mental resources backing them up: often people who normally exhibit great self-control will sometimes 'snap' their self-control and buy something entirely on impulse (Aidla, 2018; Moes et al., 2021; Vohs and Faber, 2003; Zhang et al., 2018), where factors and dimensions of extraversion, conscientiousness and neuroticism are found consistently to predict impulse buying (Thompson and Prendergast, 2015).

In other words, people ensure that their behaviour is appropriate for the occasion by observing what others are doing and by acting in harmony with that behaviour. Rather like the inexperienced traveller who watches others to see what the local customs are, people take cues from those around them in order to ensure polite behaviour. Low self-monitors are more likely to behave according to some inner drive, and may even prefer to be seen as being different from the rest of humanity; high self-monitors are more likely to conform with those around them, and are therefore more susceptible to appeals to be fashionable.

Some products are transformational, in other words they allow people to change who they are. For example, cosmetic surgery, correspondence courses and self-improvement books all offer people the opportunity to change their self-concept. Identity-related perceptions form the basis for choosing such products and for evaluating their success (or otherwise). People will also decide whether or not their self-concept can accommodate the changes (Kleine et al., 2009). For example, someone who is considering doing a **MOOC** will evaluate the course on the basis of perceived weaknesses in his or her self-concept, but will also consider whether doing the course will result in a self-concept that is equally less than ideal. Perhaps the individual recognises a need to take a course in computer science and online security (for self-actualising reasons) but does not want to be thought of as a 'nerd'.

MOOC
Massive open online course aimed at unlimited participation and open access via the web

CONSUMER BEHAVIOUR IN ACTION: SELF-LEARNING

Back in October 2011, Stanford professors launched three free online courses, open to the public. One by one, these courses went massive, with enrolments topping 100,000 students each. Soon the media was calling these courses MOOCs, short for massive open online courses. Since then, more than 900 universities around the world have launched free online courses. In addition to the larger global MOOC platforms (Coursera, edX, FutureLearn), many national governments around the world have launched their own country-specific MOOC platforms, including India, Italy, Israel, Mexico and Thailand.

After a decade of popularisation, a total of 220 million students have signed up for at least one course on one of the MOOCs platforms, and 40 million did so in 2021 alone (excluding China). MOOCs and MOOC platforms are still growing, even after the crazy 'Year of the MOOC' prompted by the pandemic and travel restrictions in 2020.

Dysmorphia
Deformity or abnormality in the shape or size of a specific part of the body

Zoom dysmorphia
A feeling of unhappiness or dissatisfaction about one's looks exacerbated by looking at oneself on camera all day

People's decisions to undergo drastic transformations (for example, cosmetic surgery) are also influenced in different ways by the people around them and the situations they find themselves in (as we've already seen earlier). For example, in the case of teenage girls contemplating cosmetic surgery, support from family tends to reduce the need for the surgery, whereas support from friends (especially through social media platforms) tends to increase it (Maes and de Lenne, 2022; Pentina et al., 2009; Zhao, 2022). Yet with midlife women, research conducted by Dunaev et al. (2018) indicated that lower weight and appearance esteem were associated with more positive cosmetic surgery attitudes. Notwithstanding the above, the global pandemic – and new way of working – has triggered a new disorder: **Zoom dysmorphia**. The coronavirus (Covid-19) pandemic increased popularity of videoconferencing saw a massive shift toward virtual living where individuals found themselves staring at their own video scrutinising their appearance and potentially developing dysmorphic concerns (Pino, 2022).

PERSONALITY

Personality is the collection of individual characteristics that make a person unique, and which control an individual's responses and relationship with the external environment. It is a composite of subordinate processes, for example attitude, motivation and perception. It is the whole of the person, and is the system that governs behaviour rather than the behaviour itself. However, the concept of personality is actually abstract but can be described in terms of personal traits. Thus, the elements that make up personality are called **traits**. Considerable research effort has been made towards linking individual personality traits to buying behaviour, but with limited success. This is despite the apparent logic that people would buy products that reflect their personality traits (for example, outgoing flamboyant people might be expected to buy more colourful clothing). In fact, there is some evidence that personality relates to new product (innovation) purchasing behaviour, as we saw earlier in Chapter 3; there is also some evidence that the degree to which someone is influenced by what other people think affects some buying behaviour. Overall, though, it is the total personality that dictates buying behaviour rather than each individual trait (Chatterjee et al., 2018).

Trait
A component of personality

Personality has the following features:

1. It is *integrated*. That is to say, all the factors making up the personality act on each other to produce an integrated whole.
2. It is *self-serving*. The characteristics of personality facilitate the attainment of needs and goals. In other words, the personality exists to meet its own needs.
3. Personal characteristics are *individualistic* and unique, in degree and intensity as well as presence. Although many personal characteristics are shared with other people, the possible number of combinations of traits is huge, and therefore each individual is different. This is what makes each person a separate and unique being.
4. Personality is *overt*. External behaviour is affected by personality. In other words, the personality can be observed (albeit indirectly) and deduced from the person's behaviour.

5. Personality is *consistent*. Once a person's basic personality has been established, it will change only slowly and with some difficulty; for practical purposes, an individual consumer's personality will stay constant throughout the buying process.

It is difficult for marketers to take a standardised approach because people are individuals, yet the exigencies of the business world require standardisation. For this reason, many attempts have been made to establish groupings of personality types, which can be approached with a standardised offering. This is one of the bases of segmentation (the process of dividing the market into target groups of customers with similar needs; Leckelt et al., 2022). For this reason, and of course for the purposes of treating abnormal personalities, there is a long history of studying personality (Cooper, 2015; Davies, 2003; Pennington, 2018).

APPROACHES TO STUDYING PERSONALITY

There are four basic approaches:

1. *The psychoanalytic approach.* Here the emphasis is on psychoanalysis, or studying the processes and events that have led to the development of personality traits. The focus is on the individual. This approach is typified by Freudian psychiatry, which seeks to help patients to confront the life events that have shaped their personalities.
2. *Typology.* Here the individuals are grouped according to recognised personality types.
3. *Trait and factor theories.* The individual traits of personality can be examined as factors making up the whole person, and each trait can be categorised.
4. *Psychographics.* Consumers are measured using their behavioural tendencies in order to infer personality traits.

The Freudian approach is very much centred on the individual. Here the psychologist asks the patient or subject to talk about anything regardless of logic, courtesy, self-defence, etc.; this is termed free association. A Freudian would analyse these statements in terms of id, ego and superego.

According to Freud, the **id** is the underlying drive of the psyche. It is the source of the most basic, instinctive forces that cause people to behave in particular ways, and operates below the conscious level: it may be responsible for the compulsive behaviour exhibited by some individuals. There is some evidence to show that compulsive behaviour such as buying lottery tickets and scratch cards is linked to other compulsive behaviour such as smoking, and negatively linked to agreeableness and intellectual dimensions of personality (Balabanis, 2002; Rein and Eysenck, 2018). The **ego** is the conscious self, the part of the mind that makes the day-to-day decisions that lead to the satisfaction of the id; the **superego** is an internalised parent, the conscience that holds us back from selfish gratification of the id's needs. The superego also operates mostly below the conscious level, and is the 'brake' on behaviour; in a sense, the ego is constantly making compromises between the id's demands and the superego's restraints. This is shown in Figure 6.4.

Id
The unconscious part of the mind responsible for basic desires

Ego
The conscious self

Superego
The component of mind that acts as a restraint on behaviour

In simple terms, the id acts like a spoilt child, demanding instant gratification regardless of consequences; the superego acts like a stern parent, urging self-restraint and devotion to duty, and the ego acts like a good lawyer, arranging compromises and settlements between the two parties which will not lead to bankruptcy. Hedonic needs (which we studied in the previous chapter) largely derive from the id, so advertising with a hedonic appeal is intended to strengthen the id's demands and encourage the ego to find in favour of the id. Some advertising also weakens the effects of the superego – marketers might suggest that life is too short to listen to your conscience all the time, for example.

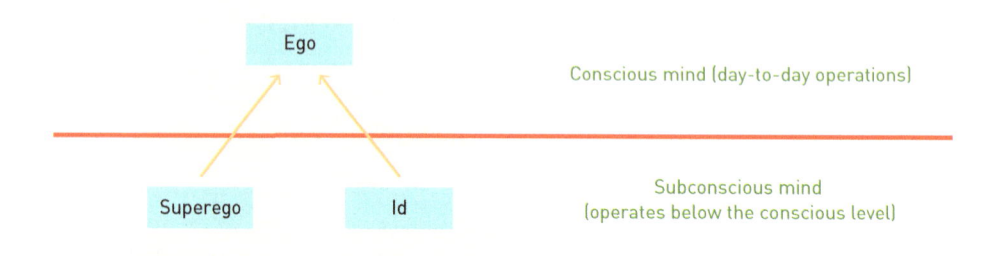

FIGURE 6.4 The id, the ego and the superego

The Freudian approach led to motivation research, which purported to explain the underlying reasons for buying. Motivation research was at its most popular in the 1950s and was, for a time, believed to be able to predict consumer behaviour in terms of basic drives that supposedly came from the id. Some of the claims made for motivational research now seem fairly ridiculous to us; for example, it was claimed that crunching cornflakes appealed to the killer instinct because it sounds like crunching animal bones, that baking a cake is a substitute for giving birth, convertible cars were thought to be a substitute for a girlfriend, and so forth. Motivational research became somewhat discredited because of the extravagant claims made, but still has something to say to marketers. Finding out what people really think, as opposed to what they say they are thinking, enables marketers to address people's underlying needs and wants much more accurately.

Without wishing to turn this chapter into one that investigates research methods, it is worth noting some of the research methods that help uncover 'motivation'. Top of the list here, and one that is still quite widely used, is the **depth** (or **guided**) **interview**. A small number of respondents (50 or fewer) are interviewed without the use of a formal list of questions. Interviewees are encouraged to express their innermost thoughts and feelings about the object of the research (perhaps a new product). The interviewer needs considerable skill to keep the interview on course without leading the interviewee into expressing beliefs that are not his or her actual beliefs: it is easy to give the interviewee the impression that there is a 'right' answer.

A variation on this is the **focus group**, in which a group of ten or so respondents are invited to discuss their feelings and motivations collectively. The advantage of this method is that the respondents will tend to stimulate each other, and therefore there is less risk of the interviewer introducing **bias** into the results: the problem

---

Depth (guided) interview
Open-ended interviews conducted with a small sample of respondents in order to assess their innermost thoughts and feelings

Focus group
A group of people assembled for the purpose of gathering their collective views about a given issue

Bias
The factor that affects the processing of information as a result of the pre-existing mindset

is that people may be reluctant to express attitudes that are embarrassing or might show them in a bad light.

FIGURE 6.5 Cartoon projective technique

Projective tests are widely used in psychological counselling and psychiatry, and occasionally have applications in market research. They are based on the assumption that the individual may sometimes have difficulty in answering questions directly, either because the answers would be embarrassing or because the answers do not readily come to mind. In effect, a projective technique requires the respondent to say what somebody else might think about a given topic. Sometimes this is done by showing the respondent a cartoon strip of people in a relevant situation: sometimes the respondent is asked to complete a sentence, or perhaps will be asked to draw a picture describing his or her feelings about the attitudinal object. In all cases the intention of the research is to allow the respondents to convey their innermost feelings in a non-personal way.

In Figure 6.5, the person on the left is expressing an opinion that may be controversial: the respondent in the research is asked to fill in what the person on the right might say in response. In theory, the respondent will fill in his or her own opinion, but without the social risk of expressing the opinion openly. This method is particularly useful for uncovering hidden attitudes, perhaps where the individual has an attitude that might be regarded as antisocial or offensive.

Motivational researchers tend to be interested in the id, claiming that this dictates the individual's basic drives. The assumption is that knowledge of the id's demands will enable marketers to shape arguments for the ego to use in overcoming the superego's restraining influence.

From a marketing viewpoint, research of this nature allows firms to determine people's real attitudes to topics such as excessive drinking, cosmetic surgery or sexual imagery in advertising. All these topics have caused people to feel embarrassed and to avoid answering truthfully – but marketers need to get to the truth if they are to address people's real needs without causing offence. Evidence published by Stedman et al. (2018) suggested that training with traditional projective tests seemed to have declined at all levels. However, other recent research shows that it is very much alive and kicking in a variety of sectors (Farzin et al., 2020; Spry and Pich, 2021).

TYPE APPROACH

Freud was the earliest of the scientific psychologists. In subsequent years, alternative theories to Freud's developed. The followers of Jung categorise people (in addition to Freudian belief) as **introverts** (preoccupied with themselves and the internal world) or **extroverts** (preoccupied with others and the outside world). This was

Projective test
A research technique whereby respondents are asked to give an opinion of what they think someone else's attitude or feelings might be on a given topic

Introvert
Someone who is withdrawn from other people

Extrovert
Someone who demonstrates his or her personality traits in a strongly overt or obvious manner to other people

an early attempt to classify people into broad types, and this process has continued ever since, with different researchers discovering different ways of grouping people according to personality types.

Seminal academic texts have defined people across three dimensions (Horney, 1945):

1. *Compliant*. Moves towards people, has goodness, sympathy, love, unselfishness and humility. Tends to be over-apologetic, over-sensitive, over-grateful, over-generous and over-considerate in seeking love and affection.
2. *Aggressive*. Usually moves against people. Controls fears and emotions in a quest for success, prestige and admiration. Needs power, exploits others.
3. *Detached*. Moves away from people. Conformity is repugnant to the detached person. Distrustful of others, these people are self-sufficient and independent, and value intelligence and reasoning.

There is empirical evidence to show that these categorisations have some effect on people's buying behaviour. For example, it has been shown that compliant people use more mouthwash and toilet soap, and prefer branded products; aggressive people use more cologne and after-shave. Detached people show low interest in branding (Cohen, 1967) and this is reflected in their lack of loyalty towards any particular brands. It seems likely that compliant people will be very eager to please, and reluctant to offend, which is likely to mean that they will be suitable subjects for campaigns emphasising gift-giving or caring behaviour. The problem, as always, lies in identifying these individuals.

Reisman (1953) categorised people against three characteristics, in terms of the sources of their basic drives:

1. *Inner-directed* people are essentially driven from within, and are not too concerned with what other people think.
2. *Other-directed* people get their motivation and take their cues from other people.
3. *Tradition-directed* people get their cues and motivations from the past, from traditional beliefs and sources. These people are nowadays in a very tiny minority.

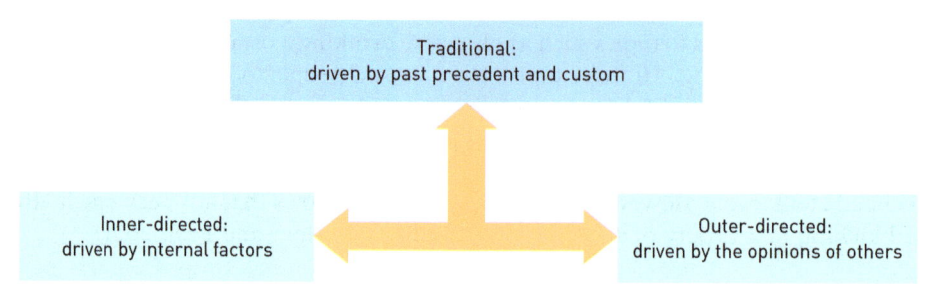

Traditional: driven by past precedent and custom

Inner-directed: driven by internal factors

Outer-directed: driven by the opinions of others

FIGURE 6.6 Reisman's typologies

Reisman's categories (see Figure 6.6) have been used in the past for marketing purposes. Inner-directeds, for example, were shown to be innovators for cars and foodstuffs (Donnelly, 1970; Tunc, 2018), whereas outer-directeds have tended to be fashion victims (Zinkhan and Shermohamad, 1986). There appears to be a change in the social paradigm, however, which is turning these views in a different direction. Broadly speaking, it would appear that more and more people are becoming inner-directed. This has led to a shift in the prevailing social paradigm away from the basically conformist attitude of the Victorian era towards a more individualistic, free-thinking society. Once again we should assume that most people are on a continuum. To some extent we are all driven by all three factors: Reisman's model is intended to show that some people may lean more towards one type of influence than towards others.

The mother and daughter team of Kathryn Briggs and Isabel Myers later developed the Myers–Briggs Type Indicator, shown in Figure 6.7 (Briggs and Myers, 1962), with four personality dimensions:

1. Extrovert/introvert.
2. Sensing/intuitive.
3. Thinking/feeling.
4. Judging/perceptive.

The combinations can define people into 16 different types; for example, an extrovert-sensing-feeling-judging person is warm-hearted, talkative, popular and likes harmonious relationships. An introvert-intuitive-thinking-judging person is likely to be quiet, intelligent, cerebral and reclusive.

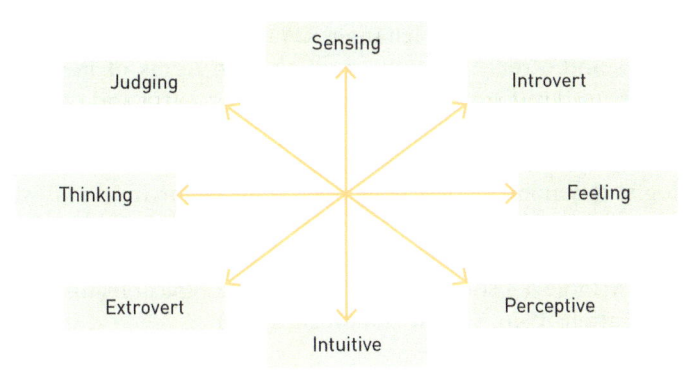

FIGURE 6.7 Myers–Briggs Type Indicator

Note yet again that most of us are on a continuum in terms of the Myers–Briggs dimensions. Relatively few people would be at the extremes of any of the dimensions, but the model does provide us with a means of categorising people in broad terms.

This shift in the social paradigm is having several effects: first, the fashion market has fragmented and almost anything goes, often with marketers suffering from ethical lapses (Sheth and Sisodia, 2015). Second, marketing practice is undergoing a paradigm shift from a transactional to a relationship orientation (Hollensen, 2016). Third, there is an increase in the tendency for people to espouse causes and work towards altruistic goals, even in the face of opposition from the Establishment. The shift in the social paradigm is coming about as a result of increased wealth and security in the Western world; as consumers move up Maslow's Hierarchy of Needs (see Chapter 5) more of them are operating at the self-actualising level (McNulty, 1985). The movement towards a more inner-directed population gave rise to the VALS typology described in Chapter 5.

Overall, the type approach has much to offer marketers. There is little doubt that personality type affects buying behaviour, and since such types are easily identified and are easy to appeal to through marketing communications, it is not difficult to approach these groups, typically by using models.

TRAITS AND FACTORS

Personality is composed of traits, or individual 'atoms' of personality. These individual predispositional attributes exert influences on behaviour, so the traits must be identified before people can be typed or classified.

Traits tend to be enduring facets of personality. In other words, traits tend not to change much over time, and even when they do change they tend to do so rather slowly. Those that might tend to change with age are: anxiety level (which tends to go down as the individual gets older), friendliness (which can change either way) and eagerness for novelty (which tends to go down) (for further information on this you should read Goleman [1987], Roberts and DelVecchio [2000] and Roberts et al. [2006]). A few traits may vary throughout life, but studies show that adult personalities do not vary significantly as a person ages. This is not to say that behaviour and attitudes never change, merely that the underlying personality tends to stay very much the same. Changing roles, responsibilities and circumstances have much more effect on behavioural changes (Franklin-Luther and Volk, 2022). For instance, Roberts and Mroczek (2008) show that 'in terms of mean-level change, people show increased self-confidence, warmth, self-control and emotional stability with age'.

The psychologist Raymond Cattell developed a 16-factor trait analysis which has proved useful in defining personality types. Each factor has a high and low range, so that people can be ascribed a position along the continuum between low and high across each factor. Table 6.3 shows the factors and the typical features of someone at either extreme (Cattell, 1946; Cattell and Mead, 2008).

The study of individual traits as they relate to buying behaviour seems unlikely to produce concrete results. This is probably because personality is interdependent; studying a few traits in isolation gives an insufficiently complete view of the whole person. However, a combination of hierarchically arranged traits has been linked to the propensity to undergo cosmetic surgery or to use tanning studios (Mowen et al., 2009). Traits are clearly interrelated, but given the number of traits that have been identified (several thousand, according to some authors), the interrelationships are likely to be complex, especially as people exhibit the different traits to a greater or lesser degree. A meta-analysis of how trait self-control relates to a wide range of behaviours has been conducted by de Ridder et al. (2012) and makes for interesting reading. One last area to mention here is what Keyes et al. (2015) call positive reciprocity. When one increases self-acceptance (liking most parts of one's personality), and also increases social integration (belonging to a community) (Wellman and Gulia, 1999), 'this may cause improvements in personality as reflected in increased extraversion and less neuroticism' (Keyes et al., 2015).

TABLE 6.3 16 personality factor (PF) trait analysis

Low-range descriptors	Primary factor	High-range descriptors
Impersonal, reserved, detached, distant, cool, formal, aloof	Warmth	Warm, easy-going, participating, likes people, outgoing, attentive to others, kindly
Concrete thinking, less intelligent, lower general mental capacity, unable to handle abstract problems	Reasoning	Abstract thinking, more intelligent, bright, higher general mental capacity, fast learner
Reactive emotionally, changeable, affected by feelings, emotionally less stable, easily upset	Emotional stability	Emotionally stable, adaptive, mature, faces reality calmly
Deferential, cooperative, avoids conflict, submissive, humble, obedient, easily led, docile, accommodating	Dominance	Dominant, forceful, assertive, aggressive, competitive, stubborn, bossy
Serious, restrained, prudent, taciturn, introspective, silent	Liveliness	Lively, animated, spontaneous, enthusiastic, happy-go-lucky, cheerful, expressive, impulsive
Expedient, non-conforming, disregards rules, self-indulgent	Rule consciousness	Rule-conscious, dutiful, conscientious, conforming, moralistic, staid, rule-bound
Shy, threat-sensitive, timid, hesitant, intimidated	Social boldness	Socially bold, venturesome, thick-skinned, uninhibited
Utilitarian, objective, unsentimental, tough-minded, self-reliant, no-nonsense, rough	Sensitivity	Sensitive, aesthetic, sentimental, tender-minded, intuitive, refined
Trusting, unsuspecting, accepting, unconditional, easy	Vigilance	Vigilant, suspicious, sceptical, distrustful, oppositional
Grounded, practical, prosaic, solution-oriented, steady, conventional	Abstractedness	Abstract, imaginative, absent-minded, impractical, absorbed in ideas
Forthright, genuine, artless, open, guileless, naive, unpretentious, involved	Privateness	Private, discreet, non-disclosing, shrewd, polished, worldly, astute, diplomatic
Self-assured, unworried, complacent, secure, free of guilt, confident, self-satisfied	Apprehension	Apprehensive, self-doubting, worried, guilt-prone, insecure, worrying, self-blaming
Traditional, attached to familiar, conservative ideas, respecting traditional ideas	Openness to change	Open to change, experimental, liberal, analytical, critical, free-thinking, flexible
Group-oriented, affiliative, a joiner and follower, dependent on others	Self-reliance	Self-reliant, solitary, resourceful, individualistic, self-sufficient
Tolerates disorder, unexacting, flexible, undisciplined, lax, self-conflict, impulsive, careless of social rules, uncontrolled	Perfectionism	Perfectionistic, organised, compulsive, self-disciplined, socially precise, exacting willpower, control, self-sentimental
Relaxed, placid, tranquil, torpid, patient, composed, low drive	Tension	Tense, high energy, impatient, driven, frustrated, over-wrought, time-driven

Source: US 16PF (2009).

16PF® is a trademark and registered trademark of The Institute for Personality and Ability Testing, Inc. (IPAT). IPAT is a wholly owned subsidiary of Performance Assessment Network, Inc. (PAN). © Copyright 2009 Institute for Personality and Ability Testing, Inc. (IPAT). All rights reserved. Reproduced with kind permission of IPAT and PAN.

Psychographics
Using behavioural tendencies to infer personality traits

PSYCHOGRAPHICS

Psychographics is sometimes known as lifestyle studies, since it is concerned with people's values and approaches to life. Essentially, it is a quantitative study of consumer lifestyles for the purpose of relating those lifestyles to the consumers' purchase behaviour. For example, somebody who has a 'green' set of values is likely to have an eco-friendly lifestyle (Strizhakova et al., 2021), which in turn means that the individual will be more likely to buy a bicycle than a car, and perhaps lean more towards being a vegetarian than eating red meat (Kuesten et al., 2022), and so forth. These ethical values can be powerful forces in decision-making (Dane and Sonenshein, 2015; Fraj and Martinez, 2006; Shaw et al., 2005). By knowing what a person's basic lifestyle is, we can make a fair prediction as to their purchasing behaviour, and the kind of products, promotions and technology (Kamal Basha et al., 2022) that will most appeal to that individual.

The psychographics approach to personality study combines the strengths of motivation research on the one hand with those of trait and factor theories on the other. The assessment of lifestyle often involves very lengthy and involved studies of large samples of the population; the Target Group Index annual research programme, part of Kantar Media Group and more recently the Kantar Worldpanel, deals in consumer knowledge and insights based on continuous consumer panels. They ask people (approximately 700,000 people across 60 countries) to respond to a multitude of lifestyle statements. From this survey, market monitoring, advanced analytics and other tailored market research solutions, researchers at Kantar can identify different lifestyles and analyse the attitudes behind what people buy and what they consume, and consequently predict different purchasing patterns.

An example of this approach is the VALS breakdown referred to in Chapter 5. A UK equivalent to the VALS breakdown (already shown in Chapter 5) was developed by Taylor Nelson, as shown in Table 6.4. The relative percentages of each group are likely to have changed in the intervening 30 years, of course – as noted earlier, there is a trend towards greater inner-directedness.

Psychographics approaches have in common that they all try to predict behaviour from knowledge of lifestyle and attitudes. The drawback with this approach is that the necessary research is complex, time-consuming and ultimately relies heavily on the judgement of the researchers to decide which factors are appropriate to a particular lifestyle.

TABLE 6.4 Lifestyle types

	Lifestyle type	Characteristics	% of population
Sustenance-driven groups; motivated by the need for security	Belonger	People who believe in the Establishment, traditional family values and patriotism. Averse to change	19%
	Survivor	People who are fighting a 'holding action'; accept authority, hard-working, quiet, traditional. Strong class consciousness	16%
	Aimless	There are two main categories: young unemployed whose main motivation is short-term 'kicks', and the very old, whose motivation is simply day-to-day existence	5%

	Lifestyle type	Characteristics	% of population
Outer-directed group	Conspicuous consumer	Interested in material possessions, taking cues from reference groups (friends, family). Followers of fashion	18%
Inner-directed groups; motivated by self-actualisation	Social resister	Caring group, motivated by ideals of fairness and a good quality of life at the societal level. Altruistic, concerned with social issues like ecology and nuclear disarmament	11%
	Experimentalist	Materialistic and pro-technology, individualistic and interested in novelty	14%
	Self-explorer	Motivated by self-expression and self-realisation. Tolerant, able to think big and look for global, holistic solutions	16%

Source: Adapted from McNulty (1985). Reproduced by kind permission.

CRITICAL REFLECTION

Human decision-making is biased by unconscious mental processes, or shortcuts, that typically allow us to make fast, smart decisions but can sometimes cause us to make seemingly irrational choices. One of these biases is the status quo bias, which is our preference for the current state of affairs. Our intuitive response to new technology like electric vehicles (EVs) is often to ignore or reject it, rather than take a risk on a new, unknown option.

Understanding biases like this can help explain the choices people make and can even help us influence those choices. Because we don't always act rationally, changing people's behaviour is less about changing their minds and more about changing how you frame a choice so that it aligns with how people's minds work. Automotive makers need to make the decision of buying an EV an intuitive and emotionally rewarding choice, not just one that ticks the boxes on range numbers or CO_2 emission comparisons.

The growth in EVs seems almost unstoppable. EV registrations in the UK in 2020 saw 125% growth and leading auto manufacturers such as Ford have announced plans to increase investment in EVs. Globally, too, the signs look promising as reports find that sales of EVs across the world grew by 40% last year.

However, if EVs are going to become the norm, more needs to be done. A significant number of consumers are still unsure about the practicalities of these vehicles and haven't yet switched their gasoline or diesel car for an electric one. In fact, research carried out by Ofgem found that 38% of people in the UK have concerns about short battery life and range, and 36% are worried about having nowhere to charge their car.

Planned infrastructure and technological improvements will, therefore, help pave the way for mass EV adoption. Battery technology that reduces range anxiety, a network of charging stations that speed up and simplify charging, and vehicle prices that compare favourably with internal combustion engine vehicles will all undoubtedly nudge people towards electric.

One of the reasons we prefer the status quo is that we're 'cognitive misers', with limited time and energy to focus on every decision. In other words, it's easier to stick with what we've always done without considering other options!

Source: Adapted from Leighton (2021). For more data and insights, visit Automotive World: www.automotiveworld.com.

The psychographics approach appears to have strong potential to tell us about what people will buy, since clearly most purchases are related to a chosen lifestyle.

Finally, it would be remiss of us to end a chapter on the self and personality without giving a mention to the selfie. People's propensity for photographing themselves and posting the pictures online has become the norm worldwide: the word has recently been included in the Oxford Dictionary Online, showing an acceptance by the Establishment.

There are mixed views about whether taking a selfie is tantamount to self-objectifying or is perhaps even narcissistic. There's no doubt however that *Brand Selfie* is with us to stay for some time (Hartmann et al., 2021). A study by Fox and Rooney (2015) examined the relationship between selfie posting, photo editing and personality. They looked at this from the perspective that there could be three other traits at work here. The first of these is narcissism, which is the notion that some individuals are extremely self-centred to the point of having a grandiose view of themselves (Raskin and Terry, 1988).

© iStock.com/swissmediavision

They also have a need to be admired by others around them in the physical as well as the virtual world (Hong et al., 2022). Second, there is psychopathy – an impulsive state with a lack of empathy (Jonason and Krause, 2013). Third, there is an element of Machiavellianism: being manipulative with disregard for others' needs (Christie and Geis, 1970; Liu and Keane, 2021). Some of the findings from Fox and Rooney (2015) are consistent with other research that says that both narcissism and low self-esteem are related to greater Facebook use (Mehdizadeh, 2010). This said, even more recent research (Sorokowski et al., 2015) indicates that there are many motivations for selfie posting other than showing off. For instance, 'naked loan selfies' are a Chinese internet phenomenon in which naked selfies taken by young women are used as a form of collateral in peer-to-peer loaning systems. These are techno-social entities that are enacted through specific online networks and practices (Liu and Keane, 2021). We also have 'data selfies': representations of self through personal quantitative data, from graphs of Tinder dating outcomes, through to the story of brain surgery told through daily step counts (Robards et al., 2021). This is of course in addition to the use of the selfie in applications such as forensic dental identification (Reesu and Brown, 2022) and possible contributions in human identification (Naidu et al., 2022). So perhaps it is a little early to accuse all those who post selfies on Facebook of being narcissistic, self-obsessed psychopaths.

SUMMARY

In this chapter we have looked at what constitutes people's self-concept and personalities. We have also looked at role-playing, and have looked at some of the ways these elements affect consumers' buying behaviour.

KEY POINTS

- Self-concept is concerned with one's feelings about oneself.
- Self-concept is learned, stable, purposeful and unique.
- As wealth increases, more people are becoming inner-directed.
- High self-monitors take their cues from others; low self-monitors take their cues from an inner drive.
- Personality is made up of traits; so far several thousand possible traits have been identified.
- Personality is a self-serving, individualistic, unique, overt and consistent gestalt.

HOW TO IMPRESS YOUR EXAMINER

You may be asked to compare the various type approaches to classifying personalities. Note that these type theories are not necessarily mutually exclusive: it would be perfectly possible to classify people across each of the types, because the typologies are based on combinations of traits, and the same traits might be combined in different ways in order to create a typology.

REVIEW QUESTIONS

1. Why are personality traits an important concept for marketers?
2. Why is self-concept such a useful way of segmenting markets?
3. What might be the impact of increased inner direction on fashion in the future?

(Continued)

4. How might high self-monitors respond to an increase in inner direction in the rest of the population?
5. How might the Myers–Briggs Type dimensions be used by marketers for a perfume company?
6. What are the marketing implications of the possible self?
7. What are the marketing implications of the gender perception of brands?

CASE STUDY: DOVE SELF-ESTEEM PROJECT

Unilever began the Dove Self-Esteem Project to empower young people and build body confidence through workshops and support materials. It combines their work with leading experts in psychology, health and body image with a vision of a world where positive body image equals positive self-esteem, and beauty is a source of confidence.

When people lose confidence in their body image, we know that many lose confidence in themselves, and this can affect their self-esteem, well-being and even mental health.

The Dove Beauty & Confidence report, for example, shows that eight in ten girls opt out of important life activities, such as trying out for a team or joining a club at school, if they don't feel good about the way they look. Seven in ten girls stop themselves from eating when they are worried about their appearance, or otherwise put their health at risk by not seeing a doctor. For adult women, it's an incredible nine in ten.

In 2020, they announced a new commitment: to empower 250 million young people by 2030 through Dove Self-Esteem Project education programmes. Since 2005, their Dove Self-Esteem Project has reached around 82 million young people, and grown to become the world's biggest provider of self-esteem education. More than 3 million parents and mentors have used their content, and over 1 million teachers have delivered a Dove self-esteem workshop. Their new commitment means more countries, more creative ways to engage audiences and many more young people feeling confident in their own skin.

And it's not just about building self-esteem. They're building their business too. Research shows a direct link between awareness of the Dove Self-Esteem Project and brand equity.

The Dove Self-Esteem Project reaches young people by offering free confidence-building workshops for classrooms and educational activities for parents, mentors and youth leaders. They work with world-renowned body image experts and leading universities to develop evidence-based tools. The positive impact of these efforts has been proven by various academic studies.

© iStock.com/swissmediavision

They've joined forces with Emmy Award-winning actor, producer and writer Lena Waithe, renowned production company ATTN, and rising director Tiffany Johnson to create the exclusive five-part series, *Girls Room*. Following the lives of five best friends: Melba, Minnie, Thelma, Gloria and Carlotta, the series explores the moments girls share in bathrooms. *Girls Room* tackles the pain and power of female adolescence through the eyes of five girls as they face the challenges of growing up in today's social media world. The series is based around those moments spent in bathrooms – the girls' room. Nearly 300,000 people have watched it so far.

Dove's latest Reverse Selfie film and campaign aim to stop the damage social media pressure and retouching apps are having on girls' self-esteem. Research they conducted in the US with girls aged 10–17 revealed that pushed by the pressure of social media, a staggering 80% of girls have already used a retouching app to distort the way they look online by age 13.

Research-driven and academically validated, Dove's *Confidence Kit* offers a wide range of materials, including practical suggestions that girls can put in place, such as curating their feed to ensure what they see is appropriate and empowering. It also includes conversation starters that can help parents and girls evaluate the reality of what they see on social media. It was used over 50,000 times in 2021.

For nearly a decade, they've also been working with the World Association of Girl Guides and Girl Scouts (WAGGGS) to get their message across to more young women. Their *Free Being Me* and *Action on Body Confidence* programmes have reached over 7 million young people in more than 125 countries, and they're aiming to reach over 9 million by the end of 2025. Examples of actions include a virtual advocacy event called Journey to Self-Esteem, which gave girls the opportunity to speak out about body image issues that they feel passionate about, alongside Dove's influencer partners. They've also formed the *Dove Youth Board* – bringing together young leaders from Women Deliver, WAGGGS and PLAN – to capture the voice of young people in their corporate strategy, programme development and advocacy and help challenge the state of body image in society today.

Dove's partnership with UNICEF brings together the scale and specialised skills of UNICEF with the expertise and experience of the Dove Self-Esteem Project. Together, they're aiming to help 10 million young people boost their self-esteem. In 2021, Dove introduced new education modules. These have been tested by academics and, starting in Indonesia and Brazil, they're being taught as part of UNICEF's wider adolescent life skills programmes for 10–18-year-olds in secondary schools and after-school programmes. They reached over 330,000 people in 2021.

They're also taking concrete action towards beauty inclusiveness. Through the CROWN Act, for example, they're campaigning to end hair discrimination and to create a more equitable and inclusive beauty experience for Black women and girls. Through the efforts of the CROWN Coalition, federal law has changed to ban hair discrimination in schools and workplaces in the US. Now they've brought their campaign to the UK too, supporting the UK's first Black hair code for schools and workplaces, known as the Halo Code.

One in four of us will experience mental health issues at some point in our lives. Dove, as well as a number of their other brands such as CLEAR, have recognised how they can play a role in supporting people's well-being.

Source: Adapted from Unilever Dove Supporting Self-Esteem and Wellbeing report. For more data and insights, see the references for this case study below.

(Continued)

REFERENCES

www.unilever.com/files/origin/a2ea4ad672fa04bc2344595f1470a2318899b21c.pdf/global-beauty-confidence-report-infographic.pdf

www.dove.com/uk/dove-self-esteem-project/our-mission/girls-room.html

www.unilever.com/news/news-search/2021/behind-the-selfie-reversing-the-damage-of-digital-distortion/?utm_source=NCReview230421&utm_medium=Email&utm_campaign=NewsCentre

www.dove.com/uk/stories/campaigns/confidence.html

www.dove.com/uk/dove-self-esteem-project/self-esteem-resources-for-youth-groups.html

www.wagggs.org/en/what-we-do/action-body-confidence/

www.dove.com/us/en/dove-self-esteem-project/our-mission/dove-youth-board.html

CASE STUDY QUESTIONS

1. What actions and activities make you feel purposeful?
2. Why might the Dove campaign resonate so much with its buyers?
3. How does age influence self-esteem?
4. How do beauty product adverts affect consumer self-esteem?
5. How can individuals (the self) overcome pressure from the media to look a certain way?

FURTHER READING

For an interesting and wider insight into the issues discussed in the chapter case study, see Michelle and Kelly Skeen's book called *Just as You Are: A Teen's Guide to Self-Acceptance and Lasting Self-Esteem* (Oakland, CA: New Harbinger, 2018).

Concepts of the Self, by Anthony Elliott (Cambridge: Polity Press, 2007), gives an overview of the key arguments in self-concept. It's a straightforward, lively account, which gives the counter-arguments as well as the theories, so that the various thinkers are linked together well.

Otto Kroeger and Janet M. Theussen's book *Type Talk: The 16 Personality Types*, 10th edn (New York: Bantam Doubleday Dell, 1989), gives a lot of applied examples of the Myers–Briggs Type Indicator. This is a very useful book in understanding why people behave the way they do.

MORE ONLINE

For additional materials that support this chapter and your learning, please visit:

https://study.sagepub.com/sethna5e

REFERENCES

Aidla, A. (2018) Improving personal sales performance by considering customer personality traits. *Journal on Business Review*, 4 (4): 4.

Baker, S.L., McCabe, S.D., Swithers, S.E., Payne, C.R. and Kranz, S. (2015) Do healthy, child-friendly fruit and vegetable snacks appeal to consumers? A field study exploring adults' perceptions and purchase intentions. *Food Quality and Preference*, 39: 202–8.

Balabanis, G. (2002) The relationship between lottery ticket and scratchcard buying behaviour, personality and other compulsive behaviours. *Journal of Consumer Behaviour*, 2 (1): 7–22.

Banister, E.N. and Hogg, M.K. (2003) Possible selves? Identifying dimensions for exploring the dialectic between positive and negative selves in consumer behaviour. *Advances in Consumer Research*, 30: 149–50.

Bartikowski, B. and Walsh, G. (2015) Attitude toward cultural diversity: A test of identity-related antecedents and purchasing consequences. *Journal of Business Research*, 68 (3): 526–33.

Bartoli, C., Nosi, C., Mattiacci, A. and Sfodera, F. (2022) Consumer self-concept in the cyberspace: How digitization has shaped the way we self-disclose to others. *Journal of Strategic Marketing*: 1–22. https://doi.org/10.1080/0965254X.2022.2056501

Bashir, A.M., Bayat, A., Olutuase, S.O. and Abdul Latiff, Z.A. (2018) Factors affecting consumers' intention towards purchasing halal food in South Africa: A structural equation modelling. *Journal of Food Products Marketing*, 25 (1): 26–48.

Baumeister, R.F. (1999) *The Self in Social Psychology*. Philadelphia, PA: Psychology Press.

Belk, R. (2003) Shoes and self. *Advances in Consumer Research*, 30: 27–33.

Belkin, S. and Sheptak, R.D.Jr (2018) Talking bodies: Athletes and tattoos as nonverbal communication. *Sport Journal*. http://thesportjournal.org/article/talking-bodies-athletes-tattoos-as-nonverbal-communication/ (accessed 31 July 2018).

Bharti, M., Suneja, V. and Bharti, M. (2022) Mindfulness as an antidote to conspicuous consumption: The mediating roles of self-esteem, self-concept clarity and normative influence. *Personality and Individual Differences*, 184: 111215.

Brendl, C.M., Chattopadhyay, A., Pelham, B.W., Carvalho, M. and Prichard, E.T. (2003) Are brands containing name letters preferred? *Advances in Consumer Research*, 30 (1): 151–2.

Briggs, K. and Myers, I. (1962) *Manual: The Myers–Briggs Type Indicator*. Princeton, NJ: Educational Testing Service.

Cattell, H.E.P. and Mead, A.D. (2008) The sixteen personality factor questionnaire (16PF). In G. Boyle, G. Matthews and D.H. Saklofske (eds), *The Sage Handbook of Personality Theory and Assessment, Vol. 2: Personality Measurement and Testing*. Los Angeles, CA: Sage. pp. 135–78.

Cattell, R.B. (1946) *The Description and Measurement of Personality*. New York: World Books.

Chatterjee, K., Adhikary, K., Sen, S. and Kar, S. (2018) Identification and analysis of factors affecting consumer behavior in fast moving consumer goods sector. *Business Perspectives – Aims and Scope*, *17* (1): 1–17.

Christie, R. and Geis, F.L. (1970) *Studies in Machiavellianism*. New York: Academic Press.

Clark, R.A., Goldsmith, R.E. and Goldsmith, E.B. (2008) Market mavenism and consumer self-confidence. *Journal of Consumer Behaviour*, *7* (3): 239–48.

Cohen, J.B. (1967) An interpersonal orientation to the study of consumer behaviour. *Journal of Marketing Research*, *4* (3): 270–8.

Connor, S., Edvardsson, K., Fisher, C. and Spelten, E. (2021) Perceptions and interpretation of contemporary masculinities in Western culture: A systematic review. *American Journal of Men's Health*, *15* (6). https://doi.org/10.1177/15579883211061009

Consiglio, I. and van Osselaer, S.M.J. (2022) The effects of consumption on self-esteem. *Current Opinion in Psychology*, *46*: 101341.

Cooper, C. (2015) *Individual Differences and Personality*, 3rd edn. Abingdon: Routledge.

Dane, E. and Sonenshein, S. (2015) On the role of experience in ethical decision making at work: An ethical expertise perspective. *Organizational Psychology Review*, *5* (1): 74–96.

Davies, M.F. (2003) Confirmatory bias in the evaluation of personality descriptions: Positive test strategies and output interference. *Journal of Personality and Social Psychology*, *85* (4): 736–44.

de Ridder, D.T.D., Lensvelt-Mulders, G., Finkenauer, C., Marijn Stok, F. and Baumeister, R.F. (2012) Taking stock of self-control: A meta-analysis of how trait self-control relates to a wide range of behaviors. *Personality and Social Psychology Review*, *16* (1): 76–99.

Donnelly, J.H. Jr (1970) Social character and the acceptance of new products. *Journal of Marketing Research*, *7* (February): 111–13.

Dunaev, J.L., Schulz, J.L. and Markey, C.N. (2018) Cosmetic surgery attitudes among midlife women: Appearance esteem, weight esteem, and fear of negative appearance evaluation. *Journal of Health Psychology*, *23* (1): 59–66.

Essa Al Lily, A. (2022) Sexmentality. *Cogent Social Sciences*, *8* (1). https://doi.org/10.1080/23311886.2022.2100183

Farzin, M., Vazifehdust, H. and Hamdi, K. (2020) Projective techniques for understanding cyber-market mavenism in social network sites. *Revista Brasileira de Gestão de Negócios*, *22* (3): 729–49.

Fox, J. and Rooney, M.C. (2015) The Dark Triad and trait self-objectification as predictors of men's use and self-presentation behaviors on social networking sites. *Personality & Individual Differences*, *76*: 161–5.

Foxall, G. (1980) *Consumer Behaviour: A Practical Guide*. London: Routledge.

Fraj, E. and Martinez, E. (2006) Influence of personality on ecological consumer behaviour. *Journal of Consumer Behaviour*, *5* (May–June): 167–81.

Franklin-Luther, P. and Volk, A.A. (2022) The links between adult personality, parental discipline attitudes and harsh child punishment. *Journal of Family Trauma, Child Custody & Child Development*, *19* (1): 3–23.

Goldring, D., Gong, B. and Gironda, J.T. (2022) Mavens at work: Brand commitment and the moderating role of market mavens on social media engagement. *Journal of Promotion Management*, 28 (3): 261–87.

Goleman, D. (1987) Basic personality traits don't change, studies say. *New York Times*, 18 June.

Green, R., Delfabbro, P.H. and King, D.L. (2020) Avatar- and self-related processes and problematic gaming: A systematic review. *Addictive Behaviors*, 108: 106461.

Green, R., Delfabbro, P.H. and King, D.L. (2021) Avatar identification and problematic gaming: The role of self-concept clarity. *Addictive Behaviors*, 113: 106694.

Harrington, A.G. and Overall, N.C. (2021) Women's attractiveness contingent self-esteem, romantic rejection, and body dissatisfaction. *Body Image*, 39: 77–89.

Hartmann, J., Heitmann, M., Schamp, C. and Netzer, O. (2021) The power of brand selfies. *Journal of Marketing Research*, 58 (6): 1159–77.

Hollensen, S. (2016) *Global Marketing*. Harlow: Pearson Education.

Horney, K. (1945) *Our Inner Conflict*. New York: W.W. Norton.

Hong, S., Kim, B. and Lee, S. (2022) Too close to like? How social media influencers recast personal space between selfies and Instagram users. *Communication Studies*, 73 (2): 119–35.

Jonason, P.K. and Krause, L. (2013) The emotional deficits associated with the Dark Triad traits: Cognitive empathy, affective empathy, and alexithymia. *Personality & Individual Differences*, 55: 532–7.

Jung, K. and Lee, W. (2006) Cross-gender brand extensions: Effects of gender of the brand, gender of the consumer, and product type on cross-gender extensions. *Advances in Consumer Research*, 33: 67–74.

Kamal Basha, N., Aw, E.C.-X. and Chuah, S.H.-W. (2022) Are we so over smartwatches? Or can technology, fashion, and psychographic attributes sustain smartwatch usage? *Technology in Society*, 69: 101952.

Keyes, C.L., Kendler, K.S., Myers, J.M. and Martin, C.C. (2015) The genetic overlap and distinctiveness of flourishing and the big five personality traits. *Journal of Happiness Studies*, 16 (3): 655–66.

Khan, S., Fazili, A.I. and Bashir, I. (2022) Constructing generational identity through counterfeit luxury consumption. *Journal of Product & Brand Management*, 31 (3): 415–37.

Kiani, I. and Laroche, M. (2019) From desire to help to taking action: Effects of personal traits and social media on market mavens' diffusion of information. *Psychology & Marketing*, 36 (12): 1147–61.

Kim, M.-Y. and Son, M. (2021) What determines consumer attitude toward green credit card services? A moderated mediation approach. *Sustainability*, 13: 10865.

Klein, J.G. (2003) Calories for dignity: Fashion in the concentration camp. *Advances in Consumer Research*, 30: 34–7.

Kleine, R.E., III, Schultz, S. and Brunswick, G.J. (2009) Transformational consumption choices: Building an understanding by integrating social identity and multi-attribute attitude theories. *Journal of Consumer Behaviour*, 8 (1): 54–70.

Kuesten, C., Dang, J., Nakagawa, M., Bi, J. and Meiselman, H.L. (2022) Japanese consumer segmentation based on general self-efficacy psychographics data collected in a phytonutrient supplement study: Influence on health behaviors, well-being, product involvement and liking. *Food Quality and Preference*, 99: 104545.

Laureti, T. and Benedetti, I. (2018) Exploring pro-environmental food purchasing behaviour: An empirical analysis of Italian consumers. *Journal of Cleaner Production*, 172: 3367–78.

Leckelt, M., König, J., Richter, D., Back, M.D. and Schröder, C. (2022) The personality traits of self-made and inherited millionaires. *Humanities & Social Sciences Communications*, 9 (1): 1–12.

Leighton, J. (2021) Overcoming behavioural bias is key to electric vehicle uptake. www.automotiveworld.com/articles/overcoming-behavioural-bias-is-key-to-electric-vehicle-uptake/ (accessed 2 September 2022).

Lin, J.-H.T., Wu, D.-Y. and Yang, J.-W. (2022) Corrigendum: Exercising with a six pack in virtual reality: Examining the Proteus effect of avatar body shape and sex on self-efficacy for core-muscle exercise, self-concept of body shape, and actual physical activity. *Frontiers in Psychology*, 13: 857059.

Lin, X., Featherman, M., Brooks, S.L. and Hajli, N. (2018) Exploring gender differences in online consumer purchase decision making: An online product presentation perspective. *Information Systems Frontiers*, 21: 1187–201.

Liu, J. and Keane, H. (2021) Naked loan selfies: Becoming collateral, becoming pornography. *New Media & Society*, 23 (12): 3616–33.

Lund, K. and Kappelgaard, L. (2018) Motivation in self-monitoring processes: Evaluation of ecological momentary storytelling. In *Proceedings from the 16th Scandinavian Conference on Health Informatics 2018*. Aalborg, Denmark, August 28–29. No. 151. Linköping: Linköping University Electronic Press. pp. 29–37.

Maes, C. and de Lenne, O. (2022) Filters and fillers: Belgian adolescents' filter use on social media and the acceptance of cosmetic surgery. *Journal of Children and Media*. https://doi.org/10.1080/17482798.2022.2079696

McNulty, W.K. (1985) UK social change through a wide-angle lens. *Futures*, August.

Mehdizadeh, S. (2010) Self-presentation 2.0: Narcissism and self-esteem on Facebook. *Cyberpsychology, Behavior, and Social Networking*, 13: 357–64. doi: 10.1089/cyber.2009.0257

Meltzer, L. (2018) *Executive Function in Education: From Theory to Practice*. New York: Guilford Publications.

Moes, A., Fransen, M., Fennis, B., Verhagen, T. and van Vliet, H. (2021) In-store interactive advertising screens: The effect of interactivity on impulse buying explained by self-agency. *Journal of Research in Interactive Marketing*, 16 (3): 457–74.

Mokhtar, I., Osman, I., Setapa, F. and Zambahari, S.R. (2015) A qualitative study on the determinants of Islamic credit card ownership and usage. In R. Hashimand Abdul and A.B. Majeed (eds), *Proceedings of the Colloquium on Administrative Science and Technology*. Singapore: Springer. pp. 423–35.

Mowen, J.C., Longoria, A. and Sallee, A. (2009) Burning and cutting: Identifying the traits of individuals with an enduring propensity to tan and to undergo cosmetic surgery. *Journal of Consumer Behaviour*, *8* (5): 238–51.

Naidu, D., Franco, A. and Mânica, S. (2022) Exploring the use of selfies in human identification. *Journal of Forensic and Legal Medicine*, *85*: 102293.

Nantel, J. and Strahle, W. (1986) The self-monitoring concept: A consumer perspective. *Advances in Consumer Research*, *13*: 83–7.

Nuttall, P. (2009) Insiders, regulars and tourists: Exploring selves and music consumption in adolescence. *Journal of Consumer Behaviour*, *8* (4): 211–24.

Oakley, A. (2015) *Sex, Gender and Society*. Farnham: Ashgate Publishing.

Okubo, M. and Ishikawa, K. (2019) The big warm smile of cheaters: Lateral posing biases and emotional expressions in displaying facial trustworthiness. *Laterality*, *24* (6): 678–96.

Oláh, L.S., Kotowska, I.E. and Richter, R. (2018) The new roles of men and women and implications for families and societies. In *A Demographic Perspective on Gender, Family and Health in Europe*. Cham: Springer Nature. pp. 41–64.

Orth, U. and Robins, R.W. (2022) Is high self-esteem beneficial? Revisiting a classic question. *American Psychologist*, *77* (1): 5–17.

Parmelee, M. (2022) Don't want to lose your Gen Z and Millennial talent? www2.deloitte.com/uk/en/insights/topics/talent/deloitte-millennial-survey.html (accessed 29 October 2022).

Patrick, K. and Xu, Y. (2018) Exploring Generation Y consumers' fitness clothing consumption: A means-end chain approach. *Journal of Textile & Apparel Technology & Management*, *10* (3): 1–15.

Pennington, D. (2018) *Essential Personality*. Abingdon: Routledge.

Pentina, I., Taylor, D.G. and Voelker, T.A. (2009) The roles of self-discrepancy and social support in young females' decisions to undergo cosmetic procedures. *Journal of Consumer Behaviour*, *8* (4): 149–65.

Perry, V.G. (2001) Antecedents of consumer financing decisions: A mental accounting model of revolving credit usage. *Advances in Consumer Research*, *28*: 1–13.

Pino, O. (2022) Is Zoom dysmorphia a new disorder? *Acta Bio-Medica: Atenei Parmensis*, *92* (6): e2021303.

Qasim, D., Mohammed, A.B. and Liñán, F. (2018) The role of culture and gender in e-commerce entrepreneurship: Three Jordanian case studies. In *Entrepreneurship Ecosystem in the Middle East and North Africa (MENA)*. Cham: Springer Nature. pp. 419–32.

Raskin, R. and Terry, H. (1988) A principal-components analysis of the Narcissistic Personality Inventory and further evidence of its construct validity. *Journal of Personality & Social Psychology*, *54*: 890–902.

Reesu, G.V. and Brown, N.L. (2022) Application of 3D imaging and selfies in forensic dental identification. *Journal of Forensic and Legal Medicine*, *89*: 102354.

Reeves, M. (2018) A contemporary rite of passage into adulthood. In *Surviving, Thriving and Reviving in Adolescence*. Singapore: Springer International. pp. 139–51.

Rein, M. and Eysenck, H. (2018) *Dimensions of Personality*. Abingdon: Routledge.

Reisman, D. (1953) *The Lonely Crowd*. New York: Doubleday.

Robards, B., Lyall, B. and Moran, C. (2021) Confessional data selfies and intimate digital traces. *New Media & Society, 23* (9): 2616–33.

Roberts, B.W. and DelVecchio, W.F. (2000) The rank-order consistency of personality traits from childhood to old age: A quantitative review of longitudinal studies. *Psychological Bulletin, 126* (1): 3.

Roberts, B.W. and Mroczek, D. (2008) Personality trait change in adulthood. *Current Directions in Psychological Science, 17* (1): 31–5.

Roberts, B.W., Walton, K.E. and Viechtbauer, W. (2006) Patterns of mean-level change in personality traits across the life course: A meta-analysis of longitudinal studies. *Psychological Bulletin, 132* (1): 1.

Schaefer, L.M., Burke, N.L., Calogero, R.M., Menzel, J.E., Krawczyk, R. and Thompson, J.K. (2018) Self-objectification, body shame, and disordered eating: Testing a core mediational model of objectification theory among White, Black, and Hispanic women. *Body Image, 24*: 5–12.

Schmitt, J. and Rasolofoarison, D. (2015) Disentangling individual and contextual shopping motivations. In M. Conway Dato-on (ed.), *The Sustainable Global Marketplace: Proceedings of the 2011 Academy of Marketing Science (AMS) Annual Conference*. Developments in Marketing Science. London: Springer International. pp. 176–80.

Schwemmer, C. and Ziewiecki, S. (2018) Social media sellout – The increasing role of product promotion on YouTube. www.researchgate.net/profile/Carsten_Schwemmer/publication/323547570_Social_Media_Sellout_-_The_Increasing_Role_of_Product_Promotion_on_YouTube/links/5a9c2ddcaca2721e3f32168a/Social-Media-Sellout-The-Increasing-Role-of-Product-Promotion-on-YouTube.pdf (accessed 20 April 2018).

Schwinger, M., Trautner, M., Pütz, N., Fabianek, S., Lemmer, G., Lauermann, F. and Wirthwein, L. (2022) Why do students use strategies that hurt their chances of academic success? A meta-analysis of antecedents of academic self-handicapping. *Journal of Educational Psychology, 114* (3): 576–96.

Shaw, D., Grehan, E., Shiu, E., Hassan, L. and Thomson, J. (2005) An exploration of values in ethical consumer decision-making. *Journal of Consumer Behaviour, 4* (3): 185–200.

Sheth, J.N. and Sisodia, R.S. (2015) *Does Marketing Need Reform? Fresh Perspectives on the Future*. Abingdon: Routledge.

Snyder, M. (1974) Self-monitoring of expressive behaviour. *Journal of Personality and Social Psychology, 34*: 526–37.

Sorokowski, P., Sorokowska, A., Oleszkiewicz, A., Frackowiak, T., Huk, A. and Pisanski, K. (2015) Selfie posting behaviors are associated with narcissism among men. *Personality and Individual Differences, 85*: 123–7.

Spry, L. and Pich, C. (2021) Enhancing data collection methods with qualitative projective techniques in the exploration of a university's brand identity and brand image. *International Journal of Market Research*, 63 (2): 177–200.

Stedman, J.M., Essery, J. and McGeary, C.A. (2018) Projective personality assessment: Evidence for a decline in training emphasis. *SIS Journal of Projective Psychology & Mental Health*, 25 (1): 54–9.

Strizhakova, Y., Coulter, R.A. and Price, L.L. (2021) The fresh start mindset: A cross-national investigation and implications for environmentally friendly global brands. *Journal of International Marketing*, 29 (4): 45–61.

Stokburger-Sauer, N.E. and Hoyer, W.D. (2009) Consumer advisors revisited: What drives those with market mavenism and opinion leadership tendencies and why? *Journal of Consumer Behaviour*, 7 (3): 100–15.

Thompson, E.R. and Prendergast, G.P. (2015) The influence of trait affect and the five-factor personality model on impulse buying. *Personality and Individual Differences*, 76: 216–21.

Tunc, T.E. (2018) The 'Mad Men' of nutrition: The drinking man's diet and mid-twentieth-century American masculinity. *Global Food History*, 4 (2): 189–206.

Tuncay, L. (2006) Men's responses to depictions of ideal masculinity in advertising. *Advances in Consumer Research*, 33: 64.

Ulrich, I. and Tiisier-Desbordes, E. (2018) 'A feminine brand? Never!' Brands as gender threats for 'resistant' masculinities. *Qualitative Market Research: An International Journal*, 21 (3): 274–95.

US 16PF (2009) Administrator's manual. In G. Boyle, G. Matthews and D.H. Saklofske (eds), *The Sage Handbook of Personality Theory and Assessment, Vol. 2: Personality Measurement and Testing*. Los Angeles, CA: Sage. pp. 135–78.

Vicente-Molina, M.A., Fernández-Sainz, A. and Izagirre-Olaizola, J. (2018) Does gender make a difference in pro-environmental behavior? The case of the Basque Country University students. *Journal of Cleaner Production*, 176: 89–98.

Visinescu, L.L., Sidorova, A., Jones, M.C. and Prybutok, V.R. (2015) The influence of website dimensionality on customer experiences, perceptions and behavioral intentions: An exploration of 2D vs. 3D web design. *Information & Management*, 52 (1): 1–17.

Vohs, K. and Faber, R. (2003) Self-regulation and impulsive spending patterns. *Advances in Consumer Research*, 30: 125–6.

Walker, B.A. (1992) New perspectives for self-research. *Advances in Consumer Research*, 19: 417–23.

Wang, Y.Y., Shanmugam, M., Hajli, N. and Bugshan, H. (2015) Customer attitudes towards internet banking and social media on internet banking in the UK. In N. Hajli (ed.), *Handbook of Research on Integrating Social Media into Strategic Marketing*. Hershey, PA: IGI Global. pp. 287–302.

Wellman, B. and Gulia, M. (1999) Net surfers don't ride alone: Virtual communities as communities. In P. Kollock and M. Smith (eds), *Communities and Cyberspace*. New York: Routledge. pp. 1–27.

Westerlund, H. and Partti, H. (2018) A cosmopolitan culture-bearer as activist: Striving for gender inclusion in Nepali music education. *International Journal of Music Education*, *36* (4). https://doi.org/10.1177/0255761418771094

Wood, N., Chaplin, L.N. and Solomon, M. (2009) Virtually me: Youth consumers and their online identities. *Advances in Consumer Research*, *36*: 23–4.

Zhang, K.Z., Xu, H., Zhao, S. and Yu, Y. (2018) Online reviews and impulse buying behavior: The role of browsing and impulsiveness. *Internet Research*, *28* (3): 522–43.

Zhao, W. (2022) The influence of media exposure on young women's intention to undergo cosmetic surgery: A third person perspective. *Atlantic Journal of Communication*, *30* (2): 146–58.

Zickfeld, J.H. and Schubert, T.W. (2018) Warm and touching tears: Tearful individuals are perceived as warmer because we assume they feel moved and touched. *Cognition and Emotion*, *32* (8): 1691–9.

Zinkhan, G.M. and Shermohamad, A. (1986) Is other-directedness on the increase? An empirical test of Reisman's theory of social character. *Journal of Consumer Research*, *13* (June): 127–30.

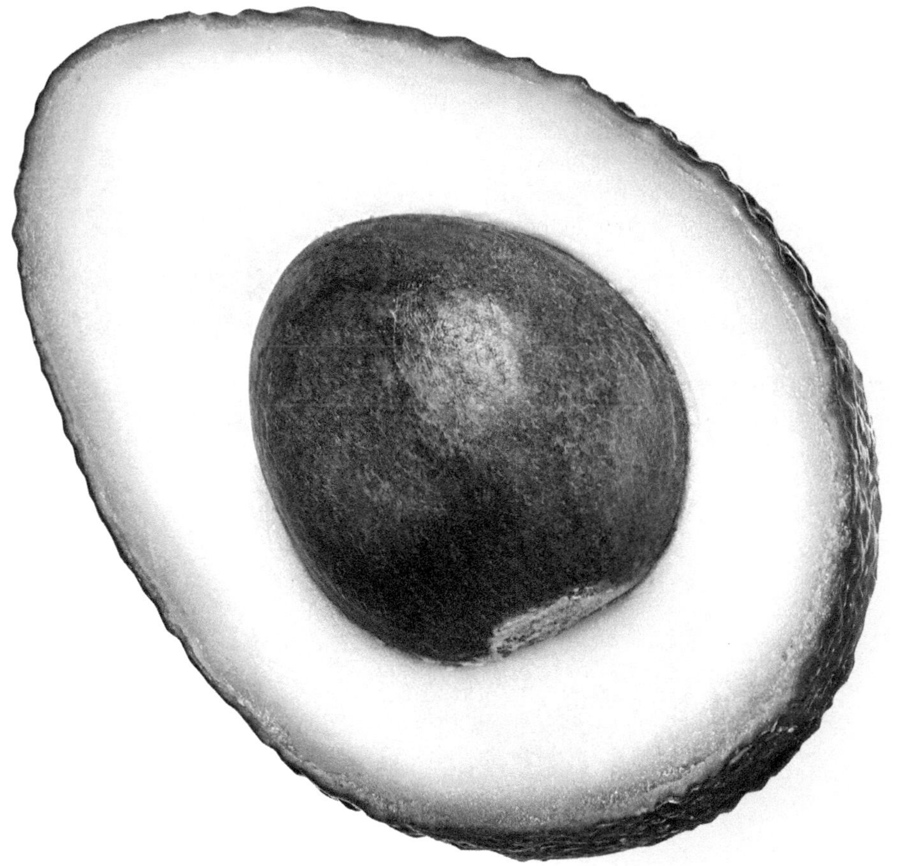

PART ONE CONSUMER BEHAVIOUR IN CONTEXT

- **Chapter 1** Understanding Consumer Behaviour
- **Chapter 2** Decisions, Behaviours and Interactions
- **Chapter 3** Consumption in B2C vs. B2B
- **Chapter 4** Consumer Technology and Innovation

PART TWO CONSUMERS AS INDIVIDUALS (THE PSYCHOLOGICAL ISSUES)

- **Chapter 5** Drive, Motivation and Hedonism
- **Chapter 6** The Self and Personality
- **Chapter 7** Perception
- **Chapter 8** Learning and Knowledge
- **Chapter 9** Attitude Formation and Change

PART THREE CONSUMERS AS SOCIAL ACTORS (THE SOCIOLOGICAL ISSUES)

- **Chapter 10** Reference Groups
- **Chapter 11** Age, Gender and Familial Roles
- **Chapter 12** Culture and Social Mobility
- **Chapter 13** Ethical Consumption
- **Chapter 14** Sustainable Consumption

CHAPTER 7
PERCEPTION

LEARNING OBJECTIVES

After reading this chapter you should be able to:
- Explain the role of analysis and synthesis in perception.
- Explain the role of synergy in creating a perceptual impression.
- Understand the problem created for marketers by selectivity.
- Explain how past experience affects perception.
- Describe Weber's Law.
- Describe the relationship between perception and reality.
- Explain the conscious and unconscious aspects of perception.
- Explain the difference between internal and overt perceptual responses.
- Discuss subliminal advertising.
- Explain the role of colour in perception.

CHAPTER CONTENTS

Introduction
Elements of perception
Creating a world-view
How we process data in our head
Culture and perception
Using our ears to eat
Environmental influences
Perception and store atmospherics
Perception and consumers' characteristics and behaviour
Combining factors
Subliminal perception
Colour
Passing off, brandalism and subvertising
Summary
Key points
How to impress your examiner
Review questions
Case study: Using consumer insight to understand consumer perceptions in higher education
Further reading
References

More online: https://study.sagepub.com/sethna5e

INTRODUCTION

How we as consumers analyse the environment around us and develop a picture of the world is of great interest to marketers. Ensuring that the company's brands become part of the world-view of the potential consumers is the main purpose of marketing communications; understanding perception processes is what puts the product there.

Perception is the keystone of building knowledge, not just about products and everything associated with them but also about everything else in the world. Although it is common to refer to perception as if it were somehow different from the truth, this is not the case: perceptions may differ between individuals, but for each person their own perception *is* the whole truth. This is sometimes difficult to remember – but in fact, our whole experience of the world happens inside our heads, filtered by our senses and moderated by our previous experiences within any given environment.

ELEMENTS OF PERCEPTION

Perception is a process of converting sensory input into an understanding of how the world works (Kenyon and Sen, 2015) and increasingly on how the effects of artificial intelligence are perceived by consumers (Chen et al., 2021). Because the process involves combining many different sensory inputs, the overall result is complex to analyse; for example, people often judge fabrics by touch, but memory and confidence in the evaluation is improved if the 'touch' input is reinforced with verbal information (d'Astous and Kamau, 2010). Human beings have considerably more than five senses. Apart from the basic five (touch, taste, smell, sight, hearing) there are sense of direction, sense of balance, a clear knowledge of which way is down, and so forth. Each sense is feeding information to the brain constantly, and the amount of information being collected would seriously overload the system if one took it all in. The brain therefore selects from the surroundings and cuts out anything that seems or is irrelevant in a given situation.

In effect, the brain makes automatic decisions as to what is relevant and what is not. Even though there may be many things happening around you, you are unaware of most of them; for example, experiments have shown that some information is filtered out by the optic nerve even before it gets to the brain. People quickly learn to ignore extraneous noises; for example, as a visitor to someone else's home you may be sharply aware of the noise from the dishwasher, whereas your host may be entirely used to it and unaware of it except when making a conscious effort to check that the machine is still cycling.

There are eight main conventions regarding perception, as shown in Table 7.1.

TABLE 7.1 Conventions about perception

Convention	Explanation
Perception is about more than the substantive part of the message	Messages may be expressed directly in words, but the observer 'reads between the lines' and creates new meanings from what is seen or read
The law of similarity says that we interpret new information in a similar way to information we already hold	If we read a news report on a website we trust to be accurate, we will tend to assume that the news report is also accurate
Expectations	If we expect a particular sequence of events, or a particular message, then we tend to see that message and interpret accordingly
'Figure–ground' relationships influence interpretation	An individual will interpret a printed message differently according to which part of the image is interpreted as the message and which part as the background

Convention	Explanation
The Law of Closure	This means that people can only obtain the whole message if they have all the components of the message. This particularly applies in advertisements that are intended to intrigue consumers: an advertisement that contains a puzzle or a visual joke will not be understood by the observers unless they are in possession of enough information to infer the punch line
The Law of Continuity	Gestalt perception is based on the idea that the elements of the overall message form a continuum rather than a set of separate elements. In other words, even when a particular stimulus (for example an advertisement) is composed of music, speech, pictures and moving images the person watching it will still form an overall impression. Of course, someone who is asked to analyse an advertisement will be able to separate out the various elements, but in normal behaviour few people would do this
The whole is greater than the sum of its parts	When the message consists of a number of elements, the elements often combine to create a stronger message
Colour influences perception	Because human beings have a well-developed colour sense, colours are often influential in creating an overall image of a product. This may be due to the need, in prehistoric times, for hunter-gatherers to assess the ripeness or nutritional value of fruit

Perception is, in part, a process of analysis in which the outside world is filtered and only the most important or interesting (as defined by the individual) items come through. Therefore, the information entering the brain does not provide a complete view of the world.

In Figure 7.1, most of the stimuli surrounding the individual are filtered out. The remaining stimuli are combined and interpreted, then included with memory and imagination to create an overall perception.

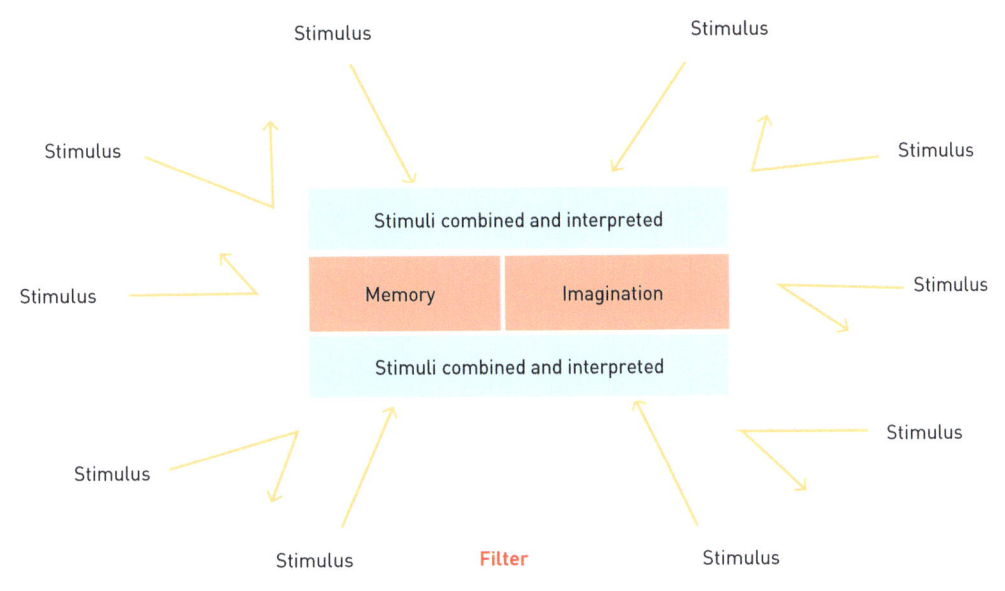

FIGURE 7.1 Selectivity and synthesis

> ## CRITICAL REFLECTION
>
> If perception is reality, are we imagining most of the world? Over 50 years ago, some research was conducted by Bugelski and Alampay (1961). In their experiment, half of the people were shown pictures of animals in black and white and the other half were shown pictures of humans in black and white. Then they showed every person an ambiguous picture and asked what the people saw. Most of the people who saw the animal pictures before usually said they saw a rat, while the people who saw pictures of humans before usually said they saw an old man with glasses. The reason that this happened is because they were used to seeing a human or animal since they had seen so many already and this caused them to have a perceptual set on the ambiguous picture.
>
> Fast-forward 40 years and we still believed what we thought we knew to be true. Research by Professor Patrali Chatterjee of Rutgers University (2001) showed that consumers patronising a familiar retailer, either online or in-store, are less receptive to negative word of mouth information and seek less information. In short, they will not accept any negativity about a product/brand with which they are very happy. They know what they know, and that's all there is to it!
>
> Fast-forward another almost 20 years and we see the hysteria created by some streetwear hyped-clothing brands with over-inflated prices due to limited supply, and 'fake news' flooding into media coverage from every perspective, sometimes leading to very controversial decisions (for example, Brexit – the UK's vote to leave the EU).
>
> In all these examples, there is an element of **hyper-reality**: what was initially simulation or 'hype' suddenly becomes real.

Hyper-reality
An inability of consciousness to distinguish reality from a simulation of reality

CREATING A WORLD-VIEW

The perception process is a social-psychological phenomenon. It involves cue selection and cue interpretation, and combining these cues to create an overall impression. Warr and Knapper (1968) identified six components of perception, as follows:

1. Stimulus.
2. Input selector.
3. Processing centre.
4. Consumer's current state.
5. Consumer's stable characteristics.
6. Response.

The stimulus is the object that is being perceived. In this sense, the object could be a person, an innovation, an event, a situation, a blog or anything that catches the individual's attention. For marketers, the stimulus on offer is likely to be a brand, a product, an e-retail shop or a marketing communication.

When the individual constructs a world-view, he or she assembles information to map what is happening in the outside world. Any gaps (and there will, of course, be plenty of these) will be filled in by using imagination and experience. The cognitive map is therefore not a 'photograph'; it is (at least in part) a construct of the imagination. This mapping will be affected by the following factors:

1. **Subjectivity**. This is the existing world-view within the individual, and is unique to that individual. People have differing views of the world – this is what makes being a human being so much fun, because we argue a lot – and this means that we interpret any incoming stimuli differently according to who we are.

2. **Categorisation**. This is the 'pigeonholing' of information, and the prejudging of events and products. This can happen through a process known as **chunking** whereby the individual organises information into chunks of related items (Miller, 1956). For example, a picture seen while a particular piece of music is playing might be chunked as one item in memory, so that the sight of the picture evokes the music and vice versa.

3. **Selectivity**. This is the degree to which the brain is selecting from the environment. It is a function of how much is going on around the individual, and also of how selective (concentrated) the individual is on the current task. Selectivity is also subjective; some people are a great deal more selective than others. Research shows that people judge the authenticity of Irish-themed pubs by the behaviour of the employees and the patrons rather than from the decor, showing that people are being selective in the factors they use to judge the pub (Munoz et al., 2006).

4. **Expectations**. These lead individuals to interpret later information in a specific way. For example, look at this series of numbers and letters:

A	13	C	D	E	F	G	H	I
10	11	12	13	14	15	16	17	18

    In fact, the number 13 appears in both series, but in the first series it may well be interpreted as a B because that is what the brain is being led to expect.

5. **Law of Primacy**. Past experience leads us to interpret later experience in the light of what we already know. This is called the Law of Primacy by psychologists. For example, adverts shown early in ad breaks generate greater brand recall than those in later slots (Li, 2010). Sometimes sights, smells or sounds from our past will trigger off inappropriate responses; the smell of bread baking may help recall aromas emanating from a village bakery from 20 years ago, but in fact the smell could have been artificially generated by a commercial aerosol spray near the supermarket's bread counter.

An example of cognitive mapping as applied to perception of product quality might run as follows. The individual uses the input selector to select clues and assign values to them. For quality, the cues are typically price, brand name and retailer name. Most of us, rightly or wrongly, assume that a higher-priced product will be better quality, and also that a well-known brand name will be better than a generic product;

Subjectivity
Judging everything from a personal viewpoint

Categorisation
The pigeonholing of information in order to prejudge events and products

Chunking
The learning process by which pieces of information are grouped by the brain

Selectivity
The part of perception that deals with rejecting unnecessary stimuli

Expectations
The existing information and attitudes that cause people to interpret later information in a specific way

Law of Primacy
First experiences affect the interpretation of later experiences

although the retailer name is less significant, it still carries some weight. For example, many consumers would feel confident that a major London department store such as Fortnum and Mason's would sell higher-quality items than the local corner shop, but might be less able to distinguish between own-label products from rival supermarket chains such as Aldi and Lidl.

The input selector is the mechanism by which the individual selects cues from the stimulus and assigns a meaning to each one. The input selector takes the various environmental factors and processes them one at a time: the processing centre has the task of integrating the cues to generate an overall perception. The input selector and the processing centre are not actually separate functions: they almost certainly operate at the same time, because the cues are delivered simultaneously or at least very closely after one another. For example, someone seeing an online advertisement for an e-cigarette might remember the shape but not the make, or might remember the background detail of the advertisement (the environment in which the e-cigarette is being smoked, perhaps) and remember nothing about the product itself. It has been shown that people perceive a task as being more difficult if the instructions on how to do it are written in a hard-to-read font (Cushing and Bodner, 2022; Song and Schwarz, 2009). It becomes even more difficult if the instructions are hidden and impossible to read without first opening the packaging, as is the case sometimes with packaged meat and cooking instructions.

This is a perennial problem in marketing communications. Knowing which cues people most often select is clearly of great interest, especially if we are considering a specific factor such as quality. In some cases people judge quality on the basis of price, in other cases on the physical attributes of the product, but the consensus view is that the use of an extrinsic cue such as price and intrinsic cues such as physical and performance attributes depend on prior knowledge (Rao and Monroe, 1988). As consumers become more familiar with the product's intrinsic attributes, price becomes less important as a surrogate for judging quality. In some cases, products are consumed almost entirely for their symbolic value: in some emerging economies, such as China, products are often bought simply because they are Western brands (Long et al., 2022; Wu, 2022). According to a report by Bloomberg (2022), and in relation to Chinese consumers, 'they've got money to burn, eschew foreign labels, and are driven by a swelling sense of nationalism that can ensnare even the biggest global brands'. Recent work by Kapferer and Valette-Florence (2022) challenges the popular belief among luxury practitioners and researchers that Millennials are a homogeneous and disruptive generation of consumers.

CONSUMER BEHAVIOUR IN ACTION: CHINESE CONSUMER AND E-COMMERCE

The global press is full of stories about how China is set to become an economic superpower (see for instance *Chindia Rising: How China and India Will Benefit Your Business*, by Professor Jagdish Sheth, 2008). Fast-forward 10 years and we now know that Chinese consumers are a key nationality driving the growth of, for instance, the luxury market, which it is estimated will be worth €390 billion in sales by 2025

(Bain & Company, 2018). With the rapid expansion of the consumer market and the development of digital technologies, China's e-commerce industry continues to be all the rage across the country. The Chinese market ranks at number one worldwide for its retail e-commerce sales. In 2021, e-commerce in China contributed more than half of the country's retail sales. However, you really need to have a look at some of the other figures and the popular websites to start to understand the impact that Chinese consumers are having on the global economy. There is certainly huge opportunity; China is one of the most lucrative countries for foreign brands to start selling in. According to Alexa (which ranks sites based primarily on tracking a sample of internet traffic), Taobao (which is similar to eBay and is China's largest consumer-to-consumer portal) and its parent company Alibaba have now overtaken Amazon as the world's most popular e-commerce platform. Alibaba has a market capitalisation of more than $260 billion. Shoppers are spending longer on Taobao, too. On average, visitors spend more than 8 minutes per day compared to the average of 7 minutes 40 seconds that visitors spend on Amazon.com.

© iStock.com/William_Potter

The number comparisons don't end there. Online sales penetration in China is the highest in the world, with 989 million people in China online and the majority of them accessing the web using a mobile device (with more than 80 million going online in the wake of the coronavirus pandemic). Taobao has over a billion products for sale on its website, and on National Singles Day (celebrated on 11 November 2021) Taobao sold a record $61 billion worth of products compared to Cyber Monday 2021 in the USA, which only generated $10.7 billion across all its access points – and its first ever year-on-year decline.

Then there is the visual perception aspect. The difference between Amazon and Taobao is very easy to see. To consumers who are used to shopping on Amazon, their perception of the Taobao site is that it looks a mess – with products being crammed into every crevice on the screen. Conversely, to Chinese consumers the Amazon site is just too sparse and therefore they cannot make any decent comparisons of products, without wasting time going backwards and forwards between screens.

One final point to consider here is that Chinese consumers are seemingly not attracted by lifestyle, so the wider environment within which we would 'frame' the product using a lifestyle backdrop for advertisements is of little consequence to Chinese consumers. They don't want to see the product being used in situ – they just want to see the product. This said, it is therefore surprising that the Chinese view e-commerce as a leisure activity. Shopping online, receiving super-efficient service and then waiting for that neat package to be delivered is a very important part of the whole e-commerce process which the Chinese consumer relishes.

The processing centre is likely to be influenced by the individual's *current state*. The current state includes factors such as mood, motivation, goals and the physical state of the individual at the time the cues come along. A mood is transitory: it will pass, no matter how strongly it is felt at the time. When we are in a good mood we tend to feel favourably towards more cues, whereas if we are in a bad mood we tend to be negative about cues. This is partly responsible for the halo effect (or horns effect) in which we tend to think that if one thing is bad about something, everything is bad about it. If people feel a momentary disgust with a company or a product this will carry over into future decisions, changing the status quo (Han and Lerner, 2008). Positive moods tend to create less elaboration (i.e. people think less when they are in a good mood, as seen in Petty and Cacioppo's [1986] 'elaboration likelihood model') and decisions are often made much more automatically than would normally be the case (Batra and Stayman, 1990). There is evidence that marketing messages that express positive outcomes are much more effective than those that stress negative outcomes, presumably because the former create good moods whereas the latter create fearful or worried moods (Lien et al., 2018; Zhao and Pechmann, 2006). On the other hand, sad expressions on the faces of victims generate greater charitable donations (Baberini et al., 2015) (see also, for example, post-flooding in Pakistan in 2022), perhaps because donors feel the need to change the unpleasant feelings that arise from seeing the charity's advertisements (Manesi et al., 2019; Small and Verrochi, 2008).

HOW WE PROCESS DATA IN OUR HEAD

Individuals process information in individual ways, of course: neuro-linguistic programming theory tells us that some people prefer to process visual information, some prefer auditory information and yet others prefer tactile or **kinaesthetic** processing. Most of us are on a continuum on which we absorb and process cues from all three areas: it is simply that we prefer one route over another.

Kinaesthetic
A learning style in which learning takes place by the students carrying out physical activities

Visual processors are likely to respond better to advertising with strong graphics or visual content. Auditory processors prefer the spoken word or music. Kinaesthetic processors prefer to touch or try out products, so would be most likely to respond to advertising that offers a trial or free sample. For instance, Kumon Wembley Central (a Maths and English study centre based in London) sees an average 30% rise in uptake during their post-summer free trial sessions. As shown in Figure 7.2, most people fit somewhere inside a triangle formed by the three processing methods, favouring one or another but still able to process information in all three ways.

Thus we need to start to investigate what influences our choice of the processing methods. There are five main influences on perceptual mapping, as shown in Figure 7.3.

The information is subjective in that people base decisions on the selected information. Each of us selects differently from the environment, and each of us has differing views. In the case of distinguishing between rival supermarket chains, each individual will have a slightly different view of the supermarkets concerned. If this were not so, we would rapidly develop a situation in which only one supermarket chain existed. The individual's previous experience also has a bearing – for example, research shows that adolescents who live in areas where there are high levels of drug use and sexual promiscuity over-estimate their own knowledge of these things (Parker et al., 2006).

PERCEPTION

```
Kinaesthetic processors          Visual processors

              Individuals fit somewhere
                inside the triangle

                  Auditory processors
```

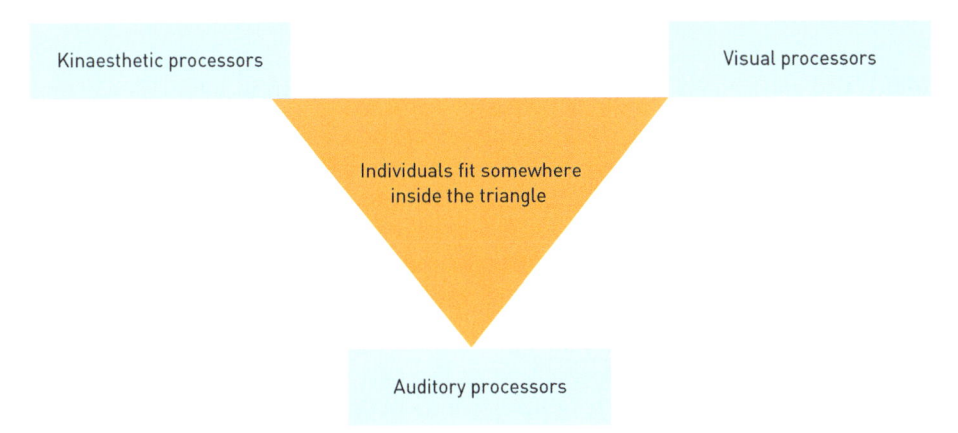

FIGURE 7.2 Information processing types

BRAND EXPERIENCES: A TRIP THROUGH THE MIGHTY AMAZON

There is a perception amongst some that Jeff Bezos, founder and former CEO of Amazon Group of Companies, and currently their Executive Chairman, is leading Amazon to dominate the world. Do you think that's an exaggeration? Well let's examine the influence he has on our lives – in all sorts of ways. If you've used IMDb.com (one of the largest movie websites in the world) to figure out who that one actor you recognise in that movie is, you've been helped by Jeff. Audible.com sells and produces audio entertainment, information and educational programming on the internet, and is famed for advertising on hundreds of podcasts. Goodreads, an online community with book reviews, recommendations and discussions is in the 350 most trafficked websites in the world, whilst Twitch.tv is a live streaming video platform that focuses on video gaming, e-sports competitions and other gaming-related events. And with over 80 million monthly visitors, that's a lot of interaction! Two other areas in which there is a perception that Amazon is making tidal waves are robotics and fast-moving consumer goods. Amazon Robotics makes robots for various tasks, including moving around products in Amazon's 'Fulfillment Centers', as well as working on drone delivery technology. All good stuff considering that Amazon are now the proud owners of 'Whole Foods Market', a $13.7 billion acquisition of the organic grocery chain. Oh, and as if that wasn't enough, Amazon also bought Zappos in 2009 – a leading footwear and apparel website whose big hook is that you can return your shoes up to a full year after buying them, as long as they're in good condition! So their customer service is second to none and driven by their CEO (Tony Hsieh) who is famed for his bestseller entitled *Delivering Happiness*, which details how he runs Zappos with happiness in mind.

So? Is your perception of Amazon now veering towards the words 'world domination'? You may be right!

CULTURE AND PERCEPTION

Culture also plays a part in perception – people who come from countries where the architecture is based on circles and cylinders (for example, rural Zambia) rather than squares and boxes sometimes have difficulty interpreting two-dimensional pictures, because they have had less experience in understanding perspective. Equally, culture affects the ways in which people interpret gestures, pictures, tones of voice and many other signals – for example, in many Indian languages a question is indicated by the use of a falling tone at the end of the sentence, whereas in English it is indicated by a rising tone. For an English speaker, someone speaking with a falling tone at the end of a sentence would sound as if they are making a flat statement, which in some contexts may sound strange or even offensive, leading to a false perception of the speaker. This false perception can also be true of many young people who have developed a habit of speaking with an 'upward inflection' – or a rising tone at the end of each sentence they speak, which makes them sound as if they are continually asking questions. The voice is of course a highly salient cue in the perception of gender, making the voice an enormously important aspect of gender presentation, particularly for those who are transitioning from one gender role, identity or presentation to another (Zimman, 2018).

Categorise

Placing products together based on information, for example quality

Information about quality will be pigeonholed, or **categorised**, so that products from different categories might be placed next to each other in the cognitive map. For example, an individual may put Jaguar in the same category as BMW, but might also include Bose or Pure in the same grouping. It is common to hear people refer to a product as 'the Rolls-Royce of...' whichever product category is under consideration – denoting that Rolls-Royce is the comparison point of all brands.

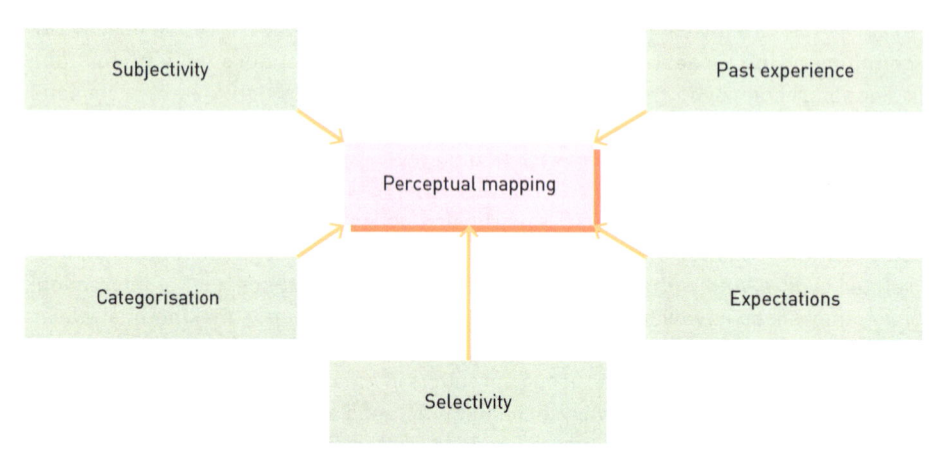

FIGURE 7.3 Influences on perceptual mapping

Selectivity will depend on how much is going on in the environment, on the individual's interest and motivation regarding the subject area, and on the degree of concentration the individual has on the task in hand. People with a highly developed ability to concentrate select less from the environment, because they are able to 'shut out' the world much more. And for those who don't have that natural ability, technology comes to their aid in the form of Bose QC45 noise-cancelling headphones, which help to 'shut out' the world!

Expectations of quality play a huge part: if the individual is expecting a high-quality item, he or she will select evidence that supports that view and tend to ignore evidence that doesn't.

Past experience will also play a part in quality judgement. If the consumer has had bad experiences of Chinese products, this might lead to a general perception that Chinese products are poor quality.

Price has a strong effect on people's assessment of products. Researchers have shown that people's confidence in guessing the 'right' price for an article varies according to how many zeroes there are in the stated price – the more zeroes, the greater the confidence in the guess (Thomas et al., 2010). People tend to think that a bargain is a better bargain if they also think that the marketers have made a mistake; in other words if people think the product has been accidentally marked at the wrong price they will tend to see it as a better bargain than if the marketers are explicit about the offer (Bardhi and Eckhardt, 2010). An example here is jacksflightclub.com started by Jack Sheldon. Airline pricing systems are complex. Once an airline sets a fare it goes into a database, and then perhaps into another one that feeds online travel agents and partner airlines, so any single mistake as a result of a currency conversion, or fuel surcharge or airport tax (and occasionally a manual error!) means that it goes out into the massive system that is international air fare pricing. But here's the key; in that lies discounts for travellers. So Sheldon has a computer program that scours every fare on every route by every airline waiting for the cost of a seat to fall – usually thanks to an unannounced flash sale or a 'mistake fare'. They then send out an email to their 1 million+ members, who benefit from fares such as London to Seville for just £30!

The downside from a marketer's viewpoint is that price could sometimes have a negative effect on perceived value and on willingness to buy (but clearly not for jacksflightclub members!). The problem therefore lies in knowing how big a price reduction will increase sales without leading to a negative perception of quality. **Weber's Law** states that the size of the least detectable change depends on the size of the stimulus. This means that a very intense stimulus will require a bigger change if the change is to be perceived by the consumer. For example, £1 off the price of a bar of Lindt chocolate is a substantial discount of almost 50%, and would attract attention in advertising; £1 off the price of a BMW would go completely unnoticed. Clearly at this level of intensity (a price of a few pence compared with a price of thousands of pounds) Weber's Law may not work very precisely, but in the middle range of prices the Law appears to work well. Incidentally, reducing the price from £10 to £9.99 is very noticeable even though the actual reduction is only 0.01% of the initial price. The important element here is that the reduction should be noticeable.

Weber's Law also applies to product differentiation. The Law can be applied to determine how much better the product has to be for the difference to be noticeable, or conversely to determine how similar the product needs to be to be indistinguishable from the leading brand. Branding is all about perception. The marketer's aim is to develop the most favourable perception possible of the brand through working with its strengths, whether the brand's strength lies in its quality, its price competitiveness or any other area. Developing a suitable brand personality means encouraging people to imbue the brand with human characteristics – which means assembling a range of stimuli to create an overall image.

Weber's Law
The size of the least detectable change will depend on the size of the stimulus

USING OUR EARS TO EAT

Since the turn of the 21st century, we have seen a proliferation of studies that emanate from the intersection of neurophysiology, cognitive neuroscience and psychophysics – which according to Charles Spence (2015) 'highlight the multisensory nature of human perception'. Using senses that (at first sight) appear to be unrelated to the primary senses to which the product relates can be extremely powerful: for example, the 'snap, crackle and pop' of Rice Krispies relates sound to the brand (Scott et al., 2022), whereas one would normally expect a food product to be primarily concerned with flavour and (perhaps) texture. People are prepared to pay more for food that is well-presented – up to 140% more in some cases (Payne and Wansink, 2010) – or indeed where there is a perception of positive effects of health consciousness through buying organic food (Konuk, 2018).

What essentially we are referring to here is the interaction of audition, aroma, vision, touch and flavour (Spence, 2015). Anyone who has eaten crisps will know that it's virtually impossible to do so without making a noise. Some experiments have been conducted in the use of multisensory brands. Sound can most definitely impact on the experience one has with food and drink (Stuckey, 2012), especially a **sonic logo** (Scott et al., 2022). Researchers have named this 'eating with our ears' (Spence, 2015). Think of the crunch of Walkers Extra Crunchy Crisps (which featured an advertisement with the pop star Lionel Richie) or the bubbles and fizz of the Moët & Chandon champagne campaign with Scarlett Johansson. In fact, Zampini and Spence (2004) conducted an experiment where respondents graded the sound emanating from individually biting into 180 Pringles. The sounds (both volume and frequency) had been manipulated by a computer, which resulted in participants believing that the crisps had come from different packets and were at different stages of freshness and staleness! A similar experiment was recently carried out with apples too (Demattè et al., 2014). Spence (2015) has also written about the sound of 'carbonation', 'creaminess', 'crunch' and 'squeaky' foods such as halloumi cheese. In Ehrenbergh-Bass speak, a sonic logo is a distinctive asset in its own right. A good sonic logo is sophisticated, detailed and, most importantly, has a story and a reason to exist. When a sonic logo has a story, it feels like part of a wider brand ecosystem. It fits with the colours and the creative because it's been designed this way. It speaks the same language as these other assets. But also, it stands on its own. Just like any good visual logo, a sonic logo with a story has grown a pair of legs. It has a legacy and tells us about a brand in a matter of seconds. This means it can live on the radio, TV and wherever else, regardless of what comes before it – whether that's a piece of branded music, a licensed track or just silence. As examples of sonic logos that trigger positive perceptions in many minds, think about the sounds for TED, McDonald's, Apple and O2. If you're unfamiliar with them (!) go and find them online. Conversely, with aroma in mind, a lot of research, observations and studies around the world have shown that various smells have an impact on people's changing moods, preferences and emotions (Berčík et al., 2021). Nike found that people who tried out their trainers in a floral-scented room preferred them to the same trainers when they tried them in a non-scented room (Lindstrom, 2005). Obviously if the fragrance is an inherent part of the product (for example, soap) any changes in the fragrance will have a profound effect on perception of the brand, even when the primary function of the brand is unaffected (Milotic, 2003). So how much does the physical environment affect our perception of a product/service, and in turn our ability to make purchase decisions?

Sonic logo

An audible version of a visual logo and a fully-fledged piece of brand work

ENVIRONMENTAL INFLUENCES

The environment refers to the physical surroundings in which decision-making takes place. It includes physical objects (the products themselves, the display stands in stores and even the stores themselves), spatial relationships (the location of products in stores, the amount of space available within the stores, the location of the stores) and the behaviour of other people within the environment.

For example, the shopping experience in an upmarket department store such as Harrods in London, El Corte Inglés in Madrid or Bungalow 8 in Mumbai is a great deal different from the shopping experience in markets such as Brick Lane in London, the Rastro market in Madrid or the Chor Bazaar in Mumbai. The actual goods on offer may even be the same in many cases, but the level of service, the behaviour of fellow shoppers and the general atmosphere will be totally different, as of course will be the prices.

Figure 7.4 shows some of the relationships between elements of the environment. The level of service, decor, presence or absence of music, and the other customers in the store all affect the store's brand image, but other factors over which the store management has little or no control will also affect the functional environment, which in turn affects the buying behaviour of the individual shoppers.

Macro-environmental factors

- Political issues
- Economic factors
- Geographical conditions
- Climate
- 'Green' factors

Micro-environmental factors

- Current conditions in-store
- Level of service
- In-store music
- Current weather conditions
- Other customers
- Store decor

Functional environment

Brand image of the store

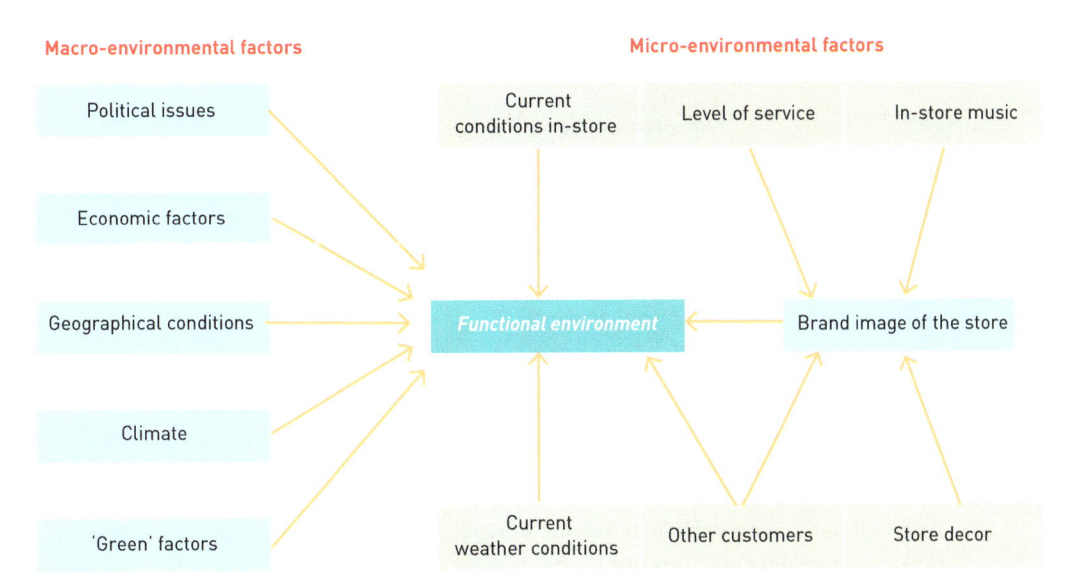

FIGURE 7.4 Elements in the environment

PERCEPTION AND STORE ATMOSPHERICS

At a more subtle level, people may be influenced by factors such as music played within the store, use of colour in the store and the perceived social **class** of other store users. For a marketer, the difficulty lies in assessing which factors are crucial, and how those factors might affect different people; some people like to have music playing in-store, for example, whereas others are irritated by it. Likewise, some people enjoy the buzz and bustle of shopping in a street market, whereas others might find it distracting or even threatening.

Class
The social and economic grouping of individuals

Atmospherics
The factors that create the overall ambience in a retail environment

Proxemics
The use of physical space to convey a perceptual stimulus

Kinesics
The interpretation of non-verbal communications related to body movement

Paralanguage
Communication carried out in a manner other than through words

The concept of store **atmospherics** was first described by Kotler (1973). Atmospherics are all the factors that make up the atmosphere and general 'feel' of a retail store: the decor, the music, the temperature and humidity, and so forth. There are three factors in the information processing of store atmospherics: proxemics, kinesics and paralanguage (see Figure 7.5).

Proxemics refers to the use of physical space in conveying a perceptual stimulus. In a retail environment, for example, a shop assistant might stand too far away (which might be interpreted as dislike for the customer) or too close (suggesting a threatening invasion of personal space). **Kinesics** is about body language, eye contact and gesture: greater eye contact between buyers and sellers would indicate positive feelings between them. **Paralanguage** refers to the way words are used, for example the use of 'here' and 'this' is more positive than using 'there' and 'that'. Some other sound cues such as yawning, speaking too loudly or too softly, or speaking too quickly or too slowly also convey messages about how the individual feels about the product.

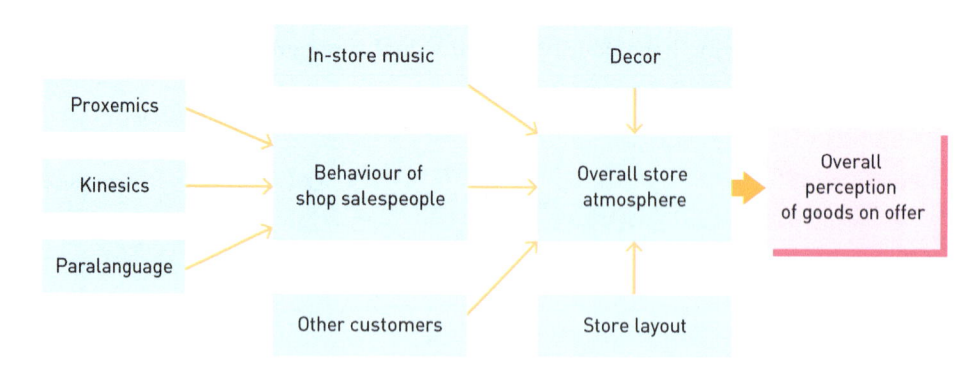

FIGURE 7.5 Perception and store atmospherics

CRITICAL REFLECTION

Do we all behave in a particular way for a reason? We are all aware that body language makes a great deal of difference to communications. Gestures and subtleties of facial expression can completely change the meaning of words used. Yet most of this happens without us even being aware of it. We operate on gut feeling – we get a sense of when someone is lying, for example, without necessarily being able to say what particular facial expression or gesture gave the game away. Body language coaches will often teach that standing 'openly' is a sign of welcoming – they call this 'open assertion' – a way of both your body and voice talking clearly and assertively but neither dominating nor submitting. Then there is the 'match and move'. Starting off by reflecting the stances – matching body language and employing a similar verbal style. This, coupled with perhaps 'leaning in' a little, helps to create an emotional bond. But beware... lean in too far and you're in danger of invading 'personal space'!

So how can we possibly expect to train shop assistants to behave in a particular way? Aren't we liable to make poor play-actors out of them, and thus give customers the impression that we are lying to them? Or should we skip the assistant and move directly to programming the retail robot (as we saw in Chapter 4)?

Or maybe we should just hire nice people to begin with? Well, retailers have become adept at training their staff to use tricks of the trade and make subtle moves which use body language to influence their customers. For instance, raising eyebrows or tilting the head slightly to show surprise, smiling to show a liking of the customer and regular soft eye contact that shows a caring attitude are among many others which are designed to engage the consumer on a variety of levels. Companies such as Disney have taken customer service to an even higher level by utilising their very own educational establishment, the Disney Institute. Their 2014 report 'The Secret to Delighting Customers? Put Employees First' makes for very interesting reading (and can be found at https://disneyinstitute.com/blog/2014/01/the-secret-to-delighting-customers-put-employees-first-/233/).

© iStock.com/ÖzgürDonmaz

Another example is the way in which store atmospherics are manipulated to generate perceptions about the products on offer – music played in-store will tend to increase purchases of hedonic products (Lee and Thomas, 2010).

Moods can be manipulated to an extent by store atmospherics (Basu et al., 2022), which in turn affect purchasing behaviour (Zaheer et al., 2022) – moods also affect processing of information from advertising (Bakamitsos and Siomkos, 2004). Brand extensions are received more favourably if the individual is in a good mood (Greifeneder et al.,

2007), and even the way the message is framed can affect perception: researchers found that smokers who read that almost 1000 people die of smoking every day found the message more powerful than saying that 440,000 people a year die of smoking. This is because the shorter time-frame means that the message has more immediacy (Chandran and Menon, 2003). Time-frames may have other effects – positive cues are often overrated when considering a future event because people broaden the range of factors they take into account when considering the future (Grant and Tybout, 2003). Dates are regarded as abstract, whereas time intervals are concrete: in other words, 'six months' interest-free credit' not only sounds a great deal better than 'interest-free credit until 30 November' (LeBoeuf, 2006), but also means that the recipient of the message doesn't have to work out the timescales.

Atmospherics go a long way towards determining whether a customer remains in the store longer, spends more (or less) money and returns at a later date. Since Kotler, researchers have taken two basic approaches to researching atmospherics. The first approach concentrates on the factors that make up store atmosphere, whereas the other approach regards atmosphere in a holistic way and concentrates instead on its effects on consumers. Under the first approach, studies have been made of colour and lighting (Bellizzi et al., 1983; Tazehmahaleh et al., 2022), social factors (Baker et al., 1992; Liu-Thompkins et al., 2022), music and lighting (Kellaris and Kent, 1992; Yang et al., 2022), crowding (Eroglu and Harrell, 1986; Santini et al., 2021), social distancing (Chang, 2021) and point-of-purchase displays (Philips and Bradshaw, 1990; Rizzi et al., 2022). There are two common findings in these studies: first, that manipulating these various elements correctly can result in outcomes favourable to the retailer, that is, people stay in the store longer and spend more money; and second, that these elements affect people's physical and psychological states, and hence their behaviour.

The second main thrust of research, an examination of the kind of effects atmospherics have on people, has produced some interesting results. Several researchers have used the Mehrabian–Russell Environmental Psychology Model (M–R model) to explain some of the features of store atmospherics (Mehrabian and Russell, 1974). The M–R model says that environmental stimuli lead to emotional states (e.g. pleasure or arousal), which then lead to approach or avoidance responses. The opposite is also true, in that the big five factors of personality (openness, conscientiousness, extroversion, agreeableness and neuroticism) themselves can also have a moderating effect on a person's consumption emotions (Jani and Han, 2015). In a study of music shops in Hong Kong, researchers were able to expand and modify the model to provide the example shown in Figure 7.6 (Tai and Fung, 1997).

The left-hand box in the model refers to the information rate. This is the degree to which the shopper is exposed to novelty and surprise – the more novel the environment, the greater the information rate. Likewise, the more complex the environment the higher the information rate. Mehrabian and Russell (1974) postulate that an individual's propensity to develop approach or avoidance behaviours is a function of three elements – pleasure (or displeasure), arousal (or boredom) and dominance (or submission). In the study of music stores, the researchers found that information rates have a marked effect on arousal, but not necessarily on pleasure: in other words customers did not necessarily like having a high information rate, even though they found it stimulating or exciting. The researchers further found that in-store behaviour contributed more to the pleasure of the experience, so from a marketer's viewpoint it would seem sensible to allow people plenty of latitude to examine goods, interact with staff, and so forth.

The environment as perceived by the consumers themselves is called the functional (or perceived) environment (Block and Block, 1981). The functional environment will be different for each individual, because individuals differ in their knowledge, beliefs, experience and (of course) preference. Since marketers generally deal with groups of people rather than individuals, subtle differences and idiosyncrasies are likely to be ignored in favour of creating a generally acceptable environment for the target group of customers.

Figure 7.7 shows some of the elements of the functional environment. The macro-environment affects everything else, including the store and its branding: store decor, music, service levels and other customers all affect the store's brand image, but the

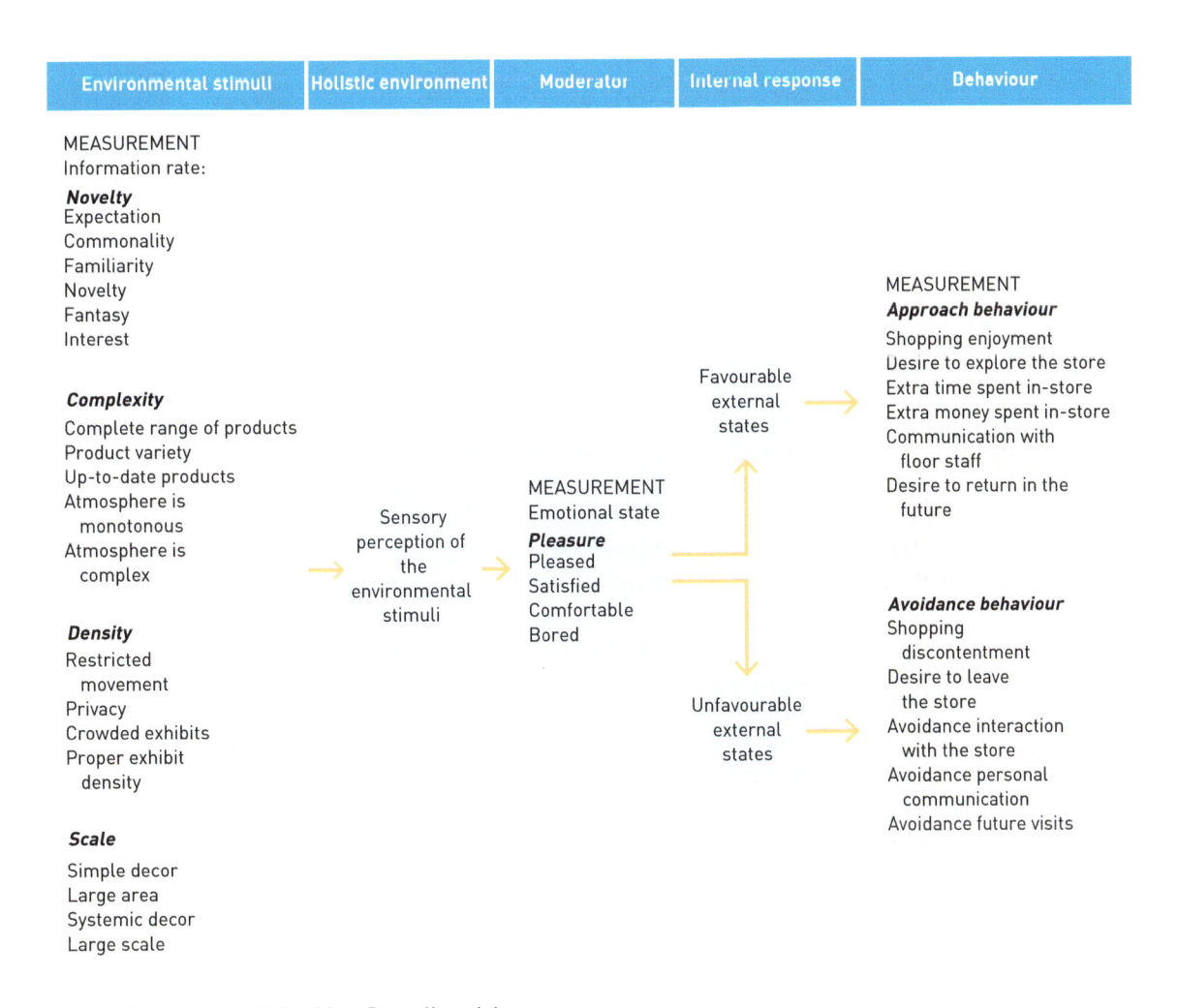

Environmental stimuli	Holistic environment	Moderator	Internal response	Behaviour
MEASUREMENT Information rate: **Novelty** Expectation Commonality Familiarity Novelty Fantasy Interest **Complexity** Complete range of products Product variety Up-to-date products Atmosphere is monotonous Atmosphere is complex **Density** Restricted movement Privacy Crowded exhibits Proper exhibit density **Scale** Simple decor Large area Systemic decor Large scale	Sensory perception of the environmental stimuli	MEASUREMENT Emotional state **Pleasure** Pleased Satisfied Comfortable Bored	Favourable external states Unfavourable external states	MEASUREMENT **Approach behaviour** Shopping enjoyment Desire to explore the store Extra time spent in-store Extra money spent in-store Communication with floor staff Desire to return in the future **Avoidance behaviour** Shopping discontentment Desire to leave the store Avoidance interaction with the store Avoidance personal communication Avoidance future visits

FIGURE 7.6 Adapted Mehrabian–Russell model

behaviour and number of other customers also affect the functional environment directly. The current conditions in the store (crowding, social distancing, cleanliness, availability of assistants) and the current weather (whether it is hot, rainy, cold) have a direct bearing on the functional environment. There are of course many other factors that may affect the individual: situational factors such as time pressures, physical interrupts such as hunger or thirst, and so forth. Since the functional environment is subjective, the individual's personality, tastes, moods and behaviour act as moderating factors. Added to all of this, we now find another layer of atmospherics related to mobile apps (Zaheer and Rizwan, 2022). Lee and Kim (2019) in their study of 216 US mobile shoppers found that consumers with a higher need for mobile app atmospherics tended to experience increased entertainment gratification and reduced irritation in using mobile apps. Thus, the consumer need for mobile app atmospherics played a significant role in predicting the intention to reuse mobile apps for apparel shopping, along with entertainment gratification and mobile irritation.

FIGURE 7.7 The functional environment

CRITICAL REFLECTION

Does it sound to you as if the functional environment is really difficult to deal with? Well, that's subjective, as it's easily affected by factors over which we have absolutely no control and it changes with every passing minute. So why do we bother? Why not just pile everything up on the counter and hope people buy it? (There are of course some retailers who do that, without naming names!)

Maybe that's a bit of an exaggeration, though. Maybe we should influence the bits we can influence, and live with the bits we can't influence. At least we'll be able to make some difference to people's perceptions! Take for example the use of digital signage and video screens by the world famous London retailer Harrods of Knightsbridge. They have over 150 screens located in their windows, which are undoubtedly adding to the store's atmospherics but will also allow the retailer to generate a substantial media income from companies and brands who are eager to advertise and therefore be 'associated' with the Harrods brand. In fact, over 67% of customers in a Pickcel (2022) survey said that they often buy products based on the retail stores' digital signage visuals.

BRAND EXPERIENCES: BANGING DIGITAL SIGNAGE

Jo Malone harnessed digital signage to create an engaging retail experience for customers by encouraging them to combine various fragrances in the store. Instead of overloading their target audience with product information, they used visual language to explain each scent. Customers could simply pick a bottle of perfume off the shelf to see an elegant representation of the fragrance. They could also identify complementary aromas and combine them to create a customised vial. As a result, they were able to achieve 25% higher product lift and 16 times the return on investment. They were also able to capture customer attention with the stunning visual representation of different scents, which meant that they could also educate prospective buyers on the essential oils and aroma compounds used in each perfume.

Another example is when an innovative concept was presented in Adidas's German headquarters at AG, Herzogenaurach. The Adidas Virtual Footwear Wall – that blended digital signage technology and user experience – was launched as a pre-booking campaign for the F50 miCoach football boot. It left customers thrilled with its immersive, virtual product experience. The digital wall allowed customers to explore the shoe's 360-degree model with an interactive touch display and an immersive sound experience. They could inspect shoes inside out, rotate, zoom in and analyse every tiny detail. This campaign garnered excellent traction for Adidas's latest product and ensured a successful launch that hit all sales targets.

Finally, you've probably heard of K-Pop, but have you heard of K-Beauty? Aritaum is a Korean franchise beauty store with a laser focus on skincare and on-trend colour collections. It houses several famous brands like Laneige, Innisfree and Happy Bath. With thousands of stores located in countries like Korea, China and North America, Aritaum has established itself as a one-stop destination for K-Beauty trends. Despite this solid offline presence, it hasn't been able to tap into the market fully. The shops introduced interactive technology to entice their walk-in customers to increase store engagement and brand recall. From a touchable mirror display to AR content, Aritaum pulled out all the stops to improve in-store experiences with digital signage. Customers could get in-depth skin examinations and consultations for free with IOPE Bio Lab's skin health machine. Several 'beauty mirrors' helped customers virtually try on Laneige make-up products with a tablet linked to the brand's mobile app. They analysed skin tone to recommend the most suitable make-up products for each customer. The store is also fitted with photo booths and 'digital skincare bars', which provide product information and reviews to users on the spot. Users can scan a QR code and add it to their purchase wish list to buy the product.

The subjective nature of the functional environment can be problematical in an international context, because there are often marked differences between individuals in different countries; even with the European Union this is a problem, despite the relative similarities between member states in terms of wealth, aspirations and product availability (Askegaard and Madsen, 1995). Because of this, it is tempting for marketers to treat each country as a separate segment, whereas in fact this can be inappropriate since new transnational segments are appearing as people travel more (Brunso et al., 1996). There are four consumer styles that have been identified that transcend national boundaries (McCarty et al., 2007):

1. *Price-sensitive consumers.* These are people who check prices, shop around for special offers and are not brand-loyal.
2. *Variety-seekers.* These people like to try new things and are the first to buy new products.
3. *Brand-loyal consumers.* These people buy known brands, and are likely to be brand-loyal even when this costs more; they are less likely to check prices or shop around for bargains.
4. *Information-seekers.* These people exchange information with other people, are more receptive to advertising and will try new products but tend to stick to known brands.

Other styles identified in the research differed across cultural boundaries – German consumers are less brand-loyal and more price-sensitive than consumers from some other countries, but they tend to enjoy shopping more than the French do, for example.

In the context of consumer behaviour, the environmental factors can be divided into **macro-environmental** factors – or the uncontrollables, such as climate, the current weather conditions, economy, politics, geography and so forth; and **micro-environmental** factors – or controllables, such as the shop assistant, the store's cleanliness and decor, and the other shoppers. Each of these factors is relevant: macro-environmental factors will dictate what people need to buy in terms of clothing, housing, transport and so forth, as well as what they are able to buy either as a result of their wealth or as a result of legal restrictions or requirements. Micro-environmental factors influence decision-making at the point of purchase: people are unlikely to linger in noisy, crowded or dirty stores, and they become frustrated if there are long queues at checkouts (Park et al., 1989).

Macro-environment
Environmental elements that are common to all firms in a given industry, and are largely uncontrollable

Micro-environment
Those elements of the environment that affect the individual firm, and which could be controlled

PERCEPTION AND CONSUMERS' CHARACTERISTICS AND BEHAVIOUR

A consumer's stable characteristics are the basic factors about an individual that do not change, or change only slowly. Gender, personality, social class, age, educational level and intelligence all affect perception. For example, work by Pfefferbaum et al. (2015) reviewed children's reactions to disasters and the personal and situational factors that influence their reactions. Such differences can and do produce differences in the accuracy of interpretation of cues, and also in the selection of cues. Therefore, wide differences in processing ability (Henry, 1980), numeric ability (Callison et al., 2015) and consequently in perception itself should be expected between different individuals.

Some demographic variables may be responsible for the misunderstanding of cues; however, although the stable characteristics of the consumer might be expected to have a strong effect on perception, the interplay of the various factors is such that researching the effect of each one proves difficult. So far, therefore, research has been somewhat inconclusive on this issue.

Responses are not necessarily overt or external. In terms of perception, a response can just as easily be internal and non-behavioural. The perceptual response has three components: affection, attribution and expectancy (see Figure 7.8).

Affection is about emotional responses. In ordinary language, affection implies a positive response, but in psychology affection merely describes any emotional effect, whether positive or negative. Such responses to a given stimulus might be liking, sympathy, fear, respect, disapproval, disgust and so forth. An affective response is what we refer to when we talk about gut feeling or instinct: it is not a rational response, but that does not necessarily mean that it is wrong or ill-conceived.

Attribution is about applying a certain characteristic to an object. For example, someone who is scowling might be perceived as being angry. It is possible that the person is actually deep in thought about a problem that has just arisen, but the observer has attributed the characteristic of anger based on the cue of the facial expression. The same process happens when people are confronted with a product or brand: they attribute characteristics to it based on the cues received.

Expectancy is about what the individual thinks the object will do. In the case of the scowling person, the observer might expect that the person will shout or even become violent. In marketing, expectancy is what leads people to believe that a well-known brand is better than the generic brand, even though the formulation is the same. One of the best-known examples of this is analgesics (pain killers). Branded aspirin actually works better than generic aspirin, even though the active ingredient (acetylsalicylic acid) is identical in each case.

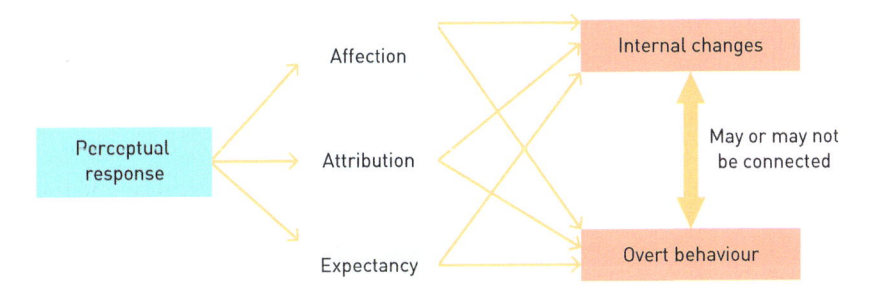

FIGURE 7.8 Perceptual responses

COMBINING FACTORS

The processing centre combines the various cues to create an overall impression. This is likely to include attribution, expectation and affection components, but there are three basic models which seek to explain how this happens in practice. These are as follows:

1. *The linear additive model* (Figure 7.9). This states that the **inferences** from each cue will build towards an overall perception. This means that the implications that attach to a particular characteristic will become stronger with the addition of each cue, regardless of how intense each cue is. For instance, work by Hu et al. (2015) examined the influence of the physical characteristics of houses on prices at different levels and found that a larger number of rooms, a bigger overall footprint and the fact that a house has been well-maintained and repaired are factors contributing to an increase in the price of a house. In other words, a strong cue will not be weakened by a subsequent weak cue.

Inference

Extra detail added to a message by a recipient, based on meta-analysis of the message

2. *The linear averaging model* (Figure 7.10). This is a refinement on the previous model, since it assumes that the implication of a particular characteristic will be strengthened or weakened by subsequent cues, according to their strength. This means that the quality of the information may be more important than the quantity of the information, so that marketers who try to provide people with very large amounts of positive information may find that the effect is weakened if people regard some of the information as being less interesting than other information. Salespeople generally understand this phenomenon well: they are trained to find out first what the customer is interested in about the product, then to talk only about those aspects. While there is some (rather old) research evidence to show that the linear averaging model fits the facts better than the linear additive model (Anderson, 1965), there is also some recent evidence that supports the theoretical usage of generalised linear mixed models (Iwasaki and Brinkman, 2015).

3. *The configural model* (Figure 7.11). Linear models have the underlying assumption that the meaning of each cue remains the same when other facts are revealed. This is not necessarily the case: as cues are brought together, the meanings of previous cues are likely to be revised in the light of the new information. The configural model is intended to address this issue. The problem with this model is, of course, that it is virtually impossible to calculate what may or may not happen in a particular individual's mind as a result of being presented with a number of cues, and it is even difficult to know what will happen across a target audience of potential customers, which makes advertising difficult. This said, neuroscience is making vast progress towards exactly that.

As with any models, all three of the above are simplifications of reality, and therefore do not tell the whole story. It seems likely that people perceive the whole of a given object, rather than breaking it down into individual cues, but this (naturally) varies according to circumstances. Someone choosing to give to a charity will have many questions and be persuaded by many cues. Their own interests or life experiences, whether it's a registered charity or not, an awareness of campaigns, emergency needs following a natural disaster, and the charity's administrative costs will all contribute to an individual's philanthropic choices.

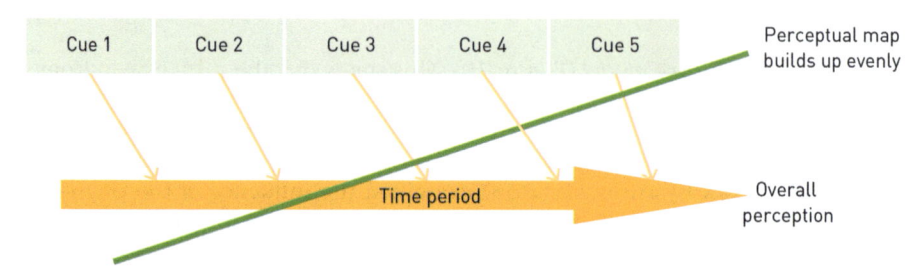

FIGURE 7.9 Linear additive model

PERCEPTION

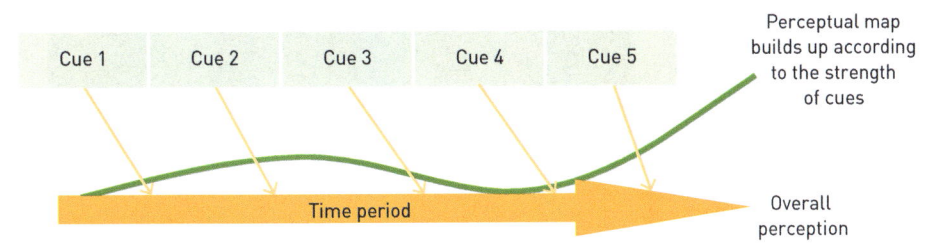

FIGURE 7.10   Linear averaging model

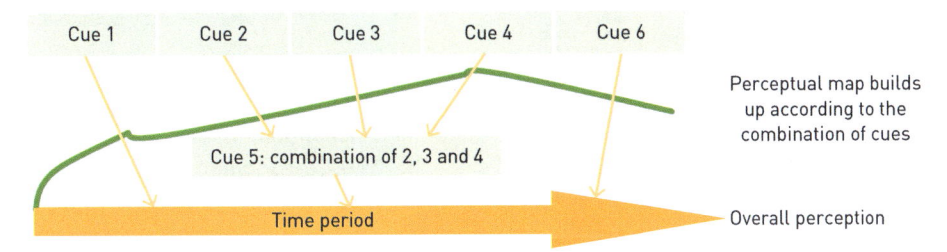

FIGURE 7.11   The configural model

CONSUMER BEHAVIOUR IN ACTION: IS YOUR BRAIN WIRED?

Your smartphone can already take instructions from you using software such as Siri and Google Assistant. But could you imagine a world in which your smartphone could read your mind, or is this still confined to science fiction movies? Imagine that you decided to delete a message and just at the moment that you decide to move your finger to delete it, it is already gone!

Well, guess what? Science fiction has become science fact for one human in California. Aflalo et al. (2015) have reported the case of a tetraplegic individual (called 'EGS') who volunteered to have his brain implanted with two small silicon chips that allow researchers to read his intentions directly from his brain activity. The chips, initially developed at the University of Utah, are now commercially available and approved for human use by the US Food and Drug Administration and consist of a matrix of 96 microscopic electrodes that can record the activity of about 100 nerve cells at the same time.

The fantasy is indeed becoming reality.

Researchers at Human Systems Lab in Canada have recently focused their attention on the development of machine vision systems. These systems sense overt biological signals – for example, the direction of eye gaze or heart rate – to estimate cognitive states like distraction or fatigue. A case can be made that these devices hold undeniable benefits in certain situations, such as driving. Human factors like distracted driving, which ranks among the top contributors of road fatalities, could be all but eliminated following an adequate introduction of these systems. Proposals to mandate the use of these devices are being introduced worldwide. A different yet equally important

(Continued)

application is the one proposed by none other than Elon Musk's Neuralink corporation. In a December 2021 appearance at the *Wall Street Journal*'s CEO Council Summit, Musk portrayed a very-near future where brain implants will help patients suffering from paralysis regain control of their limbs through a brain implant. While the concept and, in fact, the reality of brain–computer interfaces have existed since the 1960s, the thought of an implanted device having direct access to the brain is disconcerting, to say the least. It's not only these devices' ability to create a direct bridge between the human brain and the outside world that is frightening: what is questionable is what will happen to the data being harvested and who will have access to those data?

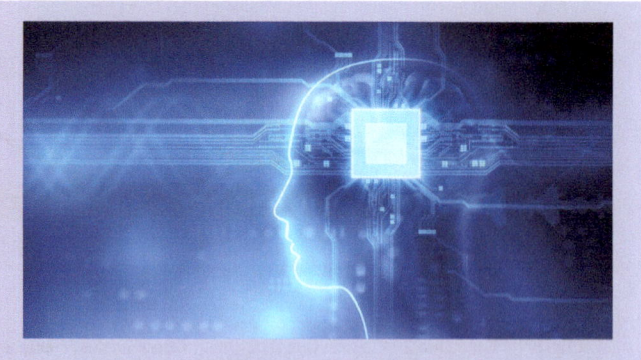

© iStock.com/Petrovich 9

Source: Adapted partially from The Conversation (2022).

Of course, we rarely have complete information about anything. Our brains are proactive in filling in the gaps – neuroscience has demonstrated that we continuously generate predictions about what to expect in the environment around us (Bar and Neta, 2008). Communications technology and the plethora of data (sensor networks, RFID tags, surveillance cameras, unmanned aerial vehicles and geo-tagged social-media posts) that we can now tap into (sometimes also known as 'big data') mean that the environment around us will foresee our every move. Computerised sensing and broadcasting abilities are being incorporated into our physical environment, creating the 'Internet of Things', which will telegraph where we've been and where we are going. It seems that we are poised to travel towards a future where these data streams will be integrated into services we receive, platforms and programs that we engage with and will provide a very large window into the lives, and futures, of billions of people.

Equally, the purchase of a brand of biscuits is unlikely to involve the same level of analysis. Few people would trouble to read the list of ingredients and the nutritional information on the packet, or ask a friend's advice, or go online and investigate the company's history and manufacturing methods.

An interesting area of research, therefore, is to try to find out what rules people use at particular times. Sometimes people will use a linear rule, at other times they might use a configural method, and at still other times people might use a combination of rules to form an overall opinion.

It may be that the more utilitarian aspects of the product are judged against a linear set of rules, whereas the hedonic or affective aspects are judged against the configural model (Holbrook and Moore, 1981).

SUBLIMINAL PERCEPTION

Perception is not necessarily a conscious process. Much of what happens in our minds happens below the conscious level (see Chapter 6), and we know that often people have a 'gut feeling' about something without being able to define why. Some of us have had the experience of helplessly falling in love at first sight – with people or with products. This happens without our having any real facts to go on, and without our having any way of analysing the reasons.

Subliminal perception has a controversial history in marketing. During the 1950s it was claimed that subliminal advertising, as it was called, could make people do things they otherwise would not do. The theory was that brief exposure to a message (for example, flashing 'Drink Cola' onto a cinema screen during a film) would cause people to experience a sudden mysterious desire to drink cola. The theory was that the message would appear and disappear much too quickly for the input selector mechanism to operate, so the message would bypass the normal perceptual safeguards and enter the person's consciousness unedited (see Figure 7.12). These claims were so powerful that subliminal advertising was banned in some countries and was regulated in others; in fact, the general air of paranoia in the 1950s may have contributed to the scare, since there is little evidence to support the claims made for subliminal advertising.

Subliminal perception
Perception that occurs below the conscious level

Wilson Key has published several books on the subject of subliminal perception in advertising (Key, 1973, 1976, 1980, 1989), in which he claims that advertisers have airbrushed-in words such as 'U Buy' into the shadows around a bottle of rum, and various sexual images in advertisements for cigarettes and even cake mix. In 1957, Vance Packard published a book called *The Hidden Persuaders* in which he analysed the various ways in which the media industry manipulates opinion; he included subliminal advertising in his analysis (Packard, 1957). However, in both cases the authors have been criticised for failing to produce solid evidence, and for making too many unsupported assumptions.

The evidence for and against subliminal perception, at least as far as marketing goes, is mixed to say the least. There is some evidence that drive and behaviour may be influenced (Hawkins, 1970), and there is also some evidence that flashing brand names onto cinema screens has impact when the stimulus is related to right-brain processing (Cuperfain and Clarke, 1985). Other studies have failed to find any evidence for subliminal perception (Beatty and Hawkins, 1989; Gable et al., 1987; Kelly, 1979). Much more recent work has focused on identifying an apparent window of subliminal perception which arises in humans under specific stimulus conditions (Sandberg et al., 2022) as well as revisiting the central question of whether observed effects result from non-conscious processing rather than from some stimuli being consciously perceived by participants which are missed due to error in the awareness measurement (Goldstein et al., 2022).

Subliminal perception, and from that subliminal advertising, is supposed to work in the same way as self-hypnosis mpegs (video files) or YouTube videos. Such videos are often sold and distributed as a means of losing weight, giving up smoking and so forth, yet there is no evidence that they have any effect whatsoever (Anon., 1991). People's attitudes towards subliminal perception are ambivalent – on the one hand, people tend to fear it, since they are afraid that marketers (and others) might use it to manipulate them unfairly, and on the other hand people often hope that it does work when they buy self-hypnosis recordings (Spencer et al., 2003). In many instances, however, it can be seen as just clever design. Take for example the world's most prestigious cycling event, the Tour de France. Its logo has been in existence since 1903, and a closer look shows that the R in 'ouR' and the orange circle make up an image of someone riding a bicycle.

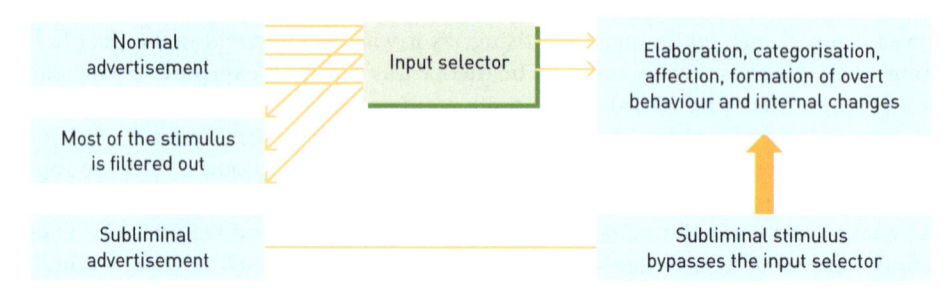

FIGURE 7.12 Subliminal advertising

CRITICAL REFLECTION

When does a nudge become a shove? **Nudges** have been controversial, to say the least (Gane, 2021; McGrew et al., 2022). For some years now, and certainly over the past decade, behavioural insights have been used by governments to improve policies in areas that include health, savings, finance, highway safety, employment, discrimination, the environment and consumer protection (Biswal et al., 2022; Halpern, 2015; OECD, 2017; SBST, 2016; Sunstein, 2013; Sunstein and Reisch, 2017). The forms that these take are varied: mandates, incentives and bans. But a prominent set of behaviourally informed tools also includes information, warnings, reminders, social norms and default rules (Thaler and Sunstein, 2008). These tools steer people in certain directions without imposing significant costs. In the academic literature there is a continuing debate over their use (Bubb and Pildes, 2014; Conley, 2012; Halpern, 2015; Thaler, 2022), and practically speaking, more than 150 governments worldwide make use of nudges to influence consumer behaviour and consumer choices (Einfeld and Blomkamp, 2022; OECD, 2017; Sousa Lourenco et al., 2016; Sunstein, 2016).

Nudges
Choice-preserving interventions that steer people's behaviour in specific directions while still allowing them to go their own way

Even if subliminal advertising were shown to work, it seems probable that it would be ineffective. First, different people have different perception thresholds, so some people might be aware that the message has flashed onto the screen. Second, there is a very high risk of misunderstanding; after all, people frequently misunderstand or misinterpret advertising that is in plain language, so the potential for missing the point in an advertisement that is flashed onto a cinema screen for a fraction of a second must be very much greater. Finally, the selective nature of perception means that most stimuli are ignored or rejected by the input selector, even when the stimulus is strong. The fleeting nature of subliminal messages is likely to mean that they never register with the observer. This view accords with Weber's Law (which we saw earlier in this chapter).

COLOUR

Colours are used to attract attention (Liu et al., 2022), but they also convey particular emotions and meanings. These meanings are culturally specific – for example, in Japan white is the colour of funerals, whereas in the USA and most of Europe it is black; in China, bright colours symbolise high quality, whereas in the UK they are often associated with low-price, low-quality articles. Consumers have a preference for colour and form which varies from one product category to another (Reddy et al., 2015). Dantec et al. (2022) noted that specific olfactory properties like freshness and lightness were found to be associated with natural odour, whilst the colours green, white and yellow were reliably associated with natural products. In the same study (Dantec et al., 2022), culture and product categories appeared to modulate associations between colours and natural products and expected intensity of natural products' odour and colour. A study by Madden et al. (2000) found that red is perceived as hot, active and vibrant across all cultures, while black and brown are perceived as sad and stale. Black and brown are also perceived as formal in Brazil, Colombia, China and Taiwan, and as masculine in Austria, Hong Kong and the USA.

Table 7.2 shows some common colour perceptions, particularly as they relate to packaging and advertising.

TABLE 7.2 Colour perceptions

Colour	Perceived meaning
Yellow	A strong attention-grabber, yellow often symbolises summer. It works well as a background colour for black print, because it makes the print stand out, but it can sometimes be perceived as 'cheap and cheerful'. Some people associate yellow with warmth, novelty or caution
Orange	Orange is a sociable colour, but in packaging it is mainly used for products (such as orange juice) that actually contain oranges. Some products (and many billboard posters) use Dayglo orange as an attention-grabber; in the UK, this bright orange colour is still successfully used by low-cost airline easyJet
Red	This is a strong attention-grabber because it can stand for most human emotions. It is often regarded as hot, exciting, passionate and strong
Purple	Purple was formerly associated with royalty, and it has retained an upmarket image. Because it is the most expensive colour to reproduce, and has poor resistance to fading, its use in packaging is limited
Blue	Blue is rarely associated with food packaging, because very few foods are blue. It is commonly used to denote coolness or cleanliness, and it is often perceived as having authority and commanding respect. This is why many countries use blue as the colour for police uniforms

(Continued)

TABLE 7.2 (Continued)

Colour	Perceived meaning
Green	The rise of environmentalism has increased the use of green for packaging and advertising. It carries connotations of naturalness, security and calmness
Pink or magenta	Pink has stereotypically been regarded as a feminine colour, so it has been widely used in cosmetics, but in recent years it has been used for baby products and some categories of household goods
White	In most European countries and the USA, white is the colour of purity and cleanliness. In Japan and India, however, it is the colour of mourning
Brown	In food packaging, brown usually denotes strong flavours such as pickles and sauces, or coffee and chocolate. For gardening products, it conveys a rich earthiness
Black	Black is usually associated with death, but combined with gold it can denote exclusivity and premium prices
Grey	Grey can symbolise sadness, transition, compromise, depression, boredom and monotony, but in recent years it has become a fashionable colour for high-tech products and modern design

Colours have a strong effect on perception. Research conducted in the 1960s showed that people believed that coffee from a dark brown container was stronger than coffee from a blue container, and that coffee from a yellow container was weak in both flavour and aroma (Dichter, 1964). In fact, the coffee in each container was identical. This research is not generalisable across cultures, and it also suffers from the major weakness that (not unnaturally) respondents will try to find a difference between the coffees if they are asked to do so. Having said that, the differences that Dichter found were remarkably consistent between the respondents, with 87% of them agreeing that the coffee from the yellow container was too weak. Fifty years later, a series of experiments conducted by Risso et al. (2015) investigated the association between the colour of a container and the liquid inside – in this case mineral water. In the first experiment respondents perceived the water as more carbonated when contained in a blue or red glass, rather than in a white glass. In another of the experiments, respondents preferred to choose a white glass for still water and blue or red for sparkling water. Had people been inventing differences simply to please the researcher, the differences would have been much less consistent. In packaging colour often has a profound effect on people's perceptions of the actual product: for example, Heinz use turquoise for their baked bean cans (even though most other Heinz cans have different colours) as turquoise makes the beans look brighter orange when the can is opened.

These perceptions may not, of course, translate well into all countries or cultures. In some cases, colour may be a fashion statement – Goths wear black, for example. The naming of colours is a crucial factor in the marketing of products such as paint and fabrics. Names such as midnight blue, dawn pink, apple green or corn yellow have a positive effect on consumer perception because there is an underlying assumption that the information must be useful in some way, which leads people to put a positive 'spin' on the colour name (Miller and Khan, 2003). Chung and Saini (2022) have demonstrated that perceived hierarchy (high vs. low) from bundled products depends on the darkness of their colour (darker vs. lighter). Experiments show that consumers infer a darker-coloured product as a higher hierarchical product, relative to the otherwise identical lighter-coloured product of the same hue and saturation. Each year has its 'fashionable' colours – for 2006 it seemed to be white and gold, but in 2018 Pantone reported that their top ten colours included Red Pear, Martini Olive and Crocus Petal, with Pantone 18-3838 Ultra Violet being their Colour of the Year (Pantone, 2018). Covid-19 has reshaped the way we see colours, trends and certainly the fashion industry. We're now more digitised and looking for harmonious escapes. Enter the 2023 Colour of the Year! At the time of going to press, it was reported that this will probably be 'Digital Lavender'... it signifies stability, serenity and digital escapism – things that apparently we are all looking for. Lavender is gender-inclusive and a neutral tone that may be readily accepted by all generations and celebrated by Gen Z. The **Rainbow Flag** (commonly the Gay Pride Flag and the LGBT Pride Flag) was designed to reflect the diversity of these communities by assigning a specific meaning to each of the colours (pink/sexuality, red/life, orange/healing, yellow/sunlight, green/nature, turquoise/magic, blue/serenity, violet/spirit). In recent years there have been variations and iterations of the Pride Flag, also known as the **Progress Pride Flags**, which have had a mixed reception. These iterations predominantly exist in order to be inclusive for the 2SLGBTQ+ communities.

Colour, and colour theory (Eliassen, 2021), also has a dramatic effect on search times for products (see Figure 7.13). Bright colours and contrasting colours make a product stand out, but people also use colour as a way of identifying brands rapidly (Jansson et al., 2004). Product colour is more important among young adults than older age groups and it is more important to females than males (Akcay et al., 2012). Companies often therefore adopt a corporate colour, or a colour denoting specific brands in the range. Coca-Cola uses red and white, Heinz uses red for its range of soups, and so forth. In the UK, firms have (in recent years) been able to include corporate colours in their trade mark registration, so that, for example, the shade of green used by BP on its forecourts is now protected by law. This does not mean that other people cannot use the same shade of green, but it would mean that other oil companies would not be able to use it as part of their forecourts if the result might be to confuse the public into thinking that they were actually buying from BP. So far there has been very little litigation based on infringements of corporate colours, although Orange and easyGroup did dispute the use of the colour orange for mobile telephone networks and the low-cost airline respectively. In 2012, Cadbury's won a legal case stopping other chocolate firms from using their purple colour and effectively tried to trademark the purple colour (Pantone 2865c) of its Dairy Milk bars. In 2013, Nestlé won an appeal overruling the court decision.

Rainbow Flag

A flag which is a symbol of lesbian, gay, bisexual, and transgender (LGBT) pride and LGBT social movements

Progress Pride Flag

A flag which is a symbol of two-spirit, lesbian, gay, bisexual, transgender, queer or questioning and additional sexual orientations and gender identity (2SLGBTQ+) social movements

Attention grabbing → Use of colour in packaging and advertising ← Fashion statement

Brand recognition → Use of colour in packaging and advertising ← Cues about product characteristics

FIGURE 7.13   Colour in marketing

PASSING OFF, BRANDALISM AND SUBVERTISING

Deliberate attempts to confuse consumers are called 'passing off', because one company is trying to *pass off* its products as being from the other company. This is illegal in most countries, since it is obviously against consumer interests as well as against the interests of the brand owner.

Connected concepts are 'brandalism' and 'subvertising', which have been defined as 'a movement with the stated aim of rebelling against the visual assault of media giants and advertising moguls who have a stranglehold over messages and meaning in our public spaces' (Smith-Anthony and Groom, 2015). In the article the authors describe subvertising as activists developing spoofs, parodies and other message-changing/obscuring alterations, which they then use through the brand's own marketing channels to make a statement against the brand itself (Smith-Anthony and Groom, 2015). It is not uncommon to see artwork that comments on consumerism, cultural values, debt, the environment, body image or specific political messages placed over existing billboards at bus stops and other public spaces. Lekakis (2017) terms this 'culture jamming'. This develops an interesting conflict between the two parties involved: on the one hand the free expression rights of the *subvertisers* and on the other the brand owners and their intellectual property rights.

SUMMARY

From a marketing viewpoint, the fact that perception is so nebulous and individual a thing is probably helpful in the long run. People's views of products and services rely heavily on perceived attributes, some of which have no objective reality; the difficulty for marketers lies in knowing what will be the general perception of the members of the market segments with whom they are attempting to do business.

Perception is, most definitely, an individual thing. The way one person selects and interprets information will be very different from the way someone else selects and interprets the same basic cues. This chapter has dealt with the processes that lead up to the formation of a view of the world: the selection, processing and interpretation of information and the subsequent keying-in of new information to existing knowledge are what enable us to understand our surroundings and deal with problems.

KEY POINTS

- Perception is both synthetic and analytic.
- Stimuli combine synergistically to create the whole impression.
- Selectivity is a key issue in perception, and is a key problem for marketers.
- Past experience contributes to the way new stimuli are interpreted as well as to the overall impression.
- Changes in the stimulus will go undetected if the stimulus is a large one.
- Perception and reality are not intrinsically different.
- Most perception happens below the conscious level.
- Perceptual responses may be internal or overt.
- Subliminal advertising is unlikely to be effective.
- Colour speeds up search times, as well as attracting attention.

HOW TO IMPRESS YOUR EXAMINER

You may be asked to explain the process of developing a world-view. You should be very clear about the synthetic aspects of perception as well as the analytic aspects: perception is not about misunderstanding the world, it is about creating a useable working model of the world on which to base decisions. There is a very strong link between perception and learning, and this should also be understood. As always, real-life examples help to show that you understand the theory.

REVIEW QUESTIONS

1. What effect does selectivity have on an integrated marketing communications campaign?
2. How might colour perceptions be complicated in a global market?
3. Why is subjectivity a problem for marketers?
4. How do internal responses create problems for marketers?
5. What is the difference between the linear additive model and the linear averaging model?
6. Explain Weber's Law.
7. What is the difference between kinaesthetic processing and visual processing?
8. What is the Law of Primacy?
9. What is the role of expectancy in branding?
10. What are the arguments for the effectiveness of subliminal advertising? What are the arguments against?

CASE STUDY: USING CONSUMER INSIGHT TO UNDERSTAND CONSUMER PERCEPTIONS IN HIGHER EDUCATION

Perception (being the keystone of building knowledge) is, most certainly, individual, and therein lies the challenge for marketers. How can marketers better understand their existing and future customers and how can they better understand (and influence) the general perception of their target audiences?

If the main purpose of marketing communications is to ensure that a company's brands become part of the world-view of potential consumers, the question becomes how can organisations use consumer insights to better understand the customer and customer perceptions?

As consumers' usage of digital media and social media platforms continues to grow, organisations must continuously seek new ways to track, analyse and interpret consumer behaviour and consumers' individual perceptions, at scale. Given the

(Continued)

heightened interest within the business community, the higher education sector needs to fully prepare their students to understand and use data analytics. To this end, Kaye Nightingale (Assistant Professor, Regent's University London) has incorporated Brandwatch for Classrooms (which has been specifically designed for educators and researchers) into the MSc Digital Marketing & Analytics (MSc DMA) module 'Consumer Intelligence' to give students hands-on access to the Consumer Research platform from Brandwatch.

For the final term of the MSc DMA students are required to either write a dissertation or to undertake a real consultancy project related to some aspect of digital marketing analytics. The conversation below (with the Research Team of three students: Axl Dreesen, Sheymaa Ali Zakariya and Lea Trøan) relates to a university in the Netherlands.

KN: What was the aim of the project and how was it connected with consumer behaviour?

Research Team: The key aim of the research was to establish new ways of working and to help establish a better way to identify, reach and engage with prospective university students. The project aimed to shed light on the possible causes of the client university's problems and how to improve and control them. To achieve this objective, an investigative approach was used to find out additional information about the target market and how to reach and engage with prospective students and their parents.

KN: In what ways was social listening, analytics and consumer intelligence relevant?

Research Team: Often social listening, analytics and intelligence is mentioned collectively, however it is important to establish the difference. Social media analytics refers to the analysis of data while social media intelligence is the insight obtained from the analysis of social media data.

Digital consumer intelligence (DCI) allows organisations to get a perspective on how and why consumers behave in a specific way. There are now consumer intelligence platforms that allow organisations to tailor their relationships with consumers to meet their strategic needs. According to Giles Palmer (CEO of Brandwatch), DCI *'is a way of taking data around consumers, behaviours, thoughts and actions and making intelligent sense of it which Brandwatch does using modern techniques, AI basically, whilst being data safe and secure and making sure that we don't step over privacy boundaries'*. DCI can be loosely defined as the accumulation of data, by gaining insight into the psychology behind the desires, needs and wants of a consumer to purchase items they might not necessarily know they want. This in turn allows companies to tap into the consumers' thoughts and understand their buying behaviour, to gain visibility on market trends in real time.

KN: How was using Brandwatch valuable as part of your data analysis?

Research Team: Brandwatch (Consumer Research) allowed us to look further into the organisation's brand and the community that developed around it. Brandwatch yields interesting insights about target customers' emotions, location, time of activity, platform and much more. The platform allows conclusions and insights to be narrowed down to the original sources (e.g. a tweet or Reddit thread). It can be used to see positive trends or threats before they are published by the media. Therefore, Brandwatch allows an organisation to take back control over the narrative about their brand. To summarise, it helps to identify, target, reach and engage people in and surrounding the community.

KN: What are some of the key benefits (for your client) of Brandwatch for HE administrators?

Research Team: Brandwatch (for HE administrators) has been specifically tailored to make data analysis as straight-forward as possible for those in the HE sector. Indeed, Emily Markham (Higher Education Specialist with Brandwatch) confirmed that *'Brandwatch does all the work, thus, administrators who are not familiar with query writing can easily find digested information, diagrams and graphs that are easy to extract from the platform. It is possible for institutions to tell Brandwatch about up to ten competitors, whose conversations and data can be benchmarked against the conversations of the target institution. The data is segmented into over 450 different categories to find specific areas that are relevant to the institution. We have regular check-ins with all our institutions, people can reach out to me at any time to make sure that the data provided is the most relevant data'* (Emily Markham, Brandwatch).

KN: Are there longer-term goals that you think Brandwatch could help with?

Research Team: Additionally, it is envisaged that the client university can replicate our work in a longitudinal, iterative approach to yield more insights and lower their cost per acquisition by implanting changes gained from the aforementioned insights.

KN: Did using Brandwatch (and other tools) help you to better understand consumer behaviour and perceptions?

Research Team: Yes. Using tools such as Google Analytics and Hootsuite Impact (to track the return on investment made on social media) offers valuable insights into social accounts and would help the client university to show data in a compelling manner. Furthermore, if the client university were to link their social accounts to social listening tools / consumer insight tools such as Brandwatch they would better understand what sentiments and emotions their posts create.

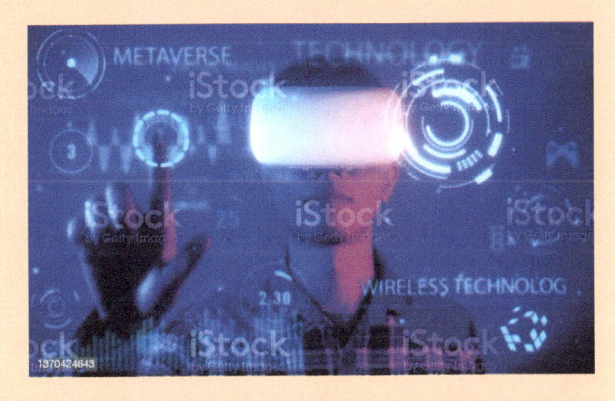

© iStock.com / hakule

CONCLUSION

Overall, this case study has demonstrated the importance of using Brandwatch for classrooms to enable students to gain hands-on experience and for universities to

(Continued)

use Brandwatch for HE administrators to gain essential market insights. In addition, the conversation above demonstrates how the research team have then used that knowledge to explore and interpret consumer insights on behalf of the client university. It is clear that using consumer intelligence will enable organisations to better understand consumer behaviour and consumer perceptions of brands and products as a vital part of their marketing and business activities.

CASE STUDY QUESTIONS

1. In what ways does using social media analytics help organisations to better understand their existing and future customers?
2. How does digital consumer intelligence help organisations ensure that an organisation's brand(s) become part of the world-view of potential consumers?
3. How can organisations use consumer insights to better understand customer perceptions?
4. How can marketers use social media to influence and nudge consumers in a specific direction?
5. What are the ethical considerations relating to consumer insight (into the psychology behind the desires, needs and wants of a consumer) leading to purchases they might not necessarily know they want?

FURTHER READING

www.brandwatch.com – Today's brands need to adapt quickly to make it to tomorrow. If you want to understand and engage with your customers at the speed of social, you should take a peek into the world of Brandwatch – the social suite built for our fast-moving world.

For a paper on brand perceptions, read L. Salciuviene, P. Ghauri, P. Streder and C. De Mattos (2010) Do brand names in a foreign language lead to different brand perceptions? *Journal of Marketing Management, 26* (11–12): 1037–56.

For more on political marketing and in particular the management of perceptions, see J. Klostermann, C. Hydock and R. Decker (2021) The effect of corporate political advocacy on brand perception: An event study analysis, *Journal of Product and Brand Management, 31* (5), 780–97.

The perception of the ideal woman in advertising has been a somewhat controversial topic in recent years. The following paper may help to pick out the issues: S. Feiereisen, A.J. Broderick and S.P. Douglas (2009) The effect and moderation of gender identity congruity: Utilising 'real women' advertising images, *Psychology & Marketing, 26* (9): 813–43.

If you're interested in the perception processes concerned with vision, a very clear and easy-to-read book on the subject is *Basic Vision: An Introduction to Visual Perception*, by Robert Snowden, Peter Thompson and Tom Trosciano (Oxford: Oxford University Press, 2012).

For a clear, well-written, basic overview of perception theory you might like *Perception: Theory, Development and Organisation*, by Paul Rookes and Jane Willson (London: Routledge, 2000). The book is actually intended for A-level Psychology students, but it covers the major theories well and is very readable.

MORE ONLINE

For additional materials that support this chapter and your learning, please visit: https://study.sagepub.com/sethna5e

REFERENCES

Aflalo, T., Kellis, S., Klaes, C., Lee, B., Shi, Y., Pejsa, K., Shanfield, K., Hayes-Jackson, S., Aisen, M., Heck, C., Liu, C. and Andersen, R.A. (2015) Decoding motor imagery from the posterior parietal cortex of a tetraplegic human. *Science*, *348* (6237): 906–10.

Akcay, O., Sable, P. and Dalgin, M.H. (2012) The importance of color in product choice among young Hispanic, Caucasian, and African-American Groups in the USA. *International Journal of Business and Social Science*, *3* (6): 1–6.

Anderson, N.H. (1965) Averaging versus adding as a stimulus combination rule in impression formation. *Journal of Experimental Psychology*, *70*: 394–400.

Anon. (1991) Self-help tapes are worthless, study says. *San Jose Mercury News*, 25 September.

Askegaard, S. and Madsen, T.K. (1995) European food cultures: An exploratory analysis of food related preferences and behaviour in European regions. MAPP Working Paper no. 26. Aarhus: Aarhus School of Business.

Baberini, M., Coleman, C.-L., Slovic, P. and Västfjäll, D. (2015) Examining the effects of photographic attributes on sympathy, emotions, and donation behavior. *Visual Communication Quarterly*, *22* (2): 118–28.

Bain & Company (2018) Global personal luxury goods market expected to grow by 6–8 percent to €276–281b in 2018, driven by strong rebound in China. Press Release. www.bain.com/about/media-center/press-releases/2018/bain-spring-luxury-report-2018/ (accessed 15 July 2018).

Bakamitsos, G. and Siomkos, G. (2004) Context effects in marketing practice: The case of mood. *Journal of Consumer Behaviour*, *3* (4): 304–14.

Baker, J., Levy, M. and Grewal, D. (1992) An experimental approach to making retail store environmental decisions. *Journal of Retailing*, *68*: 445–61.

Bar, M. and Neta, M. (2008) The proactive brain: Using rudimentary information to make predictive judgements. *Journal of Consumer Behaviour*, *7* (4/5): 319–30.

Bardhi, F. and Eckhardt, G.M. (2010) Market-mediated collaborative consumption in the context of car sharing. *Advances in Consumer Research*, *37*: 66–7.

Basu, R., Paul, J. and Singh, K. (2022) Visual merchandising and store atmospherics: An integrated review and future research directions. *Journal of Business Research*, *151*: 397–408.

Batra, R. and Stayman, D.M. (1990) The role of mood in advertising effectiveness. *Journal of Consumer Research*, *17* (September): 203–14.

Beatty, S.E. and Hawkins, D. (1989) Subliminal stimulation: Some new data and interpretation. *Journal of Advertising*, *18* (3): 4–8.

Bellizzi, J.A., Crowley, A.E. and Hasty, R.W. (1983) The effects of colour in store design. *Journal of Retailing*, *59*: 21–45.

Berčík, J., Gálová, J., Vietoris, V. and Paluchová, J. (2021) The application of consumer neuroscience in evaluating the effect of aroma marketing on consumer preferences in the food market. *Journal of International Food & Agribusiness Marketing*, 1–22. https://doi.org/10.1080/08974438.2021.1989102

Biswal, D., Singh, M. and Bahinipati, C.S. (2022) Covid-19 in India: Reflections from behavioral economics. *Journal of Developing Areas*, *56* (3): 383–91.

Block, J. and Block, J.H. (1981) Studying situational dimensions: A grand perspective and some limited empiricism. In D. Magnusson (ed.), *Toward a Psychology of Situations: An International Perspective*. Hillsdale, NJ: Lawrence Erlbaum. pp. 85–102.

Bloomberg (2022) China's Gen Z has the power to make or break Western brands. www.bloomberg.com/news/features/2022-05-24/china-s-gen-z-has-the-power-to-make-or-break-western-brands (accessed 29 October 2022).

Brunso, K., Grunert, K.G. and Bredahl, L. (1996) An analysis of national and cross-national consumer segments using the food-related lifestyle instrument in Denmark, France, Germany and Great Britain. MAPP Working Paper no. 35. Aarhus: Aarhus School of Business.

Bubb, R. and Pildes, R.H. (2014) How behavioural economics trims its sails and why. *Harvard Law Review*, *127*: 1593–678.

Bugelski, B.R. and Alampay, D.A. (1961) The role of frequency in developing perceptual sets. *Canadian Journal of Psychology*, *15*: 205–11.

Callison, C., Gibson, R. and Zillmann, D. (2015) Effects of differences in numeric ability on the perception of adversity risk to others and self. *Journal of Media Psychology*, *25* (2): 95–104.

Chandran, S. and Menon, G. (2003) When am I at risk? Now, or now? The effects of temporal framing on perceptions of health risk. *Advances in Consumer Research*, *30*: 106–8.

Chang, T.-S. (2021) Social distancing in retail: Influence of perceived retail crowding and self-efficacy on employees' perceived risks. *Journal of Retailing and Consumer Services*, *62*: 102613.

Chatterjee, P. (2001) Online reviews: Do consumers use them? In M.C. Gilly and J. Meyers-Levy (eds), *NA – Advances in Consumer Research*, Vol. 28. Valdosta, GA: Association for Consumer Research. pp. 129–33.

Chen, H., Chan-Olmsted, S., Kim, J. and Sanabria, I.M. (2021) Consumers' perception on artificial intelligence applications in marketing communication. *Qualitative Market Research: An International Journal*, *25* (1): 125–42.

Chung, M. and Saini, R. (2022) Color darkness and hierarchy perceptions: How consumers associate darker colors with higher hierarchy. *Psychology & Marketing*, *39* (4): 820–37.

Conley, S. (2012) *Against Autonomy: Justifying Coercive Paternalism*. New York: Cambridge University Press.

Conversation, The (2022) Smart devices can now read your mood and mind. https://theconversation.com/smart-devices-can-now-read-your-mood-and-mind-leading-to-a-new-set-of-concerns-about-technology-and-consent-174946 (accessed 18 May 2022).

Cuperfain, R. and Clarke, T.K. (1985) A new perspective of subliminal perception. *Journal of Advertising*, *14* (1): 36–41.

Cushing, C. and Bodner, G.E. (2022) Reading aloud improves proofreading (but using Sans Forgetica font does not). *Journal of Applied Research in Memory and Cognition*. https://doi.org/10.1037/mac0000011

d'Astous, A. and Kamau, E. (2010) Consumer product evaluation based on tactile sensory information. *Journal of Consumer Behaviour*, *9* (3): 206–13.

Dantec, M., Allain, H., Yvert, N., Sigrist, J., Bensafi, M. and Lafraire, J. (2022) Olfactory attributes and colors associated with naturalness. *Food Quality and Preference*, *98*: 104495.

Demattè, M.L., Pojer, N., Endrizzi, I., Corollaro, M.L., Betta, E., Aprea, E., Charles, M., Biasioli, F., Zampini, M. and Gasperi, F. (2014) Effects of the sound of the bite on apple perceived crispness and hardness. *Food Quality and Preference*, *38*: 58–64.

Dichter, E. (1964) *Handbook of Consumer Motivations: The Psychology of the World of Objects*. New York: McGraw-Hill.

Einfeld, C. and Blomkamp, E. (2022) Nudge and co-design: Complementary or contradictory approaches to policy innovation? *Policy Studies*, *43* (5): 901–19.

Eliassen, M.M. (2021) Color theory. Online: *Salem Press Encyclopedia*. Great Neck Publishing: Research Starters.

Eroglu, S. and Harrell, G.D. (1986) Retail crowding: Theoretical and strategic implications. *Journal of Retailing*, *62*: 346–63.

Gable, M., Wilkens, H.T., Harris, L. and Feinberg, R. (1987) An evaluation of subliminally embedded sexual stimuli in graphics. *Journal of Advertising*, *16* (1): 26–31.

Gane, N. (2021) Nudge economics as libertarian paternalism. *Theory, Culture & Society*, *38* (6): 119–42.

Goldstein, A., Sklar, A.Y. and Siegelman, N. (2022) Accurately measuring nonconscious processing using a generative Bayesian framework. *Psychology of Consciousness: Theory, Research, and Practice*. https://doi.org/10.1037/cns0000316

Grant, S.J. and Tybout, A.M. (2003) The effects of temporal framing on new product evaluation. *Advances in Consumer Research*, *30*: 1.

Greifeneder, R., Bless, H. and Kuschmann, T. (2007) Extending the brand image on new products: The facilitative effect of happy mood states. *Journal of Consumer Behaviour*, *6* (January–February): 19–31.

Halpern, D. (2015) *Inside the Nudge Unit: How Small Changes Can Make a Big Difference*. London: WH Allen.

Han, S. and Lerner, J. (2008) When the status quo turns sour: Robust effects of incidental disgust in economic transactions. *Advances in Consumer Research*, *35*: 153.

Hawkins, D. (1970) The effects of subliminal stimulation on drive level and brand preference. *Journal of Market Research*, 7 (August): 322–6.

Henry, W.A. (1980) The effect of information processing ability on processing accuracy. *Journal of Consumer Research*, 7 (June): 42–8.

Holbrook, M.P. and Moore, W.I. (1981) Feature interactions in consumer judgement of verbal versus pictorial presentations. *Journal of Consumer Research*, 8 (June): 103–13.

Hu, Y., Zhao, K. and Lian, H. (2015) Bayesian quantile regression for partially linear additive models. *Statistics and Computing*, *25* (3): 651–68.

Iwasaki, Y. and Brinkman, S.F. (2015) Application of a generalized linear mixed model to analyze mixture toxicity: Survival of brown trout affected by copper and zinc. *Environmental Toxicology and Chemistry*, *34* (4): 816–20.

Jani, D. and Han, H. (2015) Influence of environmental stimuli on hotel customer emotional loyalty response: Testing the moderating effect of the big five personality factors. *International Journal of Hospitality Management*, *44*: 48–57.

Jansson, C., Marlow, N. and Bristow, M. (2004) The influence of colour on visual search times in cluttered environments. *Journal of Marketing Communications*, *10* (September): 183–93.

Kapferer, J.-N. and Valette-Florence, P. (2022) The myth of the universal Millennial: Comparing Millennials' perceptions of luxury across six countries. *International Marketing Review*, *39* (2): 149–65.

Kellaris, J.J. and Kent, R.J. (1992) The influence of music on consumers' temporal perceptions: Does time fly when you're having fun? *Journal of Consumer Psychology*, *1*: 365–76.

Kelly, J.S. (1979) Subliminal imbeds in printing advertising: A challenge to advertising ethics. *Journal of Advertising*, 8 (Summer): 43–6.

Kenyon, G.N. and Sen, K.C. (2015) The perception process. In G.N. Kenyon and K.C. Sen (eds), *The Perception of Quality*. London: Springer. pp. 41–50.

Key, W.B. (1973) *Subliminal Seduction*. Englewood Cliffs, NJ: Signet.

Key, W.B. (1976) *Media Sexploitation*. Englewood Cliffs, NJ: Prentice-Hall.

Key, W.B. (1980) *The Clam-Plate Orgy and Other Subliminals the Media Use to Manipulate Your Behaviour*. Englewood Cliffs, NJ: Prentice-Hall.

Key, W.B. (1989) *The Age of Manipulation: The Con in Confidence, the Sin in Sincere*. New York: Henry Holt & Co.

Konuk, F.A. (2018) Antecedents of pregnant women's purchase intentions and willingness to pay a premium for organic food. *British Food Journal*, *120* (7): 1561–73.

Kotler, P. (1973) Atmospherics as a marketing tool. *Journal of Retailing*, *49* (Winter): 48–64.

LeBoeuf, R.A. (2006) Discount rates for time versus dates: The sensitivity of discounting to time-interval description. *Advances in Consumer Research, 33*: 138–9.

Lee, L. and Thomas, M. (2010) Music and consummatory focus: How background music changes preferences. Working paper. www.johnson.cornell.edu/Faculty-And-Research/Profile/id/mkt27 (accessed 25 July 2015).

Lee, Y. and Kim, H.Y. (2019) Consumer need for mobile app atmospherics and its relationships to shopper responses. *Journal of Retailing and Consumer Services, 51*: 437–42.

Lekakis, E.J. (2017) Culture jamming and Brandalism for the environment: The logic of appropriation. *Popular Communication, 15* (4): 311–27.

Li, C. (2010) Primacy effect or recency effect? A long-term memory test of Super Bowl commercials. *Journal of Consumer Behaviour, 9* (1): 32–44.

Lien, C.H., Wu, J.J., Hsu, M.K. and Wang, S.W. (2018) Positive moods and word-of-mouth in the banking industry: A moderated mediation model of perceived value and relational benefits. *International Journal of Bank Marketing, 36* (4): 764–83.

Lindstrom, M. (2005) Sensing and opportunity: Sensory appeal. *The Marketer, 10* (February): 6–11.

Liu, S.Q., Wu, L.L., Yu, X. and Huang, H. (2022) Marketing online food images via color saturation: A sensory imagery perspective. *Journal of Business Research, 151*: 366–78.

Liu-Thompkins, Y., Khoshghadam, L., Attar Shoushtari, A. and Zal, S. (2022) What drives retailer loyalty? A meta-analysis of the role of cognitive, affective, and social factors across five decades. *Journal of Retailing, 98* (1): 92–110.

Long, F., Bhuiyan, M.A., Aziz, N.A. and Rahman, M.K. (2022) Predicting young Chinese consumers' intentions to purchase Western brands: Structural model analysis. *PloS One, 17* (5): e0267563.

Madden, T.J., Hewett, K. and Roth, M.S. (2000) Managing images in different cultures: A cross-national study of colour meanings and preferences. *Journal of International Marketing, 8* (4): 90–107.

Manesi, Z., Van Lange, P.A., Van Doesum, N.J. and Pollet, T.V. (2019) What are the most powerful predictors of charitable giving to victims of typhoon Haiyan? Prosocial traits, socio-demographic variables, or eye cues? *Personality and Individual Difference, 46*: 217–25.

McCarty, J.A., Horn, M.I. and Szenasy, M.K. (2007) An exploratory study of consumer style: Country differences and international segments. *Journal of Consumer Behaviour, 6*: 48–59.

McGrew, S., Raskoff, S. and Berkman, B.E. (2022) When not to ask: A defense of choice-masking nudges in medical research. *Journal of Health Care Law & Policy, 25* (1): 1–48.

Mehrabian, A. and Russell, J.A. (1974) *An Approach to Environmental Psychology.* Cambridge, MA: MIT Press.

Miller, G.A. (1956) The magical number seven, plus or minus two: Some limits in our capacity for processing information. *Psychological Review, 63*: 81–97.

Miller, S.G. and Khan, B. (2003) Shades of meaning: The effects of novel colour names on consumer preferences. *Advances in Consumer Research*, *30*: 11–13.

Milotic, D. (2003) The impact of fragrance on consumer choice. *Journal of Consumer Behaviour*, *3* (2): 179–91.

Munoz, C.L., Wood, N.T. and Solomon, M.R. (2006) Real or blarney? A cross-cultural investigation of the perceived authenticity of Irish pubs. *Journal of Consumer Behaviour*, *5* (May–June): 222–34.

OECD (Organisation for Economic Co-operation and Development) (2017) Use of behavioural insights in consumer policy. OECD Science, Technology and Innovation Policy Papers no. 36, January 2017. Paris: OECD Publishing.

Packard, V. (1957) *The Hidden Persuaders*. New York: Pocket Books (reissued Ig Publishing, 2007).

Pantone (2018) New York Fashion Week Fall/Winter 2018. www.pantone.com/color-intelligence/color-of-the-year/color-of-the-year-2018 (accessed 30 September 2018).

Park, C.W., Iyer, E.S. and Smith, D.C. (1989) The effects of situational factors on in-store grocery shopping behaviour: The role of store environment and time available for shopping. *Journal of Consumer Research*, *15* (March): 422–33.

Parker, A.M., Fischhof, B. and deBruin, W.B. (2006) Who thinks they know more – but actually knows less? Adolescent confidence in their HIV/AIDS and general knowledge. *Advances in Consumer Research*, *33*: 12–13.

Payne, C. and Wansink, B. (2010) What is beautiful tastes good: Visual cues, taste and willingness to pay. *Advances in Consumer Research*, *37*: 49–50.

Petty, R.E. and Cacioppo, J.T. (1986) The elaboration likelihood model of persuasion. *Advances in Experimental Social Psychology*, *19*: 123–205.

Pfefferbaum, B., Jacobs, A.K., Griffin, N. and Houston, J.B. (2015) Children's disaster reactions: The influence of exposure and personal characteristics. *Current Psychiatry Reports*, *17* (7): 1–6.

Philips, H. and Bradshaw, R. (1990) How customers actually shop: Customer interaction with the point of sale. *Journal of the Market Research Society*, *35*: 51–62.

Pickcel (2022) 80 mind-boggling digital signage statistics, facts, trivia and infographics. www.pickcel.com/blog/digital-signage-statistics-trends-and-infographics/ (accessed 5 June 2022).

Rao, A.R. and Monroe, K.B. (1988) The moderating effect of price knowledge on cue utilization in product evaluations. *Journal of Consumer Research*, *15* (September): 253–64.

Reddy, S.M., Chowdhury, A., Charkrabarti, D. and Karmakar, S. (2015) Role of colour and form in product choice and variation of preferences across product categories: A review. In *ICoRD'15, Research into Design across Boundaries*, Vol. 2. New Delhi: Springer India. pp. 631–40.

Risso, P., Maggioni, E., Olivero, N. and Gallace, A. (2015) The association between the colour of a container and the liquid inside: An experimental study on consumers' perception, expectations and choices regarding mineral water. *Food Quality and Preference*, *44*: 17–25.

Rizzi, F., Gigliotti, M., Runfola, A. and Ferrucci, L. (2022) Don't miss the boat when consumers are in-store! Exploring the use of point-of-purchase displays to promote green and non-green products. *Journal of Retailing and Consumer Services*, *68*: 103034.

Sandberg, K., Del Pin, S.H., Overgaard, M. and Bibby, B.M. (2022) A window of subliminal perception. *Behavioural Brain Research*, *426*: 1–14.

Santini, F.O., Ladeira, W.J., Pinto, D.C., Herter, M.M., Mattila, A.S. and Perin, M.G. (2021) Retail crowding: Meta-analysis of contextual and cultural moderators. *Marketing Intelligence & Planning*, *40* (1): 57–71.

SBST (Social and Behavioral Sciences Team) (2016) *2016 Annual Report*. National Executive Office of the President, Science and Technology Council, Washington, DC. https://sbst.gov/download/2016%20SBST%20Annual%20Report.pdf (accessed 31 July 2018).

Scott, S.P., Sheinin, D. and Labrecque, L.I. (2022) Small sounds, big impact: Sonic logos and their effect on consumer attitudes, emotions, brands and advertising placement. *Journal of Product & Brand Management*, *31* (7): 1091–103.

Sheth, J.N. (2008) *Chindia Rising: How China and India will Benefit Your Business*. New Delhi: India Professional.

Small, D.A. and Verrochi, N.M. (2008) 'The Face of Need: Reactions to Victims' Emotion Expressions', in A. Y. Lee and D. Soman (eds), *NA - Advances in Consumer Research*, Vol 35. Duluth, MN : Association for Consumer Research. pp. 109–11.

Smith-Anthony, A. and Groom, J. (2015) Brandalism and subvertising: Hoisting brands with their own petard? *Journal of Intellectual Property Law & Practice*, *10* (1): 29–34.

Song, H. and Schwarz, N. (2009) Safe and easy or risky and burdensome? Fluency effects on risk perception and effort prediction. *Advances in Consumer Research*, *36*: 10–11.

Sousa Lourenco, J., Ciriolo, E., Rafael Rodrigues Vieira De Almeida, S. and Troussard, X. (2016) *Behavioural Insights Applied to Policy: European Report 2016*. No. EUR 27726 EN, Joint Research Centre (JRC), Brussels.

Spence, C. (2015) Eating with our ears: Assessing the importance of the sounds of consumption to our perception and enjoyment of multisensory flavour experiences. *Flavour*, *4* (1): 3.

Spencer, S.J., Strahan, E.J. and Zanna, M.P. (2003) Subliminal priming and choice. *Advances in Consumer Research*, *30*: 151–3.

Stuckey, B. (2012) *Taste What You're Missing: The Passionate Eater's Guide to Why Good Food Tastes Good*. London: Free Press.

Sunstein, C.R. (2013) *Simpler: The Future of Government*. New York: Simon & Schuster.

Sunstein, C.R. (2016) The council of psychological advisers. *Annual Review of Psychology*, *67*: 713–37.

Sunstein, C.R. and Reisch, L.A. (2017) *The Economics of Nudge*, 4 vols. London: Routledge.

Tai, S.H.C. and Fung, A.M.C. (1997) Application of an environmental psychology model to in-store buying behaviour. *International Review of Retail, Distribution and Consumer Research*, 7 (4): 311–37.

Tazehmahaleh, K.A., Godazgar, H., Smet, K.A.G. and Hanselaer, P. (2022) Multi-channel LED luminaires: An object-oriented approach for retail lighting based on the SOR framework. *Sustainability*, 14: 5994.

Thaler, R.H. (2022) The end of Nudge and the beginning of The Behavioral Code? *Regulation & Governance*, 16 (3): 974–8.

Thaler, R.H. and Sunstein, C.R. (2008) *Nudge: Improving Decisions about Health, Wealth, and Happiness*. New Haven, CT: Yale University Press.

Thomas, M., Morwitz, V. and Pyone, J.S. (2010) The precision effect in numbers: How processing fluency of numbers influences response confidence. *Advances in Consumer Research*, 37: 151–2.

Warr, P.B. and Knapper, C. (1968) *The Perception of People and Events*. London: Wiley.

Wu, Z. (2022) Crafting inconspicuous luxury brands through brand authenticity in China. *Frontiers in Psychology*, 13. https://doi.org/10.3389/fpsyg.2022.826890

Yang, S, Isa, S.M., Wu, H., Thurasamy, R., Fang, X., Fan, Y. and Liu, D. (2022) Effects of stores' environmental components on Chinese consumers' emotions and intentions to purchase luxury brands: Integrating partial least squares-structural equation modeling and fuzzy-set qualitative comparative analysis approaches. *Frontiers in Psychology*, 13: 840413.

Zaheer, N. and Rizwan, M. (2022) Engaging the customers through social mobile application experience. *IBA Business Review*, 17 (1): 69–84.

Zaheer, N., Arif, M., Shoukat, A. and Rizwan, M. (2022) Not without you: Role of shopping pal and store atmospherics in impulse buying. *Sustainable Business and Society in Emerging Economies*, 4 (1): 33–44.

Zampini, M. and Spence, C. (2004) The role of auditory cues in modulating the perceived crispness and staleness of potato chips. *Journal of Sensory Studies*, 19 (5): 347–63.

Zhao, G. and Pechmann, C. (2006) Regulatory focus, feature positive effect, and message framing. *Advances in Consumer Research*, 33: 100.

Zimman, L. (2018) Transgender voices: Insights on identity, embodiment, and the gender of the voice. *Language and Linguistics Compass*, 12 (8): e12284.

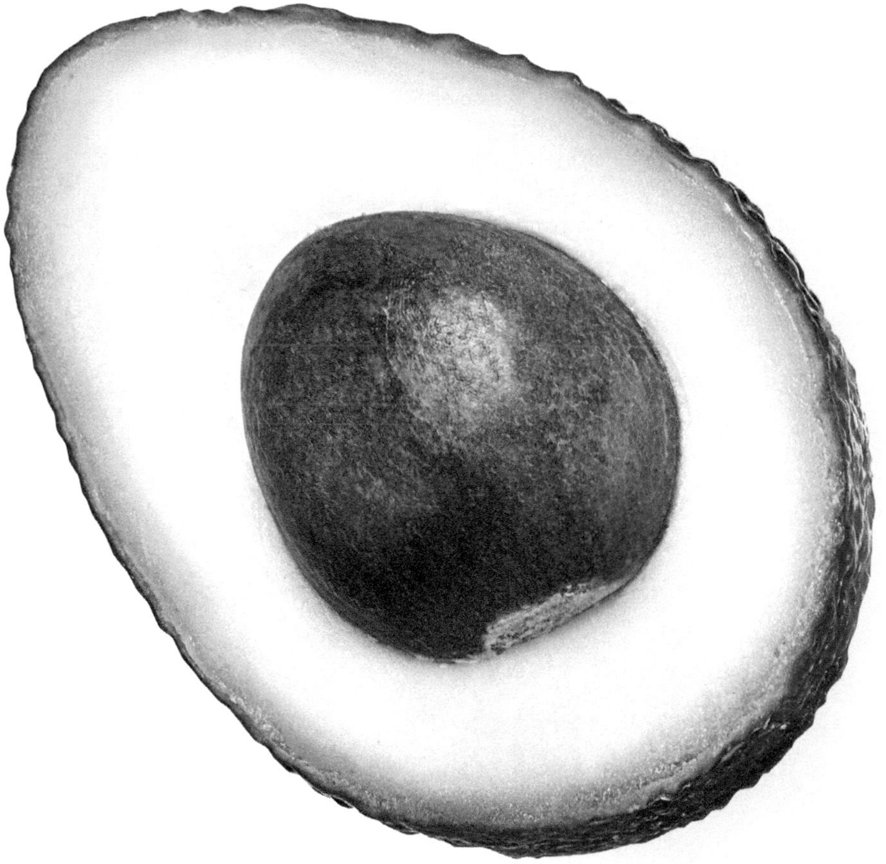

PART ONE CONSUMER BEHAVIOUR IN CONTEXT

Chapter 1 Understanding Consumer Behaviour
Chapter 2 Decisions, Behaviours and Interactions
Chapter 3 Consumption in B2C vs. B2B
Chapter 4 Consumer Technology and Innovation

PART TWO CONSUMERS AS INDIVIDUALS (THE PSYCHOLOGICAL ISSUES)

Chapter 5 Drive, Motivation and Hedonism
Chapter 6 The Self and Personality
Chapter 7 Perception
Chapter 8 Learning and Knowledge
Chapter 9 Attitude Formation and Change

PART THREE CONSUMERS AS SOCIAL ACTORS (THE SOCIOLOGICAL ISSUES)

Chapter 10 Reference Groups
Chapter 11 Age, Gender and Familial Roles
Chapter 12 Culture and Social Mobility
Chapter 13 Ethical Consumption
Chapter 14 Sustainable Consumption

CHAPTER 8
LEARNING AND KNOWLEDGE

LEARNING OBJECTIVES

After reading this chapter you should be able to:
- Explain what constitutes learning and what does not.
- Explain the role of classical conditioning.
- Describe how operant conditioning works.
- Describe how cognitive learning can be used by marketers.
- Understand the role of motivation in learning.
- Show how experiential learning is more effective than vicarious learning.
- Describe the various components of consumer knowledge and their importance to marketers.

CHAPTER CONTENTS

Introduction
Defining learning
Studying learning
The need for knowledge
Sources of consumer knowledge
Summary
Key points
How to impress your examiner
Review questions
Case study: WSUP and Global Handwashing Day
Further reading
References

More online: https://study.sagepub.com/sethna5e

INTRODUCTION

If you believe that learning is just about what happens in a classroom, think again. Most behaviour is learned as a result of external experiences (André et al., 2022; Zheng and Ding, 2022); most of what people know (and almost certainly many of the things they are most proud of knowing) they learned outside school (Steils et al., 2019). People learn things partly through a formalised structure of teaching (or of self-teaching, perhaps through online learning) and partly through an unconscious process of learning by experience (Hémar-Nicolas et al., 2022; Jiang et al., 2022). These experiential learnings can be enhanced with other sensory interventions such as music. Studies in psychology and consumer research demonstrate that music has positive short-term effects on spatial-temporal reasoning and sensorial response (Anderson and Krasnozhon, 2021).

Consumption habits, in particular, are learned. British people were not born with a liking for fish and chips, any more than a Parsee is born with a liking for dhansak or an Australian for Vegemite. Learning is highly relevant to marketing, since consumers are affected by the things they learn, and much consumer behaviour is actually based on the learning process (read more about how reference groups [Chapter 10] and familial roles [Chapter 11] both affect learning).

Persuading consumers to remember the information they see in advertisements is a major problem for marketers; for example, between 1978 and 1983 a series of humorous advertisements were produced for Cinzano vermouth. The adverts starred Joan Collins and Leonard Rossiter, and were widely screened throughout the UK, yet they were ineffective in increasing sales of the product (www.leonardrossiter.com/Cinzano.html). The reason for this was made clear when market research discovered that most consumers thought the ads were for Martini vermouth, Cinzano's main competitor. The underlying reason, however, is that humour in advertising appears to impair memory for products but enhance memory for the advertisement itself (Hansen et al., 2009), and therefore sometimes consumers negatively evaluate humour in advertising (Paramita et al., 2022).

This chapter is about the ways in which the brain orders and stores information.

DEFINING LEARNING

Learning is defined as 'the behavioural changes that occur over time relative to an external stimulus condition' (Onkvisit and Shaw, 1994). According to this definition, activities are changed or originated through a reaction to an encountered situation. We can therefore say that someone has learned something if, as a result, their behaviour changes in some way. The factors involved in learning are shown diagrammatically in Figure 8.1: existing behaviour is modified by events, information and stimuli, and new behaviour results in future.

The main conditions that arise from the definition are as follows:

1. There must be a change in behaviour (response tendencies).
2. This must result from an external stimulus.

Learning has not taken place under the following circumstances:

1. *Species response tendencies*. These are instincts, or reflexes; for example, the response of ducking out of the way when a stone is thrown at you does not rely on your having learned that stones are hard and can hurt your body.
2. *Maturation*. Behavioural changes often occur in adolescence due to, for example, hormonal changes, but again these are not a result of learning.
3. *Temporary states of the organism*. While behaviour can be, and often is, affected by tiredness, hunger, drunkenness, etc., these factors do not constitute part of a larger learning process (even though learning may result from those states – the drunk may learn to drink less in future).

4. *Damage to the brain.* Changes in behaviour due to surgery, disease or injury are obviously not a result of any learning taking place.

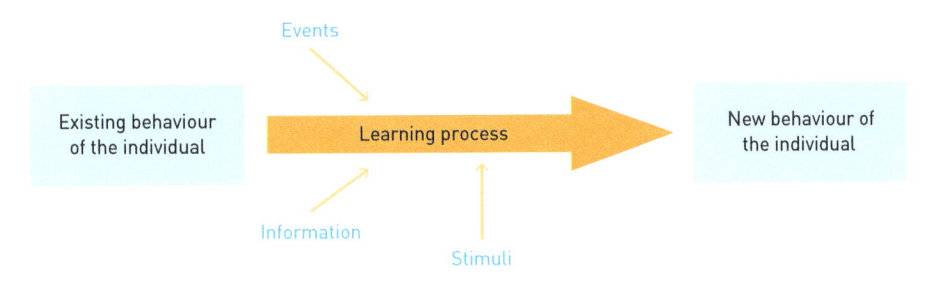

FIGURE 8.1 Learning

STUDYING LEARNING

There are two main schools of thought as regards the study of learning: first, the stimulus–response approach, which further subdivides into classical and operant conditioning, and second, cognitive theories where the conscious thought of the individual enters into the equation.

CLASSICAL LEARNING THEORY

The classical theory of learning was developed by, among others, the Russian researcher Pavlov (1927). Pavlov's famous experiments with dogs demonstrated that automatic responses (reflexes) could be learned. What Pavlov did was present a dog with an **unconditioned stimulus** (in this case, meat powder), knowing that this would lead to an **unconditioned response** (salivation). At the same time Pavlov would ring a bell (the conditioned stimulus). After a while the dog would associate the ringing of the bell with the meat, and would salivate whenever it heard the bell, without actually seeing any meat. This mechanism is shown in Figure 8.2.

Classical conditioning like this occurs with humans: many smokers associate having a cup of coffee with having a cigarette and find it difficult to give up smoking without also giving up coffee (even when **vaping**!). Likewise, the use of popular music in advertisements (Liu et al., 2022) is an example of classical conditioning. Repeated exposure to the advertisement leads the individual to associate the music with the product. This leads to two results: first, if the consumer likes the music, that extends to liking the product; and second, the consumer will tend to think of the product whenever she or he hears the music. Assuming the song used actually becomes (or is already) a hit, the company will obtain some free exposure whenever the song is played on the radio. Likewise, there is a relationship between background music and consumers' shopping behaviour based on consumers' mood-behaviour and alertness (Esfidani et al., 2022); Christmas music played in retail shops during December tends to create a mood in which consumers are more likely to buy presents and seasonal items.

Unconditioned stimulus
A stimulus that occurs without the intervention of an experimenter

Unconditioned response
A natural response to stimulus

Classical conditioning
The learning process characterised by repeating a stimulus at about the same time as a given behaviour occurs, with the aim of creating a permanent association between the stimulus and the behaviour

Vaping
The action or practice of inhaling and exhaling vapour containing nicotine and flavouring produced by a device designed for this purpose

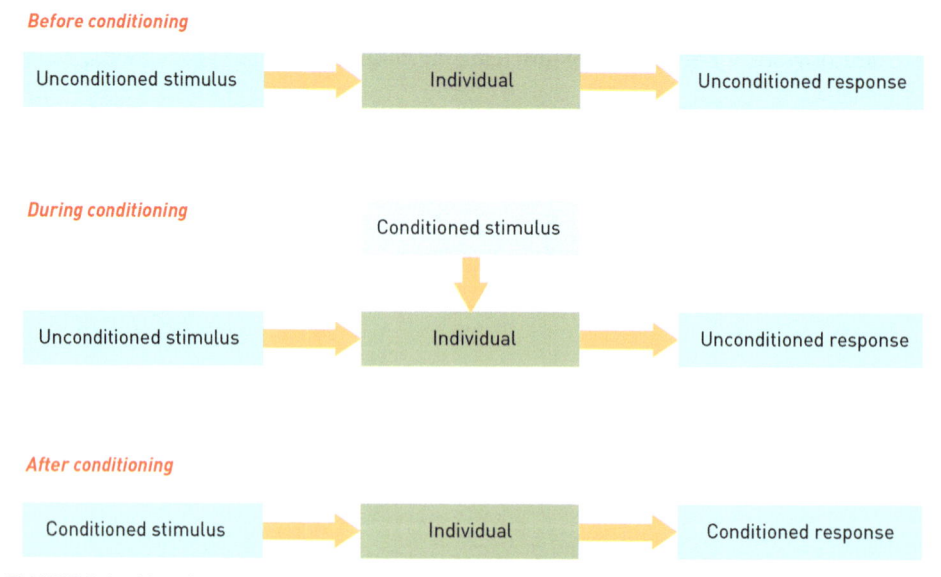

FIGURE 8.2 Classical conditioning

Before conditioning

Unconditioned stimulus → Individual → Unconditioned response

During conditioning

Conditioned stimulus ↓
Unconditioned stimulus → Individual → Unconditioned response

After conditioning

Conditioned stimulus → Individual → Conditioned response

Conditioned response

The behaviour that results from classical conditioning

For this to work it is usually necessary to repeat the stimulus a number of times in order for the **conditioned response** to become established. The number of times the process needs to be repeated will depend on the strength of the stimulus and the receptiveness (motivation) of the individual. Research has shown that, although conditioning has been reported for a single conditioning event (Gorn, 1982), perhaps as many as 30 pairings may be required before conditioning is maximised (Kroeber-Riel, 1984).

Before conditioning, the unconditioned stimulus feeding into the brain causes the unconditioned response. During the conditioning both the conditioned stimulus and the unconditioned stimulus are presented, so that after conditioning the conditioned stimulus alone will produce the response.

Behaviours influenced by classical conditioning are thought to be involuntary. If the doorbell rings, it is automatic for most people to look up, without consciously thinking about whether somebody is at the door. Most people are familiar with the start of recognition that sometimes occurs if a similar doorbell is rung during a TV drama, or perhaps upon hearing the classic WhatsApp ping tone. Classical conditioning also operates on the emotions: playing Christmas music will elicit memories of childhood Christmases, and advertisements evoking nostalgic feelings will generate warmth towards the product. For instance, department stores such as John Lewis and Marks and Spencer have, for a few years now, been competing every Christmas to see who can produce the most emotionally charged advert that will lead to prescribed feelings of desire, care and family, and ultimately to the act of consumption. Television is still a key player in the 'affect economy' and a successful exploiter of catchy emotions (Gorton, 2007). However, there is a darker, more poignant reaction to these types of adverts too – usually from those whose knowledge base of experience is very different and cannot relate to the cosy and comfortable and congenial family life that some of these adverts portray. We see this in political advertising which exists to recruit the support of voters by evoking feelings of being 'moved or touched' (Grüning and Schubert, 2022).

Another factor in the effectiveness of classical conditioning is the order in which the conditioned stimulus and the unconditioned stimulus are presented (see Figure 8.3). In **forward conditioning** the conditioned stimulus comes before the unconditioned stimulus. This would mean that the product would be shown before the music is played.

In **backward conditioning** the unconditioned stimulus comes before the conditioned stimulus. Here the music would be played before the product is shown. **Simultaneous conditioning** requires both to be presented at the same time.

Forward conditioning
A circumstance where the conditioned stimulus comes before the unconditioned stimulus

Backward conditioning
A situation in which the unconditioned stimulus is presented before the conditioned stimulus

Simultaneous conditioning
In classical conditioning, a state of affairs whereby the conditioned stimulus and the unconditioned stimulus are presented at the same time

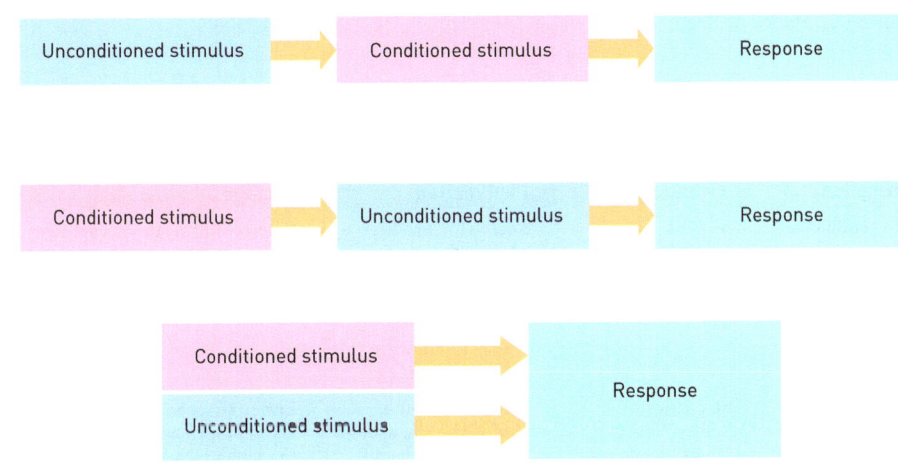

FIGURE 8.3 Ordering of stimuli

It appears that forward conditioning and simultaneous conditioning work best in advertising (McSweeney and Bierley, 1984). This means that it is usually better to present the product before playing the popular tune, or to play both together; the responses from this approach are usually stronger and longer-lasting. If classical conditioning is being used, clearly the broadcast media will be better-suited since it is easier to control the order in which the stimuli are presented; with print media this is not necessarily the case. For example – for those who still read physical newspapers – not everybody reads newspapers from front to back. Many people would start with the sports pages (at the back) and work forward, or perhaps read the headlines on the front pages then go straight to the TV pages before coming back to the local news. In an online version, we have the ability to completely focus on our particular area of interest without having to read through material in which we're uninterested. So technology and search functions have made it easier for avid sports fans to simply look for the 'sports' tab on news websites. Even if the conditioned stimulus and unconditioned stimulus are placed in the same ad on the same page, it is still possible that the reader's eye will be drawn to each stimulus in the wrong order; in other words, people do not necessarily read each page from top to bottom, either – and especially when scrolling using the flick of a finger is so easy!

Extinction
The process of forgetting a conditioned reflex

Generalisation
The tendency for a conditioned stimulus to lead to a wider than intended set of conditioned reflexes

For these reasons the print media are not as effective for classical conditioning as are the broadcast media such as the web, radio and TV, where the order of presentation of the stimuli is controllable.

Extinction occurs when the conditioned stimulus no longer evokes the conditioned response. This occurs in the ways shown in Table 8.1.

Generalisation happens when a stimulus that is close to the existing one evokes the same response. Pavlov found that a sound similar to the bell he used could also stimulate salivation, and it is often the case that a similar brand name can evoke a purchase response. A very common tactic in marketing is to produce similar packaging to that of one's competitor in order to take advantage of the generalisation effect. For an example of this, observe the remarkable similarity in packaging between Tesco Gold instant coffee (£2.99 for 200g) and Nescafé Gold Blend instant coffee (£7.49 for 200g).

TABLE 8.1 Extinction

Reason for extinction	Example	Explanation	Techniques to avoid extinction
The conditioned stimulus is encountered without the unconditioned stimulus	The product is shown without the background music	Seeing the product without the music tends to reduce the association of the music with the product; other stimuli will replace the music	Ensure that all the advertising uses the same music, or imagery associated with the music
The unconditioned stimulus is encountered without the conditioned stimulus	The background music is heard without the product being present	In this case, other stimuli may be evoked by the music; it will become associated with something other than the product	Either ensure that the music is not played anywhere other than when the product is being shown, or ensure that the product is available when the music is played. For example, if the product is a drink to be sold in nightclubs, ensure that the clubs have an ample supply of the drink being advertised

Discrimination
The process by which people distinguish between stimuli

Discrimination is the process by which we learn to distinguish between stimuli, and only respond to the appropriate one. Consumers quite quickly learn to distinguish between brands, even when the design of the packaging is similar. Advertisers will often encourage discrimination by pairing a positive unconditioned stimulus with their own product, but not with the competitor's product. For example, the HSBC slogan 'The world's local bank' conveys a clear image of a bank with worldwide experience coupled with familiarity with local customs and banking practice. Other banks are clearly excluded from this slogan. Even greater discrimination occurs when the competitor's product is paired with a negative unconditioned stimulus, for example by using phrases such as 'Unlike our competitors, we do not charge you a service fee'. NatWest Bank in the UK advertised the fact that customers wouldn't be put through to an offshore call centre (Campaign, 2004).

Classical conditioning is responsible for many repetitive advertising campaigns, and for many catchphrases that are now in common use. Some advertising fosters this, such as the 'Does exactly what it says on the tin' campaign for Ronseal Woodstain, which has resulted in the slogan entering the English language, at least amongst UK-based viewers.

> **BRAND EXPERIENCES: GEN Z ASKS NIKE 'D'YA GET ME?'**
>
> Oh yeah, they *get* them! During the 2019 Oscars, Nike released its 'Dream Crazier' advert narrated by Serena Williams. Within the first 24 hours of its release, the ad was trending on Twitter with millions of views and was quickly embraced by Gen Z celebrities like Chloe x Halle and Zendaya, which boosted its reach to more than 30 million views, 445,000 likes and 190,000 retweets. More than any other brand, Nike has captured the Gen Z zeitgeist and is regularly rated as the top clothing brand among teens.
>
> So what is it that Nike is doing so well? Well in short, Nike is bullish about its creative content. Gen Z has grown up in the golden age of premium content. They expect Netflix-like quality in every type of viewing experience, including ads. Intrusive banners or pre-roll/mid-roll ads won't be effective. Nike doesn't just know its audience. It actually listens to them. When Nike's Kaepernick ad went live, social data showed the brand received a surge of Instagram followers and Facebook and Twitter likes.

Classical conditioning assumes that the individual plays no active role in the learning process. Pavlov's dogs did not have to do anything in order to be 'conditioned', because the process was carried out on their involuntary reflex of salivation. Although classical conditioning does operate in human beings, people are not usually passive in the process; the individual person (like most higher animals) is able to take part in the process and cooperate with it or avoid it. This process of active role-playing is called **operant conditioning**.

Operant conditioning
The learning process in which the learner is rewarded for a correct action, and in which the learner plays an active role

OPERANT CONDITIONING

Here the learner will conduct trial-and-error behaviour to obtain a reward (or avoid a punishment). Burris F. Skinner (1953) developed the concept in order to explain higher-level learning than that identified by Pavlov. The difference between Pavlov's approach and the operant conditioning approach is that the learner has choice in the outcome; the modern view of classical conditioning is that it also involves a cognitive dimension. In other words, Skinner is describing a type of learning that requires the learner to do something rather than be a passive recipient of a stimulus. The modern view is that even Pavlov's dog would have thought 'Here comes dinner' when the bell rang.

The basis of operant conditioning is the concept of reinforcement. If someone buys a product and is pleased with the outcome of using it, then he or she is likely to buy the product again. This means that the activity has had a positive reinforcement, and the consumer has become 'conditioned' to buy the product next time. The greater the positive reinforcement, the greater the likelihood of repeat purchase.

CRITICAL REFLECTION

How active are people in learning? Do we really seek out knowledge and consider everything that comes our way? Or does most of it go in one ear and out the other? Or is technology perhaps negating the need to learn and thus questioning the relevance of teaching itself? (A calculator exists for those who can't do basic mathematics – audio books for those who can't read – and satnav for those who can't find their way around a map.) Game-based learning uses an actual game to teach knowledge and skills, learning in much the same way as children learn in nursery or kindergarten: through play (Neck et al., 2018). A learning game is usually a completely self-contained unit, meaning that there is a definitive start, game-play and ending. Educational video games are hypothesised to be good environments for promoting learning (Bainbridge et al., 2022). Learners know they are engaged in a game activity, and know that, in the end, there will be a winner. Of course, games can deliver different types of learning content in different settings. Game-based learning is, however, different from **gamification**, which does not typically occur in a classroom. It is a formal structure, and often it is delivered to a learner's computer, tablet or smartphone in 2- to 5-minute increments. Engagement with the content can take place when and wherever the learners happen to be. Interestingly, there is also an expectation that the content will be distributed over time, and thus the learning is not meant to take place in one setting.

How many times have you been able to answer (say) a quiz question without having any idea where that nugget of information came from? How often do you say, 'Oh, that's common knowledge'. So were you born knowing this stuff? Games such as Trivial Pursuit are based on this kind of mental fluff – useless facts that just happen to have lodged in your brain, not through repetition (classical conditioning) nor through operant conditioning, but just through some kind of alien implanting process.

As an example, there are now thousands of people around the world who are actively engaged in playing the Cashflow Board Game, a game developed by Robert Kiyosaki (author of *Rich Dad Poor Dad* (2011) – a book about investing for financial independence). They believe that by actively playing the game, in relatively safe and controlled conditions, they will undergo a process of learning (through both classical and operant conditioning) which they can then replicate in real life. This has become so popular that it is possible to find a group (through www.meetup.com) to play with in most cities around the world.

© iStock.com/cyano66

Gamification
The application of typical elements of game playing (e.g. point scoring, competition with others, rules of play) to other areas of activity, typically as an online marketing technique to encourage engagement with a product or service

If the reward works, the consumer will try to think of a way to make it even better: if a little will help, a lot will cure. This can lead to over-indulgence in food or alcohol, or indeed almost any other pleasurable activity. Typically this will happen if the consumer's need cannot be totally met by the product, but will be helped; a person with a serious psychological problem may well find that alcohol helps to numb the daily thoughts, but isn't a cure. An increasing intake of alcohol will never result in a complete meeting of the person's psychological needs because eventually sobriety will begin to set in again.

An example of operant conditioning is the growth of loyalty programmes from retailers, for example the Tesco Club Card. Customers who remain loyal to Tesco Retail by collecting points are sent extra discounts and offers and redeeming points with Tesco's partners, and also their purchasing behaviour can be traced through the electronic point-of-sale systems so that offers can be targeted at those Tesco customers who will really be interested in them.

Airline loyalty schemes saw huge growth in the early part of the century, although this growth has levelled off more recently. Most of these are aimed at reinforcing the frequent flyers, whose loyalty is desirable since they are likely to be the most profitable customers. The airlines offer limited free flights to their most regular customers, and for many business travellers these free flights (usually taken later for personal travel) offer an attractive reason for choosing the same airline every time. Loyalty cards are especially attractive to business customers because their flights are often paid for by their firms, so they are less likely to have to shop around for cheap deals.

BRAND EXPERIENCES: THE STARBUCKS CARD

The Starbucks Card is slightly different from other loyalty cards, in the sense that you need to load it up with cash before you use it. Once you've got cash on your card, you use it to pay for your purchases and you'll earn 'Stars' for every beverage you buy. These Stars stack up and, once you've collected enough, you'll earn a reward – including free coffee. And, thanks to a recent change, Stars are now based on how much you spend rather than the number of transactions you make. Now, you'll earn three Stars for every £1 you spend. What you get for your Stars depends on what 'level' you're on. Once you make your first transaction with your Starbucks Card, you'll become a Green Level member, which means you get a free drink for every 150 stars. Once you earn 450 stars within a 12-month period, you've reached Gold Level. You'll receive the same as Green Level members, but each time you purchase a drink in-store, you'll be able to add some extras to it for free. Free extras include selected syrups, extra shots of espresso, whipped cream and non-dairy alternatives (or a combination of them all). As a Gold member, you can also enjoy a free birthday drink!

Once you become a 'Gold Level' member, you have to keep earning at least 450 stars a year to maintain access to your extra benefits. There's also the added pressure to shop at Starbucks, as you have to top up the card with money in advance. This means you're committing to spending a certain amount there. Plus, if your account's inactive for two years, your stars will expire. Essentially, this card is probably only worth getting if you tend to use Starbucks a lot anyway.

The problem with this type of loyalty scheme is that it is perfectly feasible for people to carry loyalty cards for several stores (or join the Frequent Flyer clubs of several airlines – AAdvantage, Executive Club, Iberia Plus, Miles and More, Flying Blue, etc.) and thus reap the rewards without actually having to remain loyal to any supplier. In effect, people have been taught to play the system, gaining the benefits without actually having to contribute anything.

CONSUMER BEHAVIOUR IN ACTION: LEARNING THROUGH PLAY IN FOREST SCHOOLS

Young children learn and develop skills quickly. They are always seemingly playing and experimenting; but unbeknown to them, they are learning. They are also beginning to get a sense of their own identity and how they may be different from others, such as noticing gender differences. Some children benefit from being at a nursery or playgroup at this age. Here, organised activities help develop their learning in an informal setting. The philosophy of Forest School is to encourage and inspire individuals of any age through positive outdoor experiences. By participating in engaging, motivating and achievable tasks and activities in a woodland environment each individual has an opportunity to develop intrinsic motivation as well as sound emotional and social skills. These skills, through self-awareness, can be developed to reach personal potential. Forest School has demonstrated success with children of all ages who visit the same local woodlands on a regular basis and, through play, have the opportunity to learn about the natural environment, how to handle risks, and most importantly to use their own initiative to solve problems and cooperate with others. Forest School programmes run throughout the year for about 36 weeks, going to the woods in all weathers (except for high winds). Children use full-sized tools, play, learn boundaries of behaviour – both physical and social – establish and grow in confidence and self-esteem, and become self-motivated.

Children, and increasingly adults too, need time to thoroughly explore their thoughts, feelings and relationships. This time and reflective practice develop understanding of the world, the environment and everything within it through the use of emotions, imagination and senses. Over the past decade, one of the major training providers for this particular type of learning (Forest Schools Education, 2018) has successfully taken the Forest School approach to using natural spaces and has applied it to not only forest, woodland and park land, but the shoreline with Beach Schools and the Australian and New Zealand landscape

© iStock.com/Morsa Images

> with Bush Schools. Forest Schools Education have developed foundational courses to meet the needs of some of those who are passionate about the value of children's education being able to quickly access outdoor learning, with courses such as Outdoors And Up For It! and the Certificate of Outdoor Learning. The learning and knowledge team is made up of people for whom nature has been a central element of their life, and who have been countryside rangers, outdoor centre managers, expedition guides, freelance instructors and have experience in a depth and breadth of experience in working with all age groups in the outdoors, for personal, social and emotional development.

Figure 8.4 charts three forms of operant conditioning. In the first example, positive reinforcement, the individual receives a stimulus and acts upon it. This action works, and the individual gets a good result; this leads to the behaviour being repeated if the same antecedent stimulus is presented at a later date. For example, if you are in a long queue at a retailer such as IKEA you might notice that the customer service counter is empty or even the self-service counter, and go there to make your purchases instead of the usual tills. This enables you to leave the store more quickly, and so if you find yourself in a long queue in IKEA again at some time, you are likely to try the same tactic once more.

The second example in the diagram shows a negative stimulus: this time the operant behaviour relieves the problem, and again the individual has learned how to avoid bad consequences when faced with a difficulty.

The third example shows how punishment fits into the learning process. If the operant behaviour leads to a bad result, for example the customer service counter won't serve you and you lose your original place in the queue, you will not try that tactic again. The problem with punishment as a motivator, in this example, is that it may lead to the individual not shopping at IKEA again. (Revisit Chapter 5 for the discussion on pain avoidance.)

Operant conditioning does not necessarily require a product purchase; marketers will frequently give away free samples in the hope that a positive experience from using the product will encourage consumers to purchase in future (for example, wee drams of malt whisky given out at the airport, or new flavours of coffee outside Starbucks). Likewise, car dealers always offer a test drive; some go even further, and allow the customers and their families to borrow a car for the weekend in order to get a very clear reinforcement of the car's merits (for instance, the Audi Philippines strapline encouraging a test drive says: 'The Audi Driving Weekend: Take Control and Take Off' – www.autodeal.com.ph/articles/car-news-philippines/audi-ph-hold-test-drive-event-in-bgc-weekend).

Operant conditioning is helpful in explaining how people become conditioned, or form habits of purchase; however, it still does not explain how learning operates when people become active in seeking out information. To understand this aspect of learning, it is necessary to look at the cognitive learning process.

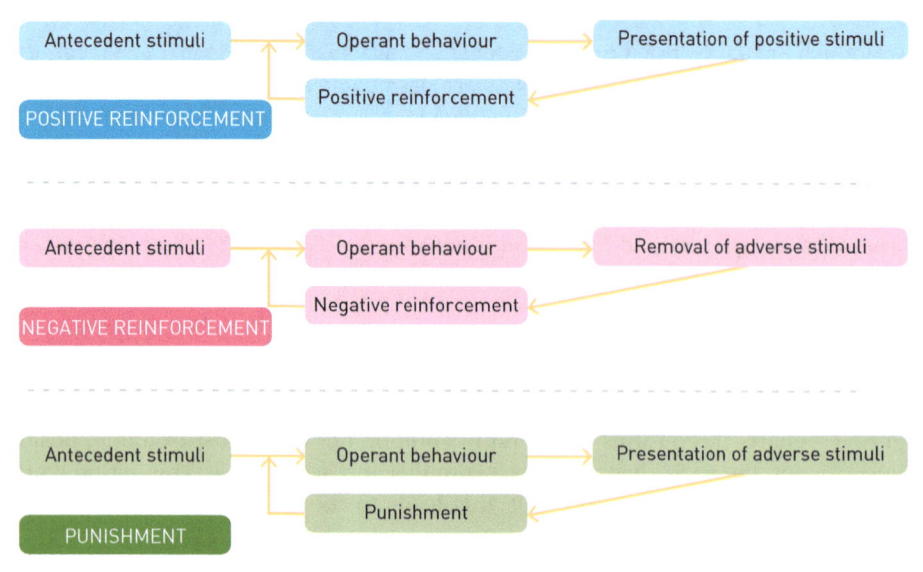

FIGURE 8.4 Operant conditioning

Source: Adapted from Widrick (1986). Reprinted with permission from the American Marketing Association.

COGNITIVE LEARNING

Not all learning is an automatic response to a stimulus. People analyse purchasing situations taking into account previous experiences, and make evaluative judgements. Learning is part of this, both in terms of informing the process as a result of earlier experiences, and also in terms of the consumer's approach to learning more about the product category or brand.

Cognitive learning
Acquiring and retaining new information through a conscious effort or thought

When considering **cognitive learning**, the emphasis is not on *what* is learned (as in stimulus–response theories) but on *how* it is learned. Classical learning and operant conditioning theories suppose that learning is automatic; cognitive learning theories assume that there is a conscious process going on. This is true in many cases of consumer behaviour.

The classical and operant theories assume that what goes on inside the consumer's head is a 'black box', in that we know that a given stimulus will prompt a particular response, but for most practical purposes we have no real way of knowing what is

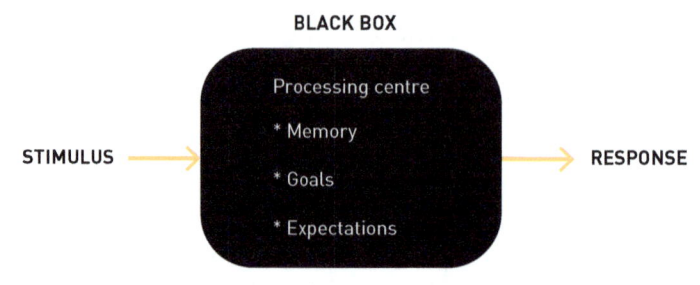

FIGURE 8.5 Cognitive learning

happening inside the black box. Within the cognitive learning paradigm, however, we are concerned with what happens inside the box, and we try to infer what is going on by analysing behaviour and responses from the individual. Figure 8.5 illustrates this.

The black box contains the cognitive processes; the stimulus is considered in the light of the individual's memory of what has happened in the past when presented with similar stimuli, his or her assessment of the desirable outcome and an assessment of the likely outcome of any action. Following this processing, the individual produces a response.

Cognitive learning expertise has five aspects, summarised in Figure 8.6.

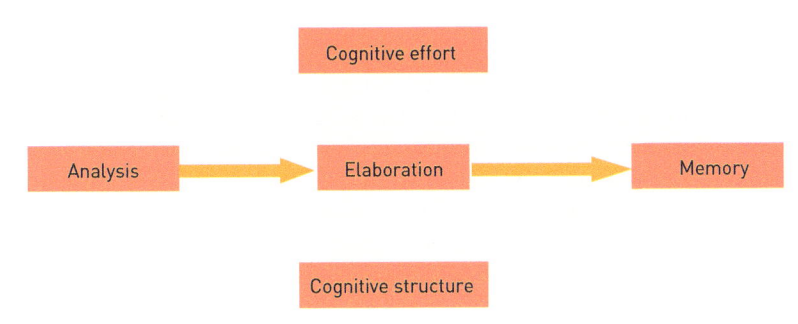

FIGURE 8.6 Factors in cognitive learning

Cognitive effort is the degree of effort the consumer is prepared to put into thinking about the product offering. This will depend on such aspects as the complexity of the product, the consumer's involvement with it and the motivation for learning. Making a complex decision can often lead to forgetting not only what the decision was, but in some cases forgetting that a decision has been made (Norton and Chance, 2008). Most of us are familiar with making a choice from a packed restaurant menu, then forgetting what it was we had ordered by the time the food arrives.

Cognitive structure is about the way the consumer thinks, and the way the information is fitted into the existing knowledge.

The *analysis* of information is first concerned with selecting the correct, relevant information from the environment, and second with interpreting the information correctly in order to obtain a clear action plan.

Elaboration is the structuring of the information within the brain, and adding to it from memory in order to form a coherent whole.

Memory is the mechanism by which learned information is stored. In fact, nothing is ever truly forgotten; information will eventually become irrecoverable by the conscious mind (forgotten), but the brain still retains the information and can be stimulated to recall it, either by hypnosis or by association of ideas.

Cognitive learning processes are important to marketers since they are helpful in predicting consumer responses to advertising. Stephen J. Hoch and Young-Won Ha

Cognitive effort
The amount of work needed to consider a course of action or understand a set of issues

Cognitive structure
The way the individual thinks, and the way new information is fitted into existing knowledge

Elaboration
The structuring of information within the brain, relating it to existing memory

(1986) say that consumers view advertisements as tentative hypotheses about product performance that can be tested through product experience, and this perspective has been added to by Sumpradit et al. (2015), who note that negative attitudes can often interfere with the processing of the message content. Early learning about a product will affect future learning; this is called the Law of Primacy (see Chapter 7). For this reason, first impressions count for a great deal.

According to Hoch and Ha (1986), advertising will tend to be ignored if there is unambiguous objective evidence to hand; if you can test the product for yourself, advertising has only a small effect. If the evidence is ambiguous or unobtainable at first hand (as is often the case), advertising might sway you, and in fact advertising appears to have dramatic effects on consumers' perceptions of quality. For example, it is possible for somebody to visit the Apple Store to play with a new iPhone before making a commitment to buy. Thus, advertising plays a small part in computer purchase, only serving to alert the consumer to what is available within the current technology. Conversely, somebody spending a similar amount on a package holiday or booking an Airbnb apartment has no chance to try out the holiday or the apartment before buying it, and is therefore more likely to be swayed by the advertising or other communications (brochures, salespeople, other peer-to-peer customer reviews, etc.). One of the main considerations for a consumer in that position is the reputation of the service provider (or the star-rating of the Airbnb accommodation owner), since the consumer is, after all, buying a promise.

Learning from experience is a four-stage process, as Table 8.2 shows. In most cases people prefer to learn by experience, especially for major product purchases; few people would buy a car without having a test drive first, and still fewer would buy one online unless they were people with previous direct experience of the car. It is for this reason that online retailers have a no-quibble money-back guarantee; if this were not the case, few people would be prepared to buy online rather than visit a high street shop where they can see and feel the goods. It's interesting to note here that when most people are buying a house – usually the single largest purchase that they will make in their life – there is no chance of 'living in the property' in order to learn from experience, and they will probably only make two or three visits prior to making an offer to purchase.

TABLE 8.2 Learning from experience

Stage	Explanation	Example	Marketing response
Hypothesising	Developing a rough estimate as to what's happening or what's available	Getting information from a friend, or reading some advertising material; trawling through blogs/websites	Have clearly written and informative blogs and websites, don't use too much jargon, especially if your product is a complex one, or can be 'test-driven'
Exposure	Having a look at the product, trying one out, getting direct experience of it	Visiting a retailer or outlet to try the product and ask questions about it	Ensure that the product is on display, and allow plenty of opportunity for hands-on testing

Stage	Explanation	Example	Marketing response
Encoding	Making sense of the information	Translating the jargon into something comprehensible, perhaps getting some clarification; understanding what the product is and does in terms that fit in with previous experience	Have salespeople who can explain things in lay terms, and who don't frighten off the customer by using too much technical language. Ensure that any chatbots you use are sophisticated enough to decipher the customer needs/requirements
Integration	Fitting the new information into the existing knowledge bank	Thinking about the new information gained about the product and discarding previous misconceptions	Ensure that customers feel able to come back for further explanations if they still have problems. Make sure that customers understand everything before leaving the outlet

There are also three moderating factors in the cognitive learning process:

1. *Familiarity* with the domain. This is the degree to which the consumer has pre-existing knowledge of the product category. For example, an IT enthusiast would go through a different, and probably shorter, learning curve for buying a new laptop than would a complete novice. Familiarity with the components of a brand name make it more memorable (Blackston and Lebar, 2015). People tend to choose more often the recognised option over the unrecognised one (Anglada-Tort et al., 2022).

2. *Motivation* to learn. If the purchase is an important one, or the possible effects of making a mistake would be serious, the consumer is likely to be highly motivated to obtain as much information as possible. In the customer–brand relationship, people also appear to remember advertising better if they either love or hate the advert (Jabeen et al., 2022); neutral advertising is quickly forgotten (Küster and Eisend, 2016).

3. *Ambiguity* of the information environment. If the information is hard to get, contradictory or incomprehensible, this will hinder the learning process. Sometimes consumers give up on the process if this is the case. Researchers at Carnegie Mellon University found that individuals tend to be averse to risk and ambiguity when uncertainty (or other circumstances) makes the information gap unpleasant to think about. Yet when an information gap happens to be pleasant, an individual may seek to take a gamble by providing exposure to it (Golman et al., 2015).

Table 8.3 illustrates these moderating factors in terms of classifying readiness to learn from experience.

If someone is highly motivated to learn (for example, a Syrian who has committed to studying for an MBA degree in the UK might be highly motivated to learn English), the learning process is most susceptible to management. The individual would probably want to follow a formal course of study (evening classes or a distance learning course) and would welcome help in managing the learning process. If the individual

Flicking
Also called zapping. Using a remote control device to avoid advertisements by switching to another channel

already speaks a little English, but has decided to study in Aberystwyth in Wales, the motivation to learn Welsh might also be strong, but familiarity with the domain (learning a foreign language) might cause the individual to form beliefs that are unrealistic (for example, believing that the process will be easier than it actually is).

People whose motivation to learn is low are obviously less likely to want their learning managed, or indeed to manage it themselves. If the person is unfamiliar with the domain, he or she is unlikely to be interested in learning at all; if, on the other hand, the domain is all too familiar, complacency sets in and the person is likely to say 'I already know all that stuff' and thus will have no interest in managing learning. Motivation has an effect on the tendency to flick TV advertisements by *channel hopping* – if the advertisement is unpleasant or uninformative, the advert is more likely to be zapped, but at higher levels informativeness and pleasantness are incompatible because of a reduced motivation and ability to process information (Elpers et al., 2002). Of course, when online, loading each app up takes time, so channel hopping is slower than with a 'real' TV.

If people are unable to learn much by experience, the situation becomes ambiguous; if learning by experience is the main way of learning, the situation is unambiguous but learning is difficult to manage. From the viewpoint of marketers, encouraging people to learn about products is easiest when the individuals are motivated to learn, and where the situation is ambiguous and therefore needs careful explanation.

Cognitive lock-in occurs when there is a high cognitive cost either in obtaining information or in switching providers. This happens on the internet: people tend to stick with the sites they are familiar with rather than going to the trouble of learning how to navigate a new site, especially if the initial setting up or the ongoing usage is difficult (Cheung et al., 2015; Murray and Haubl, 2002; Zauberman, 2002). It has been found that habit exhibits a significant moderating effect on the relationship between alternative attractiveness and continuous intention (Cheung et al., 2015).

TABLE 8.3 Managing the learning process

How motivated are people to learn?	What do consumers already know?	How much can experience teach?	
		Little (high ambiguity)	A lot (low ambiguity)
Highly motivated to learn	Unfamiliar with the domain	Learning is most susceptible to management	Learning is spontaneous, rapid and difficult to manage
	Familiar with the domain	Formation of superstitious beliefs is possible. Existing beliefs inhibit suggestibility	
Weakly motivated to learn	Unfamiliar with the domain	Learning is slow to start and difficult to sustain, but is susceptible to management	Learning is difficult to initiate and, once started, is difficult to manage
	Familiar with the domain	Complacency inhibits initiation of learning, so experience is unresponsive to management	

Source: Hoch and Deighton (1989). Reprinted with permission from *Journal of Marketing*, published by the American Marketing Association.

> ### CONSUMER BEHAVIOUR IN ACTION: HABITUAL MASK WEARING
>
> Through the Covid-19 pandemic we were told that protective facial masks reduce the spread of Covid-19 infection and save lives. Yet a substantial number of people have been resistant to wearing them. Considerable effort has been invested in convincing people to put on a mask, if not for their own sake then for those more vulnerable. Social and cognitive psychologists know that use and liking go both ways: people use what they like, and they like what they use. Dudarev et al. (2022) asked whether positive attitudes towards facial masks were higher in those who had been wearing them longer. They asked participants in a diverse sample (N = 498 from five countries and more than 30 US states) to rate how attractive and emotionally arousing masks and other objects associated with Covid-19 were in comparison to neutral objects, as well as reporting on their mask-wearing habits. To confirm reliability of findings, the experiment was repeated in a subset of participants 8–10 weeks later. The findings showed that regular use of protective masks was linked to their positive appraisal, with a higher frequency and a longer history of wearing a mask predicting increased mask attractiveness. Practically, they imply that societal measures to encourage mask wearing may have contributed to positive emotional appraisals in those who put them on, whether due to personal choice or societal pressure.

Incidentally, people who respond most favourably to online advertising are those with a high motivation to learn, high social escapism and high internet ability due to its perceived informativeness (Zhou and Bao, 2002). Moreover, the social capital derived from participating in online social networks (Cruz, 2021) also contributes to having a positive impact in response to advertising (Pinho and Soares, 2015). Evidently a desire to learn affects the ways people learn as well as their capacity for learning.

Cognitive theories recognise that consumers influence the outcome in an active manner, so the learning process is not always easy for an outsider (i.e. a marketing person) to manage. This may be part of the reason why new products fail so frequently; weak motivation to learn about new products leads to difficulty for marketers in starting the learning process.

Cognitive learning can also be viewed as having five elements, as shown in Figure 8.7.

1. **Drive.** As seen in Chapter 5, drive is the stimulus that impels action. It is strong, internal and general. The impulse to learn can be driven by a fear of making an expensive mistake, or by a desire to maximise the benefits of the purchase.
2. **Cue.** This is some external trigger that encourages learning. It is weaker than a drive, is external and is specific. For example, a public service such as the Health and Safety Executive might exhort employers to send for a leaflet on safety in the workplace. Sometimes firms will use advertisement retrieval cues to trigger responses.
3. **Response.** This is the reaction the consumer makes to the interaction between a drive and a cue. With luck, this results in a sale; but humans learn, and will base future purchases on their concrete experience of the product rather than on the marketer's cues.

Cue
An external trigger that encourages learning

Response
The reaction the consumer has to the interaction between a drive and a cue

Reinforcement
The process of consolidating classical conditioning

Retention
The stability of learned material over time

4. **Reinforcement.** Purchase response should be rewarded with a positive experience of the product. The object of reinforcement is to get consumers to associate the product with certain benefits.

5. **Retention.** This is the stability of the learned material over time, or in other words how well it is remembered. For example, advertising jingles have very high retention. People can often recall jingles that have not been broadcast for 30 years or more (for example, people often remember the original Nokia ringtone or the theme tune to Sesame Street). This is particularly true for advertisements that were popular when the individual was a child. (The opposite of retention is extinction.) In the current climate, it is trendy TikTok videos which seem to be remembered by users, especially in areas such as the impacts of sudden destination popularity through social media (Wengel et al., 2022).

Cognitive learning usually involves some form of reasoning – people need to think about what they are seeing or hearing in order to remember the information. If the person has a low involvement with the product or brand, it will take a long time for the information to sink in, whereas if the individual has a high involvement with the product the information is processed and absorbed much more effectively, presumably because the person is thinking about the product much more (Krugman, 1965). Current examples of such high online and internet involvement have led to issues of internet addiction (Wiegman and van Schie, 1998). Recently, there has been some extremely interesting work investigating how adults and adolescents have learnt about and adopted coping strategies in response to cyber aggression and cyber victimisation (Fulantelli et al., 2022; Marganski and Melander, 2018; Mishna et al., 2018; Navarro et al., 2018; Wright, 2015).

Advertising clutter
Excessive information, especially applied to advertising; a situation in which the recipient is presented with a large number of stimuli at the same time

Part of the problem for marketers is that they have little or no control over how people think about the messages they are shown. For example, an advertisement may be designed to be as interesting as possible in order to cut through **advertising clutter** and attract attention, but the people who see the ad may become more interested in the cleverness of the advertising than they are in the brand (Pieters et al., 2002). This is exemplified by the Cinzano adverts mentioned earlier in the chapter – enjoyment of a clever and entertaining advertisement detracted from people's understanding of what was actually being advertised. The reasoning process is shown in Figure 8.8: the stimulus is followed by a reasoning process, which may lead either to retaining the information or forgetting it, according to how interested the individual is in the subject matter.

A further possibility for cognitive learning is vicarious learning, in which we learn from the experiences of others; other consumers, other competitors or teams within which one works (Myers, 2021). This is an extremely useful way of learning since it requires much less effort and risk than learning directly by trial and error. It requires either direct observation (watching what happens to someone else when they buy a product or behave in a particular way) or effective communication (as when someone describes their learning experiences). Because human beings are excellent communicators compared with most other species, we are particularly good at vicarious learning. In the marketing context, advertisers use models to show how products are used, and to show (or describe) the benefits of using a specific product. Having said that, learning by doing is generally much more effective than vicarious learning – imagine how far you would get in learning to drive a car if all you were ever allowed to do was observe other drivers and read an instruction book (partly why there are two parts to the UK's driving test: theory and practical!).

FIGURE 8.7 Five elements of cognitive learning

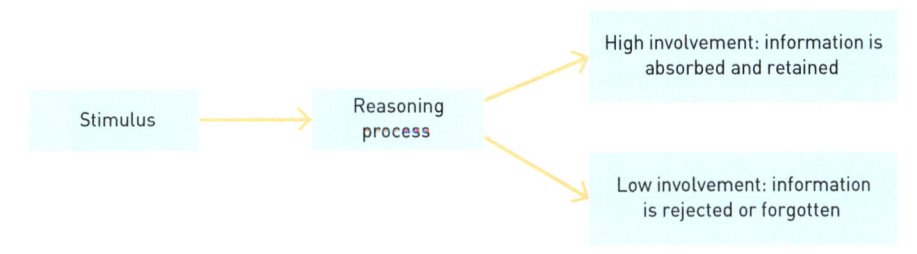

FIGURE 8.8 Reasoning and cognitive learning

CRITICAL REFLECTION

So learning by doing is more effective than thinking about things. If that's so, why do we still sit in classrooms, read books and (eventually) get a degree or other qualification? Why don't we do all our learning at work? Whatever happened to getting oneself apprenticed at 14 and spending 7 to 10 years becoming a master craftsperson?

Most of us can remember assignments we have written a great deal better than we can remember any lectures we attended – and we can remember how to play cricket, football, netball, hockey and so forth a great deal better than we can remember Shakespeare's plays (unless we acted in them, of course). So much for schoolroom lessons!

Maybe it's just about motivation to learn, but maybe there is something wrong with the way the

© iStock.com/skynesher

(Continued)

> education system operates – perhaps sitting through an hour-long monologue delivered by someone in a beige cardigan is not the best way to learn!
>
> Enter the 'flipped classroom'! Many educators are fast running away from the traditional lecture-then-seminar-then-homework model. Instead, they provide the learners with lots of pre-class materials (content-based videos, readings and possibly even assessments). Then in class, the content and learning is reinforced with practical hands-on activities. So you, as a student, hold responsibility for your learning by increasing engagement and therefore, by default, attendance as well. The educator has more of a role as a facilitator here rather than a professor.

Learned responses are never truly unlearned. The brain remembers (stores) everything, but rather like a computer with a faulty hard-drive it may not always be able to recall (retrieve) everything. Also, the human memory is huge; the *Encyclopaedia Britannica* contains around 12,500 million characters, but the brain has approximately 125,000,000 million characters in storage capacity; this is enough storage to hold 10,000 *Encyclopaedia Britannica*s.

THE NEED FOR KNOWLEDGE

The purpose of learning about products is mainly to reduce risk. The more one knows about the product and the product category, the lower the level of risk, as shown in Figure 8.9. In many cases, less knowledgeable buyers will ask a more knowledgeable friend to help in making the purchase. In some cases, people will spend considerable time researching information about the product category and individual brands (this is mainly true where there is high involvement with the product or where there is a high risk).

Lack of knowledge may lead to a purchase that is inappropriate; for example, an inexperienced car buyer might miss a sign of potential engine problems, whereas more experienced and knowledgeable buyers would not. Knowledgeable people have a better understanding of what attributes to look for, and how to evaluate the product against those attributes (Alba and Hutchinson, 1987).

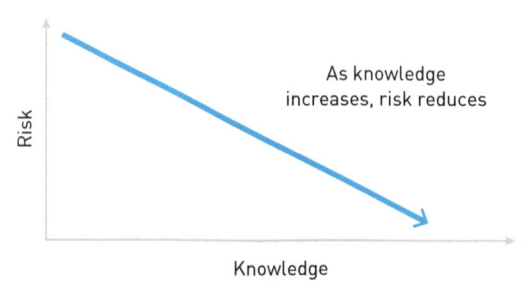

FIGURE 8.9 Knowledge and risk

The key point here, however, is that people understand that they need to know about the products they buy, especially when a major commitment is involved. This means that there is a motivation to learn, arising from a need for knowledge (see Chapter 5).

This need is met through the same ways as any other need – goals are set, heuristics are developed and the process is as subject to interrupts and dissonance as the actual purchase itself.

CRITICAL REFLECTION

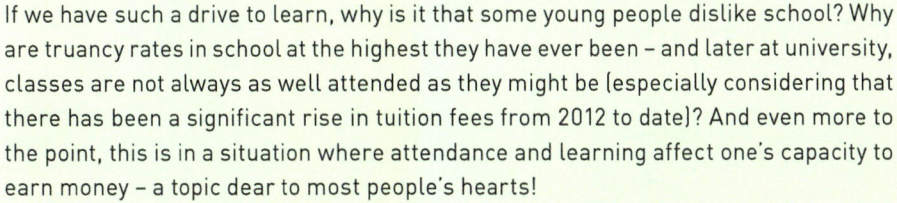

If we have such a drive to learn, why is it that some young people dislike school? Why are truancy rates in school at the highest they have ever been – and later at university, classes are not always as well attended as they might be (especially considering that there has been a significant rise in tuition fees from 2012 to date)? And even more to the point, this is in a situation where attendance and learning affect one's capacity to earn money – a topic dear to most people's hearts!

Perhaps it isn't so much that we don't want to learn as that we don't want to be told what to learn? So is there a problem with the way that we are taught? Can you see the traditional classroom coming to an end, in favour of new ways of learning, such as, for instance, MOOCs (which we read about in Chapter 6)?

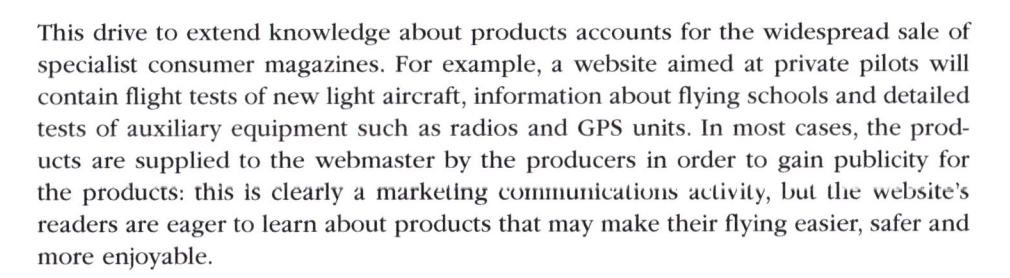

This drive to extend knowledge about products accounts for the widespread sale of specialist consumer magazines. For example, a website aimed at private pilots will contain flight tests of new light aircraft, information about flying schools and detailed tests of auxiliary equipment such as radios and GPS units. In most cases, the products are supplied to the webmaster by the producers in order to gain publicity for the products: this is clearly a marketing communications activity, but the website's readers are eager to learn about products that may make their flying easier, safer and more enjoyable.

Each individual has many different types of knowledge, as shown in Figure 8.10. This is far from being a comprehensive list of an individual's knowledge categories, but some knowledge in each category will relate to marketing issues. The main types of knowledge of interest from a marketing point of view are as follows:

1. *Product knowledge.* This subdivides into *product category knowledge* and *brand knowledge*. Product category knowledge is the information an individual remembers about all the possible solutions to the need problem.
2. *Purchase knowledge.* This is about how to buy, what things cost and where to buy from.
3. *Consumption* or *usage knowledge*. This is about how to use the product, how to dispose of whatever is left after use, what the risks are in using the product and what will be done with the product at the **end of life (EOL)**.
4. *Persuasion knowledge.* This is an understanding of the goals and tactics of people who might be trying to persuade us to buy – in the main, this is knowledge about marketers, but it includes knowledge about friends, review websites, etc. who might be recommending a product or service to us.

End of life (EOL)

A term used to indicate that a product has come to the end of its useful life and where a vendor stops marketing, selling and sustaining it (there may also be a responsibility and requirement for the original-equipment manufacturer to dispose of the product in a sustainable way)

5. *Self-knowledge.* This is knowledge about one's own needs, including knowledge about one's own failings. For example, an adult deciding to learn how to play the piano will be well aware of his or her lack of knowledge about the instrument, and therefore be more prepared to watch instructional videos on YouTube or www.onlinepianist.com, get piano lessons and extra coaching and, of course, to practise, practise, practise.

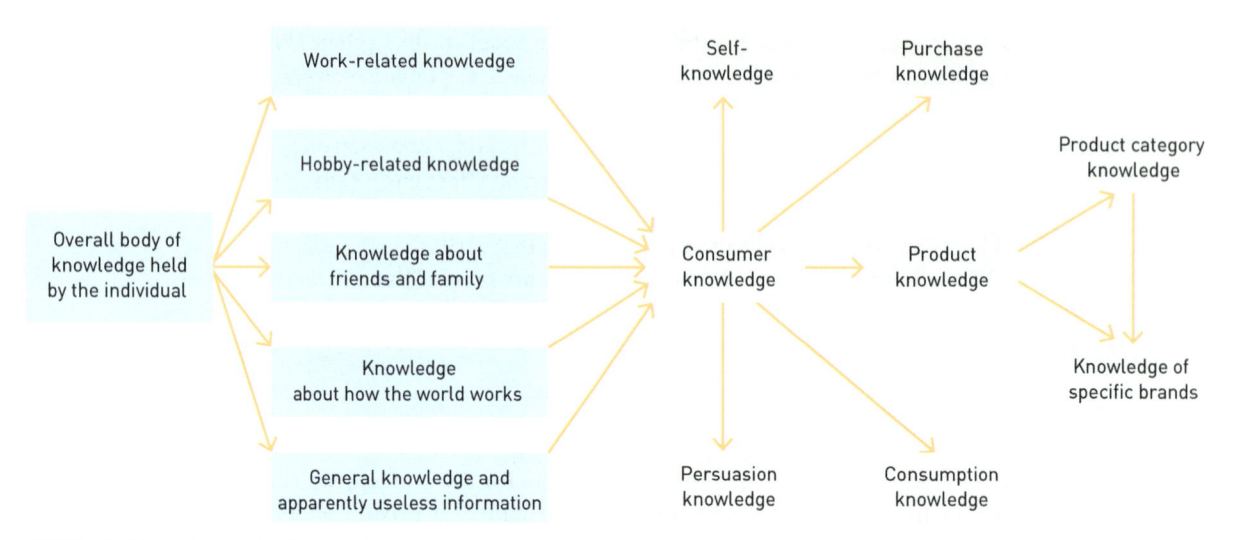

FIGURE 8.10 Categorising knowledge

PRODUCT CATEGORY KNOWLEDGE

This type of product knowledge is fairly general. For example, we all know what a television set is, and broadly we all know how to operate one, and know what it will do for us in terms of entertainment. Relatively fewer of us would know the difference between a QD OLED, OLED, QLED, LED and 4K LCD screens! Few of us would really understand the technicalities of how digital TV works, even though this is the only available TV system in the UK. If we head into the technical detail of ultra high definition and 4K resolution, almost all of us would be lost. Someone who has basic product knowledge is called a product **novice**; someone who has a large amount of product knowledge is a product expert. (So, for instance, an enthusiast or expert will know that, technically speaking, ultra high definition is actually a derivation of the 4K digital cinema standard, but while the local multiplex cinema shows movies in the native 4096 x 2160 4K resolution, the ultra HD consumer format has a slightly lower resolution of 3840 x 2160.) Those who have large amounts of product or market knowledge and enjoy sharing this knowledge with others are called market mavens (see Chapter 6).

Knowledge about these different factors would be chunked in the individual's memory under the category of 'TV sets'. For most people information is frequently cross-referenced, so that information about the microchips might also be contained in the category of 'things I know about electronics' or, in some cases, 'things I deal with at work'.

Novices
Customers who have purchased the product for the first time within the last 90 days

Product expert knowledge is shown in Figure 8.11 on the following page. A product expert would also have extensive knowledge of the members of a product category (the brands). A product expert would be able to judge unknown product attributes by reference to known attributes (for example, knowing that the product's components are reliable would give an indication of the longevity of the product as well as its reliability), and would influence acceptance of a price for a product since the expert would be aware of the prices of competing products. Knowledge influences responses to salespeople, which places a burden on salespeople to judge quickly and accurately how much the prospective customer already knows.

BRAND KNOWLEDGE

Brand knowledge is concerned with what people know about a specific product within the general product category. From a marketing viewpoint, the starting point of brand knowledge is whether people remember the brand at all (van Reijmersdal, 2011). The next level is whether people associate the brand strongly with the product category (Koll et al., 2022) – further increases in knowledge about the brand may follow, but without knowing that the brand exists and that it relates to a particular product there is no chance whatever that the brand will be included in the consideration set.

To test whether individuals have this level of knowledge, market researchers have two main tools. The first is a *recall test*, which tests top-of-the-mind awareness. Respondents might be asked to list all the breakfast cereals they can think of, for example, and the researcher would be able to tell first whether the brand being tested is included in the list, and second where it stands in relation to the other brands. Michel (2022) discusses how plumbers, for instance, may use *leave behinds* or low-cost items that you give to customers to promote your brand following service calls (or that they give away during home shows and other events) to aid brand recall. The second method is a *recognition test*, in which people are shown a list of brand names and are asked to say which ones they recognise. The problem with this test is that people may claim to recognise brands they have never heard of rather than appear to be ignorant; sometimes researchers will include fictitious brands in the list to test for this.

The tests are used for different circumstances. A recall test might be useful for testing advertising effectiveness or to determine the product's position in consumers' perceptual maps. A recognition test might be more useful when testing merchandising success, since it is important that people recognise the brand when they see it in-store.

Both recall and recognition are enhanced when the brand has a strong symbol attached to it. The three stripes of Adidas, the smell of a Zippo lighter or the McDonald's sound tag are all powerful symbols, each in a different way. Each one provokes instant recognition, and a clear image of what the product is and what it does.

Symbol
A method of converting thought into something that can be transmitted as a message

Encouraging people to learn about brands is a major part of advertising, and certainly of the more information-based, cognitive approaches to advertising. Many sales promotions are aimed at increasing people's knowledge about brands, encouraging them to learn more; for example, the tourist boards of countries sometimes run informative advertisements about their countries, linked to a competition for which the prize is a holiday in the country. In order to win the prize, participants have to complete a questionnaire about the country, which means that they need to view the website and read the advertisement to find out the answers. For instance, VisitScotland previously ran a campaign offering 4000 pairs of foot passenger tickets for a free return trip to one of 23 Scottish islands. Their 2022 campaign entitled 'Keep Scotland Unspoiled' speaks to their target markets by using social media, local radio and digital marketing to educate, inspire and inform people about issues such as water safety, camping, littering and the need to adhere to the Scottish Outdoor Access Code.

Brand associations (see Figure 8.12) are the connections people make between the brand and other concepts (Blackwell et al., 2005; Koll et al., 2022). Brand associations include beliefs and perceptions about what the brand will do, in other words, the consumption benefits. Brand associations are important to marketers because they tend to influence the degree to which consumers will adopt the product, and also the degree to which they will accept brand extensions and recommend the product to others (Belen del Rio et al., 2001; Osorio et al., 2022). The higher the consumer's perception of brand quality, the more likely he or she is to recommend the brand (no surprises there) and also to buy brand extensions. Some very important work in this area has recently been conducted by Chen et al. (2015), and their paper makes for very interesting reading: the authors were able, through neuro-imaging techniques, to identify the areas of the brain involved in processing brand data and to predict which brand the individual is thinking about based on brand associations and brain activity. This type of work, which has focused on 'cataloguing brain regions associated with marketing stimuli', has really advanced the application of neuroscientific methods to consumer research (Birknerová et al., 2022; Jayadatta et al., 2021; Mashrur et al., 2022; Micu et al., 2021).

Brand extensions may be in products that have some related production similarities, so that one might assume that a firm that is good at making the first product would also be good at making the other. Saab have played on this assumption in their advertising: since the company manufactures fighter aircraft as well as cars, it might be reasonable to assume that the engineering capabilities within the company would be high. Conversely, there is absolutely no reason to suppose that Virgin would be good at running airlines, commissioning new rock bands, running an insurance company and launching spacecraft. Yet the fact that the Virgin brand appears on the products is apparently seen as a signal of quality, and people who have been happy with one Virgin product seem to accept that other Virgin products will have similar quality values.

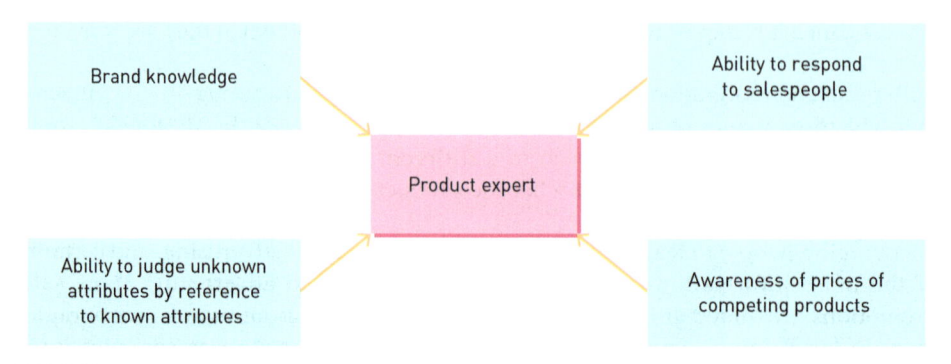

FIGURE 8.11 Product expert knowledge

Developing appropriate brand associations for new products is an especially challenging task. An almost equally challenging task is that of moving an existing product into a new market, and this is precisely the problem firms have when they move to e-commerce and online trading. A brand that is well known in its home market might be entirely unknown in the rest of the world, so apart from the logistical problems of arranging physical distribution, the firm faces the challenge of establishing a consistent brand image across a wide spectrum of foreign media, channels and cultures.

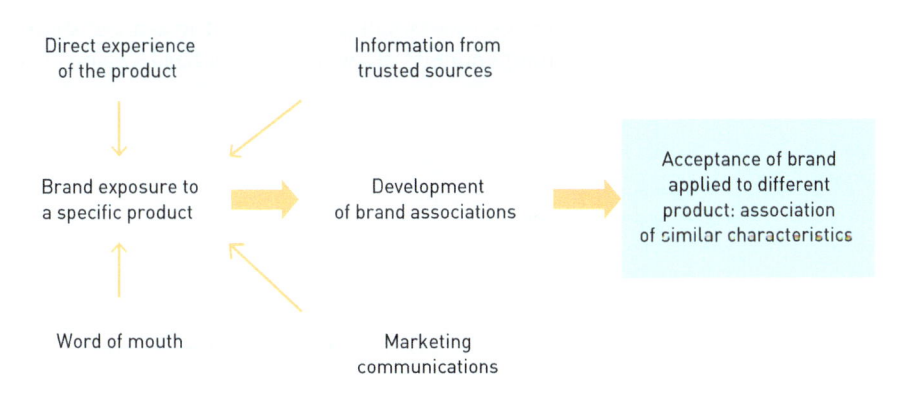

FIGURE 8.12 Brand association

PURCHASE KNOWLEDGE

Purchase knowledge is the information people have about buying products. This includes where the product can be bought (the distribution channel), whether discounts apply at some times or in some places, how much the product should cost and what the procedure/process is for buying the product.

Price is an important issue, because it is the measure of what the consumer has to give in return for the product benefits. This judgement is made not only on the basis of the cost of the brand from different sources, but also on the cost of products that provide similar benefits (Rao and Sieben, 1992). If one has little knowledge of the pricing within the product category, one might assume that a reasonable price is far too high (or be delighted to find that the actual price is lower than expected). In some cases, marketers (and especially salespeople) will try to give an impression that the price will be higher than it actually is, in order to delight the customer with the real price. This is called **price conditioning**. For example, a salesperson selling fitted kitchens might, at an early stage of the presentation, suggest that the new kitchen might cost £20,000 or more. When the actual price turns out to be only £18,000 the customer is delighted, but if the customer had been expecting a price of £6000 the delight would have been replaced by an entirely different feeling.

Price conditioning
Managing the expectations of a potential customer regarding price

It is useful if marketers gain knowledge of what people perceive is a reasonable price for a product (see Chapter 7). This will be a combination of what people believe is reasonable when they see the actual product, and what people already know about the price of competing products (see Figure 8.13). Relative price knowledge is what people know about one price relative to another (Monroe et al., 2015). For example, one American study found that people thought that buying books online was about 3% cheaper than buying them from a bricks-and-mortar retailer, whereas in fact the price difference was an average 10% cheaper online (Tedeschi, 2005). The likelihood is that the price difference will be even greater now that people have more search engines available to make price comparisons, that they sometimes buy used books, that occasionally there is an option to 'rent or borrow' (through a book club), or that they may just buy an e-book. Indeed, e-commerce was once the land of discounts and cheaper goods, but during the pandemic recovery this too has become a steady source of inflation (Tanzi, 2021).

```
Knowledge of what
competing products cost  ──►
                                Relative price perception
Perception of the value of the
product under consideration ──►
```

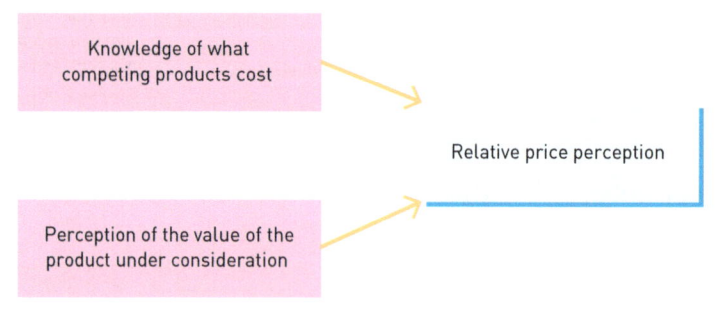

FIGURE 8.13 Relative price information

Marketers may decide prices (at least in part) on how well informed they believe customers to be about competitors' prices. If the products are rarely purchased, consumers will be unlikely to have very precise knowledge of prices (although this is a major motivator for customers to learn about prices before committing to a purchase). A further factor would be the ease of finding out about prices – in the case of home improvements, for example, it might prove extremely time-consuming to obtain quotes from different contractors, even if the contractors are willing to provide quotes (which they are often unprepared to do, given that this is a time-consuming activity for them and most builders have more than enough work as it is). In this respect, the internet represents something of a threat to marketers since, as we've seen already with the books example above, price comparisons are relatively easy to make, especially in such areas as booking flights or buying insurance.

BRAND EXPERIENCES: THE GREAT INTERNATIONAL BOOK EXCHANGE

There have recently been a number of posts doing the rounds on various social media platforms to do with The Great International Book Exchange. The message says 'Hi, I'm looking for people to participate in a huge, international book exchange. You can be anywhere in the world. All you have to do is send a copy of your favourite book (just one) to a stranger (I'll send you their details in a private message). You'll receive a max of 36 books back to keep; they'll be favourite books from strangers around the world! If you'd like to take part, comment 'IN' below and I'll send you all the details!' Now on the face of it (and let's not judge a book by its cover!) it sounds too good to be true... You buy one book, send the offer to six of your friends and you will soon receive dozens of books in return. However, because it's likely a pyramid scheme, the 36 book exchange you probably heard about on Facebook is one offer you should refuse. You'll receive a letter in the mail or a social media invite asking you to buy one book, send it on to a stranger on a list you receive via mail or email, then add your name to the bottom of the list, and, lastly, send the invitation letter on to six friends or acquaintances. The letter promises that if you follow the directions, you will receive 36 free books within 2 weeks. The book exchange is similar to other suspicious gift-exchange programmes, such as the Secret Sister Gift Exchange and Secret Wine Bottle Exchange, and what's wrong with it is that it shares characteristics of pyramid schemes. Pyramid schemes ask you to invest a certain amount of money or to buy a gift in order to join a club. The hope is that you'll receive compensation far greater than your initial contribution. But the mathematical odds aren't in your favour. Most pyramid schemes grow exponentially and only benefit the first few groups of people to join the offer.

For instance, for a scheme that requires six new recruits per member, by the time the pyramid reaches level 10, it would require 10,077,696 people to keep going. By level 10, about 97% of the people who participate will not get their free books.

But because of the high number of new recruits needed to keep a pyramid scheme going, they often collapse after only three or four rounds. Instead of a bonanza of books or windfall of money, you stand very little chance of recouping your initial payment, never mind reaping the benefits promised to you.

The victims are the people at the bottom of the pyramid – that is, those who joined later than others are given false hope and are much less likely to benefit. Hint: They're the suckers who enrich those who joined before them.

Many people who start such pyramid schemes also find ways to 'game' the system, such as by creating false names they seed throughout the list to multiply their chances of winning money or gifts.

© iStock.com/monkeybusinessimages

Other untrustworthy people who join later may add their name to the top of the list, instead of the bottom, thereby continually pushing the names of those who play by the rules further to the bottom.

And there are other people who won't follow the instructions correctly and won't bother to send the book – or the money or other gift – as instructed in their invitation, thereby causing a break in the chain.

Knowing when to buy is also an important part of purchase knowledge. In some cases purchases are seasonal – for example, flights are cheaper at off-peak times, and so also is hotel accommodation. For those with the flexibility to travel at any time, there are considerable savings to be made. Buying in advance may also save money. The advantages of having purchase knowledge are shown in Figure 8.14 – the individual is able to make much better decisions from a basis of knowing about the purchase factors and parameters.

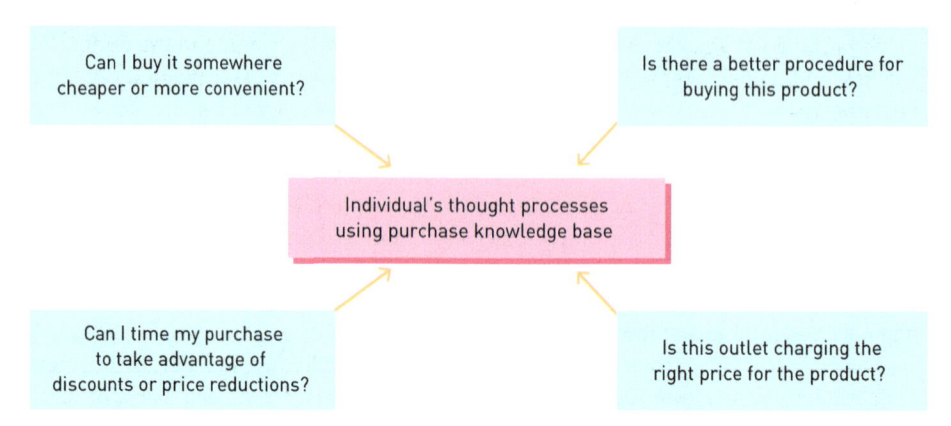

```
Can I buy it somewhere                          Is there a better procedure for
cheaper or more convenient?                          buying this product?

                    Individual's thought processes
                    using purchase knowledge base

Can I time my purchase                           Is this outlet charging the
to take advantage of                             right price for the product?
discounts or price reductions?
```

FIGURE 8.14 Advantages of having purchase knowledge

Another example is consumer electronics. Most people are well aware that when a new product is launched the price is high – for example, domestic drones started off priced in the thousands of pounds, but prices have dropped dramatically as the drones have gained in popularity. Partly this is due to reduced manufacturing costs on longer production runs, and partly it is due to the need for manufacturers to recoup development costs, but it is also due to manufacturers knowing that some people are prepared to pay a premium price for the pleasure of being the first to own a new, exciting product.

Knowing where to buy the product is a more complex issue than it once was, due to the increasing number of possible channels – online and offline retail outlets and resellers – from which products can be purchased. Fifty years or so ago retailers were much more specific in the range of products they carried: stationers only sold stationery, chemists only sold medicines and so forth. Items such as soy sauce or spices are often cheaper from specialist Chinese or Indian grocers than they are from supermarkets, for example. In addition, someone may need a specific product and have no knowledge of where to buy it – specialist products for motor or building work might not be available from normal hardware stores, but might instead need to be bought from specialist outlets or ordered from the manufacturers (OEMs – original-equipment manufacturers). In these circumstances manufacturers need to be sure that people are aware of where the products can be bought.

CONSUMPTION KNOWLEDGE

This type of knowledge is the information consumers have about how a product's benefits can be obtained in use. Lack of such knowledge would mean that people would be unlikely to buy the product in the first place: mobile telephones suffered from this problem for some time, since people found the networks, tariffs and choices confusing (many still do). Other high-tech products suffer from similar problems – many people, for instance, don't use all the facilities available on their smart TVs: on-demand video, web browsers, media streamers, networking and coaxial digital connections. A product that is used incorrectly is unlikely to perform to the required standard, which in turn is likely to lead to consumer dissatisfaction or even injury (Staelin, 1978).

As shown in Figure 8.15, ignorance about the correct use of the product can lead to two outcomes: either the consumer uses the product incorrectly, which leads to dissatisfaction with the product's performance, or the consumer reads the producer's information about the product (the manual) and learns how to use the product correctly (assuming that the manual is written in a language that the consumer can read!). This should lead to satisfaction. In some cases, consumers effectively re-invent the product, failing to use it according to the manufacturer's instructions, but are still satisfied with the performance. The final possibility is that the consumer knows how to use the product, uses it according to the instructions and is thus satisfied with the product.

At an obvious level, it is difficult to sell cars to people who do not have driving licences (unless of course they are going to employ the services of a chauffeur!), and difficult to sell computers to people who have no idea how to use one (unless you are selling to a CEO of a company with an existing IT department). At a more subtle level, there may be uses for the product which are not obvious to consumers – using baking powder for deodorising fridges is a well-known example, but using bath oil to remove tar spots from cars or white vinegar as a general household cleaning agent is less obvious. Whether a manufacturer would want to promote this use for bath oil or vinegar is doubtful, but consumers do invent novel ways of using products and this knowledge enters the product experts' minds even when it is not put there by the producers.

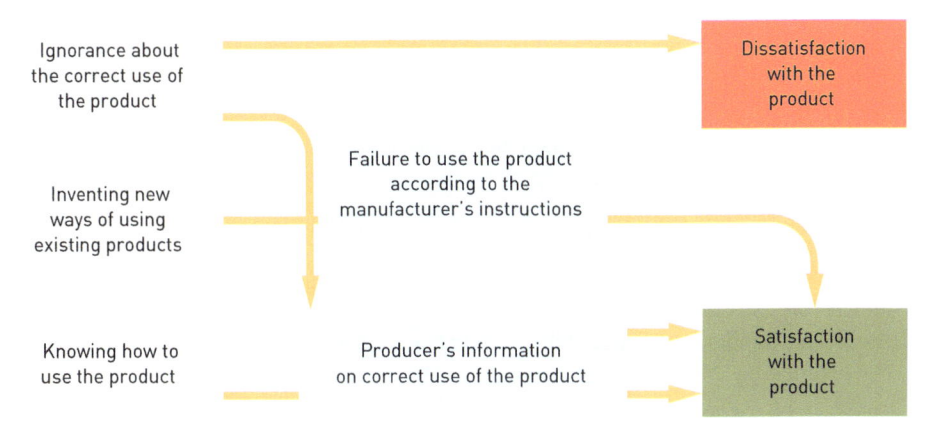

FIGURE 8.15 Consumption knowledge

BRAND EXPERIENCES: LEARNING AT THE HUMAN LIBRARY

The Human Library, or 'Menneskebiblioteket' as it is called in Danish, was created in Copenhagen in the spring of 2000 by Ronni Abergel and his brother Dany and colleagues Asma Mouna and Christoffer Erichsen. The original event was open 8 hours a day for 4 days straight and featured over 50 different titles. The Human Library is a non-profit learning platform that has hosted personal conversations designed to challenge stigma and stereotypes. It creates a safe space for dialogue where topics are discussed openly between the human books and their readers. All of the human books are volunteers with personal experience with their topic. The Human Library is a place where difficult questions are expected, appreciated and answered. The broad selection of books at the original event provided readers with ample choice to challenge their stereotypes, and so more than a thousand readers took advantage, leaving books, librarians, organisers and readers stunned at the reception and impact of The Human Library. One of the creators, Ronni Abergel, realising the potential of the idea, decided after the first event to begin to work to promote the idea to potential new organisers. Since then he has founded the Human Library Organization and produced a guide to new organisers with the Nordic Council of Ministers and the Council of Europe. He has travelled to many countries to help train new local organisers, plan launch events and present the idea to interested organisations and public authorities. Today it is estimated that The Human Library has been presented in more than 80 countries around the world, most of them in partnership with local organisers. Despite a very positive response, the first few years were a slow process. In 2008 the concept reached the USA and Canada, and since then it has spread with ever-increasing pace. In 2018 The Human Library premiered in Kenya, Panama and Botswana, to name just a few. Today their concept exists in more than 85 countries worldwide, known as the 'Human Library Organization'. The Human Library is present in Asia, Africa, Australia, North and South America, and Europe. The concept and method are trademark registered in Denmark and many other countries, in order to preserve and protect The Human Library's quality and uniqueness regardless of its global existence. The organisation's headquarters are located in Copenhagen, from where the global work is coordinated and cooperation agreements with local partners are made and managed; most events are planned and held in cooperation with local organisers in the different countries. In addition to the headquarters Copenhagen is also home to one of the four Danish book depots, the other three are in Esbjerg-Varde, Århus and Odense. A book depot is a gathering of volunteer books and librarians who frequently visits libraries, schools, high schools, festivals, etc. A book depot often services a town or region. The Human Library has found its calling in different areas of the civil society. In Denmark the platform is used as a part of the education of new social workers at the Institute of Social Work in Copenhagen. In the United States medical students from Thomas Jefferson University also participate in a Human Library. At a corporate level it's about creating an inclusive work environment, and increasing employees' ability to benefit from the great diversity that especially global companies are characterised by. Therefore some of the biggest companies in the world collaborate with The Human Library. This includes companies like Daimler, Heineken, eBay, Microsoft and Eli Lilly.

Source: Adapted from The Human Library (2022). More data and insights from The Human Library can be found at www.humanlibrary.org.

PERSUASION KNOWLEDGE

Persuasion knowledge is what people know about the goals and tactics of those trying to persuade them (Binder et al., 2022; Eisend, 2015). The seminal model developed by Friestad and Wright (1994) remains one of the most influential theories in this area. People are often sceptical about the motives of marketers, with good reason: marketers are not in business to do consumers a bit of good, they are in business for their own ends, and aim to manage the exchange between consumers and the firm. Perceiving themselves as being immune to 'undesirable persuasion' helps to protect and enhance consumers' self-esteem (Petty and Cacioppo, 2018). Since most of us resent being managed, we tend to seek out information about marketing tactics in order to strengthen our own negotiating position.

In recent years people have become more marketing aware, and marketing jargon is commonly heard from people who are not marketers. Understanding how marketers (and perhaps especially salespeople) operate has been shown to affect consumers' opinions of marketer sincerity adversely (Brown and Krishna, 2004). A study by Bearden et al. (2001) showed that people were able to make the following statements about their understanding of persuasion:

1. I know when an offer is 'too good to be true'.
2. I can tell when an offer has strings attached.
3. I have no trouble understanding the bargaining tactics used by salespeople.
4. I know when a marketer is pressuring me to buy.
5. I can see through sales gimmicks used to get consumers to buy.
6. I can separate facts from fantasy in advertising.

This clearly has implications for the marketing approach. Marketers cannot naively assume that consumers can be led around on a leash or can be easily persuaded by glib sales patter: people are suspicious, and are able to see through many marketer-induced ploys.

SELF-KNOWLEDGE

This area of knowledge (which we partially examined in Chapter 6) is about the individual's understanding of their own mental processes (Alba and Hutchinson, 2000; Andrades and Dimanche, 2018; Vazire and Solomon, 2015). People who understand their own strengths and weaknesses, as well as what they like and do not like, are in a better position to make realistic purchasing decisions than people who are not in touch with their own personalities. Self-knowledge and also self-referencing (Turk et al., 2015; Weiss, 2022) are important to market researchers, since much commercial market research is based on self-reports by consumers. For example, Balogh et al. (2015) examined the self-knowledge, attitudes and perceptions of Hungarian car drivers towards biofuels, on the basis that the development of biofuels may provide considerable emission savings and at the same time are socially and environmentally acceptable; therefore support measures need to be based on the sustainable performance of biofuels, in terms that are acceptable to users. Gulzari et al. (2022) have conducted a similar and more recent study investigating the role of environmental protection attitude, subjective norms, perceived functional quality, post-rental service quality, price value and willingness-to-pay regarding consumers' intentions for electric vehicles.

SOURCES OF CONSUMER KNOWLEDGE

People gather information about products from a large number of sources, both personal and impersonal. The sources may be controlled (or at least influenced) by marketers, or may be entirely independent.

Marketer-controlled sources include the following:

- Salespeople.
- Service people.
- Paid product endorsers (for example, athletes who recommend sports equipment).

These would be classified as **personal sources** of information, since they are provided by people.

Non-personal sources that are controlled by marketers would include the following:

- The products themselves.
- Point-of-purchase materials.
- Advertising (online and offline).
- Review websites/vlogs/blogs.
- E-catalogues/industry forums.
- Corporate websites.
- Directories such as www.yell.com.

Non-marketer influences may also be personal or impersonal. Personal sources would include family and friends, work colleagues, other shoppers, market mavens and other influential people (reviewers, bloggers, vloggers, YouTubers, etc.). Impersonal sources would include non-corporate websites, TV and radio shows, books, government reports and the press.

People are naturally suspicious of marketer-controlled information sources, but will use them and will often base most of their decision-making on the rival claims of different producers. Word of mouth and impartial articles in newspapers and magazines are trusted much more, because people feel that there is no purpose to be served by the source lying to them. It is for this reason that marketers try to influence word of mouth, word of mouse (see Sethna et al. [2013] for more information) and the opinions of journalists (who are, after all, powerful influentials).

The most useful source of information is, of course, consumption of the product itself. Actually using a product and forming a judgement about it is clearly far and away the best route for gaining information.

Personal sources
Sources of involvement derived from means–end knowledge stored in the individual's memory

Sometimes a lack of knowledge can be an advantage. Research shows that giving people a surprise (i.e. providing information for which there are no antecedents) can lead to them evaluating a brand higher than people to whom the information was not a surprise (Vanhamme and Snelders, 2003).

SUMMARY

Learning is something that we all do, every day of our lives, and the bulk of what we learn comes from outside the classroom. Learning comes about in many ways: sometimes it happens subconsciously, as in the case of classical conditioning; sometimes it requires conscious effort, as in cognitive learning. We never really forget anything we have learned, however.

From a marketing viewpoint, how people find out about products and brands, and more especially what drives people to do so, is the basis of our thinking when developing communications strategies. How people store the information in memory, and where they store it, are the basis of our communications strategies. Even though some people zap advertisements, we do have a natural desire to learn, and we also have considerable pressures on us to know about the products we buy – the downside of not knowing varies from losing our money, through social embarrassment, to physical injury.

KEY POINTS

- Learning is behavioural change over time relative to an external stimulus.
- Classical conditioning is largely involuntary on the part of the learner.
- Operant conditioning assumes that the learner has choice in the process: 'good' behaviour is reinforced by reward, 'bad' behaviour is reduced by punishment.
- Cognitive learning involves conscious thought and effort.
- Motivation is a key factor in all learning.
- Learning by experience is more powerful than learning vicariously.
- Consumer knowledge breaks down into product knowledge, purchase knowledge, consumption knowledge, persuasion knowledge and self-knowledge.

HOW TO IMPRESS YOUR EXAMINER

You are likely to be asked to compare theories of learning and how they relate to advertising. If you can provide real examples of repetitive advertising (classical learning), interactive websites (operant learning) and viral advertising in which a game is played or something similarly active (cognitive learning), you will show that you understand the theory and can apply it in practice.

REVIEW QUESTIONS

1. How might a marketer use music in classical conditioning?
2. What methods of operant conditioning are available to marketers?
3. What is the role of cognitive learning in major purchases?
4. How might a marketer motivate a consumer to learn about a product?
5. How can learning by experience be used in selling high-value products such as stereo systems?
6. How might mavens be recruited for a word of mouth campaign?
7. What effect does persuasion knowledge have on marketing communications?
8. How can self-knowledge be enhanced by marketers?
9. How can marketers encourage people to improve their purchase knowledge?
10. What should marketers do to ensure that consumers have adequate consumption knowledge?

CASE STUDY: WSUP AND GLOBAL HANDWASHING DAY

Yes, that's a thing! In fact, 15 October is the day. Global Handwashing Day is an international handwashing promotion campaign to motivate and mobilise people around the world to improve their handwashing habits. In Chapter 3 we read about the amazing work that WSUP.com (Water and Sanitation for the Urban Poor) is doing around the world. Well, during Covid-19, they've gone into overdrive. Quite simply, on Global Handwashing Day, the need for everyone to be able to wash their hands with soap has never been clearer. The devastating effects of the Covid-19 pandemic have shown the importance of universal hand hygiene as the simplest and most effective way to prevent the spread of a virus. For low-income communities around the world, the simple act of washing your hands with soap could save countless lives from Covid-19. Handwashing has saved millions of people from diseases like cholera, diarrhoea and dysentery, and yet over 40% of the world's population lacks access to basic handwashing facilities – including 900 million school-aged children. WSUP has been working to reach those urban communities most at risk from Covid-19, where high population density and lack of access to handwashing facilities mean the virus has the potential to spread quickly. They are using their long-standing relationships with water service providers to help them reach communities with messaging about handwashing and hygiene, soap and hand sanitiser and to adapt communications channels to meet the long-term challenges of the pandemic. By working this way, they have already reached hundreds of thousands of people in low-income urban areas across Ghana and Kenya since the outbreak of Covid-19. Where local lockdowns have been in effect in Ghana, WSUP has worked alongside the Community Water and Sanitation Agency (CWSA) to reach low-income communities remotely through community radio stations, a key communications channel in Ghana. Representatives from CWSA have taken part in radio and online interviews ahead of Global Handwashing Day to discuss handwashing and its importance in helping Ghanaians prevent the spread of Covid-19. This has ensured that crucial messaging around handwashing and good hygiene has reached communities where Covid-19 restrictions have meant face-to-face communication is not possible. WSUP has also been working with CWSA and local authorities in Accra, Kumasi and Tamale to identify locations for new handwashing stations. This has enabled low-income residents to practise the positive hygiene behaviours promoted on Global Handwashing Day. A top priority has been to ensure that all segments of the population have the ability to access information and understand the specific risks around Covid-19. In Kenya, community groups have reported that inaccurate understanding of how the disease is transmitted has led to people with disabilities being unfairly stigmatised, because of the false beliefs that these groups of people are more likely to be infected than other groups. WSUP has worked with the Association for the Physically Disabled of Kenya and other community-based organisations to run *train the trainer* sessions on handwashing and good hygiene, helping increase understanding of how best to protect against Covid-19. As well as focusing on handwashing, WSUP has been seeking ways to minimise risk of transmission through improved hygiene more generally. In Kenya, WSUP has been working with water service providers to strengthen and extend the online services they offer to customers in low-income areas. This has reduced the risk of Covid-19 transmission as customers do not need to visit utility offices to pay bills and utility staff do not need to visit households to conduct meter readings. These improved online services will also enable new customers to sign up to services online and existing customers to quickly report leaks or burst pipes in the network. Once in place, these remote service systems will provide long-term support to utilities and their customers, ensuring essential water services can continue during the pandemic.

CASE STUDY QUESTIONS

1. What are your personal perspectives on the importance of events such as Global Handwashing Day?
2. In what ways does the work at WSUP provide experiential learning opportunities and why is this beneficial for the learner?
3. How does the WSUP model enable cognitive learning to take place?
4. Why are community groups important in the process of acquiring knowledge in learning?
5. What part do online resources play here in acquiring self-knowledge about one's own role?

FURTHER READING

Think Again: The Power of Knowing What You Don't Know... (New York: Random House, 2021). The way we think shouldn't be taken for granted – and the skill of leaders to be more conscious of how they think and how to think again is a key skill. Adam Grant unpacks how to be 'thinking like a scientist' and how to find the 'joy in being wrong'. Intrigued?

(Continued)

A paper by Y.-P. Chen, L. Nelson and M. Hsu (2015) From 'where' to 'what': Distributed representations of brand associations in the human brain, *Journal of Marketing Research*, 52 (4): 453–66, is a fascinating read and represents an important advance in the application of neuroscientific methods to consumer research, moving from work focused on cataloguing brain regions associated with marketing stimuli to testing and refining constructs central to theories of consumer behaviour.

Contemporary Theories of Learning: Learning Theorists... In Their Own Words, edited by Knud Illeris (Abingdon: Routledge, 2009), is a useful book of essays in which leading learning theorists explain their ideas. If you are interested in learning about how people learn, this book provides an excellent overview.

The Power of Regret: How Looking Backwards Moves Us Forward... by Dan Pink. Known for his book *Drive*, which examines what motivates people, Dan Pink has embarked on an exploration of one of the biggest human emotions that drives both personal and professional lives: *regret*. Leading with a mantra of 'no regrets' is nonsense, and each of us should be using this important emotion to make better decisions, improve performance and find greater meaning.

Soap, Sex and Cigarettes: A Cultural History of American Advertising, by Juliann Sivulka (Boston, MA: Wadsworth Publishing Inc., 2011), provides an entertaining view of how advertising has both created and been created by American society. The book shows how advertising has helped Americans learn how to be American – and, of course, the same processes have gone on in other countries.

Human Memory: Theory and Practice, by Alan Baddeley (Hove: Psychology Press, 1997), is about the mechanisms of memory. It covers the interconnectedness of learning, knowledge and memory, and explores three different types of memory.

Advertising and the Mind of the Consumer: What Works, What Doesn't, and Why, by Max Sutherland (London: Kogan Page, 2000), explains how exposure to advertising builds up in people's memories. The author uses a lot of anecdotes and real-life examples, as well as an entertaining writing style to get the point across.

MORE ONLINE

For additional materials that support this chapter and your learning, please visit:

https://study.sagepub.com/sethna5e

REFERENCES

Alba, J.A. and Hutchinson, J.W. (1987) Dimensions of consumer expertise. *Journal of Consumer Research*, 13 (March): 411–54.

Alba, J.A. and Hutchinson, J.W. (2000) Knowledge calibration: What consumers know and what they think they know. *Journal of Consumer Research*, 27 (September): 123–56.

Anderson, J.L. and Krasnozhon, L.A. (2021) Effect of the use of music on definitional knowledge in an introductory statistics course: Evidence from a Pareto chart activity. *Decision Sciences Journal of Innovative Education*, 19 (4): 265–74.

Andrades, L. and Dimanche, F. (2018) Co-creation of experience value: A tourist behaviour approach. In N. Prebensen, J.S. Chen and M. Uysal (eds), *Creating Experience Value in Tourism*. Wallingford: CABI. pp. 83–97.

André, Q., Reinholtz, N. and Langhe, B.D. (2022) Can consumers learn price dispersion? Evidence for dispersion spillover across categories. *Journal of Consumer Research*, 48 (5): 756–74.

Anglada-Tort, M., Schofield, K., Trahan, T. and Müllensiefen, D. (2022) I've heard that brand before: The role of music recognition on consumer choice. *International Journal of Advertising*. https://doi.org/10.1080/02650487.2022.2060568

Bainbridge, K., Shute, V., Rahimi, S., Liu, Z., Slater, S., Baker, R.S. and D'Mello, S.K. (2022) Does embedding learning supports enhance transfer during game-based learning? *Learning and Instruction*, 77: 101547.

Balogh, P., Bai, A., Popp, J., Huzsvai, L. and Jobbágy, P. (2015) Internet-orientated Hungarian car drivers' knowledge and attitudes towards biofuels. *Renewable and Sustainable Energy Reviews*, 48 (August): 17–26.

Bearden, W.O., Hardesty, D.M. and Rose, R.L. (2001) Consumers' self-confidence: Refinements in conceptualisation and measurement. *Journal of Consumer Research*, 28 (June): 121–34.

Belen del Rio, A., Vacquez, R. and Iglesias, V. (2001) The effects of brand association on consumer response. *Journal of Consumer Marketing*, 18: 410–25.

Binder, A., Stubenvoll, M., Hirsch, M. and Matthes, J. (2022) Why am I getting this ad? How the degree of targeting disclosures and political fit affect persuasion knowledge, party evaluation, and online privacy behaviors. *Journal of Advertising*, 51 (2): 206–22.

Birknerová, Z., Miško, D., Ondrijová, I. and Čigarská, B.N. (2022) Analysis of consumer awareness of neuromarketing. *TEM Journal*, 11 (2): 870–5.

Blackston, M. and Lebar, E. (2015) Constructing consumer-brand relationships to better market and build businesses. In S. Fournier, M. Breazeale and J. Avery (eds), *Strong Brands, Strong Relationships*. Abingdon: Routledge. pp. 376–92.

Blackwell, R.D., Miniard, P.W. and Engel, J.F. (2005) *Consumer Behaviour*, 10th edn. Mason, OH: Thomson South-Western.

Brown, C.L. and Krishna, A. (2004) The skeptical shopper: A metacognitive account for the effects of default options on choice. *Journal of Consumer Research*, 31 (December): 529–39.

Campaign (2004) Contact centres: Call centres that talk brands. *Campaign Magazine*. www.campaignlive.co.uk/article/contact-centres-call-centres-talk-brands/218633 (accessed 15 April 2018).

Chen, Y.P., Nelson, L. and Hsu, M. (2015) From 'where' to 'what': Distributed representations of brand associations in the human brain. *Journal of Marketing Research*, 52 (4): 453–66.

Cheung, C.M., Zheng, X. and Lee, M.K. (2015) How the conscious and automatic information processing modes influence consumers' continuance decision in an e-commerce website. *Pacific Asia Journal of the Association for Information Systems*, 7 (2): 25–40.

Cruz, G.L. (2021) Human, social, and intellectual capital in the COVID-19 era: Establishing the agenda. Framing, plausibility, and verifiability in the repositories. *Conexión, 16.* doi: 10.18800/conexion.202102.006

Dudarev, V., Manaligod, M.G., Enns, J.T. and Todd, R.M. (2022) In the hands of the beholder: Wearing a COVID-19 mask is associated with its attractiveness. *Quarterly Journal of Experimental Psychology, 75* (4): 598–615.

Eisend, M. (2015) Persuasion knowledge and third-person perceptions in advertising: The moderating effect of regulatory competence. *International Journal of Advertising, 34* (1): 54–69.

Elpers, J.W., Wedel, M. and Pieters, R. (2002) The influence of moment-to-moment pleasantness and informativeness on zapping TV commercials: A functional data and survival analysis approach. *Advances in Consumer Research, 29*: 57–8.

Esfidani, M.R., Rafiei Samani, S. and Khanlari, A. (2022) Music and consumer behavior in chain stores: Theoretical explanation and empirical evidence. *International Review of Retail, Distribution & Consumer Research, 32* (3): 331–48.

Forest Schools Education (2018) What are Forest Schools? http://forestschools.com/what-are-forest-schools/ (accessed 19 July 2018).

Friestad, M. and Wright, P. (1994) The persuasion knowledge model: How people cope with persuasion attempts. *Journal of Consumer Research, 21* (1): 1–30.

Fulantelli, G., Taibi, D., Scifo, L., Schwarze, V. and Eimler, S.C. (2022) Cyberbullying and cyberhate as two interlinked instances of cyber-aggression in adolescence: A systematic review. *Frontiers in Psychology, 13*: 1–21.

Golman, R., Loewenstein, G. and Gurney, N. (2015) Information gaps for risk and ambiguity. *SSRN.* http://dx.doi.org/10.2139/ssrn.2605495

Gorn, G.J. (1982) The effects of music in advertising on choice behaviour: A classical conditioning approach. *Journal of Marketing, 46* (Winter): 94–101.

Gorton, K. (2007) Theorizing emotion and affect feminist engagements. *Feminist Theory, 8* (3): 333–48.

Grüning, D.J. and Schubert, T.W. (2022) Emotional campaigning in politics: Being moved and anger in political ads motivate to support candidate and party. *Frontiers in Psychology, 12*: 1–15.

Gulzari, A., Wang, Y. and Prybutok, V. (2022) A green experience with eco-friendly cars: A young consumer electric vehicle rental behavioral model. *Journal of Retailing and Consumer Services, 65*: 102877.

Hansen, J., Strick, M., van Baaren, R.B., Hooghuis, M. and Wigboldus, D.H. (2009) Exploring memory for product names advertised with humour. *Journal of Consumer Behaviour, 8* (2/3): 135–48.

Hémar-Nicolas, V., Pantin-Sohier, G. and Gallen, C. (2022) 'Do you eat insects?' Acceptance of insects as food by children. *Journal of Consumer Marketing, 39* (5): 505–22.

Hoch, S.J. and Deighton, J. (1989) Managing what consumers learn from experience. *Journal of Marketing, 53* (April): 1–20.

Hoch, S.J. and Ha, Y. (1986) Consumer learning: Advertising and the ambiguity of product experience. *Journal of Consumer Research*, *13* (September): 221–33.

Jabeen, F., Kaur, P., Talwar, S., Malodia, S. and Dhir, A. (2022) I love you, but you let me down! How hate and retaliation damage customer-brand relationship. *Technological Forecasting & Social Change*, *174*: 121183.

Jayadatta, S., Shivappa, S.J. and Ramanjaneyalu, N. (2021) Applications, challenges, promises and potential role of neuromarketing as an emerging tool of market research. *International Journal of Management & Information Technology*, *6* (2): 1–14.

Jiang, K., Qin, M. and Li, S. (2022) Chatbots in retail: How do they affect the continued use and purchase intentions of Chinese consumers? *Journal of Consumer Behaviour*, *21* (4): 756–72.

Kiyosaki, R.T. (2011) *Rich Dad Poor Dad*. Scottsdale, AZ: Plata Publishing.

Koll, O., von Wallpach, S. and Uzelac, B. (2022) Stakeholder-oriented brand management: A Venn-diagram approach to monitor brand associations. *European Management Journal*. https://doi.org/10.1016/j.emj.2022.03.004

Kroeber-Riel, W. (1984) Emotional product differentiation by classical conditioning. *Advances in Consumer Research*, *11*: 538–43.

Krugman, H.E. (1965) The impact of television advertising: Learning without involvement. *Public Opinion Quarterly*, *29*: 349–56.

Küster, F. and Eisend, M. (2016) Time heals many wounds: Explaining the immediate and delayed effects of message sidedness. *International Journal of Advertising*, *35* (4): 664–81.

Liu, G., Abolhasani, M. and Hang, H. (2022) Disentangling effects of subjective and objective characteristics of advertising music. *European Journal of Marketing*, *56* (4): 1153–83.

Marganski, A. and Melander, L. (2018) Intimate partner violence victimization in the cyber and real world: Examining the extent of cyber aggression experiences and its association with in-person dating violence. *Journal of Interpersonal Violence*, *33* (7): 1071–95.

Mashrur, F.R., Rahman, K.M., Miya, M.T.I., Vaidyanathan, R., Anwar, S.F., Sarker, F. and Mamun, K.A. (2022) An intelligent neuromarketing system for predicting consumers' future choice from electroencephalography signals. *Physiology & Behavior*, *253*: 113847.

McSweeney, F.K. and Bierley, C. (1984) Recent developments in classical conditioning. *Journal of Consumer Research*, *11* (September): 619–37.

Michel, M. (2022) 17 great leave behinds: Build brand recall with customers. *Plumbing & Mechanical*, *40* (5): 16.

Micu, A., Capatina, A., Micu, A.-E., Geru, M., Aivaz, K.A. and Muntean, M.C. (2021) A new challenge in digital economy: Neuromarketing applied to social media. *Economic Computation & Economic Cybernetics Studies & Research*, *55* (4): 133–48.

Mishna, F., Regehr, C., Lacombe-Duncan, A., Daciuk, J., Fearing, G. and Van Wert, M. (2018) Social media, cyber-aggression and student mental health on a university campus. *Journal of Mental Health*, *27* (3): 222–9.

Monroe, K.B., Rikala, V.M. and Somervuori, O. (2015) Examining the application of behavioral price research in business-to-business markets. *Industrial Marketing Management*, 47: 17–25.

Murray, K.B. and Haubl, G. (2002) The fiction of no friction: A user skills approach to cognitive lock-in. *Advances in Consumer Research*, 29: 11–18.

Myers, C.G. (2021) Performance benefits of reciprocal vicarious learning in teams. *Academy of Management Journal*, 64 (3): 926–47.

Navarro, R., Larrañaga, E. and Yubero, S. (2018) Differences between preadolescent victims and non-victims of cyberbullying in cyber-relationship motives and coping strategies for handling problems with peers. *Current Psychology*, 37 (1): 116–27.

Neck, H.M., Neck, C.P. and Murray, E.L. (2018) *Entrepreneurship: The Practice and Mindset*. Thousand Oaks, CA: Sage.

Norton, M. and Chance, Z. (2008) Decision amnesia: Why taking your time leads to forgetting. *Advances in Consumer Research*, 35: 55–8.

Onkvisit, S. and Shaw, J.J. (1994) *Consumer Behaviour, Strategy and Analysis*. New York: Macmillan.

Osorio, M.L., Centeno, E., Cambra-Fierro, J. and del Castillo, E. (2022) In search of fit or authenticity? A product-type consumer decision in celebrity brand extensions. *Journal of Product & Brand Management*, 31 (6): 841–53.

Paramita, W., Septianto, F. and Nasution, R.A. (2022) The interactive effects of moral identity and humor on advertising evaluations: The mediating role of disgust. *International Journal of Advertising: The Review of Marketing Communications*, 41 (7): 1263–81.

Pavlov, I.P. (1927) *Conditioned Reflexes*. London: Oxford University Press.

Petty, R.E. and Cacioppo, J.T. (2018) *Attitudes and Persuasion: Classic and Contemporary Approaches*. Abingdon: Routledge.

Pieters, R., Warlop, L. and Wedel, M. (2002) Breaking through the clutter: Ad originality and familiarity effects on brand attention and memory. *Advances in Consumer Research*, 29: 89–90.

Pinho, J.C. and Soares, A.M. (2015) Response to advertising on online social networks: The role of social capital. *International Journal of Consumer Studies*, 39 (3): 239–48.

Rao, A.R. and Sieben, W.A. (1992) The effect of prior knowledge on price acceptability and the type of information examined. *Journal of Consumer Research*, 19 (September): 256–70.

Sethna, Z., Jones, R. and Harrigan, P. (2013) *Entrepreneurial Marketing: Global Perspectives*. Bingley: Emerald Publishing.

Skinner, B.F. (1953) *Science and Human Behaviour*. New York: Macmillan.

Staelin, R. (1978) The effects of consumer education on consumer product safety behaviour. *Journal of Consumer Research*, 5 (June): 30–40.

Steils, N., Crié, D. and Decrop, A. (2019) Online consumer learning as a tool for improving product appropriation. *Journal of Retailing and Consumer Services*, 46: 51–7.

Sumpradit, N., Bagozzi, R.P. and Ascione, F.J. (2015) 'Give me happiness' or 'Take away my pain': Explaining consumer responses to prescription drug advertising. *Cogent Business & Management, 2* (1): 1–27.

Tanzi, A. (2021) Inflation spreads to online retail, once a haven of discounts. www.bnnbloomberg.ca/inflation-spreads-to-online-retail-once-a-haven-of-discounts-1.1683882 (accessed 29 October 2022).

Tedeschi, B. (2005) Cheaper than it seems. *New York Times*, 10 January.

Turk, D.J., Gillespie-Smith, K., Krigolson, O.E., Havard, C., Conway, M.A. and Cunningham, S.J. (2015) Selfish learning: The impact of self-referential encoding on children's literacy attainment. *Learning and Instruction, 40* (December): 54–60.

van Reijmersdal, E.A. (2011) Mixing advertising and editorial content in radio programmes: Appreciation and recall of brand placements versus commercials. *International Journal of Advertising: The Quarterly Review of Marketing Communications, 30* (3): 425–46.

Vanhamme, J. and Snelders, D. (2003) What if you surprise your customers – will they be more satisfied? Findings from a pilot experiment. *Advances in Consumer Research, 30*: 48–56.

Vazire, S. and Solomon, B.C. (2015) Self- and other-knowledge of personality. In M. Mikulincer, P. Shaver, M.L. Cooper and R.J. Larsen (eds), *APA Handbook of Personality and Social Psychology, Vol. 4: Personality Processes and Individual Differences*. Washington, DC: American Psychological Association. pp. 261–81.

Weiss, J.K. (2022) Examining engagement and self-referencing across the duration of narrative processing. *Psychology of Popular Media, 11*(1): 102–108. https://doi.org/10.1037/ppm0000308

Wengel, Y., Ma, L., Ma, Y., Apollo, M., Maciuk, K. and Ashton, A.S. (2022) The TikTok effect on destination development: Famous overnight, now what? *Journal of Outdoor Recreation and Tourism, 37*: 100458.

Widrick, S.M. (1986) Concept of negative reinforcement has place in classroom. *Marketing News, 20*: 48–9.

Wiegman, O. and van Schie, E.G.M. (1998) Video game playing and its relations with aggressive and prosocial behaviour. *British Journal of Social Psychology, 37* (3): 367–78.

Wright, M.F. (2015) Emerging adults' coping strategies: Longitudinal linkages to their involvement in cyber aggression and cyber victimization. *International Journal of Cyber Behavior, Psychology and Learning, 5* (2): 1–14.

Zauberman, G. (2002) Lock-in over time: Time preferences, prediction accuracy and the information cost structure. *Advances in Consumer Research, 29*: 8–10.

Zheng, Q. and Ding, Q. (2022) Exploration of consumer preference based on deep learning neural network model in the immersive marketing environment. *PloS One, 17* (5): e0268007.

Zhou, Z. and Bao, Y. (2002) Users' attitudes towards web advertising: Effects of internet motivation and internet ability. *Advances in Consumer Research, 29*: 71–8.

PART ONE CONSUMER BEHAVIOUR IN CONTEXT

Chapter 1 Understanding Consumer Behaviour
Chapter 2 Decisions, Behaviours and Interactions
Chapter 3 Consumption in B2C vs. B2B
Chapter 4 Consumer Technology and Innovation

PART TWO CONSUMERS AS INDIVIDUALS (THE PSYCHOLOGICAL ISSUES)

Chapter 5 Drive, Motivation and Hedonism
Chapter 6 The Self and Personality
Chapter 7 Perception
Chapter 8 Learning and Knowledge
Chapter 9 Attitude Formation and Change

PART THREE CONSUMERS AS SOCIAL ACTORS (THE SOCIOLOGICAL ISSUES)

Chapter 10 Reference Groups
Chapter 11 Age, Gender and Familial Roles
Chapter 12 Culture and Social Mobility
Chapter 13 Ethical Consumption
Chapter 14 Sustainable Consumption

CHAPTER 9

ATTITUDE FORMATION AND CHANGE

LEARNING OBJECTIVES

After reading this chapter you should be able to:

- Describe what is meant by attitude.
- Explain how attitudes can be inferred from behaviour.
- Explain why behaviour cannot be assumed from knowing attitude.
- Describe the components of attitude.
- Explain the role of salient beliefs in forming attitudes.
- Explain the purpose of attitudes.
- Explain the relationship between attitude and behaviour.
- Describe the factors that determine the strength of attitude.
- Explain the difference between public and private attitudes.
- Show the effect of situation on attitude.
- Explain the role of changing beliefs in changing attitudes.
- Explain how emotions are important in changing attitudes.
- Describe the various complaint behaviours that arise from post-purchase dissatisfaction.

CHAPTER CONTENTS

Introduction
Defining attitude
Dimensions of attitude
Attitude formation
Attitude measurement
Functions of attitudes
Attitude and behaviour
The duality of private vs. public attitudes
Attitude vs. situation
Attitude towards adverts vs. attitude towards the brand
General vs. specific attitudes
Changing attitudes
Cognitive dissonance
Summary
Key points
How to impress your examiner
Review questions
Case study: Changing attitudes to education: Multiverse
Further reading
References

More online: https://study.sagepub.com/sethna5e

INTRODUCTION

Attitudes are what put us in the right position for behaviour. We each have attitudes towards many things – our friends, families, employers, possessions, money, government policies, other people's behaviour and so forth. Our differing attitudes are (in part) the differentiators between us as human beings, and since attitudes are the precursor to any consumption behaviour they are of great interest to marketers, both in terms of finding out what they are and in seeking to change them.

DEFINING ATTITUDE

Attitude can be defined as 'a learned tendency to respond to an object in a consistently favourable or unfavourable way' (Onkvisit and Shaw, 1994). In consumer behavioural terms, it is a customer's thoughts and feelings towards a brand (Pauwels, 2015). Whether a product will be bought or not depends to a large extent on the consumer's attitude towards it, and therefore much marketing effort is expended on finding out what consumers' attitudes are to product offerings, and in seeking to change those attitudes where appropriate and achievable. With consumers cautious of Covid-19, managers are forced to adapt to changes in attitudes with regard to consumer behaviour, government regulations and disrupted supply chains (Taillon et al., 2022).

To break down the definition and make it easier to handle:

- Attitude is learned, not instinctive.
- It is not behaviour; it is a predisposition towards a particular behaviour.
- It implies a relationship between a person and an object. The object of the attitude could be another person, an institution or a physical article; 'object' is used here in the sense of 'an objective'.
- Attitudes are fairly stable; they do not change much with physical states or circumstances. For example, if someone's preferred painkiller is ibuprofen, that attitude remains whether or not the individual has a headache. The behaviour (actually taking the tablets) may not happen, but the attitude remains.
- The relationship between a person and an object is not neutral. It is a vector, having both direction and intensity; if you express an attitude about something, you either like it or you do not. If you are neutral about it, or indifferent, you would say you don't have any attitude towards it.

Attitude has to be inferred from statements or behaviour; it is intangible and not directly observable. In other words, although we can observe and measure behaviour, we have to ask people about their attitudes to various things, and hope that their replies are honest ones. This can cause difficulties if we are researching a sensitive topic.

The formation of attitude is based on experience of the object, normally direct experience; driving a particular make of car, or trying a particular brand of beer, will lead to the formation of an attitude. The individual builds up a mental picture (perception) of the object, and forms an attitude accordingly. First impressions are important, since they influence our later information gathering (see Chapter 8) – this is why people behave in a positive and approval-seeking manner on a first date (or a first meeting), so that the other person forms a favourable attitude. Both psychology and marketing researchers have highlighted a number of attitudinal metrics (see Table 9.1) over the past few years. We'll be taking a look at attitude measurement a little later in this chapter, but it's important to have some of these in the back of your mind as you read further, so here are nine metrics which have been adapted from Verhoef et al. (2015):

Attitude
A learned tendency to respond to an object in a consistently favourable or unfavourable way

TABLE 9.1 Attitudinal metrics

Trust	Customers' confidence in the quality and reliability of the services provided (Garbarino and Johnson, 1999). A more formal definition might be 'a binary relation between two entities: one entity's confidence, belief and expectation that another entity will act or intend to act beneficially' (Xiu and Liu, 2005) – the role played by consumer trust on website loyalty, for instance (Flavián et al., 2006)
Satisfaction	An overall evaluation/appraisal based on the customer's total purchase and consumption expectation and experience within the relationship (Anderson et al., 1994) and regarding a product's performance and a brand's behaviour as a relationship partner (Odekerken-Schroder et al., 2003)
Commitment	The extent to which a customer believes that an ongoing relationship with the company is so important as to warrant maximum efforts at maintaining it (Morgan and Hunt, 1994) and in conveying those positive experiences to others (Babin et al., 2015), and being supportive of the relationship longevity in terms of faithfulness and willingness to make small sacrifices (Aaker et al., 2004)
Payment equity	Customers' perceived fairness of the price paid for their consumed products or services (Bolton and Lemon, 1999)
Value equity	The customer's objective assessment of the utility of a brand based on perceptions of what is given up for what is received. Sub-drivers of value equity include quality, price and convenience
Brand equity	The customer's subjective and intangible assessment of the brand, above and beyond its objectively perceived value. Sub-drivers of brand equity include brand awareness, customer brand perceptions/associations and perceptions of brand ethics
Relationship equity	The customer's assessment of interactions with the brand, above and beyond objective and subjective assessments of the brand. Sub-drivers of relationship equity include salesperson and serviceperson relationships, loyalty programmes, customer communities and knowledge of the customer
Net promoter score	The percentage of promoters minus the percentage of detractors
Loyalty intentions	The extent to which customers intend to remain loyal to a firm

CRITICAL REFLECTION

So attitudes form through experience. And yet we often base our beliefs on very limited experience, do we not? Is this some weakness in the human brain? Or is it, perhaps, a sign of one of our great talents – the ability to develop a working hypothesis, and assess the risk, based on limited data? We all know that technology continues to advance at a phenomenal rate. This makes some technophobes somewhat nervous, and trying to change their attitude is a tough call. This is unless, of course, they experience a 'need'! So here's an example. Let's say recent flash floods in your village have rendered you unable to leave your house for 3 days and your 9-month-old baby has a worryingly high temperature and won't stop crying. Or you're hiking through a forest and your knee starts to swell up, go red and is severely itching as, evidently, you've been bitten by something. The good news is that, in both of these situations, you'd be able to see a doctor via your smartphone and there is every possibility that the doctor may even

(Continued)

be able to prescribe medication, wherever you are (whether you are able to access the medication is a different story!). Telehealth and telemedicine are not only more convenient, but are bringing the cost of healthcare down and thus are less expensive. (Apps such as 'Cliniko', 'doctorondemand', 'healthtap', 'livehealthonline', amongst others, will all generally let you see a doctor via a video call.)

If people still need convincing to change their attitudes, enter the world of gamification (which we saw earlier in Chapter 8!). There are a number of commentators who have recently written about the economic and societal impact of gaming (see, for example, Deterding et al., 2011; McGonigal, 2011; Reeves and Read, 2009) and most recently its impact through the Covid-19 pandemic (Savolainen et al., 2022). And the large number of downloads of popular apps such as Swarm by Foursquare, Facebook and Angry Birds have added to the societal interest in gamification to such an extent that the concept of playing 'games' has been added to other areas of our life. Marketers are now trying to change user attitudes using apps in areas such as healthcare (see 'fitocracy'), developing loyalty and engagement for TV channels (see 'Beamly') and environmental awareness (see 'changingice', 'earthnow' and 'offset').

© iStock.com/AndreyPopov

Synthetic
That which is constructed from disparate components. In perception, an overall view derived from grouping together a set of stimuli

Some experience is indirect: recommendations and the communicated experiences of friends or relatives are important when forming attitudes towards objects of which we don't have direct experience. This can sometimes lead to superstitious beliefs and prejudices due to the *synthetic* nature of perception. If your friends and peers have all told you that a particular film is boring, you are likely to maintain that attitude, even if you have not seen the film yourself. Negative attitudes are often formed in this way. Marketing communications generally can help a lot here by providing additional sources of information (think advertising and public relations, which both have a particularly important role in this since they are activities that can form and change attitudes).

There is a perceptual component in attitude. The manner in which an object is perceived is affected by the consumer's stable characteristics (personality, intelligence, previous knowledge, culture, gender, etc.) and by current characteristics, such as mood, state of the organism, etc.

DIMENSIONS OF ATTITUDE

Attitude has three dimensions, as shown in Figure 9.1, and Table 9.2 explains the relationship between each of these components.

ATTITUDE FORMATION AND CHANGE

It is important to note that attitude and behaviour are separate things. Simply because an individual has a particular attitude about something does not mean that the individual will act on the attitude. For example, someone might hear that his bank is investing in a country with an oppressive regime. This is cognition. He may think that this is unethical; he does not like the bank doing this (affect). He therefore decides to move his account elsewhere (conation). Conation may not always lead to behaviour; our ethical bank customer may have second thoughts later and decide to leave the account where it is, perhaps on the basis that switching to another bank is just too complicated. Other factors often prevent us from taking the course of action we had originally planned.

Cognition
Thought processes: the element of attitude derived from conscious thought or knowledge

Affect
The emotional element of attitude

Conation
The behavioural intentions that arise from attitudes

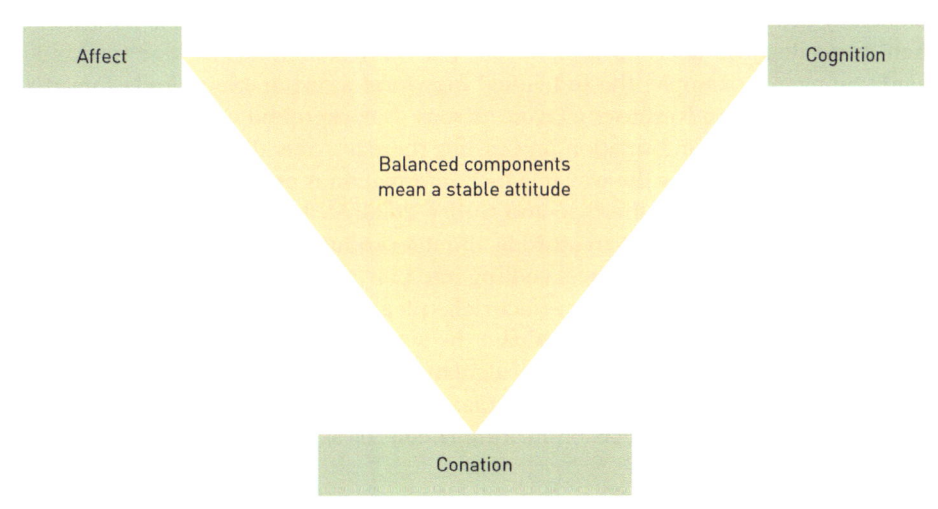

FIGURE 9.1 Dimensions of attitude

(Affect — Cognition — Conation: Balanced components mean a stable attitude)

TABLE 9.2 Dimensions of attitude

Dimension	Definition	Explanation	Example
Cognition	The perceptual component of attitude	This is the individual's awareness, knowledge, beliefs and images of the attitudinal object. It is the conscious, thinking part of attitude	An individual's attitude towards a car may be composed of comparative information, e.g. the Toyota Prius is cheaper to buy and run than the Volkswagen Golf, but the Golf holds its value better. These are the facts (or beliefs) informing the attitude
Affect	The evaluative component of attitude	These are the emotions, the feelings of like and dislike which do not always have a basis in objective fact	Drivers frequently have affective relationships with their first cars. The car is given a name, and often the driver will speak to it
Conation	Behavioural intention	Conation is about what we intend to do about the attitudinal object: whether to approach it, reject it, buy it, etc. It is not the actual behaviour, merely an intention	Having formed an attitude about a car ('I love the bodywork, it really looks great, and it does 45 to the gallon as well'), the consumer forms an intention ('I'm going to take out a loan and buy one'). This intention is the conation

The three elements are interrelated in a complex way. Purchase intentions relate to beliefs and brand evaluations, and likelihood of buying a brand has been shown to be influenced by attitudes towards advertising as well as attitudes towards brands (Homer and Yoon, 1992; Mohan et al., 2018; Safeer et al., 2021).

The traditional view of attitude is that affect towards an object is mediated by cognition; in other words, emotional responses about something are controlled to a marked extent by rational evaluation. This was challenged by Zajonc and Markus (1985), who assert that affective responses do not have to be based on prior cognition. There are individual differences in affective, cognitive and neural responses to interpersonal and social motivation (Stavrou, 2022) and people can develop a 'gut feel' about something without conscious evaluation (as can be the case with decision-making for luxury products [Bowen and Bowen, 2018]), and even on limited information, then rationalise the decision afterwards. This may sometimes be due to classical conditioning; for example, the individual may form a favourable attitude towards a product because the advert uses a favourite song as background music (see Chapter 8). Affect also influences information processing: there is a 'meddling-in' effect in which cognition is influenced by the way in which information is processed, which is in turn influenced by emotions (Albertson and Guiler, 2020; Mishra et al., 2006; Schmeichel et al., 2018). In fact, forming an attitude about a product might start with any of the three components, with the others coming into play afterwards. Also, if the outcome of any action is expected to be affect-rich (pleasurable, unpleasant, emotionally moving, etc.) the individual will evaluate the action by its effect on feelings. Affect-poor outcomes trigger evaluation by calculation (Hsee and Rottenstreich, 2002). In other words, putting a strong emotional bias into marketing communications is likely to lead to emotion-based decision-making (Kemp et al., 2020; McClain et al., 2022; Peplak et al., 2017).

Although it may seem illogical or dangerous to form an attitude without first finding out a lot about the attitudinal object, most people are familiar with the feeling of having 'fallen in love' with a hopelessly impractical purchase. Likewise, most people are familiar with the feeling of having taken an instant dislike to somebody without first getting to know the person. This is illustrated in Figure 9.2.

Affect: Falling in love with the product ⟷ Cognition: Learning about the product

Conation: Trying out the product

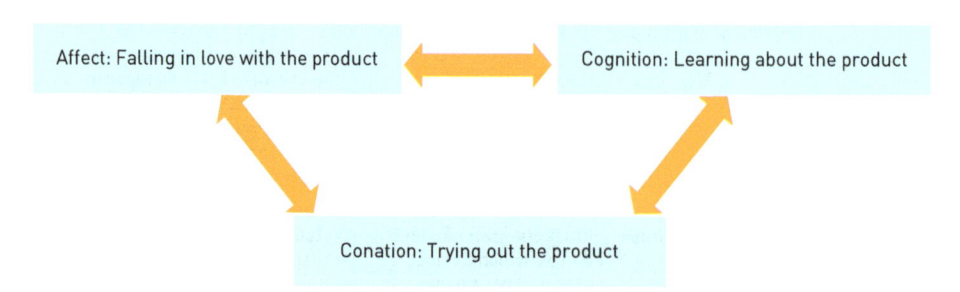

FIGURE 9.2 Starting points for attitude formation

Attitude contains components of belief and opinion, but it is neither. Attitude differs from *belief* in that belief is neutral, not implying good or bad. Belief is concerned with the presence or absence of an attribute, and is usually based on a judgement of the available evidence. Attitude contains an element of affect, and evaluates whether the existence of an attribute will result in satisfaction or dissatisfaction. For example, a consumer might believe that a Tesla is an eco-friendly, reliable and well-engineered car but have no particular feelings about this either way. Conversely, another consumer might feel that the Tesla is an excellent and desirable car, precisely because it is eco-friendly, reliable and well-engineered.

Attitude differs from *opinion* in that opinion is an overt, vocalised expression of an attitude. Attitude can also be expressed non-verbally (facial expressions, body language, etc.), or indeed may not be expressed at all. While opinions may arise from attitudes (i.e. be expressed as the result of an attitude) and attitudes may arise from hearing the opinions of others, the two are in fact separate entities.

ATTITUDE FORMATION

A more complete model of the formation of attitudes about brands shows that it is a somewhat complex process. Figure 9.3 gives an overview of the complete process. The diagram begins with the consumer's needs, both utilitarian (practical) and expressive (emotional). This feeds into the consumer's motivation to process information, as does advertising; motivation and exposure feed into the processing, but the consumer also needs to have the ability and the opportunity to process the information.

Within the processing 'black box' the consumer's level of processing is affected by attention and capacity for processing; in other words, by the degree of interest the consumer has, and his or her ability to process the information. The result of the processing is both cognitive and affective, feeding into the formation of attitudes about the brand.

Situational variables surrounding the brand or product will also affect the attitude formation process. For example, an unpleasant salesperson or an inconveniently located outlet may affect the way we perceive brands. Exposure to advertising stimuli plays a major part in encouraging learning and the formation of attitudes, but the main drive comes (as always) from the consumer's needs (Berger and Mitchell, 1989). Pre-existing attitudes may colour the formation of attitudes about a particular situation. Researchers have found that people can be categorised according to their attitudes about Christmas, Navroz, Diwali and Eid, for example; these attitudes are themselves formed by attitudes about religion, about gift-giving and about commercial influences (Choudhury, 2019; Gurau and Tinson, 2003). Likewise, people who are materialistic will get into debt to fund their purchases even if their incomes are very low (Ponchio and Aranha, 2008; Rocha, 2021), and this is especially true when looking at the impact of social media intensity and materialism (Pellegrino et al., 2022; Thoumrungroje, 2018).

Consumers acquire **salient beliefs** about products. Because the cognitive system can only hold a relatively small number of facts in the mind at once, the salient beliefs are the ones that are used by the consumer to make a judgement. Usually the salient beliefs will be those that the consumer holds to be most important, but they may be merely the ones that have been most recently presented (Fishbein and Ajzen, 1975; Youn et al., 2021).

Salient belief
A belief that is key in the formation of an attitude

A consumer's overall attitude towards an object is a function of many attributes of the object. The attitude forms as a result of the consumer's strength of feeling, or the strength of the salient beliefs, about the attributes and also the evaluation of those beliefs. Table 9.3 shows an example of a belief set about a restaurant. The question marks represent areas where the consumer has no knowledge, or has the knowledge but is not taking it into consideration. In other words, only the salient beliefs are taken into account.

This *multi-attribute attitude model* attempts to explain how the consumer's salient beliefs help to form the final attitude. The attributes listed are integrated to form an overall attitude; in this example, the consumer will form an attitude about the restaurant as to whether it is a good restaurant or a bad one. The attitude may be qualified in some way: the restaurant may be regarded as a good one for vegans, but a bad one for carnivores, or perhaps as a good one for a quick meal when one doesn't feel like cooking, but a bad one for special occasions.

Attitude formation is clearly affected by context: conation in particular may be affected by the feasibility of carrying out a particular behaviour, or the need to modify it to take account of what is happening around the individual (Bless et al., 2002).

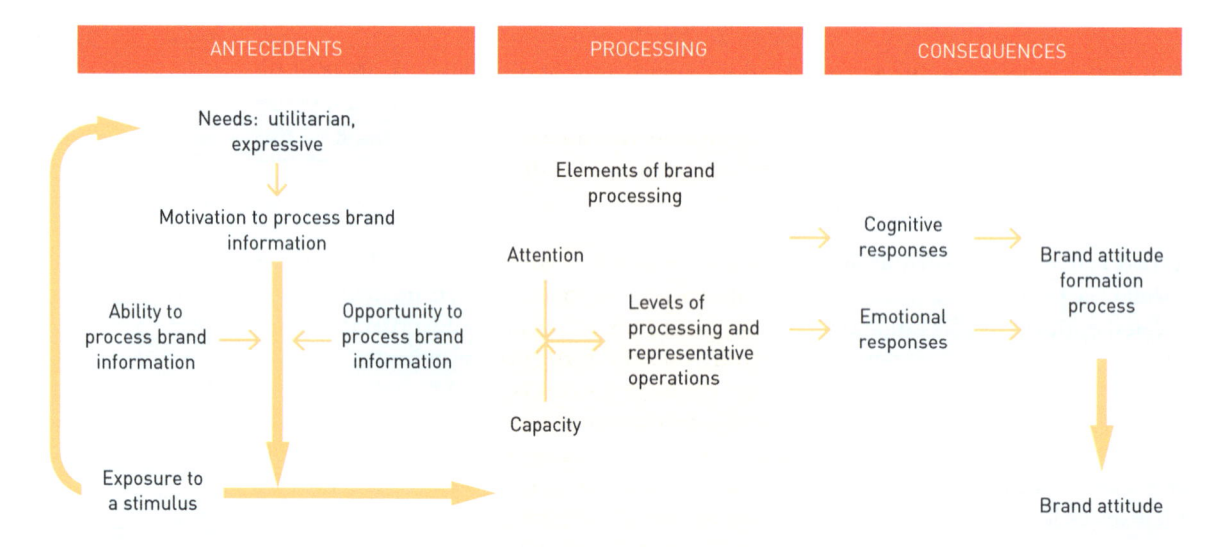

FIGURE 9.3 Attitude formation

Source: McInnis and Jaworski (1989). Reprinted with permission from *Journal of Marketing*, published by the American Marketing Association.

TABLE 9.3 Example of a belief set

Attribute	Strength of salient belief (out of 10)	Level of importance (out of 10)
Convenient parking	5	7
Good food	6	8
Friendly waiters	?	4

Attribute	Strength of salient belief (out of 10)	Level of importance (out of 10)
Availability of vegan food	8	10
Keto friendly	?	8
Pleasant decor	7	5
Clean cutlery	3	7
Reasonable prices	?	3
Open on Wednesday	?	5

ATTITUDE MEASUREMENT

Measuring attitudes is clearly a subject of some interest to marketers, since attitudes play such a major role in consumer purchasing behaviour. It is obviously of importance for manufacturers to know what the consumer's attitude is to the product, but it is difficult to quantify. This is because attitude contains elements of both cognition and affect. Here are two contrasting models for attitude measurement: the Rosenberg model and the Fishbein model.

The *Rosenberg model* (Rosenberg, 1960) says that an individual's attitude towards an object represents the degree and direction of the attitudinal effect aroused by the object. Put more simply, attitude is composed of a *quantity* of feeling and a *direction*, and has two main components:

1. **Perceived instrumentality**. This is the subjective capacity of the object to attain the value in question, in other words the usefulness of the object.
2. **Value importance**. This is the amount of satisfaction the person derives from the attainment of a particular value. More simply, this is the importance of achieving the result that the consumer is hoping to achieve by buying and using the object of the attitude.

Perceived instrumentality means the degree to which the person believes that the product will work as it is supposed to. Value importance is the degree to which getting the job done is important to the consumer.

Theoretically, perceived instrumentality and value importance are actually independent, and taken separately they don't predict responses well, but taken together they are good predictors of behaviour that is illustrative of attitude.

The *Fishbein model* (Fishbein, 1980) takes a different perspective on the problem by focusing on the consumer rather than on the product. For Fishbein, attitudes can be predicted from beliefs and evaluation. Belief is the probability that the object possesses a particular attribute; evaluation is whether that attribute attracts or repels. This is not compatible with the value importance concept in the Rosenberg model.

In this model, the consumer's belief in the product's capabilities replaces the perceived instrumentality aspect. For example, it may be useful for a car to have a large boot (Rosenberg model), but whether a particular car's boot is large or not is a relative term and relies on the consumer's beliefs (Fishbein model). Furthermore, the belief

Perceived instrumentality
The degree to which an action or product is thought to be useful in a practical way

Value importance
The level of satisfaction the individual gains from the achievement of a particular value

that a car's boot is large does not necessarily mean that the prospective owner will like that attribute (Fishbein model). This will depend on how important the attribute is to the customer (Rosenberg model).

Combining the two models, there are three distinct aspects of the importance of attitude:

1. Perceived instrumentality.
2. Evaluative aspect (affect).
3. Value importance.

These are illustrated in Figure 9.4. Examples of these aspects are as follows:

1. I believe the Range Rover Autobiography is the most comfortable car in its class.
2. I like comfort and speed.
3. Comfort and speed are very important to me.

Note that the second two are not identical. Someone can like something without it being very important to him or her.

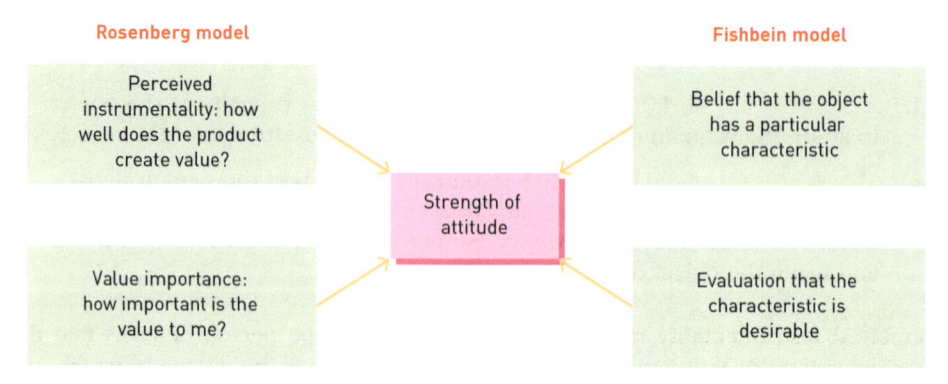

FIGURE 9.4 Strength of attitudes

FUNCTIONS OF ATTITUDES

Attitudes have a function in helping consumers make decisions about their purchasing practices, and also serve other functions according to the individual's circumstances. Four main categories of function have been identified, as shown in Table 9.4 (Locander and Spivey, 1978).

These functions of attitude may not all be present at the same time: a given attitude may only serve one or two of these functions, while still being valuable. The relationship between them is illustrated in Figure 9.5. In some cases, the **ego-defensive function** and the **value-expressive function** might conflict with each other. If the individual has beliefs that go against the majority, the ego-expressive function may not protect the person from attacks by others. Equally, having attitudes that accord with those of other people may conform well with the ego-defensive function.

Ego-defensive function
The function of attitude which enables the individual to maintain stability of the conscious self

Value-expressive function
The factor in group behaviour that allows the members to display their own beliefs and attitudes

ATTITUDE FORMATION AND CHANGE

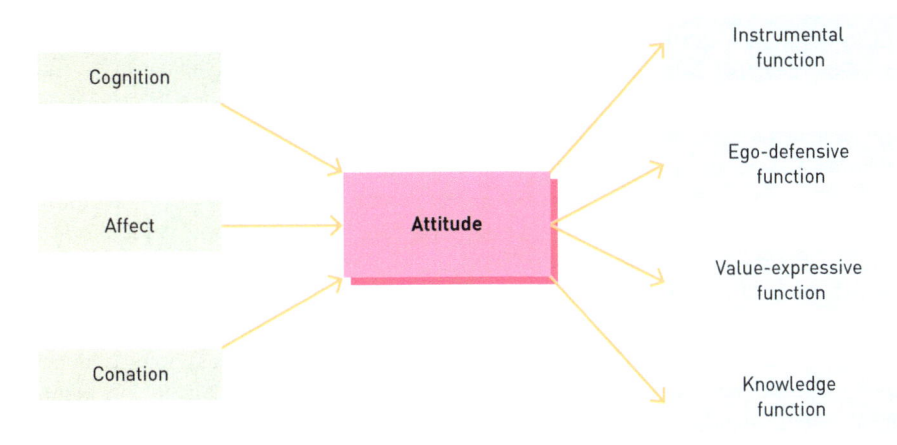

FIGURE 9.5 Functions of attitudes

TABLE 9.4 Functions of attitudes

Function	Definition	Explanation	Example
Instrumental function	The individual uses the attitude to obtain satisfaction from the object	The individual thus aims to maximise external reward while minimising external punishment	An individual might develop an attitude towards a particular cycling club because his or her friends are members and the facilities are good
Ego-defensive function	Protects against internal conflicts and external dangers	Here the attitude shields the individual from his or her own failings	Someone who is unable to understand how to use the product might have the attitude that manufacturers make products too complex
Value-expressive function	Opposite of ego-defensive; the drive for self-expression	The attitudes expressed often go against the flow of opinion	Most radical political viewpoints are examples of the value-expressive attitude in action
Knowledge function	The drive to seek clarity and order	Related to the need to understand what the object is all about. Comes from the belief that if you know what you like and dislike, decision-making is easy	Somebody who has an interest in audio-visual systems is likely to visit websites about them, to go to exhibitions, to engage in online forums and to discuss them with friends so as to know what the latest products are

BRAND EXPERIENCES: FROM SONG TO SCREEN

Assume that you're an agent working with pop stars in the UK. Would you be tempted to suggest that your client makes a movie? After all, other agents have suggested it to their clients – One Direction, Katy Perry and Justin Bieber have all had this suggestion made.

(Continued)

This is often a quick way to leverage a star's fame to generate earnings from box-office receipts – and in most cases the stars sing in the movie, which generates record sales. In some cases it works fine – The Beatles made *Hard Day's Night* and *Help!*, which were considerable successes, but went on to make *Magical Mystery Tour* and *Yellow Submarine*, both of which virtually disappeared without trace. Later outings by the individual band members were equally poorly received: John Lennon's films (with Yoko Ono) scarcely saw the light of day, and Paul McCartney's *Give My Regards to Broad Street* sank like a stone. The greatest success has probably been Ringo Starr's voice-overs for *Thomas the Tank Engine*. Madonna, The Spice Girls, Britney Spears and Mariah Carey have all made films that have been listed among the Top Ten Worst Films of All Time. Newsday said of Madonna's *Swept Away*: 'New ways of describing badness need to be invented to describe exactly how bad this movie is.' The biopic *Amy* (about Amy Winehouse) has, by all accounts, been a sad disappointment, although Lady Gaga did very well at the box office with *A Star is Born* in 2018. *Bohemian Rhapsody* – a foot-stomping celebration of Queen, their music and their extraordinary Zarathustrian lead singer Freddie Mercury – opened in cinemas in late 2018 and within 3 weeks had reached global box office sales of nearly $400 million. In total it has amassed revenues of over $910 million against a production budget of about $52 million.

So why does this happen? No doubt these people are talented individuals, capable of holding an audience's attention and capable of performing a role. They already have a substantial fan base, most of whom are likely to go to see the movie. They have good, capable managers, and they already know the entertainment business.

Is it, perhaps, that we have already developed an attitude towards these stars as singers and musicians, and find it hard to relate to them when they are playing a part? The Beatles' two successful movies both showed them purely as a band, to some extent mocking their own success and image, whereas the flops showed them acting a part. Fans want to see their idol, not someone who looks like the idol but is actually supposed to be somebody else! The willing suspension of disbelief is essential for enjoying a night at the cinema, and somehow this is damaged if one is unable to believe in the lead character. Rami Malek had his work cut out with emulating Freddie Mercury but did incredibly well in helping to develop a believable attitude.

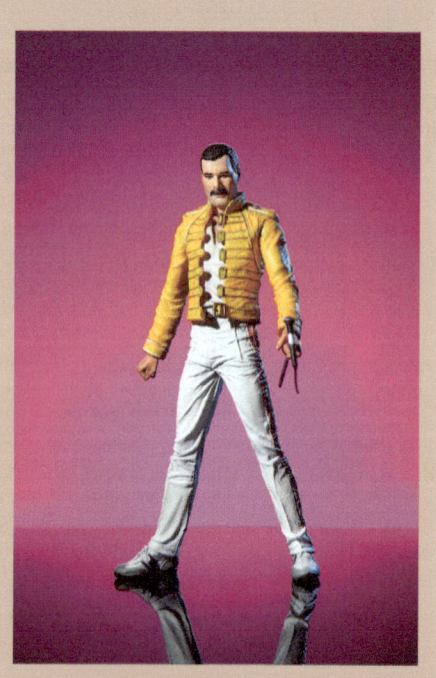

© iStock.com/muratkoc

ATTITUDE AND BEHAVIOUR

The *theory of reasoned action* (Ajzen and Fishbein, 1980) says that consumers consciously evaluate the consequences of alternative behaviours, and then choose the one that will lead to the most favourable consequences. Figure 9.6 shows the four main components of the theory – behaviour, intention to behave, attitude towards the behaviour and subjective norm. The subjective norm is the component that reflects the social pressures the individual may feel to perform (or avoid performing) the behaviour being contemplated.

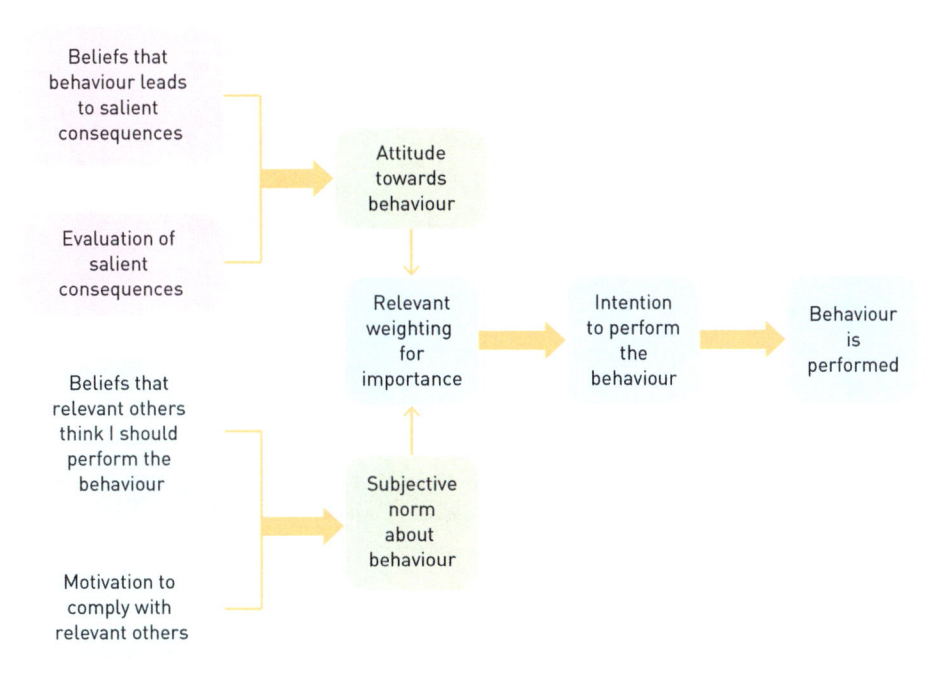

FIGURE 9.6 The theory of reasoned action
Source: Fishbein (1980). Reprinted with permission from the American Marketing Association.

The individual's beliefs about the behaviour and the evaluation of the possible main consequences will combine to produce an attitude about the behaviour. At the same time, the individual's beliefs about what other people might think, and the degree to which he or she cares about what other people think, go towards developing a subjective norm about the contemplated behaviour. The individual will then weigh the relative importance of the attitude and the norm, and will form an intention of how to behave. This may, in turn, lead to the behaviour itself.

The theory of reasoned action assumes that consumers perform a logical evaluation procedure for making decisions about behaviour, based on attitude towards the behaviour, which in turn derives from attitudes towards the product or brand.

Logically, attitude should precede behaviour. In other words, we would expect that someone would form an attitude about something, then act on that attitude. In fact, much of the evidence points the other way. It appears in some cases that people behave first, and form attitudes afterwards (Fishbein, 1972).

An extension of the theory of reasoned action is the theory of planned behaviour, shown in Figure 9.7 (Ajzen, 1988; Ajzen and Madden, 1986). Planned behaviour assumes that the individual also takes account of the ease or difficulty of performing the planned behaviour, in other words the degree of control the individual has over the behaviour and its outcomes. This depends in part on past experience, and in part on the anticipation of future obstacles.

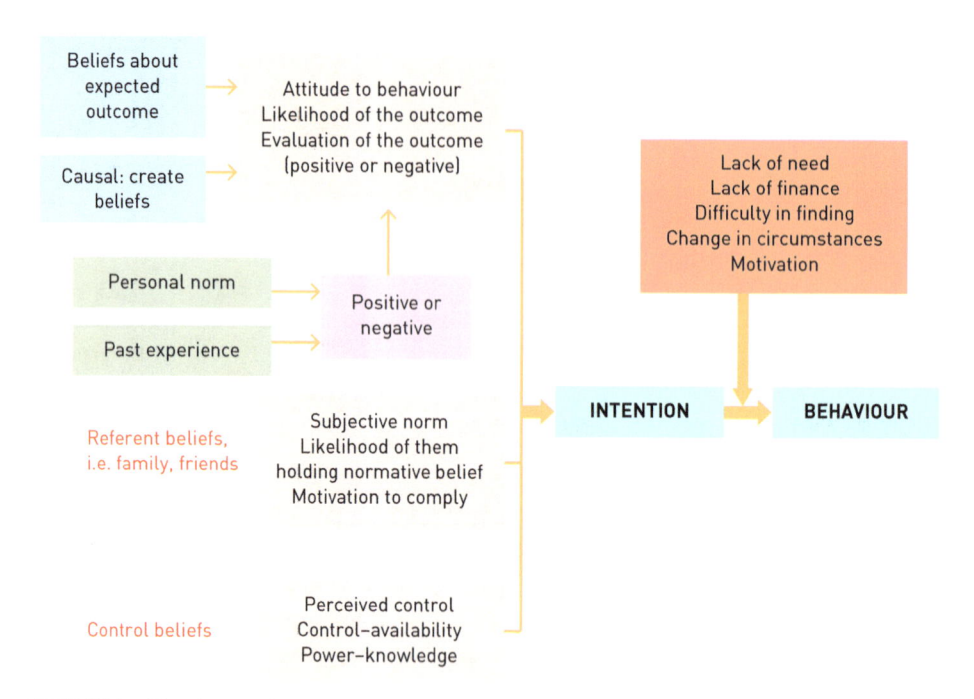

FIGURE 9.7 The theory of planned behaviour

Essentially, the model attempts to predict behaviour based on conation (intent to commit the behaviour). The overall attitude towards the behaviour is predicted by the salient beliefs about the behaviour and its possible outcomes, and the subjective norm is determined by the individual's beliefs about what salient others (friends and family) would think about the behaviour, coupled with the level of motivation to comply with the views of others. For example, it appears that women and men have very different attitudes towards genetically modified (GM) foods: women tend to distrust the science (a conative factor) and also tend to have ethical views about GM (an affective factor). In fact, religion, scientific background, education, age, gender and environmental values all impact upon attitudes towards GM foods (Castéra et al., 2018; Hudson et al., 2015; Martin-Collado et al., 2022).

Marketing efforts often encourage people to try (experience) products first, then form attitudes; free samples, test drives, demonstrations and coupons are all more powerful in forming attitude and behaviour consistency than are advertisements (Hilken et al., 2022; Levy and Gendel Guterman, 2021; Smith and Swinyard, 1983). Attitudes formed without trial experience are probably weak and easily changed. In this context, the classic Pepsi Challenge represents a way of persuading people that Pepsi is better than Coca-Cola. Each summer stands are set up in shopping malls and at seaside resorts and passers-by are offered the chance to compare Pepsi with

Coke in a blind taste test. Part of the reason for this is that the two drinks do, in fact, taste very similar, and without the visual cue of the packaging the consumers often cannot tell the difference between the two. Since Pepsi has a smaller market share than Coke, the company only needs half of the respondents to prefer the Pepsi in order to gain a greater market share than it currently holds. In fact, there is a slight preference for Pepsi, since around 65% of people state that they prefer it in blind taste tests, often to their surprise.

Trial of a product is so much more powerful than advertising in forming favourable impressions that car manufacturers are prepared to give special deals to car rental companies and driving schools in the hope that hirers and learners will buy the same model at a later date.

It may not matter greatly whether attitude precedes behaviour or not. Attitude is not always followed by the proposed behaviour; most people are familiar with having proposed doing something, then doing something else instead. This may be because attitude and behaviour are not always consistent. For example, a smoker may take the attitude that smoking is unhealthy and antisocial, but may still not give up smoking an e-cigarette. Dieting is a similar example: even though an overweight person may believe that being fat is unhealthy and unattractive, losing weight may not be the end result. Many other examples abound; in Freudian terms, the attitude may have come from the superego, but the demands of the id result in a failure to act (see Chapter 6).

In fact, it seems more likely that, at least regarding fast-moving consumer goods (FMCG), the process of attitude formation and behaviour are interwoven. Figure 9.8 illustrates this. In this model there is a feedback loop that allows the consumer to re-evaluate and reconsider his or her attitudes. The formation of attitude is thus seen as a dynamic process, with the behaviour itself forming part of the process.

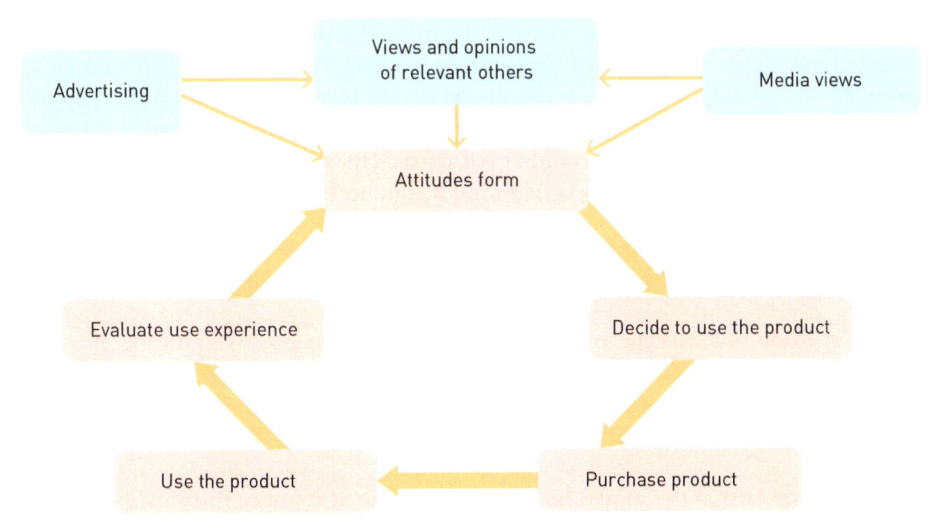

FIGURE 9.8 The cycle of attitude and behaviour

THE DUALITY OF PRIVATE VS. PUBLIC ATTITUDES

Often people hold attitudes that they are reluctant to admit to in public. This is particularly true in recent years due to an increase in the requirement to be **politically correct** (PC). This makes attitude measurement difficult because respondents will give a rational or acceptable answer rather than a true one. Few people would be prepared to admit openly that they have racist, sexist or ageist attitudes, for example, yet it is undoubtedly the case that many people harbour such attitudes.

In marketing terms, people are often reluctant to admit to buying products that are embarrassing (or illegal). Many people would be reluctant to admit, for instance, that they enjoy pornography, and therefore it is easier to sell such products over the internet than it is to sell them through retail outlets. The internet, at least for the moment, preserves the anonymity of the customer (Arca and Hewett, 2021; article19.org, 2015; Simioni et al., 2021).

Clearly there are implications for market research, since any questions that enquire into these attitudes are likely to meet with evasive answers or just plain lies. Most people will have some private attitudes and some opposing public attitudes, and therefore measurement of these private attitudes can best be carried out by using projective techniques such as sentence completion or cartoon tests. These research techniques were discussed in Chapter 6.

Often people's private attitudes do not have a logical basis and are very subjective; thus the individuals concerned are even more reluctant to admit to holding those views. Sometimes there is a reluctance to express an opinion when it has no logical basis. Attitude, as we have seen, has a strong affective component.

ATTITUDE VS. SITUATION

During the 1930s, in a hotel in the South of France, a strange ceremony was acted out daily. One of the Romanoff princes (from the Russian royal family) would ask his chauffeur to mash up a plate of strawberries and then eat them. This ceremony took place every day, even when the strawberries had to be specially flown in for the purpose. The reason was that the prince loved the smell of strawberries, but was allergic to them and therefore couldn't eat them. His attitude towards the 'product' therefore could not result in his consuming it, due to his medical situation.

In Figure 9.9, the thwarted conation feeds back information to the cognition element of attitude, which may cause a slight shift in the attitude itself.

Positive attitude towards the product may not equate to positive attitude about the *purchase* of the product. A consumer may have a strong positive attitude towards light-coloured clothes, but not buy them because she works in the city and light-coloured clothes show the dirt.

Fishbein suggests that the model be modified to take account of this (Fishbein, 1972). The attitude to be measured should, under the extended model, be the attitude towards performing a given act (e.g. purchase or consumption) rather than an attitude towards the object itself. The evidence is that this model is a better predictor of

Political correctness

Commonly abbreviated to PC, it is an ordinarily pejorative term used to criticise language, actions or policies seen as being excessively calculated not to offend or disadvantage any particular group of people in society

purchasing behaviour than merely measuring attitudes towards the brands themselves, but of course there is greater complexity involved in understanding why a consumer has a particular attitude, since more variables are involved.

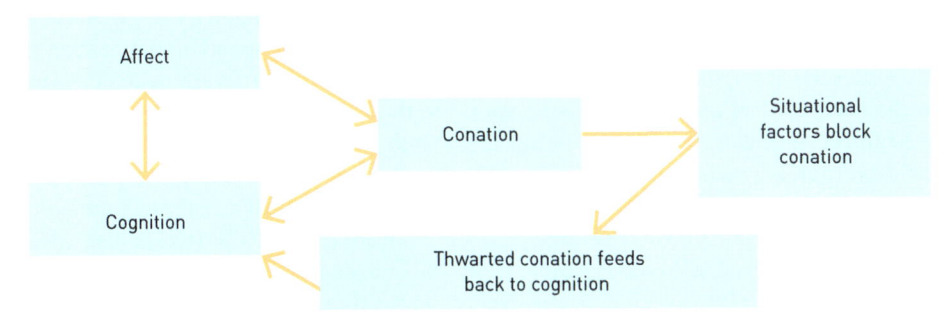

FIGURE 9.9 Effect of situation on attitude

CRITICAL REFLECTION

Presumably if one had an attitude that was permanently thwarted by one's situation, the attitude would have to change. For example, most of us have academic subjects we dislike – many people do not enjoy maths, for example. Yet we often have to study something we dislike in order to be given a particular qualification, or as the precursor to studying something we do like.

Does this ever make us like the actual subject or is it that we simply like the outcome? How can we maintain an attitude in the face of its unpleasant aspects?

Attitudes can be changed due to situational changes. For example, following the Covid-19 pandemic and numerous job losses (i.e. a sudden drop in disposable income) people had to rethink whether, for example, that subscription to Sky TV was too expensive and thus a luxury, even if it was seen as good value for money previously. Intentions can be checked against later performance by means of garbage analysis or self-report: Cote, McCullough and Reilly found that 'behaviour-intention inconsistency is partly attributable to unexpected situations' (Cote et al., 1985).

ATTITUDE TOWARDS ADVERTS VS. ATTITUDE TOWARDS THE BRAND

An individual may love the ads and hate the product, or vice versa. Although there is an assumption that a positive attitude towards the advertisement will lead to a positive attitude about the product, the two are actually separate hypothetical constructs (Mitchell, 1986).

This is because the attitude towards the brand is affected by many more factors than the advertisement, whereas attitude towards the advertisement is only affected by the ad itself. The perception of the brand is much more likely to have a major cognitive element in it, whereas most advertising is intended to produce an affective response.

Early evidence suggested that liking the advertisement relates to whether the product is meaningful and relevant to the consumer at the time (Biel, 1990). This has been corroborated by Zhu and Chen (2015). They note that even though in 2013 over $5 billion were spent by US companies on social media advertising, a Gallup survey has said that those advertisements had no influence on the majority of consumers' buying decisions. Zhu and Chen (2015) further argue that for social media marketing to be effective it needs to be congruent and aligned with the different needs of social media users. Social media advertising spend in the United States currently stands at $63 billion, so clearly needs are being met. There is also some evidence that food and beverage advertisements are more likeable than non-food advertisements (Biel and Bridgwater, 1990; Gauthier et al., 2020). Liking the advertisement will tend to spill over into liking the product, and the combination of the two is also likely to lead to an increase in sales (Biel, 1990; Kidd and Loxton, 2018; Stapel, 1991). This situation can be reversed in the case of some financial services products (e.g. insurance) because the advertising is often of the 'cautionary tale' type in which the advertisement shows what can go wrong if the individual does not buy the insurance. This naturally means that the advertisement is unpleasant and worrying (Shafer et al., 2018). Of course at the other end of the spectrum we see that if there is repeated consumption of both products and experiences, this may well lead to a reduction in enjoyment over time. This is commonly referred to as 'satiation'. Where this happens, we are likely to see a production of dissonance in consumers (Dootson et al., 2018; Palcu et al., 2019), especially those with an active identity. This is so because the reduced enjoyment with identity-consistent products conflicts with their identity (Chugani et al., 2015; Coleman et al., 2020).

Perhaps not surprisingly, people who have a high need to justify their decisions rationally (that is, people with a high need for cognition) are less likely to be swayed by their liking for the advertisement. People with a low need for cognition tend to like products that are advertised in a likeable way (Raziq et al., 2018; Reinhard and Messner, 2009).

Other factors in creating an attitude might include the way the message is framed – emphasising the cost of a better product rather than its higher quality may result in a poorer perception of the product and a lower propensity to buy it (Gamliel, 2010). This may be because people experience losses more intensely than they experience gains of the same magnitude (Kahneman and Tversky, 1979).

GENERAL VS. SPECIFIC ATTITUDES

It is necessary to look at specific attitudes when attempting to predict behaviour. It is possible to hold one attitude generally, but an opposing attitude in a specific case; for example, it is possible to dislike children while still loving one's own children, or to like wine in general but dislike Pinot Grigio. For marketers, the important attitude to measure is, of course, the attitude to the specific *brand* rather than the attitude to the product class as a whole (Filieri et al., 2021).

Having said that, there is an issue regarding brand switching (Roy et al., 2022). If a consumer has a generally negative attitude about a product class, but will use a specific brand within that class, it may be possible to switch the consumer towards another brand similar to the one that is already acceptable (Ajiwinanto et al., 2021). Consumers may already be prepared to do this in the event that the desired brand is out of stock, as has recently been the case with technology products (Hanifati and Salehudin, 2021); the difficulty lies in knowing why the individual consumer has made the decision to keep to only one brand of a class of products which he or she dislikes.

CHANGING ATTITUDES

Attitudes derive from consumer need, and from beliefs. People select salient beliefs (the beliefs that are most relevant to their individual needs) and build attitudes towards products based around those beliefs, for example towards female genital mutilation; a social norm embedded in the patriarchal system (Agboli et al., 2022). Superstitious beliefs have been shown to affect attitudes towards novelty-seeking (Afshani and Sheikhalishahi, 2021; Hernandez et al., 2008), especially with consumers in many parts of the world who eat insects – about 2000 species of insects are known to be consumed by different ethnic groups (Chow et al., 2021; Ghosh et al., 2018; Nyberg et al., 2021).

The model is useful to marketers in that it helps when devising strategies for changing consumer attitudes. There are four ways of changing attitudes, as follows:

1. *Add a new salient belief.* For example, a restaurant might point out that it offers music played by a jazz pianist on Saturday nights. This would be a new fact for the consumer to take into account.

2. *Change the strength of a salient belief.* If the belief is a negative one, it can be discounted or played down; if it's a positive one, it can be given greater importance. If a customer has a low level of belief in the cleanliness of the cutlery in a particular restaurant, but a high evaluation of this attribute, then the restaurant needs to address this point specifically in its promotional messages. The restaurant might, for example, make a point of telling customers that the cutlery is specially checked before it reaches the table. In some Chinese restaurants, chopsticks are delivered to the table in paper sleeves: although the chopsticks have been used many times, putting the sleeves on after they have been washed reassures the customers.

3. *Change the evaluation of an existing belief.* A customer may have a low evaluation of the prices in a restaurant, perhaps being more concerned about enjoying a romantic evening than about getting a cheap meal. The restaurant could increase the evaluation of this attribute by pointing out that the low prices mean that the customer can come more often (although this could result in an attitude that it's not as special), or treat friends to a meal without breaking the bank.

4. *Make an existing belief more salient.* A restaurant customer might not regard friendliness of the waiters as a salient attribute. The restaurant could therefore emphasise that it makes a big difference to the enjoyment of the evening if the waiters are pleasant.

Using a contrasting example, a Chinese restaurant in Wardour Street, London, called Wong Kei, was once famous for the rudeness of its staff, and had acquired the dubious accolade of being London's rudest restaurant. Restaurant-goers would be shouted at ('*Go upstairs!*' or '*Sit down there*') and the general communications were levied with quite some disdain. This, however, was actually seen as a salient attribute, almost an event and tourist destination in itself, since it contrasted so much with other restaurants, and was viewed as characterful. Thirty years later and attitudes have changed, even at Wong Kei's, with a renovation taking place in 2014 and the new owners dismissing the previous forms of 'differentiation' – as presumably, the joke was wearing thin by then.

If the three components of attitude (cognition, affect and conation) are in balance, it is difficult to change the attitude because the attitude becomes stabilised. For example, if somebody is becoming overweight, believes that this is a bad thing and therefore diets, the attitude is stable and would be difficult to change. If, on the other hand, the same person is overweight, believes that it is bad but just somehow never gets round to dieting, it is relatively easy to tempt the person to a snack or two. In the latter case, the attitude is inconsistent because the conation does not match with the affect and cognition. Changing a person's beliefs can be an effective route to attitude change (see Figure 9.10).

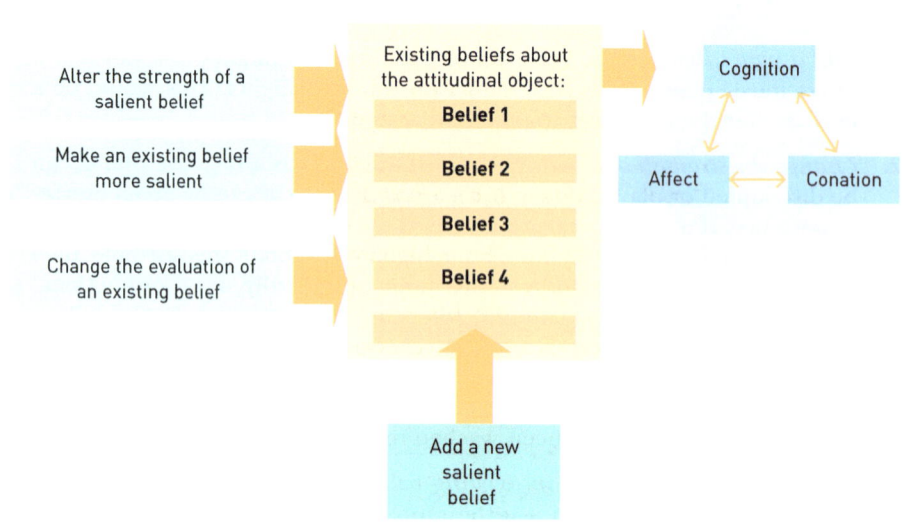

FIGURE 9.10 Changing beliefs

Inconsistency between the three components of attitude may come about when a new stimulus is presented. New information might affect the cognitive or conative aspects or a bad experience might change the affective aspects. When the degree of inconsistency between the three components exceeds a certain tolerance level, the individual will be compelled to undertake some kind of mental re-adjustment to restore stability (see Figure 9.11). This can come about through three main defence mechanisms:

1. Stimulus rejection.
2. Attitude splitting.
3. Accommodation to the new attitude.

ATTITUDE FORMATION AND CHANGE

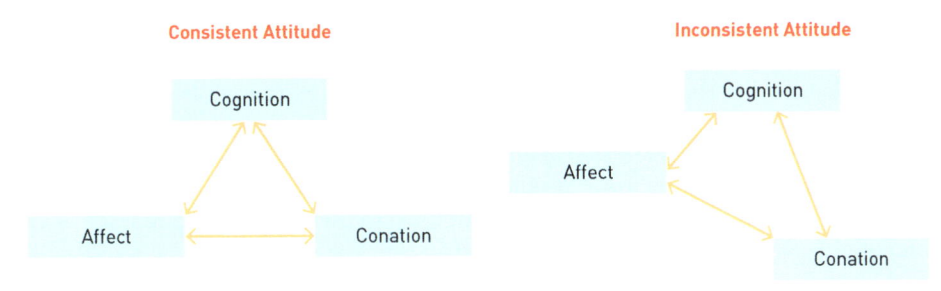

FIGURE 9.11 Consistent vs. inconsistent attitude

Stimulus rejection means that the individual discounts the new information (Marques et al., 2022). For example, an overweight person might reject advice that slim people live longer than overweight people, on the grounds that the research does not examine people who used to be fat but are now slim and have kept the weight off. By rejecting the new information, the individual is able to maintain the status quo as regards the cognitive element of attitude. Sometimes stimuli are rejected simply because they come from a marketing source – there is evidence that consumers remember products that have been placed in movies and TV shows, but will often reject them because of a feeling of being manipulated (Bhatnagar and Aksoy, 2004; Kivak, 2022). There is further evidence of this from the perspective of brand prominence on **advergamers'** brand recall (Chiu, 2019; Raimondo et al., 2022; Vashist, 2018). Likewise, teenagers tend to respond better to new media rather than to traditional mass media (Brennan et al., 2010).

> **Stimulus rejection**
> The process of protecting an attitude by ignoring information that conflicts with it
>
> **Advergaming**
> A method of interactive marketing in which free downloadable computer games appear on websites (often as pop-ups) to advertise a company or product

CONSUMER BEHAVIOUR IN ACTION: CONNECTED THAILAND

The majority of Thai people access the internet via mobile phones. Thailand's population of 69.24 million is divided into 51.3% women and 48.7% men. Half of the entire population lives in highly urbanised areas. There are 92.33 million active phone numbers in Thailand. This suggests that many people in the country use more than one number. Fifty-seven million people have internet access and a whopping 98% of users browse the internet on a mobile device. Fifty-one million people use social media and 71% use a smartphone accounting for that usage. Thai people spend an average of 9 hours a day online with the average Thai user spending about 3 hours and 11 minutes on social media daily. They also stream videos online for an average of 3 hours and 44 minutes a day. Interestingly, Google is ranked as the number one website that Thai users access daily. Facebook also reigns supreme on social media sites (93% active users), which is followed by YouTube (91%), LINE (84%) and Facebook Messenger (72%). In terms of advertising access on social media, Facebook is the leading platform with 50 million people, followed by Instagram with 13 million people, Twitter with 4.7 million people, and Snapchat with 555,000 people. Thai teen attitudes are certainly being changed by the internet superhighway.

People are generally much more marketing literate nowadays, and often know what marketers are trying to do as well as understanding how they intend to do it – marketers would do well to remember this.

Attitude splitting
The process of protecting an attitude by accepting only part of a new piece of information that conflicts with the attitude

Accommodation to the new attitude
Accepting new information and using it to re-form an existing attitude

Attitude splitting involves only accepting that part of the information that does not cause an inconsistency. Here, the individual might accept that the new information is basically true, but that his or her own circumstances are exceptional. For example, if an individual finds out that the company he or she was planning to sue has gone bankrupt, this will alter the conative element of attitude since the anticipated returns from a bankrupt company are virtually nil. The individual might agree that this is *generally* the case, but decide that the circumstances to sue the directors of the company, personally, are favourable instead.

Accommodation to the new attitude means, in effect, changing the attitude to accommodate the new information. The person with a high body mass index may join a gym and start dieting, the smoker may cut down or give up altogether, the prospective litigant may just put it down to experience and cut their losses.

Whilst it was first noted back over 60 years ago, by Rosenberg (1960), that these three elements are so closely related to each other that a change in one element will usually cause a change in the others, it is still extremely valid today. New information causing a change in cognition will change the consumer's feelings about the product, which in turn is likely to change the consumer's intentions about the product.

Direct route
A route to attitude change which relies on reasoned argument: an appeal to cognition, in other words

Peripheral route
Using emotional appeals in order to change the affective component of attitude

Direct route: Works on knowledge of the object

Peripheral route: Works on feelings about the object

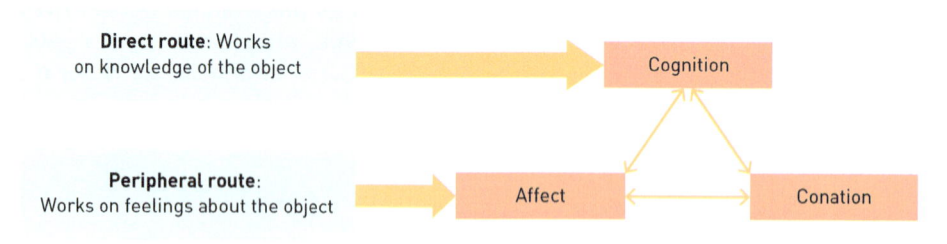

FIGURE 9.12   Peripheral and direct routes to attitude change

The *elaboration likelihood model* (Petty et al., 1983) describes two routes (see Figure 9.12) by which attitude might be changed. The **direct route** involves an appeal to the rational, cognitive element: the consumer makes a serious attempt to evaluate the new information in some logical way. The **peripheral route**, on the other hand, tends to involve the affective element by associating the product with another attitudinal object. For example, if a rock star appears in an ad for a soft drink this might cause the star's fans to change their attitudes towards the drink. This has nothing to do with the attributes of the drink, but everything to do with the attributes of the star.

BRAND EXPERIENCES: FROM SINGING TO SIPPING

Over the years there have been numerous rock stars who have turned their hand to taking part in commercials. David Bowie and Pepsi, The Rolling Stones and Kellogg's Rice Krispies cereal, The Beatles and Nike, Elton John and Sasson, Elton John and Cadbury, Bob Dylan and IBM, Ted Nugent and Energizer, The Who and Coca-Cola, Barry Manilow wrote jingles for McDonald's, Justin Timberlake and McDonald's, Led Zeppelin and Cadillac, Bon Jovi and DirecTV, Michael Jackson and Pepsi.

ATTITUDE FORMATION AND CHANGE

> There is of course a debate around whether this nurtures or neuters the rock star. The term 'rock star' itself comes with a lot of baggage. A rock star, in the traditional sense, was a free-spirited, convention-flouting artist/rebel/hero/Dionysian fertility god who fronted a world-famous band, sold millions of records and headlined stadium concerts where people were trampled in frenzies of cult-like fervour (Chocano, 2015). Yet in recent decades, the phrase has become a business buzzword to refer to any kind of virtuosity: you can be a rock star salesperson, marketer, programmer, chef and so on. Chocano noted that pretty much anyone can be a rock star these days – except actual rock stars, who are encouraged to think of themselves as brands!
>
> What do you think?

Peripheral cues such as this are not relevant to a reasoned evaluation, but because of the interdependence of the components of attitude, change will occur. In effect, the affect felt towards the star 'rubs off' on the product.

Changing existing attitudes relies heavily on market research, but in particular the teasing-out of the factors that make up the attitude can be a demanding task. This is because of the **halo effect** – the tendency for attitudes about one salient belief to colour attitudes about another. For example, if a diner had a bad meal at a restaurant, this is likely to lead to a view that everything else about the restaurant was bad, too. Likewise, a favourable view of some factors often leads to respondents reporting a favourable view of other factors.

Halo effect
The tendency for an individual to believe that every aspect of something is good, based on a belief that some aspects are good

CRITICAL REFLECTION

The halo effect is said to be the process by which attitudes about one aspect of a product (or person) tend to colour the whole perception of the product (or person). Apparently, if we think our new car is really comfortable and cosy, we will also think its fuel consumption is good.

How about the reverse case? If we think something is really bad – perhaps the car is unreliable – do we then think its performance is bad as well? Probably so, if the theory is correct. In that case, what happens if something is brought to our attention? If the rock star we loved and admired turns out to be a paedophile, do we stop liking the music? For instance, Kellogg dropped most decorated swimming Olympian Michael Phelps after a photo leaked of him inhaling from a marijuana pipe. The company insisted that Phelps' behaviour did not align with its views and announced that they would not renew his contract once it expired. After signing a contract with Swiss watchmaker Raymond Weil, actress Charlize Theron found herself in some serious watch drama when she violated the terms of her contract by wearing and being photographed in a Christian Dior watch, resulting in the company suing her for $20 million. In 2005, iconic British supermodel Kate Moss lost her modelling contracts with Burberry, Chanel and H&M, following her alleged involvement in a cocaine scandal (Kaulingfreks and Bos, 2007). Where does that leave the organisation that formerly used her in their advertising? (It's of course interesting to note that Burberry's attitude since changed, with Kate Moss having appeared in their 2015 Eau de Toilette campaigns – maybe organisations can also *suffer* from the halo effect of celebrities?)

Using the peripheral route to attitude change means working on the affective component of attitude. Research has shown that emotional appeals often work a great deal more effectively than do cognitive, logical appeals; emotional appeals (Andreu et al., 2015) also appear to have a greater effect on explicit memory, so people remember the advertisement better. Much depends on the group of individuals being studied. For example, studies have shown that campaigns to discourage smoking among teenagers work best on boys if they use emotional 'cosmetic' appeals (for example, telling boys that the smell of smoke on their clothing is repellent to girls), whereas long-term health appeals (a logical, cognitive approach) work better on teenage girls (Smith and Stutts, 2003). It has also been found that friendship support lowered the level of smoking among men but not women (Alcántara et al., 2015). Mood has an effect on the interpretation of information: people in a good mood tend to process and remember brands better (Bakamitsos and Siomkos, 2004; van Reijmersdal et al., 2015).

COGNITIVE DISSONANCE

Cognitive dissonance theory states that holding two competing cognitions leads to discomfort and an eventual readjustment (Festinger, 1957). The readjustment can take two forms: rejecting one or another of the competing cognitions, or introducing a third idea which resolves the conflict between the other two. Studies in neuroscience have used fMRI (functional magnetic resonance imaging) to prove that there is an association between dissonance and increased neural activation in key brain regions (Choi et al., 2022; de Vries et al., 2015; Ito et al., 2019; Janik et al., 2022).

The most interesting aspect of dissonance theory is that attitudes can apparently be changed more easily by offering a low reward than by offering a high reward. In a famous experiment conducted in the 1950s, researchers induced students to lie to other students about a task they were being recruited to undertake. The actual task was to place round pegs into holes, turn the pegs one-quarter turn, then remove the pegs. The students were told that this was a psychological experiment, and were then asked to recruit other students primarily by telling them how interesting and fun the task was. Since it would be difficult to imagine a more tedious task, these students obviously had to lie: the experimenters offered a recruitment reward, but some students were only offered $1 to lie, whereas others were offered $20 (a substantial sum of money in 1959). The students being paid the lower amount were found to actually believe the lie, whereas the higher-paid students simply told the lie as a lie without changing their own attitudes. The theory is that the higher-paid students justified lying on the basis that they were being well-paid for it, whereas the other students could not use this justification and therefore needed to find another reason for lying – in this case, they decided that what they were saying must be at least partly true (Festinger and Carlsmith, 1959).

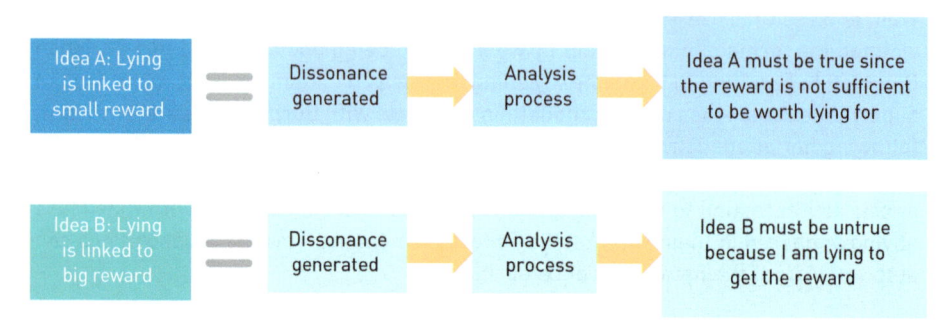

FIGURE 9.13 Cognitive dissonance

In Figure 9.13, the situation in which lying is linked to only a small reward leads to the attitude that the lie must be at least partly true, since the reward is not in itself sufficient to make lying worthwhile. In the second situation, the individual can justify lying on the basis that the reward is generous enough to justify not telling the truth, and therefore the lie remains a lie.

Cognitive dissonance is a powerful force in attitude change because the individual is, almost by definition, personally involved in the process. Reduction in dissonance always involves some kind of internal debate and (ultimately) some self-justification (Aronson et al., 1974; Vasquez et al., 2019). This happens because the individual tends to believe that the dissonance has arisen through an act or thought that is immoral or stupid. The most common manifestation of cognitive dissonance in consumer behaviour is post-purchase dissonance, in which someone who has just made an important purchase finds out that the product is not quite what was expected (see Figure 9.14).

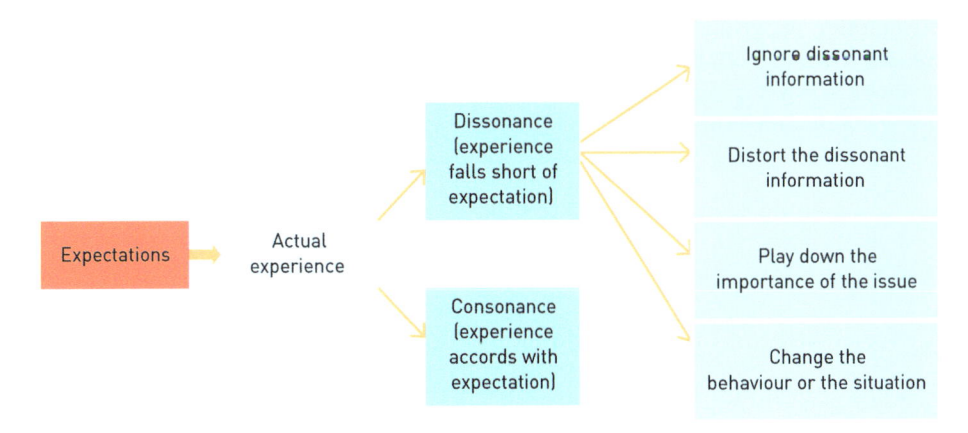

FIGURE 9.14 Post-purchase dissonance

In other words, the individual has been presented with new information that contradicts his or her pre-purchase expectations. In most cases, actual experience with the product conflicts with information obtained in the pre-purchase information search (Chakkambath et al., 2022). For example, someone buying a new flat-screen television set might have expected it to be wall-mountable, like a picture. On opening the packing, our new purchaser finds that the wall-mounting bracket makes the TV stand out 6 inches from the wall, and that this is a necessary factor because of the wiring, controls and air vents at the back of the set. At this point, the buyer has four basic choices:

1. Ignore the dissonant information and look for positive (consonant) information about the product. In the case of the TV, the buyer might just accept that the TV will stick out from the wall a bit and will instead admire the quality of the picture, the excellent soundbar, the online connectivity and so forth.
2. Distort the dissonant information. In this case our buyer might convince himself or herself that the TV really does not stand away from the wall too much after all. With some careful lighting, no one will notice.

3. Play down the importance of the issue. Here the buyer simply says that the distance from the wall is really not that important anyway.
4. Change the behaviour or the situation. Our TV buyer might take the TV back to the shop and ask for a refund, or might decide to put the TV on a table instead, and buy a picture for the wall.

For marketers, reducing or minimising post-purchase dissonance is key to avoiding complaint behaviour (Indwar and Mishra, 2022; Khraim, 2020).

SUMMARY

In this chapter we have looked at the dimensions of attitudes and how they are formed and maintained. We have also looked at ways of changing attitudes, and at some of the theories of attitude measurement.

Attitude is the starting point of all behaviour: people's attitudes inform their decision-making, create and change their motivations, and both create and are created by their consumption experiences. Marketers are always concerned with creating favourable attitudes towards both the product and the firm, and most marketing communications are aimed at developing those favourable attitudes so that consumers are not attracted by any competitor brands.

KEY POINTS

- Attitude is a learned construct that shows a person's tendency to respond to an object in a consistently favourable or unfavourable manner.
- Attitude is not neutral.
- Although attitude is not behaviour, it can be inferred from behaviour.
- Likewise, behaviour can be inferred from attitude, but the relationship is not reliable.
- Attitude is multidimensional, comprising affect, cognition and conation.
- Consumers only use salient beliefs when forming attitudes, not all the facts.
- Attitudes serve four useful purposes: instrumental, ego-defensive, value expressive and knowledge.
- Behaviour affects attitude more than attitude affects behaviour.
- The strength of an attitude is determined by perceived instrumentality, evaluative aspect and value importance.
- People may also assess the difficulty of carrying out the behaviour when establishing an attitude.
- Attitudes may be public or private.
- Situations may prevent behaviour without altering attitude.
- Beliefs are the basis of cognitive change: this type of change comes about through the direct route.
- Emotions are the basis of affective change: this type of change comes about through the peripheral route.
- Post-purchase dissonance may evoke several possible complaint behaviours.

HOW TO IMPRESS YOUR EXAMINER

You are likely to be asked how attitudes might be changed. It's very tempting just to dive into the various methods of changing attitudes without first making clear that attitudes actually are quite hard to change from the outside – more typically, attitude change comes from within, as a result of experience. You should also give a brief outline of how attitudes are formed in the first place – this will make the explanation of how to change them much easier. Then think about the current context. How have the world's attitudes towards life and consumption changed after the Covid-19 pandemic?

REVIEW QUESTIONS

1. What is the role of belief in forming attitudes?
2. How might marketers appeal to the cognitive element in attitude formation?
3. What is the difference between the ego-defensive role of attitude and the value-expressive role?
4. How might a marketer increase the strength of an attitude?
5. What is the purpose of measuring private attitudes?
6. How does situation affect attitude?
7. What processes might be important in forming attitudes?
8. What is the relationship between affect and the evaluative aspect of attitude strength?
9. What difficulties might exist when trying to infer attitude from behaviour?
10. How might beliefs be formed?

CASE STUDY: CHANGING ATTITUDES TO EDUCATION: MULTIVERSE

Multiverse, the apprenticeship startup founded by Euan Blair, son of former British prime minister Tony Blair, has become the UK's first edtech unicorn (a term for startup tech businesses that have reached a valuation of more than $1 billion) after its latest funding round gave it a $1.7 billion (£1.36 billion) valuation. The investment in Multiverse gives the 38-year-old a paper fortune of between $425 million and $850 million, while doubling the valuation of the business in less than a year. The company helps young people in the UK and US who have not been to university find apprenticeships with companies and access training.

'There has never been a more pressing time to create an alternative to university education that is equitable and inclusive and there is an incredible opportunity before

(Continued)

us to change the status quo with apprenticeships', said Blair, Multiverse's CEO. 'This funding will help us bring more people without degrees or in need of reskilling into tech careers and ultimately create a more diverse group of future leaders.'

Blair's father implemented a policy of bringing 50% of young people into higher education when he was prime minister, but his son added in a LinkedIn post that an emphasis on undergraduate degrees was not enough. 'One of the things that's so broken about the current system is it tries to pretend a three- or four-year undergraduate degree is enough to see you through a multi-decade career', he said 'We won't make the same mistake with apprenticeships. Our vision is for a system in which people can return to apprenticeships whenever they need to, to level up their career.'

Blair founded the group in 2016 with the aim of matching young adults and those looking to reskill with apprenticeships. The firm now works with more than 500 businesses including Microsoft, Visa and the investment bank Morgan Stanley. It has helped more than 8000 people go through apprenticeships in the UK and US. Of the apprentices directly placed with companies by Multiverse, 56% of those are people of colour, more than half are women and a third come from poor communities.

Multiverse are now starting to significantly change attitudes by taking on universities directly by offering debt-free degrees for apprentices as they work at firms like Rolls-Royce and Mastercard. An initial cohort of 170 students will be enrolled onto Multiverse degrees in September 2022. Elisabeth Barrett, Vice-President of Learning at Multiverse, said: 'Young people have been faced with an artificial trade-off between getting a degree or starting a career and immediately learning real-world skills. Now they can do both. We have a vision for Applied Degrees that allow people to obtain a quality education – but where a salary replaces debt. A high quality job from the start replaces the risk of being unprepared for the modern workplace by the time they graduate. And applied learning and personalised coaching replaces theoretical lectures and outdated exams. Our degrees will offer training in the areas fuelling today's economy: like data and tech. Already, our tech and computing programmes have higher employability than computer science degrees. Multiverse's degree awarding powers enable us to take this even further.'

Students will spend around a fifth of their degree with Multiverse coaches and experts in their given subject area and will be given graded assignments to complete during the three-year course.

Alongside this they will work as an apprentice at one of hundreds of businesses, such as Rolls-Royce and Mastercard, earning a starting salary of at least £18,000 per annum.

Mr Blair's company has become the first apprenticeship provider to be granted degree-awarding powers by the regulator, the Office for Students. Jean Arnold, Director of Quality at the Office for Students, said: 'We support innovation in the sector to enhance the options and quality of courses for students. We're pleased to grant degree awarding powers to Multiverse as a provider that delivers opportunities and choice to students.'

Training will be free for apprentices, who will not take on any debt as the bill is footed by the employer. The cost of tuition is covered through the apprenticeship levy, which was first introduced in April 2017 to help the Government fund their plan to deliver more apprenticeship schemes. Employers are required to pay the levy at 0.5% of their annual pay bill, if this is over £3 million. Meanwhile, smaller employers whose annual pay bill totals less than £3 million pay just 5% of the cost of their apprenticeship training while the Government pays the rest.

Source: Adapted from Blake (2022). More data and insights from *Daily Mail* can be found at www.dailymail.co.uk.

CASE STUDY QUESTIONS

1. What is the role of cognition in forming attitudes and how can we leverage technology to transform the student experience?
2. In the world that we live in now, is it the experiential learning or the certificate that is important for future careers?
3. What are the main attitudes that are being changed by Multiverse?
4. How should traditional higher education institutes respond to these new models of learning?
5. Is there enough room in the market, and the minds of the consumer, for both models to co-exist happily?

FURTHER READING

As an example of how attitude is formed in an online environment, you might enjoy C.H. Miller, J. Reardon, L. Salciuviene, V. Auruskeviciene, K. Lee and K. Miller (2009) Need for cognition as a moderator of affective and cognitive elements in online attitude toward the brand formation, *Journal of Business and Economics Research, 7* (12): 65–72.

For an interesting study in how an unpopular or counter-social attitude can affect the way an individual fits into a culture, read M. Piacentini and E.N. Banister (2009) Managing anti-consumption in an excessive drinking culture, *Journal of Business Research, 62*: 279–88. This paper is about the experiences of students who do not like to engage in heavy drinking.

For a good book on attitude and attitude change, try Greg Maio and Geoff Haddock's *The Psychology of Attitudes and Attitude Change* (London: Sage, 2009). In particular, this book explains clearly how attitudes can be used to predict behaviour.

MORE ONLINE

For additional materials that support this chapter and your learning, please visit:

https://study.sagepub.com/sethna5e

REFERENCES

Aaker, J.L., Fournier, S. and Brasel, S.A. (2004) When good brands do bad. *Journal of Consumer Research, 31*: 1–16.

Afshani, S.A. and Sheikhalishahi, Z. (2021) Socio-cultural factors related to the tendency toward superstition among women living in the suburbs of Yazd. *Alzahra University, 19* (2): 51–92.

Agboli, A., Richard, F., Botbol-Baum, M., Brackelaire, J.-L., D'Aguanno, A., Diallo, K., Mikolajczak, M., Ricadat, E. and Aujoulat, I. (2022) Changing attitudes towards female genital mutilation. From conflicts of loyalty to reconciliation with self and the community: The role of emotion regulation. *PLoS One, 17* (6). https://doi.org/10.1371/journal.pone.0270088

Ajiwinanto, M., Simanjuntak, M. and Tanjung, H. (2021) Investigating brand switching on cosmetics products: A case study of Nu Skin. *Binus Business Review, 12* (3): 241–54.

Ajzen, I. (1988) *Attitudes, Personality and Behaviour*. Milton Keynes: Open University Press.

Ajzen, I. and Fishbein, M. (1980) *Understanding Attitudes and Predicting Social Behaviour*. Englewood Cliffs, NJ: Prentice-Hall.

Ajzen, I. and Madden, T.J. (1986) Prediction of goal-directed behaviour: Attitudes, intentions and perceived behaviour control. *Journal of Experimental Social Psychology, 22* (5): 453–74.

Albertson, B. and Guiler, K. (2020) Conspiracy theories, election rigging, and support for democratic norms. *Research & Politics, 7*. https://doi.org/10.1177/2053168020959859

Alcántara, C., Molina, K.M. and Kawachi, I. (2015) Transnational, social, and neighborhood ties and smoking among Latino immigrants: Does gender matter? *American Journal of Public Health, 105* (4): 741–9.

Anderson, E.W., Fornell, C. and Lehmann, D.R. (1994) Customer satisfaction, market share and profitability: Findings from Sweden. *Journal of Marketing, 58* (3): 53–66.

Andreu, L., Casado-Díaz, A.B. and Mattila, A.S. (2015) Effects of message appeal and service type in CSR communication strategies. *Journal of Business Research, 68* (7): 1488–95.

Arca, S. and Hewett, R. (2021) Analytics on anonymity for privacy retention in smart health data. *Future Internet, 13* (11): 274.

Aronson, E., Chase, T., Helmreich, R. and Ruhnke, R. (1974) A two-factor theory of dissonance reduction: The effect of feeling stupid or feeling awful on opinion change. *International Journal of Communication Research, 3*: 340–52.

article19.org (2015) Right to online anonymity: Policy brief. www.article19.org/data/files/medialibrary/38006/Anonymity_and_encryption_report_A5_final-web.pdf (accessed 16 July 2018).

Babin, B.J., Boles, J.S. and Griffin, M. (2015) The moderating role of service environment on the customer share–customer commitment relationship. In M. Moore and R.S. Moore (eds), *New Meanings for Marketing in a New Millennium*. London: Springer International Publishing. pp. 266–71.

Bakamitsos, G. and Siomkos, G. (2004) Context effects in marketing practice: The case of mood. *Journal of Consumer Behaviour, 3* (4): 304–14.

Berger, I.E. and Mitchell, A.A. (1989) The effect of advertising on attitude accessibility, attitude confidence, and the attitude–behaviour relationship. *Journal of Consumer Research, 16* (December): 269–79.

Bhatnagar, N. and Aksoy, L. (2004) Et tu, Brutus? A case for consumer skepticism and backlash against product placements. *Advances in Consumer Research, 31*: 87–8.

Biel, A.L. (1990) Love the ad: Buy the product? *ADMAP, 299* (September): 21–5.

Biel, A.L. and Bridgwater, C.A. (1990) Attributes of likeable television commercials. *Journal of Advertising Research, 30* (3): 38–44.

Blake, E. (2022) Tony Blair's super-rich son Euan's education start-up takes on universities by offering debt-free degrees for apprentices as they work at firms like Rolls-Royce and Mastercard. *Mailonline*, 1 September 2022. www.dailymail.co.uk/news/article-11169051/Tony-Blairs-son-Euans-education-start-takes-universities-offering-degrees-apprentices.html (accessed on 15 September 2022).

Bless, H., Wanke, M. and Schwartz, N. (2002) The inclusion/exclusion model as a framework for predicting the direction and size of context effects in consumer judgments. *Advances in Consumer Research, 29*: 86–7.

Bolton, R.N. and Lemon, K.N. (1999) A dynamic model of customers' usage of services: Usage as an antecedent and consequence of satisfaction. *Journal of Marketing Research*, 36 (2): 171–86.

Bowen, G. and Bowen, D. (2018) Luxury product decision-making strategy: Leveraging social media to create the emotional component of the strategy. In W. Ozuem and Y. Azemi (eds), *Digital Marketing Strategies for Fashion and Luxury Brands*. Hershey, PA: IGI Global. pp. 289–308.

Brennan, R., Dahl, S. and Eagle, L. (2010) Persuading young consumers to make healthy nutrition decisions. *Journal of Marketing Management*, 26 (7/8): 635–55.

Castéra, J., Clément, P., Munoz, F. and Bogner, F.X. (2018) How teachers' attitudes on GMO relate to their environmental values. *Journal of Environmental Psychology*, 57: 1–9.

Chakkambath, R.S., Joseph, A.I., Maitra, R. and Jacob, J.S. (2022) Post-purchase dissonance among laptop consumers in India. *IUP Journal of Marketing Management*, 21 (2): 36–60.

Chiu, Y.-P. (2019) Do social and competitive advergames affect brand attitude in Asia? *International Journal of Electronic Commerce Studies*, 10 (1): 23–41.

Chocano, C. (2015) How 'Rock Star' became a business buzzword. *New York Times Magazine*. www.nytimes.com/2015/08/16/magazine/how-rock-star-became-a-business-buzzword.html (accessed 30 October 2022).

Choi, W.D., Kelley, T., Walden, E., McCool, B. and O'Boyle, M. (2022) Emotional dissonance among frontline hospitality employees: An exploratory study examining habituation theory using fMRI. *Journal of Hospitality & Tourism Research*, 46 (1): 174–88.

Choudhury, K. (2019) Materialism, consumerism, and religion: A Buddhist vision for nonprofit marketing. *International Journal of Nonprofit and Voluntary Sector Marketing*, 24 (3). https://doi.org/10.1002/nvsm.1634

Chow, C.-Y., Riantiningtyas, R.R., Sørensen, H. and Bom Frøst, M. (2021) School children cooking and eating insects as part of a teaching program – Effects of cooking, insect type, tasting order and food neophobia on hedonic response. *Food Quality and Preference*, 87: 104027.

Chugani, S.K., Irwin, J.R. and Redden, J.P. (2015) Happily ever after: The effect of identity-consistency on product satiation. *Journal of Consumer Research*, 42 (4): 515–34.

Coleman, N.V., Williams, P., Morales, A.C., Johar, G.V., Kirmani, A. and Argo, J.J. (2020) Retraction: Identity threats, compensatory consumption, and working memory capacity: How feeling threatened leads to heightened evaluations of identity-relevant products. *Journal of Consumer Research*, 47 (3): 472.

Cote, J.A., McCullough, J. and Reilly, M. (1985) Effects of unexpected situations on behaviour–intention differences: A garbology analysis. *Journal of Consumer Research*, 12 (September): 188–94.

de Vries, J., Byrne, M. and Kehoe, E. (2015) Cognitive dissonance induction in everyday life: An fMRI study. *Social Neuroscience*, 10 (3): 268–81.

Deterding, S., Sicart, M., Nacke, L., O'Hara, K. and Dixon, D. (2011) Gamification: Using game-design elements in non-gaming contexts. In *Proceedings of the 2011 Annual Conference Extended Abstracts on Human Factors in Computing Systems (CHIEA'11)*. Vancouver, BC. pp. 2425–8.

Dootson, P., Johnston, K.A., Lings, I. and Beatson, A.T. (2018) Tactics to deter deviant consumer behavior: A research agenda. *Journal of Consumer Marketing*, 35 (6): 577–87.

Festinger, L. (1957) *A Theory of Cognitive Dissonance*. Stanford, CA: Stanford University Press.

Festinger, L. and Carlsmith, J.M. (1959) Cognitive consequences of forced compliance. *Journal of Abnormal and Social Psychology*, 58: 203–10.

Filieri, R., Yen, D.A. and Yu, Q. (2021) #ILoveLondon: An exploration of the declaration of love towards a destination on Instagram. *Tourism Management*, 85: 104291.

Fishbein, M. (1972) The search for attitudinal–behavioural consistency. In J.E. Cohen (ed.), *Behavioural Science Foundations of Consumer Behaviour*. New York: Free Press. pp. 245–52.

Fishbein, M. (1980) An overview of the attitude construct. In G.B. Hafer (ed.), *A Look Back, A Look Ahead*. Chicago, IL: American Marketing Association. pp. 1–19.

Fishbein, M. and Ajzen, I. (1975) *Belief, Attitude, Intention and Behaviour: An Introduction to Theory and Research*. Reading, MA: Addison-Wesley.

Flavián, C., Guinalíu, M. and Gurrea, R. (2006) The role played by perceived usability, satisfaction and consumer trust on website loyalty. *Information & Management*, 43 (1): 1–14.

Gamliel, E. (2010) Message framing of products causes a preference shift in consumers' choices. *Journal of Consumer Behaviour*, 9 (4): 303–15.

Garbarino, E. and Johnson, M.S. (1999) The different roles of satisfaction, trust, and commitment in customer relationships. *Journal of Marketing*, 63 (2): 70–87.

Gauthier, C., Fornerino, M., Werle, C.O.C., Jolibert, A., Lee, M.S. and Sego, T. (2020) Social and personal values in advertising: Evidence from food advertising in South Korea. *International Studies of Management & Organization*, 50 (2): 174–200.

Ghosh, S., Jung, C. and Meyer-Rochow, V.B. (2018) What governs selection and acceptance of edible insect species? In A. Halloran, R. Flore, P. Vantomme and N. Roos (eds), *Edible Insects in Sustainable Food Systems*. Cham: Springer. pp. 331–51.

Gurau, C. and Tinson, J. (2003) Early evangelist or reluctant Rudolph? Attitudes towards the Christmas commercial campaign. *Journal of Consumer Behaviour*, 3 (1): 48–62.

Hanifati, L.N. and Salehudin, I. (2021) The effect of perceived product quality, brand personality, and loyalty on brand switching intention of technological products. *South East Asian Journal of Management*, 15 (2): 169–87.

Hernandez, M.D., Wang, Y.J., Minor, M.S. and Liu, Q. (2008) Effects of superstitious beliefs on consumer novelty seeking and independent judgement making: Evidence from China. *Journal of Consumer Behaviour*, 7 (6): 424–35.

Hilken, T., Chylinski, M., Keeling, D.I., Heller, J., de Ruyter, K. and Mahr, D. (2022) How to strategically choose or combine augmented and virtual reality for improved online experiential retailing. *Psychology & Marketing*, 39 (3): 495–507.

Homer, P.M. and Yoon, S. (1992) Message framing and the interrelationships among ad-based feelings, affect and cognition. *Journal of Advertising*, 21 (March): 19–33.

Hsee, C.K. and Rottenstreich, Y. (2002) Panda, mugger and music: On the affective psychology of value. *Advances in Consumer Research*, 29: 59–61.

Hudson, J., Caplanova, A. and Novak, M. (2015) Public attitudes to GM foods: The balancing of risks and gains. *Appetite*, 92 (September): 303–13.

Indwar, R.G. and Mishra, A.S. (2022) Emojis: Can it reduce post-purchase dissonance? *Journal of Strategic Marketing*. https://doi.org/10.1080/0965254X.2021.2013935

Ito, A., Kawachi, Y., Kawasaki, I. and Fujii, T. (2019) Effect of aging on choice-induced cognitive conflict. *Behavioural Brain Research*, 363: 94–102.

Janik, R.A., Podolak, I.T., Struski, Ł., Ceglarek, A., Lewandowska, K., Sikora-Wachowicz, B., Marek, T. and Fafrowicz, M. (2022) Neural spatio-temporal patterns of information processing related to cognitive conflict and correct or false recognitions. *Scientific Reports*, 12 (1): 1–19.

Kahneman, D. and Tversky, A. (1979) Prospect Theory: An analysis of decision under risk. *Econometrica*, 47 (2): 263–92.

Kaulingfreks, R. and Bos, R. (2007) On faces and defacement: The case of Kate Moss. *Business Ethics: A European Review*, 16 (3): 302–12.

Kemp, E., Briggs, E. and Anaza, N.A. (2020) The emotional side of organizational decision-making: Examining the influence of messaging in fostering positive outcomes for the brand. *European Journal of Marketing*, 54 (7): 1609–40.

Khraim, H. (2020) An exploratory study on factors associated with consumers' post-purchase dissonance of electric vehicles. *Innovative Marketing*, 16 (4): 13–23.

Kidd, C. and Loxton, N.J. (2018) Junk food advertising moderates the indirect effect of reward sensitivity and food consumption via the urge to eat. *Physiology & Behavior*, 188: 276–82.

Kivak, R. (2022) Persuasion. Online: *Salem Press Encyclopedia*. Great Neck Publishing: Research Starters.

Levy, S. and Gendel Guterman, H. (2021) Twofold impact of experiential marketing: Manufacturer brand and hosting retailer. *EuroMed Journal of Business*, 16 (4): 345–60.

Locander, W.B. and Spivey, W.A. (1978) A functional approach to the study of attitude measurement. *Journal of Marketing Research*, 15 (November): 576–87.

Marques, C., Correia, E., Dinis, L.-T. and Vilela, A. (2022) An overview of sensory characterization techniques: From classical descriptive analysis to the emergence of novel profiling methods. *Foods*, 11: 255.

Martin-Collado, D., Byrne, T.J., Crowley, J.J., Kirk, T., Ripoll, G. and Whitelaw, C.B.A. (2022) Gene-edited meat: Disentangling consumers' attitudes and potential purchase behavior. *Frontiers in Nutrition*, 9: 856491.

McClain, L.M., Hultgren, B.A., Geisner, I.M., Mallett, K.A., Turrisi, R. and Larimer, M.E. (2022) Emotion-based decision-making as a predictor of alcohol-related consequences in college students. *Addictive Behaviors*, 124: 107083.

McGonigal, J. (2011) *Reality is Broken: Why Games Make Us Better and How They Can Change the World*. London: Penguin.

McInnis, D.J. and Jaworski, B.J. (1989) Information processing from advertisements: Toward an integrative framework. *Journal of Marketing*, 53 (4): 1–23.

Mishra, A., Mishra, H. and Nayakankuppam, D. (2006) The meddling-in of affect in information integration. *Advances in Consumer Research*, 33: 48.

Mitchell, A.A. (1986) The effect of verbal and visual components of advertisements on brand attitudes and attitudes towards the advertisements. *Journal of Consumer Research*, 13 (June): 12–24.

Mohan, M., Brown, B.P., Sichtmann, C. and Schoefer, K. (2018) Perceived globalness and localness in B2B brands: A co-branding perspective. *Industrial Marketing Management*, 72: 59–70.

Morgan, R.M. and Hunt, S.D. (1994) The commitment–trust theory of relationship marketing. *Journal of Marketing*, 58 (3): 20–38.

Nyberg, M., Olsson, V. and Wendin, K. (2021) 'Would you like to eat an insect?' – Children's perceptions of and thoughts about eating insects. *International Journal of Consumer Studies*, 45 (2): 248–58.

Odekerken-Schroder, G., De Wulf, K. and Schumacher, P. (2003) Strengthening outcomes of retailer–consumer relationships: The dual impact of relationship marketing tactics and consumer personality. *Journal of Business Research*, 56: 177–90.

Onkvisit, S. and Shaw, J.J. (1994) *Consumer Behaviour, Strategy and Analysis*. New York: Macmillan.

Palcu, J., Haasova, S. and Florack, A. (2019) Advertising models in the act of eating: How the depiction of different eating phases affects consumption desire and behavior. *Appetite, 139*: 59–66.

Pauwels, K. (2015) Truly accountable marketing: The right metrics for the right results. *GfK Marketing Intelligence Review, 7* (1): 8–15.

Pellegrino, A., Abe, M. and Shannon, R. (2022) The dark side of social media: Content effects on the relationship between materialism and consumption behaviors. *Frontiers in Psychology, 13*: 1–15.

Peplak, J., Song, J.-H., Colasante, T. and Malti, T. (2017) 'Only you can play with me!' Children's inclusive decision making, reasoning, and emotions based on peers' gender and behavior problems. *Journal of Experimental Child Psychology, 162*: 134–48.

Petty, R.E., Caccioppo, J. and Schumann, D. (1983) Central and peripheral routes to advertising effectiveness. *Journal of Consumer Research, 10* (September): 135–46.

Ponchio, M.C. and Aranha, F. (2008) Materialism as a predictor variable of low income consumer behaviour when entering into instalment plan agreements. *Journal of Consumer Behaviour, 7* (1): 21–34.

Raimondo, M.A., Cardamone, E., Miceli, G. 'Nino' and Bagozzi, R.P. (2022) Consumers' identity signaling towards social groups: The effects of dissociative desire on brand prominence preferences. *Psychology & Marketing*. https://doi.org/10.1002/mar.21711

Raziq, M.M., Ahmed, Q.M., Ahmad, M., Yusaf, S., Sajjad, A. and Waheed, S. (2018) Advertising skepticism, need for cognition and consumers' attitudes. *Marketing Intelligence & Planning, 36* (6): 678–93.

Reeves, B. and Read, J.L. (2009) *Total Engagement: Using Games and Virtual Worlds to Change the Way People Work and Businesses Compete*. Boston, MA: Harvard Business School Press.

Reinhard, M. and Messner, M. (2009) The effects of source likeability and need for cognition on advertising effectiveness under explicit persuasion. *Journal of Consumer Behaviour, 8* (4): 179–91.

Rocha, P. (2021) It's beginning to look like a good Christmas for credit card lenders. *American Banker, 186* (217): 2.

Rosenberg, M.J. (1960) An analysis of affective-cognitive consistency. In C.I. Hovland and M.J. Rosenberg (eds), *Attitude Organisation and Change*. New Haven, CT: Yale University Press. pp. 15–64.

Roy, S.K., Sharma, A., Bose, S. and Singh, G. (2022) Consumer–brand relationship: A brand hate perspective. *Journal of Business Research, 144*: 1293–304.

Safeer, A.A., Chen, Y., Abrar, M., Kumar, N. and Razzaq, A. (2021) Impact of perceived brand localness and globalness on brand authenticity to predict brand attitude: A cross-cultural Asian perspective. *Asia Pacific Journal of Marketing and Logistics, 34* (7): 1524–43.

Savolainen, I., Vuorinen, I., Sirola, A. and Oksanen, A. (2022) Gambling and gaming during COVID-19: The role of mental health and social motives in gambling and gaming problems. *Comprehensive Psychiatry, 117*: 152331.

Schmeichel, B.J., Vohs, K.D. and Baumeister, R.F. (2018) Intellectual performance and ego depletion: Role of the self in logical reasoning and other information processing. In R.F. Baumeister (ed.), *Self-Regulation and Self-Control*. London: Taylor and Francis Group. pp. 318–47.

Shafer, P.R., Fowler, E.F., Baum, L. and Gollust, S.E. (2018) Television advertising and health insurance marketplace consumer engagement in Kentucky: A natural experiment. *Journal of Medical Internet Research, 20* (10): e10872.

Simioni, M., Gladyshev, P., Habibnia, B. and Nunes de Souza, P.R. (2021) Monitoring an anonymity network: Toward the deanonymization of hidden services. *Forensic Science International: Digital Investigation, 38*: 301135.

Smith, K.H. and Stutts, M.A. (2003) Effects of short-term versus long-term health fear appeals in anti-smoking advertisements on the smoking behaviour of adolescents. *Journal of Consumer Behaviour, 3* (2): 155–77.

Smith, R.E. and Swinyard, W.R. (1983) Attitude–behaviour consistency: The impact of product trial versus advertising. *Journal of Marketing Research, 20* (3): 257–67.

Stapel, J. (1991) Like the advertisement but does it interest me? *ADMAP*, April.

Stavrou, M. (2022) *Individual Differences in Affective, Cognitive, and Neural Responses to Interpersonal and Social Motivation: Novel Methodological Perspectives*. Unpublished PhD Thesis, Goldsmiths College.

Taillon, B.J., Mai, E. (Shirley) and Haytko, D.L. (2022) Risky business: Consumer attitudes, perceptions, and consumption behaviors during COVID-19. *Basic and Applied Social Psychology, 44* (2): 47–65.

Thoumrungroje, A. (2018) A cross-national study of consumer spending behavior: The impact of social media intensity and materialism. *Journal of International Consumer Marketing, 30* (4): 276–86.

van Reijmersdal, E.A., Lammers, N., Rozendaal, E. and Buijzen, M. (2015) Disclosing the persuasive nature of advergames: Moderation effects of mood on brand responses via persuasion knowledge. *International Journal of Advertising, 34* (1): 70–84.

Vashist, D. (2018) Effect of product involvement and brand prominence on advergamers' brand recall and brand attitude in an emerging market context. *Asia Pacific Journal of Marketing and Logistics, 30* (1): 43–61.

Vasquez, K., Oswald, D.L. and Hammer, A. (2019) Being dishonest about our prejudices: Moral dissonance and self-justification. *Ethics & Behavior, 29* (5): 382–404.

Verhoef, P.C., Kooge, E. and Walk, N. (2015) *Creating Value with Big Data Analytics: Making Smarter Marketing Decisions*. Abingdon: Routledge.

Xiu, D. and Liu, Z. (2005) A formal definition for trust in distributed systems. In J. Zhou, R.H. Deng and F. Bao Feng (eds), *Information Security, Lecture Notes in Computer Science*, Vol. 3650. Heidelberg: Springer. pp. 482–9.

Youn, H., Xu, J. (Bill) and Kim, J.-H. (2021) Consumers' perceptions, attitudes and behavioral intentions regarding the symbolic consumption of auspiciously named foods. *International Journal of Hospitality Management, 98*: 103024.

Zajonc, R.B. and Markus, H. (1985) Must all affect be mediated by cognition? *Journal of Consumer Research, 12* (December): 363–4.

Zhu, Y.Q. and Chen, H.G. (2015) Social media and human need satisfaction: Implications for social media marketing. *Business Horizons, 58* (3): 335–45.

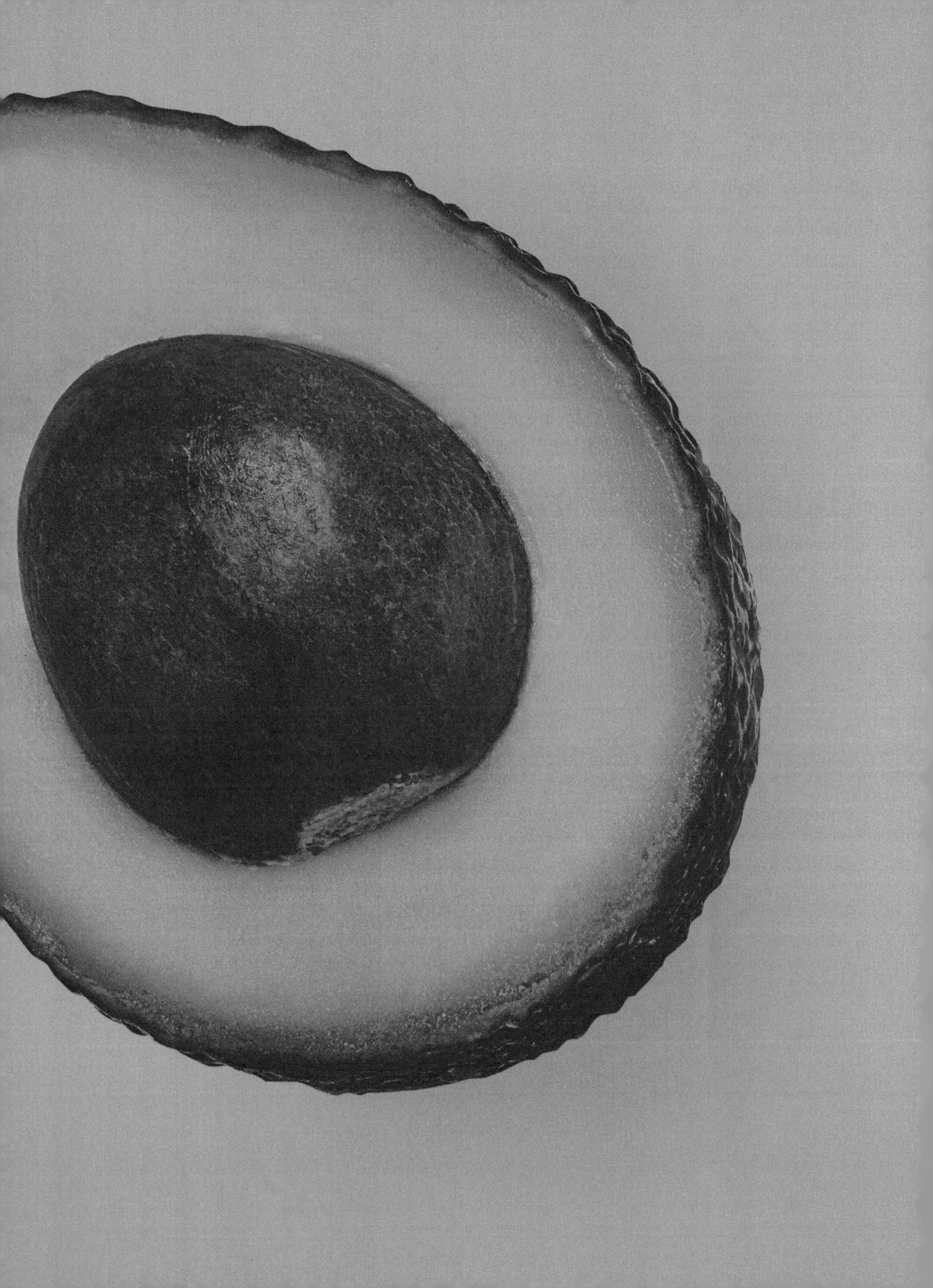

PART THREE

CONSUMERS AS SOCIAL ACTORS (THE SOCIOLOGICAL ISSUES)

10	Reference Groups	381
11	Age, Gender and Familial Roles	417
12	Culture and Social Mobility	461
13	Ethical Consumption	501
14	Sustainable Consumption	541

Although people are individuals, they act in groups. Human beings are herd animals, and rely heavily on each other for support, advice, practical help, entertainment and security. Thus this third section in the book takes a look at some of the sociological issues that consumers are subjected to and are influenced by.

Chapter 10 is about the types of group of which we are members. These groups have a great influence on us as sources of information, as 'sanity checks' to ensure that we are behaving appropriately, and as support systems for us in our daily lives. Each group influences us in different ways, and each has its own role in helping us to function effectively as human beings.

Chapter 11 is devoted to an investigation of age, gender and the most influential group of all – the family. It is through our families that we first learned to behave appropriately, and as we get older and have children of our own we are influenced by their needs (as well as having a role in teaching them to be effective consumers, regardless of where they lie on the gender scale). However the family is defined, and however humanity might change the structure of what is considered to be the family, the closeness of kinship and shared consumption will always ensure that families are at the heart of what makes us what we are.

Chapter 12 takes a look at how the social environment in which we live and behave is affected by our notions of culture and social mobility. These are usually derived from the people around us, and form the basis for our social behaviour as well as our understanding of who we are as individuals. This naturally affects our purchase behaviour, since we buy things that tend to validate our status.

Chapter 13 is on ethical consumption, which is, as a subject matter, still in its relative infancy. This is an area that remains to be fully embraced by all societies in all communities. The ethics of consumerism are continuously being influenced by the ever-evolving ways in which we acquire and consume things. This chapter takes a brief look at some of the key issues that are facing consumers currently.

Finally, Chapter 14 delves into sustainable consumption briefly. *Briefly* because, like ethical consumption, the area of sustainable consumption is evolving and developing as you sit and read this. We take a look at some of the main drivers behind sustainability and sustainable consumption, who it currently benefits, and why it's vitally important for the future of planet Earth.

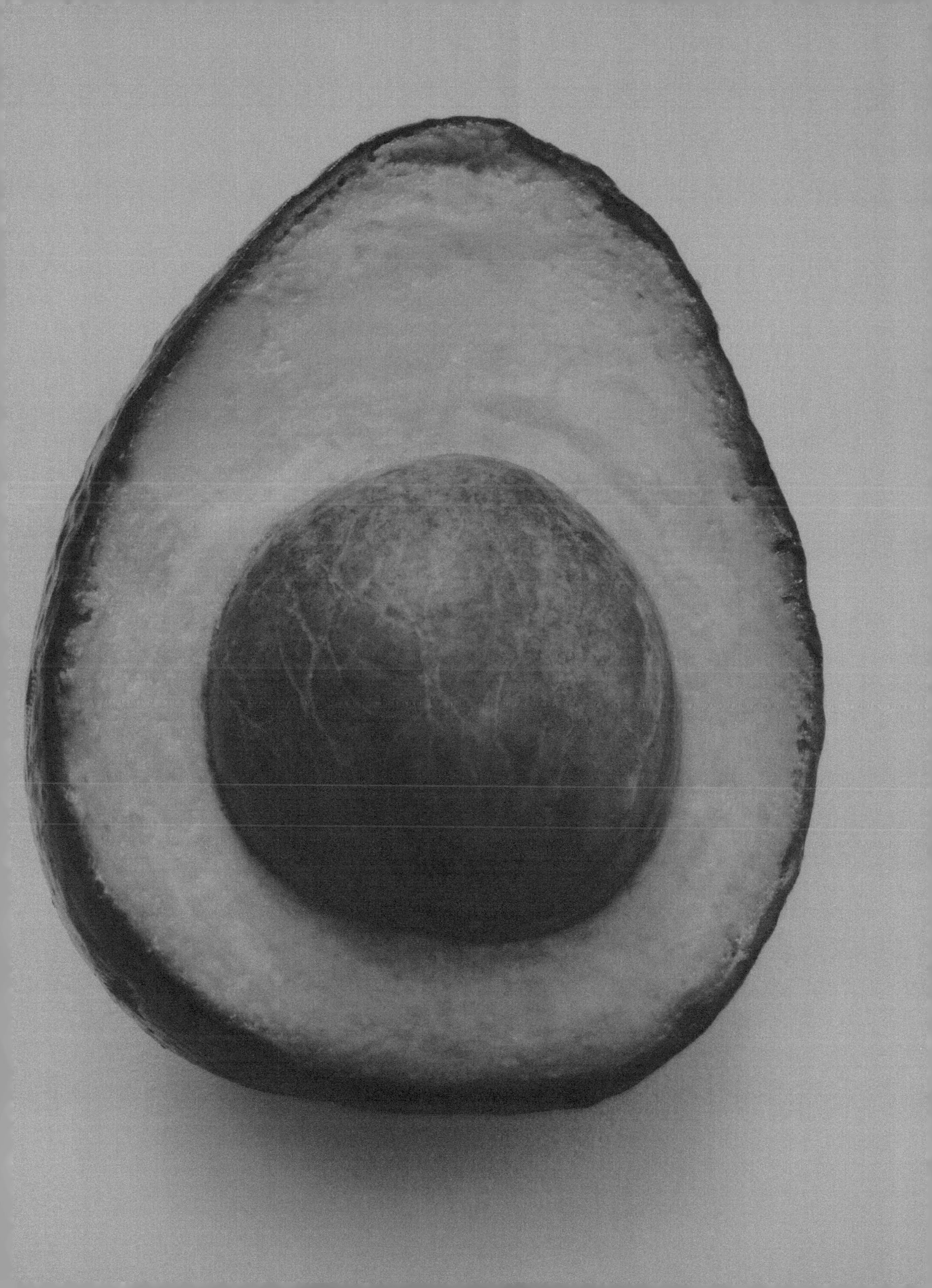

PART ONE   CONSUMER BEHAVIOUR IN CONTEXT

Chapter 1 Understanding Consumer Behaviour
Chapter 2 Decisions, Behaviours and Interactions
Chapter 3 Consumption in B2C vs. B2B
Chapter 4 Consumer Technology and Innovation

PART TWO   CONSUMERS AS INDIVIDUALS (THE PSYCHOLOGICAL ISSUES)

Chapter 5 Drive, Motivation and Hedonism
Chapter 6 The Self and Personality
Chapter 7 Perception
Chapter 8 Learning and Knowledge
Chapter 9 Attitude Formation and Change

PART THREE   CONSUMERS AS SOCIAL ACTORS (THE SOCIOLOGICAL ISSUES)

Chapter 10 Reference Groups
Chapter 11 Age, Gender and Familial Roles
Chapter 12 Culture and Social Mobility
Chapter 13 Ethical Consumption
Chapter 14 Sustainable Consumption

CHAPTER 10
REFERENCE GROUPS

LEARNING OBJECTIVES

After reading this chapter you should be able to:

- Explain how reference groups influence individual members.
- Explain what is meant by normative compliance.
- Describe the main drivers for normative compliance.
- Explain the role of word of mouth communication.
- Describe ways of handling complaints.
- Explain the importance of email communication.

CHAPTER CONTENTS

Introduction
Formation of reference groups
Influence of reference groups
Modelling
Mechanisms of personal influence and word of mouth
The emergence of word of mouse
Summary
Key points
How to impress your examiner
Review questions
Case study: The taste of Brexit
Further reading
References

More online: https://study.sagepub.com/sethna5e

INTRODUCTION

Human beings are social animals: we form ourselves into groups, and in fact most of us are members of several different groups, formed for different purposes. In most cases we join groups because we can achieve more as part of a group than we can as individuals, but there are some groups that we belong to without ever having made a voluntary decision to join. Examples are our gender group, our ethnic or racial group and our family group. Because the family, age and gender are such important groups they have a chapter to themselves (see Chapter 11); this chapter deals with other groups that affect consumption.

Groups have considerable influence on our buying behaviour, either because we need to own certain items in order to join the group (there is no point in joining a golf club if one does not own a set of golf clubs, for example, although the loud check trousers are usually optional), or because we have joint consumption within the group for the purposes of saving ourselves time, money or effort. For example, members of a yacht club are able to share facilities such as berthing, a club house, maintenance facilities and so forth, and many members also share a yacht.

Sociology
The study of human behaviour in groups

Sociology is the study of human behaviour in groups, so much of the research into groups comes from sociologists rather than from marketing academics. Marketers are, of course, mainly interested in how group behaviour affects attitude formation (Chapter 9), eventual decision-making (Chapter 2) and purchasing behaviour.

FORMATION OF REFERENCE GROUPS

Reference group
A group of people who act as the yardstick for our behaviour

A group is two or more persons who share a set of norms and whose relationship makes their behaviour interdependent. A **reference group** is a person or group of people that significantly influences an individual's behaviour (Bearden and Etzel, 1982; Lee and Fortuny, 2022). The reference groups provide standards or norms by which consumers judge their attitudes and behaviour.

Originally, groups formed for the purpose of cooperating on survival activities. Because human beings could cooperate in such activities as hunting, food-gathering and defence from predators, we were able to increase the chances of survival for the species as a whole. Interestingly, this still appears to hold true; social researchers have reported that social isolation and loneliness are associated with increased mortality (Lennartsson et al., 2022; Steptoe et al., 2013), with rates between 50% and 300% higher than people who are strongly integrated into groups (Koretz, 1990). For all of human history we have cooperated with each other to survive and prosper, and we continue to do so for both practical and social reasons.

Most people prefer to fit in with a group (to a greater or lesser extent). This is either through politeness or through a desire not to be left outside the group. Particularly with groups of friends, people will 'go along with the crowd' on a great many issues, and will tend to adopt the group norms regarding behaviour and attitudes. The process starts from an early age – children as young as 8 are aware of the importance of having the right brands of food in their lunch boxes, and this awareness becomes stronger as they grow older (Roper and La Niece, 2009). Children in Brazil are able to recognise cigarette logos at an even earlier age (Borzekowski and Cohen, 2013).

Experiments conducted by Solomon Asch in 1951 demonstrated this in a graphic manner. In the experiment, subjects were asked to judge the lengths of different lines. The lines were displayed on a large board, and each person was seated with a group of strangers who were also supposed to be making judgements about the line lengths. In fact the strangers were Asch's assistants who had been instructed to agree with each other about the length of each line, but to make errors; the experimental subjects consistently agreed with these errors, even though the errors were sometimes glaringly obvious. Respondents did not make the same mistakes when there were no other people present, however. It appears from this that the fear of seeming foolish or of being the odd one out is enough to make the individual doubt the evidence of his or her eyes, or at the very least to lie about the evidence (Asch, 1951).

Responses to group pressures may, in some circumstances, be gender-specific (Zitelny et al., 2022). Fisher and Dube (2003) found that men and women respond differently to emotional advertising depending on whether other people are present. Specifically, women show the same emotional responses to advertisements whether other people are present or not, whereas men are affected by the presence of others, especially if the emotional response is regarded as gender-specific. For example, an advertisement that causes someone to shed tears would cause the same response in a woman whether or not other people were around, whereas a man would be more likely to suppress this response if others were present (even if he were to shed a tear when in private). This said, more recent research has investigated male athletes and masculinity, and has found that even though the populist belief of men compressing their emotional expression and experience is still prevalent, this does not mean that it is either 'typical [or] ideal masculinity in contemporary dominant culture' (MacArthur and Shields, 2015). Although the psychological states of athletes were negatively affected during the Covid-19 pandemic, there is a lack of studies examining the psychological impact on athletes according to age, sports discipline and contact requirement of the sport. Lima et al. (2022) have addressed this by evaluating the psychological effects of the Covid-19 pandemic on elite athletes. They conclude that the mental health status of team sport athletes was relatively protected, whereas individual contact sports athletes were highly affected. The psychological states of individual contact sports athletes should be monitored closely, and necessary psychosocial support should be provided to create coping strategies.

Perception of what is fair and what is not also seems to be influenced by social interaction with the group one happens to be in at the time (Carlson and Sally, 2002). For example, when associating with a group of middle-class professionals one might perceive welfare payments as unfair, since they are paid for by hard-working taxpayers; in the company of a more left-wing group, one might perceive welfare payments as unfair because they do not provide enough money for a dignified and comfortable lifestyle.

CRITICAL REFLECTION

Are we easily influenced by our friends? Do we really go along with things that easily? Is it so straightforward to lead people around by the nose? If so, how come we get into arguments with our friends? How come we have so many people who are prepared to stand up against the general flow of opinion and disagree?

Asch's experiment might just show that students try to please their lecturers, or that people try to give the 'right' answers in situations that look a lot like exams. Or maybe the results are good, but only when we are in the company of strangers – does our natural politeness (and fear of embarrassment, or worse still public humiliation) make us wary of arguing with someone we know nothing about?

And is this further exemplified if we are in the company of robots?

In an early episode of the popular television programme *Dr Who* there were the now infamous Daleks (a race of malignant and malicious pepperpot-esque robots) which zipped around the place voicing 'exterminate, exterminate'. They were supposedly driven by some form of cultural xenophobia – a 'dislike of the unlike' that caused them to seek to exterminate all other life forms in the universe. Brandstetter et al. (2014) rightly ask the question of whether we will regard robots as mindless machines, as subservient, or as peers? The current development of 'human-like' social robots

(Continued)

(Breazeal, 2004; Edwards and Edwards, 2022; Kanda et al., 2004; Shaw-Garlock, 2009) may well lead to a future where they are actively involved in our lives – from teaching young children basic education to helping with household chores to maybe even working in marketing! In December 2015, scientists at Nanyang Technological University in Singapore introduced the world to 'Nadine', a socially intelligent, human-looking robot who has a personality, possesses moods and displays emotions. The humanoid 'receptionist's' creator, Professor Nadia Thalmann, predicted that 'physical social robots such as Nadine are poised to become more visible in offices and homes in future'. Brandstetter et al. (2014) set out to recreate and expand upon the Asch experiment to see whether robots could create conformity by means of group pressure. Their analyses demonstrated that participants behaved significantly differently when among robot peers than among human peers and that individuals clearly interpret robot peers differently from human peers.

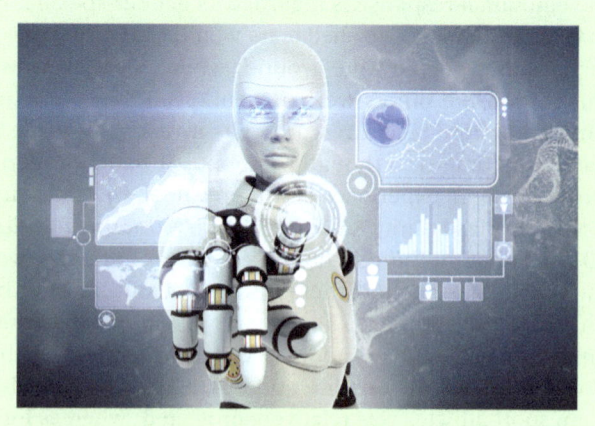

The influence of artificial agents on our lives is continuously changing. Recent literature shows that the presence of such agents will be more pervasive in our social environments, leaving the open question of whether humans will perceive these agents as possible social partners. Hence, a novel challenge arises in understanding whether humans will deploy socio-cognitive mechanisms similar to the ones activated in human–human interaction to understand and predict the behaviour of these new entities (Marchesi, 2021).

Will we, however, succumb to social pressure from robots?

Reference groups fall into many possible groupings; the following list is not intended to be exhaustive.

Primary group

The group of people we see daily, and to whom we feel closest

Secondary group

A group of people whom we do not necessarily see every day, and who are not our closest friends, but to which we belong nonetheless

Primary groups are composed of those people we see most often: friends, family and close colleagues. A primary group is small enough to permit face-to-face interaction on a regular basis, and there is cohesiveness and mutual participation which results in similar beliefs and behaviour within the group. Because people tend to choose friends who think in similar ways and have similar interests, the primary group is often very cohesive and long-lasting. Possibly the strongest primary group is the family, but primary groups might be close friends, colleagues at work or people with whom we share a hobby.

Secondary groups are composed of people we see occasionally, and with whom we have some shared interest. For example, a trade association or a sports club would constitute a secondary group. These groups are correspondingly less influential in shaping attitudes and controlling behaviour, but can exert influence on behaviour within the purview of the subject of mutual interest. For example, if you are a member of a cycling club, you may be persuaded to take part in a sponsored bike ride, or perhaps a protest in favour of creating more cycle lanes. Within a secondary group, primary groups will sometimes form; there will often be groups of special friends whose shared interests go beyond those of the rest of the secondary group. For example, a cycling enthusiast might have a close friend with whom he cycles regularly: the friends might be members of a cycling club and arrange with a few other members of the club to go on an evening out. In this example the friends are a primary group, but met through a secondary group (the cycling club) and formed a new primary group to enjoy a different shared interest (the evening out).

Aspirational groups are the groups the individual wants to join. See for example work done by Vaadal and Ravn (2021) on the ambivalent futures among Norwegian 'top girls'. These groups can be very powerful in influencing behaviour, because the individual will often adopt the behaviour of the aspirational group in the hope of being accepted as a member. People who feel excluded because of some kind of stigma (perhaps having extremely visible facial tattoos or being from a seemingly poor background) or indeed because of the colour of their skin (Pittman, 2020) or their sexual orientation (Nölke, 2018) will modify their consumption patterns (either buying specific products or reducing their consumption of other products) in order to conceal or reduce the stigma (Crosby and Otnes, 2010). Sometimes the aspirational group will be better off financially, or will be more powerful; the desire to join such groups is usually classed as ambition. For example, a humble young office worker, studying part-time for a Chartered Marketer qualification, may dream of one day becoming the Chief Marketing Officer. Advertising commonly uses images of aspirational groups, implying that use of a particular product will move the individual a little closer to being a member of an aspirational group.

Aspirational group
A group of individuals which one wishes to join

Dissociative groups, on the other hand, are those groups that the individual does not want to be associated with. Like a backpacker who does not want to look like a typical tourist, or a Marxist who would not want to be mistaken for a capitalist, the individual tries to avoid dissociative groups. This can have a negative effect on behaviour; the individual would rather avoid certain products or behaviours than be taken for somebody from the dissociative group. Like aspirational groups, the definition of a group as dissociative is purely subjective; it varies from one individual to the next.

Dissociative group
A social group to which one does not wish to belong

Formal groups have a known list of members, very often recorded somewhere. An example might be a professional association like, for instance, the Chartered Institute of Marketing (CIM), or a club. Usually the rules and structure of the group are laid down in writing; there are rules for membership, and members' behaviour is constrained while they remain part of the group. However, the constraints usually only apply to fairly limited areas of behaviour; for example, the CIM lays down a code of practice for marketers in their professional dealings, but has no interest in what its members do as private citizens. Membership of such groups may confer special privileges, such as job advancement or use of club facilities, and may lead to responsibilities in the furtherance of the group's aims.

Formal group
A group of people with a known, recorded membership and a set of (usually written) rules of membership

Informal group
A group of people that has no recorded membership and no written rules

Informal groups are less structured, and are typically based on friendship. An example would be an individual's circle of friends, which only exists for mutual moral support, company and sharing experiences. Although there can be even greater pressure to conform than would be the case with a formal group, there is no written set of rules. Often informal groups expect a more rigorous standard of behaviour across a wider range of activities than would a formal group; such circles of friends are likely to develop rules of behaviour and traditions that are more binding than written rules.

Automatic group
A group of people to which an individual belongs by reason of race, gender or other non-changeable factor

Category group
See Automatic group

Automatic groups are those groups to which one belongs by virtue of age, gender, culture or education. These are sometimes also called **category groups**. Although at first sight it would appear that these groups would not exert much influence on members' behaviour, because they are groups that have not been joined voluntarily, it would appear that people are influenced by group pressure to conform. For example, when buying clothes older people are sometimes reluctant to look like 'mutton dressed as lamb' or dressing 'inappropriately as compared to their age'. It would certainly look somewhat odd if an older gentlemen walked into the golf club wearing clothes that made him look like Dr Dre. Also, membership of some racial groups can influence behaviour because of the associated physical characteristics: some cosmetics are specifically designed for skin and hair types that are genetically determined (see, for example, www.imancosmetics.com).

Virtual community
A group of people with common goals and interests who interact via electronic media

Virtual communities (Hiltz and Wellman, 1997; Ridings et al., 2002) are a phenomenon brought about as a result of chatrooms on the internet (Okleshen and Grossbart, 1998). The term virtual community was coined by media scholar Howard Rheingold in 1993 for the first edition of his book *The Virtual Community: Homesteading on the Electronic Frontier*. Rheingold used the term to describe his participation in a variety of early internet communities. A virtual community (VC), or 'online community', is a collection of people who gather together online to engage in shared interests. Different platforms in cyberspace allow people to form such communities. Online gaming sites, chatrooms and social media platforms are all examples of VCs that allow people to actively engage with one another. VCs are a digital outgrowth of humanity's interest in forming relationships, even in virtual settings. Such communities enable people to express themselves without the constraints of national boundaries or distance (Bullard, 2022). The communication is virtual rather than face-to-face, which means that people can (in effect) be whoever they say they are. These virtual groups work together on tasks supported by communications technologies (Lipnack and Stamps, 2000). Such internet communities are based on social interactions that can often be more open and uninhibited than would be the case in a real space rather than a virtual space (Fischer et al., 1996). This allows people to express views that might be controversial, and of course since the chatrooms are not geographically based, people with unusual interests (such as collecting rare whiskies or building light aircraft) are able to share information much more easily, reducing the time and cost of travelling (Baskerville and Nandhakumar, 2007) as well as helping to foster a work–life balance (Fonner and Roloff, 2010). Satisfaction with virtual communities such as forums, **blogs** and chatrooms comes from interactions with the members: the organisers of chatrooms have little influence over this (Langerak et al., 2004). On the one hand, the platforms allow individuals to discuss issues of common interest, and to share information about

Blog
Short for web log – a publicly accessible personal journal

whatever topics interest them (however obscure). On the other hand, they open up possibilities for people to misrepresent themselves, perhaps for social purposes (for example to appear more interesting or desirable), or perhaps for sinister purposes such as fraud or paedophilia.

There are four types of virtual community, as follows (Muniz and O'Guinn, 2001):

- *Brand communities*. These are groups who have a shared interest in a specific brand, for example owners of a particular motorcycle or classic car. These groups share experiences, help each other with obtaining accessories, spare parts, etc., and offer each other advice when things go wrong.
- *Communities of interest*. Typically these are hobby sites for people who share an interest such as a sport, or a professional interest.
- *Fantasy communities*. These are based on games, whether fantasy games or ordinary games, such as chess or bridge.
- *Relationship communities*. These are based on common shared problems and experience, for example support groups for people with mental illness, victims of crime or action groups who campaign for reform.

The above categories of group are not mutually exclusive. A dissociative group could also be an informal one, a formal group can be a secondary group (and often is) and so forth. For example, one may not wish to become friends with a group of drunken hooligans (who see themselves as an informal group of friends having a good time). Likewise, the golf club could be a place of refuge to which one retreats to have a quiet drink with like-minded people, as well as a place where golf is played.

Figure 10.1 shows how an individual might be a member of several groups, each one with different purposes, members and characteristics. Each group develops a set of shared knowledge and behaviours (this is called social constructivism) and therefore the individual will behave (and even think) differently when interacting with each separate group. In some cases the groups will fall into more than one classification: for the person in Figure 10.1, the Chartered Institute of Marketing is both a formal group (with a known set of members) and a secondary group (one that he relates to occasionally, because he has a professional interest). Social constructivism suggests that we are created as individuals through our social interactions with members of groups to which we belong – this contrasts somewhat with the psychological theories of personality discussed in Chapter 6.

INFLUENCE OF REFERENCE GROUPS

Reference groups affect people in several ways. First, groups tend to modify members' behaviour through a process of socialisation. This is a learning process for the individual, leading to an understanding of which behaviours are acceptable within the group and which are not. Gong et al. (2022) have recently asked a pertinent question – 'Will green parents have green children?' – the basic premise of the work being to investigate the relationship between parents' and early adolescents' green consumption values (there is more on this in Chapter 14). For example, there may

Socialisation

The process of becoming an effective and integrated member of society by attaining and replicating norms, customs and ideologies in order to maintain continuity

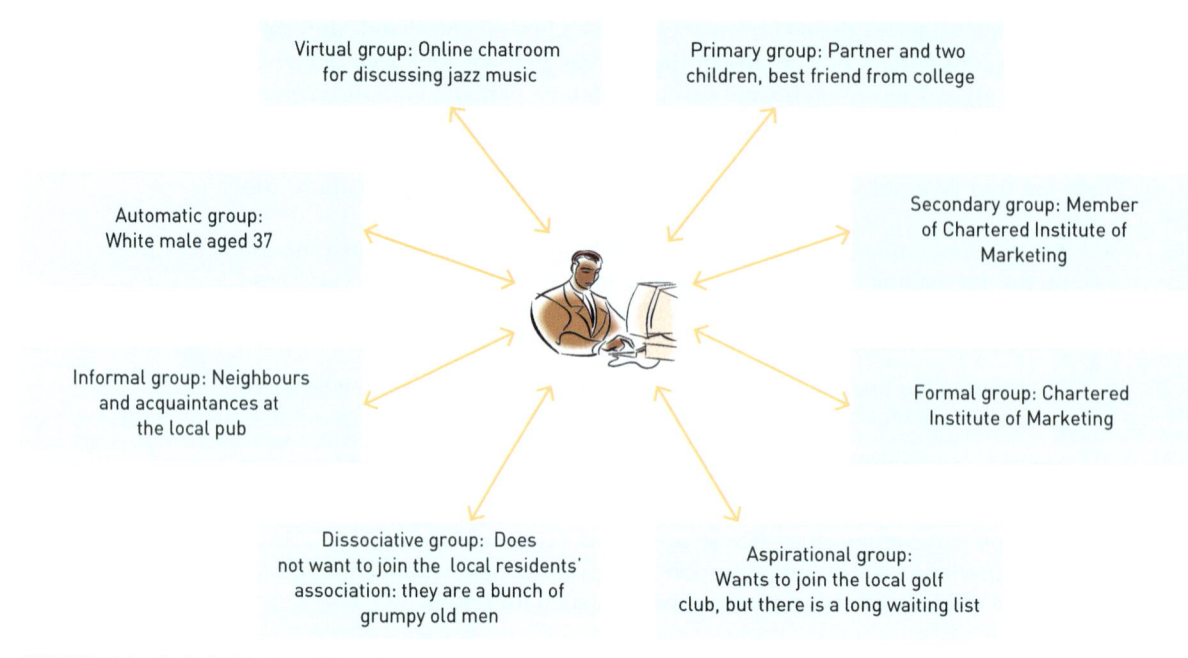

FIGURE 10.1 An individual and his reference groups

- Virtual group: Online chatroom for discussing jazz music
- Primary group: Partner and two children, best friend from college
- Automatic group: White male aged 37
- Secondary group: Member of Chartered Institute of Marketing
- Informal group: Neighbours and acquaintances at the local pub
- Formal group: Chartered Institute of Marketing
- Dissociative group: Does not want to join the local residents' association: they are a bunch of grumpy old men
- Aspirational group: Wants to join the local golf club, but there is a long waiting list

be a formal set of rules laid down by a golf club regarding care of the greens, dress codes, behaviour in the clubhouse and so forth, but it is the existing members who will advise new members on which rules are essential and which are often ignored. More importantly, the existing members will advise new members on behaviour that is expected but is not in the written rules – for example, buying a round of drinks when one scores a hole in one. Spending time with friends is an important way of learning what is appropriate and what is not, which may be one of the reasons why adolescent females spend a lot of time shopping with friends (Haytko and Baker, 2004). Shopping also provides a shared activity for the adolescent which develops social education, companionship and an understanding of what is safe and what is not in the adult world.

CRITICAL REFLECTION

Ask yourselves the following question... 'If shopping has become a hobby, and more particularly an educational experience for young teenage girls, do marketers think they've absolutely struck gold?' But how true is it that young girls behave in this way? Haytko and Baker's (2004) research was conducted in the USA, where 'going to the mall' is inbuilt within the culture. But does it apply in Europe, or elsewhere in the world?

Would most European shopping malls be happy for gangs of teenagers to be hanging around anyway? Surely the situation in Europe or the rest of the world is different culturally? For instance, research suggests that young people in Taiwan are certainly taking their reference from their counterparts in the rest of the world. A study by Wu et al. (2015) found that Asian consumers not only consumed large swathes of media commentary, but were also greatly inspired by female celebrities. And when it came to discussing luxury fashion brands with friends, this was an enjoyable yet very serious business. Commentators around the world are noting that 'marketers should be communicating appeals to an aspirational lifestyle in both traditional and social media' (Wu et al., 2015). But how much mileage does this actually have when we know that consumers are increasingly interacting with smart technologies and this may well have an impact on both other human interactions as well as in shopping mall loyalty (Ameen et al., 2022)?

Second, people develop a self-concept through their interactions within groups. How we see ourselves is a result of how others see us: feedback from others is the basis of our understanding of who we are. This is particularly apparent when the group has a specific purpose, such as supporting a football team: supporters often wear uniforms to show which team they support, thus identifying with the group and also projecting their own identity, not only to the group but to any other observers. This is a way of blending one's personal identity with the culture surrounding the team (Oliver, 1999). Marketers use this aspect of group behaviour to sell uniforms; it is also a feature of celebrity endorsement – by using a particular product, the individual associates him- or herself with the celebrity.

Third, groups affect people through **conformity**. This is a change in beliefs or actions based on group pressures (Marton-Alper et al., 2022; Wijenayake et al., 2022). There are two types of conformity: compliance and acceptance. **Compliance** happens when an individual goes along with the behaviour of the group without really accepting its beliefs. For example, someone who is not a football supporter might accompany a friend to a match and cheer on the friend's team without actually having any long-term interest in the team's fortunes. Compliance is common in the workplace. Acceptance occurs when the individual not only adapts their behaviour, but also adapts their beliefs to come into line with the group. This might happen if the non-supporter finds that the experience was so exciting, and the team played so well, that he or she decides to become a supporter. Acceptance also commonly occurs through religious conversions. Overall, conformity can be considered as behaviour one adopts by observing others when confronted with membership of a new group; it is most likely to occur when the costs of conforming are outweighed by the advantages. Advantages might include self-esteem, acceptance by an aspirational group, companionship, practical benefits such as the potential for earning or saving money and so forth (Homans, 1961). More recently, our societies have also seen an increase in cyber aggressive behaviours such as non-consensual image sharing, nasty comments and social exclusion, which frequently take place on WhatsApp. These behaviours often involve group processes, where adolescents conform to peers' behaviours. WhatsApp is pre-eminently suited for group-communication among adolescents, and, thus, may facilitate conformity to such behaviours (Bleize et al., 2021).

Fourth, people use groups for social comparison. We evaluate ourselves by comparing our performance with others (Leung and MacDonald, 2022) – for example, when we consider our wealth or our social standing we compare ourselves with people whom we consider to be our equals in other respects. Comparisons are not necessarily made with groups with whom we have personal contact; for example, a lawyer might

Conformity
The social pressure to behave in similar ways to other people

Compliance
Adherence without belief: acquiescence

compare his or her salary with what other lawyers earn, or alternatively might make the comparison with other professionals such as doctors or accountants. If the groups are similar, the individual has greater confidence in the comparison (Jansen et al., 2022; Tesser et al., 1988), but people generally value differing views when they are themselves confident in their own ability and opinions (Wheeler et al., 1969). This may explain why some people opt for cosmetic surgery (breast implants, liposuction, or a nose job, etc.) whereas other people are apparently quite happy to live with physical 'imperfections' (Lyu et al., 2022).

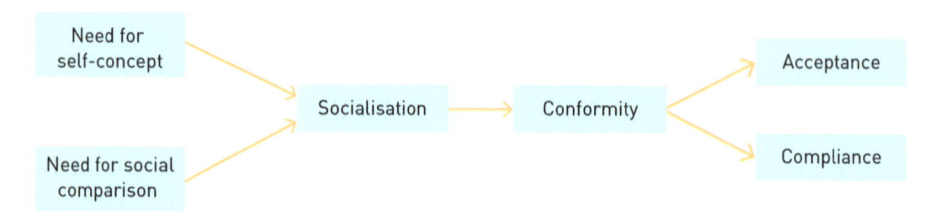

FIGURE 10.2 Modifying behaviour through groups

In Figure 10.2 the need for social comparison and self-concept drives the socialisation process. These are the reasons why people are prepared to accept socialisation. The result of socialisation is conformity, either by acceptance or by compliance.

TABLE 10.1 Effects of reference groups on consumer choice

Type of influence	Definition	Explanation	Example
Normative compliance	The pressure exerted on an individual to conform and comply	Works best when social acceptance is a strong motive, strong pressures exist from the group and the product or service is conspicuous in its use	Street gangs share common characteristics such as wearing distinct clothing, specific jackets or other uniforms. The members want to be accepted, the pressure to wear the jacket is great and the jacket itself is a conspicuous badge of membership. The Los Angeles Police Department have a web page about how gangs are identified: www.lapdonline.org/newsroom/los-angeles-police-department-2009-gang-initiatives-january-2009/
Value-expressive influence	The pressure that comes from the need for psychological association with a group	The desired outcome is respect from others; this pressure comes from the need for esteem, rather than from the need to belong	The city worker in his pinstripe suit and the lumbersexual hipster in his flannel shirt, well-groomed beard, covered in tattoos and wearing jeans are both seeking respect from others by expressing a set of values in the way they dress
Informational influence	The influence arising from a need to seek information from the reference group about the product category being considered. Small groups tend to exercise more influence (Soll et al., 2010)	People often need to get expert advice and opinion about their product choices. This can often be provided by the appropriate reference group	Many professional organisations and trade bodies offer their members free advice about useful products for their businesses. Clearly a recommendation on, say, computer software for a hairdressing business would be well received if it came from the Hairdressers Federation

The mechanisms by which reference groups affect consumer behaviour are shown in Table 10.1 and diagrammatically in Figure 10.3.

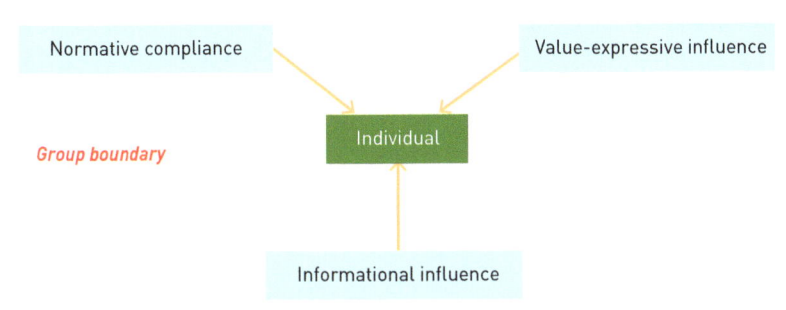

FIGURE 10.3   Mechanisms for controlling behaviour

Of the above three influences, **normative compliance** is probably the most powerful. The source of normative compliance lies in operant conditioning (Lin and Shek, 2022); the individual finds that conforming behaviour results in group approval and esteem, whereas non-conforming behaviour results in group disapproval. Eventually the 'good' behaviour becomes automatic and natural, and it would be difficult to imagine any other way of doing things (see Chapter 8 for more on operant conditioning). For example, materialistic people are often stigmatised by groups, whereas people who enjoy experiential consumption are not. This, in time, results in behaviour modification (Van Boven et al., 2009).

The principles of good moral behaviour are not absolutes; they are the result (in most cases) of normative compliance with a reference group (Khan and Kalra, 2022). Normative compliance may be less important now than it used to be, for four reasons. First, the influence of the extended family (grandparents, parents, aunts and uncles) may be reducing as people move away from their home towns, and second there is strong evidence that people are becoming more inner-directed (McNulty, 1985; Trompenaars and Hampden-Turner, 2012). Third, the reduction in face-to-face interaction may be leading to this move away from normative compliance; increasingly people communicate by impersonal means such as text messages and email. Whether this is a cause of the paradigm shift or one of its effects is difficult to decide at present. Fourth, there is a weakening of respect for social norms, generated by a feeling of alienation from society. This is called anomie by sociologists (Durkheim, 1951; Hövermann et al., 2015; Sârbu et al., 2022). Some people have little or no respect for rules made by other people, and conform grudgingly or not at all, because they do not feel that they have a position within society as a whole.

Normative compliance
The force that compels people towards agreeing with the rest of the group

BRAND EXPERIENCE: ANOMIE IN BREXIT

Although support for Britain's withdrawal from the EU in the 2016 referendum emanated from all sections of society, it was much stronger and prevalent among specific socio-economic and demographic cohorts, namely older citizens, people who had received

(Continued)

> a minimal formal education in their youth and those on low incomes. These were the citizens who had benefited the least, and whose communities had suffered the most, from four decades of deindustrialisation, globalisation, neoliberalism and apparent neglect or abandonment by politicians in Westminster and the London-centric national media. Leave voters (Brexiteers) were also notable for the extent to which they shared five social, cultural and political attitudes, characteristics or experiences, all beginning with the letter 'a': anomie, alienation, austerity, authoritarianism and atavism. Only by examining these five aspects can we fully comprehend the fears, frustrations, grievances and resentments which underpinned support for Leave in the referendum, and why these characteristics were very strongly concentrated in specific sections of British society.
>
> *Source*: Dorey (2022).

Of course, the pressure to conform will only work on someone who has a strong motivation to be accepted. If the pressure is coming from an aspirational group, this is likely to be the case; if, on the other hand, the pressure is coming from a dissociative group, the reverse will be the case and the individual will not feel under any pressure to conform. For example, most law-abiding citizens would comply with instructions from the police, and would usually go out of their way to help the police. Criminals, on the other hand, might avoid helping the police even in circumstances where their own crimes were not at issue.

The conspicuousness of the product or service is also crucial to the operation of normative compliance. For example, if all your friends vote for the Conservative Party in the UK general election, you might be under some pressure to do likewise; but since the ballot is secret nobody will know if you vote Labour instead, so there is little pressure for normative compliance. Similarly, if your friends all drink Stella Artois lager you may feel under pressure to do the same, but might be happy with a supermarket own-brand when you're having a beer in the back garden at home. Conspicuous behaviour carries its own downside, though – the more conspicuous the behaviour, the more embarrassing it becomes if the group does not acknowledge the signal (Han and Nunes, 2010).

Advertisers often appeal to the need to belong to an aspirational group. Advertising that shows desirable groups having a good time together, all thanks to the product, are so common that they are regarded as clichés. Typically, products with a social element such as beer, entertainment and some food products are advertised in this way.

The reference group will not exert influence over every buying decision. Even in circumstances where group influence does come into play, people will be influenced by other variables such as product characteristics, standards of judgement and conflicting influences from other groups. Table 10.2 shows some of the determinants of reference group influence.

REFERENCE GROUPS

TABLE 10.2 Determinants of reference group influence

Determinant	Definition	Explanation	Example
Judgement standards	The criteria used by the individual to evaluate the need to conform	Judgement standards are objective when the group norms are obvious and when the group approach is clearly the sensible course of action. The standards are subjective when it is not clear which is the most sensible course of action	Decisions of the ruling party in government are often portrayed as being unanimous; in the UK, the Conservative Party is famous for presenting a united front, and individual members of the Cabinet therefore believe it is important to conform. The Labour Party, on the other hand, has a tradition of public debate and therefore its Shadow Cabinet is more likely to disagree in public, since members do not see a need to conform
Product characteristics	The features of the product that are salient to the group influence	The two main characteristics necessary for group influence to work are that the product should be visible, and that it should stand out (non-universal ownership)	A member of a judo club will be proud to wear the black belt, since it not only denotes a high level of expertise, but is not available to other members unless they achieve the same level
Member characteristics	The traits of the group member which make him or her more or less susceptible to group pressures	People vary considerably in the degree to which they are influenced by pressures from the group. Some people remain fairly independent, whereas others conform habitually. Personality, status and security all seem to play major roles in determining whether an individual will conform	It transpires that university students are much more likely to conform with group norms than are housewives (Manz and Sims, 1981). This is possibly because university students are young, and often away from home, and thus have a greater need to belong
Group characteristics	The features of the group which influence individuals to conform	The power of the group to influence the individual varies according to size, cohesiveness and leadership. Once the group is bigger than three members, the power to influence levels off. This is probably because the group has difficulty reaching a consensus. Likewise, the stronger the leadership the greater the influence, and the greater the cohesiveness the stronger the influence, because the group reaches a clear decision	Many smokers take up the habit as a result of peer group pressure when they are aged around 12 or 13. If a child's friends are strongly anti-smoking, there is likely to be much less of an influence and therefore uptake
Role model	An individual whose influence is similar to that of a group	A role model is a hero, a star or just somebody the individual respects and admires, and wishes to imitate	Many young women seek to imitate top models by extreme dieting, to the extent that the Madrid fashion week banned all models with a body mass index below 18; Milan threatened to follow suit (BBC News, 2006). During the 1930s, when Clark Gable took off his shirt in a movie and showed that he was not wearing a vest, sales of vests plummeted because it became non-macho to wear one

MODELLING

Role model
An individual who acts as a reference point for judging one's own behaviour

Modelling was briefly discussed in Chapter 5, with regard to motivation and pain avoidance. The effectiveness of the role model in modelling behaviour will depend on the personal characteristics of the role model (see Figure 10.4) or indeed as a result of voice pitch or hand gestures which can elicit a stronger emotional response (Rodero, 2022). *Attractive* models will be imitated more than unattractive ones; *successful-looking* models are given more credence than unsuccessful-looking ones; and a model who is perceived as being *similar* to the observer is also more likely to be emulated (Baker and Churchill, 1977). Somewhat more recent neuro-psychological research has shown that average-looking celebrity models produce high levels of electrodermal response; in other words, they create the strongest physical effect on the observer (Gakhal and Senior, 2008; Zuckerman, 1988).

There is also some evidence to show that observers are more likely to identify with role models who have some difficulty in completing the modelled task (Manz and Sims, 1981). There has, of course, been debate about whether crime shows on TV encourage people to copy the behaviour that is shown in the programmes; according to the theory, modelled behaviour will be copied if the observer feels able to identify with the role model. Presumably, therefore, a programme showing young working-class men making a living from selling hard drugs might encourage other young working-class men to do the same. However, the saving grace of this scenario is that the role model must also be seen to be successful and attractive – and in most TV dramas and movies the criminal is shown as being, ultimately, unsuccessful.

Whilst some have noted that it is beneficial to 'stand on the shoulder of giants' when choosing role models with which to shape a career (García-Martínez, 2021), other research has shown that sometimes role models can be too good to be true (Contín-Pilart and Larraza-Kintana, 2015) – Superman turns out to be too super, so that people who compare themselves to Superman are less likely to volunteer to help others, simply because they feel that they do not measure up to the role model (Nelson and Norton, 2005).

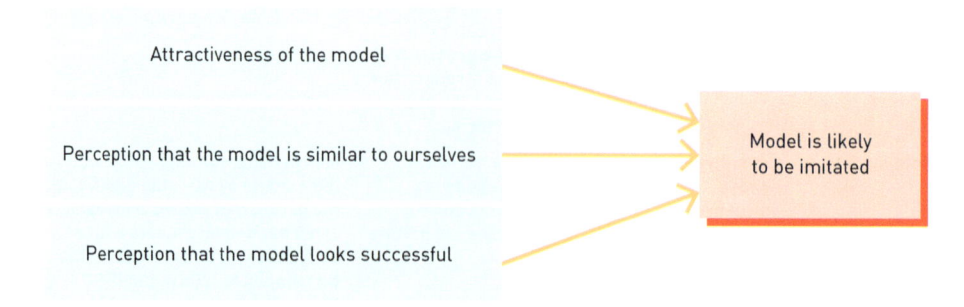

FIGURE 10.4 Factors in modelling

MECHANISMS OF PERSONAL INFLUENCE AND WORD OF MOUTH

Personal influence is commonly conducted via word of mouth. The classic definition of word of mouth was proffered by Arndt (1967): 'Oral person to person communication between a receiver and a communicator whom the person perceives as non-commercial, regarding brand, product or a service'.

Word of mouth communication is informal, and is conducted between individuals, neither of whom is a marketer. Word of mouth is therefore conducted without the ulterior motive of profiting from a sale; the non-commercial perception is dominant. Word of mouth becomes increasingly more influential compared to well-researched sources of product information such as *Which?* magazine as a result of consumers being somewhat cynical about the true independence of third party advice (Sethna et al., 2013).

Groups and individuals obviously have a strong influence on people's attitudes and behaviour through word of mouth; there are three main theories regarding the mechanisms whereby this personal influence is exerted. The history of the theory is not so much one of advancing knowledge about the mechanisms involved, but is rather a history of the way society has changed in the period in which the theories were evolving.

Trickle-down theory says that lower-class people often imitate upper-class people (Veblen, 1899). Influence is transmitted down from the wealthier classes to the poorer classes, as the poorer groups in society seek to 'better themselves' (d'Aura, 2020; Hammad et al., 2019; Srivastava et al., 2021). In fact, trickle-down is rarely seen in industrialised, wealthy countries like the UK because new ideas are disseminated overnight by the mass media and copied by chain stores within days. This is particularly true of clothing fashions, and the punk revolution in the mid-1970s was an example of 'trickle-up', where the fashion came up from the poorer classes. What is replacing trickle-down theory is **homophilous influence**, which refers to transmission between those of similar age, education, social class, etc. – in other words, those who already have a lot in common (Barnett et al., 2022). The 'commonality' (from the perspective of influence) is prolific when one considers the use of Twitter, YouTube and Instagram on which consumers share information about what they've bought and why.

Another area in which trickle-down theory can be observed is in the cult of celebrity (Ahluwalia and Miller, 2022): famous people are frequently imitated, and marketers use this to their advantage by obtaining celebrity endorsements of products. Soap operas play an influential role here, because they mimic group life in the real world, so much so that people often associate themselves with the cast of a soap opera in the same way as they would with a real group of people. This has given rise to the popularity of reality television shows, the cast members of which have become 'celebrities' in their own right (see for example *Made in Chelsea*, *The Only Way is Essex* and *Gogglebox*). This can affect people's aspirational consumption patterns (Russell and Stern, 2006) and occasionally lead to controversies (Misra, 2022).

Two-step flow theory says that new ideas flow from the media to 'influentials' who then pass the information on to the rest of society (Lazarsfeld et al., 1948). When this theory was first formulated in the late 1940s and early 1950s it probably had a great deal of truth in it, and there is still evidence for this view; certainly in the **diffusion** of innovative high-tech products there is strong evidence for it. However, there is a weakening of this mechanism due to the preponderance of mass media. In the 1940s most homes did not have TV and there was no commercial radio in the UK; the availability of commercial information was therefore more restricted to the wealthy. Also, two-step flow assumes that the audience is passively waiting for the information to be presented, whereas in fact people actively seek out information about new things by asking friends and relatives and by looking for published information. A comparison of two-step flow theory and trickle-down theory is shown in Figure 10.5.

Trickle-down theory
The belief that innovations are adopted by wealthy, educated people first and eventually 'trickle down' to people in lower socio-economic groups

Homophilous influences
The transmission of ideas between people of similar standing in the community

Diffusion
The process of adoption of an innovation throughout the market

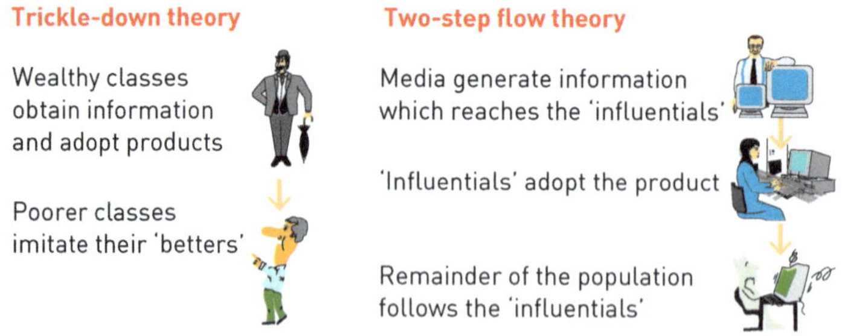

Trickle-down theory

Wealthy classes obtain information and adopt products

Poorer classes imitate their 'betters'

Two-step flow theory

Media generate information which reaches the 'influentials'

'Influentials' adopt the product

Remainder of the population follows the 'influentials'

FIGURE 10.5 Mechanisms of personal influence

CONSUMER BEHAVIOUR IN ACTION: BRITAIN... A LOVE ISLAND?

Britain, like many other countries, has seen an explosion of 'reality TV shows'. Amongst some of the most popular are *Celebs go Dating*, *Too Hot to Handle*, *Naked Attraction*, *Teen Mom*, *Ex on the Beach* and finally the one which perhaps gives the most feral pleasure to millions of viewers, *Love Island*, a dating show in which ten singles (five men and five women) try to find true love whilst parading around a sunny villa wearing virtually nothing, goaded by a lack of contact with the outside world... oh and a distinct lack of single beds! Indeed, such is the influence of the show that following a spate of intensely heavy smoking by the contestants, Lord Storey asked his peers in the House of Lords 'What message does that say to young people?' In addition, the show has, in one guise or another, been accused of racism, fatphobia, sexism, ageism and heteronormativity. Then there's sadly the fact that two former contestants and a former host, Caroline Flack, have committed suicide.

It would seem that in the early 21st century we are well beyond the forelock-tugging attitude of our Victorian forebears. The plethora of 'I'm a Celebrity' TV shows, where C-list 'celebrities' whom very few have heard of put themselves into embarrassing situations, demonstrates that people still have an interest in what the pseudo-famous have to say. Or is it simply that we like to see the once-famous fall heavily? Some may not have much respect for the opinions of the aristocracy, but there are other opinion leaders around – rock stars, TV stars, professional footballers and so forth.

Turning our attention to the island's other love... that of food! Even the subtle aristocracy of the TV chef has an influence on what we eat. Take for example the BBC's TV series called *The Incredible Spice Men*. Cyrus Todiwala and Tony Singh, a couple of Indian-born celebrity chefs, travelled around the UK trying to convince the great British public that British food needs 'spicing up'. Apparently the British palate has struggled with things such as clove, ginger and cumin. And so we see everything from chilli and cinnamon ice cream to the indelibly staple fish and chips being spiced. Even though the psychology of our taste buds dictates that we have a natural dislike for things that are different, guess what... we lapped it up! Perhaps first impressions can be wrong... it turns out that these media influentials have changed our opinions on spice.

The multistage interaction model (see Figure 10.6) agrees that some people are more influential than others, but also recognises that the mass media affect both influentials and seekers. The influential doesn't mediate the information flow, as the two-step model suggests, but rather acts as a mechanism for emphasising or facilitating the information flow. Within the model there is a continuous dialogue between marketers, seekers and influentials, with many stages of influence before the new idea is adopted or rejected. If there are several influentials, their influence is very much stronger if they occupy a number of different positions in the network rather than being at the top of the network (Stephen and Berger, 2009). This may be because the person being influenced receives the message several times, meaning there is redundancy in the communication.

Clearly it is important for marketers to identify who the influential people are likely to be, and much research has been carried out into this area. Table 10.2 shows the main characteristics of influentials which have been identified so far. This is probably not an exhaustive list, nor will it be generally applicable to all cases.

Influentials (and market mavens – see Chapter 6) like to pass on their knowledge, and there are several reasons for doing this.

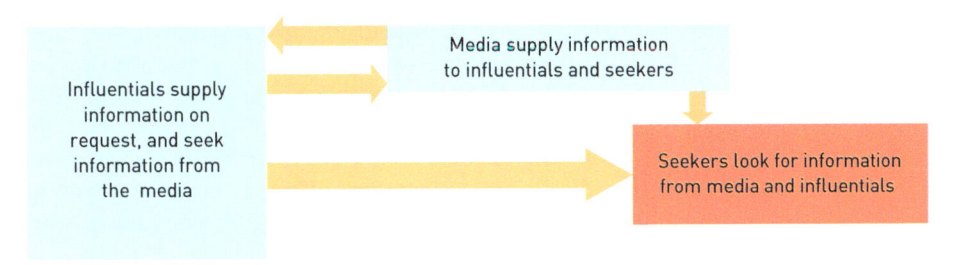

FIGURE 10.6 Multistage interaction model

Involvement is a major force. The influential is usually very interested in the product category, and wants to share the excitement with others; mavens also have a high need for variety (Goldring et al., 2022; Schneider and Huber, 2022; Stokburger-Sauer and Hoyer, 2009). An audio-visual entertainment enthusiast who buys a new *Pivetta Opera Only* will want to tell friends and colleagues all about it as soon as possible using social media. And why wouldn't you? The Italian designer Andrea Pivetta's ludicrous 120,000-watt amplifier stands a whopping 2.4m tall and weighs a colossal 1.5 tonnes – that's as much as a caravan. Though this is sure to give you much better sound. When powered on, the 12-sided, aircraft aluminium prism opens up in seven distinct sections to reveal all the electronics. But the most redeeming (can I use that word here?) feature is its price tag – $2.2 million. Perhaps telling other people acts as an outlet for the pleasure of owning such equipment.

Self-enhancement is about airing one's superior knowledge. People like to appear to be 'in the know' – perhaps being able to say 'I own a Pivetta Opera Only – the world's finest and most state-of-the-art amplifier'. Appearing to be a connoisseur, whether of fine wines, works of art, classic cars or technology, is something many influentials, and especially mavens, strive for. People often ask a friend or relative to help when choosing a gift for a third party, especially where the gift-giving might be risky (where little is known about the third party, or where a lot of importance is placed on the gift). This usually increases the social bonding between the giver and the adviser (Lowrey et al., 2004).

Concern for others often precipitates influence. The genuine desire to help a friend to reach a good decision often prompts the expert to say, 'OK, I'll come with you when you go to buy that car'. This factor works most strongly when there is a strong link between the individuals concerned, and when the influential has been very satisfied with the product or service concerned. People with high levels of altruism are especially likely to help (Kaikati and Ahluwalia, 2010) and thus further instigate prosocial behaviour (Pfattheicher et al., 2022). This can have a very direct effect on consumption: there is evidence that people often feel guilty about buying themselves a treat, but if a free gift for someone else is included, the guilt is very much reduced or even disappears altogether (Lee and Corfman, 2004). This implies that firms in the 'treat' or 'luxury' business would do well to offer an extra little something to 'give to a friend'. Laphroaig Whisky Distillers do this: periodically they ask established customers ('Friends of Laphroaig') to pass on the names and addresses of three friends, to whom the distillery sends a small bottle of the whisky. Naturally, people are asked to obtain permission from their friends before passing on their details, but the promotion is successful on two fronts: it rewards the loyalty of the existing customer, and it brings the whisky to the attention of the friends. People generally enjoy giving gifts to their friends and sharing good fortune – people who are given gift vouchers enjoy the vouchers more when it involves sharing with a friend (Norton et al., 2010).

The main practical lesson from this is that 'bring a friend' promotions should reward the friend rather than the original customer: offering someone a free gift for introducing a friend does not work as well as offering a gift to any friends who are introduced.

Message intrigue is the factor concerned with comments about advertising messages. If an advertisement is particularly humorous or intriguing, people will discuss it; this enhances the message by repetition. In the USA, Donald Trump turned the presidency into a live-action reality television series comprising a chaotic blend of televised and tweeted intrigue (Jordan and Dykes, 2022). Advertisements for Guinness have often used this approach. One such advertisement shows Gareth Thomas (former Wales rugby captain) talking about how his teammates were there for him when he needed them. In the advert, called 'Never Alone', we hear Gareth talk about his life on the rugby field, and the hard times he faced. The viewer assumes that he is talking about the game being gruelling, but half way through the advert we find that Gareth is actually referring to the psychological battle he faced as he harboured the secret of

---

Self-enhancement
The practice of airing one's superior knowledge in order to create a better image

Message intrigue
The element of a message which arouses the interest of a recipient

his sexuality. He had not told his fans, or the crowd, or his team – the closest people to him, whom he calls his family – about the fact that he is gay, for fear of people rejecting him. The advert subtly intimates that there is a perception associated with men who play rugby, and thus young men take their 'reference' from such portrayals; by implication, it would not be acceptable to have a gay rugby player. The advert ends with the words 'Gareth Thomas. Thought he was alone. Always part of a team. Guinness – made of more'. With music by Ludovico Einaudi playing in the background, it is not only emotionally gripping, but the fact that it was aired just before the start of the Rugby World Cup meant that people were more likely to watch it, remember it and continue to make the connections between rugby and Guinness.

Dissonance reduction is about reducing doubts after making a major purchase (see Chapter 9). As word of mouth, or word of mouse (Sethna et al., 2013) influence, this can be good or bad; sometimes the influential will try to reassure him- or herself by telling everybody (the volume relates to the number of people to which the message is relayed) about the good points of the product; more often, though, the disappointed customer will use word of mouth/mouse to complain bitterly and explain how the wicked manufacturer has cheated him or her. This is sometimes a way of passing the responsibility over to the supplier rather than admitting that the influential has made a bad decision or a bad choice.

Dissonance
A mental state that arises when outcomes do not match with expectations

The forces driving influentials are summarised in Figure 10.7.

Tinderitis
The harmful side effect of incessant use of the smartphone app Tinder. Often diagnosed by a flat battery, blowing your data allowance or a ruined index finger or thumb tendon

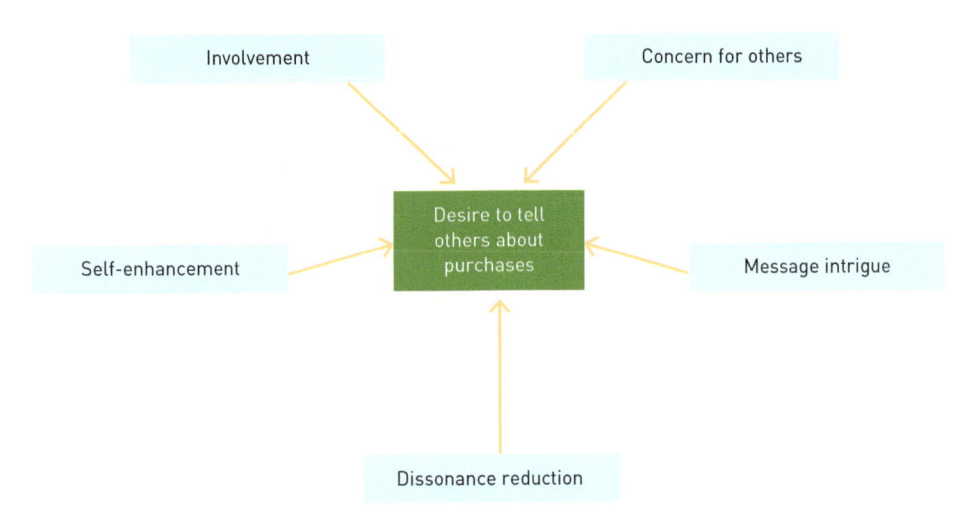

FIGURE 10.7 Forces driving influentials

BRAND EXPERIENCE: TINDERITIS

Yes apparently that's a thing – according to the Urban Dictionary (2022). Interestingly, most of the reasons influentials have for passing on what they know are selfish ones. They want to show off their knowledge, pass on an interesting bit of gossip, reassure

(Continued)

themselves that they made the right decision by persuading someone else to make the same choice and so forth.

Only occasionally, apparently, are they motivated by concern for others – passing on a good tip to a friend, in this case. Does this tell us that people are essentially selfish? Or should we give people credit for getting their kicks by being helpful rather than destructive? And what do we actually mean by 'being helpful'?

Take Tinder, for instance. It's a location-based social discovery application that facilitates communication between mutually interested users. The dating app allows users to chat with their matches. It was launched in 2012 and currently has 75 million users, of which 78% are men and 22% are women – and 30% of its users are married. Tinder has registered over 60 billion matches. What makes Tinder different from its competition is that it was among the first 'swiping apps', where the user uses a swiping motion to choose between the photos of other users: swiping right for potentially good matches and swiping left on a photo to move to the next one. Over 1.6 billion left and right swipes are registered on Tinder every day, and more than 30 million matches are made each day on the app; 95% of Tinder users meet their matches within a week. Tinder has over 6.03 million paid subscribers and it made $1.2 billion in 2020. They donated $100,000 for a dream wedding of an LGBTQ couple. Not only is Tinder available in 190 countries, it is also available in 40+ different languages. It is the most popular dating app in the USA. In the fall semester of 2015, the good folks at Tinder posted a blog entitled 'Most right-swiped campuses 2015: Did yours make the list?' Statistics for the top 50 universities in the USA for right-swipes are shown for both girls and boys, thus passing on 'good tips' about where the rest of the like-minded reference group believes the '**buff tings**' are. By 'being helpful' Tinder has amassed a fortune and in August 2021 it was said, by Morgan Stanley, to be worth $42 billion.

© iStock.com/jpgfactory

Buff ting
A British slang phrase for people who are very attractive, glamorous and good-looking

Overall, word of mouth/mouse influence is much stronger than advertising or other marketer-produced communications. For marketers, then, the problem lies in knowing how to use word of mouth to its best advantage. Table 10.3 offers some comparisons and strategies.

It is not usually possible to rely entirely on word of mouth, but marketers should take steps to stimulate it as a promotional tool. Advertising that provokes word of mouth about the advert itself can be very powerful – research shows that a very creative advertisement that prompts people to tell others about it leads to a much greater intention to purchase after the other people see the advertisement for themselves (Moldovan and Lehmann, 2010). In other words, someone who is told about a very exciting or entertaining advertisement will be prompted to look out for the advert, and is then much more likely to buy the product. Sometimes marketers are able to encourage word of mouth by giving influential people a product sample and asking them to blog about their experiences with the product. Most people in that position will accept, embrace, ridicule or apologise for accepting the role as a marketing tool, and very few ignore their role by not mentioning in the blog that they were given the product (Kozinets et al., 2008).

If the company is in a position to be able to identify influentials, it is well worthwhile offering to lend them the product (or even give them it, if the cost is low enough) so that they can be stimulated into talking about it to friends. Advertising should be interesting and involving, perhaps even controversial, so that debate ensues. Although it is not true to say that any word of mouth will be good for a company, it is certainly true to say that controversy and debate will always increase brand awareness, even when it does not enhance brand image. For example, Harveytiles (a brand of Harvey Roofing Products Ltd, a South African roofing tile manufacturer) produces advertisements that are extremely controversial. The slogans use religious references ('A roof without Harveytiles is like being burnt in hell without a saviour: Only heaven is covered with Harveytiles') that have proved to be extremely offensive to the committed Christians of Zambia. The result has been that everyone in Zambia has heard of Harveytiles, but of course this does not necessarily mean that people will buy the product. Some people undoubtedly boycott the product because of the religious references.

Another way of stimulating word of mouth is to allow people to try out the product. As mentioned earlier, car manufacturers usually give exceptionally generous discounts to car hire companies, taking the view that hirers might well be tempted to buy the same model at a later stage, and are also very likely to talk about the vehicle to others.

Marketing theorists have not taken word of mouth seriously as there is a perception among marketers that one cannot plan, monitor and control word of mouth. But if one looks at this through an entrepreneurial marketing lens (Sethna et al., 2013), one would assume that marketers would take this activity seriously, as the majority of small and medium-sized enterprises use word of mouth recommendations as their main source of new business (Stokes and Nelson, 2013).

TABLE 10.3 Word of mouth

Strong influence	Weak influence	Tactical suggestions
Seeker initiates conversation with source	Source initiates conversation with seeker	Advertising could emphasise the idea of 'Ask the person who owns one'. Network marketers could emphasise a more advisory role for their salespeople rather than a strongly proactive approach
Negative information	Positive information	Because marketers are uniformly positive about the product, the seeker is more alert to any negatives. The essential thing for marketers to do is to ensure that any complaints are dealt with immediately and thoroughly
Verbal communication is stronger for thinking and evaluation	Visual communication is stronger for awareness and stimulation of interest	Where appropriate, marketers could encourage satisfied customers to show their friends the product; this tactic is often used for home improvement sales, where customers are paid a small reward or commission for introducing friends to the product. This is also the basis for party-plan selling, e.g. Tupperware and Ann Summers

CONSUMER BEHAVIOUR IN ACTION: WORD OF MOUTH SELLS WORDS

Dan Brown's climb to fame was far from meteoric. He failed at several careers before getting into writing – and even then his earlier books hardly set the world on fire. Yet everyone needs to learn their craft, and eventually Dan hit the jackpot with *The DaVinci Code*, published in 2003.

The book, which puts forward the theory that Jesus married Mary Magdalene and had children by her, was not exactly a great work of literature, but it caught the public imagination. Initially the publishers planned only a short print run – based on the sales of Dan's other books, it seemed unlikely that the book would be a runaway bestseller. The rest, of course, is history: the book has to date sold in excess of 100 million copies, and in 2022 became an epic stage thriller touring in the UK.

So how come this book sold so much better than expected? The publishers certainly didn't hype the book – after all, they weren't expecting to sell it in large enough numbers to justify a big publicity campaign. The answer lies in word of mouth. People told people about the book, and those people told other people, and so the process went on until everybody had heard of it.

Research by Nielsen Bookscan in 2005 showed that a large number of best-selling books have achieved success this way – *Captain Corelli's Mandolin*, *Eats, Shoots & Leaves* and *The Lovely Bones* were all cited as million-plus sellers that had succeeded almost entirely on personal recommendation.

As a result, the World Book Day organisers ran a campaign encouraging people to recommend a book to a friend – another resounding success!

© iStock.com/DarioRota

THE EMERGENCE OF WORD OF MOUSE

In recent years word of mouth has been supplemented by the use of the internet, email communications and of course social media. Collectively, they have contributed to the creation of a new channel of communication which has been referred to as 'word of mouse' (Sethna et al., 2013).

BRAND EXPERIENCE: GILLETTE'S 2019 #THEBESTMENCANBE

The provocative hashtag-led campaign that got thousands of people talking on social media was Gillette's 2019 campaign #TheBestMenCanBe. The video-based social media campaign was created in the wake of #MeToo and aimed to challenge traditional male stereotypes and encourage positive behaviour. It disregarded the brand's shaving products and instead addressed themes of toxic masculinity, misogyny and sexual harassment. Gillette's video showed various situations involving boys and men, from men making derogatory comments toward women to young boys fighting each other, intending to encourage others to make better choices. The divisive advert sparked serious debate with some viewers applauding the brand's stance on this social issue and others viewing the ad as an attack on men. Among the negative responses was a tweet from an outspoken British journalist, Piers Morgan, accusing the brand of virtue-signalling: 'I've used Gillette razors my entire adult life but this absurd virtue-signalling PC guff may drive me away to a company less eager to fuel the current pathetic global assault on masculinity.' Other responses saw the campaign as a catalyst for positive change with one Twitter user writing 'Thank you, Gillette, for standing out and keeping the conversation going' and another stating 'I don't even use Gillette but I may start using it after this… great job, great message, great delivery.' Although opinions were divided on the campaign, which immediately went viral and now has 3 million views on YouTube, overall, it seems that feedback was positive, encouraging 65% more purchase intent. The original post gained 203k retweets, 76.3k quoted tweets and a staggering 513.3k likes on Twitter, revealing how powerful brand campaigns that tackle social issues can be. However, given the backlash received around a razor company attempting to virtue-signal, it's important for brands to consider whether they have the authority to make comments in these areas and whether the end goal of the campaign justifies the means.

E-communications are a fast and powerful communications medium, but more importantly they provide a semi-permanent record of what was said, so that communications can contain facts and figures that can be referred to later. Encouraging people to communicate with each other about products has become a growth area for e-marketing, and is a feature of many websites. The decision to forward a message implies that the individual endorses it: the person's involvement in the product is of course important, but the decision to forward a message seems to depend much more on the amount of traffic between the individuals concerned (Harvey et al., 2011).

The power of word of mouse, however, has grown exponentially with the rapid adoption of all things 'mobile' and m-commerce (mobile-commerce) related. This is partly because many consumers are comfortable with the convenience of buying on their mobile devices (iPhones, tablets, etc.) and it is thought that over a quarter of all e-commerce traffic stems from a mobile device. The prolific use of smartphones has meant that communications using chatrooms, blogs, vlogs, cross-platform mobile messaging apps (for example WhatsApp, WeChat, LINE, Viber, Tango) and virtual

Vlog
Short for video log – a blog that includes video clips

gaming are leading the way in the world of m-commerce. From a societal perspective, there are some commentators who believe that fourth-tier cities in emerging economies may not even experience the traditional bricks-and-mortar shopping and retail outlets, mainly due to the convenience and increasing sophistication of mobile shopping. Virtual communities are extremely powerful in promoting products – they frequently ask each other for specific recommendations about products (WeChat currently has over 1.2 billion active users). Young consumers have been shown to develop online personalities, which may differ from their real personalities but which act in very similar ways in terms of group behaviour.

CONSUMER BEHAVIOUR IN ACTION: OLDER REFERENCES

Are we in danger of assuming that it's really only 'young' people who make their opinions count? Are they the only trendsetters? Well, if you were to believe all the media stories about vloggers, you'd be forgiven when taking that stance.

The media is awash with the names of Millennials who transmit their daily dosage of performing prowess on YouTube channels – live and direct from their bedrooms – to millions of adoring fans over whom they have influence – or some might say a stranglehold. One of the top vloggers among this group is Zoella (Zoe Sugg), who reigns supreme with over 10 million subscribers and 1.11 billion views of her videos. Her contemporaries are, among others, people such as Danisnotonfire (Dan Howell), who generally makes videos about his own escapades, and Selena Gomez, who seems to be the resident fashion and make-up maven. So influential is this group of people that vloggers even have their own physical magazine now called *Oh My Vlog!* It's similar in style to teen mags about boy bands, but it is aimed at the YouTube generation. Some people have questioned whether such an 'archaic' form of communication is right for the audience – to which the publishers have said, 'Well, you can't print out a vlog and stick it up on your bedroom wall, can you?', which is a fair point.

In reality, it's not all about the Millennials. There is a lot to be said about age and experience, and some over 50s are eager to play the YouTube game. Admittedly their view and subscriber scores are not as impressive as those of younger people, but they are still yielding an influence over a substantial number of people. Take, for instance, 'Elle is for Living'. She talks about her passions and her life, whether it's product testing, or sharing beauty and style tips – she has an opinion on everything. And with over 5.49 million views and in excess of 31,000 subscribers, it seems that there is an interested audience. Then there's 'Wheaten Beauty' – a 50-something university academic whose vlog is crammed full of beauty tips which she records both in the morning and at night. With thousands of subscribers and over 216,000 views, there's a considerable following developing, even more so as her videos talk about her involvement with **Influenster**. Influenster is a product discovery, testing and review platform that uses social media analytics to measure its users' influence on social media. In essence, what the people at Influenster do is quantify its users' influence via 'social impact', which tracks the number of friends, followers or subscribers a user has. Based on the impact score (the higher the better) and the demographic, the user can then be invited into campaigns that Influenster is running for various consumer branded products. The brands offer complementary products or digital rewards to the Influenster member. Once they've

Influenster
Is a product discovery and reviews platform that uses social media analytics to measure its users' influence on social media

received the shipment and tested the product, all they have to do is create a vlog, share their thoughts with their followers (although there is no obligation to do either) and complete a survey. The more they do, the more chance there is of unlocking a badge of honour – 'expert' or 'lifestyle', part of a gamification type of system to encourage usage and the creation of content. The more content, the more views – and thus the greater the possibility for greater impact. By their own admission, Influenster enables members to compare products and then allows the mavens to guide members on how products can be adopted and integrated into their own life.

It's worth noting that mainly due to the elements of gamification and the way in which Influenster is structured, the response rates to their surveys have regularly achieved over 82% return. This is indeed quite an achievement and has totally eclipsed the research industry average.

Social networking sites that focus around celebrities often generate a very strong sense of togetherness and belonging, amounting to a tribal situation, despite having no reality outside cyberspace (Hamilton and Hewer, 2010).

Online communities provide support and help for their members in the same way as offline, face-to-face groups. Online communities on Facebook often 'nudge' each other towards buying particular products (Harris and Dennis, 2011), and online communities can be very powerful in raising brand commitment (Kim et al., 2008). A study of a slimming website revealed that there are three main types of participant: Passive Recipients obtain high levels of informational and emotional support, but communicate passively; Active Supporters are much more proactive in communication, and obtain high levels of support; and Casual Browsers communicate passively and receive little support (Ballantine and Stephenson, 2011). Sometimes online communities can be damaging for marketers. Counter-brand and alter-brand behaviour is easily facilitated in cyberspace: users can develop dangerous opposition, or even their own products that compete directly with firms, without the need for corporate involvement.

Web forums used to be used by companies to attract new customers and to provide an outlet for people's discussions about products. People used such sites as information sources, and as ways of validating their self-concept as being knowledgeable, or as 'insiders'. But social media have taken the space of the once-loved online bulletin board.

SUMMARY

There is little doubt that word of mouse will grow as access to the internet and the World Wide Web spreads throughout the world. In fact, it could even be the case that the mouse has had its day, and that it's the 'power of the finger' which currently rules our life. That said, we're also seeing a move towards voice-command mobile devices which (bizarrely) may bring us back to vocal delivery of messages (word of mouth), but web-enabled viral marketing is likely to be an increasing force for the foreseeable future.

In this chapter we have looked at some of the interpersonal factors that influence purchasing behaviour. In particular, we have looked at the groups and individuals who most influence consumers, and at the ways the influence is exerted. Finally, we have looked at ways marketers can use these interpersonal factors to improve customer relations and customer loyalty.

KEY POINTS

- Most people are members of several reference groups, all of which influence the individual in different ways.
- Normative compliance is probably the most powerful influence on behaviour.
- Conspicuousness is the most crucial product characteristic for normative compliance.
- Word of mouth spreads because the informant (influential) likes to talk about the products concerned.
- Complaints can be turned to the marketer's advantage by generous handling.
- Word of mouse is likely to be a growth area in marketing communications in the 21st century.

HOW TO IMPRESS YOUR EXAMINER

You are likely to be asked to compare different types of reference groups and/or explain your answer – for instance, that peer groups sometimes pressure people into buying the 'right' product, or that dissociative groups will tend to tarnish brand values. This not only shows that you understand the theory, it also shows that you can apply it in a marketing context.

REVIEW QUESTIONS

1. How might companies encourage word of mouth?
2. What is the role of normative compliance in fashion marketing?
3. How might peer pressure encourage people to try new things?
4. Why is word of mouse becoming more popular with companies?
5. How can companies counteract negative word of mouth?
6. How might membership of an automatic group affect buying behaviour?
7. How might membership of an automatic group affect someone's propensity to join a secondary group?
8. How might a secondary group also be a formal group?
9. What are the defining characteristics of a primary group?
10. How might a marketer make use of a virtual group?

CASE STUDY: THE TASTE OF BREXIT

Nigel Farage left a successful career as a commodities trader to go into politics after the Conservative Party signed the Maastricht Treaty, which advocated 'ever closer union' between European nations. He became a founding member of the United Kingdom Independence Party (UKIP) in 1993 and set about campaigning for Britain's EU withdrawal. In 2014, under Farage's leadership, UKIP came first in the European election topping the poll in the UK with 4.5 million votes and in doing so became the first political party since 1906 to win a national election that was not the Labour or Conservative parties. This successful result eventually forced the Conservative Party to hold a referendum on European Union membership. In June 2016, Farage was a leading figure in the campaign to leave. This gained him the name 'Mr Brexit' by Republican Presidential candidate Donald J. Trump, whom he supported at a rally on the campaign trail.

He is now encouraging people to sample his Farage Gin and try the 'taste of Brexit'.

The Brexit champion unveiled his new range of gins announcing it consists of three bottles made with 'patriotic flavours'. The red gin is flavoured with British cherries, the white gin is a classic dry style, and the blue gin is flavoured with gardenia flower giving it its trademark blue hue; mirroring the colours of Britain 'Red White and Blue'.

Clearly Nigel is trying to cash-in on the *Brand Farage* narrative. To contextualise the potential size of the 'reference group' who may well have an infinity with Farage Gin, let's look back at the numbers from the Brexit vote: 52% voted to leave the EU; 48% voted to remain in the EU.

© iStock.com / Vasil_Onyskiv

Speaking about the launch, Farage said he is planning to send a gift-wrapped bottle of his patriotic gin to the former president of the European Commission Jean-Claude Juncker in time for Christmas as well as his friend Donald Trump, if he were a drinker.

Farage said: 'Jean-Claude Juncker was a pleasant human being, despite the fact he didn't agree with my position. He deserves a bottle and one will be on its way to Luxembourg. I can't quite say the same about [European Parliament Brexit negotiator] Guy Verhofstadt, so he won't be getting one. And Donald Trump is teetotal. I hope when people give this as a present to Brexiteers it brings a big smile. And if it's given to Remainers, well I hope it makes the family laugh.'

He explained: 'A couple of years ago I happened to chance upon a retired

(Continued)

couple who decided to have a go producing gin in their garage. I looked at the process they were using and its all hand made, hand bottled, hand labelled and hand packed. It's a truly great cottage industry. We're about to have our fourth Prime Minister in six years and there is clearly much more to do. You might not yet have got the Brexit you voted for, but this stuff really is the taste of it.'

Farage added: 'I was a gin-drinking Eurosceptic in the eighties back when people said, "Nigel, you're so old fashioned". At home I will drink gin and tonic, straight. And with this range you can really experiment. The colours are so fantastic and vibrant and cocktails are a joy to make.'

In response to the launch, Remainers took to social media reminding Farage that the launch is ironic considering that gin is actually not quintessentially British, but European and has Dutch heritage, while others highlighted how his line-up simply illustrates the French flag!

Source: Adapted from Express.co.uk (2022).

CASE STUDY QUESTIONS

1. What is the role of normative compliance in a group such as the reference group?
2. What type of group is the reference group?
3. Why would the group be composed of people within a specific age group and social status?
4. What role does peer pressure play here, if at all?
5. Could the distillery have foreseen and potentially controlled any ramifications of the campaign?

FURTHER READING

For some more on gift-giving, try S. McKechnie and C. Tynan (2006) Social meaning in Christmas consumption: An exploratory study of UK celebrants' consumption rituals, *Journal of Consumer Behaviour*, 5 (2): 130–44. Also, *The Gift of Thanks: The Roots and Rituals of Gratitude*, by Margaret Visser (Boston, MA: Houghton Mifflin Harcourt, 2009), explores the other side of gift-giving – gratitude on the part of the recipient.

Ervin Goffman's *The Presentation of Self in Everyday Life* is a classic read (Harmondsworth: Penguin, 1990). It explores the ways in which we present ourselves in different group situations, and explains his 'life as theatre' analogy.

Also by Goffman, *Stigma: Notes on the Management of Spoiled Identity* (Harmondsworth: Penguin, 1990) explores another side of groups – the fate of those who are excluded. His research was carried out among people who were disfigured through birth or accident, people from racial or religious minorities, and people with mental illnesses. Goffman notes that other people tend to focus on the distinguishing feature, not on the whole personality, therefore such people become defined by their differences rather than by their similarities. This is a thought-provoking book, and often a very moving one.

For a humorous look at the fashion industry, and at our obsession with wearing the right clothes, you might like *Fashion Victim: Our Love–Hate Relationship with Dressing, Shopping and the Cost of Style*, by Michelle Lee (New York: Broadway Books, 2003). The author takes a wry look at the fashion industry, and pokes fun at some of the 'rules' of fashion ('Thou Shalt Pay More to Look Poor' being one of them). This is a fun read, with some interesting ideas underneath it.

MORE ONLINE

For additional materials that support this chapter and your learning, please visit:

https://study.sagepub.com/sethna5e

REFERENCES

Ahluwalia, P. and Miller, T. (2022) Celebrity activism. *Social Identities*, 28 (3): 293–5.

Ameen, N., Hosany, S. and Paul, J. (2022) The personalisation-privacy paradox: Consumer interaction with smart technologies and shopping mall loyalty. *Computers in Human Behavior*, 126: 106976.

Arndt, J. (1967) Role of product-related conversations in the diffusion of a new product. *Journal of Marketing Research*, 4: 291–5.

Asch, S.E. (1951) Effects of group pressure on the modification and distortion of judgements. In H. Guetzkow (ed.), *Groups, Leadership and Men*. Pittsburgh, PA: Carnegie Press. pp. 177–90.

Baker, M.J. and Churchill, G.A. Jr (1977) The impact of physically attractive models on advertising evaluations. *Journal of Marketing Research*, 14 (4): 538–55.

Ballantine, P.W. and Stephenson, R.J. (2011) Help me, I'm fat! Social support in online weight loss networks. *Journal of Consumer Behaviour*, 10 (6): 332–7.

Barnett, N.P., DiGuiseppi, G.T., Tesdahl, E.A. and Meisel, M.K. (2022) Peer selection and influence for marijuana use in a complete network of first-year college students. *Addictive Behaviors*, 124: 107087.

Baskerville, R. and Nandhakumar, J. (2007) Activating and perpetuating virtual teams: Now that we're mobile, where do we go? *IEEE Transactions on Professional Communication*, 50: 17–34.

BBC News (2006) Madrid bans waifs from catwalks. www.news.bbc.co.uk/1/hi/5341202.stm (accessed 23 July 2018).

Bearden, W.O. and Etzel, M.J. (1982) Reference group influence on product and brand purchase decisions. *Journal of Consumer Research*, 9 (September): 184–94.

Bleize, D.N.M., Tanis, M., Anschütz, D.J. and Buijzen, M. (2021) A social identity perspective on conformity to cyber aggression among early adolescents on WhatsApp. *Social Development*, 30 (4): 941–56.

Borzekowski, L. and Cohen, R. (2013) International reach of tobacco marketing among young children. *Pediatrics*, 132: 26–31.

Brandstetter, J., Racz, P., Beckner, C., Sandoval, E.B., Hay, J. and Bartneck, C. (2014) A peer pressure experiment: Recreation of the Asch conformity experiment with robots. In *Intelligent Robots and Systems (IROS 2014), 2014 IEEE/RSJ International Conference*. Chicago, IL. pp. 1335–40.

Breazeal, C.L. (2004) *Designing Sociable Robots*. Cambridge, MA: MIT Press.

Bullard, E. (2022) Virtual community (research starters). Online: *Salem Press Encyclopedia*. Great Neck Publishing: Research Starters

Carlson, K.A. and Sally, D. (2002) Thoughts that count: Fairness and possibilities, intentions and reactions. *Advances in Consumer Research*, 29: 79–89.

Contín-Pilart, I. and Larraza-Kintana, M. (2015) Do entrepreneurial role models influence the nascent entrepreneurial activity of immigrants? *Journal of Small Business Management*, 53 (4): 1146–63.

Crosby, E. and Otnes, C. (2010) Consumption as a strategy for stigma management. *Advances in Consumer Research*, 37: 28–9.

d'Aura, G. (2020) Shifting paradigms impact of technology on the diffusion of trends. *ZoneModa Journal*, 10 (2): 119–29.

Dorey, P. (2022) Explaining Brexit: The 5 A's – Anomie, alienation, austerity, authoritarianism and atavism. *Revue Française de Civilisation Britannique*, 27 (2). https://doi.org/10.4000/rfcb.9060

Durkheim, E. (1951) *Suicide: A Study in Sociology*. New York: Free Press.

Edwards, A. and Edwards, C. (2022) Does the correspondence bias apply to social robots? Dispositional and situational attributions of human versus robot behavior. *Frontiers in Robotics and AI*, 8. https://doi.org/10.3389/frobt.2021.788242

Express.co.uk (2022) Nigel Farage launches patriotic gin range promising it's the taste of Brexit. www.express.co.uk/news/politics/1663863/nigel-farage-gin-taste-of-brexit/amp (accessed 8 September 2022).

Fischer, E., Bristor, J. and Gaynor, B. (1996) Creating or escaping community? An exploratory study of internet consumers' behaviours. *Advances in Consumer Research*, 23: 178–82.

Fisher, R.J. and Dube, L. (2003) Gender differences in responses to emotional advertising: The effect of the presence of others. *Advances in Consumer Research*, 30: 15–17.

Fonner, K.L. and Roloff, M.E. (2010) Why teleworkers are more satisfied with their jobs than are office-based workers: When less contact is beneficial. *Journal of Applied Communication Research*, 38: 336–61.

Gakhal, B. and Senior, C. (2008) Examining the influence of fame in the presence of beauty: An electrodermal 'neuromarketing' study. *Journal of Consumer Behaviour*, 7 (4/5): 331–41.

García-Martínez, J. (2021) Standing on the shoulders of giants – Your mentors and role models will shape your career. *Chemistry (Weinheim an Der Bergstrasse, Germany)*, 27 (55): 13664–8.

Goldring, D., Gong, B. and Gironda, J.T. (2022) Mavens at work: Brand commitment and the moderating role of market mavens on social media engagement. *Journal of Promotion Management*, 28 (3): 261–287.

Gong, Y., Li, J., Xie, J., Zhang, L. and Lou, Q. (2022) Will 'green' parents have 'green' children? The relationship between parents' and early adolescents' green consumption values. *Journal of Business Ethics*, *179* (2): 369–85.

Hamilton, K. and Hewer, P. (2010) Tribal mattering spaces: Social networking sites, celebrity affiliations, and tribal innovations. *Journal of Marketing Management*, *26* (3/4): 271–9.

Hammad, H., Muster, V., El-Bassiouny, N.M. and Schaefer, M. (2019) Status and sustainability: Can conspicuous motives foster sustainable consumption in newly industrialized countries? *Journal of Fashion Marketing & Management*, *23* (4): 537–50.

Han, Y.J. and Nunes, J.C. (2010) Read the signal but don't mention it: How conspicuous consumption embarrasses the signaler. *Advances in Consumer Research*, *37*: 81–4.

Harris, L. and Dennis, C. (2011) Engaging customers on Facebook: Challenge for e-retailers. *Journal of Consumer Behaviour*, *10* (6): 338–46.

Harvey, C.G., Stewart, D.B. and Ewing, M.T. (2011) Forward or delete: What drives peer-to-peer message propagation across social networks? *Journal of Consumer Behaviour*, *10* (6): 365–72.

Haytko, D.L. and Baker, J. (2004) It's all at the mall: Exploring adolescent girls' experiences. *Journal of Retailing*, *80* (1): 67.

Hiltz, S.R. and Wellman, B. (1997) Asynchronous learning networks as a virtual classroom. *Communications of the ACM*, *40*: 44–9.

Homans, G.C. (1961) *Social Behavior: Its Elementary Forms*. New York: Harcourt, Brace and World.

Hövermann, A., Messner, S.F. and Zick, A. (2015) Anomie, marketization, and prejudice toward purportedly unprofitable groups: Elaborating a theoretical approach on anomie-driven prejudices. *Acta Sociologica*, *58* (3): 215–31.

Jansen, M., Boda, Z. and Lorenz, G. (2022) Social comparison effects on academic self-concepts – Which peers matter most? *Developmental Psychology*, *58* (8): 1541–56.

Jordan, L.S. and Dykes, D. (2022) 'If you don't fight like hell, you're not going to have a country': An intersectional settler colonial analysis of Trump's 'Save America' speech and other messages of (non)belonging. *Cultural Studies/Critical Methodologies*, *22* (5): 443–53.

Kaikati, A.M. and Ahluwalia, R. (2010) Word of mouth communication as helping behavior. *Advances in Consumer Research*, *37*: 127–8.

Kanda, T., Hirano, T., Eaton, D. and Ishiguro, H. (2004) Interactive robots as social partners and peer tutors for children: A field trial. *Human–Computer Interaction*, *19* (1): 61–84.

Khan, U. and Kalra, A. (2022) It's good to be different: How diversity impacts judgments of moral behavior. *Journal of Consumer Research*, *49* (2): 177–201.

Kim, J., Choi, J., Qualls, W. and Han, K. (2008) It takes a marketplace community to raise brand commitment: The role of online communities. *Journal of Marketing Management*, *24* (3/4): 409–31.

Koretz, G. (1990) Economic trends. *Business Week*, 5 March.

Kozinets, R.V., de Valck, K., Wilner, S.J.S. and Wojnicki, A.C. (2008) Opening the black box of buzzing bloggers: Understanding how consumers deal with the tension between authenticity and commercialism in seeded word-of-mouth campaigns. *Advances in Consumer Research*, 35: 49–51.

Langerak, F., Verhoef, P.C. and Verleigh, P.W.J. (2004) Satisfaction and participation in virtual communities. *Advances in Consumer Research*, 31: 56–7.

Lazarsfeld, P.F., Berelson, B.R. and Gaudet, H. (1948) *The People's Choice*. New York: Columbia University Press.

Lee, J.K. and Fortuny, E.J. de (2022) Influencer-generated reference groups. *Journal of Consumer Research*, 49 (1): 25–45.

Lee, S.N. and Corfman, K.P. (2004) A little something for me, and maybe for you too: Promotions that relieve guilt. *Advances in Consumer Research*, 31: 28–38.

Lennartsson, C., Rehnberg, J. and Dahlberg, L. (2022) The association between loneliness, social isolation and all-cause mortality in a nationally representative sample of older women and men. *Aging & Mental Health*, 26 (9): 1821–8.

Leung, P.C. and MacDonald, T.K. (2022) Please stop rubbing your relationship in my Face(book): An investigation of online romantic social comparison. *Canadian Journal of Behavioural Science / Revue Canadienne des Sciences du Comportement*, 54 (3): 182–93.

Lima, Y., Şenışık, S., Denerel, N., Hurşitoğlu, O., Balcı, G.A., Bolat, G.U. and Ergün, M. (2022) Effects of COVID-19 pandemic on the psychological states of youth and adult elite male athletes. *Spor Hekimligi Dergisi*, 57 (1): 31–7.

Lin, L. and Shek, D.T.L. (2022) Association of normative moral character and prosocial behavior – Moderators of personal moral character and sociodemographic factors. *Personality and Individual Differences*, 187: 111400.

Lipnack, J. and Stamps, J. (2000) *Virtual Teams: Working across Boundaries with Technology*. New York: Wiley.

Lowrey, T.M., Otnes, C.C. and Ruth, J.A. (2004) An exploration of social influence on dyadic gift-giving. *Advances in Consumer Research*, 31: 112.

Lyu, Z., Jiao, Y., Zheng, P. and Zhong, J. (2022) Why do selfies increase young women's willingness to consider cosmetic surgery in China? The mediating roles of body surveillance and body shame. *Journal of Health Psychology*, 27 (5): 1205–17.

MacArthur, H.J. and Shields, S.A. (2015) There's no crying in baseball, or is there? Male athletes, tears, and masculinity in North America. *Emotion Review*, 7 (1): 39–46.

Manz, C.C. and Sims, H.P. (1981) Vicarious learning: The influence of modelling on organisational behaviour. *Academy of Management Review*, 6 (1): 105–13.

Marchesi, S. (2021) *Individual and Cultural Differences in the Adoption of the Intentional Stance towards Robots*. Thesis submitted to University of Manchester. www.research.manchester.ac.uk/portal/files/216120110/FULL_TEXT.PDF (accessed 8 August 2022).

Marton-Alper, I.Z., Sobeh, A. and Shamay-Tsoory, S.G. (2022) The effects of individual moral inclinations on group moral conformity. *Current Research in Behavioral Sciences*, 3: 100078.

McNulty, W.K. (1985) UK social change through a wide-angle lens. *Futures*, August.

Misra, A. (2022) Can the celebrity speak? Controversies and the eulogistic fandom of Shah Rukh Khan. *American Behavioral Scientist*, 66 (8): 1075–90.

Moldovan, S. and Lehmann, D. (2010) The effect of advertising on word of mouth. *Advances in Consumer Research*, 37: 118–21.

Muniz, A. and O'Guinn, T. (2001) Brand community. *Journal of Consumer Research*, 27 (March): 412–32.

Nelson, L.D. and Norton, M.I. (2005) From student to superhero: Situational primes shape future helping. *Journal of Experimental Social Psychology*, 41 (4): 423–30.

Nölke, A.-I. (2018) *Viscosity of Stigma: Media Experiences, Intersectionality, and the Life-Course of LGBTQ+ Consumers*. Unpublished PhD thesis, University of Edinburgh. uk.bl.ethos.756718

Norton, M.J., Aknin, L. and Dunn, E. (2010) Putting the 'social' in prosocial spending: Interpersonal giving promotes happiness. *Advances in Consumer Research*, 37: 36–43.

Okleshen, C. and Grossbart, S. (1998) Usenet groups, virtual community and consumer behaviours. *Advances in Consumer Research*, 25 (1): 276–82.

Oliver, R.L. (1999) Whence consumer loyalty? *Journal of Marketing*, 63 (4): 33–44.

Pfattheicher, S., Nielsen, Y.A. and Thielmann, I. (2022) Prosocial behavior and altruism: A review of concepts and definitions. *Current Opinion in Psychology*, 44: 124–9.

Pittman, C. (2020) 'Shopping while Black': Black consumers' management of racial stigma and racial profiling in retail settings. *Journal of Consumer Culture*, 20 (1): 3–22.

Ridings, C.M., Gefen, D. and Arinze, B. (2002) Some antecedents and effects of trust in virtual communities. *Journal of Strategic Information Systems*, 11: 271–95.

Rodero, E. (2022) Effectiveness, attractiveness, and emotional response to voice pitch and hand gestures in public speaking. *Frontiers in Communication*, 7. https://doi.org/10.3389/fcomm.2022.869084

Roper, S. and La Niece, C. (2009) The importance of brands in the lunch-box choices of low-income British school children. *Journal of Consumer Behaviour*, 8 (2/3): 84–99.

Russell, C. and Stern, B. (2006) Aspirational consumption in US soap operas: The process of parasocial attachment to television soap opera characters. *Advances in Consumer Research*, 33 (1): 134–8.

Sârbu, E.A., Nadolu, B., Runcan, R., Tomiță, M. and Lazăr, F. (2022) Social predictors of the transition from anomie to deviance in adolescence. *PLoS One*, 17 (6): e0269236.

Schneider, S. and Huber, F. (2022) The diffusion of price-related word-of-mouth: A study exploring the role of market mavens and social ties. *Journal of Relationship Marketing*, 21 (1): 50–80.

Sethna, Z., Jones, R. and Harrigan, P. (eds) (2013) *Entrepreneurial Marketing: Global Perspectives*. Bingley: Emerald Publishing.

Shaw-Garlock, G. (2009) Looking forward to sociable robots. *International Journal of Social Robotics*, 1 (3): 249–60.

Soll, J., Larrick, R. and Mannes, A. (2010) When it comes to wisdom, smaller crowds are wiser. *Advances in Consumer Research*, 37: 94–7.

Srivastava, A., Mukherjee, D.S. and Jebarajakirthy, C. (2021) Triggers of aspirational consumption at the base of the Pyramid: A qualitative inquiry from Indian context. *Journal of Strategic Marketing.* https://doi.org/10.1080/0965254X.2021.1885476

Stephen, A. and Berger, J. (2009) Creating contagion: Cascades in spatially dispersed social networks. *Advances in Consumer Research, 36*: 36–7.

Steptoe, A., Shankar, A., Demakakos, P. and Wardle, J. (2013) Social isolation, loneliness and all-cause mortality in older men and women. *Proceedings of the National Academy of Sciences of the United States of America, 10* (15): 5797–801.

Stokburger-Sauer, N.E. and Hoyer, W.D. (2009) Consumer advisors revisited: What drives those with market mavenism and opinion leadership tendencies and why? *Journal of Consumer Behaviour, 7* (3): 100–15.

Stokes, D. and Nelson, C. (2013) Word of mouth to word of mouse. In Z. Sethna, R. Jones and P. Harrigan (eds), *Entrepreneurial Marketing: Global Perspectives*. Bingley: Emerald Publishing. pp. 243–58.

Tesser, A., Miller, M. and Moore, J. (1988) Some affective consequences of social comparison and reflection processes: The pain and pleasure of being close. *Journal of Personality and Social Psychology, 54* (1): 49–61.

Trompenaars, F. and Hampden-Turner, C. (2012) *Riding the Waves of Culture: Understanding Diversity in Global Business*, 3rd edn. London: Nicholas Brealey.

Urban Dictionary (2022) Tinderitis definition. www.urbandictionary.com/define.php?term=tinderitis (accessed 28 August 2022).

Vaadal, K. and Ravn, S. (2021) 'It feels like life is narrowing': Aspirational lifestyles and ambivalent futures among Norwegian 'top girls'. *Sociology, 55* (6): 1135–50.

Van Boven, L., Campbell, M.C. and Gilovich, T. (2009) Stigmatising materialism: On stereotypes and impressions of materialistic versus experiential consumers. *Advances in Consumer Research, 36*: 14–15.

Veblen, T. (1899) *The Theory of the Leisure Class*. New York: Macmillan.

Wheeler, L., Shaver, K.G., Jones, R.A., Goethals, G.R., Cooper, J., Robinson, J.E., Gruder, C.L. and Butzine, K.W. (1969) Factors determining the choice of a comparison other. *Journal of Experimental Social Psychology, 5* (April): 219–32.

Wijenayake, S., Berkel, N. van, Kostakos, V. and Goncalves, J. (2022) Quantifying determinants of social conformity in an online debating website. *International Journal of Human–Computer Studies, 158*: 102743.

Wu, M.S.S., Chaney, I., Chen, C.H.S., Nguyen, B. and Melewar, T.C. (2015) Luxury fashion brands: Factors influencing young female consumers' luxury fashion purchasing in Taiwan. *Qualitative Market Research: An International Journal, 18* (3): 298–319.

Zitelny, H., Dror, T., Altman, S. and Bar-Anan, Y. (2022) The relation between gender identity and well-being. *Personality & Social Psychology Bulletin, 48* (4): 495–515.

Zuckerman, M. (1988) Behavior and biology: Research on sensation seeking and reactions to the media. In L. Donohew, H. Sypher and E.T. Higgins (eds), *Communication, Social Cognition and Affect*. Hillsdale, NJ: Erlbaum. pp. 173–94.

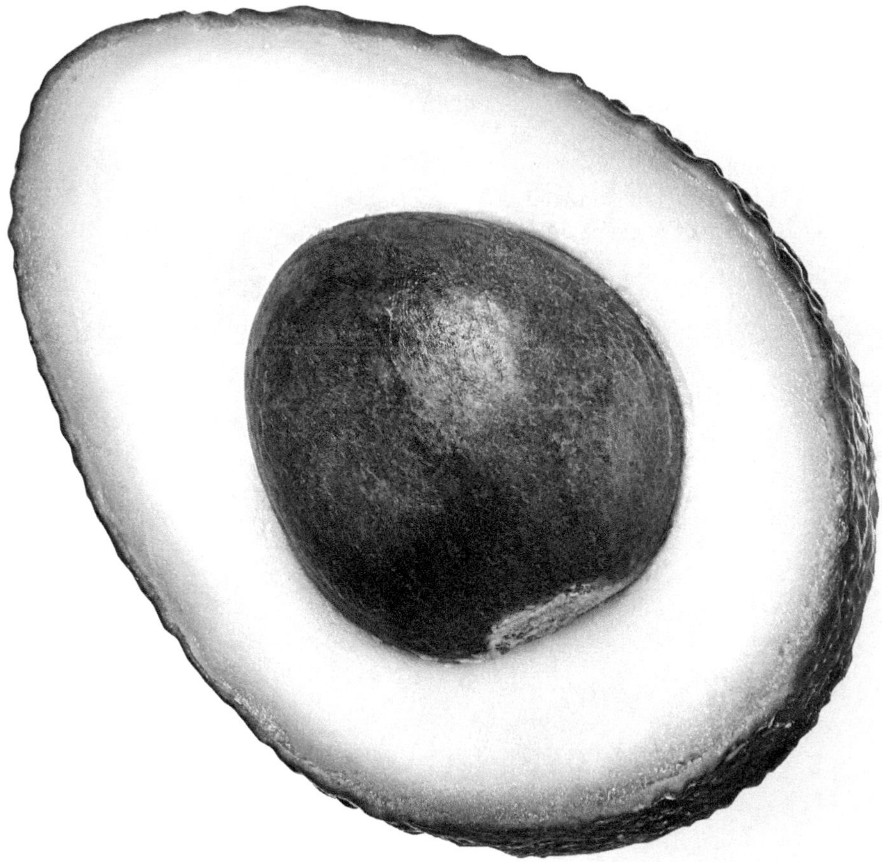

PART ONE   CONSUMER BEHAVIOUR IN CONTEXT

Chapter 1   Understanding Consumer Behaviour
Chapter 2   Decisions, Behaviours and Interactions
Chapter 3   Consumption in B2C vs. B2B
Chapter 4   Consumer Technology and Innovation

PART TWO   CONSUMERS AS INDIVIDUALS (THE PSYCHOLOGICAL ISSUES)

Chapter 5   Drive, Motivation and Hedonism
Chapter 6   The Self and Personality
Chapter 7   Perception
Chapter 8   Learning and Knowledge
Chapter 9   Attitude Formation and Change

PART THREE   CONSUMERS AS SOCIAL ACTORS (THE SOCIOLOGICAL ISSUES)

Chapter 10   Reference Groups
Chapter 11   Age, Gender and Familial Roles
Chapter 12   Culture and Social Mobility
Chapter 13   Ethical Consumption
Chapter 14   Sustainable Consumption

CHAPTER 11

AGE, GENDER AND FAMILIAL ROLES

LEARNING OBJECTIVES

After reading this chapter you should be able to:

- Describe the different definitions of family, and explain the influences on creating the definitions.
- Explain the role of culture in creating decision-making styles.
- Explain the roles of family members in decision-making.
- Describe ways in which conflict is generated and resolved.
- Describe the process by which children become effective consumers.
- Explain how brand loyalty is passed down through the generations.
- Critique family lifestyle models and explain the possible alternatives.
- Describe the roles family members take in the purchase and consumption process.

CHAPTER CONTENTS

Introduction
How old are you? (Cohorts and subcultures developed using age)
Defining families
Influence of children on buying decisions
Changing nature of the family
Gender roles
Other functions of the family
Roles in family consumption
Summary
Key points
How to impress your examiner
Review questions
Case study: The largest adolescent population in the world
Further reading
References

More online: https://study.sagepub.com/sethna5e

INTRODUCTION

Of all the reference groups we are exposed to, the family is probably the most powerful in influencing consumer decision-making. Individuals' consumption decisions tend to be greatly influenced by the people that surround them (Zorell, 2022). Almost all of us are members of families: our parents and guardians teach us how to be effective consumers from an early age, and we influence our brothers and sisters, our parents and eventually our own children in their purchasing choices.

The family has gone through many changes in structure, but still remains the most important social grouping. The reasons for this are as follows:

1. In the case of children, the parental influence is the earliest, and therefore colours the child's perception of everything that follows. In fact, the superego (see Chapter 1) is thought to be an internalised parent.
2. In the case of parents, the desire to do the best they can for their children influences their decision-making when making purchases for the family. Clear examples are the purchase of breakfast cereals and disposable nappies, where the appeal is almost invariably to do with the comfort and well-being of the baby.
3. In the case of siblings, the influence comes either as role model (where an older sibling is looked up to by a younger one) or as carer/adviser to younger siblings.
4. Families share a large part of their consumption, and thus joint decision-making often takes place by following formalised rules that control consumption behaviour within the group.

It is precisely because we value the opinions of our family members that we take their advice and often conform to their norms of behaviour. Even though the structure of families has undergone major changes in recent years, it is still true to say that the family is the basic unit of society. We'll discuss the family in more detail a little later. But before we do that, let's turn our attention to the other two constituents listed in the title of this chapter: age and gender.

HOW OLD ARE YOU? (COHORTS AND SUBCULTURES DEVELOPED USING AGE)

When English rock band The Who formed in 1964 they could not have foreseen that their second single, 'My Generation', written by guitarist Pete Townshend, would become not only the group's highest charting UK single, but also one of their most memorable. The lyrics from the first two verses emphasise the view that people in each generation go through similar experiences, and can relate to each other, but people from other generations will not share that understanding. This applies equally to events that each generation will remember as being 'my generation'; that is, particular to their 'era' (for instance London's Iranian Embassy siege in 1980, or the 9/11 attacks on New York's World Trade Center in 2001, or the Syrian humanitarian crisis in 2015, or the Covid-19 lockdowns in 2020, or the Russian invasion of Ukraine in 2022). This method of categorisation of age and time extends to, among others, food (for example wartime rationing compared with the 2008 world food price crisis), music (for example The Rat Pack, Queen, The Spice Girls or One Direction), clothing (vintage, New Romantic, post-war, anti-modern, designer) and gaming (*Pacman* arcade game in the 1980s in local chip shops compared with the versatility of eSports and The Metaverse).

In many cases, this fondness for a past event is closely linked to psychologically comforting experiences (Boym, 2001) and is called 'nostalgia' (Han and Newman, 2022; Havlena and Holak, 1991). The Online Etymology Dictionary (2022) defines nostalgia as being a 'wistful yearning for the past', and many scholars using qualitative methods have posited that nostalgic memory is usually seen in a positive light (Wildschut et al., 2006, 2010). If we think back to the earlier 2000s, our hands were glued to iPods that had click wheels, and in our down-time we couldn't get enough of playing *Tony Hawk's Pro Skater*! There are many examples from the world of advertising which use nostalgia as a backdrop (for instance, the Hovis bread advert from 1973, Microsoft's 'Child of the 90s' campaign, and LEGO's 55-year anniversary). The 2018 Super Bowl advertising featured the return of Cindy Crawford for Pepsi; Steven Tyler (a 1970s rocker travelling back in time) for Kia; and Australia showing a renewed version of the much-acclaimed 1986 film *Crocodile Dundee*! There are many reasons why this should be the case. Nostalgia creates a story where the brand can be the hero and a nostalgic advert demonstrates the idea of 'trust' of a known (and quite often loved) brand, thus simultaneously showcasing a brand's longevity too. Showing that a brand has always been a part of the culture helps to explain its relevance today.

AGE SUBCULTURES

Age subcultures exist because the members have differing attitudes and values. This is often called the **generation gap**. In some cases, people retain behaviours and attitudes that were current in their youth – this is typically the case with popular music, for example. In other cases, people change their views as they age, for example becoming more politically right wing as they become wealthier and less inclined towards radical changes.

Generation gap
A difference of attitudes and values between people of different generations, leading to a lack of understanding

Let's start with pre-adolescence. This is the stage of development which follows early childhood but precedes adolescence. This age group (10–13) are more commonly known as pre-teenagers, tweenies or sometimes tweenagers. Adolescents or teenagers (13–19) form a distinct, and often international, subculture. Combined, these two groups are important not only because of their own spending power (which can be substantial), but also because they have a strong influence on their parents' spending. Often teenagers have at least some responsibilities for the household shopping, and undoubtedly influence family choices about food brands (Lilo and West, 2022), environmental issues (Thompson et al., 2022) and media consumption (Bond, 2022; Hynes et al., 2022). The teen market is notoriously difficult to deal with, since brand preferences change with each year: each group of teenagers wants to have its own favourite brands (Biraglia et al., 2018), so that 14-year-olds are unlikely to be loyal to the same brands as their 16-year-old brothers and sisters. This means that producers need to be at the forefront of what is going on, quite often using technology as a route to this market (Mishra et al., 2018; Stalgaitis et al., 2021; Willoughby, 2015). Teenagers are often very communications-literate (technology readiness) in using a combination of both online and offline channels, and understand that they are being 'marketed to' (Mishra et al., 2018).

Baby Boomers are people born between 1946 and 1964. They are sometimes colloquially known as the 'hippie generation'. These years saw an unprecedented number of births, following on from the Second World War as soldiers returned to civilian life and began raising families. This period was also one of rising prosperity and improved healthcare, so more people survived into adulthood and had greater expectations from life. These Baby Boomers are now aged between 50 and 70 and are heading towards (or are already in) retirement: the younger of them are in their peak earning years, and the older of them often have substantial savings and pensions. They have shaped modern society (for instance Bill Clinton and Tony Blair in politics; Sting and Mick Jagger in music). They represent the largest and most affluent market in history and will continue to have a major economic and social impact for the next 30 years at least. This hippie generation have seen it all: from the swinging 60s (with sex, drugs and rock & roll) to the formation of the civil rights movement, the rise (and fall) of the dot com era, and more recently the housing bubble and subsequent global recession. Maybe this is the reason that in 2010 a British politician, David Willets (then Minister of State for Universities and Science), accusingly intimated that the Baby Boomers had thrown a 50-year-long party for which the 'bills are coming in' and it is the younger generation who will pay them. Since Baby Boomers have tended to have smaller families than did their parents, the spend per child has been much higher, and in the longer term the levels of inheritance that Baby Boomers' children will receive will also be higher. Baby busters (aka Generation X) is the label given by popular culture to the generation born between approximately 1964 and 1980. The author of this book is one! They are the children of the Baby Boomers. Members of Generation X were children during a time of shifting societal values, and as children were sometimes called the 'latchkey generation' due to reduced adult supervision as children compared to previous generations, a result of increasing divorce rates and increased maternal participation in the workforce, prior to widespread availability of childcare options outside the home. As adolescents and young adults, they were dubbed the 'MTV Generation' (a reference to the music video channel of the same name). In the 1990s they were sometimes characterised as slackers, cynical and disaffected. Some of the cultural influences on Generation X youth were the musical genres of punk, heavy metal, grunge and hiphop, and indie films. In midlife, research describes them as active, happy and achieving a work–life balance. The cohort has been credited with having an entrepreneurial spirit (Khor, 2017; Petráková et al., 2021; Winograd and Hais, 2011). Sage (2015) reported that Generation Xers dominate the playing field with respect to founding startups in the USA and Canada, with Generation Xers launching the majority (55%) of all new businesses in 2015.

Millennials (or Generation Y, and sometimes teased as Generation Why?) are generally thought to be those born between 1981 and 1996. The 21st century saw their coming of age politically, socially, economically and, obviously, technologically. The rise of mass communications and the age of the internet are both world-changing events that this generation grew up with and witnessed first-hand.

However, when one looks at the population figures a little more closely, we can see that in Europe, Millennials only account for a small percentage of the total population in several countries (for example Poland 28%, Italy 19%). This, compared to figures for people who are 50 and older, shows a very different picture (for instance, Germany 52% and Italy 51%). This is concrete evidence that we have an aging population in Europe, a phenomenon of increasing importance, and mirrored within Japan and the USA. As life expectancies increase, there are progressively more people in the over-50 age group. This is commonly called the grey market, but it should not be assumed that it is homogeneous: it is unlikely that a 55-year-old man would have a lot in common with his 80-year-old mother, at least in terms of consumer behaviour. By 2025 it is estimated that 22% of Europe's population will be aged over 65 (compared with 15.4% in 1995; European Union, 1995). The population of older people will get to an estimated 149 million people by 2050 (Europa, 2019) and this has dramatic implications for pensions, prosperity and, of course, marketing. In Japan the situation is far more serious – the birth rate is extremely low, to the point where the population is shrinking rapidly. Kyodo (2018) reported that the number of children in Japan fell for the 37th consecutive year to yet another record low. There were 15.53 million Japanese and other children in the nation as of 1 April 2018. Since then, the number has dropped to 14.7 million. That's a drop of over 800,000 in four years and the lowest figure since comparable data became available in 1950. In 2006, Dejevsky noted that by the end of the century, Japan's population is forecast to shrink from its current 130 million to less than 50 million, most of whom will be very elderly (Dejevsky, 2006), and this of course has societal as well as economic implications (Matsuno and Kohlbacher, 2018). In 2022, the population is already down to 123 million and so the numbers are moving as predicted.

The assumption has always been that these older consumers would be prime candidates for care homes, walking frames, stairlifts, hearing aids and little else. However, the rising life expectancy has been accompanied by a rise in the level of fitness of older people, due to better nutrition, healthcare, and technological and medical advancements (Nies and Leichsenring, 2018).

Today there are almost 11 million people aged 65 and over – 16% of the total population. In 10 years' time, this will have increased to almost 13 million people or 19% of the population (Centre for Ageing Better, 2022). At the younger end, most of this group are at the peak of their earning power and often have paid off their mortgages and are free of commitments to children. Their discretionary income is therefore higher than it has ever been. As we look at older members of the group, many have retired or are semi-retired and have a great deal more leisure time, while frequently enjoying generous private pensions and savings. Many older people use this time to take holidays, enjoy new hobbies, improve their education and so forth. These new activities are not necessarily those traditionally associated with elderly people: the holidays on offer in the Saga brochure are just as likely to include windsurfing, skydiving, mountaineering, skiing or motorbike holidays as they are to include bridge playing or coach tours. Some flying schools report that the majority of their students are over 50, and Open University applications from the over-60s run into the thousands. Equally, some other members of the segment fit the more traditional pattern, happy to dig the garden and perhaps do an evening class.

Marketers would be well advised to treat this age group with extreme caution. The 'age appropriateness' of a product is rarely relevant as opposed to the product benefits. The perceived age is an important consideration and can be measured using how old a person feels (feel-age) (Liu and Tang, 2022) or how old a person looks (the look-age) (Agrigoroaei et al., 2017; Barak and Schiffman, 1981). McFarlane and Samsioe (2020) demonstrated how 50+ fashion Instagram influencers contribute to the social construction of cognitive age through their aesthetic digital labours. This is far from being a homogeneous subculture.

DEFINING FAMILIES

Nuclear family
A couple and their dependent children (and maybe a dog!), regarded as a basic social unit

Extended family
A family that extends beyond the nuclear family to include grandparents and other relatives

The concept of what constitutes a family varies from one culture to another. In the UK and the USA, families usually consist of parents and their natural, adopted or fostered dependent children: this is called the **nuclear family**. In some other cultures, families might extend to grandparents, aunts, uncles and cousins all living in the same house and sharing their consumption. These **extended families** are becoming rare in industrialised countries, partly because of the mobility of workers: someone who finds a job in another part of the country is unlikely to find it convenient to take a large number of extended family members along.

Even in nuclear families there will also be influences from uncles, aunts, grandparents and cousins. While these influences are often less strong in UK households than they might be in some other countries where the extended family is more common, the influences still exist to a greater or lesser extent. For statistical purposes, Eurostat has adopted the United Nations definition of a family, which is as follows:

> *The persons within a private or institutional household who are related as husband and wife or as parent and never-married child by blood or adoption.*
> *(United Nations, 2016)*

For the purposes of the definition, couples who live together without marrying are still regarded as a family (this applies to both heterosexual and people in any 2SLGBTQIA+ relationship). On the other hand, the European Community Household Panel defines a family household more broadly as a shared residence with common housekeeping arrangements.

From a marketing viewpoint, the level of demand for many products is dictated more by the number of households than by the number of families. For example, most households in affluent countries would have a washing machine, but hardly any would have two washing machines. The relevance of families to marketing is therefore much more about consumer *behaviour* than about consumer *demand levels*.

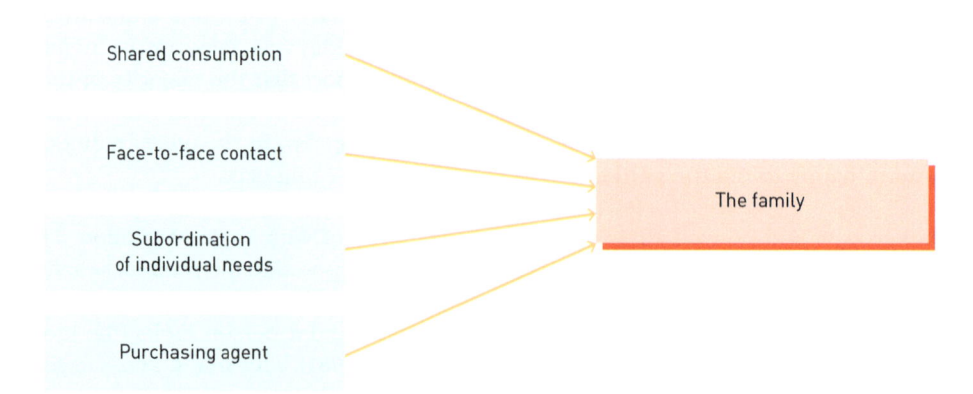

FIGURE 11.1 Defining characteristics of families

In terms of its function as a group, the family is defined (see Figure 11.1) by the following characteristics:

1. *Face-to-face contact.* Family members see each other most days, and interact as advisers, information providers and sometimes deciders. Other reference groups rarely have this level of contact.

2. *Shared consumption.* Durables such as fridges, freezers, televisions and furniture are shared, and food is collectively purchased and cooked (although a family eating together is fast becoming uncommon). Purchase of these items is often collective: children even participate in decision-making on such major purchases as cars and houses. Other reference groups may share some consumption (for example, members of a car club may hire and share particular cars), but families share consumption of most domestic items.

3. *Subordination of individual needs.* Because consumption is shared, some family members will find that the solution chosen is not one that fully meets their needs. Although this happens in other reference groups, the effect is more pronounced in families.

4. *Purchasing agent.* Because of the shared consumption, most families will have one member who does most, or all, of the shopping. Traditionally and historically this has been the mother of the family, but increasingly the purchasing agent(s) are the older children of the family – even pre-teens are sometimes taking over this role. This has major implications for marketers, since pre-teens and young teens are generally better 'connected' online than adults and are therefore more open to marketing communications via a multitude of channels. Other reference groups may well have a purchasing agent, but this is probably only for specific items rather than for all those items the group is interested in – and most informal groups would appoint a purchasing agent for occasional purposes only.

Purchasing agent
Someone who has the task of making purchases on behalf of a group

In some cases products are passed on from one generation to another as a way of preserving family identity and values (Frahm et al., 2022). Whether this means passing on great-grandmother's wedding ring or handing over the family's old car to the newly licensed eldest child, the family link is continued (Curasi, 2006); although this is not always the case, much to the distress of some families. Paul Kalmanovitz's relatives were unsuccessful in their court battle over his estate. He left virtually all of his estimated $1.2 billion estate to a charitable foundation – not to his family (Fondiller, 1996). This *passing-on* behaviour has been found in investments, with parents passing on investments and investment advice to children (Williams, 2006). Products passed on in this way can move between 'sacred' and 'profane' values (Hartman and Kiecker, 2004; Shubik, 2018). For example, Granny's wedding ring might be worn on a chain round the neck of a teenager; equally, Grandad's revered Victoria Cross (from the Second World War) might be preserved as a family heirloom. The older generation often pass on these items, complete with their history and an account of their significance, in the hope that the younger generation will continue to cherish them (Curasi, 2011).

Family decision-making is not as straightforward as marketers have supposed in the past. There has been an assumption that the purchasing agent (for example, the mother) is the one who makes the decisions, and while this is often the case, this approach ignores the ways in which the purchasing decisions are arrived at.

Wife-dominant decision-making

Decisions that are left to the female adult of the family

Husband-dominant decision-making

A situation in which the male of the household has the most power in consumption decisions

Syncratic (democratic) decision-making

In-group decision-making, the type of decision that is made on the basis of consultation

Autonomic decision-making

A type of decision that is made by the individual without recourse to others

Role specialisation is critical in family decision-making because of the sheer number of different products that must be bought each year in order to keep the family supplied. What this means in practice is that, for example, the family member responsible for doing the cooking is also likely to take the main responsibility for shopping for food. The family member who does the most driving is likely to make the main decision about the car and its accessories, servicing, fuelling and so forth; the family gardener buys the gardening products and so on.

There is a problem here with terminology. Traditionally, studies of the family have referred to the male partner as the husband, and the female partner as the wife. The increasing number of families in which the parents are not married has rendered this approach obsolete; the research reported in the next section was conducted in the 1970s, when the vast majority of parents were married. The validity and relevance of the research is not in question, since it refers to traditional roles that may or may not actually be adopted by specific families.

Four kinds of marital role specialisation have been identified: **wife dominant** where the wife has most say in the decision, **husband dominant** where the husband plays the major role (Tiwari, 2015), **syncratic** (or **democratic**) where the decision is arrived at jointly and **autonomic** where the decision is made entirely independently of the partner (Filiatrault and Ritchie, 1980). For example, the wife may have the biggest role in deciding on new curtains, the husband may have the lead role in choosing the family car, they may decide together on a home extension, and the husband alone might choose the fertiliser for the garden. Marketers need to identify which role specialisation type is typical of a target market in order to know where to aim the promotional activities. Some more recent research indicates that in the event of disagreement about a joint decision it is the man's decision which is likely to prevail (Ward, 2006). This research was conducted exclusively in Tennessee, however, which may account for at least some of the results.

Product category affects role specialisation and decision-making systems. When an expensive purchase is being considered, it is likely that most of the family will be involved in some way, if only because major purchases affect the family budgeting for other items. At the other end of the scale, day-to-day shopping for toilet rolls and ketchup entails very little collective decision-making (although it has been known for families to rebel collectively against ketchup that is not Heinz branded). But more generally, where the product has a shared usage (a holiday or a car) the collective decision-making component is likely to increase greatly. Conversely, where the product is used predominantly by one family member, that member will dominate the decision-making even when the purchase is a major one (the main chef in the family will have most influence in the decision about the new range cooker, for example).

Culture has a marked effect on family decision-making styles. Religion and nationality will often affect the way decisions are made: followers of the Zarathustrian religion closely abide by their three tenets of 'Good Thoughts, Good Words and Good Deeds', which therefore feed into their decision-making processes on a daily basis (Sethna, 2015); African cultures tend to be male-dominated in decision-making, whereas European and North American cultures show a more egalitarian pattern of decision-making (Green et al., 1983). In India, gold carries very strong family significance at weddings. The bride is thought to be purified by gifted and borrowed gold – typically her new husband's family will lend jewellery to her, as a way of binding her to the new family (Fernandez and Veer, 2004).

There are two issues here for the marketer trying to understand consumer behaviour: first, what is the effect on the marketing mix of the multi-ethnic society in Europe, and second, what is the effect when dealing internationally? This is a somewhat sensitive area, and one that marketers are still getting to grips with. There is more on general aspects of culture in Chapter 12.

The openness or closure of a society can be gauged by looking at **social mobility** (Clark et al., 2022; Longley et al. 2021). An open society will exhibit a high level of social mobility due to a low persistence of privilege from one generation to the next; a closed society will exhibit a low level of social mobility due to persistence of social position across generations (Hout, 2018; Maslen, 2022). A popular early interpretation in the 1950s by Professor Joseph Kahl (an expert on social stratification and a Professor of Sociology) supposed that social mobility arose as a result of 'four causes': technological, reproductive, immigration mobility and mobility due to the fact that 'some people slip down and make room for others to move up', later referred to as 'individual mobility'. Some theoretical aspects of this interpretation are noted by Lizama-Loyola et al. (2022), who discuss subjective experiences of social mobility, but with three different emphases: critical notions of social mobilities and inequalities, intersectional perspectives of social mobility, and educational social mobilities, or experiences of social mobilities situated in educational settings.

Social mobility
The movement of individuals, families, households or other categories of people within or between social strata in a society

The family may well adopt different roles according to the *decision-making stage*. At the problem-recognition stage of, for example, the need for new shoes for the children, the children themselves may be the main contributors. The stay-at-home parent may then decide what type of shoes should be bought, and will then be the one to whisk the children off to the shoe shop for a fitting and to buy the shoes. It is reasonable to suppose that the main user of the product might be important in the initial stages, with perhaps joint decision-making at the final purchase. These determinants of decision-making style are summarised in Figure 11.2.

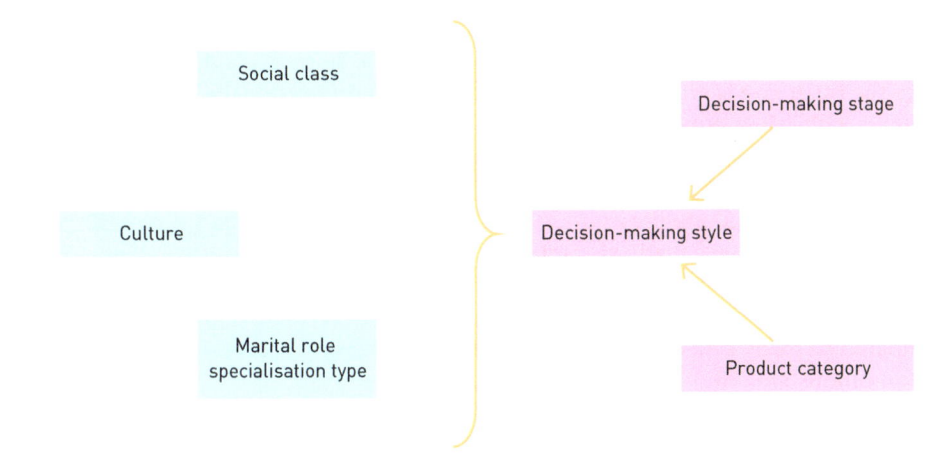

FIGURE 11.2 Determinants of decision-making style in families

Other determinants might include such factors as whether both carers are earning. In such families, decision-making is more likely to be joint because each has a financial stake in the outcome. It is now uncommon to find a situation where the family decision-making is more likely to be dominated by the sole earner, and previous research as well as more common practice amongst families suggests that where couples are both earning, they will make decisions jointly (Filiatrault and Ritchie, 1980). Males stereotypically used to dominate highly technical durable products (e.g. computing and audio-visual equipment), but in recent years this imbalance has been redressed with the emergence of the new generation of digital natives: those young people to whom all things digital and technical come as second nature.

Gender role orientation is clearly crucial to decision-making. Husbands (and wives) with conservative (many would say traditional and outdated) views about gender roles (more on this later in this chapter) will tend towards the assumption that most decisions about expenditure will be made by the husband. Even within this type of decision-making system, however, husbands will usually adjust their own views to take account of their wife's attitudes and needs. A classic example of this is in the 1964 book (and later a musical and screenplay) by Joseph Stein entitled *Fiddler on the Roof* where the father character believes that he is the dominant party who makes the decisions yet it is the mother who cleverly manipulates him to her way of thinking!

Conflict resolution tends to have an increased importance in family decision-making as opposed to individual purchase behaviour. The reason for this is that, obviously, more people are involved, each with their own needs and their own internal conflicts to resolve. The conflict resolution system is as shown in Table 11.1.

INFLUENCE OF CHILDREN ON BUYING DECISIONS

We live in an era where we expect to live longer. This, coupled with lower fertility rates, means that the share of global population under age 15 has dropped to about 26%. First-born children generate more economic impact than higher-order babies. Around 40% of babies are first-born; they are photographed more, they get all new clothes (no hand-me-downs) and get more attention all round. First-born and only children have a higher achievement rate than those born second, third, etc., and since the birth rate is falling, there are more of them proportionally. Other factors to contend with when considering familial buying decisions include service providers such as hotels, restaurants, etc. who are more likely to be able to cater for a family of four than a family of five or more – I have first-hand experience of this! At the other end of the spectrum, childlessness is also more common now than it was 30 years ago and the figure is actually rising (Sobotka, 2022; Taylor et al., 2010). Finland has been a demographic forerunner in terms of the adoption of new family forms as well as family friendly social policies. Childlessness has nevertheless grown and is high compared to many other countries. A large and increasing share of all persons who live in unions are childless (Saarela et al., 2022).

CONSUMER BEHAVIOUR IN ACTION: EAST ASIAN CHOICES

In recent decades, most economically developed East Asian countries have experienced extremely low fertility levels as well as high and rising childlessness. In Japan, Hong Kong and Singapore, about three out of ten women born in the mid-1970s remain permanently childless. This phenomenon is closely associated with the decline in marriage and the rise of lifetime singleness, and with more married women remaining without children. Among women born in the 1960s and 1970s, rising childlessness accounts for about two-thirds of cohort fertility decline in Japan, Hong Kong and South Korea. Future childlessness trends will also depend on the way East Asian societies adapt to the 'gender revolution' and changing family patterns. Key factors include greater gender equality, a greater focus on well-being among children and families, better economic prospects for young adults and labour market reform to ensure women no longer have to choose between career and motherhood (Sobotka, 2021).

Children also have a role in applying pressure on their parents to make particular purchasing decisions. The level of **pester power** generated can be overwhelming, and parents will frequently give in to the child's demands (Ekstrom et al., 1987; Lavuri and Aileni, 2022). It should be noted that this is not just a 'first world' problem. Children around the world will utilise pester power to get their way (Christino et al., 2020). O'Neill et al. (2013) did some very interesting investigation on whether pester power existed in third world communities, which are perceived to have considerably less disposable income. Results showed that over 75% of children admitted to continually making requests until they were granted. And so children rapidly become adept at negotiating with their parents, and are quite able to recognise the various responses parents will make (agreement, refusal, procrastination, negotiation) as well as the parents' reasons for their decisions. This is especially true now that there is an increase in the use of new and social media (Desrochers, 2015), and also the proliferation of online brand communities (OBCs) motivating 7–11-year-old children (Thomas et al., 2021). Children often see negotiation as a good-natured game between themselves and the parents rather than as a source of conflict as the literature tends to suggest (Lawlor and Prothero, 2011; Shivany, 2015).

Pester power
The ability of children to influence their parents by means of repetitive requests

TABLE 11.1 Conflict resolution in families

Resolution method	Explanation
Persuasion through information exchange	When a conflict occurs, each family member seeks to persuade the others of his or her point of view. This leads to discussion, and ultimately some form of compromise
Role expectation	If persuasion fails, a family member may be designated to make the decision. This is usually somebody who has the greatest expertise in the area of conflict being discussed. This method appears to be going out of fashion as greater democracy and negotiation in family decision-making are appearing

(Continued)

TABLE 11.1 (Continued)

Resolution method	Explanation
Establishment of norms	Families will often adopt rules for decision-making. Sometimes this will involve taking turns over making decisions (perhaps over which restaurant the family will go to this week, or where they will go on holiday)
Power exertion	This is also known as browbeating. One family member will try to exert power to force the other members to comply; this may be a husband who refuses to sign the cheque unless he gets his own way, or a wife who refuses to cook the dinner until the family agree, or a child who throws a tantrum. The person with the most power is called the least dependent person because he or she is not as dependent on the other family members. Using the examples above, if the wife has her own income she won't need to ask the husband to sign the cheque; if the other family members can cook they can get their own dinner; and if the family can ignore the yelling toddler long enough, eventually the child will give up

Source: Adapted from Onkvisit and Shaw (1994). Reprinted with permission.

Least dependent person
The individual within a buying group who has the highest degree of autonomy

Although the number of children as a percentage of the population has fallen in recent times, their importance as consumers has not. Apart from the direct purchases of things that children need, they influence decision-making to a marked extent. For instance, in recent years, children have become much more aware of where food comes from and what they eat, partly due to in-school health education programmes. Sometimes on-package health claims have a negative effect (perhaps due to a mistrust of marketer-generated information) but education programmes do have an effect in encouraging more healthy choices (Miller et al., 2011). However, children are well aware that 'children's food' often consists of cheap junk food (Elliott, 2011). The problem lies in translating this knowledge into action, since children still make unhealthy choices even when they know better (Dias and Agante, 2011). In Hémar-Nicolas et al.'s (2022) work they asked the question 'Do you eat insects?' and investigated the acceptance of insects as food by children. Children predominantly reject insects as food because of their sensory properties and the disgust they arouse. However, their interest in eating insect-based food is embedded within experiential contexts specific to childhood, in particular the peer group, which makes insect-eating fun and challenging, and the family, which offers a protective and reassuring setting.

When parents and children are making joint decisions about food purchase, the children will often use subtle techniques to get their own way – offering to help with the shopping reduces conflict and means they are more likely to impose their own choices, for example (Norgaard and Brunso, 2011).

Children have to be taught how to be consumers, since they will (eventually) become adults and will need to manage their money and make appropriate choices in their purchasing behaviour. Children's development as consumers goes through five stages (Figure 11.3):

1. Observing.
2. Making requests.
3. Making selections.
4. Making assisted purchases.
5. Making independent purchases.

AGE, GENDER AND FAMILIAL ROLES

```
Observing              Parental help and guidance high
    ↓
Making requests              ↕
    ↓
Making selections
    ↓
Making assisted purchases
    ↓
Making independent purchases   Parental help and guidance low
    ↓
```

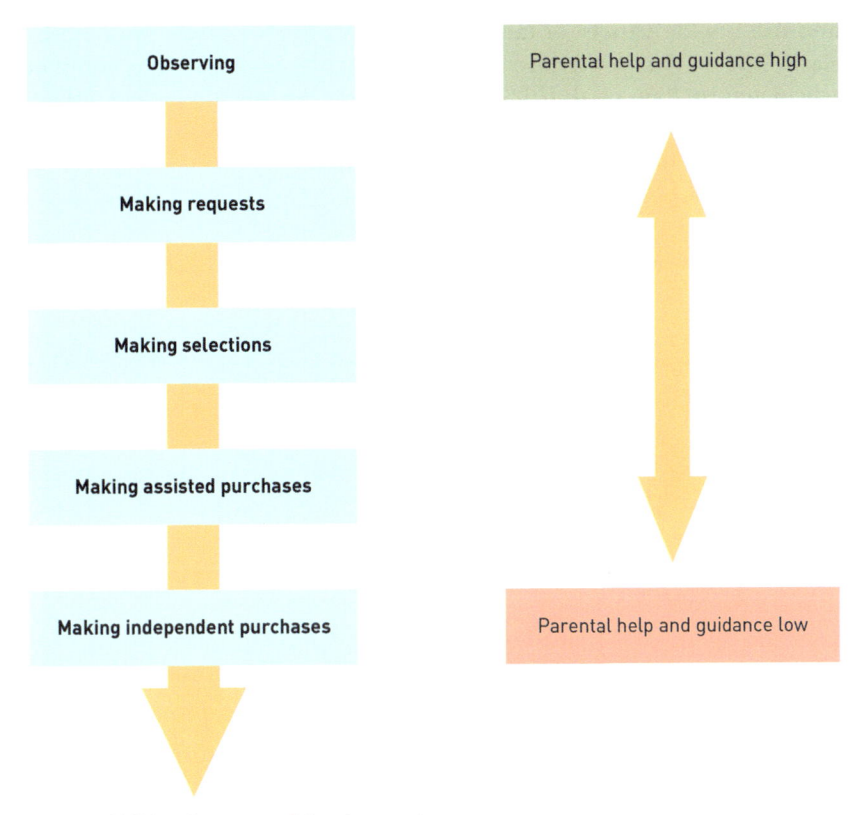

FIGURE 11.3 Children's stages of development as consumers

In the observing stage, children see how their parents go about obtaining the things they need. At this point, the child will probably not understand that money is a finite resource, but can easily understand the basic system: things that the family needs are available in shops, and they can be bought with money if you know what to do. Observation is actually more important than teaching in children's development, especially when the family has a good quality of relationship between its members (Mittal and Royne, 2010). Usually children will begin to consider ways in which they might obtain goods themselves – quite young children can grasp the idea that goods must be paid for, and they will sometimes try using a representation of 'money' (perhaps play money or tokens) to pay for things.

At a very early stage children learn to make requests. Even before being able to talk, children recognise brands and favourite products and are able to reach for them or point to them. As they grow older and more able to articulate requests (Pronovost and Scott, 2022), they can (and do) develop pester power. This means that they make insistent demands for products, sometimes throwing tantrums or continually wheedling their parents to obtain what they want. At this point parental judgement about the products' suitability and the situation context may vary – some parents will give in fairly quickly and provide the child with what he or she wants, while others will refuse to buy the product. In many cases the request becomes a basis for negotiation – the parent agrees to buy the product on condition that the child behaves in a certain way.

Children use a wide variety of tactics to influence their parents (Sun et al., 2018; Wimalasir, 2004). This sometimes has a tendency to continue into adulthood (as was articulated by Ram et al. [2022] in their study investigating social influence of adult children on parental health behaviour among South Asian immigrants living in America). These tactics are shown in Table 11.2, and the relationship between them is shown in Figure 11.4.

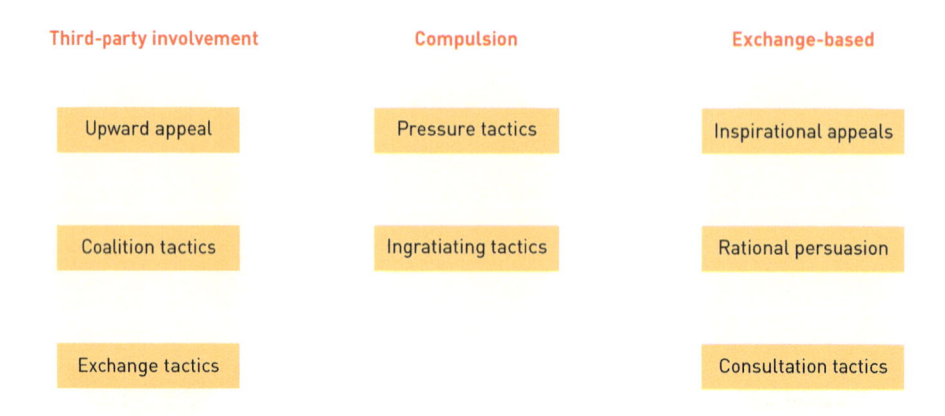

Third-party involvement	Compulsion	Exchange-based
Upward appeal	Pressure tactics	Inspirational appeals
Coalition tactics	Ingratiating tactics	Rational persuasion
Exchange tactics		Consultation tactics

FIGURE 11.4   Children's persuasion tactics

Parenting style has an obvious effect on the likely response to such requests. Broadly, there are five basic styles of parenting (Carlson and Grossbart, 1988):

1. *Authoritarians.* These parents are cold and restrictive.
2. *Authoritative.* These parents are warm and restrictive.
3. *Permissives.* These parents are warm and non-restrictive.
4. *Strict-dependent.* These parents foster dependence in their children, almost to the point of not allowing them to grow up.
5. *Indulgent-dependent.* These parents foster dependence by giving their children everything they want and need, even into adult life.

These parenting styles are not necessarily universal; in fact they happen almost exclusively in collectivist cultures (Rose et al., 2002). It is easy to see that authoritarian and authoritative parents are unlikely to yield easily to pester power, strict-dependents would not allow the child to pester, and permissives and indulgent-dependents are unlikely to need to be pestered – they would simply accede to the request the first time round. Research suggests that authoritative parenting is the most effective style (Milner, 2015).

In most cases, parents will agree to purchases subject to conditions being met. This is an important lesson, because the child needs to know that products are subject to exchange processes. Here, the parent is demonstrating that, in order to obtain benefits, there will need to be concessions in terms of behaviour. So for instance, children who've studied diligently and passed their exams have been bought holidays to Barcelona or Specialized road bikes as a reward for their 'behaviour'. Parents frequently use the promise of supplying (or withholding) products as a way of modifying the child's behaviour. There is evidence to suggest that this is culturally based in some respects: American parents apparently seek to develop autonomy (Frick et al., 2022) in their children, making them independent consumers, whereas Japanese parents maintain greater control over their children's consumption (Oh et al., 2022; Rendall et al., 2022; Yanaoka and Saito, 2022), so that the children tend to develop consumer skills at a later age (Rose, 1999).

Once children reach an age when they can understand money, parents will typically provide them with pocket money so that they can learn to make their own selections. In most cases pocket money is supplied as a fixed amount; this is so that the child can learn that money is not an infinite resource, and must be spent carefully. In other cases, pocket money might be provided as a reward for specific behaviour (for example, cleaning the car or mowing the lawn) so that the child learns the concept of working for rewards (although some parents might argue that household chores should not warrant any payment and should be done as the price of being part of the family). This is a further reinforcement of the exchange concept. In the early stages of having pocket money, parents will often help the child make choices, applying their own sense of value to the transaction. As time goes on, the child will be able to make choices alone, and will ultimately (perhaps during teenage years) become a fully-fledged consumer by spending money earned by doing odd jobs or part-time work (perhaps using goHenry, as seen in Chapter 6).

TABLE 11.2 Tactics used by children to influence their parents

Tactic	Explanation
Pressure tactics	The child makes demands and uses threats or intimidation to persuade the parents to comply with his or her request
Upward appeal	The child seeks to persuade the parent by saying that the request was approved or is supported by an older member of the family, a teacher or even a family friend
Exchange tactics	The child makes an implicit or explicit promise to provide some sort of service such as washing the car, cleaning the house or taking care of the baby in return for a favour
Coalition tactics	The child seeks the aid of others to persuade the parents to comply with his or her request, or uses the support of others as an argument for the parents to agree with him or her
Ingratiating tactics	The child seeks to get the parent in a good mood or think favourably of him or her before asking the parent to comply with a request
Rational persuasion	The child uses logical arguments and factual evidence to persuade the parent to agree with his or her request
Inspirational appeals	The child makes an emotional appeal or proposal that arouses enthusiasm by appealing to the parent's values or ideals
Consultation tactics	The child seeks the parent's involvement in making a decision

CRITICAL REFLECTION

Consuming cookies

Ofcom (2022) have made some super interesting findings recently. Nearly all children went online in 2021 (99%); the majority used a mobile phone (72%) or tablet (69%) to do so. More than a third (36%) of primary school-age children did not always have access to an adequate device for online learning at home, compared to 17% of secondary-age children. One in ten primary-age children rarely or never had access (11%), compared to 3% in secondary school. Research shows that the average British child has more chance of recognising the Nike swoosh or the Golden Arches (of the M word!) than recognising a picture of Christ, and is familiar with as many as 400 brand names by the time they reach the age of 10. Using video-sharing platforms (VSPs) such as YouTube or TikTok was the most popular online activity among children aged 3–17 (95%); while the majority chose to watch content on VSPs, 31% posted content they had made themselves, especially those aged 12–17.

TV channels are awash with adverts for all sorts of products, from sugar-infused soft drinks to oven-ready fast food to chocolate and sweets. And guess what time they're usually on-air – teatime! The timing, coupled with an inducement – a motivation to buy – means that children are most definitely going to want that product which is linked to the latest film release, etc. Among all types of online platforms, YouTube is the most widely used by children; 89% used it, compared to half using TikTok. But TikTok is more popular for posting content.

Should marketers take responsibility for inducing pester power? We hear all the time that wicked marketers are encouraging children to want the latest toys, games, gadgets and even fashions – an industry worth at least £70 million every year: advertising aimed directly at children. So are marketers to blame if the young ones then pester their parents?

© iStock.com/KQconceptsd

Of course, advertisers don't have to rely on the timing constraints of watching TV at teatime when they have the internet at their disposal. And with the internet, we get 'cookies'. No, not the eating kind, but the kind that embed themselves into your web browser to keep track of your visit to a particular website. But here's where things get a little more sinister. Cookies are now retargeting their victim. Companies such as Criteo and Vizury are seeing huge growth in business from e-commerce customers who want to woo back their online visitors. These startups target ads at people who visit e-commerce sites but move on before buying anything. Retargeting means that when they visit other sites, they will continue to see ads for products from those e-commerce sites. Vizury's online ad platform now counts around 500 million monthly users. And digitally native children who have a short attention span are prime candidates to be retargeted.

On the other hand, people do have to buy things, and marketers have been trained to 'repeat' their message a number of times before it's accepted by the consumer. It's the way the world works. Children have to learn to distinguish between advertising and programming – and they have to learn that they can't just demand anything they want in this life. So maybe marketers are carrying out a public service, educating the consumers of tomorrow and teaching children that they can't just have everything!

At this point, the individual is more likely to look to friends or role models for ideas on acceptable consumer behaviour (John, 1999). Although younger children respond best to advertising in which the spokesperson is a parental or authority figure, teenagers often buy products simply because their parents disapprove of them (Rummel et al., 2000). For example, nose rings, hair dye, army boots and an undercut with nape shaved head seem to be the fashion for 17-year-old girls at the time of writing. This is probably part of the process by which people become independent adults, and demonstrates that they are no longer children.

CONSUMER BEHAVIOUR IN ACTION: KEY ASPECTS OF CHILDREN AND CONTENT CONSUMPTION

Children today have access to much more content than even 10 years ago. The communications revolution has certainly made it much harder to monitor the behaviour of teenagers (Ghosh et al., 2018) – not that it was ever easy, of course. Each generation of teenagers takes great care to prevent their parents from knowing what they are really doing, but electronic communications have made the situation much easier for teenagers. They access the content through their online profiles. A majority of children under 13 have their own profile on at least one social media app or site; 33% of parents of 5–7s said their child had a profile, and 60% of 8–11s said they had one. More than six in ten children aged 8–17 said they had more than one profile on some online apps and sites (62%); the most common reason, overall, was having one profile just for their parents, family or friends to see. Just four in ten parents of 3–17s knew the minimum age requirement for using most social media; 42% correctly said 13. Four in ten parents of 8–11-year-olds said they would allow their child to use social media (38%). In terms of actual consumption, children still watch live television but are more likely to watch paid-for on-demand streaming services; 78% watched services like Netflix, Amazon Prime Video and Disney+, compared to 47% watching live TV. Scotland had the largest decline in broadcast viewing. It's interesting to note though that despite almost six in ten teenagers saying they used social media for news, it was the least trusted or accurate news source; 12–15s preferred to trust their family (68%) or the TV (65%) for news.

So it's only natural that hand-in-hand with the above, there are parental concerns about their children's content consumption. Seven in ten parents of children under 16 were concerned about the content their child saw online; the aspects of greatest concern were age-inappropriate content such as violence, bad language and disturbing content and sexual or 'adult' content. Parents had fewer concerns about the TV content their child watched than about online content: 46% were concerned about their child seeing bad language, violence or disturbing content on TV.

Source: Adapted from Ofcom (2022). More data and insights can be found at www.ofcom.org.uk.

Socialisation continues down the generations even after the child has become a fully independent adult, however. Some research shows that brand loyalties can be passed down from one generation to another, even for three or four generations within the same family (Mandrik et al., 2004; Olsen, 1993). The reason for this is that people enjoy using the brands that they remember from their childhood: specific brands of sauces, soups, marmalade or soft drinks commonly remain popular in the family for many years after the child has grown up and left home. In some respects the family identity is carried on through the generations by these means (Epp and Arnould, 2006). 'A finger of fudge is just enough to give your kids a treat'; 'Beans means Heinz'; 'Just one Cornetto'; 'webuyanycar.com'. These are all jingles that people of a certain age will vividly remember. This is an important consideration for three reasons: first and foremost is that advertisements really do have an impact on the young brain, which soaks up all the communication that it's exposed to; second, this memory can last for decades; third, using TV to persuade children to buy things, including sweets, is not new. There is a generation of viewers in the UK who will forever have the 'Go Compare' insurance advert, with the pseudo-opera-singer, emblazoned in their long-term memory!

CONSUMER BEHAVIOUR IN ACTION: THE BATTLE OF BRANDS – TEENAGERS AND TECHNOLOGY

Communicus, a research-based advertising consultancy in Arizona with 25 years of experience in measuring and diagnosing billions of dollars in placed advertising, found that 'child pestering' is one of the top predictors of a parent's purchase intentions to buy a wireless device for their children. Its study, *The Mobile Device Path to Purchase: Parents & Children*, found that for Apple, 'child pestering' is the top predictor, being twice as important as social media, while for Samsung it was the second predictor (first was positive word of mouth, by about 15%) in driving parental purchase intent.

''Tis the season for children to ask for the latest technology and wireless devices', said Ms Jeri Smith, President and CEO of Communicus, Inc. 'We found that "pester power" can even outweigh a parent's beliefs that a device is easy to use or has the best features and functionality.'

So, what influences children to request a particular brand? For the younger generation, Apple's brand success is based on positive word of mouth and fitting in. For Samsung, positive word of mouth and non-traditional tactics such as the 'Samsung Nation' social rewards programme have contributed positively to children requesting the brand.

Further, the study found that for children, the top predictors of requests to parents are people saying good things about Apple and it being a brand that a lot of friends have. Similarly, for Samsung, the top predictors of parental requests are Samsung social media efforts and the belief that Samsung is a brand for 'someone like me'.

Advertising (or sometimes advertising bans; Greiner and Sahm, 2018) can work to build demand for devices, but despite the large advertising budgets involved, success isn't guaranteed. In the case of Apple, children are far more impacted by social influences ('my friends have them') (Chronis-Tuscano et al., 2018; Eutsler and Antonenko, 2018) and by technological capabilities (Yan, 2018) than by advertising. Adults are impacted by Apple brand advertising when it comes to the device they are considering for themselves, but child pestering takes over as the key driver when considering a new device for their child.

Conversely, Samsung's advertising has had a more impactful push on children in boosting awareness, requests and perceptions that the brand is for 'someone like me'. Samsung's advertising is effective across kid age groups, but has shown the strongest persuasive power among younger (age 6–12) kids.

© iStock.com/DougSchneider

'When considering advertising, one of the age-old questions brands ask is whether to go negative on competitors', said Smith. 'Our study found that for Samsung and Microsoft, displaying the key attributes of their devices in a positive light was much more impactful than an Apple-bashing strategy among both adults and kids.'

Source: Adapted from communicus.com (2014). More data and insights from *The Mobile Device Path to Purchase: Parents & Children* can be found at www.communicus.com. Courtesy of Communicus.

CHANGING NATURE OF THE FAMILY

One of the changes currently occurring throughout Western Europe is the increase in the number of single-person households. In the UK, this means that in 2021 approximately 8.3 million people lived alone in the UK, an increase of around 52,000 when compared with the previous year when around 8.25 million people were estimated to be living by themselves. There is, of course, a difference between a household and a family. A further change, coming about through the tremendous increase in the divorce rate, is the growing number of single-parent families. A third major change is the worldwide shift in attitude towards having large families. In addition, more women say that they would prefer to have fewer children than was the case even 10 years ago (Doepke and Kindermann, 2016). European birth rates are below the replacement rate for the population (Cocco, 2018) – and as we saw earlier, the crisis in Japan is even worse – meaning that the population would be shrinking if it were not for immigration (at least in Europe), and with measures such as Brexit having taken place, even this is now under threat.

In Figure 11.5, the 1900 family has more children, but the other five people (those outside the family circle in the figure) remained single, like many other people at that time. From the seven people in the example, only five children are born. In 1960, a more typical family size would be three children, but many more people married and had children (only two people are outside the family circles): that was an expectation of the Baby Boom years. Nowadays, families are smaller and many people never have children at all, so in our final example the ten people in the diagram only manage four children between them. Two of the family circles contain only one child, the other one contains none, and we have two people who remain single. It should be noted that these are examples only to accentuate the point: the birth rate actually has not fluctuated quite that dramatically over the period.

The family is a flexible concept, and families go through life cycles. There have been various versions of the family life cycle, but most are based on the original work of Wells and Gubar (1966). Table 11.3 shows the stages of the family life cycle.

1900:
Typical couple has five children, but many people do not marry at all

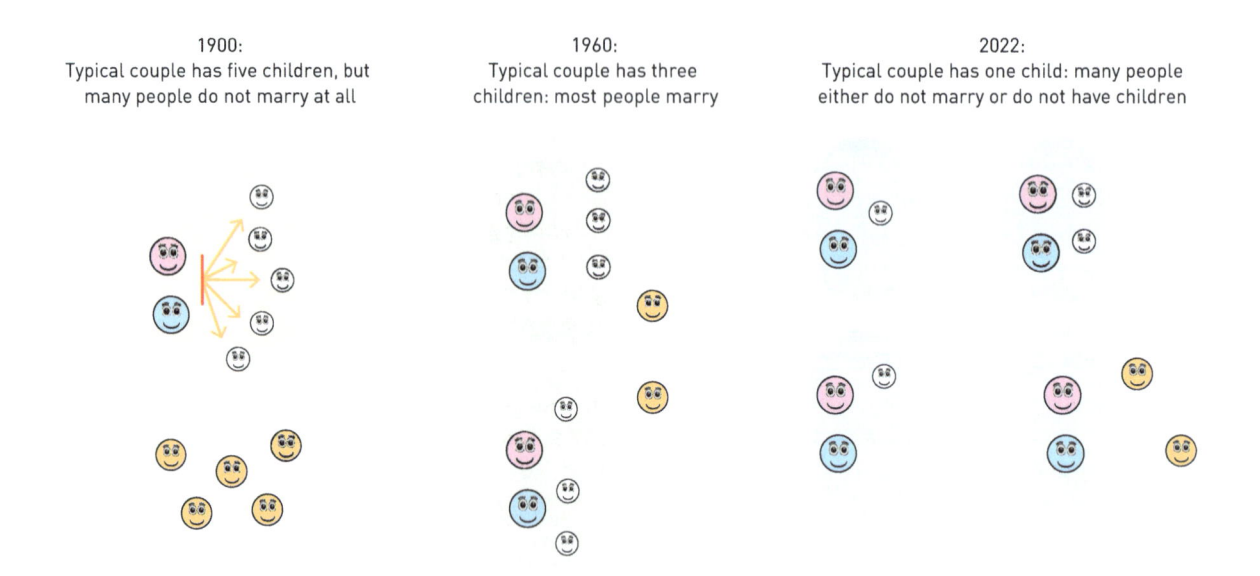

1960:
Typical couple has three children: most people marry

2022:
Typical couple has one child: many people either do not marry or do not have children

FIGURE 11.5 Effects of falling birth rate

TABLE 11.3 The family life cycle

Stage of life cycle	Explanation
Single stage	Single people tend to have low earnings, but also have low outgoings so have a high discretionary income. They tend to be more fashion- and recreation-orientated, spending on clothes, music, alcohol, eating out, holidays, leisure pursuits and hobbies, and 'mating game' products. Often they buy cars and items for their first residence away from home
Newly married couples	Newlyweds without children are usually dual-income households and therefore usually well-off. They still tend to spend on similar things to the singles, but also have the highest proportion of expenditure on household goods, consumer durables and appliances. They appear to be more susceptible to advertising
Full nest I	When the first child arrives, one parent usually stops working outside the home so family income drops sharply. The baby creates new needs that alter expenditure patterns: furniture and furnishings for the baby, baby food, vitamins, toys, nappies and baby food. Family savings decline, and usually couples are dissatisfied with their financial position
Full nest II	The youngest child is over 6, so often both parents will work outside the home. The employed spouse's income has risen due to career progression, and the family's total income recovers. Consumption patterns are still heavily influenced by children: bicycles, piano lessons, large-size packages of breakfast cereal, cleaning products, etc.

Stage of life cycle	Explanation
Full nest III	Family income improves as the children get older. Both parents are likely to be working outside the home, and both may have had some career progression; also, the children will be earning some of their own money from paper rounds, part-time jobs, etc. Family purchases might be a second car, replacement furniture, some luxury items and children's education
Empty nest I	Children have grown up and left home. Couples are at the height of their careers and spending power, have low mortgages and very reduced living costs. They often spend on luxury travel, restaurants and theatre – so they need fashionable clothing, jewellery, diets, spas, health clubs, cosmetics and hairdressing
Empty nest II	The main breadwinner has retired, so there is some drop in income. Expenditure is more health-orientated, buying appliances for sleep and over-the-counter remedies for indigestion. The couple often buy a smaller house, or move to an apartment in a retirement area or warmer country
Solitary survivor	If still in the workforce, widows and widowers enjoy a good income. They may spend more money on holidays, as well as the items mentioned in Empty nest II
Retired solitary survivor	These people have the same general consumption pattern as above but on a smaller scale due to reduced income. The individual has special needs for love, affection and security, so may join clubs, etc.

The main problem with this model is that it was originally developed in the 1960s, when couples rarely lived together without being married, there were very few single-parent families and the divorce rate was dramatically lower than it is in the 21st century. Towards the end of the life cycle (from Empty nest I onwards) it is likely that the model holds true fairly well, but it is unlikely that the earlier stages will follow the same pattern. This said, it is still important that students of consumer behaviour learn a historical perspective too in order to make sense of what is happening with our current society.

The traditional nuclear family of two parents with their own children has become a minority of households: it is more likely that a household will consist of a mother with her children from her first marriage (women account for 91% of lone parents with dependent children), a husband or partner who pays maintenance to his ex-wife for the children from his first marriage, and possibly a new child from the new partnership. Even more common is a childless home, either a single-person household or a childless couple living together: these represent more than half of all UK households. The number of families that include a couple in a legally registered partnership in the UK has increased by 3.7% in the past decade, to 12.7 million; by comparison, the number of cohabiting couple families saw an increase of 22.9% over the same period, to 3.6 million (ONS, 2022).

It may be more realistic to consider the life cycle of the individual, and link this to possible family roles and responsibilities rather than consider different possible family structures. Here are some of the life stages an individual might have:

1. *Living alone I.* This is someone who has left home, has a job and is living alone.
2. *Cohabiting, no children I.* This would be a couple who are living together without being married, and have no children.
3. *Cohabiting, with joint children.* This couple have a child or children, but are not married.

4. *Married, no children I*. Similar to 'Cohabiting, no children I' but have a legal relationship as well as a romantic one.
5. *Married, with joint children*. Similar to cohabiting, but with the legal relationship.
6. *Living alone II*. This is someone who is divorced or widowed.
7. *Cohabiting, no children II*. This couple is divorced or separated from earlier partners, and are now living together.
8. *Cohabiting, with children II*. The children may be from a previous relationship, or may not live with the couple at all, but be occasional visitors at weekends or during the week.
9. *Married, no children II*. This couple have been married before, and may or may not intend to have children together at some future time.
10. *Married, with children II*. This couple is second-time married, with children from earlier relationships who may or may not live with them.
11. *Married or cohabiting couple with grown-up children still at home*. This situation is becoming more common as single people find it harder to buy a home. These households can be extremely wealthy, since three or more adults are contributing to the overall income.

There are likely to be other, more complex, situations but each of these situations impacts on family decision-making, and (particularly in the case of cohabiting or married couples with children from previous relationships) other people who are not actually part of the family will also need to be considered (in this case, ex-partners). Working out the decision rules between the various players is likely to be difficult in these cases, and in some cases special marketing activities are in place to take account of single parents who have access rights to their children on specific days. The concept of being 'a father for half an hour in McDonald's' has become familiar, and some advertising reflects this.

The divorce–remarry cycle also means dramatic surges in income. Divorce usually means a dramatic fall in disposable income as the economies of scale in shared consumption evaporate and the individuals have to set up their own homes; this can mean a boost for businesses selling furniture, household appliances and homes, of course. Later on, though, the remarry phase often leads to a sudden sharp increase in wealth as the previously single people pool their resources. When people in their 40s remarry, having finished paying out for child maintenance and (often) now owning substantial equity in their homes, they will combine their assets and can find themselves suddenly wealthy.

GENDER ROLES

The last census in the UK (2021) showed that there are marginally more women than men in the population (30.4 million or 51% women vs. 29.1 million or 49% men) in England and Wales, largely due to two factors: greater infant mortality among boys, and greater life expectancy of women. Women's role has changed greatly over the past 30 years or so; women make more (or most) of the purchasing decisions, earn around a third of the household income and make most of the decisions regarding the home and the children.

The change in gender roles, summarised in Figure 11.6, comes from the following factors:

1. Technology means that most jobs do not require physical strength, so more careers are open to women.
2. Mass contraception has provided women with choices regarding childbearing.
3. A more ordered society has led to greater physical security; there is less need for the defence role of the male.
4. Greater accessibility to education means that women have many more choices and opportunities.

This shift in gender roles and expectations is affecting marketers, who are now changing the appeal of their advertising to meet the new conditions. For example, Flash Wipes are advertised showing a man doing the cleaning: he is portrayed as the average man, doing the cleaning and winning praise for doing so, but revealing to the audience that in fact the cleaning is really no big task. Twenty years ago such advertisements would only have been shown for comic purposes, and even now men are frequently portrayed as being incapable of doing the housework properly. Even as little as over 20 years ago, if a 'new' father told his dad that he planned to be a stay-at-home dad his father would have laughed at him because he simply came from a generation where there were very clearly defined roles for men and women. This is why in the 2004 film *Meet the Fockers* the portrayal of a man feeding his grandchild from a rubber breast (*boob*) strapped to his chest (while a little freaky) is actually quite progressive for its time. Fast-forward almost another 20 years and we're now starting to see the emergence of synthetic breast milk being produced (Sternlicht, 2022).

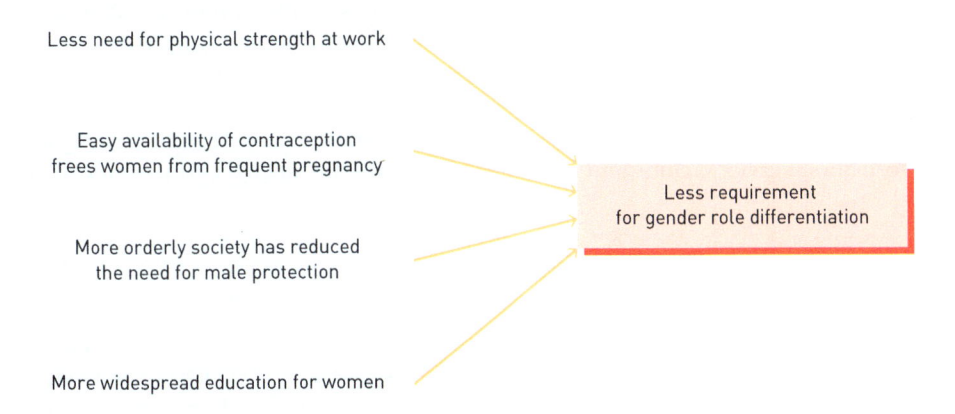

FIGURE 11.6 Drivers for gender role change

Sexual orientation affords another dimension to the definition of family. In the UK, civil partnerships between same-sex couples were introduced towards the end of 2005, and there was consequently a flurry of people in long-term relationships going through the ceremony. Registering a civil partnership in this way gives the couple the same legal status as if they were a heterosexual married couple: giving the relationship a legal status means that such partnerships have the status of being families by definition. No doubt the people concerned already felt as if they were families, and in many cases they have even had children either from previous heterosexual marriages or by adoption. The Marriage (Same Sex Couples) Act 2013 enabled same-sex couples in England and Wales to marry from 29 March 2014. It also has a number of related provisions, including for those in a civil partnership to convert that relationship to a marriage if they choose to do so and provisions that will enable a person to change their legal gender without ending their existing marriage.

Lesbian and gay people tend to be wealthier than heterosexuals (Carpenter and Eppink, 2017): lesbians continued to out-earn straight women. Specifically, the average annual earnings (pre-tax) for lesbians were $47,026 compared to $39,902 for heterosexual women. In contrast to the earlier data, however, it turns out that gay men now earn more than straight men. The average annual earnings for gay men were $59,618 compared to $57,032 for straight men. US research carried out by prideworldradio.com (2018) has concluded that LGBT households make 16% more shopping trips a year than non-LGBT households, and that in 2018 they spent on average 8% more than non-LGBT households. In fact, male same-sex households make almost 30% more shopping trips yearly. Various market research agencies have conducted surveys to try to show not just affluence, but that disproportionate levels of brand loyalty were a hallmark of gays and lesbians. This in turn meant that gay men were portrayed as being voraciously consumerist, cosmopolitan and thus well-to-do. There is no doubt that these research studies view the LGBT community from the perspective of a consumer market; it is worth noting that this is a very different perspective compared with how a social science researcher investigating poverty would look at those questions.

In the UK, disposable income from within the LGBT community is called the Pink Pound (in the US it is called the Dorothy Dollar) and is worth around £6 billion a year. Of course, marketers like to categorise people for segmentation purposes and some segments are much larger: the 'grey pound' market comprising older people amounts to nearly £320 billion a year. Nonetheless, £6 billion is a substantial market, so the 2SLGBTQIA+ communities have been targeted by some financial institutions and by information services, clubs and even holiday companies, such as Pink Pound Travel.

BRAND EXPERIENCES: BLACK BACCARA, FOSSIL AND SAKS

Gay- and women-owned indie perfume house Black Baccara knows that supporting the queer community is a year-round commitment. Founded by artist Kalliope Amorphous in 2010, Black Baccara creates herbal, gender-free fragrances for all. To celebrate Pride 2022, the brand has released a limited edition perfume oil, called Love is Love – which is described as a 'unique unisex blend' that 'opens with sugared lavender that quickly gives way to dollops of honey swirled with earthy light patchouli'. Lovely. Not only is Black Baccara celebrating Pride with its special fragrance, but it's also stated that

> 50% of the proceeds will support the work being done by New Alternatives for LGBTQ+ homeless youth.
>
> The watch and accessory brand Fossil is celebrating Pride with a multi-pronged approach. First, the brand has released a limited-edition capsule collection – which features Pride-themed products, such as watch faces, straps, charms, bracelets, purses, rings and more. Second, 100% of the proceeds will go directly to The Trevor Project, which is the world's largest suicide prevention and crisis intervention organisation for LGBTQ (lesbian, gay, bisexual, transgender, queer and questioning) young people. Fossil has pledged a minimum donation of $100,000 – meaning even if their collection doesn't sell out or make huge profits, the brand will still ensure that The Trevor Project receives the full donation amount. Third, Fossil has launched a social media campaign using the hashtag #TakeAMinute, where the brand's social profiles will serve as a platform to magnify the voices of members of the LGBTQIA+ community to its 1.2 million followers.
>
> Finally, Saks Off 5th (the less expensive sister brand to luxury department store Saks Fifth Avenue) has taken a great approach to Pride 2022. In partnership with The Phluid Phoundation (a non-profit that supports trans-led organisations and homeless queer youth at a grassroots and global level), Saks Off 5th launched 'a gender-neutral capsule' in June 2022 to celebrate queer culture. The Pride collection, which 'reinvents the rainbow and celebrates the freedom of universal love and self-expression' includes everything from scarves to hats to bags to kimonos. The collection also highlights the work of LGBTQIA+ designers, which adds to the campaign's effectiveness. Impressively, 100% of the net proceeds from sales will go to The Phluid Project – up to $100,000. In the campaign's video promo, the LGBTQIA+ community is honoured through dance – with the video spotlighting dancers of various skill sets, like Honey Balencaiga, West Dakota, Luis Dosu Carrera, Michelle Dorrance, Mila Jam, Courtney Taylor Key, Adriana Pierce and Harper Watters.

The LGBT community is estimated to account for at least 4% of the population (the exact figure is hard to determine as some members of the 2SLGBTQIA+ community still feel that they would face prejudice or hostility if they were open about their sexuality); they represent a substantial market (see Figure 11.7). No doubt some organisations feel pressure to appear gay friendly in order to access the Pink Pound, while not necessarily practising what they preach; this has become known as 'pinkwashing'. Advertising campaigns and media stories give us many examples of this.

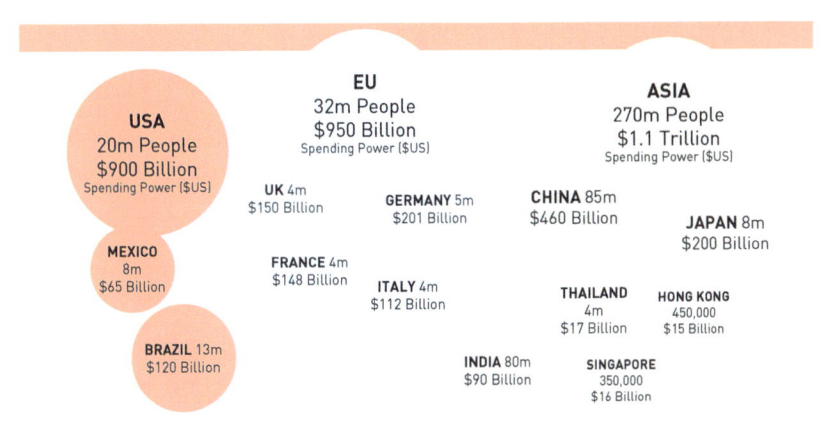

USA 20m People $900 Billion Spending Power ($US)
MEXICO 8m $65 Billion
BRAZIL 13m $120 Billion

EU 32m People $950 Billion Spending Power ($US)
- UK 4m $150 Billion
- FRANCE 4m $148 Billion
- GERMANY 5m $201 Billion
- ITALY 4m $112 Billion

ASIA 270m People $1.1 Trillion Spending Power ($US)
- CHINA 85m $460 Billion
- JAPAN 8m $200 Billion
- THAILAND 4m $17 Billion
- HONG KONG 450,000 $15 Billion
- INDIA 80m $90 Billion
- SINGAPORE 350,000 $16 Billion

FIGURE 11.7 Estimated size of the global LGBT community

Source: www.prideworldradio.com/wp-content/uploads/2018/02/maa_pwm_ssshhh_sponsor.pdf.

American retailer Target in the USA featured a gay couple in their advertising, but unfortunately for Target, the press found out that they had some time later donated cash to an anti-gay politician. Heinz ran an advert in 2008 that showed two men kissing, but decided to scrap the advert after receiving a backlash from, one presumes, the heterosexual community. This of course angered the LGBT community and made a mockery of Heinz's initial pro-gay stance. Timing is everything, and it certainly worked for the UK's suit-hire business Moss Bros. They ran an advertising campaign in 2014 entitled 'Mister and Mister' during the same week that gay marriage was legalised in the UK. Steinmetz (2014), who authored a cover story in *Time* magazine about Laverne Cox (a transgender actress, reality television star and activist), intimated that 'another civil rights movement is poised to challenge long-held cultural norms and beliefs', suggesting that the visibility that transgender people were getting was enabling them to move 'from the margins to fight for an equal place in society'. Three years on, BBC News (2017) ran a story about Nigel and Sally Rowe, who removed their 6-year-old son from his primary school on the basis that their son was confused as to why another child at the Church of England school on the Isle of Wight dressed as both a boy and a girl. This certainly gave increased 'visibility' but for all the wrong reasons; transgender has somehow now become an identifiable threat to gender normativity for some.

The UK, with its estimated 650,000 people who are 'likely to be gender incongruent to some degree' (BMA, 2022), is not alone. In the USA there has been much debate on the rights and non-discrimination laws that play a part in various transgender issues. Within the public domain, and according to the Public Religion Research Institute (2016), 53% of Americans oppose laws that require transgender individuals to use bathrooms that correspond to their assigned sex at birth rather than their current gender identity, compared to 35% who favour such laws. Laverne Cox has previously vocalised that 'bathroom bills' are not about restrooms but about 'the right to exist in public spaces'. The emotional disgust, revulsion and hatred towards individuals who do not conform to society's gender expectations, known as 'transphobia' (Robinson, K.H. et al., 2017; Robinson, M.J. et al., 2017), continues to be rife and centre stage (Hill and Willoughby, 2005). Eventually one might expect that gender role will not be an issue in advertising at all, but since advertising (at least in part) reflects society, this may still be some way off.

OTHER FUNCTIONS OF THE FAMILY

Families also provide economic well-being, emotional support and suitable family lifestyles (see Figure 11.8). Because families share consumption, the standard of living of the members is higher than would have been the case had they chosen to live separately. In some families, economic well-being is also generated by employment in the family business. Because the overall tasks within the family are divided between the members, some members might exchange earning their own money for taking on a larger role within the family, for example staying at home to care for small children.

In the majority of UK families both parents work outside the home. There is considerable debate as to whether this has a detrimental or a positive effect on children, but it certainly has a positive effect on the family's finances, increasing spending power and also (on the downside) increasing the need for labour-saving devices and behaviour, for example ready meals, childcare and children's entertainment devices, which leave the parents free to carry out other work-related tasks.

In some societies children are expected to contribute to the family's finances; in particular, teenage children are expected to work and contribute. In most Western families, teenagers would expect to retain any earnings, whereas their parents would want them either to save towards their education or adult life in general, or at least to pay something towards their upkeep, for example entertainment and perhaps clothing items.

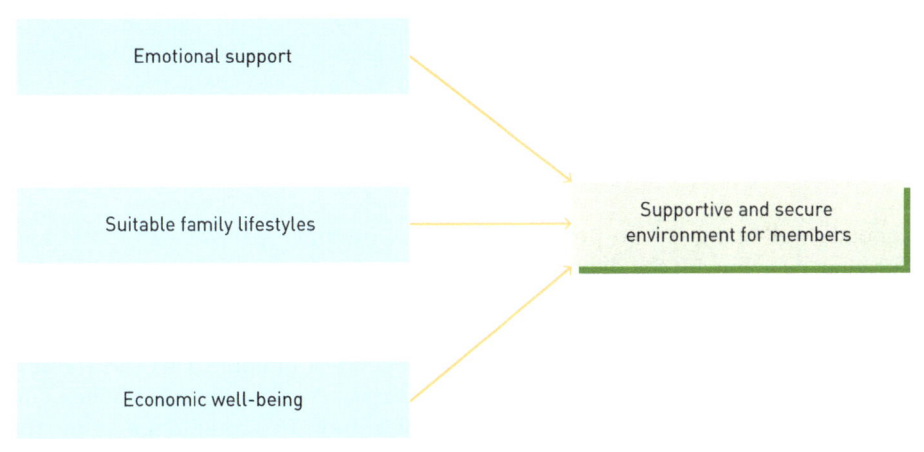

FIGURE 11.8   Other functions of the family

CONSUMER BEHAVIOUR IN ACTION: WHY IS FAMILY IMPORTANT?

Why do parents or guardians' matter? Are they important in shaping the lives of young people? Can they leave a negative effect if they get it wrong? Even back in 1966, research that was centred on *Equality of Educational Opportunity Study* (also known as the 'Coleman Study'; commissioned by the United States Department of Health, Education, and Welfare to assess the availability of equal educational opportunities to children of different race, colour, religion, and national origin) had noted that compared to most other variables, family background has the greatest influence on educational attainment. However, our society is full of examples of both parents working long hours, and where children are **latchkey kids**, or where the childcare has been sub-contracted to nannies, childminders and childcare centres. At the same time, our politicians are continually extolling the virtues of family values, and suggesting that parents should spend more time with their children. Children can be quite emotionally astute. There are only so many 'gifts' one can bring back following a 'work trip' – sometimes all the children want and value is some quality time with their parents.

(Continued)

Latchkey kid

A child who returns from school to an empty home because their parent or parents are away at work, or a child who is often left at home with little parental supervision

> It is perhaps this lack of or limited 'contact time' which then gives rise to other societal issues – a lack of exercise in young people (Anderson, 2006), which is fuelled by a nonchalant approach to eating habits (Savage et al., 2007) and even criminal behaviour and delinquency (Chung et al., 2002). It is also worth noting that the gap that parents sometimes leave in their children's lives is often filled by their friends and peers. Again, Milner (2015) points to issues such as use of drugs and smoking, early initiation of sexual behaviour, binge drinking and eating high calorie snacks, but the research notes that it is often difficult to measure the effects of peers precisely.
>
> It is of course easy to fall into a 'blame culture' and lay the responsibility at the door of the parent. What about all the other influences that a family is involved with? Johnson et al. (2009) make a very pertinent point when they assert that 'behaviour in adolescence is a function of multiple interactive influences including experience, parenting, socio-economic status, individual agency and self-efficacy, nutrition, culture, psychological well-being, the physical and built environments and social relationships and interactions'.
>
> So let's go back to basics and ask a very simple question – why is family important?

Economic well-being is also provided when, for example, parents pay for a child's education, or help with the deposit for a house. Sometimes the help goes in the other direction: grown-up children might pay for a care home, or for improvements to an elderly parent's home. In either case, marketers have a role in providing facilities for this to happen. Emotional support is a core function of families. This can comprise love and affection, but also involves moral support and encouragement. When families are unable to provide appropriate emotional support from within the group, they may turn to counselling, social care workers or even psychiatric services to provide professional help for their members.

Finally, families also help to establish suitable lifestyles (Zheng et al., 2022). Family members bear more than a physical resemblance to each other; they tend to have similar attitudes about the importance of education, about reading, about environmentalism, about home decoration, about holidays and about appropriate entertainments (sport, dining out, etc.). There is a clear association between health-promoting lifestyles and family relationships, social support and quality of life. Even though there is a trend towards family members acting independently rather than sharing activities, we return to the idea of spending 'quality time' with each other as this has recently led to a tendency to seek out activities and experiences that can be shared, especially during the Covid-19 pandemic (Martin-Storey et al., 2021). Marketers have not been slow to capitalise on this, promoting family leisure activities (for example, the PGL activity holiday), short breaks and so forth.

ROLES IN FAMILY CONSUMPTION

Within families, a great deal of decision-making is collective. Even such basic decisions as buying underwear might be shared or carried out by one member of the family on behalf of another. The traditional example would be a mother buying underwear for the children of the family, but many women buy underwear for their husbands, and it is far from unknown for husbands to buy lingerie for their wives (Hume and Mills, 2013), often as Valentine or birthday gifts.

AGE, GENDER AND FAMILIAL ROLES

Within families, consumption and purchase roles are often divided between family members. There are thought to be eight basic roles in family decision-making, as shown in Table 11.4. Depending on the type of product being considered, family members may adopt different roles for each decision. In other words, deciders are not necessarily deciders for everything – they may be deciders for some categories of product (e.g. holidays) and gatekeepers for another category (e.g. home entertainment systems). Likewise, roles often overlap, or the same person occupies more than one role.

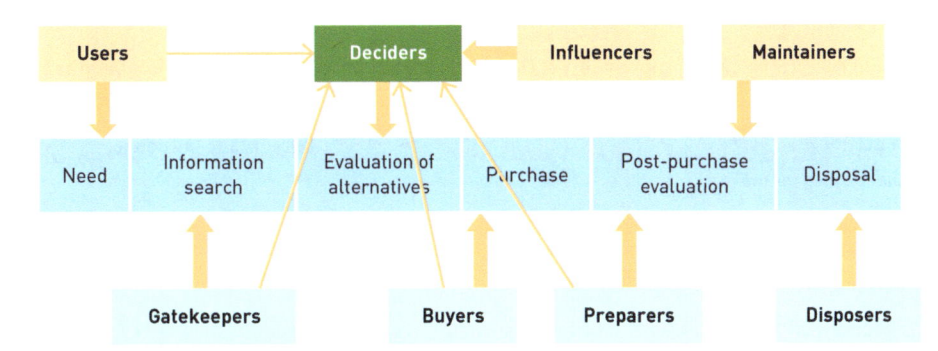

FIGURE 11.9 Family roles and decisions

In Figure 11.9 the main arrows show where each individual has a major input. The fine arrows show where the individuals have a lesser input. Obviously the same individual may have more than one role in the purchase decision.

TABLE 11.4 Roles in family decision-making

Role	Explanation
Influencers	These are the family members who perhaps have no direct involvement in the purchase or consumption of the item, but who can offer help and advice
Gatekeepers	These members control the flow of information to the others. A gatekeeper may be the person who scours the websites and reads the e-brochures or watches the advertising on TV
Deciders	These members have the final say on the product being bought or consumed. In most families, the deciders would be the parents, but this is not always the case: it depends on the product being considered
Buyers	Family members who make the actual purchase are the buyers. It may be that a decision is made to book a particular holiday, and the member with the best IT skills is given the task of booking it online
Preparers	These members transform the product into a form suitable for the others to consume it. The obvious example is cooking food, but the concept could equally apply to one of the children of the family setting up the Apple TV box to the new Smart TV
Users	The family members who will consume/use the product
Maintainers	The family members who will ensure that the product is in good condition for the others to use it. This not only applies to someone who mends the kitchen cupboards, it also applies to someone who cleans the house and does the laundry
Disposers	Members who have the job of removing the used products and packaging or arranging for the sale or trade-in of products for which the family has no further use

Preparers
Family members responsible for transforming a product into a condition suitable for other members to use it

Children appear to have a greater role in family decision-making than in the past. As children (and of course their parents) grow older, parents begin to seek the advice of their children on some aspects, particularly where new technology is concerned or where the child has acquired specialist knowledge. Research shows that parents in lower income groups are more likely to see their children as being 'consumer savvy', especially if the child is female and at the older end of the spectrum (Nancarrow et al., 2011). Parents with a 'warm' approach to parenting are more likely to learn from their children (Grossbart et al., 2002). Children themselves believe that they have considerable influence in many family purchase decisions, even including buying a car (Tinson and Nancarrow, 2005). The areas in which children believe themselves to be most important as decision-makers are shown in Table 11.5.

TABLE 11.5 How children perceive themselves to have influenced the purchase of different products

Product	Percentage influence
Casual clothes for me	91%
Trainers for me	88%
CDs for me	84%
Sweets for me	83%
Computers for me	83%
Soft drinks for me	80%
School shoes for me	80%
A family trip to the cinema	73%
Food for me for lunch at the weekend	73%
A holiday I would go on with the family	63%
Going out for a family meal	52%
A family car	37%

Research carried out in Canada indicates that children there have an even greater influence on decisions: 40% of children in one study believed themselves to be the main decision-makers with respect to choice of restaurant when eating out (Labrecque and Ricard, 2001) and in family food involvement in general (Metcalfe et al., 2018).

There is some evidence to suggest that the family's communication pattern is also related to the child's influence on the decision-making process (see Figure 11.10). Communication patterns usually fall into one or another of the following categories (Shoham et al., 2004):

1. *Pluralistic parents*. These parents encourage their children to express their ideas and preferences. Not surprisingly, these families experience the greatest influence from the children.
2. *Consensual parents*. These parents encourage their children to seek harmony, but they are influenced by the children's ideas.
3. *Protective parents*. These parents believe that 'mother knows best' and in general expect children to agree to the parents' choices.

It seems probable that children with pluralistic parents would be likely to develop consumer skills early, but they might also be the most likely to use pester power to get their own way. Children with protective parents might take longer to develop consumer skills, but would perhaps be more likely to adopt brands favoured by their parents in later life.

```
        The child's learning to be a consumer reduces
    ──────────────────────────────────────────────────▶

  [Pluralistic parents]   [Consensual parents]   [Protective parents]

    ◀──────────────────────────────────────────────────
        The child's influence on the immediate decision increases
```

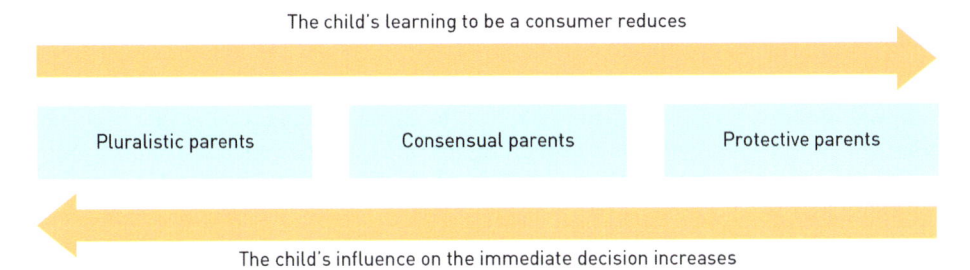

FIGURE 11.10 Communication pattern and children's influence

SUMMARY

Age, gender and the family are important factors in consumer behaviour. Families are often said to be the building blocks of society. We are influenced more by our families than by anybody else: partly this is because the influence starts at a very early age, partly it is because we spend a large part of our lives living with our families, and partly it is because our family relationships (especially those with our siblings if we have them) are the longest-lasting relationships in our lives. Marketers recognise that children – toddlers, tweenies and teenagers – all yield varying degrees of power and influence. As gender roles are continually defined and re-defined by societies in different cultures, marketing departments continually evolve their notion of what is acceptable, admissible and effective in their campaigns.

Because families share so much of their consumption, the ways in which they interact and make decisions are of great interest to marketers. Families share decision-making in many ways, and the views of family members are still important even when it is the parents who make the final decision.

There are many different patterns of family, but what they have in common is relationships by blood, marriage or adoption; shared consumption; face-to-face contact on a daily basis; emotional, economic and lifestyle support for their members; and finally, shared regard for each other's welfare.

KEY POINTS

- 'Family' has several definitions, each of which is dependent on culture and circumstances.
- Cohorts and subcultures developed using age are affected by differing attitudes and values.
- Culture has a marked effect on decision-making styles.
- All members of a family have some input into decision-making.
- Conflict is common in families because of shared consumption.
- Children (pester power) have to be taught to be effective consumers.
- The fluidity of gender roles is playing an increasingly important part in our lives.
- Brand loyalty can pass down through several generations.
- Family life cycle models are pluralistic in 21st-century society.
- Family members often adopt specific roles in the purchase and consumption process.

HOW TO IMPRESS YOUR EXAMINER

You will probably be asked about the effects of age and gender on decision-making patterns in families; and this is especially true for the influence of children. You should be able to differentiate the varying influences between the toddler, tweenie and teenager. It will gain you extra marks if you can provide the downside of decision-making, by outlining the ways in which children are influenced by their peers and by marketers. You should think about the attitudes towards changing gender roles in society. The question also implies that you should understand that decision-making, and indeed all consumption behaviour, is very much culturally driven.

REVIEW QUESTIONS

1. Why are children powerful in influencing consumption behaviour?
2. Why is the family a culturally based concept?
3. What have been the main changes in the family in recent years?
4. How might purchase roles change in the next 20 years?
5. What are the drivers for change in purchase roles?
6. How might the change in the ethnic structure of European society affect family decision-making?
7. To what degree does social class have an influence on consumer behaviour?
8. How does parenting style affect children's consumption behaviour?
9. What are the main criticisms of the family life cycle concept?
10. What are the key functions of a family?

CASE STUDY: THE LARGEST ADOLESCENT POPULATION IN THE WORLD

India has the largest adolescent population in the world, 253 million, and every fifth person is between 10 and 19 years old. India stands to benefit socially, politically and economically if this large number of adolescents are safe, healthy, educated and equipped with information and life skills to support the country's continued development.

Both adolescent girls and boys lack access to information on issues affecting their lives and have limited spaces to develop competencies crucial for active participation. Adolescent girls, especially, are exposed to multiple layers of vulnerability due to pernicious social norms affecting the value of girls, which in turn affects their ability to move freely and to make decisions affecting their work, education, marriage and social relationships.

About 43% of girls drop out before completing secondary education due to household responsibilities, marriage, child labour, limited relevance of education for employment and employability, distance to school and/or lack of sanitation facilities at the school. Menstruation disrupts the lives of girls in ways that are unimaginable in many countries. At least 42% of girls in India use cloth rather than disposable sanitary napkins.

Child marriage, a deeply rooted social norm, provides glaring evidence of widespread gender inequality and discrimination. Estimates suggest that each year, at least 1.5 million girls under 18 get married in India, which makes it home to the largest number of child brides in the world – alone accounting for a third of the global total.

Girls who become pregnant as adolescents are at a higher risk of maternal and newborn disease and death. About 9% of adolescent girls aged 15–19 years old in rural areas, and 5% in urban areas, have begun childbearing. Babies born from an adolescent mother are at an increased risk of being stunted in early childhood. This further leads to cognitive and physical deficits in young children and reduces productivity in adults.

Critical game changers in leveraging the potential of adolescents in India include postponing marriage, improving the health and nutritional status of adolescent girls, and generating better education, skill development, work and citizenship opportunities for adolescent girls and boys.

The solution?

UNICEF, in collaboration with the Government of India, seeks to include India's 253 million adolescents as active participants, rather than passive beneficiaries, in the process of their empowerment. They are the leaders of today, not tomorrow. The aim is to develop their skills and bring their voices more prominently into the public domain so that they can influence policies and programmes concerning them now and in the future.

© iStock.com / pixelfusion3d

The aim is to institutionalise adolescent participation through formal platforms at the block, district, state and national level and through informal platforms such as youth-led networks. To strengthen adolescent participation an equal number of girls and boys must participate. Engaging peer support leaders is key to adolescent participation and skilling. The focus is also on ensuring adolescents have opportunities to develop employable skills, both in school and out of school.

UNICEF is supporting the Ministry of Human Resource Development to develop an action plan for girls' education and out of school children. This will be integrated in the education curriculum and pedagogy from age 3 to 19 years in all states. UNICEF also supports state governments in rolling out their action plans for girls' education and out of school children, as well as in developing skills frameworks.

Their aim is social policy that best supports the adolescent transition to adulthood, such as integrating technical and non-cognitive skills competencies for a better transition to work, providing information on market opportunities and linking training

(Continued)

programmes to tangible workforce chances. Such policies would also protect adolescents from child marriage, child labour, civil strife and other harmful influences.

UNICEF engages with various youth-led networks and is building the capacity of district administrations and community structures to raise awareness on adolescents' rights through reference groups and by creating adolescent-centric, experience-based learning tools.

They work with key influencers, constituencies such as parliamentarians, faith-based organisations, media, private sector and community structures so that they have the capacities and skills to engage adolescent girls, boys, parents and community influencers to improve the well-being of adolescent girls and boys everywhere.

Source: Adapted from UNICEF (2022). For more information see unicef.org.

CASE STUDY QUESTIONS

1. How will UNICEF's work help social mobility?
2. Will empowerment here lead to conflict within families, and if so, how can this be managed?
3. Can India do this alone or is there an international effort required?
4. How important is the part that education plays?
5. What are the likely outcomes if UNICEF succeeds in its efforts?

FURTHER READING

Surrounded by Idiots: The Four Types of Human Behaviour (or, How to Understand Those Who Cannot Be Understood), by Thomas Erikson (New York: St. Martin's Essentials, 2019). Do you ever think you're the only one making any sense? Or tried to reason with your partner with disastrous results? Do long, rambling answers drive you crazy? Or does your colleague's abrasive manner get your back up? You are not alone. Thomas Erikson helps you to understand how people function and why we often struggle to connect with certain types of people.

For more information about breastfeeding and its benefits to society, please visit www.llli.org/. You could also visit the National Health Service webpage for the health benefits to consumers: www.nhs.uk/conditions/pregnancy-and-baby/pages/why-breastfeed.aspx#close.

If you want to know more about dealing with children who misbehave, you might like *Raising Your Spirited Child: A Guide for Parents Whose Child is More Intense, Sensitive, Perceptive, Persistent and Energetic*, by Mary Sheedy Kurcinka (New York: Harper Perennial, 1992). This American book might seem a bit 'worthy' but it does have some very good advice and techniques for dealing with children who get upset easily, or who challenge their parents.

There are many anthropological texts on childrearing practices in different cultures. An example is the rather scholarly *Turkish Mothers' Attitudes to Child-Rearing Practices*, by Gokce Tekin (Cambridge: Proquest/UMI Dissertation Publishing, 2011). It is in fact a PhD thesis, so can be hard going, but it shows how childrearing practices can vary greatly according to cultural differences.

For a look at the other face of marketing to children, Ed Mayo and Agnes Nairn's book *Consumer Kids: How Big Business is Grooming Our Children for Profit* (London: Constable, 2009) reveals some of the alleged tactics used by large corporations to target children. The book is maybe a little one-sided, but it certainly is thought-provoking and raises a number of ethical issues.

Another cautionary tale comes from Juliet Schor. Her book *Born to Buy: The Commercialised Child and the New Consumer Culture* (New York: Simon and Schuster, 2006) outlines some American marketing practices (many of which would be illegal in the UK and indeed in most of Europe). These include an educational TV channel available only in schools in which commercials are embedded in the teaching materials. Scary stuff – and something that certainly goes against the tenets of responsible marketing.

A comprehensive look at the theory of communication within families comes from *Communication in Family Relationships*, by Patrick Noller and Mary Ann Fitzpatrick (Englewood Cliffs, NJ: Prentice-Hall, 1993). A note of caution, however – although English is a universal language, there are marked differences between American culture and those of other English-speaking countries (not to mention non-English-speaking countries). Since family life is very culture-specific, theories developed in the USA may not apply elsewhere – so use your own judgement as well!

MORE ONLINE

For additional materials that support this chapter and your learning, please visit:

https://study.sagepub.com/sethna5e

REFERENCES

Agrigoroaei, S., Lee-Attardo, A. and Lachman, M.E. (2017) Stress and subjective age: Those with greater financial stress look older. *Research on Aging*, *39* (10): 1075–99.

Anderson, S. (2006) How does exercise cause asthma attacks? *Current Opinion in Allergy and Clinical Immunology*, *6* (1): 37–42.

Barak, B. and Schiffman, L.G. (1981) Cognitive age: A nonchronological age variable. In K.B. Monroe (ed.), *Advances in Consumer Research*, Vol. 8. Ann Arbor, MI: Association for Consumer Research. pp. 602–6.

BBC News (2017) Parents remove son from school in pupil gender row. www.bbc.co.uk/news/uk-england-hampshire-41224146 (accessed 9 January 2017).

Biraglia, A., Metastasio, R. and Carroll, A. (2018) Self-categorization theory and perception of coolness: An explorative study among British teenagers. *Rassegna di Psicologia*, *34* (2): 47–57.

BMA (British Medical Association) (2022) Managing patients with gender dysphoria. www.bma.org.uk/advice-and-support/gp-practices/gp-service-provision/managing-patients-with-gender-dysphoria (accessed 10 May 2022).

Bond, R. (2022) Social network determinants of screen time among adolescents. *Social Science Journal*, 59 (2): 236–51.

Boym, S. (2001) *The Future of Nostalgia*. New York: Basic Books.

Carlson, L. and Grossbart, S. (1988) Parental styles and consumer socialisation of children. *Journal of Consumer Research*, 15 (June): 77–94.

Carpenter, C.S. and Eppink, S.T. (2017) Does it get better? Recent estimates of sexual orientation and earnings in the United States. *Southern Economic Journal*, 84 (2): 426–41.

Centre for Ageing Better (2018) Greater support needed for older workers as number of over 50s in the UK workforce reaches record 10 million. www.ageing-better.org.uk/news/number-over-50s-uk-workforce-10-million (accessed 18 April 2018).

Christino, J.M.M., Cardozo, E.A.A., Silva, T.S. and Mazzini, C. (2020) Children's pester power, packaging and unhealthy food preference. *Young Consumers*, 21 (1): 35–55.

Chronis-Tuscano, A., Danko, C.M., Rubin, K.H., Coplan, R.J. and Novick, D. (2018) Future directions for research on early intervention for young children at risk for social anxiety. *Journal of Clinical Child & Adolescent Psychology*, 47 (4): 655–67.

Chung, I.-J., Hill, K.G., Hawkins, J.D., Gilchrist, L. and Nagin, D. (2002) Childhood predictors of offense trajectories. *Journal of Research in Crime and Delinquency*, 39: 60–91.

Clark, S.M., Hack-Polay, D. and Bal, M. (2022) Social mobility and promotion of officers to senior ranks in the Royal Navy: Meritocracy or class ceiling? *Armed Forces & Society*, 48 (1): 92–114.

Cocco, F. (2018) Highest fertility rates in Europe still below 'replenishment level'. *Financial Times*. www.ft.com/content/d54e4fe8-3269-11e8-b5bf-23cb17fd1498 (accessed 31 July 2018).

communicus.com (2014) Pester power. www.communicus.com/2014/12/17/pester-power-communicus-advertising-study-shows-children-significant-influence-parents-wireless-purchases/ (accessed 10 August 2015).

Curasi, C. (2006) Maybe it IS your father's Oldsmobile: The construction and preservation of family identity through the transfer of possessions. *Advances in Consumer Behaviour*, 33: 83.

Curasi, C. (2011) Intergenerational possession transfers and identity maintenance. *Journal of Consumer Behaviour*, 10 (2): 111–18.

Dejevsky, M. (2006) Japan: A country in crisis? *The Independent*, 26 August.

Desrochers, D.M. (2015) Advertising to children in traditional and new media. *Journal of Children and Media*, 9 (2): 272–5.

Dias, M. and Agante, L. (2011) Can advergames boost children's healthier eating habits? A comparison between healthy and non-healthy food. *Journal of Consumer Behaviour*, 10 (3): 152–60.

Doepke, M. and Kindermann, F. (2016) Why European women are saying no to having (more) babies. VOX CEPR Policy Portal. https://voxeu.org/article/why-european-women-have-few-babies (accessed 16 August 2018).

Ekstrom, K.M., Tansuhaj, P.S. and Foxman, E. (1987) Children's influence in family decisions and consumer socialization: A reciprocal view. *Advances in Consumer Research*, *14*: 283–7.

Elliott, C. (2011) It's junk food and chicken nuggets: Children's perspectives on 'kids' food' and the question of food classification. *Journal of Consumer Behaviour*, *10* (3): 133–40.

Epp, A.M. and Arnould, E.J. (2006) Enacting the family legacy: How family themes influence consumption behaviour. *Advances in Consumer Research*, *33*: 82–6.

Europa (2019) Ageing Europe. https://ec.europa.eu/eurostat/documents/3217494/10166544/KS-02-19%E2%80%91681-EN-N.pdf/c701972f-6b4e-b432-57d2-91898ca94893 (accessed 9 May 2020).

European Union (1995) *The Population of the EU on 1 January 1995*. Statistics in Focus. Population and Social Conditions No. 8. Luxembourg: Office for Official Publications of the European Communities.

Eutsler, L. and Antonenko, P. (2018) Predictors of portable technology adoption intentions to support elementary children reading. *Education and Information Technologies*, *23* (4).

Fernandez, K.V. and Veer, E. (2004) The gold that binds: The ritualistic use of jewellery in an Indian wedding. *Advances in Consumer Research*, *31*: 55.

Filiatrault, P. and Ritchie, J.R.B. (1980) Joint purchasing decisions: A comparison of influence structure in family and couple decision-making units. *Journal of Consumer Research*, *7* (September): 131–40.

Fondiller, D.S. (1996) Family jewels. *Forbes*, *157* (7): 16.

Frahm, L.B., Laursen, L.N. and Tollestrup, C. (2022) Categories and design properties of inherited long-lasting products. *Sustainability*, *14*: 3835.

Frick, A., Brandimonte, M.A. and Chevalier, N. (2022) Understanding autonomous behaviour development: Exploring the developmental contributions of context-tracking and task selection to self-directed cognitive control. *Developmental Science*, *25* (4): 1–15.

Ghosh, A.K., Badillo-Urquiola, K., Rosson, M.B., Xu, H., Carroll, J.M. and Wisniewski, P.J. (2018) A matter of control or safety? Examining parental use of technical monitoring apps on teens' mobile devices. In *Proceedings of the 2018 CHI Conference on Human Factors in Computing Systems*. New York: ACM. p. 194.

Green, R.T., Leonardi, J., Chandon, J., Cunningham, I.C.M., Verhage, B. and Strazzieru, A. (1983) Societal development and family purchasing roles: A cross-national study. *Journal of Consumer Research*, *9* (4): 436–42.

Greiner, T. and Sahm, M. (2018) How effective are advertising bans? On the demand for quality in two-sided media markets. *Information Economics and Policy*, *43*: 48–60.

Grossbart, S., Hughes, S., McConnell, P.S. and Yost, A. (2002) Socialisation aspects of parents, children and the internet. *Advances in Consumer Research*, *29*: 66–70.

Han, M. and Newman, G.E. (2022) Seeking stability: Consumer motivations for communal nostalgia. *Journal of Consumer Psychology, 32* (1): 77–86.

Hartman, C.L. and Kiecker, P. (2004) Jewellery: Passing along the continuum of sacred and profane meanings. *Advances in Consumer Research, 31*: 53–4.

Havlena, W.J. and Holak, S.L. (1991) The good old days: Observations on nostalgia and its role in consumer behavior. In R.H. Holman and M.R. Solomon (eds), *NA – Advances in Consumer Research*, Vol. 18. Provo, UT: Association for Consumer Research. pp. 323–9.

Hémar-Nicolas, V., Pantin-Sohier, G. and Gallen, C. (2022) 'Do you eat insects?' Acceptance of insects as food by children. *Journal of Consumer Marketing, 39* (5): 505–22.

Hill, D.B. and Willoughby, B.L.B. (2005) The development and validation of the genderism and transphobia scale. *Sex Roles: A Journal of Research, 53* (7–8): 531–44.

Hout, M. (2018) The politics of mobility. In M. Hout (ed.), *Generating Social Stratification: Toward a New Research Agenda*. London: Taylor and Francis. pp. 293–316.

Hume, M. and Mills, M. (2013) Uncovering Victoria's Secret: Exploring women's luxury perceptions of intimate apparel and purchasing behaviour. *Journal of Fashion Marketing and Management: An International Journal, 17* (4): 460–85.

Hynes, K., Lannin, D.G., Kanter, J.B., Yazedjian, A. and Nauta, M.M. (2022) Do materialistic adolescents ruminate more about their social media posts? *Youth & Society, 54* (5): 766–87.

John, D.R. (1999) Consumer socialization of children: A retrospective look at twenty-five years of research. *Journal of Consumer Research, 26* (December): 183–213.

Johnson, S.B., Blum, R.W. and Giedd, J.N. (2009) Adolescent maturity and the brain: The promise and pitfalls of neuroscience research in adolescent health policy. *Journal of Adolescent Health, 45* (3): 216–21.

Khor, P. (2017) A phenomenological study of the lived experiences of the Generation X and Y entrepreneurs. *Sinergi: Jurnal Ilmiah Ilmu Manajemen, 7* (2). doi: 10.25139/sng.v7i2.363

Kyodo, J. (2018) Japan's child population shrinks to 15.53 million, setting another record low. *The Japan Times*, 4 May. www.japantimes.co.jp/news/2018/05/04/national/number-children-japan-falls-37th-year-hit-new-record-low/#.W_MBfjj7SUk (accessed 24 July 2018).

Labrecque, J. and Ricard, L. (2001) Children's influence on family decision-making: A restaurant study. *Journal of Business Research, 54* (November): 173–6.

Lavuri, R. and Aileni, V.R. (2022) TV advertisements: Assessing the moderating effect of children's pester power on parents' purchase decision. *Journal of Promotion Management, 28* (5): 625–49.

Lawlor, M. and Prothero, A. (2011) Pester power: A battle of wills between children and their parents. *Journal of Marketing Management, 27* (5/6): 561–81.

Lilo, E.A. and West, A. (2022) 'OMG, I get like 100 teaspoons of sugar a day!' Rural teens' grasp of their beverage consumption habits. *Community Health Equity Research & Policy, 42* (4): 367–73.

Liu, W. and Tang, W. (2022) Effects of age-appropriate mobile app use behavior on subjective well-being of young elderly. *Security and Communication Networks, 2022*: 3209804.

Lizama-Loyola, A., Sepúlveda, D. and Vanke, A. (2022) Making sense of social mobility in unequal societies. *Sociological Research Online, 27* (1): 95–100.

Longley, P.A., van Dijk, J. and Lan, T. (2021) The geography of intergenerational social mobility in Britain. *Nature Communications, 12* (1): 1–8.

Mandrik, C.A., Fern, E.F. and Bao, Y. (2004) Intergenerational influence in mothers and young adult daughters. *Advances in Consumer Research, 31*: 697–9.

Martin-Storey, A., Dirks, M., Holfeld, B., Dryburgh, N.S.J. and Craig, W. (2021) Family relationship quality during the COVID-19 pandemic: The value of adolescent perceptions of change. *Journal of Adolescence, 93*: 190–201.

Maslen, J. (2022) Do the Conservatives believe in social mobility? *Political Quarterly, 93* (1): 104–11.

Matsuno, K. and Kohlbacher, F. (2018) Firms' (non) responses: The role of ambivalence in the case of population aging in Japan. *Long Range Planning.* https://doi.org/10.1016/j.lrp.2018.02.006

McFarlane, A. and Samsioe, E. (2020) #50+ fashion Instagram influencers: Cognitive age and aesthetic digital labours. *Journal of Fashion Marketing & Management, 24* (3): 399–413.

Metcalfe, J.J., Fiese, B.H. and STRONG Kids 1 Research Team (2018) Family food involvement is related to healthier dietary intake in preschool-aged children. *Appetite, 126*: 195–200.

Miller, E.G., Seiders, K., Kenny, M. and Walsh, M.E. (2011) Children's use of on-package nutritional claim information. *Journal of Consumer Behaviour, 10* (3): 122–32.

Milner, M. (2015) *Freaks, Geeks, and Cool Kids: Teenagers in an Era of Consumerism, Standardized Tests, and Social Media.* Abingdon: Routledge.

Mishra, A., Maheswarappa, S.S. and Colby, C.L. (2018) Technology readiness of teenagers: A consumer socialization perspective. *Journal of Services Marketing, 32* (5): 592–604.

Mittal, B. and Royne, M.B. (2010) Consuming as a family: Modes of intergenerational influence on young adults. *Journal of Consumer Behaviour, 9* (4): 239–57.

Nancarrow, C., Tinson, J. and Brace, I. (2011) Profiling key purchase influencers: Those perceived as consumer savvy. *Journal of Consumer Behaviour, 10* (2): 102–10.

Nies, H. and Leichsenring, K. (2018) Concepts and strategies of quality assurance in care for older people. In T. Boll, D. Ferring and J. Valsiner (eds), *A Volume in Advances in Cultural Psychology: Constructing Human Development.* Charlotte, NC: Information Age Publishing. pp. 347–72.

Norgaard, M.K. and Brunso, K. (2011) Family conflicts and conflict resolution regarding food choices. *Journal of Consumer Behaviour, 10* (3): 141–51.

O'Neill, T., Vigar-Ellis, D. and Paterson, S. (2013) Pester power in low income families. In K. Kubacki (ed.), *Ideas in Marketing: Finding the New and Polishing the Old, Development in Marketing Science*. London: Springer International Publishing. p. 600.

Ofcom (2022) Children and parents: Media use and atttudes report. www.ofcom.org.uk/__data/assets/pdf_file/0024/234609/childrens-media-use-and-attitudes-report-2022.pdf (accessed 18 March 2022).

Oh, D.D., Barger, M.M. and Pomerantz, E.M. (2022) Parents' math anxiety and their controlling and autonomy-supportive involvement in children's math learning: Implications for children's math achievement. *Developmental Psychology*. https://dx.doi.org/10.1037/dev0001422

Olsen, B. (1993) Brand loyalty and lineage: Exploring new dimensions for research. *Advances in Consumer Research*, *20*: 575–9.

Onkvisit, S. and Shaw, J.J. (1994) *Consumer Behaviour: Strategy and Analysis*. New York: John Wiley.

Online Etymology Dictionary (2022) Definition of nostalgia (n.). www.etymonline.com/search?q=nostalgia (accessed 13 August 2022).

ONS (Office for National Statistics) (2022) Families and households in the UK: 2021. www.ons.gov.uk/peoplepopulationandcommunity/birthsdeathsandmarriages/families/bulletins/familiesandhouseholds/2021#:~:text=The%20number%20of%20families%20that,same%20period%2C%20to%203.6%20million (accessed 23 March 2022).

Petráková, Z., Okręglicka, K., Maňák, R. and Fialová, V. (2021) Generation disparities on the perception of SMEs business risks. *International Journal of Entrepreneurial Knowledge*, *9* (2): 32–48.

prideworldradio.com (2018) Sssshhh! Can you keep a secret? www.prideworldradio.com/wp-content/uploads/2018/02/maa_pwm_ssshhh_sponsor.pdf (accessed 31 July 2018).

Pronovost, M.A. and Scott, R.M. (2022) The influence of language input on 3-year-olds' learning about novel social categories. *Acta Psychologica*, *230*: 103729.

Public Religion Research Institute (2016) Majority of Americans oppose laws requiring transgender individuals to use bathrooms corresponding to sex at birth rather than gender equality. www.prri.org/research/poll-lgbt-transgender-bathroom-bill-presidential-election/ (accessed 9 January 2017).

Ram, A., Dave, S.S., Lancki, N., Moran, M., Puri-Taneja, A., Mammen, S., Kanaya, A.M. and Kandula, N.R. (2022) Social influence of adult children on parental health behavior among South Asian immigrants: Findings from the MASALA (Mediators of Atherosclerosis in South Asians Living in America) study. *Ethnicity & Health*, *27* (3): 639–57.

Rendall, S., Dodd, H. and Harvey, K. (2022) Controlling feeding practices moderate the relationship between emotionality and food fussiness in young children. *Appetite*, *178*: 106259.

Robinson, K.H., Smith, E. and Davies, C. (2017) Responsibilities, tensions and ways forward: Parents' perspectives on children's sexuality education. *Journal of Sex Education*, *17* (3): 333–47.

Robinson, M.J., Van Esch, C. and Bilimoria, D. (2017) Bringing transgender issues into management education: A call to action, learning and education. *Academy of Management, 16* (4): 300–13.

Rose, G.M. (1999) Consumer socialization, parental style, and developmental timetables in the United States and Japan. *Journal of Marketing, 63*: 105–19.

Rose, G.M., Dalakis, V., Kropp, F. and Kamineni, R. (2002) Raising young consumers: Consumer socialization and parental style across cultures. *Advances in Consumer Behaviour, 29*: 65.

Rummel, A., Howard, J., Swinton, J.M. and Seymour, D.B. (2000) You can't have that! A study of reactance effects and children's consumer behaviour. *Journal of Marketing Theory and Practice, 8* (1): 38–45.

Saarela, J., Hardy, M. and Skirbekk, V. (2022) Childlessness among heterosexual partnered individuals: Register-based evidence from the Finnish cohorts born 1952–1966. *Journal of Comparative Family Studies, 53* (2): 189–215.

Sage (2015) Survey report 2015 state of the startup. www.sage.com/na/~/media/site/sagena/responsive/docs/startup/report (accessed 24 July 2018).

Savage, J., Fisher, J.O. and Birch, L. (2007) Parental influence on eating behavior: Conception to adolescence. *Journal of Law, Medicine & Ethics, 35* (1): 22–34.

Sethna, Z. (2015) Entrepreneurial marketing and the Zarathustrian entrepreneur: Thoughts, words and deeds. In *Academy of Marketing AM2015 Conference Proceedings*. Limerick, Ireland.

Shivany, S. (2015) Resolving methods for parent–children conflict engaged by the TV-commercials in the post-war market. *New Media and Mass Communication, 35*: 56–65.

Shoham, A., Rose, G.M. and Bakir, A. (2004) The effect of family communication patterns on mothers' and fathers' perceived influence in family decision making. *Advances in Consumer Behaviour, 31*: 692.

Shubik, M. (2018) Who gets what, when and how? Power, organization, markets, money and the allocation of resources. Cowles Foundation Discussion Paper No. 3018. https://cowles.yale.edu/sites/default/files/files/pub/d30/d3018.pdf (accessed 4 June 2018).

Sobotka, T. (2021) World's highest childlessness levels in East Asia. *Population & Sociétés, 595*: 1–4.

Stalgaitis, C.A., Jordan, J.W., Djakaria, M. and Saggese, D.J. (2021) Social branding framework to address smoking among alternative peer crowd teens. *Journal of Social Marketing, 11* (3): 189–203.

Steinmetz, K. (2014) Laverne Cox talks to TIME about the transgender movement. *TIME Magazine.* http://time.com/132769/transgender-orange-is-the-new-black-laverne-cox-interview/ (accessed 9 January 2017).

Sternlicht, A. (2022) Two women-led startups look to solve baby-formula crisis with synthetic breast milk. www.forbes.com/sites/alexandrasternlicht/2022/05/22/two-women-led-startups-look-to-solve-baby-formula-crisis-with-synthetic-breast-milk/?sh=799b3ab141c8 (accessed 1 June 2022).

Sun, Q., Lou, V.W. and Law, B.M. (2018) Validating the effectiveness scale of children's familial influencing behavior within three-generational relationships. *Research on Social Work Practice*, *28* (4): 482–92.

Taylor, P., Livingston, G., Cohn, D., Wang, W., Velasco, G. and Hinze-Pifer, R. (2010) *Childlessness Up among All Women; Down Among Women with Advanced Degrees*. Pew Research Center. http://assets.pewresearch.org/wp-content/uploads/sites/3/2010/11/758-childless.pdf (accessed 19 July 2018).

Thomas, R.J., White, G.R.T. and Samuel, A. (2021) Exploring the motivations to participate in an online brand community: A study of 7–11-year-old children. *European Journal of Marketing*, *55* (8): 2308–43.

Thompson, R., Fisher, H.L., Dewa, L.H., Hussain, T., Kabba, Z. and Toledano, M.B. (2022) Adolescents' thoughts and feelings about the local and global environment: A qualitative interview study. *Child & Adolescent Mental Health*, *27* (1): 4–13.

Tinson, J. and Nancarrow, C. (2005) The influence of children on purchases. *International Journal of Marketing*, *47* (1): 5–27.

Tiwari, S. (2015) Exclusion of Madheshi women in decision making. *Academic Voices: A Multidisciplinary Journal*, *4*: 68–72.

UNICEF (2022) Adolescent development and participation. www.unicef.org/india/what-we-do/adolescent-development-participation#:~:text=India%20has%20the%20largest%20adolescent,between%202010%20to%2019%20years (accessed 30 September 2022).

United Nations (2016) Households and families. http://unstats.un.org/unsd/demographic/sconcerns/fam/fammethods.htm (accessed 14 February 2016).

Ward, C.B. (2006) He wants, she wants: Gender, category and disagreement in spouses' joint decisions. *Advances in Consumer Research*, *33*: 117–23.

Wells, W.D. and Gubar, G. (1966) The life cycle concept in marketing research. *Journal of Marketing Research*, *3* (November): 353–63.

Wildschut, T., Sedikides, C., Arndt, J. and Routledge, C. (2006) Nostalgia: Content, triggers, functions. *Journal of Personality and Social Psychology*, *91*: 975–93.

Wildschut, T., Sedikides, C., Routledge, C., Arndt, J. and Cordaro, F. (2010) Nostalgia as a repository of social connectedness: The role of attachment-related avoidance. *Journal of Personality and Social Psychology*, *98*: 573–86.

Williams, T.P. (2006) Money and meaning: The role of social bonds and capital in inter vivos gifting. *Advances in Consumer Research*, *33*: 84–5.

Willoughby, J.F. (2015) Effectiveness of a social marketing campaign promoting use of a sexual health text service by teens. *Journal of Health Communication*, *20* (10): 1206–13.

Wimalasir, J.S. (2004) A cross-national study on children's purchasing behaviour and parental response. *Journal of Consumer Marketing*, *21* (4): 274–84.

Winograd, M. and Hais, M. (2011) *Millennial Momentum: How a New Generation is Remaking America*. New Brunswick, NJ: Rutgers University Press.

Yan, Z. (2018) Child and adolescent use of mobile phones: An unparalleled complex developmental phenomenon. *Child Development, 89* (1): 5–16.

Yanaoka, K. and Saito, S. (2022) The development of learning, performing, and controlling repeated sequential actions in young children. *Topics in Cognitive Science, 14* (2): 241–57.

Zheng, X., Xue, Y., Dong, F., Shi, L., Xiao, S., Zhang, J., Xue, B., Qian, Y., Zhu, H., Man, Q. and Zhang, C. (2022) The association between health-promoting-lifestyles, and socioeconomic, family relationships, social support, health-related quality of life among older adults in China: A cross sectional study. *Health and Quality of Life Outcomes, 20* (1): 64.

Zorell, C.V. (2022) Central persons in sustainable (food) consumption. *International Journal of Environmental Research and Public Health, 19*: 3139.

PART ONE   CONSUMER BEHAVIOUR IN CONTEXT

Chapter 1   Understanding Consumer Behaviour
Chapter 2   Decisions, Behaviours and Interactions
Chapter 3   Consumption in B2C vs. B2B
Chapter 4   Consumer Technology and Innovation

PART TWO   CONSUMERS AS INDIVIDUALS (THE PSYCHOLOGICAL ISSUES)

Chapter 5   Drive, Motivation and Hedonism
Chapter 6   The Self and Personality
Chapter 7   Perception
Chapter 8   Learning and Knowledge
Chapter 9   Attitude Formation and Change

PART THREE   CONSUMERS AS SOCIAL ACTORS (THE SOCIOLOGICAL ISSUES)

Chapter 10   Reference Groups
Chapter 11   Age, Gender and Familial Roles
Chapter 12   Culture and Social Mobility
Chapter 13   Ethical Consumption
Chapter 14   Sustainable Consumption

CHAPTER 12
CULTURE AND SOCIAL MOBILITY

LEARNING OBJECTIVES

After reading this chapter you should be able to:

- Explain what the constituent parts of the social environment are.
- Understand what is meant by culture.
- Explain how subcultural factors colour our purchasing behaviour.
- Describe the difference between high-context cultures and low-context cultures.
- Discuss some approaches to studying culture and consumer culture theory.
- Understand the problems raised for people who move from one culture to another by discussing acculturation.
- Describe how social class distinctions have changed in the last 50 years, to take account of social mobility.

CHAPTER CONTENTS

Introduction
Culture
Subcultures
Social mobility (aka class)
Summary
Key points
How to impress your examiner
Review questions
Case study: Hopscotch Women's Centre
Further reading
References

More online: https://study.sagepub.com/sethna5e

INTRODUCTION

This chapter is about the contexts within which behaviour takes place. Individual decision-making always occurs within a social, cultural or environmental context, since human beings interact and need to consider the responses of others. Also, the physical environment within which decisions are made can affect the outcomes dramatically: some environments are conducive to paying higher prices, or buying more of a specific type of product, whereas others encourage greater thrift.

The social environment includes all the behavioural inputs received from other people. In some cases, these may be direct interactions (a conversation with a salesperson, advice from a friend, an encounter with someone unpleasant) and in other cases they may be indirect (observing how a friend negotiates with a vendor, seeing a banner advert on a website, seeing how other people act in a new social situation either offline or online).

The social environment can also be divided into macro- and micro-environments. The macro-environment has three components: culture, subculture and social class. Each of these has profound influences on behaviour because they have been powerful drivers in the formation of attitudes, beliefs and values. Although people from the same cultural background differ considerably among themselves, there will still be similarities. Each of these elements will be dealt with in more detail later in this chapter.

Subculture
A set of beliefs and attitudes which, while part of a main culture, represents a distinctly separate set

Culture provides the social environment within which people live. This chapter also considers what happens when people change culture (Neville and Schneider, 2021), or when their own culture shifts around them (Bao et al., 2022; Madani, 2022); in addition it considers the variations within a culture that is called **subculture**. In the latter part of this chapter, we also take a closer look at social mobility, associated with '*class*'; this somewhat ambiguous concept has been a talking point for sociologists for many years.

As shown in Figure 12.1, the micro-social environment comprises the face-to-face social interactions we have with our friends, work colleagues, family and others in the groups of which we are members. These micro-environmental interactions have been dealt with already in Chapters 10 and 11. The macro-environment comprises those factors that are common to everyone living within the same country or region; in other words, those factors that affect us all.

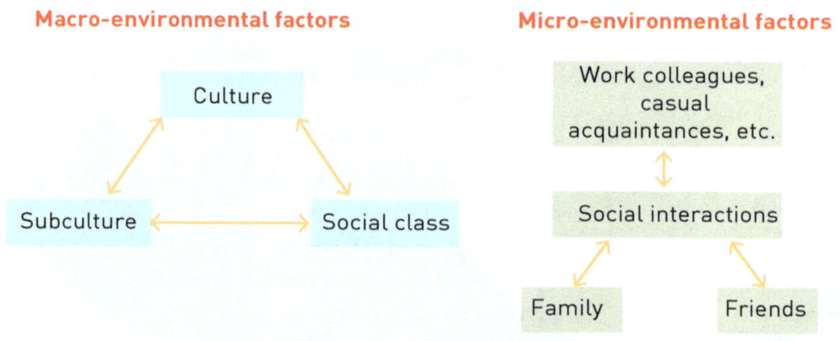

FIGURE 12.1 The social environment

CULTURE

Culture is the set of shared beliefs, attitudes and behaviours associated with a large and distinct group of people. Culture is learned, but it is often so deeply ingrained in people that they imagine that the rules of their particular society or group have the status of natural laws. As a result, culture is one of the main drivers of behaviour and influences almost everything we do, including, of course, our consumption behaviour.

The main elements of culture, summarised in Figure 12.2, are as follows:

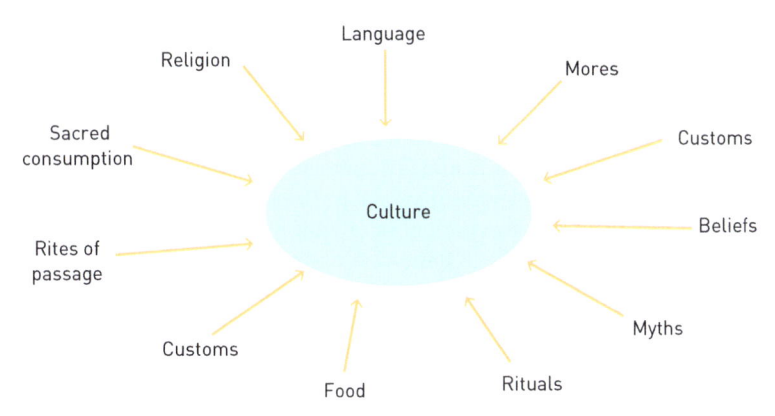

FIGURE 12.2 Elements of culture

- *Religion*. Religious beliefs colour people's behaviour in many ways, from laying down rules about which foods are permissible and which are not, through to disposal of the dead (Panikkar, 2018). For example, it is frowned upon for a deceased Zarathustrian to be buried. The religious dictate is that if death is the temporary triumph of evil over good, then by using burial as a method of disposal, one is defiling the Earth (made by God and thus 'good') for 35 years or more.
- *Language*. Language and culture are synonymous (Alqarni, 2022). Language clearly affects purchasing behaviour in many ways. First, the ability to understand and act on marketing communications relies not only on understanding the specific language but also on understanding specific words and sentence constructions within the language. For example, slang terms and puns might not be accessible to all the observers of the communication, and communications written in dialect might not be understood by non-native speakers of the language. Second, some products (such as books and newspapers) may not be of any use to someone who does not understand the language in which they are written. The market for books in Welsh, for example, is confined to Wales and parts of Argentina, with few (if any) sales elsewhere. The structure and rules of languages can affect consumer perceptions: in languages where brand names acquire gender (Spanish and French, for example) this will affect consumer perception of the product as being either masculine or feminine. In languages that include a neuter gender (English and Greek are examples) this is not an issue unless the marketer deliberately uses a masculine or feminine ending on the brand name (Yorkston and deMello, 2004).
- *Customs*. These are norms of behaviour handed down from the past. And whilst there is nostalgia and heritage intertwined, sometimes we lose culture based on our 'accelerated times' (Berliner, 2020). Some customs grow out of religious beliefs (many of the traditions associated with Christmas have come from Christian belief, although some are pagan or pre-Christian), while others come from traditions associated with climate or shared experiences. For example,

throughout most of southern Spain villages and towns celebrate the Fiesta of 'Moros y Cristianos', which refers to the overthrow of the Moorish invaders, who had occupied the region between 722 and 1492 AD. The date varies in each village, as each village overthrew its Moors on a different date, but for most it is a spectacular celebration involving fireworks (symbolising the fighting and also the traditional destruction of remaining ammunition to show that the shooting really is over) and a great deal of dancing and partying throughout the night.

- *Food*. Food is strongly linked to culture (e.g. Saint Pol and Hébel, 2021). While cheese is regarded as an essential part of any meal in France, and each region of the country produces several distinct examples, in Japan it is regarded as being as appealing as sour milk and is a somewhat exotic food, even though it is nowadays available in most supermarkets. In Britain, people will not eat insects (remember the example of experiences of eating insects from Chapter 9?) but will happily eat prawns, while in Zambia deep-fried caterpillars are a delicacy. In Mexico, the tortilla has a cultural significance that is bound up in what it means to be a Mexican, but (paradoxically) there is an underlying belief that everything emanating from the USA is better than anything Mexican: there is evidence that even American tortillas are considered to be somehow better than Mexican ones (Gabel and Boller, 2003). In India and Pakistan, it is quite normal to fry cutlets made of sheep's brains! These differences in taste are explained by culture rather than by random differences in taste between individuals: behaviours tend to be shared by people from the same cultural background.

- *Mores*. Mores are customs with a strong moral incentive. Moral development has several contributors, for example, religion, economics and culture (Pawlak et al., 2021). In most societies, cannibalism is regarded as immoral and is not part of the cultural mores; in other societies (most of them in the past) cannibalism is not only moral but is regarded as a necessary and respectful way of dealing with dead people. Violation of mores often results in strong reactions from other members of the culture – in some cases these can be abusive or even violent, while in other cases the law becomes involved and the individual receives a formalised punishment. In many countries, the media portrayal of the police treatment of Black people is fast becoming a more of sorts. There is certainly deep unrest concerning the types of cases that are being realised.

- *Conventions*. These are norms regarding the conduct of everyday life, for instance the way in which individuals avoid disagreement and conflict in order to maintain social equilibrium or react to the creation of age-friendly communities and environments that can support older residents' health, well-being and quality of life (Brossoie et al., 2022). For example, in the UK a dinner guest would normally be expected to bring a bottle of wine, and many dinner guests would also bring flowers; in Hawaii people would bring small snacks called *puu-puus*. From a verbal perspective, some spoken phrases are conventional – for instance when someone asks you 'How are you?', they are usually expecting the answer, 'Fine, thanks' rather than an actual description of your current circumstances, or a detailed health report, etc. Table manners, appropriate clothing for formal occasions and rules about when it is permissible to make a noise (for example, play loud music) and when it is not are also examples of conventions. As an exercise to test conventions, try saying 'Hi' to random people on the London Underground, or even try to strike up a conversation (!)… it's just not the done thing as Brits like to sit in silence.

Mores
Elements of a culture

- *Myths*. A myth is a story that contains symbolic elements expressing the shared emotions and ideals of a culture. The outcome of a myth might illustrate a particular moral pathway, and it thus serves to provide a guideline to the world (Kuznetsov, 2022). An example might be the 'urban myths' that often circulate by email, to warn people of inappropriate behaviour or to provide entertainment. Take for example a truly modern urban myth, Slender Man. It started life in an online competition to Photoshop pictures but to include a supernatural element. One particular entrant to the competition added a suited, faceless, unnaturally tall figure into two black and white photos which were copied and distributed virally over the net. Since then, millions of authors, mostly online, have shared and spread the story on websites such as Creepypasta. The Slender Man's speciality is to abduct people, often children, who seem to willingly go with the figure never to be seen again, making him a terrifying version of the Pied Piper.

- *Rituals*. A ritual is a set of symbolic behaviours that occur in a fixed sequence (Hajdas et al., 2022). For example, weddings follow a fairly well-defined path in most cases, and there are many rituals attached to sporting events such as football matches. The singing of specific songs, the consumption of specific foods or beverages (few football fans would watch the match while drinking a glass of Chardonnay wine – beer is the ritual drink) and the wearing of specific clothing are all ritualistic. Many people have grooming rituals (brushing one's hair numerous times each day, showering to a specific pattern and so forth), which serve to transform the individual from the private persona to the public persona. Gift-giving is another example of a ritual – in most Western cultures, gifts should be wrapped in attractive paper and should contain an element of surprise, the price tag should be removed and the recipient has to look pleased to receive the gift. Deviation from this ritual causes discomfort for one or the other party to the transaction. In China, on the other hand, giving a gift imposes an obligation on the recipient to do the other person a favour at some time or to reciprocate; over-effusive thanks for a gift can be interpreted as an attempt to avoid this obligation.

- *Rites of passage*. A rite of passage is an event or a set of behaviours that moves an individual from one state to another (Devi and Singh, 2021). The Freshers Ball at university is an example, as is the traditional 21st birthday party, which of course relates to the time when 21-year-olds were regarded as full adults. This has been diluted somewhat by changes in legislation, which now confers full responsibilities and rights at different stages during an individual's teenage years. In Japan, where the **age of majority** is 20, there is a special public holiday dedicated to those who will reach age 20 during that year. Some rites of passage are more individual in nature: marriage ceremonies or divorce proceedings are rites of passage between the single and married states, but may occur at almost any stage in the individual's adult life, or may not occur at all. Rites of passage are important to people as statements of status, and new rites are invented periodically to take account of new situations: legislation in the UK now allows marriage between couples of the same sex, and at a more mundane level there are definite rituals that are observed when someone changes job. Sadly, there are some rites of passage which are abhorrent in our world. Female circumcision, the partial or total cutting away of the external female genitalia, has been practised for centuries in parts of

Age of majority
The threshold of adulthood as it is conceptualised (and recognised or declared) in law

Africa, generally as one element of a rite of passage preparing young girls for womanhood and marriage. Often performed without anaesthetic under septic conditions by lay practitioners with little or no knowledge of human anatomy or medicine, female circumcision can cause death or permanent health problems as well as severe pain. Despite these grave risks, its practitioners look on it as an integral part of their cultural and ethnic identity, and some perceive it as a religious obligation. Since the late 1990s, so-called 'alternative rites of passage' (ARPs) have gained popularity in Kenya as a strategy to end female genital mutilation (FGM). ARPs promise to end FGM while respecting indigenous cultures by mimicking the 'traditional' initiation ritual but with the omission of the physical cut (Hannelore Van Bavel, 2021).

- *Sacred consumption.* Some places are set apart as special because something of great significance happened there. So what becomes sacred to the consumer? And therefore what are the implications for marketers (Schindler and Minton, 2022)? In some cases these places have mystical or religious significance, for example Stonehenge (UK), Persepolis (Iran) or Machu Picchu (Peru), while in other cases the place might have no religious significance as such but acquires sacred qualities. A prime example is the Principality Stadium in Cardiff, UK, the national stadium for Welsh rugby union. The actual pitch is often referred to as 'the hallowed turf' and there have been numerous attempts (some successful) to scatter the ashes of deceased Welsh rugby fans on the pitch.

These elements of culture are common to all cultures, but vary in type and importance between cultures. For some cultures, religion is almost the defining factor: Islamic states that operate under Sharia law as laid down in the Koran, and countries such as Spain where fiestas, public holidays and many aspects of daily life are conducted with reference to the Catholic Church, are prime examples.

To an extent, national characteristics can be identified. The most famous (and widely taught) study of national characteristics is that of Hofstede (1980). This research reported on a study of 6000 respondents in 66 countries, all of whom worked for IBM. Hofstede initially identified four cultural dimensions, as follows:

1. *Individualism vs. collectivism.* This is the degree to which the culture values individualism and individual freedom above that of the group.
2. *Uncertainty avoidance.* This is the degree to which the culture adheres to rules and customs to avoid risk.
3. *Power distance.* This is the degree to which power is centralised in the culture.
4. *Masculinity–femininity.* This is the degree to which the culture exhibits 'masculine' qualities of assertiveness, achievement and wealth acquisition rather than the 'feminine' attributes of nurturing, concern for the environment and concern for the poor.

Hofstede later revisited the data and the problem, and came up with a fifth dimension. This is long-term vs. short-term orientation, and is a dimension that is particularly relevant to cultures where perspectives of 'time' are very different (for example

China) from that experienced in, say, the UK. Very recent studies include examination of indulgence vs. restraint, the sixth dimension of Hofstede's cultural framework, at the individual level (Heydari et al., 2021).

These categorisations, summarised in Figure 12.3, are interesting, and may be useful for planning the overall tone of a communications campaign, but it would be dangerous to make assumptions about individuals based on these broad generalisations. The average Taiwanese may be more collectivist than the average American, but the most individualistic Taiwanese is likely to be a great deal more individualistic than the most collectivist American.

Hofstede's research has been widely criticised for several reasons. First, the research was conducted with IBM employees, and since IBM has a strong corporate culture it seems likely that this will have affected the results. Second, Hofstede was concerned mainly with work-related values rather than with consumer behaviour, yet the research has often been used to justify marketing communication activities. Third, the actual survey was conducted in the late 1960s, around 50 years ago, and the world has become considerably more globalised since then – recent research shows that the opening up of China has resulted in markedly changed attitudes to, for example, cosmetic surgery, formerly the prerogative of Western societies (Lindridge and Wang, 2008). Even then, though, the same research showed that participants were encouraged to undergo plastic surgery because of the interplay of traditional Chinese hierarchies of family and society.

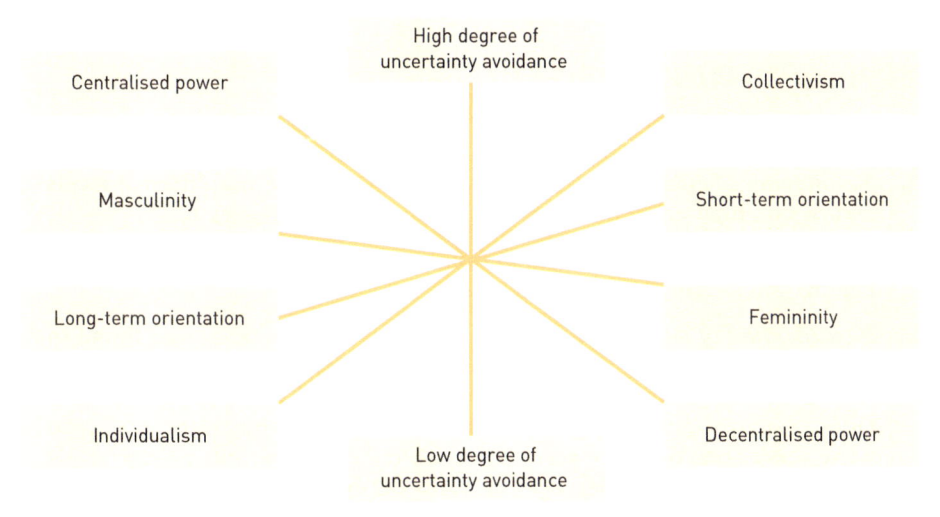

FIGURE 12.3 Dimensions of culture

CRITICAL REFLECTION

Hofstede might be getting a critical hammering these days (Lux et al. [2021] note that examining culture from a cognitive perspective is a challenge to traditional values-based approaches and that existing measures based on this framework are methodologically problematic and warrant renewal), but there is little doubt that

(Continued)

different cultures do generate different behaviours and attitudes – that's sort of the point! So why can't we identify and classify these differences? Is it a fear of being politically incorrect? Or is it just that these differences are notoriously difficult to pin down? And what about our new 'online' cultural presence – has that developed organically or has it also been the subject of manipulation by marketers?

Although we have far greater technical capabilities now than Hofstede had 50 years ago, maybe it's just that we are daunted by the prospect of carrying out a research project on an even bigger scale, for fear of what we may uncover. And don't even get me started on '**cancel culture**'! 'Cancel culture' is a term about which opinion is divided, especially on the internet (Lokhande and Natu, 2022). Initially meant to call out the wrong doings of the people in powerful positions and hold them accountable for their actions, it is now also seen as a tool for further exploitation of marginalised people (Kaufmann, 2022). On a final note, remember that 'freedom of speech' is the architecture of a free society. Censorship and an emerging 'cancel culture' have a profound impact on freedom of speech in the age of social media. Liberty interests advance through the use of language; language constructs and builds structures of thought that allow a free people to govern themselves. Democratic governance depends upon these twin pillars: freedom of thought and freedom of speech. In a free and democratic society, diversity of thought is buttressed through the freedom to engage in reasoned discourse, debate and dissent. Censorship threatens 'this architecture of a free society and speech suppression through "cancel culture" acts as a handmaiden of illiberalism and intolerance' (Hidy, 2021).

Cancel culture
Used to refer to a form of ostracism in which someone is thrust out of social or professional circles – whether it be online, on social media or in person. Those subject to this ostracism are said to have been 'cancelled'.

APPROACHES TO STUDYING CULTURE

There are three main approaches to studying culture, which are as follows:

1. *Taxonomies of culture.* This involves dividing cultures into different levels and/or into high-context or low-context cultures (see Figure 12.4).

2. *Lifestyle analysis.* This involves examining the way people live within the culture and looking for commonalities.

3. *Identification of cultural universals.* These are aspects of culture found in all societies. For example, all cultures use some form of bodily adornment (tattooing, cosmetics, jewellery, clothing, etc.). All cultures have sexual taboos (who is 'permissible' for sexual activity and who is not, and even what sexual practices are acceptable), all cultures have gift-giving rituals and all cultures have differences in status between members.

High-context cultures are those in which norms of behaviour and values are deeply embedded in the members of the culture, and thus do not need to be explained in any specific way (Hofstede, 1980). Members communicate easily (Fang et al., 2022) because they share the same basic beliefs and reference points – there is no need to explain, so people can communicate non-verbally relatively easily. Characteristics of high-context cultures are as follows:

- Communication is rapid and efficient within the group, but rapidly breaks down with outsiders because the group members find it harder to explain matters that they think of as obvious.

- Behaviour within the group is stable and predictable.
- The nature of the group is such that outsiders are likely to stereotype the group, as this is the only way they have of understanding the culture.
- All parties within the group share much the same perceptual field.

High-context culture
- Communication is rapid, but only within the group
- Behaviour within the group is stable and predictable
- Group members share the same perceptual field
- Outsiders are likely to stereotype the group

Low-context culture
- Members use clear messages to communicate
- Members' attitudes, perception and behaviour patterns change frequently
- Members are individualistic rather than collectivistic

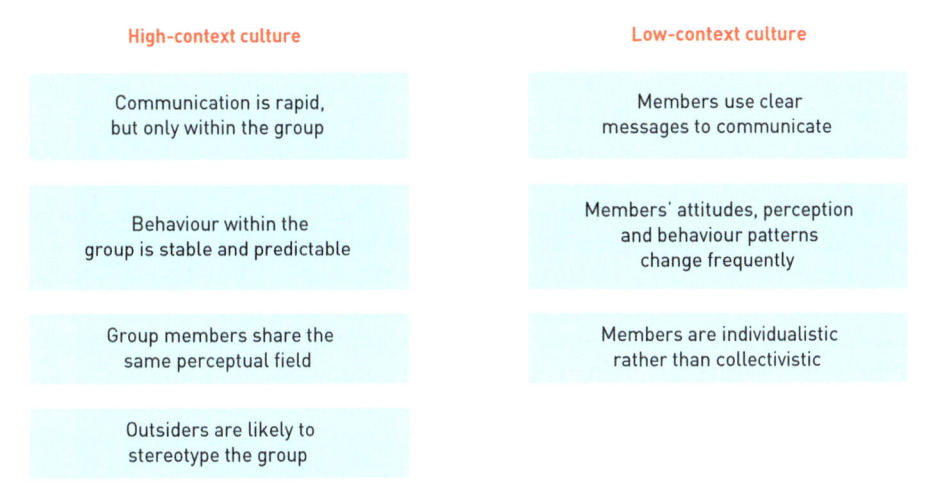

FIGURE 12.4 High-context vs. low-context cultures

High-context cultures are therefore totalitarian (Emery et al., 2021), orthodox and conservative. There is little room for personal expression or change, but each member has a clear (and perhaps reassuring) understanding of their role and responsibilities as well as what they can expect from the other members of the culture. Rigidity gives a degree of security in a high-context culture.

Low-context cultures are much less rigid (Vila-Lopez et al., 2022), but require more effort of their members. They have the following features:

- They are individualistic rather than collectivistic.
- Members communicate using clearly coded messages.
- Members' values, attitudes, perceptions and patterns of behaviour are diverse and liable to change quickly.

The USA and most of Western Europe have low-context cultures, because of mass migrations and world travel, which have combined to expose the members of the cultures to many diverse cultural influences. Countries such as Japan, which have relatively few foreigners living in them, tend to have high-context cultures.

The degree to which people are ethnocentric affects behaviour as well. **Ethnocentrism** is the belief that one's own culture is the 'right' one, and others are mere copies. It has been shown that ethnocentric people are much more likely to be loyal to products from their own countries; by the same token, people who are culturally sensitive (i.e. understand and respect other cultures) are more open to buying imported products (Achabou et al., 2021; Lu Hsu and Han-Peng, 2008; Nguyen et al., 2008). If the local identity is more accessible than the global one,

Ethnocentrism
The belief that one's own culture is 'correct' and other cultures are derived from it

local products will be preferred (and vice versa). In other words, the easier it is to understand and access local products, the more likely they will be preferred over global ones (Zhang and Khare, 2009).

CONSUMER CULTURE

Consumer culture theory and its proponents cannot be defined easily (Cronin and Fitchett, 2022). There are a number of theoretical perspectives of 'culture' which, when combined as a group, start to investigate how consumers interact with the markets that they find themselves in (Patsiaouras, 2022). Researchers are interested in this heterogeneous set of representations and shared values. However, Zaltman (2003) notes that consumer cultures develop as a result of appeals to our emotions, and that we are often unaware of the influence that our unconscious has on our thinking. This is so much so that apparently only about 5% of our thinking (cognition) is of a higher-order consciousness (Ludwig, 2022) and the vast majority happens beneath our levels of awareness (Zaltman, 2003). Arnould and Thompson (2005) noted that consumer culture represents a 'social arrangement in which the relations between lived culture and social resources and between meaningful ways of life and the symbolic and material resources on which they depend are mediated through markets'. Thus consumption, apart from being a somewhat central social phenomenon, is very much linked to motivation, and in a wider sense the consumption of culture itself. So for researchers, there is a very strong element of needing to understand the entire cycle that surrounds consumption, from acquiring an item, through possessing it, to consumption and finally to disposition. We need to understand the dynamics that are driving these consumption cycles in order to be able to theorise about them.

Going back to the seminal article by Arnould and Thompson (2005), which really put consumer culture theory on the academic map, we see that they had suggested four distinct areas which could contribute to theory building:

Ethnicity
The cultural background of the individual

1. *Socio-historic pattern of consumption.* The institutional and structural forces that shape people's consumption patterns. For instance, social mobility (which we'll look at a little later in this chapter), a person's gender or maybe even the effects of their ethnicity on consumption behaviour.
2. *Consumer identity.* This is all about the individual and how she or he shapes their self-identity using market-related resources, and how these vary from person to person depending on where they are in the world.
3. *Marketplace cultures.* How the relationship between the marketplace itself and the consumers develops networks and cultural communities. In the world with which we are familiar, this manifests itself in what we know as subcultures (for instance, communities of practice, brand communities, etc.).
4. *Consumers' interpretive strategies.* How consumers receive messages (verbal and non-verbal) and then how they are reinterpreted to consume resources in their own lives.

The cult of consumerism identified in Chapter 5 has an effect on the wider culture in which it sits. It can be considered as a subculture: people who consume particular brands can be defined by the brand (for example, people who enjoy the TV series *Star Trek* sometimes define themselves as Trekkies, and people who have been swiped 'right' by others using the dating app Tinder are known as Tinderites, according to the online Urban Dictionary (2022).

Problems with consumer culture have been identified, however. First, consumer (marketplace) culture tends to erode national cultures because the culture associated with specific brands becomes more important than the 'naturally occurring' cultural identity of the individual. For example, there is strong evidence for a worldwide 'youth' culture based on consumption of music (via MTV and others) and fashion items. This culture means that young people worldwide tend to wear similar clothing and listen to similar music rather than wearing the clothing typical of their countries and listening to traditional music. Second, consumer culture creates superficial social interactions and encourages people to be competitive rather than cooperative. Third, consumerism is regarded as bad for the environment because it encourages excessive use of natural resources (see Chapter 13).

These criticisms do not in fact stand up very well (Miller, 1995), since people do still take pleasure in individual narcissistic tendencies (Hart and Stekler, 2022; Lambert et al., 2014) and in retaining the traditions of their own region and family background (Sethna, 2015). The criticisms do indicate, however, that the consumer society is not necessarily an unmitigated force for good in the world. No doubt debate will continue on this topic.

Tinderite
A 'date' (sexual partner) who has been swiped right (to signify approval) on the Tinder app

CONSUMER BEHAVIOUR IN ACTION: GIFTS IN A POST-PANDEMIC WORLD

Everybody likes receiving a gift – but people seem to like giving gifts as well, especially to oneself (d'Astous and Mouakhar, 2022)! Every human culture contains some kind of gift-giving behaviour, from small gifts to oil the wheels of our working lives to major gifts to family and friends on special occasions. We give gifts as a way of apologising, as a symbol of respect, as a 'thank you' or because we feel obligated to by social conventions. Gift-giving can also be seen from the perspective of a professional services firm offering **pro bono** services (McColl-Kennedy et al., 2015).

Although gift-giving is common to all cultures, the connotations of some gifts can be different in different cultures. For example, in China it is common practice for someone to give a small gift to a superior, or someone in power. The gift is not intended to influence the person especially, although it is intended as an ice-breaker; if the superior then makes a decision that goes against the gift-giver, there would not be any special feeling of resentment. However, to a Westerner these gifts look suspiciously like bribes. In the West, one might offer a gift after the business has been concluded, but even this is fraught with social risks: one does not tip one's superiors. In Western cultures, it is more likely that the gifts would come from the superior to the subordinate, not the other way round.

The gift-giving market was, like all others, drastically changed by the lockdowns of the Covid-19 pandemic. However, as opposed to many sectors that suffered devastating blows through lack of customers, this is one industry that easily adapted to using the

(Continued)

Pro bono
Latin phrase for professional work undertaken voluntarily and without payment as a public service

internet as its means of maintaining stability during a tumultuous time. For gifting companies to stay afloat, they have to keep up to date with the current consumer trends and market statistics. This helps them to meet the demands of consumers and stay ahead of the game. Like many other industries, the Covid-19 pandemic pushed shoppers online to buy their gifts when the holiday season came along. This caused a huge spike in online sales, with shoppers having spent almost £148.5 billion online during the holiday shopping season. That's a 45.2% increase from the same time the previous year. Hootsuite and We Are Social nailed it down with their Digital 2021 Snapshot report, which shows that, by April of 2021, the number of social media users reached 4.33 billion. Most interestingly, 27% of those users were looking for inspiration for things to do or buy, while 26.5% were actively looking for products to purchase.

The personalised gift market is booming, with 85% of gift buyers saying that personalisation is one of the biggest factors that determine the perfect gift. The market for personalised gifts was valued at £23.32 billion in 2020. Personalised gifts allow customers to write their own little messages, include the receiver's name, send a gift video or choose the wrapping they want the retailer to use. Giving customers this ability to customise the perfect gift for their friends or family creates a loyalty and appreciation that keeps them coming back to your business.

According to a report by CNBC (2020), it seems people are taking more time to seek out meaningful gifts, and the shopping season started earlier this year as people were looking for things to look forward to. On Etsy, an e-commerce site that features handmade goods, crafts and other unique items, searches for custom or personalised gifts increased by 156% when compared to the same time the previous year. So many people really struggled during the lockdowns, and witnessing that, most people really want to offer meaningful gifts that go beyond practical, or fun, purposes. They want something to show how much they care, and that they are there for each other, despite the distances between them, as noted in Etsy's Christmas trend report of 2020 (Etsy, 2020).

© iStock.com/ozgurdonmaz

In many Western cultures, the period around Christmas is the main time of year for exchanging gifts. Typically, people aim to spend about the same amount on each other (so as to avoid embarrassment) and sometimes even agree an approximate figure beforehand. For small children, parents maintain that the gifts do not in fact come from the parents at all, but from Santa Claus (also known as Papa Noel, Père Nöel, Kris Kringle, Sinter Klaas, Babbo Natale, Joulupukki and many other names). The gifts are supposed to be a surprise, although among adults people often ask each other what would be a suitable present. Recipients of the gifts have to look surprised and pleased as they open the gifts on Christmas Day (for the UK and USA, or at Epiphany, or on Christmas Eve, or whatever date is appropriate to the local culture), even if they knew in advance what the gift was, or (worse) if it is something they do not want. All this is regarded as normal, polite behaviour.

A study by Joel Waldfogel (1993) showed that the giving of gifts at Christmas destroyed anything up to 30% of the monetary value of the gift. This was because the recipient of the gift frequently ascribed a cash value to it well below the actual price paid by the donor. What Waldfogel's research did not take into account is all the social aspects of the gift itself – the choosing, the wrapping, the performance rituals attached to the actual exchange of presents. For most people, it seems that these are far more important than the actual gift itself.

In Technavio's industry analysis (Technavio, 2021), they estimate that the global gift market was worth roughly £46 billion in 2019, and is expected to grow with a compound annual growth rate of 2% to reach around £50.5 billion by 2024. The personal gifts market alone was estimated at £19 billion during 2020, despite the drastic changes brought by the Covid-19 pandemic. The market for personalised gifts is expected to grow at a rate of 7.7% between now and 2027 to reach an estimated value of almost £32 billion.

SUBCULTURES

Subcultures are distinctive groups of people within a society who share common cultural meanings, behaviours and environmental factors. Although a subculture shares most of the mainstream culture within which it is embedded, its members have a distinct and identifiable set of behavioural norms, customs, scripts and so forth which distinguish them from the rest of the culture. In some cases, the subculture requires members to buy specific items, and members will often not buy items from outside the subculture (Bush et al., 2017; O'Connor and Portzky, 2015; Richardson and Turley, 2006).

Subcultures could be based on age or gender type (see Chapter 11), ethnic background or special interests. For example, Goth culture is distinct from mainstream UK culture, but has a distinct set of behaviours and beliefs (O'Connor and Portzky, 2015). Likewise, second-generation immigrant populations often develop subcultures that are combinations of the new country's culture and elements from the parents' home country culture (Özbek et al., 2021). Bi-cultural consumers often switch between the two cultures and make different judgements depending on which cultural context they happen to be 'switched' to at the time (Chattaraman et al., 2010).

Some subcultures are defined by the ways they interpret messages: these are called interpretive communities (Kates, 2002; Pulvera, 2021). For example, a subculture of conspiracy theorists would tend to interpret all official statements as evidence of a cover-up. An anti-globalisation interpretive community would respond with deep suspicion or even hostility to any marketing messages, which makes marketing to such communities difficult; however, they are still consumers.

In Figure 12.5 the main culture's beliefs are shared by the subcultures but each subculture has beliefs and behaviours that lie outside the mainstream. Often the behaviours associated with the subculture can create problems for its members as members of the mainstream culture see them as outsiders or rebels, and therefore a threat to the mainstream.

GEOGRAPHIC SUBCULTURES

Geographic subcultures can be very significant for marketers. Most countries have geographic subcultures: Friesland in the Netherlands has a distinct language and traditions; Bavarians regard themselves as culturally different from the neighbouring 'Prussians' (and often feel closer to their Austrian neighbours in Salzburg than they do to their fellow Germans in Stuttgart). In the UK, Wales and Scotland regard themselves as separate countries, and have different food, language and customs from those of England, and Ulster (Northern Ireland) has a different culture from both the UK of which it is legally a part, and Ireland of which it is historically and physically a part. The significance for marketers lies in the possibilities for causing offence – for a Welshman, Wales is not, and never has been, part of England. There is also a positive significance in terms of recognising the differences between the subcultures, perhaps by referring to local events or using local dialects in advertising. For example, some major supermarkets in the UK offer locally sourced products in their stores and have signage in a dual language (for instance stores in Wales show signage in both Welsh and English).

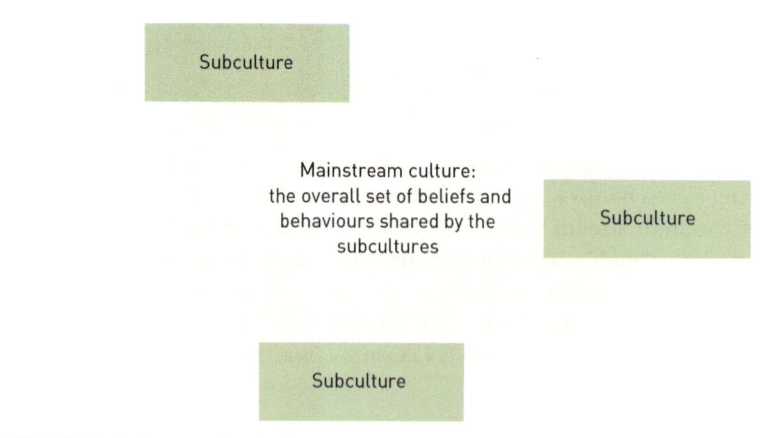

FIGURE 12.5 Culture and subculture

ETHNIC SUBCULTURES

The transient nature of populations means that cultural identities move with people (Akaliyski et al., 2021; Gillespie et al., 2022). Ethnic subcultures are a growing group, not just within Europe but globally also (Irvine, 2022). The populist definition of ethnicity is that of Bulmer (1996):

> *An ethnic group is a collectivity within a larger population having real or putative common ancestry, memories of a shared past, and a cultural focus upon one or more symbolic elements which define the group's identity, such as kinship, religion, language, shared territory, nationality or physical appearance. Members of an ethnic group are conscious of belonging to an ethnic group.*

CONSUMER BEHAVIOUR IN ACTION: THE AGE SUBCULTURE

Old age is a great time to sit back and enjoy your life. You are much wiser, people's opinions do not easily fluster you, you are much more comfortable in your own skin, your kids have left home and you have the freedom to do all the things you want to do

(Aging.com, 2022). But apparently many older people are not ready for the rocking-chair and daytime TV just yet. We see plenty of people in their 50s, 60s and even 70s joining the gym, taking flying lessons, canoeing up the Amazon and generally behaving like teenagers. Therein lies a clue about the perspective that our societal culture holds about older people; the physical attractiveness might have disappeared, and they are no longer either literally or metaphorically 'sexy'. Yet over the past 20 years we have seen rising divorce rates resulting in many more older people using dating services and engaging in activities (nightclubs, singles holidays, etc.) that are stereotypically seen as the domain of young people. Our culture (the media, press, general society) is fixated with 'youth culture'. Most adverts, TV shows and films are populated with healthy-looking, fresh-faced young characters, as opposed to older people. Does that mean that our culture values these young people with their sexual attractiveness more than older people? Is 'old' always going to be seen in a negative light?

Who is to say that a 60-year-old cannot or should not be going out dancing, or that a 70-year-old should not be trekking to Machu Picchu, or even that an 80-year-old should not be sky-diving? Perhaps there is no such thing as an age-related product.

Take for example a very dear family friend, Aunty Gul. She's always been an active person (did her first abseil well into her 70s). Following a serious road traffic accident in which she almost lost her life, she luckily managed to survive but not before an amputation of one leg. Despite the extreme hardship that she's undergone, and at the age of 82, she recently did an exhilarating outdoor climb over the world famous roof of the O2 Arena, and then decided she wanted to abseil from the 17th floor of The Royal London Hospital in order to fundraise for the London Air Ambulance service, without whom she wouldn't be alive today. Older people are indeed an inspiration! Go Aunty Gul!

© iStock.com/Srabin

Perhaps we should ignore age altogether in our planning – yet marketers have only recently started to understand the vast differences that exist in this supposedly homogeneous group of people who are all labelled as 'old'. A 55-year-old is very different from an 85-year-old in attitudes and consumption patterns.

Of course physically, not all older people are going to be as fit (and determined) as Gul, or as fit as they were when they were younger, and mentally things can begin to deteriorate as well – greater experience might be a fine thing, but when you can't remember what you came upstairs for, experience may not help a lot. That is a very different life stage from those who are fit, active, financially buoyant and wanting to live life.

So perhaps there will still be a few things we can sell specifically to older people – if only we can get them out of their convertible!

This said, ethnic marketing is much more advanced in the USA, probably because the USA is composed of a wide variety of cultures, whereas within Europe ethnic minorities account for less than 15% of the 770 million people who inhabit the continent. These groups are growing as migration continues, and tend to fall into two main groups: those who have emigrated from their country of origin, and are therefore perhaps best considered as members of their home-country culture, and those whose parents came from another country but who were born in the host country. The latter group often develops a distinct culture that is part way between their parents' national culture and the culture of the host country. Ethnicity is measured in the UK Census and other official data sets (for instance the UK's Labour Force Survey) by asking individuals to select among categories that may include nationality (Chinese, Indian, Irish), broader geographic or ancestral categories (African, Asian, Arab), colour (e.g. White, Black), and combinations of these ('White Irish', 'White British'), including explicitly 'mixed' categories ('White and Black Caribbean') (Afkhami, 2012; Gov.uk, 2022). In the UK, the British government includes a question about religious affiliation, since for many people religion is one of the most important defining characteristics of their identity. When such questions are asked in conjunction with those about 'ethnic grouping', they can complement each other and allow for a more distinct picture of a population. Research conducted in Canada, for example, showed that Muslim women used the *hijab* (the head-covering material used by some Muslim women) as a way of indicating that they are traditional and therefore religiously *respectable* when using an online dating service (Zwick and Chelariu, 2006). This is a distinct move away from the cultural origins of the *hijab* in the Middle East, which historically showed a willingness to comply with religious norms of conduct. But even this is changing. The death of Mahsa Amini on 16 September 2022, three days after her arrest by the so-called morality police in Tehran, prompted the spread of large-scale protests in Iran, unprecedented in terms of both their geographic range and the diverse social backgrounds of the demonstrators. The movement has extended to large and small cities outside Tehran, including Kurdish areas – where Amini came from – and youth from across the socio-economic and educational spectrum have taken part. As the protests intensified, videos of women cutting their hair and burning their *hijabs* spread, acts which served as both an expression of anger directed towards the morality police who they claim are responsible for Mahsa Amini's death, and a rejection of the policy of compulsory *hijab* more generally.

The UK's 2021 Census provided some interesting facts about religious effects on culture in the UK (see Table 12.1).

TABLE 12.1 Ethnic groups and religion in the UK (taken from the UK 2021 Census)

1	As in the 2011 Census, the most ethnically diverse region in England and Wales was London, where 40.2% of residents identified with either the Asian, Black, Mixed or Other ethnic groups
2	Out of all regions, London had the smallest percentage of White British people, at 44.9%, and the North East had the highest percentage, at 93.6%
3	People from the White ethnic group were more likely to live in the South East than any other region, with 16.2% doing so; people from the Black, Asian, Mixed and Other ethnic groups were more likely to live in London than any other region, with 58.4%, 35.9%, 33.1% and 49.9% doing so respectively

4	81.5% of the general population lived in an urban location, and 18.5% lived in a rural location – the ethnic groups most likely to live in an urban location were Pakistani (99.1%), Bangladeshi (98.7%) and Black African (98.2%)
5	Newham in London was the local authority where people from the White ethnic group made up the lowest percentage of the population (at 29.0%); eight out of the ten most ethnically diverse local authorities were in London
6	In 2011, the profile of religious affiliation in England and Wales was skewed, with the majority of the population identifying as Christian or having no religion
7	In 2011, the category of people with no religion had the highest proportion of people who were economically active, Christians and Muslims the lowest. Jewish people had the highest level of employment and Muslim people the highest level of unemployment
8	The main reason for Christians being economically inactive was retirement, for Muslims economic inactivity was mainly because they were students, or because they were looking after the home or family

There is a final point to be made about the religious category in the Census. As in 2011, the 2021 Census contained a 'write-in' question where respondents had identified themselves as belonging to 'other religions'. Apart from some newly encouraged entries such as Spiritualist, Taoist, Zoroastrian, etc., there were some rather intriguing entries also. At the time of going to press, the definitive 2021 figures haven't been released as yet, but in 2011 we apparently had amongst us people who are firm believers of Satanism (<2k), Shamanism (<700), Scientology (<2.5k) and over 176,000 adherents of the Jedi Knight religion!

Clearly these groups have specific purchasing behaviour: specific foods to meet religious restrictions or personal tastes, non-Christian greetings cards, clothing, cooking utensils, products from the country of origin, and occasionally *Star Wars* memorabilia. In 2013, a do-it-yourself enthusiast even built a working prototype of a Jedi light sabre and posted various videos on YouTube showing the invention cutting through paper, tape, cardboard and even melting a ping-pong ball. Thankfully, legislation in most countries prevents the sale of such devices.

On the other hand, most immigrants are happy to embrace at least some aspects of the host country culture, and in some cases deliberately seek out local products as a way of expressing a desire to integrate (Bann, 1996). Equally, migrant groups sometimes identify themselves around cultural factors from the country of origin – religion is especially powerful in this context. It has been shown that Sikhs in Britain use conspicuous consumption of their religion to establish their identity, while Muslims tend to reject Western cultural values of consumption while embracing British liberalism (Lindridge, 2009).

How these groups should be addressed by marketers is a matter for considerable thought. At present, advertising largely ignores ethnic minorities, and attempts to include minorities (or advertise directly to them) have sometimes been interpreted as patronising or even offensive (Sudbury and Wilberforce, 2006). Part of the difficulty here is that what some people regard as offensive can be regarded as totally acceptable by others: the UK Advertising Standards Authority, which responds to examples of offensive advertising, will take action even if a relatively small number of people complain. This may cause advertisers to avoid the issue by not including ethnic minorities in their advertising at all.

A SCHEMA FOR CULTURAL CLASSIFICATION OF ETHNIC MINORITIES

Many academic commentators have written about identity (Erikson, 1968; Goodson and Cole, 1994; McCormick and Pressley, 1997). They have all recognised the two defined parts of the person's identity – the personal and the professional – of which the latter's development depends very much upon an individual's interaction with the wider environment (Weinberger and Shefi, 2012) and the context within which it takes place (Gee, 2001), and also takes into account the period of time over which it takes place (Connelly and Clandinin, 1999). This all supports the idea that identities are a complex and ever-changing entity, which Beijaard et al. (2004) noted is in a state of flux, change and evolution through the life cycle.

For instance, understanding ethnic entrepreneurship (Low and MacMillan, 1988) and ethno-cultural values is a necessary step to understanding ethnic minority markets and the driving forces behind ethnic entrepreneurial activity in those markets (Chen and Tan, 2009; Down, 2010; Drori et al., 2009). However, it has been noted by Bjorn Bjerke and Claes Hultman (2013) that 'existing … research … excludes, for instance, female entrepreneurs and ethnic minorities and what is referred to as the cultural sector'. Consequently, there is a need to provide a schema for identifying ethnic subcultures as a result of ethnic immigration into Britain (Bagwell, 2008; McPherson, 2008; Panayiotopoulos, 2008; Rusinovic, 2008), and the 'theory of acculturation' does exactly this (Cabassa, 2003; Faber and O'Guinn, 1987; Penloza, 1989). The degree to which individuals from ethnic minorities differ in their behaviour from the rest of society depends largely on their degree of **acculturation**. For marketers, consumer acculturation is clearly of more interest: this refers to the process of becoming a skilled consumer in a different culture or subculture (Penloza, 1989).

Acculturation
The process of adopting a new culture

Acculturation measures the social, physical and psychological exchanges between individuals from different cultures when there is continuous contact (Ryder et al., 2000). However, the literature poses two versions of this theory. It is described by Khairulla et al. (1996) as 'a process in which ethnic consumers move along a theoretic continuum from low acculturation, where they maintain the cultural values of their ethnic origin, to the other extreme, high acculturation, where they have adopted the cultural values of the dominant culture'. This theory proposes a single continuum that conceptualises a one-dimensional construct (Gordon, 1995). This is of great interest to a marketer using this as a segmentation tool, because of the depth to which it has the potential to change a person's buying preferences and patterns, and consequently consumption behaviour and attitudes towards the local media (O'Guinn and Faber, 1986). However, a number of scholars (Berry, 1997; Marín and Gamba, 1996; Ryder et al., 2000; Teske and Nelson, 1974) have argued that both the adherence to the practices of the host culture as well as maintenance of the original culture should be investigated as independent dimensions, hence bi-directional and reciprocal.

These two perspectives have contributed to the sociological (Brubaker, 2001), social psychological (Lambert, 1967; Rudmin, 2003, 2009; Rudmin and Ahmadzadeh, 2001) and anthropological literature (De Vos, 1995). Ward (2001) coined the term 'ABCs of acculturation', as it involves 'Affective, Behavioural and Cognitive' changes. As regards ethnic entrepreneurs and the application of the theory of acculturation, De Vos (1995, in Rudmin, 2009) argued that 'ethnicity is essentially subjective and symbolic, and that ethnic identity is in competition with other identities depending on the contextual and temporal focus of the individual'. Segal and Sosa (1983) had, 20 years previously, illustrated through their *acculturation influence group model* that ethnic minority groups could be identified and understood much more coherently if the degree of acculturation was ascertained. Based on this work by Segal and Sosa (1983), Nwankwo and Lindridge (1998) devised a framework with four broad classifications for 'identifying levels of acculturation and possible variations even within a subculture' of the ethnic entrepreneur (see Table 12.2). They clarified that their framework is based on 'exposure and adaptation to the dominant Caucasian culture', as opposed to age. Furthermore, their hypothesis was that an Indian entrepreneur who 'has lived in Britain all his/her life is likely to display a higher level of acculturation to the Caucasian culture than one who has only recently arrived'.

In sum, even with the tools as described above, there are various limitations of acculturation, not least of all the difficulty with 'defining and operationalizing culture' (Sam and Berry, 2006).

TABLE 12.2 Acculturation framework for ethnic entrepreneurs

Cluster 1: Least acculturated
- More at ease with items closely related to their own culture
- Tend to live in close-knit family groups and ethnic dwelling areas
- Low-income and blue-collar workers
- Very limited knowledge of the host country language
- Do not accept the dominant culture as relevant to their lifestyle
- Are not motivated to adjust to their new environment
- Behaviour heavily influenced by native culture
- Poorly educated (based on Western-style education systems)
- Dress mainly in their ethnic clothes
Cluster 2: Moderately acculturated
- Have a working knowledge of the host country language
- Prefer to speak in their native language
- Behavioural patterns are predominantly influenced by their subculture's values
- Combine some characteristics of clusters 1 and 3
Cluster 3: Most acculturated
- Fluent in both the host country's language and their native tongue
- At ease in a predominantly host country environment
- Live in areas not predominantly ethnic oriented
- Their behavioural patterns are largely driven by the dominant culture
- Have some pride in their ethnic background
Cluster 4: Totally acculturated
- Fluent only in the host country language
- Have little knowledge of their ethnic culture
- Likely to be born in the host country
- View themselves as members of the host culture and have patriotic feelings towards the host country only
- Ignorant of and not motivated to understand their own ethnic background

Source: Adapted from Nwankwo and Lindridge (1998). Reused by permission.

The degree to which someone can adapt to the new culture will depend on the level of cultural interpenetration he or she experiences (Moftizadeh et al., 2021). The more the individual interacts socially with members of the host culture, the more he or she is able to adapt. This does not necessarily mean giving up one's original cultural norms and

Adoption

The process of incorporating an innovating product/ritual/custom into one's daily life

beliefs; it does mean understanding and being sympathetic to the cultural norms and beliefs of the host culture (Andreasen, 1990). In some cases, migrant populations use consumption as a way of integrating with the host country (Tan et al., 2021) – buying a locally made car, eating local food, moving out of immigrant neighbourhoods and home ownership by buying a house in an area populated by the host society, and so forth (Hughes, 2010). This partial **adoption** of the host culture helps migrants to feel part of their new society.

Another way of looking at acculturation is using Oberg's (1960) somewhat sequential four stage model:

1. *Honeymoon stage*. The individual is fascinated by the culture or subculture, but because interpenetration is shallow and superficial, there is very little acculturation. The honeymoon stage is typical of tourists travelling in another country: on their return from holiday, they may feel a desire to go and live in the country, having only seen the positive aspects of life there.

2. *Rejection stage*. After further cultural interpenetration, the individual realises that previous cultural norms are not adequate for dealing with the new culture, and that new norms and behaviours will need to be adopted. Often people become hostile to the new culture at this point, seeing the drawbacks rather than the advantages. Cultural conflicts are at a maximum in this stage.

3. *Tolerance stage*. Here the interactions have increased to the point where the individual accepts the new culture with all its drawbacks. This stage is reached by a process of cultural interpenetration, learning more about the new culture and reducing the level of cultural conflict.

4. *Integration stage*. At this stage the individual has made the necessary adjustments, valuing the new culture for its good qualities while still retaining important elements of the old culture. The new culture is seen as a perfectly viable way of life, as valid in its own way as the old culture.

In Figure 12.6, the individual's initial degree of happiness with the new culture is high in the honeymoon stage, as is motivation to learn about the culture: actual knowledge of the culture (and therefore ability to function well within it) is low. At the rejection stage, satisfaction with the culture drops dramatically, as does motivation to learn, but ability to function is still rising. With the tolerance stage comes a renewed interest in the culture, and also greater satisfaction with it. Finally, in the integration stage the individual is functioning well, knows about the culture and is consequently much happier within the culture. The initial disappointment at the rejection stage may account in part for the fact that the majority of immigrants return home within a few years. Interestingly, according to Vignola (2015), the migration processes that Europe is learning to handle due to the Syrian conflict are just 'economic liberalisation of borders and their security arrangements'.

CULTURE AND SOCIAL MOBILITY

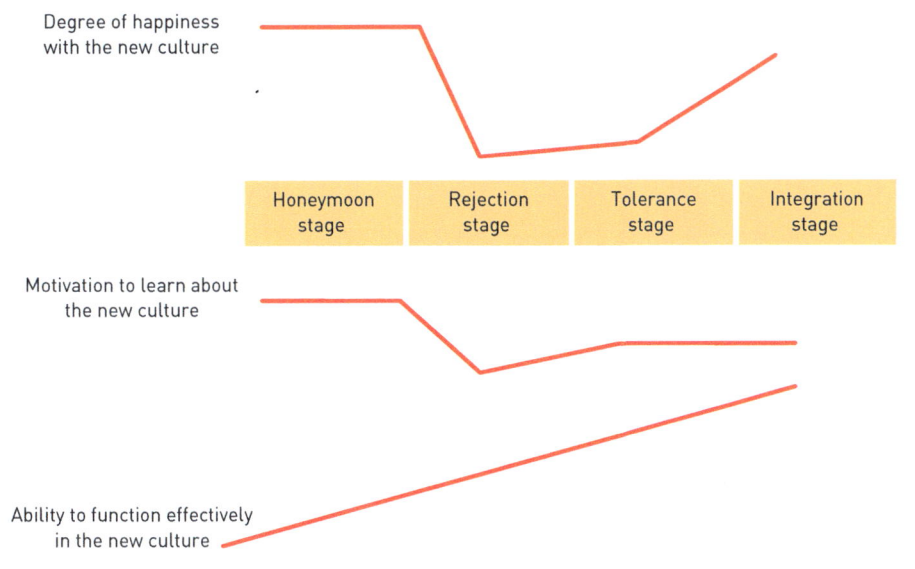

FIGURE 12.6 Stages in acculturation

Recent research by Williams (2015) has indicated the existence of cultural fractures caused by crossing borders (Davies and Fitchett, 2004) and the cultural diversity that brings both in person (Jusik, 2022; Ng Tseung-Wong et al., 2022) and online (Wood et al., 2022). These are as follows:

- **Emotional fracture.** This can lead to feelings of loneliness and lack of a support infrastructure from friends and family left behind, or could be characterised by a willingness and ability to make new friends in the new country.
- **Symbolic fracture.** This is characterised by running out of things to say in everyday conversation, not knowing what the appropriate greetings for different people are, and a difficulty in 'reading the signs' to understand what people are thinking or feeling. There is also a difficulty in understanding how people socialise in the new country.
- **Functional fracture.** This is about the ease or difficulty of carrying out functional tasks such as opening a bank account, using trains and buses, or buying and preparing food.
- **Culture shock.** This is how life in the new country differs from expectations.
- **Consumer behaviour.** This is the gap between what one would buy at 'home' and what one buys in the 'new, host country'.
- **Demographic fracture.** This is the disparity between the socio-economic structure one was part of in the old culture, and the socio-economic structure in which one finds oneself in the new culture. Sometimes immigrants move down the social scale, sometimes up, depending on the relationship between the host country and the old country.

Emotional fracture
The sense of loss of emotional support encountered when moving from one culture to another

Symbolic fracture
The disparity between old and new communication paradigms encountered when moving from one culture to another

Functional fracture
The disparity between old and new systems for daily living encountered when moving from one culture to another

Culture shock
The discomfort that arises from being displaced from one's normal cultural milieu

Consumer behaviour
Activities undertaken by people in the process of obtaining, using and disposing of goods and services for personal use

Demographic fracture
The disparity between old and new socio-economic structures, encountered when moving from one culture to another

SOCIAL MOBILITY (AKA CLASS)

Aristocracy
The highest class in certain societies, typically comprising people of noble birth holding hereditary titles and offices

Some sociologists regard class as being one of the central concepts of the discipline, yet it is seemingly an ill-defined and ambiguous concept (Rao et al., 2022). For non-sociologists the concept of class is now very much outmoded: at the beginning of the 20th century, around 75% of people in industrialised countries were manual workers of one sort or another, quite clearly distinct in behaviour and wealth from the better-educated white-collar workers and, of course, the aristocracy. As machines have largely taken over from muscle power, education has become universal, the services sector dominates, and differential taxation has eroded differences of wealth – the differences between 'working class' and 'middle class' are almost undetectable. Even aristocrats now work for a living. So perhaps social mobility is a better descriptor for the movement between social strata in society.

According to Nightingale (2012), cited in Marcinczak et al. (2015), using socio-economic status as a tool to sort residents 'is as old as the history of urbanisation'. In the 1911 Census in the UK, the government decided to record socio-economic groupings for the first time. The system used (known as the Joint Industry Committee for National Readership Surveys; JICNARS) is shown in Table 12.3.

This system of classification worked fairly well for several decades, but shifts in social patterns made much of its assumptions irrelevant: Table 12.3 assumes that incomes are lower further down the scale, but in the 21st century plumbers earn more than doctors (at least in much of Western Europe) and changing patterns of working life mean that today's labourer is tomorrow's film star, and film stars become politicians (notable examples include Ronald Reagan, Arnold Schwarzenegger and Glenda Jackson). There are three different types of resource that consumers draw upon (social, economic and cultural capital) when competing for status (Bourdieu, 1984). The basic lifestyles and indeed standards of living do not vary greatly between the groups – Group D individuals probably still own cars and have foreign holidays, even if Group A individuals run bigger cars and go to more exotic destinations. The classification is still used in a great deal of published market research. Partly this is because it is familiar to researchers, and partly it is because researchers sometimes need to make comparisons with previous studies; but it is well known that the system is seriously flawed.

TABLE 12.3   UK socio-economic groupings (JICNARS)

Social grade	Social status	Head of household's occupation
A	Upper middle class	Higher managerial, administration or professional
B	Middle class	Intermediate managerial, administrative or professional
C1	Lower middle class	Supervisory or clerical, junior managerial, administrative or professional
C2	Skilled working class	Skilled manual workers
D	Working class	Semi-skilled and unskilled manual workers
E	Lowest level of subsistence	Unemployed, casual or lowest-grade workers, state pensioners

TABLE 12.4 The Socio-Economic Classification System

1	Higher managerial and professional occupations
	1.1 Large employers and higher managerial occupations
	1.2 Higher professional occupations
2	Lower managerial and professional occupations
3	Intermediate occupations
4	Small employers and own account workers
5	Lower supervisory and technical occupations
6	Semi-routine occupations
7	Routine occupations
8	Never worked and long-term unemployed
9	Students and those whose occupations cannot be adequately described in any above category

In 2001 the UK government introduced an alternative classification method – the Socio-Economic Classification System. This classification system has nine categories, the first of which can be subdivided. The categories are shown in Table 12.4.

Although this classification system is a better reflection of 21st-century society, it still suffers from a number of weaknesses common to all such classification systems. First, it does not take account of the possibility of rapid social movement: someone might change occupations very rapidly, without (presumably) changing lifestyle very much. Equally someone might change lifestyle rapidly without officially changing occupation – a teacher who decides to leave an inner-city school for a less stressful life in the country would be an example. Third, the classification usually refers to the head of the household, which might have been a reasonable concept in 1911 but which has many possible interpretations now. In 1911, the head of the household would almost certainly have been the father of the family, the main (and probably only) earner. In 2019, several people in the household are likely to be earning, and decision-making is likely to be shared in many different ways.

There is, of course, more to social mobility than occupation. Mobility implies a movement of position in the power hierarchy. Early sociologists such as Karl Marx and Max Weber examined social class (see Figure 12.7). Marx saw class as being essentially about the power to set the prevailing intellectual climate. He said that 'The ideas of the ruling class are, in every epoch, the ruling ideas, i.e. the class which is the ruling material force of society, is at the same time its ruling intellectual force' (Marx and Engels, 1848). Weber defined class in terms of life chances (Weber, 1946). For Weber, a class is a group of people who have in common a specific causal component of their life chances which is represented by possession of goods and opportunities for income, and which operates under the conditions of the commodity or labour markets. In other words, the individual's class is determined by the opportunities presented to that individual in terms of earning opportunities and the level of possession of goods.

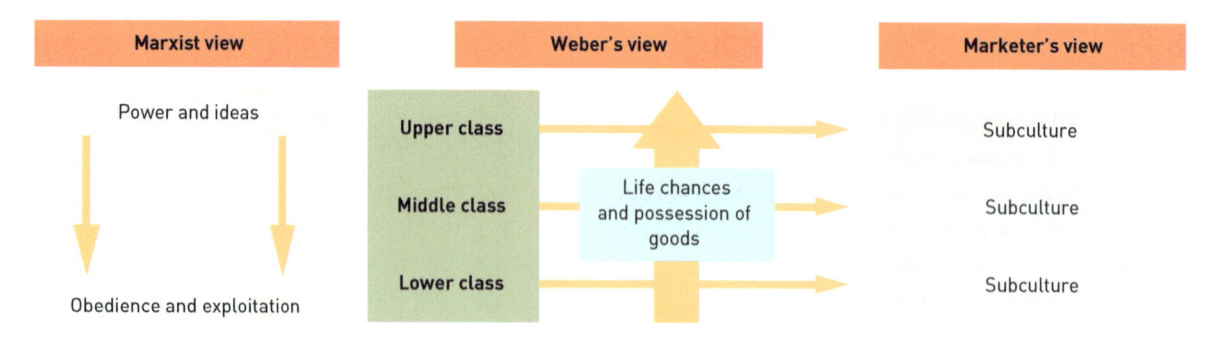

FIGURE 12.7 Studying social class

More recent studies (Loughnan et al., 2014) about people from working-class backgrounds (or the 'poor' as they were referred to by both Jahoda [1999] and Papa [2021]) have shown that there is a tendency for views on social class to perceive people of low socio-economic status in a very dehumanising way. This is often 'regardless of whether people share the same ethnic or racial categories of their more advantaged peers' (Loughnan et al., 2014). This perspective is not restricted to any one geographic region: examples exist for different parts of the world, from the USA to Australia. For instance, the term 'white trash' is used in the USA and denotes low socio-economic status White people in rural environments as violent, coarse, dirty, stupid and sexually unrestrained (Spencer and Castano, 2007; Wray, 2006). Jones (2011) describes the UK equivalent of this stereotyped urban group (known as 'chavs') as feckless, crude, unintelligent and criminal. In Australia, a similar grouping of suburban people are called 'bogans' (Nichols, 2011). The commonality, according to Loughnan et al. (2014), is that they are all 'predominantly white, contain both men and women and they are all stereotyped as bestial'.

This of course gives us a glimpse into the many issues that arise with looking at social class as a measure. For instance, Liu et al. (2016) have found that most of the existing literature on social mobility and its interaction with say, masculinity, is focused on the heterosexual, be that the single male or those in couples, families and marriages. Having said that, the literature investigating the intersection between the lesbian, gay, bisexual and transsexual communities and social mobility is indeed growing (Whitcomb and Walinsky, 2013).

BRAND EXPERIENCE: CLASSY TV

Is it still realistic to talk about social class at all? Can we really predict someone's behaviour based on how they earn a living? And if we take more factors into account, are we really looking at social class, or are we defining people in different ways? Well, if you use television programmes as a yardstick or a measure of the idiosyncratic way in which it feeds culture, one can see an embarrassing overabundance of drivel which is reflective of a population. Take for instance the British fascination with using programmes to poke fun at either end of the spectrum, from using the rich in a rather liberal elite way (*Secret Millionaire*, *Posh People: Inside Tatler*, *Made in Chelsea*, *You Can't*

Get the Staff, *Rich, Russian and Living in London*) to using the poor as an endless carnival of the impoverished-on-display (*Benefit Street*, *Britain's Hardest Grafter*, *The Briefcase*). And if that's not enough, there are programmes that compare one against the other (*Rich House, Poor House*). This type of reality TV has been referred to as 'poverty porn'. And it doesn't get any better Stateside either. The US TV airways are crammed full of continuous adverts for diets, followed by adverts for an inordinate amount of food, followed by comical contraptions on which to exercise, perhaps to ease the conscience from the earlier overconsumption.

And this is all supposedly for our viewing pleasure. But let's step back in history for just a second. Rome's ancient blood sports (viewed by thousands) were ways of keeping citizens and communities aligned. In Medieval times, fear and humiliation through thousands of executions helped stabilise communities. Are the TV programmes (mentioned earlier) and others like them the twenty-first-century equivalent of keeping people pigeonholed?

A survey by YouGov (2017) made some interesting revelations about what Britons thought about the class system: however, with a sample size of fewer than 1700 people, is this really representative of the Great British public? Is the world that we live in obsessed with social class and status? Well social class is more than a bit problematic – it's riddled with issues! People move up and down the social scale, they find it hard to define their own social class never mind anybody else's, and changes in the structure of society in general mean that we have trouble now identifying classes anyway. Why is it that the good people of Britain insist on identifying which school a 70-year-old man attended in any news story about him? Arise Sir Snobbery x-public and y-grammar school! Why is it that our friends in the USA are greatly allured by fame and fortune?

In short, given that people in the 21st century are not only individuals but are also extremely individualistic, is social class a concept that still has any relevance or should we be thinking about eradicating class and embracing the ease with which opportunities are presented to us to become *socially mobile*?

It would appear that an individual's consumption pattern is as much a determining factor of social class as it is the result of social class. Those individuals who are able to accumulate possessions and improve their opportunities to earn money can move up the social scale, if they choose to do so. For example, a bricklayer would clearly be classified as working class (skilled manual worker). Yet if that same bricklayer saves some capital and sets up his own business, he could eventually become a wealthy property developer or house builder. His basic attitudes and values might change a little during this process, and *he* would probably still define himself as working class. This type of social mobility has become more common as class barriers break down and educational opportunities increase.

From the viewpoint of marketers, social class is more a reflection of the existence of a set of subcultures based on the education level, occupational requirements and economic power of the individual members. In this context, marketers use class-related imagery in advertising in order to highlight the subculture and involve the consumer. Social mobility takes reference from a set of subcultures because the distinctions are generally agreed upon within the main culture, and the members of each stratum share most of their meanings and behaviours. The assumption is that people from one social stratum are less likely to mix socially with people from other social strata, preferring the company of members who reflect their own values and status (see for example 'consumption patterns of society' as depicted in programmes such as *Made in Chelsea* or *The Only Way Is Essex*).

Thus social class is measured in two basic ways. People can be asked which social class they belong to (self-assignment), or their social class can be inferred from objective criteria. In market research the latter approach is much more common, but in most cases respondents are only asked about their income, occupation and education level. Certainly there is likely to be some discrepancy between self-assignment and an objective measure in cases where there has been upward social mobility – an individual who comes from a working-class background but who has become educated, professional and wealthy might still self-assign him- or herself to the working-class category.

More useful geodemographic measures have emerged in recent years, such as **ACORN** and **MOSAIC**. These measures work by classifying people according to the area in which they live. As we have already seen, due to the diversity of the population and social mobility, even these measures are struggling now to reflect the population with any accuracy.

Increasing social mobility and a steady reduction in wealth concentration are eroding the old distinctions between classes.

SUMMARY

Consumer behaviour (and indeed all behaviour) happens against a backdrop of cultural and social mobility factors. These vary from place to place and from time to time, and some of these variations are greater than others, but as consumers we have to learn to operate within the culture we inhabit and the transient nature of social mobility that we are afforded.

ACORN
A Classification of Residential Neighbourhoods

MOSAIC
A system for geodemographic classification of households which applies the principles of geodemography to consumer household and individual data collated from a number of government and commercial sources.

KEY POINTS

- The social environment can be divided into macro- and micro-environments where the macro-environment has three components: culture, subculture and social class.
- Culture provides the social environment within which people live.
- Cultural factors colour all our behaviour, not just our purchasing behaviour.
- Consumer culture theory starts to investigate how consumers interact with the markets in which they find themselves.
- Subcultures are distinctive groups of people within a society who share common cultural meanings, behaviours and environmental factors.
- Moving from one culture to another is almost always problematic in terms of learning to be a consumer.
- Class now has a very limited relevance to marketing activities, and social mobility continues to erode the old distinctions between classes that were valid 50 years ago.

HOW TO IMPRESS YOUR EXAMINER

Questions about culture will definitely benefit from giving examples of how culture affects purchasing behaviour. You should be very wary of ethnocentrism – the belief that your own culture is the 'right' one – because this will make you sound patronising. You should be able to critique Hofstede's findings as well.

Class is an outdated concept. So it is worthwhile mentioning social mobility (which is transient by nature) and how it has become a *game-changer*.

REVIEW QUESTIONS

1. What are the core components of the social macro-environment?
2. What might be the problems for someone emigrating from a low-context culture to a high-context culture?
3. What might be the problems for someone emigrating from a high-context culture to a low-context culture?
4. What are some of the main constituent elements of culture?
5. How might social mobility affect consumption behaviour?
6. What special marketing approaches might be useful at traditional gift-giving times?
7. What are the main problems with the JICNARS system of social classification?
8. What special difficulties might arise for a firm seeking to export products to a high-context culture?
9. What are the main criticisms of Hofstede's work?
10. How should marketers approach marketing to a subculture?

CASE STUDY: HOPSCOTCH WOMEN'S CENTRE

hopscotch WOMEN'S CENTRE

iStock.com/PixelsEffect

Can we envision nurturing a culture and developing a society where all women are empowered, connected, well and safe, so that they can achieve their full potential?

There are of course many thousands of silent warriors (individual and group) in the world who are battling for this to happen. One such organisation is Hopscotch Women's Centre, in London. They serve communities with two key pillars of services in mind:

(Continued)

- Offering a series of charitable services for women and girls who are under the influences of inequalities and abuse.
- Providing care at home through their Hopscotch Homecare service.

THEIR STORY

Hopscotch was first formed after the Second World War, when a very war-torn Camden community had to rebuild itself. A childcare facility, 'Hopscotch', was formed, so that parents could get on with the work of rebuilding the housing and economy of the borough.

Since then, in one form or another, Hopscotch has existed to support the citizens of the borough. In 1998, Save The Children asked Hopscotch to become official, and formulate a programme specifically to support women and families from Bangladeshi communities.

In 2020 Hopscotch Asian Women's Centre rebranded completely, including a name change which became the more inclusive Hopscotch Women's Centre. They now offer a series of services for all women from all communities who are caught between gender and race inequity, throughout London.

WOMEN'S SERVICES

Hopscotch's charitable work is centred around women and girls who are under the influence of inequalities, poverty, unemployment, mental health issues, isolation and abuse.

Since 1998, Hopscotch has been a safe space for minoritised ethnic women and their families in their times of need, having helped over 16,000 women out of poverty, abuse and into employment. Their elder women's services and youth provision specifically have given hundreds of women and girls a place away from isolation and abuse, moving towards friendship and positive mental health.

As well as this, they are consistently increasing their outreach to strengthen access to their support via a wrap-around service, to be there for every woman who needs them. These services include domestic abuse help, welfare and benefits advice, job skills training, better employment opportunities, mental health and refugee advocacies.

The whole service covers areas of London which lack in culturally appropriate support through floating one-stop shops which wrap around women in need, with them in the centre.

DOMESTIC ABUSE HELP

Trained domestic abuse advocates are available to help and listen to everyone. Working with complex needs cases, in a trauma-informed way, their overarching goal is to help build autonomy in women whilst finding the best support for the people suffering and for any children involved to be safe from harm. Peer-led awareness-building workshops develop understanding of types of abuse across minoritised ethnic communities to prevent violence from developing within families.

WELFARE AND BENEFITS ADVICE

A team of welfare advisers are on hand to help sort out problems with benefits, universal credit, housing and more. They run excellent workshops on developing awareness around overcoming welfare issues and ways to build financial independence.

JOB SKILLS TRAINING

Hopscotch runs workshops which are designed to increase confidence, improve English and develop computer skills. Sessions are online and face to face with staff from the very communities they serve who are experienced in helping service users prepare for work or training.

Their *Better Employment* project is specifically for those in low paid employment and wanting to improve their job prospects and reduce their risk of in-work poverty. Their *Better Employment* facilitators are fantastic in guiding service users to build the confidence to achieve work with a higher salary, greater progression chances or with more flexibility.

REFUGEE ADVOCACIES

The specialist team of *Hopscotch Advocates*, with lived experience, work with refugees in Camden. They support both 121 and in groups to help adjust to life in the UK, providing trauma-informed, specialist support for all the issues that inevitably come up.

HOMECARE

Hopscotch's second pillar is founded on a vision which is to make sure that they are there for every vulnerable adult who needs their care – in a safe, person-centred and compassionate way. The three areas of support that they cover in Homecare are support for the elderly, dementia care and live-in care.

The benefits of the Hopscotch Homecare service can be far reaching. By helping with tasks like dressing, cooking and domestic chores, the dedicated carers can make daily routine that bit easier. Regular visits from the team of care workers can also improve self-esteem, by increasing independence and reducing reliance on family and friends.

ELDERLY CARE

Elderly Care exists for those who are of advanced age (or have a family member who is) or find performing everyday tasks difficult due to an illness, injury or disability. Hopscotch's care workers provide the extra support needed to live independently at home.

DEMENTIA CARE

Over 850,000 people in the UK have a form of dementia, and one in three people over the age of 65 will have the condition. Almost everybody will know of someone with dementia. It's important that the right support and care is available for those who have dementia, and for those who are living with or caring for a loved one with the disease. At Hopscotch Homecare, there is specialist support to help people with dementia to continue living at home safely. The help extends out to families through what is a tough time. Staff are trained to deal with the challenging behaviours that may come with dementia progression with care, compassion and professionalism.

LIVE-IN SUPPORT

At Hopscotch Homecare, around-the-clock care can be provided for those who may need this level of support to continue living in their own home and community. A

(Continued)

dedicated team of live-in care workers will provide the necessary level of support in a person-centred way.

For all provided services, Hopscotch bears their Quality Commitment. A high standard of care provision is reached, and they continually invest greatly in their services. The service is approved by Camden Council for Home Care provision and is Care Quality Commission (CQC) inspected. All carers are DBS checked, fully insured and trained to a high standard, with ongoing professional development training.

Adhering to 15 different CQC Training standards, as specified in the Care Certificate, both field carers and office staff undergo training every year with additional specialist training regularly throughout the year.

HOW CAN YOU GET INVOLVED TO HELP SUPPORT THEIR WORK, AND TO DEVELOP YOURSELF AT THE SAME TIME?

ARE YOU AN ORGANISATION OR A BUSINESS?

If you are an organisation or a business that understands and supports their vision and mission, they want to hear from you. They'd love to partner up to reach more minoritised women and provide robust support for them.

VOLUNTEER FOR HOPSCOTCH

Consider bringing your expertise to them as a volunteer. They are always looking for those with experience and compassion to spend time with their team and service users and make a difference to their workload.

© iStock.com Stock photo ID:1137116212

FUNDRAISE!

With so many ways to raise money for Hopscotch, they've got everything you need to make it happen, your way. Whether you want to go it alone or do something with your university, work, sports club or place of worship, you'll find lots of fundraising inspiration and have lots of fun at the same time!

CASE STUDY QUESTIONS

1. How does a charity like Hopscotch benefit the local community?

2. What are the needs of the beneficiaries at Hopscotch and how has this changed as a result of Covid-19?

3. Where does the support that Hopscotch provides to its community fit into the wider context of social mobility?

4. How might the rebranding have influenced the increased income Hopscotch has seen since 2020?
5. What might the next 10 years look like for Hopscotch?

FURTHER READING

Culture& – Check out their website (www.cultureand.org). Culture& is an independent arts and education charity formed in 1988 and based in London who work in partnership with arts and heritage institutions and artists to develop programmes that promote diversity in the workforce and expand audiences.

Consumer Culture Theory, edited by Russell Belk and John Sherry Jr (Greenwich, CT: JAI Press, 2007), is the outcome of a major conference on consumer culture theory. It contains papers from a wide range of authors, on a wide range of aspects of consumer culture. For some cutting-edge theory it's hard to beat, although it is somewhat academic in its style.

Consumer Behaviour and Culture: Consequences for Global Marketing and Advertising, by Marieke de Mooij (Thousand Oaks, CA: Sage, 2003), gets right to the heart of the problem of culture and marketing. Marieke de Mooij makes the point that the theories that come from the USA do not necessarily apply elsewhere in the world – and ethnocentrism is always hovering in the wings ready to trap the unwary.

Multicultural Perspectives in Consumer Behaviour, edited by Maria G. Piacentini and Charles Cui (London: Routledge, 2012), is another edited collection of papers from a wide variety of authors. The book was originally a special edition of the *Journal of Marketing Management*, so it is a rigorous and academic book, with papers from the UK, Greece, Austria, Germany and China.

Consumer Culture and Postmodernism, by Mike Featherstone (London: Sage, 2007), locates consumer culture in the context of global climate change, and further displaces the 'West' from centre stage.

For something a little more out of the ordinary, you might like *Material Culture and Consumer Society: Dependent Colonies in Colonial Australia*, by Mark Staniforth (New York: Kluwer, 2003). This is actually a book about underwater archaeology, but the author examines how material goods served to link early colonists to the home country, to distinguish themselves from the indigenous population, to help establish their own social relationships in terms of wealth and position, and to reassure the colonists about their place in the world.

MORE ONLINE

For additional materials that support this chapter and your learning, please visit:

https://study.sagepub.com/sethna5e

REFERENCES

Achabou, M.A., Dekhili, S. and Hamdoun, M. (2021) How the country of origin cue affects consumer preference in the case of ecological products: An empirical study in two developing countries. *Journal of Strategic Marketing.* https://doi.org/10.1080/0965254X.2021.2004207

Afkhami, R. (2012) *Ethnicity: Introductory User Guide*. ESDS Government, January 2012 update.

Aging.com (2022) The way of living: Being happy and healthy at an old age. https://aging.com/the-way-of-living-being-happy-and-healthy-at-an-old-age/ (accessed 1 September 2022).

Akaliyski, P., Welzel, C., Bond, M.H. and Minkov, M. (2021) On 'nationology': The gravitational field of national culture. *Journal of Cross-Cultural Psychology*, *52* (8/9): 771–93.

Alqarni, A.M. (2022) Hofstede's cultural dimensions in relation to learning behaviours and learning styles: A critical analysis of studies under different cultural and language learning environments. *Journal of Language & Linguistics Studies*, *18*: 721–39.

Andreasen, A.R. (1990) Cultural interpenetration: A critical consumer research issue for the 1990s. In M.E. Goldberg, G. Gorn and R.W. Pollay (eds), *Advances in Consumer Research*, Vol. 17. Provo, UT: Association for Consumer Research. pp. 847–9.

Arnould, E.J. and Thompson, C.J. (2005) Consumer culture theory (CCT): Twenty years of research. *Journal of Consumer Research*, *31* (March): 868–82.

Bagwell, S. (2008) Transnational family networks and ethnic minority business development: The case of Vietnamese nail-shops in the UK. *International Journal of Entrepreneurial Behavior and Research*, *14* (6): 377–94.

Bann, G. (1996) Race for opportunity. *New Impact Journal*, December 1996/January 1997: 8–9.

Bao, H.-W.-S., Cai, H. and Huang, Z. (2022) Discerning cultural shifts in China? Commentary on Hamamura et al. (2021). *American Psychologist*, *77* (6): 786–8.

Beijaard, D., Meijer, P.C. and Verloop, N. (2004) Reconsidering research on teachers' professional identity. *Teaching and Teacher Education*, *20*: 107–28.

Berliner, D. (2020) *Losing Culture: Nostalgia, Heritage, and Our Accelerated Times*. New Brunswick, NJ: Rutgers University Press.

Berry, J.W. (1997) Immigration, acculturation and adaptation. *Applied Psychology: An International Review*, *46* (1): 5–33.

Bjerke, B. and Hultman, C.M. (2013) The role of marketing rationale and natural business start-ups. In Z. Sethna, R. Jones and P. Harrigan (eds), *Entrepreneurial Marketing: Global Perspectives*. Bingley: Emerald Publishing. pp. 63–88.

Bourdieu, P. (1984) *Distinction: A Social Critique of the Judgement of Taste* (trans. R. Nice). London: Routledge.

Brossoie, N., Hwang, E., Song, K., Jeong, J.W. and Young-Woo, K. (2022) Assessing age-friendliness: Individualistic vs. collectivistic cultures. *Journal of Aging & Social Policy*, *34* (2): 311–34.

Brubaker, R. (2001) The return to assimilation? Changing perspectives on immigration and its sequels in France, Germany, and the United States. *Ethnic and Racial Studies*, *24*: 531–48.

Bulmer, M. (1996) The ethnic group question in the 1991 Census of Population. In D. Coleman and J. Salt (eds), *Ethnicity in the 1991 Census: Demographic Characteristics of the Ethnic Minority Populations*. London: HMSO. pp. 33–62.

Bush, V., Bush, A.J., Oakley, J. and Cicala, J.E. (2017) The sales profession as a subculture: Implications for ethical decision making. *Journal of Business Ethics*, *142* (3): 549–65.

Cabassa, L.J. (2003) Measuring acculturation: Where we are and where we need to go. *Hispanic Journal of Behavioural Sciences*, *25* (2): 127–46.

Chattaraman, V., Rudd, N.A. and Lennon, S.J. (2010) The malleable bicultural consumer: Effects of cultural contexts on aesthetic judgements. *Journal of Consumer Behaviour*, *9* (1): 18–31.

Chen, W. and Tan, J. (2009) Understanding transnational entrepreneurship through a network lens: The theoretical and methodological considerations. *Entrepreneurship Theory and Practice*, *33* (5): 1079–91.

CNBC (2020) Shoppers seek out personalized thoughtful holiday gifts to feel connected during pandemic. www.cnbc.com/2020/11/16/holiday-2020-shoppers-seek-out-more-meaningful-gifts-amid-pandemic-.html (accessed 19 July 2021).

Connelly, F.M. and Clandinin, J. (1999) *Shaping a Professional Identity: Stories of Educational Practice*. New York: Teachers College Press.

Cronin, J. and Fitchett, J. (2022) Consumer culture theory and its contented discontent: An interview with Søren Askegaard. *Journal of Marketing Management*, *38* (1/2): 127–44.

d'Astous, A. and Mouakhar, K.D. (2022) Self-gift giving and satisfaction with life: A behavioural tendency perspective. *International Journal of Consumer Studies*, *46* (1): 268–78.

Davies, A. and Fitchett, J. (2004) Crossing culture: A multi-method enquiry into consumer behaviour and the experience of cultural transition. *Journal of Consumer Behaviour*, *3* (4): 315–30.

De Vos, G.A. (1995) Ethnic pluralism: Conflict and accommodation. In L. Romanucci-Ross and G.A. De Vos (eds), *Ethnic Identity: Creation, Conflict and Accommodation*, 3rd edn. London: AltaMira Press. pp. 15–47.

Devi, B. and Singh, D. (2021) Silko's narrative negotiation of the Rain Man's Rites of the Passage. *Explicator*, *79* (4): 160–5.

Down, S. (2010) *Enterprise, Entrepreneurship, and Small Business*. Thousand Oaks, CA: Sage.

Drori, I., Honig, B. and Wright, M. (2009) Transnational entrepreneurship: An emergent field of study. *Entrepreneurship Theory and Practice*, *33* (5): 1001–22.

Emery, C.R., Wu, S. and Chan, K.-L. (2021) A comparative study of totalitarian style partner control in Seoul and Beijing: Confucian sex role norms, secrecy, and missing data. *Journal of Interpersonal Violence*, *36* (7/8): NP4443–67.

Erikson, E.H. (1968) *Identity, Youth and Crisis*. New York: W.W. Norton and Company.

Etsy (2020) Marketplace insights: 2020 Christmas trends. www.etsy.com/au/seller-handbook/article/marketplace-insights-2020-christmas/925709481071 (accessed 15 August 2021).

Faber, R. and O'Guinn, T. (1987) Ethnicity, acculturation and the impact of product attributes. *Psychology and Marketing*, 4: 121–34.

Fang, X., Sauter, D.A., Heerdink, M.W. and van Kleef, G.A. (2022) Culture shapes the distinctiveness of posed and spontaneous facial expressions of anger and disgust. *Journal of Cross-Cultural Psychology*, 53 (5): 471–87.

Gabel, T.G. and Boller, G.W. (2003) A preliminary look into the globalization of the tortilla in Mexico. *Advances in Consumer Research*, 30: 135–41.

Gee, J.P. (2001) Identity as an analytic lens for research in education. In W.G. Secada (ed.), *Review of Research in Education*, Vol. 25. Washington, DC: American Educational Research Association. pp. 99–125.

Gillespie, A., Seff, I., Caron, C., Maglietti, M.M., Erskine, D., Poulton, C. and Stark, L. (2022) 'The pandemic made us stop and think about who we are and what we want': Using intersectionality to understand migrant and refugee women's experiences of gender-based violence during COVID-19. *BMC Public Health*, 22 (1): 1469.

Goodson, I.F. and Cole, A.L. (1994) Exploring the teachers' professional knowledge: Constructing identity and community. *Teacher Education Quarterly*, 21 (1): 85–105.

Gordon, M. (1995) Assimilation in America: Theory and reality. In A. Aguirre and E. Baker (eds), *Notable Selections in Race and Ethnicity*. Guilford, CT: Dushkin. pp. 91–101.

Gov.uk (2022) Ethnicity facts. www.ethnicity-facts-figures.service.gov.uk/style-guide/ethnic-groups (accessed 1 September 2022).

Hajdas, M., Radomska, J., Szpulak, A. and Silva, S.C. (2022) Conflicting consumer cultures, shopping rituals, and the challenges of measuring consumer-based brand equity. *Journal of Marketing Theory & Practice*. https://doi.org/10.1080/10696679.2022.2080714

Hannelore Van Bavel, P. (2021) The 'Loita Rite of Passage': An alternative to the alternative rite of passage? *SSM: Qualitative Research in Health*, 1: 100016.

Hart, J. and Stekler, N. (2022) Does personality 'Trump' ideology? Narcissism predicts support for Trump via ideological tendencies. *Journal of Social Psychology*, 162 (3): 386–92.

Heydari, A., Laroche, M., Paulin, M. and Richard, M.-O. (2021) Hofstede's individual-level indulgence dimension: Scale development and validation. *Journal of Retailing and Consumer Services*, 62: 102640.

Hidy, K.M. (2021) The speech gods: Freedom of speech, censorship, and cancel culture in the age of social media. *Washburn Law Journal*, 61 (1): 99–161.

Hofstede, G. (1980) *Culture's Consequences*. Beverley Hills, CA: Sage.

Hughes, M.U. (2010) From resistance to integration: Changing consumer acculturation practices of immigrants. *Advances in Consumer Research*, 37: 10–14.

Irvine, J.M. (2022) *Marginal People in Deviant Places: Ethnography, Difference, and the Challenge to Scientific Racism*. Ann Arbor, MI: University of Michigan Press.

Jahoda, G. (1999) *Images of Savages: Ancient Roots of Modern Prejudice in Western Culture*. London: Routledge.

Jones, O. (2011) *Chavs: The Demonization of the Working Class*. London: Verso.

Jusik, P. (2022) Systemic oppression and cultural diversity: Putting flesh on the bones of intercultural competence. *Transactional Analysis Journal*, *52* (3): 209–27.

Kates, S. (2002) Doing brand and subcultural ethnographies: Developing the interpretive community concept in consumer research. *Advances in Consumer Research*, *29*: 43.

Kaufmann, E. (2022) The new culture wars: Why critical race theory matters more than cancel culture. *Social Science Quarterly*, *103* (4): 773–88.

Khairulla, D., Tucker, F. and Tankersley, C. (1996) Acculturation and immigrant consumers' perceptions of advertisements: A study involving Asian-Indians. *International Journal of Commerce and Management*, *6* (34): 81–104.

Kuznetsov, I.V. (2022) Mythology of myth as the foundation of postmodern culture. *Вестник Кемеровского Государственного Университета (Bulletin of the Kemerovo State University)*, *24* (1): 42–9.

Lambert, A., Desmond, J. and O'Donohoe, S. (2014) Narcissism and the consuming self: An exploration of consumer identity projects and narcissistic tendencies. In J.W. Schouten, D.M. Martin and R.W. Belk (eds), *Consumer Culture Theory: Research in Consumer Behaviour*, Vol. 16. Bingley: Emerald Publishing. pp. 35–57.

Lambert, W.E. (1967) A social psychology of bilingualism. *Journal of Social Issues*, *13* (2): 91–109.

Lindridge, A.M. (2009) Acculturation, religion and consumption in normative political ideology. *Advances in Consumer Research*, *36*: 16–19.

Lindridge, A.M. and Wang, C. (2008) Saving 'face' in China: Modernization, parental pressure, and plastic surgery. *Journal of Consumer Behaviour*, *7* (6): 496–508.

Liu, W.M., Colbow, A.J. and Rice, A.J. (2016) Social class and masculinity. In Y.J. Wong and S.R. Wester (eds), *APA Handbook of Men and Masculinities*. Washington, DC: American Psychological Association. pp. 413–32.

Lokhande, G. and Natu, S. (2022) 'You are cancelled': Emergence of cancel culture in the digital age. *IAHRW International Journal of Social Sciences Review*, *10* (2): 252–9.

Loughnan, S., Haslam, N., Sutton, R.M. and Spencer, B. (2014) Dehumanization and social class. *Social Psychology*, *45* (1): 54–61.

Low, M.B. and MacMillan, I.C. (1988) Entrepreneurship: Past research and future challenges. *Journal of Management*, *14* (2): 139–61.

Lu Hsu, J. and Han-Peng, N. (2008) Who are ethnocentric? Examining consumer ethnocentrism in Chinese societies. *Journal of Consumer Behaviour*, *7* (6): 436–47.

Ludwig, D. (2022) The functional contributions of consciousness. *Consciousness and Cognition*, *104*: 103383.

Lux, A.A., Grover, S.L. and Teo, S.T.T. (2021) Development and validation of the Holistic Cognition Scale. *Frontiers in Psychology*, *12*: 551623.

Madani, R. (2022) The new image of Saudi cultural shift; MDL Beast music festival; Saudi Vision 2030. *Cogent Arts & Humanities*, *9* (1): 2105511.

Marcinczak, S., Musterd, S., Van Ham, M. and Tammaru, T. (2015) Inequality and rising levels of socio-economic segregation: Lessons from a pan-European comparative study. In T. Tammaru, S. Marcinczak, M. van Ham and S. Musterd (eds), *Socio-Economic Segregation in European Capital Cities: East Meets West*. Abingdon: Routledge. pp. 358–82.

Marín, G.S. and Gamba, R.J. (1996) A new measurement of acculturation for Hispanics: The Bidimensional Acculturation Scale for Hispanics (BAS). *Hispanic Journal of Behavioral Sciences*, *18* (3): 297–316.

Marx, K. and Engels, F. (1848) *The Manifesto of the Communist Party*. London: The Communist League.

McColl-Kennedy, J.R., Patterson, P.G., Brady, M.K., Cheung, L. and Nguyen, D. (2015) To give or not to give professional services to non-paying clients: Professionals' giving backstory. *Journal of Service Management*, *26* (3): 426–59.

McCormick, C.B. and Pressley, M. (1997) *Educational Psychology: Learning, Instruction, Assessment*. Longman: New York.

McPherson, M. (2008) HRM practices and systems within South-Asian small businesses. *International Journal of Entrepreneurial Behavior and Research*, *14* (6): 414–39.

Miller, D. (1995) Consumption as the vanguard of history. In D. Miller (ed.), *Acknowledging Consumption*. London: Routledge. pp. 1–57.

Moftizadeh, N., Zagefka, H. and Barn, R. (2021) Majority group perceptions of minority acculturation preferences: The role of perceived threat. *International Journal of Intercultural Relations*, *84*: 41–51.

Neville, L. and Schneider, B. (2021) Why is it so hard to change a culture? It's the people. *Organization Development Review*, *53* (1): 41–6.

Ng Tseung-Wong, C., Dandy, J. and Lane, M. (2022) Perceived diversity norms, cultural identity styles and bicultural identity consolidation in two bicultural groups in Australia. *International Journal of Psychology/Journal International de Psychologie*, *57* (3): 363–71.

Nguyen, T.D., Nguyen, T.T.M. and Barrett, N.J. (2008) Consumer ethnocentrism, cultural sensitivity, and intention to purchase local products: Evidence from Vietnam. *Journal of Consumer Behaviour*, *7*: 88–100.

Nichols, D. (2011) *The Bogan Delusion: Myths, Mischief and Misconceptions*. Melbourne, VIC: Affirm Press.

Nightingale, C.H. (2012) *Segregation: A Global History of Divided Cities*. Chicago, IL: University of Chicago Press.

Nwankwo, S. and Lindridge, A. (1998) Marketing to ethnic minorities in Britain. *Journal of Marketing Practice: Applied Marketing Science*, *4* (7): 200–16.

O'Connor, R.C. and Portzky, G. (2015) The association between Goth subculture identification, depression, and self-harm. *The Lancet Psychiatry*, 2 (9): 766–7.

O'Guinn, T. and Faber, R. (1986) Acculturation: The impact of divergent path on buyer behaviour. In R. Lutz (ed.), *Advances in Consumer Research*, Vol. 13. Provo, UT: Association for Consumer Research. pp. 579–83.

Oberg, K. (1960) Cultural shock: Adjustment to new cultural environments. *Practical Anthropologist*, 7: 177–82.

Özbek, M., Bohn, A. and Berntsen, D. (2021) A tale of two cultural life scripts: Do young second-generation Turkish immigrants versus young Danes in Denmark perceive life through different cultural lenses? *Memory*, 29 (3): 778–92.

Panayiotopoulos, P.I. (2008) Turkish immigrant entrepreneurs in the European Union: A political-institutional approach. *International Journal of Entrepreneurial Behavior and Research*, 14 (6): 395–413.

Panikkar, R. (2018) *Cultures and Religions in Dialogue*, Vol. 2. Maryknoll, NY: Orbis Books.

Papa, V. (2021) The new working (poor) class. Self-employment and in-work poverty in the EU: A supranational regulatory strategy. *Italian Labour Law E-Journal*, 14 (2): 41–58.

Patsiaouras, G. (2022) Marketplace cultures for social change? New social movements and consumer culture theory. *Journal of Marketing Management*, 38 (1/2): 17–47.

Pawlak, M., Payne, D., Corey, C. and Zingoni, M. (2021) Nexus of religion, economic model and culture: Impacts on moral development. *Journal of Business & Management*, 27 (2): 69–108.

Penloza, L. (1989) Immigrant consumer acculturation. In T.K. Srull (ed.), *Advances in Consumer Research*, Vol. 16. Provo, UT: Association for Consumer Research. pp. 110–18.

Pulvera, D.M. (2021) Filipino BIGBANG fandom: A textual analysis of online fandom community activities. *Media Asia*, 48 (4): 271–94.

Rao, T., Yang, S., Yu, F., Xu, B. and Wei, J. (2022) Perception of class mobility moderates the relationship between social class and prosocial behaviour. *Asian Journal of Social Psychology*, 25 (1): 88–102.

Richardson, B. and Turley, D. (2006) Support your local team: Resistance, subculture and the desire for distinction. *Advances in Consumer Research*, 33: 175–80.

Rudmin, F.W. (2003) Critical history of the acculturation psychology of assimilation, separation, integration and marginalization. *Review of General Psychology*, 7: 3–37.

Rudmin, F.W. (2009) Catalogue of acculturation constructs: Descriptions of 126 taxonomies, 1918–2003. *Online Readings in Psychology and Culture*, 8 (1). http://dx.doi.org/10.9707/2307-0919.1074.

Rudmin, F.W. and Ahmadzadeh, V. (2001) Psychometric critique of acculturation psychology: The case of Iranian migrants in Norway. *Scandinavian Journal of Psychology*, 42: 41–56.

Rusinovic, K. (2008) Moving between markets? Immigrant entrepreneurs in different markets. *International Journal of Entrepreneurial Behavior and Research, 14* (6): 440–54.

Ryder, A.G., Alden, L.E. and Paulhus, D.L. (2000) Is acculturation unidimensional or bidimensional? A head to head comparison in the prediction of personality, self-identity and adjustment. *Journal of Personality and Social Psychology, 79* (1): 77–88.

Saint Pol, T. de and Hébel, P. (2021) Practices and representations of snacking in a highly standardized food culture: The scenario in France. *Food Quality and Preference, 93*: 104245.

Sam, D.L. and Berry, J.W. (eds) (2006) *The Cambridge Handbook of Acculturation Psychology*. Cambridge: Cambridge University Press.

Schindler, R.M. and Minton, E.A. (2022) What becomes sacred to the consumer: Implications for marketers. *Journal of Business Research, 151*: 355–65.

Segal, M. and Sosa, L. (1983) Marketing to Hispanic community. *California Management Review, 26* (1): 120–34.

Sethna, Z. (2015) Entrepreneurial marketing and the Zarathustrian entrepreneur: Thoughts, words and deeds. In *Academy of Marketing AM2015 Conference Proceedings*. Limerick, Ireland.

Spencer, B. and Castano, E. (2007) Social class is dead, long live social class! Stereotype threat among low socioeconomic status individuals. *Social Justice Research, 20*: 418–32.

Sudbury, L. and Wilberforce, F. (2006) The portrayal of black people in UK television advertising: Perception and reality. *Journal of Consumer Behaviour, 5* (September–October): 465–76.

Tan, J., Xu, H., Yu, J. and Radu, V. (2021) Consumption and savings of migrants in China – social cohesion perspective. *Ekonomska Istraživanja, 35* (1): 4029–46.

Technavio (2021) Gifts retailing market by product, distribution channel and geography – forecast and analysis 2021–2025. www.technavio.com/report/gifts-retailing-market-industry-analysis (accessed 10 March 2022).

Teske, R.H.C. and Nelson, B.H. (1974) Acculturation and assimilation: A clarification. *American Ethnologist, 1*: 351–67.

Urban Dictionary (2022) Tinderite. www.urbandictionary.com/define.php?term=tinderite (accessed 16 August 2022).

Vignola, M. (2015) Crossing the border: Migration flows in the Mediterranean area. *Nómadas: Revista Crítica de Ciencias Sociales y Jurídicas, 39* (3): 127–39.

Vila-Lopez, N., Boluda, I.-K. and Marin-Aguilar, J.T. (2022) Improving residents' quality of life through sustainable experiential mega-events: High- versus low-context cultures. *Journal of Hospitality & Tourism Research, 46* (5): 979–1005.

Waldfogel, J. (1993) The deadweight loss of Christmas. *American Economic Review, 83* (5): 1328–36.

Ward, C. (2001) The ABCs of acculturation. In D. Matsumoto (ed.), *The Handbook of Culture and Psychology*. Oxford: Oxford University Press. pp. 411–45.

Weber, M. (1946) Class, status, party. In H.H. Gerth and C. Wright Mills (eds), *From Max Weber*. Oxford: Oxford University Press. pp. 180–95.

Weinberger, Y. and Shefi, P. (2012) Professional identity formation through narrative research: How much the personal and the professional are intertwined. *International Journal of Learning*, 18 (11): 261–76.

Whitcomb, D.H. and Walinsky, D.J. (2013) Lesbian, gay and bisexual issues, social class, and counseling. In W.M. Liu (ed.), *The Oxford Handbook of Social Class in Counseling*. New York: Oxford University Press. pp. 446–65.

Williams, D. (2015) *Leadership for a Fractured World: How to Cross Boundaries, Build Bridges, and Lead Change*. Chicago, IL: Berrett-Koehler Publishers.

Wood, A., Kleinbaum, A.M. and Wheatley, T. (2022) Cultural diversity broadens social networks. *Journal of Personality and Social Psychology*. https://doi.org/10.1037/pspi0000395

Wray, M. (2006) *Not Quite White: White Trash and the Boundaries of Whiteness*. Durham, NC: Duke University Press.

Yorkston, E. and deMello, G. (2004) Sex sells? The effects of gender marking on consumers' evaluations of branded products across languages. *Advances in Consumer Research*, 31: 148–51.

YouGov (2017) How Britain voted at the 2017 general election. https://yougov.co.uk/topics/politics/articles-reports/2017/06/13/how-britain-voted-2017-general-election (accessed 19 August 2022)

Zaltman, G. (2003) *How Customers Think: Essential Insights into the Mind of the Market*. Boston, MA: Harvard Business School Press.

Zhang, Y. and Khare, A. (2009) Consumers' local–global identity: Measurement. *Advances in Consumer Research*, 36: 43–4.

Zwick, D. and Chelariu, C. (2006) Mobilising the hijab: Islamic identity negotiation in the context of a matchmaking website. *Journal of Consumer Behaviour*, 5 (July–August): 380–95.

PART ONE　CONSUMER BEHAVIOUR IN CONTEXT

Chapter 1　Understanding Consumer Behaviour
Chapter 2　Decisions, Behaviours and Interactions
Chapter 3　Consumption in B2C vs. B2B
Chapter 4　Consumer Technology and Innovation

PART TWO　CONSUMERS AS INDIVIDUALS (THE PSYCHOLOGICAL ISSUES)

Chapter 5　Drive, Motivation and Hedonism
Chapter 6　The Self and Personality
Chapter 7　Perception
Chapter 8　Learning and Knowledge
Chapter 9　Attitude Formation and Change

PART THREE　CONSUMERS AS SOCIAL ACTORS (THE SOCIOLOGICAL ISSUES)

Chapter 10　Reference Groups
Chapter 11　Age, Gender and Familial Roles
Chapter 12　Culture and Social Mobility
Chapter 13　Ethical Consumption
Chapter 14　Sustainable Consumption

CHAPTER 13
ETHICAL CONSUMPTION

LEARNING OBJECTIVES

After reading this chapter you should be able to:

- Define and categorise ethics.
- Understand the part that morality plays in ethical consumption.
- Explain why consumers sometimes use 'boycott' as a strategy.
- Describe the role of environmental pressure groups.
- Describe and analyse the recycling or disposal choices available to a consumer at the end of a product's life cycle.
- Elaborate on the relationship with ethics and the online environment.

CHAPTER CONTENTS

Introduction
Definitions and categories
Ethics and the person
Ethics and the public
Disposal and recycling
Summary
Key points
How to impress your examiner
Review questions
Case study: If ethics meets efficiency: Healthcare in India
Further reading
References

More online: https://study.sagepub.com/sethna5e

INTRODUCTION

This chapter is about the ethics of consumerism.

The United Nations (2022) Department of Economic and Social Affairs forecast that on 15 November 2022 the world's population would have reached 8 billion people. By 2050, the population figures for people living on Earth will be nearly 10 billion. More than half of the projected increase in the global population between 2022 and 2050 is expected to be concentrated in just eight countries: the Democratic Republic of Congo, Egypt, Ethiopia, India, Nigeria, Pakistan, the Philippines and the United Republic of Tanzania. One important facet of population growth is the greying of human populations. When growth rate falls, and fewer babies are born, the average age of the population shifts toward older people. Many industrialised nations are realising the effects of an aging population, such as a decline in the working-age population and a surge in healthcare costs. Over 20% of the population of 17 countries consists of persons 65 years or older. The decline in the working-age population results in a supply shortage of qualified workers. Nations with a large senior population depend on a smaller group of people to pay for higher health costs, pension benefits and other publicly funded programmes.

In 2020, there were 727 million people aged 65 or older. This number is expected to more than double by 2050. That fact, in itself, brings with it a host of issues. First of all, the obvious one of a decline in the working-age population. A rapidly aging population means there are fewer working-age people in the economy. This leads to a supply shortage of qualified workers, making it more difficult for businesses to fill in-demand roles. An economy that cannot fill in-demand occupations faces adverse consequences, including declining productivity, higher labour costs, delayed business expansion and reduced international competitiveness. In some instances, a supply shortage may push up wages, thereby causing wage inflation and creating a vicious cycle of a price/wage spiral.

To compensate, many countries look to immigration to keep their labour forces well supplied. While countries such as Australia, Canada and the UK are attracting more highly skilled immigrants, integrating them into the workforce can be a challenge because domestic employers may not recognise immigrant credentials and work experience, especially if they were obtained in countries outside of North America, Western Europe and Australia.

Secondly, an aging population equates to an increase in healthcare costs. Given that demand for healthcare rises with age, countries with rapidly aging populations must allocate more money and resources to their healthcare systems. Healthcare spending as a share of GDP (gross domestic product) is already high in most advanced economies; one challenge that advanced economies face is to ensure that when they increase spending, healthcare outcomes actually improve. Additionally, the healthcare sector in many advanced economies faces similar issues, including labour and skills shortages and increased demand for at-home care. All of these cost escalators can make it more difficult for existing systems to handle the increased prevalence of chronic diseases, while also addressing the needs of large and growing senior populations.

Third, and as a combination of the first two, we'll experience an increase in the dependency ratio. This is where countries with large elderly populations depend on smaller pools of workers in which to collect taxes to pay for higher health costs, pension benefits and other publicly funded programmes. This is becoming more common in advanced economies where retirees live on fixed incomes with much smaller tax brackets than workers. The combination of lower tax revenue and higher spending commitments on healthcare, pension and other benefits is a major concern for advanced industrialised nations.

Fourth, an economy with a significant share of seniors and retirees has different demand drivers than an economy with a higher birth rate and a larger working-age population. For example, rapidly aging populations tend to have greater demands for healthcare services and retirement homes. Although this is not necessarily negative, economies may face challenges transitioning to markets that are increasingly driven by goods and services linked to older people.

New consumption patterns will be formed by new middle classes, natural resources such as oil will be scarce, climate change will result in our planet Earth becoming warmer.

We and other consumers around the world, whether from developed or developing societies and economies, are becoming increasingly aware of the part that ethics plays both in the acquisition (through monetary decisions we make) and the consumption of products on an everyday basis. This is because we have **ethical consumption** values, of some kind or another. It is about making the connections between a product, where that product originated and in what context it has been produced. It requires YOU to think before you shop, to consider just how your lifestyle affects other people and communities, as well as the environment. An ethically informed consumer realises that when they buy something, they are not only buying the product. For example, some people buy organic food and calculate the 'food miles' their produce has travelled to reach them (thus determining the carbon footprint that those food miles have left) in a bid to satisfy values of environmental friendliness. Others check to see whether or not the clothes they buy have been manufactured in a **sweatshop** somewhere by 12-year-old girls working 12-hour shifts in an inhumane factory, because human rights as well as working conditions and wage rates are of importance to them. Others are conscious about whether their energy consumption is from renewable sources or not.

Ethical consumption
Refers to a values-based approach to purchase and consumption which puts the onus on the consumer to exercise their choice as they deem fit

Sweatshop
A factory or workshop, especially in the clothing industry, where manual workers are employed at very low wages for long hours and under poor conditions

DEFINITIONS AND CATEGORIES

Ethics is defined by the Oxford English Dictionary as 'the discipline dealing with what is good and bad and with moral duty and obligation'. It adds: 'ethics has been called the science of the ideal of human character'. The second definition reads: 'The principles of conduct governing an individual or group'.

A deeper study takes us to the field of philosophy, and there we see ethics as a branch of normative science as distinguished from the formal sciences. The history of thought in Western civilisation begins with Greece. The earliest consideration of ethics began in the 5th century BCE, and since then the Greek schools of ethics, early Christian ethics, ethics after the Reformation and ethics since Darwinism have all developed. In the late 1700s a number of people began petitioning the UK's government for better factory working conditions. The result, in 1802, was the Factory and Health and Morals Act. Although it significantly pre-dated the concept of ethical consumption as we know it today, it was arguably the first significant social justice movement of modern times. Ethical consumption in its contemporary form began to take shape in the 1950s, as 'fair trade' initiatives began across North America. The 'hippy' movement of the 1960s encouraged individuals to think of themselves not only in terms of family, work and their community, but as consumers in their own right. As people grew more aware of the ethical implications of buying one product and not another, the ethical consumption model began to form in earnest. The first alternative trading organisation was established in the Netherlands in the 1960s and was called SOS Wereldhandel – 'Wereldhandel' meaning 'world trade' and SOS standing for 'Support Underdeveloped Regions'. More recently it has been seen that ethics should mean complete participation in the life of society with the freedom to express one's nature. As to what is good and what is bad, each school of ethics has its own definition, from cynicism to existentialism. We have lists of prescriptions and proscriptions, do's and don'ts; in fact we have books that run into several thousand pages each, as well as tests judging the willingness to pay as penance in the demand for ethical consumption (Goff, 2021).

For the most part, marketers and consumers do not make a deep study of philosophy, however. Liebe et al. (2014) succinctly summarise our most recent thinking on ethical consumption by saying that it can be defined as:

> *purchase decisions by persons concerned with not only the price of products and services, but also with the political, social and environmental consequences of their purchases.*

The current driver behind businesses adopting ethical business practices in industry has to be, and indeed actually is, the customer: the ethical consumer (Reczek et al., 2022). Work by Bendell (1998) first mooted an element of 'citizenship' in the consumerist perspective. In a simplistic way, businesses are merely satisfying the consumers' wants and needs, but in fact we've been seeing a growth in the popularity of ethical consumption since the late 1980s, when society started to frown upon the exuberant and indulgent lifestyle of the yuppie with his Golf GTI 16v and weekends away in New York using Concorde.

People started to become a lot more aware of the 'choices' they had through information published in magazines and guidebooks (Brower et al., 1999; Harrison et al., 2005; Jackson, 2006). The interests of the early proponents of this movement were firmly centred on areas such as certified timber, and organic and Fairtrade agriculture such as bananas and coffee. Unsurprisingly there was also a significant interest in cosmetics products, which instigated the growth of organisations such as The Body Shop (see the 'consumer behaviour in action' example below). Although some academics (Zadek et al., 1998) had reported early on that ethical consumption would be the norm among the masses, it is not the norm yet. That said, the 'movement' is slowly making its way into society as a way of living. Mainstream retailers are eager to provide us with information about their ethical retailing, and as consumers we have access to material from organisations such as www.eartheasy.com or www.thegreenguide.com, online and app-based tools which enables consumers to retrieve evaluations of the health, environmental and social impacts of consumer products such as toys, food and detergents. For example, a consumer might avoid a brand of canned chopped tomatoes because it's lined with BPA-containing plastic whereas the competitor's cans are not. This is clearly something the company would like to know. Wouldn't you like to know?

One final perspective is that of the distinction between unethical behaviour and selfishness. If we talk about 'Ethical consumption' or 'Fairtrade', then we must consider whether 'Unethical consumption' and 'Unfair trade' also exist? And if they do exist, what constitutes them? Can we assume that any product not carrying the Fairtrade logo has been unfairly traded? While this chapter will not go into detail on some of these aspects, it is worth noting where the boundaries lie. There is no easy answer to this question. The subjective nature of ethical consumption means that there is often disagreement over what makes a product ethical, and it is just as difficult to establish which products are unethical. What we already know is that generally speaking, all the research to date on this area tends to investigate situations in which individuals perform unethical actions to benefit themselves (Dubois et al., 2015), hence the aspect of selfishness. This begs the question of how to define ethical behaviours. Jones (1991) took a social psychology perspective on this and noted that unethical behaviour is any action that is illegal or morally unacceptable to the larger community. However, even this is debatable as social norms within different societies vary, and thus what individuals see as moral or immoral could be quite subjective (Ayal and Gino, 2011; Monin and Jordan, 2009). This approach could encompass a number of variables, from lying and cheating (Brass et al., 1998; Gino and Bazerman, 2009; Treviño et al., 2006) to general dishonesty (Mazar et al., 2008). Ethics are essentially values and are dependent on context. There are, however, certain basic ethical standards which are universal: for example, it can never be considered justifiable to subject workers to slave-like conditions, nor can trade in 'blood diamonds' or illegal logging be regarded as in any way ethical. So, there appear to be certain obvious production methods that are distinctly unethical, although many grey areas exist – for example, let's say that you live 10 km away from work, in a remote village: you could, with some effort, cycle to and from work every day. Yet, if you chose to drive instead – would this be considered unethical?

CONSUMER BEHAVIOUR IN ACTION: SIMPLY LUSHCIOUS

Founded in 1976 by the late British environmental and human rights campaigner Dame Anita Roddick, The Body Shop started as a small shop in Brighton selling just 25 products. The Body Shop was the first mainstream UK retailer to put a real emphasis on natural ingredients that were ethically sourced and not tested on animals. In its day, The Body Shop was a true pioneer in bringing cruelty free and ethically sourced skincare and body products to the British consumer, and it is hard to imagine how we managed without it. In 2006, it was controversially sold to the cosmetics giant L'Oréal. This is, of course, a subjective view, but walk into one of their stores now and you are likely to be confronted with fussy, brash packaging and an array of artificial aromas. So has this particular retailer lost its way?

Lush, on the other hand, is a handmade cosmetics company set up in 1995 by husband and wife team Mark and Mo Constantine and four of their friends. It began in Poole, Dorset (where it still has its headquarters). The company uses fruit and vegetables, essential oils and some synthetic ingredients in its products, and like The Body Shop guarantees no animal testing on any products.

Walk into one of their 951 stores across 49 countries (106 in the UK) and you are greeted by enthusiastic staff. It has a knack for communicating its ethical messages to consumers in a lively and imaginative way – both in-store and online – such as its recent campaign to encourage shoppers to return plastic bottle tops. Consumers love the approach. They can return the empty black pots from the cosmetics products

(Continued)

they'd bought earlier, in exchange for a face mask. These pots are made from a sturdy polypropylene plastic which Lush recycles and thereby works towards a closed loop and, eventually, a self-sustainable plastic supply.

In the beginning, Lush inventors discovered that creating solid products without water meant they could do away with excess packaging and keep products self-preserving. Their soap, shampoo bars, bubble bars and bath bombs have gone on to become global bestsellers; and in 2013 global sales of their solid shampoo prevented 9 million plastic bottles ending up in landfill. The company continually tries to invent ways to reduce packaging and plastics, and makes sure that they recycle and reuse from the factory to the shop floor. This said, they have never liked to call themselves an ethical company. They find the term rather a difficult concept, because it seems to them that it is used to describe companies who try not to damage people or planet with their trade practices – when surely this should not be regarded as 'ethical' but as normal business-as-usual. They believe that all business should be ethical and all trade should be fair. Individual companies should not stand out simply by not being damaging or unfair. No company should be trading from an unethical position, and society has a right to expect as the norm fairness and resource stewardship from the companies that supply them. They always wish to conduct their business so that all people who have contact with them, from their ingredients suppliers through to their staff and customers, benefit from their contact with Lush and have their lives enriched by it. They say that no company is perfect and they strive daily to get closer to the ideal vision that all Lush people share:

> *We will always want and demand more from Lush, so that our business practices match our own expectations, our staff and customer expectations and the needs of the planet.*

Their black pots have been through a few transformations; at first they were imported from overseas, and in 2010 they found a local supplier close to their Poole factory where they make their cosmetics. This not only reduces freight and transportation costs of the pots, but also allows them to support the local economy. So, when customers return their pots, they already know it's not the end of the road for these robust little guys, who are sent on to be thoroughly cleaned, heated and remoulded, and turned back into new pots for freshly made creams, scrubs, masks and shampoos.

© iStock.com/ChrisGramly

But it goes beyond the black pots. Lush makes full use of its platform often and doesn't shy away from taking bold stands on societal and political issues – which has earned the brand both praise and censure over the years. Most recently, Lush stopped posting to many of its social media accounts and won't return until the platforms in question (Facebook, Instagram, TikTok and

Snapchat) 'take action to provide a safer environment for users'. Instead, the brand will be investing in 'new ways to connect and build better communication channels elsewhere' (https://weare.lush.com/press-releases/lush-is-becoming-anti-social/).

How this innovative 'Anti-Social Media Policy' will affect the brand has yet to be seen. However, for now, Lush will remain on platforms like Twitter, YouTube and Pinterest – where it feels that users' rights are better protected. Clearly, this is a brand that sticks by its ethics in marketing.

As of late 2021, Lush stores reopened for consumers – but with a few caveats. In US locations, customers were required to adhere to local mask mandates, all samples were removed from the floor, and only a limited number of people were allowed inside at the same time.

Lush also asked that all visitors wash their hands upon entering and exiting the store and keep 'at least a bathtub's distance' between themselves and other customers. At least they're trying to keep the situation as light as possible.

CATEGORIES OF ETHICAL CONSUMER

Over the past 40 years, researchers have used a variety and combination of segmentation variables (behavioural, demographic, environmental and psychographic) to try to categorise consumers in order to chart their position on a continuum of ethical consumption. This has of course been a difficult exercise since quite often it is difficult to identify particular segments in the marketplace (Paco and Raposo, 2009). Some mediators, moderators and consumer profiles based on ethical priorities have been identified (Casais and Faria, 2022).

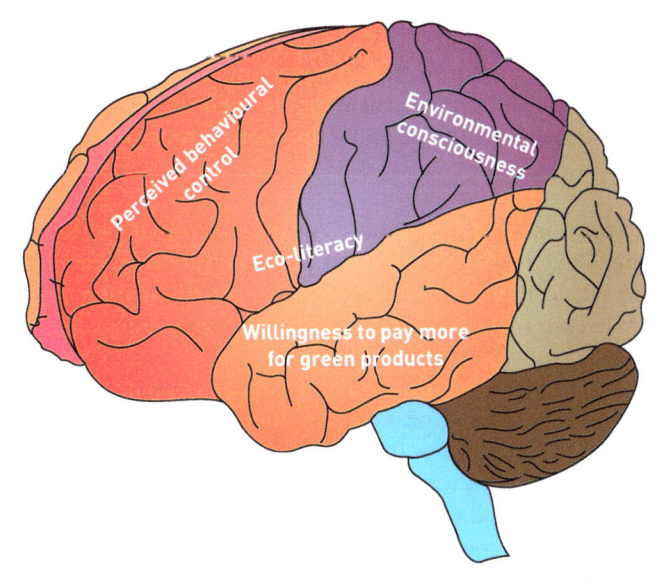

FIGURE 13.1 Variables determining environmental preferences and practices

Source: Adapted from Modi and Patel (2013).

Humphery (2011) and Littler (2008) had both noted that 'ethical consumption' as a term does not refer to a clearly defined set of practices, but rather has become a convenient umbrella phrase for a range of tendencies within contemporary consumer economies. Previous research on sustainability and health-related product labels has sought to develop segmentation frameworks based on consumers' self-reports. However, consumers are likely to overstate the effect that these labels have on their purchasing behaviour. Moreover, existing consumer segmentation frameworks do not distinguish among product labels based on whether they offer public benefits (e.g. environmental benefits, animal welfare, social equity) vs. private benefits (e.g. cost savings, health benefits) vs. both (Sarti et al., 2018). As Modi and Patel (2013) rightly surmise (see Figure 13.1), researchers in this area will regularly return to a handful of variables that determine where a consumer sits on the continuum. Let's start with **eco-literacy**. The concept of eco-literacy is useful in assessing the level of environmental knowledge that a consumer has (Popovic et al., 2020). (For example, Al Mamun et al. [2018] investigated the willingness to pay for environmentally friendly products among low-income households in Malaysia.) The more knowledge one has about the effects of particular types of consumption, and indeed the production ecosystem (Snow, 2020), the more one can make an informed and conscious choice, leading to environmental consciousness. There is evidence to suggest that environmental consciousness is therefore more closely allied to purchasing behaviour than any socio-demographic measures (Mataracı and Kurtuluş, 2020; Sohn et al., 2022; Yang et al., 2021), which means that people will often change their purchasing behaviour based on their knowledge of, and therefore their attitudes towards, what is more environmentally friendly (Hartmann and Ibanez, 2006) or greener (Peattie, 2001). This naturally leads to a person's perception about how much their individual behaviour will actually make an impact on the overall environment. Those people who demonstrate a deep, passionate and proactive attitude towards being eco-friendly are said to have a high perceived behavioural control (de Pelsmacker et al., 2002). Unsurprisingly, there is research (Guath et al., 2022; Laroche et al., 2001; Wan et al., 2018; Wu et al., 2017) to suggest that these people will pay more for eco-friendly products.

In the midst of the uptake of ethical consumerism, Roper Starch Worldwide (1997) attempted to categorise the green consumer, as seen in Table 13.1. It is interesting to note that we see here the insertion of the word 'green' to denote an interest in the 'environment'.

At around the same time, the National Consumer Council (which has since been subsumed by the Citizens Advice Bureau) published its own categorisation of 'UK Green Consumers' (see Table 13.2) by segmenting the population depending on how green their purchasing, recycling and consumption behaviour was.

It seems that in recent years the individual consumer's perspective has evolved from one that initially assumed that ethical consumption was all about 'less is more' to one that appreciates that there are ways in which their habitual consumption patterns can be made more eco-friendly. Research carried out by Whan (2010) in 17 countries has confirmed that our individual consumer preferences are only a reflection of the fact that we are increasingly becoming more concerned about the environment (see also work by Hidalgo-Crespo et al. [2022] on behaviours and attitudes and their influence on energy use). Yin et al. (2018) further corroborated this with their research on consumers' adoption of a public bicycle-sharing scheme.

This 'reflection' can be even further embedded in this context by using the past as a yardstick. The political and social commentator Professor David Starkey (2015) noted that 'the culture of the past will lay the ground for the future'. There are numerous

---

Eco-literacy

The environmental knowledge that a consumer has

examples from the past that we can draw upon to learn about the future (Bryant and Mitchell, 2021; Leow and Krishnaswamy, 2021; Sharma, 2021), not least the English author and philosopher Geoffrey Chaucer, who wrote the following lines in his poem entitled 'Parlement of Foules' (The Parliament of Birds):

> *For out of old fields, as the saying goes,*
>
> *Comes all the new grain garnered year by year,*
>
> *And speaking truly, out of old books flows,*
>
> *All the new knowledge men learn to revere.*

TABLE 13.1 Early categories of ethical consumers

Percentage of population	Segment name	Description
28%	Basic Browns	• People who do not believe that action can make a difference • May have lower educational attainment than other groups
26%	Sprouts	• Middling levels of concern about the environment • Have some green tendencies but not completely translated into behaviour
24%	Grousers	• People who have quite poor environmental behaviour • Often indulge in making excuses for their own lack of ethical consumption and are all too ready to blame others
11%	Greenbacks Greens	• People who are willing to pay higher prices for green goods (often equating a higher price for supposedly greener qualities)
11%	True-Blue Greens	• These people are the most active of green consumers • Will regularly take the lead and will often be seen at the forefront of the movement

Source: Adapted from Roper Starch Worldwide (1997).

TABLE 13.2 National Consumer Council's 'UK Green Consumers'

Percentage of population	Segment name	Description
26%	Sceptics	• The sceptics doubt they can influence the environment and think most environment symbols on products are merely a marketing ploy
19%	Affluent Greens	• These are committed buyers of environmentally friendly products even though they think that such products are expensive. They regularly recycle household waste. They are also generally wealthy and mostly female
19%	Recyclers	• These people recycle particular products – paper, glass and cans – more than any other group. However, they avoid environmentally friendly products and cannot be described as green shoppers
19%	Careful Spenders	• This group are thrifty with energy use but are the group least likely to recycle. They do not seem to be motivated by any environmental issues
17%	Young Greens	• These people have low incomes, and are recyclers. Their commitment to buying green products is second only to the affluent greens

Source: Adapted from National Consumer Council (1997).

ETHICS AND THE PERSON

Here we look at the individual's consumption, which is often entwined with morality. We also look at positive and negative ethical purchase behaviour, and finally consumer action in the form of boycotts.

MORAL LIVES – COMPASSION IN CONSUMPTION?

In the years surrounding both the First and Second World Wars, consumers naturally developed ethical and political concerns and were seen very much as 'citizen-consumers' as opposed to 'customer-consumers' (Bendell, 1998; Cohen, 2003; Frank, 1985; Trentmann, 2006), and to a certain degree we, in the 21st century, are moving back towards that stance (Ma, 2021; Ranchordás, 2018; Thiel and Moser, 2018). As consumers in households, our current thinking on issues of, for instance, environmental pollution (Awasthi et al., 2018; Rieuwerts, 2015; Sultana et al., 2022; Xu et al., 2022), food scarcity (Fennis et al., 2022; Findlay and Yeoman, 2015; Folwarczny et al., 2022; Nooghabi et al., 2018; Siddiqui et al., 2022) and inequality among consumers (Crockett, 2022; Fernandes and Calamote, 2015; Gibson-Davis and Percheski, 2018) is that these areas certainly do impact on our daily lives. The UK in terms of income inequality is ranked among the highest in Europe (Berisha et al., 2021). Over the past 25 years, there has been an increase of about 25% more 'households' in the UK and thus households account for the majority of energy consumption. It is of no surprise then that these sorts of figures have far-reaching implications for the environment. In our role as consumers of goods and services, we are essentially voting (making choices) with our pockets. Each time we make a purchase, we are contributing towards a company's profits and giving that company (and its work practices) a thumbs up. When you buy a piece of clothing, the label won't state on it that it's been manufactured in a sweatshop in Bangladesh, nor will the fruit and vegetables you buy indicate that they have been unfairly traded – but this doesn't change the fact that these products may well be unethical. Pleading ignorance doesn't change this either – it still means that every cent contributed towards these practices is a vote in favour of continuing them.

By not shopping ethically, are we making a choice to perpetuate injustice and unsustainable growth models? There is a positive justification for ethical consumption. Supporting ethical businesses and initiatives can act as an agent of broad social and economic change. Buying fairly traded products begins to help in the readjustment of the trade imbalance between rich and poor states; ensuring that your furniture has been made with reclaimed timber encourages furniture makers to divert more resources towards such timber and less towards unsustainable and sometimes illegal logging practices.

Guilt may be a factor in buying and consumption decisions. It is probable that at least some people go through a mental checklist (Table 13.3) each time they buy something.

TABLE 13.3 The guilt checklist of ethical consumption

Tick if the item we're about to buy is:	✓
Free-range	
Fairtrade	
Locally grown	
Environmentally friendly	
Low on food miles	
Non-sweatshop	
Carbon neutral	
Animal-cruelty free	
Recyclable	
Sustainable	
All of the above	

Guilt can be a compelling force when it comes to moderating consumer appetite for products and services, and guilt appeals have been found effective in stimulating ethical consumption behaviours in Western cultures (Chen and Moosmayer, 2020). For instance, out-of-season exotic foods that have travelled thousands of miles, or quick-dry clothing, or perhaps even something as mundane as 2-in-1 shampoo/conditioner render consumers partially responsible for some bad things around the world: environmental destruction, animal cruelty and human exploitation. Pre-knowledge of these factors may lead to the individual's self-image being tarnished, to quiet contentment, or perhaps feelings of guilt.

Sometimes these value statements are in conflict with each other. Sometimes the individual is unable to afford the 'ethical' option, or perhaps the 'not-tested-on-animals' moisturiser is based on petrochemicals and packaged in plastic. Research conducted by the School of Oriental and African Studies (SOAS, 2014) at the University of London found that Fairtrade certified coffee, tea and flowers do not improve the lives of the very poorest rural people in Ethiopia and Uganda. According to the SOAS website, their lead researcher, Professor Cramer, had this to say:

> The British public has been led to believe that by paying extra for Fairtrade certified coffee, tea and flowers they will 'make a difference' to the lives of poor Africans. Careful fieldwork and analysis in this four year project leads to the conclusion that in our research sites Fairtrade has not been an effective mechanism for improving the lives of wage workers, the poorest rural people.

There are of course two sides to every story, and even though the SOAS research is seemingly robust, Fairtrade International (2014) published their own statement about the research:

> While we were given an opportunity to comment at an earlier stage in their report writing process, we are disappointed to see that the final report has not properly taken account of the many issues we raised, particularly regarding

what we view as the report's generalised conclusions, unfair representation of data and lack of attention to the specific interventions of the Fairtrade system when attributing their conclusions to Fairtrade or other factors affecting the experiences of waged workers. While we have already taken action on specific issues we have been made aware of, the SOAS data and findings therefore warrant further scrutiny and analysis.

This paradox then also leads us to question whether wealth and social class affect ethical behaviour, or put in another way, 'Are the rich less ethical than the poor?' (Dubois et al., 2015; Jain et al., 2022). These authors' results showed that high social class does not inherently lead to unethical behaviour but instead predicts tendencies to behave selfishly. In contrast, low social class can lead to unethical behavior, but more so when it benefits others (see Chapter 12 for more on culture and social mobility). Interestingly, people with lower socio-economic status have less **nepotistic intentions** than richer people (Jain et al., 2022). Vanderhaegen et al. (2018) found that Fairtrade standards improve either productivity and farm incomes or biodiversity and carbon storage, but fail to eliminate trade-offs between socio-economic and environmental outcomes, even when combined in multiple certifications.

Regardless of where people are on the social mobility continuum, working out what is most important to the individual should take priority when scrutinising ethical values and consumption. This could then help in making more consistent purchasing decisions and avoiding unconscious hypocrisy (take for instance the fuel hungry 4x4 driven by a city dweller who compensates by filling it with premium 'more cleaner' petrol, or the same person who uses large quantities of Nespresso coffee pods – which take between 150 and 500 years to decompose in a landfill – before going to the supermarket and using jute bags-for-life.

The Ethical Superstore offers consumers a choice so that they can make a decision about value judgements from their own beliefs about what things are important to them. Sometimes there will be conflict, so a vegan may not buy a leather purse, but equally someone who doesn't worry about where their raw materials come from will be very happy to have a Fairtrade leather purse.

Ultimately the choices people make in their buying decisions create the coherent moral position within which consumer behaviour operates. Within this, people use 'trade-offs' to pacify their consciences, remembering all the occasions when they have been 'good' (being environmentally friendly) and using these to justify the times when they have not been so environmentally friendly. When rationalising their behaviour, people use a technique called confirmation bias. This enables them to accept information that fits with their current beliefs or decisions, and filter out or simply ignore information that doesn't. The reality is that adjusting behaviour to do what is morally right more often, if not all the time, tends to require some uncomfortable self-appraisal.

Preference is very important. Thirty years ago Fairtrade coffee was usually poor quality, but people drank it because it was politically the right thing to do, not because they enjoyed it. Now there are many good-quality Fairtrade coffees, so that a consumer doesn't have to sacrifice flavour and aroma, and can choose based on the moral

Nepotistic intentions

Favouritism shown to relatives or close friends by those in power argument in favour of Fairtrade. The choices exist because the Fairtrade producers (who want to sell more) have the benefits of improved production methods, wider markets and 'supported entrance' into the market. For each of us there are different things that motivate and excite us, whether it's a leather purse, or vegetarian food, or buying products that support trade in Palestine or Syria, and there will be different reasons for adopting those positions.

Fairtrade is an external benefit to a person many thousands of miles away, and this market has grown, despite the global recession; meanwhile the market for organic produce, which is actually a 'me benefit' – namely, 'I don't want to put anything bad inside me' – has fallen since early 2010. Fairtrade has flourished over the past 20 years, benefiting the early pioneers, but big business is now dressing itself up in the same clothes and taking up the standards that ethical organisations were adhering to many years ago.

Fairtrade is a contentious issue in some parts of the developing world, where producers are saying that it's of dubious benefit and has been imposed on them by Western NGOs and charities. What some producers want is to be running big corporates and development themselves. Some research suggests that Colombian coffee producers were making more money selling under the Colombian coffee brand than they were through the Fairtrade coffee brand because they were getting a share of the brand equity. Companies such as Divine Chocolate have come along where the producers own a substantial chunk of the business, so they get to share in the brand and the brand value.

BRAND EXPERIENCES: KAO CORPORATION

Since its foundation in 1887, Kao – a Japanese chemicals and cosmetics company – has always put their customers first. This spirit reflects in their Environmental, Social and Governance strategy known as Kirei.

Kirei means *'living a beautiful life inside and out'*. It has three principles:

- Making my every day more beautiful.
- Making thoughtful choices for society.
- Making the world healthier and cleaner.

Kao doesn't just *talk-the-talk* but it certainly walks too!

Their mission is 'to create a world where all life can coexist and flourish'. To this end, they consider sustainability as the only path forward. As a company they are dedicated to protecting future lives and aim to make a positive contribution to everyday life, to society and to the planet. Kao creates high-value-added products that enrich the lives of consumers around the world. Through a portfolio of over 20 leading brands such as Attack, Bioré, Goldwell, JERGENS®, John Frieda®, Kanebo, Laurier, Merries and Molton Brown, Kao is part of the everyday lives of people across the globe.

Combined with their chemical division, which contributes to a wide range of industries, Kao generates about 1400 billion yen in annual sales. Using leftover material from extracting edible palm oil, they developed Bio IOS, a sustainable surfactant to be used in cleaning products. Kao Corporation is constantly developing products that encourage consumers to use refill packs and concentrated products, aiming for zero waste.

PERSONAL ETHICAL CONSUMPTION

One of the early proponents of ethical purchase behaviour and accountability was Smith (1990). Smith asked a very direct and pertinent question that marketers still discuss today: 'Can businesses abandon the axiom that the customer is always right when consumers start questioning the ethics of business practices?' Much of Smith's early work focused on the negative aspects of disengaging with organisations by boycotting certain products that were deemed to be an unethical purchase due to environmental unfriendliness. However, there are also many positive aspects of ethical purchase behaviour (see Figure 13.2). The three broad areas that dominate ethical consumerism are shown in Figure 13.3. Each has both a positive and negative dimension.

My ethical purchases
Positive – should I buy products with ethical characteristics?
Negative – should I avoid buying or even boycott products that have unethical characteristics?
Consumer Action – Should I use lobbying or direct action to make my point?

FIGURE 13.2 The ethical consumer's choices
Source: Adapted from Tallontire et al. (2001).

CRITICAL REFLECTION

So what part does the 'individual' in the household play? What about the 'moral-self'? Do we have an awareness about how we perceive ourselves as moral actors in the world? Do we echo what others in the 'group' are saying, or are we, as Bauman (1995) said, 'behaving like a kind of lonely rebel and daring to act morally on behalf of others'? And whatever happened to those other perhaps traditional and institutional moralities as dictated to us by the likes of any religious institution, our families and/or our local community? Have they been eroded?

There are some commentators who propose that the primary moral consideration for shoppers should not be to consume differently (the positive way of consuming)

ETHICAL CONSUMPTION

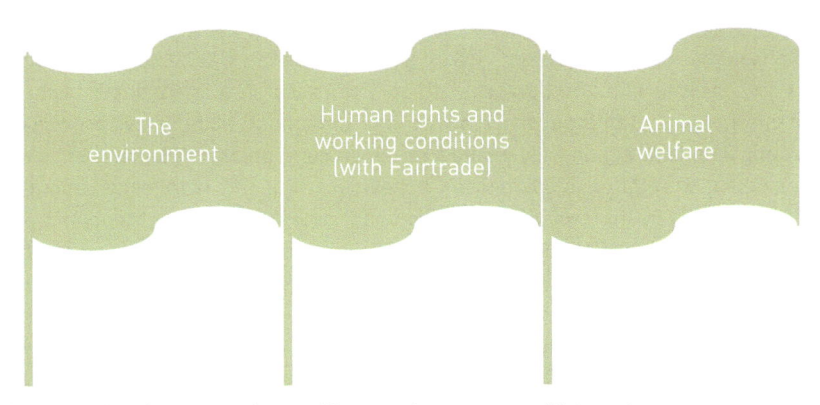

- The environment
- Human rights and working conditions (with Fairtrade)
- Animal welfare

FIGURE 13.3 Ethical consumerism and its constituent areas of interest

but to consume less, and that that which is consumed should cause as little harm as possible. For the past few years, many countries have been in economic recession, forcing people to lead more austere lives. Wholesale natural gas prices started increasing in 2021 as countries reopened from their pandemic lockdowns, causing a global spike in demand. Russia's invasion of Ukraine in late February 2022, and the resulting energy crunch, has only pushed prices further up. Western countries have banned Russian coal and oil imports, and Europe is desperately trying to wean itself off Russian natural gas. June 2022 was the first month on record that the UK did not import any fuel from Russia, traditionally one of its major suppliers, according to data released by the Office for National Statistics. Eye-watering prices have caused 29 smaller energy suppliers in the UK to go bust since last summer. Those that have survived have passed on much of the cost to their customers.

Reducing overall consumption seems to suggest making a virtue of austerity – a lot of people will be consuming less, not because they want to be ethical consumers but because they do not have enough money to consume as they would wish.

BRAND EXPERIENCES: STUDENT SAVIOURS OF ETHICAL CONSUMERISM

When it comes to personal behaviours to reduce environmental harm, it would seem that students are leaps and bounds ahead of the majority of the population: 86% said that they take reusable bags when they go shopping, and 81% use refillable water bottles to reduce waste. When buying food and drink the most important ethical/environmental issues are the way goods are packaged, animal testing, Fairtrade and free range. In terms of buying alcohol, packaging is also important, as is whether or not the product is Fairtrade or locally produced.

Over three-quarters want to see stronger action from government, saying they would support a tax on suppliers and manufacturers based on the amount of non-recyclable packaging they use!

(Continued)

> The National Union of Students (NUS) asked more than 1000 students about their views on consumerism and business ethics. The research was conducted with NUS Extra cardholders to find out more about their shopping habits, views on corporate behaviour and what action they would like to see companies, NUS and their student unions taking. In relation to businesses' behaviours, students were asked about what was most important to them. The top five factors were: human rights, being paid a living wage, animal welfare, air pollution and climate change – reflecting the broad range of students' commitments to ethics and justice. Two-thirds of respondents said their purchasing had been influenced by ethical or environmental standards in the last year. Respondents look for technology goods that are recyclable and energy efficient, as well as being generally environmentally friendly. Quality is also sought out, which could be seen as desire for longer-lasting products. When seeking to buy travel and holidays, the carbon footprint is noted as an important environmental issue. Then again, their main considerations were price, budget and quality – understandably, especially since many students are under severe financial strain.
>
> Finally, respondents expressed their conviction that knowledge is power, with a majority wanting more information on the ethical and environmental credentials of the products available in their student union shops and catering outlets – along with these venues stocking a wider range of ethical products. Respondents also spontaneously said they would like to see NUS working better with companies and businesses who supply their student unions in terms of using less packaging, and recycling more. They would also like to be better informed of the ethical credentials of suppliers.
>
> *Source*: Adapted from NUS (2018). The full case can be found at https://sustainability.nus.org.uk/our-research/articles/here-s-what-students-think-about-ethical-consumerism.

Global warming is expected to raise temperatures by between 2.5 and 10 degrees Fahrenheit this century (NASA, 2018), which is potentially catastrophic to the living world and to its people: this may be the greatest moral problem that we face. Global climate change has already had observable effects on the environment. Glaciers have shrunk, ice on rivers and lakes is breaking up earlier, plant and animal ranges have shifted and trees are flowering sooner. Effects that scientists had predicted in the past would result from global climate change are now occurring: loss of sea ice, accelerated sea-level rise and longer, more intense heatwaves. However, most people do not share any sense of panic about consumption, and still think that economic growth is a good thing, not least in helping raise living standards for more poor people. Environmental arguments are therefore unlikely to get governments elected to pursue non-growth policies.

CONSUMER ACTION AND THE BIG BOYCOTT

White list
A list containing details of product manufacturers who treat their workers fairly

This is nothing new. As a society we have been doing this for many years, and it is even more prevalent before and after times of war when quite often there is a scarcity of products available. The turn of the century saw the rise of the National Consumer League in the USA. These consumer groups wanted to gain social justice by exerting pressure on companies by boycotting the purchase of products and/or engaging in public protests to bring about wider awareness of ethical issues. One of the by-products of their endeavours was to produce what became known as '**white lists**' (Glickman, 1999; Strasser et al., 1998).

On the other hand, letting companies know when their behaviour is not acceptable is crucial. Social media are often used to influence companies who are desperate to maintain a good public image, reflecting ethical values. For example, Nestlé used to purchase their palm oil from plantations that were causing the destruction of orangutan habitat, but following a Greenpeace campaign, closely followed by widespread support on social media, Nestlé changed its decision and are now purchasing from sustainable sources only. Consumer boycotts seem to work, and money can be a moral agent as well as a means of exchange: consumers might boycott coffee shops who avoid paying their taxes (as happened to Starbucks in the UK), but boycotting may be more about political posturing than about a coherent moral crusade. For instance, the Starbucks political campaign probably did a lot more to shame Starbucks into making an apparent change than the actual buying decisions.

Things don't change. During 2022, whilst the UK was gripped by a major energy crisis, and with prices set to soar out of control, a campaign was launched urging 1 million consumers to stop paying their energy bills from October in protest at record price hikes. Run by a group of activists who were operating anonymously for fear of repercussions from energy firms, the *Don't Pay* campaign (https://dontpay.uk/) launched in June and within a matter of days gathered 4000 social media followers, and over 180k people have pledge to 'stirke' by withholding payment for the energy bills. They said they were hoping for a rerun of the *poll tax protests* that helped bring down Margaret Thatcher's government when 17 million people refused to pay. The manifesto, emblazoned in black and yellow on the group's website, said: 'Millions of us won't be able to afford food and bills this winter. We cannot afford to let that happen. We demand a reduction of bills to an affordable level. We will cancel our direct debits from 1 October if we are ignored.'

ETHICS AND THE PUBLIC

In this section we look at the wider impact that ethical consumption has on global societies and therefore, in turn, on organisations. It is certainly true that we as consumers use our buying power to ensure that organisations remain accountable to us as ordinary citizens and to society (Frank, 2018). Consumers are able to exercise choices (for example, what characteristics of nursing homes are most valued by consumers? [Moore et al., 2018]), but can exercise very little in the way of 'power of restraint'. An individual might give up driving a car and ride a bicycle instead, but unless that's taking place in a political context in which the government is reducing the road space allocated to cars and increasing the road space for bicycles (like they have in both Beijing and Copenhagen [Zhao et al., 2018]), all the individual is doing is opening up road space for someone else to occupy. This means that the power of restraint on other people's actions is limited, because individuals cannot prevent other people from behaving unethically.

PRESSURES ON FIRMS

While companies are coming under increasing consumer pressure, ethical consumers also need to think carefully about the strategies they employ. For example, following the clothing factory fires and subsequent building collapses in Bangladesh which killed 300 workers and injured nearly 1000 more, there were many calls for boycotts of Bangladesh-made items (for instance from customers of H&M and Nautica), but some commentators pointed out that such a move by Western consumers would devastate the struggling nation's economy and affect mainly women, who make up the bulk of the garment industry's workforce, particularly harshly. In their book *Half the Sky*, authors Kristof and WuDunn (2010) make a case for how factory work in Bangladesh has really liberated women there. Activists were instead persuading consumers to look for brands that had signed up to a new Bangladesh accord, which insisted on safe working conditions.

Websites such as the EarthEasy (www.eartheasy.com), Environmental Working Group (www.ewg.org) and Greener Choices (www.greenerchoices.org) aim to make the impacts of consumer consumption transparent for us as consumers, especially those who are time and resource poor. In a similar way, smaller organisations and even many Fortune 500 companies lack the time, money and market drivers to conduct a traditional life cycle assessment (LCA). Without a measurement tool such as LCA, companies that are asked to improve their environmental performance are lost. They may spend extensive resources on an initiative that produces little return while ignoring easier targets. Earthster (sustainablepackaging.org) aims to give life cycle evaluation and publishing power to all companies by helping them obtain a quantitative and visual understanding of the life cycle sustainability impacts of the products they buy and sell; to share the results of such an assessment with others using the web; and to make use of data shared by actors in their supply chain to obtain a more accurate assessment and to establish a dynamic sustainability reporting and assessment system.

DISPOSAL AND RECYCLING

There is one more element to post-purchase behaviour that is becoming increasingly important – the disposal of unwanted products. After a product has been used up, the consumer has the problem of disposing of whatever remains. In some cases, what is left still has value – the second-hand car market is an obvious example. In other cases, the product has been so totally used up that virtually nothing remains, as is the case with most food products. These issues have become central to the cause of environmentalism in recent years. Recycling, using products to the full and care in disposal into the environment have been near the top of the agenda, and consumer behaviour in these areas has come under considerable scrutiny.

People occasionally form strong attachments to products and find it difficult to 'let go'. Favourite clothing, a much-loved car and even now-almost-obsolete vinyl records may be kept until there is really no further possibility of using them. Such possessions are our links with our past, and giving them up removes one of the anchors of our identities (Belk, 1989). People who retain possessions have been defined as **packrats** (Kaur and Bawa, 2018), whereas people who regularly dispose of their possessions have been defined as **purgers** (Coulter and Ligas, 2003). Packrats attach more meaning to their possessions, and see themselves as thrifty: they usually do not mind giving possessions away to other people or to charities, but they hate waste. Purgers, on the other hand, think packrats are messy and disorganised, and they do not attach much significance to their possessions. Motivations for either of these behaviours are not clear-cut: hoarding in particular is an ambiguous concept (Maycroft, 2009) and one which is seen as 'extreme ownership'

Packrats
Individuals who tend to keep their possessions for a long time

Purgers
People who regularly discard their possessions

ETHICAL CONSUMPTION

(Peck and Shu, 2018). One motivation may be the sentimental value attached to the objects: mothers sometimes keep children's toys as mementos, for example, although they will throw away broken toys (Sego, 2010). Certainly if people are temporarily separated from some possessions (for example, leaving a mobile phone in a taxi, or even having to fly economy when one normally flies business class) there is a loss of self-identity (Black, 2011). In the last example the opposite is also true – that is, if one always travels in economy, and is suddenly upgraded to business class or even first class, the traveller is likely to encounter some feelings of apprehension at being in an unfamiliar environment with different rules.

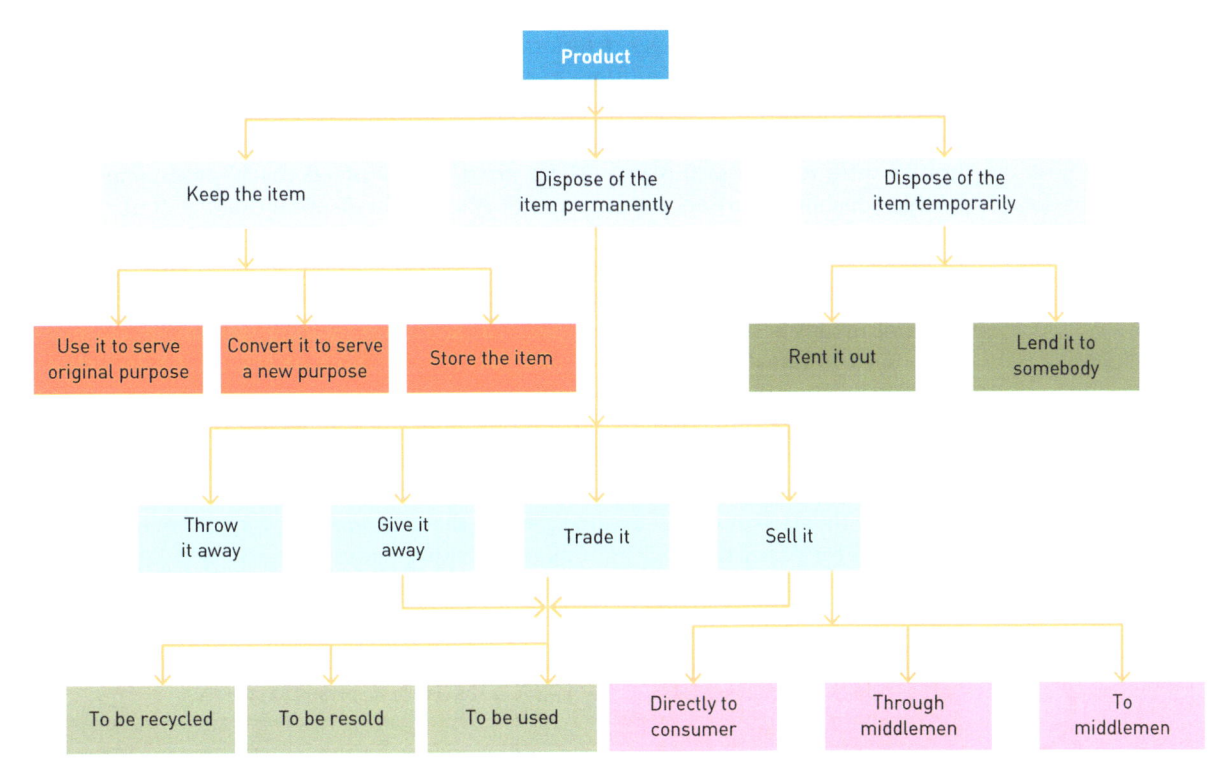

FIGURE 13.4 Disposal options

Source: Jacoby et al. (1977). Reprinted with permission from *Journal of Marketing*, published by the American Marketing Association.

No matter how assiduously some of us might try to hoard our possessions, sooner or later everything must go. When the object is no longer of any use the individual has a choice of three options, summarised in Figure 13.4:

1. *Keep the item*. This may mean putting the item away in a safe place – a loft or a garage – or it may mean re-using the product in some way. For example, an old bath might be recycled as a garden pond, or a broken radio might be incorporated into an artwork.

2. *Temporarily dispose of the item*. Christmas decorations might be put away for use the following year, for example. Equally, products might be lent to someone else, or even rented to someone. For example, someone who will be working abroad for a year might rent out his or her house rather than sell it.

3. *Permanently dispose of the item.* This could be achieved by selling the item, giving it away, putting it into the refuse disposal system, or by some other permanent means such as burning it. Trade-in can also be used – exchanging the used product as part payment for a new one greatly increases the buyer's willingness to buy (Zhu et al., 2008).

The increasing emphasis on recycling items that are no longer of any use by providing some form of incentive (Li et al., 2021) results in the recycled article being renovated, cleaned or donated as itself; for example, used spectacles can be collected and sent to developing countries to be worn by people who otherwise could not afford glasses. Since individuals' eyes deteriorate over time, everyone needs new spectacles with a different strength from time to time, so glasses that are still perfectly usable need to be disposed of. Equally, bottles can be cleaned and re-used as bottles rather than being smashed in a bottle bank and re-melted. Before the 1970s virtually all bottles were re-used in this way. There are a variety of 'takeback' programmes that enable consumer journeys for practices of sustainable disposal (Radtke et al., 2022).

Clothing, books and used household items are often contributed to charity shops, where they are sold to new users. Customers of charity shops are not necessarily short of money – some are anti-corporatist, some are looking for vintage clothing, some seek to transform their purchases into new clothing or objects. Charity shops effectively re-commoditise clothing for these buyers (Brace-Govan and Binay, 2010). This is a necessary function, because it distances the new owner from the previous wearer of the clothes – most people feel slightly uncomfortable wearing clothes of unknown provenance, but rationalise this by imagining the previous owner as being much like themselves (Roux, 2010). Clothing that is completely beyond re-use can be processed for paper-making: high-quality writing paper uses recycled fabric fibres (known in the trade as 'tramp's trousers') to strengthen the paper.

BRAND EXPERIENCES: LUXURIOUS CHARITY

Luxury department stores and charity shops might seem unlikely bedfellows. Some of us might even, reasonably, regard the endless proliferation of charity shops in the local area as a sign that our high street has taken a turn for the worse. But Selfridges Chief Executive Anne Pitcher says it's time to think again. Charity shops, she insists, could be about to play a vital role in hauling town centres – battered by the rise of online shopping and, more recently, the pandemic – back from the brink.

The goal is to work together to make sure more products are used again or recycled – and not thrown away. 'This isn't optional', says Pitcher, a lifelong retailer who rose through the ranks to run what has become one of the most impressive retail businesses in the world. 'This comes from consumer demand. Consumers are going to make their own choices and we've seen them making those choices in the last couple of years. We're all looking at ways of trying to bring a circular model into our businesses – recycling, reselling, repairing – and remember, charity shops have been doing exactly that for years.'

To force the point home, Pitcher met with charity shop bosses to deliver a call to action that the two opposite ends of the high street must work together more closely.

Selfridges, she observes, has already cleared space for projects that allowed charity shops to operate in its stores – most recently with Oxfam.

'At Selfridges Group we want to be a part of the solution', she told the audience.

'Why are we not constantly collaborating with each other? We should be working together and learning from each other to reduce waste, to increase circularity, to bring you online and to bring us to local communities. There is so much potential here for us to re-invent retail together.' She describes charity shops – impressive because they raise hundreds of millions for worthy causes – as 'hyper-local' and with 'super circularity' for their ability to find homes for stuff many might think no one wants. Selfridges can bring its skilful brand and marketing knowledge to help inspire charity chains to rejuvenate their approach and craft a more curated approach to stock categories.

The fashion press is already tweaking the conscience of shoppers. *Elle* reported recently that 'if everyone in the UK didn't buy new clothes for one day, the emissions saved would be equivalent to driving a car around the world 8,640 times'.

Fast-growing commercial firms have jumped on the theme. Websites offering second-hand products are not new but trendy online firms such as Thrift.Plus are making it more appealing to buy someone else's fashion cast-offs. Others, including Rent The Runway and Hirestreet, allow fashion fanatics to bag the best clothes for that special occasion – and then send them back for someone else to try.

Pitcher, who launched Project Earth in 2020 to 'embed' sustainability into the business, says she doesn't 'have all the answers'. But a 'deep dive' between the two industries is required to develop closer ties and practical solutions. 'We have to start somewhere and that somewhere is here', she says. 'We have to embrace new ways of thinking. It's not necessarily easy but it's important to have a curiosity about it – it's very challenging. And very exciting, by the way.'

Add to that the tide seems to be turning against the fashion industry – hardly a standard bearer for sustainability with 3.5 tons of clothing thrown away every five minutes in the UK alone. She says chains will need to be transparent. 'We banned fur in 2004 – we've been making this part of our DNA. We've signed the Fashion Pact [at the G7 in 2019] and now we've got Cop26 coming up.'

But while Selfridges' products might have a life beyond the first few wears, what about cheap, fast fashion? Some of them are also burnishing their 'sustainability' credentials while some of their products barely last the first night out. 'I think products will need to have more value in the future. They will need to be worn more than once and we have to understand what that means for customer behaviour. What is happening is that people are saying, "Yeah right, sustainability" – in a way that says they don't trust you [when firms make claims they cannot substantiate]. There's going to have to be a lot more regulation around claims companies make. I think customers are very aware of whether a claim by a retailer sits within the company's culture. There has to be an authenticity and an integrity about this. Either way, I think the consumer will decide for us.'

Source: Adapted from Craven (2021).

Some countries place a greater emphasis on recycling than do others, and there is also some debate over which recycling options are worthwhile and which are not (Gupta and Gentry, 2018). In some cases, the cost of collecting and recycling used items (including the energy used) may mean that it is less environmentally damaging to use new materials rather than attempt to recycle (van Doorn and Kurz, 2021).

There is an increasing awareness of and concern for socially responsible operations and environmental sustainability issues, and there are many discussions on the proper treatment of 'end-of-life', 'obsolete' and used items (Shi et al., 2016; Wilson and Goffnett, 2022). Under the extended producer responsibility rule in the electronics industry sector, the responsibility for the collection and further processing (such as recovery and disposal) of many end-of-life electronics products lies with the manufacturer (Atasu and Subramanian, 2012). There of course needs to be an understanding of the social determinants factors of public acceptance towards the end of life of vehicles in the automobile industry (Sitinjak et al., 2022). BMW, Renault and Fiat established a joint venture on the recovery and processing of used cars under their brands. Many companies such as Canon and Xerox in the copier and printer industry have collection and recovery programmes for their own used machines and cartridges, albeit the operations behind the used product collection programmes vary a lot in different industries. Some companies such as Canon and Xerox directly collect their used products (such as ink cartridges) from consumers using postal mailboxes.

One study showed how specific instrumental goals were linked to abstract terminal values, and thus to recycling behaviour. Lower-order goals that were identified were 'avoid filling up landfills', 'reduce waste', 're-use materials' and 'save the environment'. These were linked to terminal values of 'promote health and avoid sickness', 'achieve life-sustaining ends' and 'provide for future generations'. The perceived effort of recycling turns out to be the best predictor of whether people will actually take the trouble at all. In other words, even when people are sold on the idea of recycling and believe it to be important, difficulty in actually recycling will often outweigh their motivation to do so (Bagozzi and Dabholkar, 1994).

There is some evidence that the eagerness to recycle is levelling off somewhat and is certainly far from embedded in people's consciousness. Much depends on culture and on the availability of recycling schemes – Germans appear to be far more recycling conscious than, for example, Spaniards or Britons. There is some evidence that women are more environmentally conscious than men, but this is based on American research and may not be true for other countries (Iyer and Kashyap, 2007). These authors conclude that recycling will not succeed unless people are offered incentives and are reminded regularly about the need to recycle. Interestingly, they also found that recycling attitudes and behaviours correlate weakly with environmental attitudes and behaviours – in other words, having environmentally friendly attitudes in some areas (cycling rather than driving, using eco-friendly products) does not necessarily mean that one also believes in recycling.

There is also another popular term in this area which is 'product return and recycling' (PRR), and it is quite often used in the intimate apparel industry ('intimate' being a special category in the fashion apparel sector [Hart and Dewsnap, 2001]). As well as ticking the box for being environmentally sustainable, PRR in intimate apparel also helps enhance female consumers' health as over-used and aged bras may cause health issues (tension in shoulders and neck leads to headaches, and potentially breast-related issues). Intimate apparel retailers advise every user to continuously renew the bras and dispose of the old ones, and are well aware of the importance of doing so in a socially and environmentally responsible manner. There are programmes to provide cash incentives and encourage consumers to return old bras and buy new ones. Companies such as the Japanese luxury lingerie company Bonluxe, Wacoal and Triumph all allow consumers to return bras in exchange for cash vouchers (from US$6 to US$100) as an incentive to consumers for returning old bras. All parts of the collected bras are recycled (buckles, wires and other metallic components) by turning them into refuse paper and plastic fuel (RPF). In a 6-year period, Wacoal collected nearly 600,000 bras and helped produce nearly 60 tons of RPF.

BRAND EXPERIENCES: BRA-VO BRA-VO

In the UK, the charity Against Breast Cancer has a bra recycling scheme which takes your unwanted or unloved bras and through their network of bra banks raises vital funds for pioneering breast cancer research. The bras donated help support small businesses in Africa through their textile recovery project (giving these bras a new lease of life) as they are too expensive to produce locally. The lingerie brand Bravissimo has recycling bins for old or damaged bras/bikinis in its stores. For each tonne of bras they collect and recycle, they receive £700 to fund their research. Bras that are in a useable condition go directly to developing countries across the world. Companies can get involved too by having a bra bank in the place of work. The delivery of the bra bank and collection of bras is a free service. To maintain this they ask their supporters to confirm that they can fill at least four bra bank liners for each collection. Each liner holds approximately 100 bras, so the bank would need to be able to collect at least 400 bras and be able to keep the bank on an ongoing basis.

Smalls For All is another UK charity which accepts your new or 'gently worn' bras. It uses old, donated bras to help those living in orphanages, slums and IDP (internally displaced person) camps in Africa. They also carry out educational projects to help children in schools. If your old bra is too worn to donate, the charity will organise for the bra to be recycled. They can then use the material and metal to raise money. The money is put towards buying the people they help new knickers, as well as providing them with bras. The M&S Shwopping campaign also allows you to donate any old or unwanted bras (along with clothes and shoes) to many of their stores all over the UK. M&S says they ensure that by working with Oxfam absolutely none of those items end up in landfill and guarantees that the clothes will go where there's a demand, or are recycled. ZABRA is a free bra initiative to collect pre-owned and new bras in the UK for women in South Africa and other countries who can't afford their own. They work closely with organisations that identify situations where women can benefit from receiving bras free of charge.

© iStock.com/natalie_board

As some consumers become more environmentally friendly, they may seek to distance themselves from the materialism of modern life and take a more minimalist approach to consumption. These people experience a transformation as they dispose of their goods, deciding what to keep and what to get rid of, and move away from the profane marketplace and towards a more sacred type of consumption in which they consume only goods that fit into their new lifestyle (Cherrier, 2009). Often this disposal process helps develop a sense of community – for example, people who join clothing exchanges participate in the life of the goods by passing them on to friends (Albinsson and Perera, 2009).

Lateral recycling is the term given to selling goods on, donating them to others, or exchanging them for other items. Car boot sales (also called flea markets) exist to facilitate this process, as do charity shops. A more recent arrival in the lateral recycling market is eBay and similar websites, on which people can sell almost anything. eBay has become an international institution of its own, with people selling and buying in an almost compulsive manner – the website has rules about what can and cannot be sold, but even so some very dubious items have appeared from time to time. The existence of eBay has meant that previously worthless goods have become transformed into valuable stock-in-trade for many people (Denegri-Knott and Molesworth, 2009). Online trading of this sort creates a self-sufficient, self-regulating and self-sustaining community (Arsel, 2010).

> **Lateral recycling**
> Donating goods to others, selling them on or otherwise transferring ownership to someone who will obtain further use of the goods

CRITICAL REFLECTION

In the 1950s everything was recycled. People took bottles back to the shop and were refunded a small deposit, milk bottles were given back to the milkman (and he would get quite upset if he didn't get his bottles back) and in the countryside, food scraps were collected by pig-keepers. Ashes were spread on gardens or made into building blocks; paper and scrap wood were burned in household boilers to heat water; clothes were repaired, darned and eventually re-cut or unpicked and re-knitted to make new clothes. Newspapers were used to wrap food (notably, in the UK, fish and chips), and in some households were used as toilet paper.

© iStock.com/Kali Nine LLC

Do 21st-century consumers really think that recycling is some sort of 21st-century innovation? Sending newspapers away to be re-pulped instead of simply using them as packaging? Breaking bottles and re-melting them instead of re-using them as bottles? Packing milk in one-way, irreplaceable plastic containers instead of in multi-use glass bottles? Since the environmental movement started, we seem to have become less environmentally responsible than we were before!

Selling used products has become a lucrative business for some people – clearly antique dealers and the like can make their livings from selling off previously unwanted products, but even dedicated car boot sale attendees and eBayers can make substantial amounts of money from buying and selling. Reclaimed architectural products such as Victorian fireplaces, antique tiles, decorative roofing features, stained glass windows and so forth are often traded both online and offline. When goods are auctioned off, their previous cultural worth becomes commoditised – in other words, the history of an object becomes eroded by the fact that it is being sold, although some history still travels with the object. For many buyers, it is the history rather than the object that is important (Cheetham, 2009).

Given the huge increase in wealth in developed countries over the past 30 years or so, and the correspondingly dramatic increase both in number of possessions per household and in quantities of rubbish produced, disposal is becoming one of the hot issues of the 21st century. People can no longer simply throw things away – in the words of one researcher, there is no longer an 'away' to throw things to (Sherry, 1990). Marketers are likely to find that, if they do not address the issue of disposal and find ways to tap the potential of recycling in all its forms, they will be forced to do so by legislation. Already the European Union (largely at the instigation of Germany) is moving towards legislation that will require companies to take cradle-to-grave responsibility for their products.

SUMMARY

The environment of consumer behaviour includes the social environment as well as the physical environment. The social environment is the sum total of the human interactions that surround us, both those we are directly involved with and those we are not. Some of these interactions involve social class as well as personal behavioural preferences. Ethical consumerism has had in the past a number of negative identity connotations, and conversations often revolve around consumer 'denial', 'the cost' and/or 'inconvenience'. These variables nurture a social identity that is distinctly uncomfortable in the present day. This is in contrast to other consumers who receive a 'positive sense of self' following their ethical consumption practices: the individuals (or the *person* as seen earlier) who are now far better equipped to make the 'right choice' are far from being gullible, and may well actually be the saviour of consumption. That said, we may suffer from what managers would call 'analysis paralysis' as we're having to deal with complex ethical issues and large quantities of product information before making any buying decisions. This could lead to occasions where we might take the attitude of 'we'll do our bit'. Whether we're motivated by our desires, or whether it's to appease our friends and family (or even the wider society), we'll consume in a manner that somehow brings equilibrium into our lives; our lifestyle and consumer ethics need to be in balance.

One of the earliest examples of organised ethics is in 'religion'. Prophets of the world's religions used ethical dictates in devising plans in order to attract customers to buy into their products, services, beliefs and brands – even though they won't have consciously called it 'ethical consumerism'. For example, followers of the world's first monotheistic religion, Zarathustrianism, dated to approximately the 14th century BCE, believe in three core tenets, Humata, Hukhta, Hvarshta, which translate to Good Thoughts, Good Words and Good Deeds (Figure 13.5). This philosophy of pragmatism based on a systematic approach works very well as a foundation for summarising ethical consumerism.

Humata, Hukhta, Hvarshta
Three core tenets of Zarathustrianism, translating to Good Thoughts, Good Words and Good Deeds

> **Good Thoughts, Good Words, and Good Deeds**
>
> Three core tenets of Zoroastrianism

FIGURE 13.5 Good Thoughts, Good Words and Good Deeds (Zoroastrianism is the Greek derivative of Zarathustrianism)

KEY POINTS

- The driver behind businesses adopting ethical business practices has to be the ethical consumer.
- Ethical consumerism is not new, and has a long history dating back to the 5th century BCE.
- Social media have made it far easier for individuals to connect both with other individuals and with organisations about issues related to ethical consumption.
- Ethical consumption can be categorised using a mix of traditional variables (behavioural, demographic, environmental and psychographic) as well as contemporary variables (eco-literacy, environmental consciousness, etc.).
- Morality and compassion in consumption play a key role in the lives of individuals.
- The 'question mark' gets more of a workout than the full stop in these debates on ethical consumption, as the personal choices we each have in the buying decisions we make are still varied.
- Boycotts seem to work as the pound in your pocket can be a moral agent as well as a means of exchange.
- The disposal of unwanted products as 'ethical post-purchase consumer behaviour' is becoming increasingly important.
- There are three options for disposal: keep and store the article, dispose of it temporarily, or dispose of it permanently.
- Lateral recycling (passing the product on to someone else for re-use) is a growing phenomenon.

HOW TO IMPRESS YOUR EXAMINER

This is currently a very topical discussion, and the media are awash with examples of how companies are either getting it right or not. You should make efforts to collate a file of examples that you can call upon for different scenarios and feel comfortable in applying the categorisation of variables used to measure ethical consumption (behavioural, demographic, environmental, psychographic, eco-literacy) to those examples.

REVIEW QUESTIONS

1. Can ethical consumption always be a rational choice for consumers?
2. Which gaps exist when consumers are faced with a choice of ethical consumption or not?
3. What part do social media play in promoting ethical awareness and behaviour?
4. How can organisations affect the eco-literacy of society for their benefit?
5. Is the moral maze of ethical consumption one that an individual can navigate successfully?
6. In what situations should one boycott a product or an organisation?
7. Landfill or recycle – are the choices always so easy? What does one have to consider?
8. Why might a company encourage environmentally friendly disposal of its products?
9. What are the basic routes for disposal of used products?
10. What are the drivers for lateral recycling?

CASE STUDY: IF ETHICS MEETS EFFICIENCY: HEALTHCARE IN INDIA

The world's population crossed 8 billion in November 2022. China has the world's largest population (1.426 billion), but India (1.417 billion) is expected to claim this title in 2023.

India's mixed health system has evolved by default, not by design. India needs to make the best use of all their healthcare providers and avoid exploitation of vulnerable patients. To improve access, affordability and quality of healthcare, they need the public sector to be more responsive, the private sector to be more responsible and the voluntary sector to be more resourceful.

The first and most important maxim of the healthcare industry is *Primum non nocere*, or 'First, do no harm'. It sounds simple enough, but the healthcare industry is complex, and anyone in this demanding field faces difficult choices every day.

Commentators both inside and outside of the sector have repeatedly noted healthcare and public health must absorb and apply the efficiency-enhancing practices of business management. But are the foci different? The mantra of business management is efficiency and profit, while the mantra of healthcare and public health management must surely be efficiency, equity and ethics?

In contrast, there have been conversations between leading doctors in large private hospitals where there have been complaints about the way private hospitals have been 'ruthlessly run by management graduates who had no medical background'.

(Continued)

Supposedly 'they' lacked empathy and their only objective was to maximise profits for the investors who owned the hospital.

Word on the street is that the situation is worsening, with foreign investors gaining control of established Indian hospitals. Their representatives squeeze the doctors to generate more and more revenues, often through unnecessary tests and procedures as well as over-billing. These complaints are not new, but to hear it from a leading doctor in a private hospital who felt oppressed and revolted by the unethical practices revealed the extent to which mercenary management had derailed value-based medical practice.

In an article written by Professor Dr Reddy, he notes:

I was reminded of this when I received a WhatsApp forward of an anonymous post by 'An Indian Doctor'. A highly anguished and critical denunciation of the state of private hospital management by non-medical MBAs was the theme of that post. A sampler of the views expressed (from milder portions of that trenchant critique): 'No manager knew the sinking feeling of looking into the eyes of the un-affording patient and telling him that you have to bring more money to live'. He complained that, apart from oppressing patients, some hospitals were also charging doctors for their car parking slots!

The very same post also listed the other evils of commercialised private healthcare whose practices were being shaped by non-medical managers: doctors being criticised for partial payment exemptions granted to poor patients, with threatened deductions from their salaries; bullying on the level of revenue brought through tests and procedures, with coercion to prescribe and more of those even when unnecessary, and over-billing on the sly. The fervent appeal of the post was that doctors must regain control of hospital administration from non-medical MBAs.

After reading this WhatsApp post another doctor said, '*We cannot exonerate doctors who turned entrepreneurs and commercialised all places.*' His contention was that many hospitals were started by reputed doctors who did bring in a high quality of care. However, as they looked to attract more investments for expansion, they let financiers take control. Values receded as valuation came to the fore. Some of the medical entrepreneurs cashed in on the high market value and sold out to international and Indian businesspeople. The former had no emotional or ethical commitment to Indian patients while the latter saw the control of hospitals both as a high revenue opportunity and as a route to social and political influence. The interests of the patient did not matter any longer.

Srivastava (2019) reported a harrowing story. Farm labourer Dharmendra Meena's first year of marriage with his wife Vaijanti in northwest India was '*beautiful and carefree*'. But their first pregnancy changed everything. First came the infection during childbirth, then the stark choice presented by a visiting doctor: undergo a '*life-saving*' hysterectomy – the removal of her uterus and ovaries – or die. The couple took a loan of 100,000 rupees ($1400) to cover the procedure, trapping Dharmendra in slave labour and joining thousands of people in rural India estimated to have been duped by unscrupulous doctors into having unnecessary hysterectomies. A Thomson Reuters Foundation investigation found many women – often young – targeted by doctors whom medical experts say seek to profit by prescribing the surgery for minor ailments, with the operation and later costs driving families into debt. Having a hysterectomy brought on the menopause for Vaijanti, also a farm labourer, then aged 19, while Dharmendra was forced to work on the money lender's farm for long hours and low pay as he tried to clear his debt – becoming a victim of debt bondage. He ended up having to do other jobs and take more loans to support his wife and child, and now – seven years after the surgery – earns less than the monthly interest of 6000 rupees. *'The interest on the loan is rising every month'*, Dharmendra told the Thomson Reuters Foundation, sitting in a sparse hut next to his wife in Taroli, a village in the state of Rajasthan. *'We don't sleep any more. We fear the money lender'*, he said before Vaijanti listed their losses – the wedding jewellery they sold, her fertility, his freedom and their hopes for the future.

During the recent pandemic, the Indian health ministry had begun to recommend traditional remedies to tackle the country's Covid-19 outbreak, dismaying many Indian doctors and scientists. On 6 October, health minister Harsh Vardhan released recommendations for preventing Covid-19 and treating mild cases based on Ayurveda, India's millennia-old system of herbal medicine, triggering sharp criticism from the Indian Medical Association, a group of more than one-quarter of a million modern medicine practitioners (Pulla, 2020).

Worse still, one needs to question the medical qualifications of some 'doctors'.

In a four-month investigation, Reuters has documented the full extent of the fraud in India's medical-education system. It found, among other things, that more than one out of every six of the country's 398 medical schools has been accused of cheating, according to Indian government records and court filings.

The probe also found that recruiting companies routinely provide medical colleges with doctors to pose as full-time faculty members to pass government inspections. To demonstrate that teaching hospitals have enough patients to provide students with clinical experience, colleges round up healthy people to pretend they are sick. Government records show that since 2010, at least 69 Indian medical colleges and teaching hospitals have been accused of such transgressions or other significant failings, including rigging entrance exams or accepting bribes to admit students. Two dozen of the schools have been recommended for outright closure by the regulator (Reuters, 2015).

Paying bribes – often in the guise of 'donations' – to gain admission to Indian medical schools is widespread, according to India's health ministry, doctors and college officials. 'The next generation of doctors is being taught to cheat and deceive before they even enter the classroom', said Dr Anand Rai. He exposed a massive cheating ring involving medical school entrance exams in the central Indian state of Madhya Pradesh in 2013. Rai was given police protection after he received death threats following the bust (Reuters, 2015)

There are two broad segments of the private sector that provide healthcare. One is the unorganised private segment of individual healthcare providers (both qualified and unqualified). In the organised healthcare sector, we have the non-profit, for profit and for profiteering segments. Many in the first two segments have performed well in service provision and respected ethical norms. It is the third segment that brings disrepute to private healthcare. Currently, there is worry that many institutions in the second category are moving into the third category.

The ethos of medical practice was distinctly different before the large corporate hospitals emerged. With the advent of corporate hospitals, access to quality healthcare improved for those who could afford to pay. The poor could not afford such care, while those in the middle class who accessed high end private care suffered severe financial strain.

(Continued)

In recent decades, governments are also purchasing services from the organised private sector, through publicly financed health insurance schemes. The government provides several concessions to the private sector for establishing or expanding their facilities – land, water, electricity, customs duties, etc. There is both a need and an opportunity for the central and the regional state governments to exercise their regulatory powers to ensure ethical and cost-optimising practices by the private sector.

Overuse of healthcare, involving inappropriately induced demand, has also been a feature of health systems in the US. A recent study of 676 US healthcare systems reported that those which were overusing healthcare had more beds, had fewer primary care physicians, had more physician practice groups, were more likely to be investor owned and were less likely to include a major teaching hospital. Of these, investor ownership and lack of primary care physicians are factors particularly relevant to India.

Unfortunately, public sector healthcare providers are also treading the same path as private healthcare. Many doctors who are formally employed in government hospitals also work in private hospitals, often to the detriment of their clinical and teaching functions in the public hospitals. Up to the early 1990s, doctors working in government hospitals of many states did private practice in the evening, after their regular working hours. They never neglected patients or students during their daytime commitment to government healthcare institutions.

The growth of corporate hospitals changed that. Once government doctors started moonlighting in private hospitals during their working day, attention to patients as well as bedside clinical teaching suffered, as very little time was spent in the public hospital which was their place of duty. Is this because perhaps government doctors are not paid well, that they have to moonlight, and should they therefore also be barred from private practice? There is of course great value that dedicated time commitment brings to the quality of patient care.

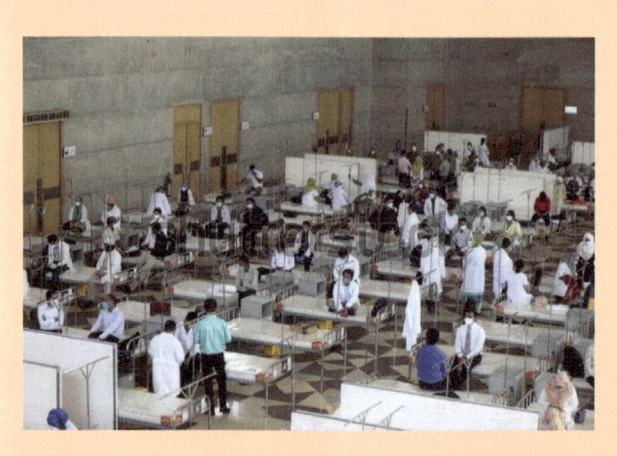

© Shutterstock: Stock Photo ID: 1805277517

The voluntary sector in India can proudly claim to have several excellent healthcare institutions. Even though some of them are labelled as private, they cross-subsidise care provided to the poor and have excellent ethical standards. However, these institutions are not geographically well distributed and do not have the financial resources to rapidly extend their reach and expand their services. Even among such institutions, those which have medical colleges attached to the hospitals or have credible post graduate training programmes tend to practise ethical, evidence-based care. Usually, their hospitals are not run by non-medical MBAs. Their management teams are led by medical doctors.

India's mixed healthcare system has evolved by default, not by design. They cannot turn the clock back. But with India set to overtake China and become the largest populated country on earth, *Mother India* needs to make the best use of all their healthcare providers to provide optimal healthcare, which avoids exploitation of vulnerable patients. To improve access, affordability and quality of healthcare in India, the public sector needs to be more responsive, the private sector to be more responsible and the voluntary sector to be more resourceful.

Source: Adapted from Reddy (2022).

CASE STUDY QUESTIONS

1. Is India's healthcare system physically prepared to become the country with the largest population in the world?
2. What questions should be asked of the government department looking after the healthcare sector?
3. Where do the lines lie between unethical behaviour, malpractice and abuse which is clearly illegal?
4. Can there ever be a happy partnership between the private and public sectors? Do you have examples from your own countries?
5. What will it take to become more responsive, responsible and resourceful – bearing in mind a population of nearly 1.5 billion?

FURTHER READING

For a review of ethical marketing practices, see a *Harvard Business Review* article by Professor Julie Irwin: Ethical consumerism isn't dead, it just needs better marketing. https://hbr.org/2015/01/ethical-consumerism-isnt-dead-it-just-needs-better-marketing.

Does the 'conscious consumer' demand transparency as they take an increasing interest in the ethical practices of those they buy from? Jessie Baker in the UK's *Guardian* newspaper takes a stance: www.theguardian.com/women-in-leadership/2015/apr/02/the-rise-of-the-conscious-consumer-why-businesses-need-to-open-up.

A Mintel report in July 2015 examined the issue of communicating ethics to different generations, as well as companies needing to improve the visibility of their CSR activity: http://store.mintel.com/the-ethical-consumer-uk-july-2015?cookie_test=true.

During the summer of 2014, environmentalists Muna Dajani and Lina Isma'il conducted research for an innovative Palestinian guidebook. The authors visited farmers, artisans and companies throughout Palestine, and wrote 100 profiles introducing their work. The result of their journey is a guidebook (*Conscious Choices: A Guide to Ethical Consumerism in Palestine*) that invites its readers to get to know the people behind the products they buy, and to build and expand their own individual network of producers: https://ps.boell.org/en/2015/05/12/conscious-choices-guide-ethical-consumerism-palestine.

MORE ONLINE

For additional materials that support this chapter and your learning, please visit:

https://study.sagepub.com/sethna5e

REFERENCES

Al Mamun, A., Fazal, S.A., Ahmad, G.B., Yaacob, M.R.B. and Mohamad, M. (2018) Willingness to pay for environmentally friendly products among low-income households along coastal peninsular Malaysia. *Sustainability*, *10* (5): 1316–35.

Albinsson, P.A. and Perera, B.Y. (2009) From trash to treasure and beyond: The meaning of voluntary disposition. *Journal of Consumer Behaviour*, *8* (6): 340–53.

Arsel, Z. (2010) Exploring the social dynamics of online bartering. *Advances in Consumer Research*, *37*: 67–8.

Atasu, A. and Subramanian, R. (2012) Extended producer responsibility for e-waste: Individual or collective producer responsibility? *Production and Operations Management*, *21* (6): 1042–59.

Awasthi, A.K., Wang, M., Awasthi, M.K., Wang, Z. and Li, J. (2018) Environmental pollution and human body burden from improper recycling of e-waste in China: A short-review. *Environmental Pollution*, *243* (Part B): 1310–16.

Ayal, S. and Gino, F. (2011) Honest rationales for dishonest behavior. In M. Mikulincer and P.R. Shaver (eds), *The Social Psychology of Morality: Exploring the Causes of Good and Evil*. Washington, DC: American Psychological Association. pp. 149–66.

Bagozzi, R.P. and Dabholkar, P.A. (1994) Consumer recycling goals and their effect on decisions to recycle: A means–end chain analysis. *Psychology and Marketing*, *11* (July/August): 313–40.

Bauman, Z. (1995) *Life in Fragments: Essays in Postmodern Morality*. Oxford: Blackwell.

Belk, R.W. (1989) The role of possessions in constructing and maintaining a sense of past. *Advances in Consumer Research*, *17*: 669–76.

Bendell, J. (1998) Citizen's cane? Relations between business and civil society. In *International Society for Third-Sector Research (ISTR) 3rd International Conference*. Geneva, Switzerland, July 8–11.

Berisha, E., Gabauer, D., Gupta, R. and Lau, C.K.M. (2021) Time-varying influence of household debt on inequality in United Kingdom. *Empirical Economics*, *61* (4): 1917–33.

Black, I.R. (2011) Sorry not today: Self and temporary consumption denial. *Journal of Consumer Behaviour*, *10* (5): 267–78.

Brace-Govan, J. and Binay, I. (2010) Consumption of disposed goods for moral identities: A nexus of organisation, place, things and consumers. *Journal of Consumer Behaviour*, *9* (1): 69–82.

Brass, D.J., Butterfield, K.D. and Skaggs, B.C. (1998) Relationships and unethical behavior: A social network perspective. *The Academy of Management Review*, *23*: 14–31.

Brower, M., Leon, W. and Union of Concerned Scientists (1999) *The Consumer's Guide to Effective Environmental Choices: Practical Advice from the Union of Concerned Scientists*. New York: Three Rivers Press.

Bryant, C. and Mitchell, M.I. (2021) The political ecology of cocoa in Ghana: Past, present and future challenges. *Natural Resources Forum*, 45 (4): 350–65.

Casais, B. and Faria, J. (2022) The intention-behavior gap in ethical consumption: Mediators, moderators and consumer profiles based on ethical priorities. *Journal of Macromarketing*, 42 (1): 100–13.

Cheetham, F. (2009) Out of control? An ethnographic analysis of the disposal of collectable objects through auction. *Journal of Consumer Behaviour*, 8 (6): 316–26.

Chen, Y. and Moosmayer, D.C. (2020) When guilt is not enough: Interdependent self-construal as moderator of the relationship between guilt and ethical consumption in a Confucian context. *Journal of Business Ethics*, 161: 551–72.

Cherrier, H. (2009) Disposal and simple living: Exploring the circulation of goods and the development of sacred consumption. *Journal of Consumer Behaviour*, 8 (6): 327–39.

Cohen, E. (2003) *A Consumers' Republic: The Politics of Mass Consumption in Post-War America*. New York: Knopf.

Coulter, R.A. and Ligas, M. (2003) To retain or to relinquish: Exploring the disposition practices of packrats and purgers. *Advances in Consumer Research*, 30: 38–43.

Craven, N. (2021) Selfridges boss: Charity shops can help save high streets… and cut waste. *Mail on Sunday*, 11 September, p. 129.

Crockett, D. (2022) Racial oppression and racial projects in consumer markets: A racial formation theory approach. *Journal of Consumer Research*, 49 (1): 1–24.

de Pelsmacker, P., Janssens, W. and Geuens, M. (2002) Environmentally friendly behaviour with respect to air pollution: The role of environmental knowledge, concern and perceived behavioural control. In M. Farhangmehr (ed.), *Proceedings of the 31st EMAC Conference*. Braga: Universidade do Minho.

Denegri-Knott, J. and Molesworth, M. (2009) I'll sell this and I'll buy them that: eBay and the management of possessions as stock. *Journal of Consumer Behaviour*, 8 (6): 305–15.

Dubois, D., Rucker, D.D. and Galinsky, A.D. (2015) Social class, power, and selfishness: When and why upper and lower class individuals behave unethically. *Journal of Personality and Social Psychology*, 108 (3): 436. http://dx.doi.org/10.1037/pspi0000008

Fairtrade International (2014) Statement on SOAS Report. www.fairtrade.net/single-view+M5a2383b864f.html (accessed 29 September 2015).

Fennis, B.M., Gineikiene, J., Barauskaite, D. and van Koningsbruggen, G.M. (2022) Acute stress can boost and buffer hedonic consumption: The role of individual differences in consumer life history strategies. *Personality and Individual Differences*, 185: 111261.

Fernandes, T. and Calamote, A. (2015) Unfairness in consumer services: Outcomes of differential treatment of new and existing clients. *Journal of Retailing and Consumer Services*, 28: 36–44.

Findlay, K. and Yeoman, I. (2015) Dr Spock's Food Festival. *Journal of Tourism Futures*, *1* (2): 148–51.

Folwarczny, M., Otterbring, T., Sigurdsson, V., Tan, L.K.L. and Li, N.P. (2022) Old minds, new marketplaces: How evolved psychological mechanisms trigger mismatched food preferences. *Evolutionary Behavioral Sciences*. doi: 10.31234/osf.io/zdrpq

Frank, D. (1985) Housewives, socialists and the politics of food: The 1917 New York cost of living protests. *Feminist Studies*, *11*: 255–85.

Frank, P. (2018) Me, my family or the public good? Do inter-role conflicts of consumer-citizens reduce their ethical consumption behaviour? *International Journal of Consumer Studies*, *42* (3): 306–15.

Gibson-Davis, C.M. and Percheski, C. (2018) Children and the elderly: Wealth inequality among America's dependents. *Demography*, *55* (3): 1009–32.

Gino, F. and Bazerman, M.H. (2009) When misconduct goes unnoticed: The acceptability of gradual erosion in others' unethical behavior. *Journal of Experimental Social Psychology*, *45*: 708–19.

Glickman, L.B. (1999) Born to shop? Consumer history and American history. In L.B. Glickman (ed.), *Consumer Society in American History: A Reader*. Ithaca, NY: Cornell University Press. pp. 1–14.

Goff, S.H. (2021) A test of willingness to pay as penance in the demand for ethical consumption. *Journal of Behavioral and Experimental Economics*, *94*: 1–12.

Guath, M., Stikvoort, B. and Juslin, P. (2022) Nudging for eco-friendly online shopping – Attraction effect curbs price sensitivity. *Journal of Environmental Psychology*, *81*: 101821.

Gupta, S. and Gentry, J.W. (2018) Evaluating fast fashion: Examining its micro and the macro perspective. In M. Heuer and C. Becker-Leifhold (eds), *Eco-Friendly and Fair*. Abingdon: Routledge. pp. 33–42.

Harrison, R., Newholm, T. and Shaw, D. (2005) *The Ethical Consumer*. London: Sage.

Hart, C. and Dewsnap, B. (2001) An exploratory study of the consumer decision process for intimate apparel. *Journal of Fashion Marketing and Management*, *5* (2): 108–19.

Hartmann, P. and Ibanez, V.A. (2006) Green value added. *Marketing Intelligence and Planning*, *24* (7): 673–80.

Hidalgo-Crespo, J., Coello-Pisco, S., Reyes-Venegas, H., Bermeo-Garay, M., Amaya, J.L., Soto, M. and Hidalgo-Crespo, A. (2022) Understanding citizens' environmental concern and their pro-environmental behaviours and attitudes and their influence on energy use. *Energy Reports*, *8*: 103–9.

Humphery, K. (2011) The simple and the good: Ethical consumption as anti-consumerism. In T. Lewis and E. Potter (eds), *Ethical Consumption: A Critical Introduction*. Abingdon and New York: Routledge. pp. 40–53.

Iyer, E.S. and Kashyap, R.K. (2007) Consumer recycling: Role of incentives, information and social class. *Journal of Consumer Behaviour*, *6*: 32–47.

Jackson, T.E. (2006) *The Earthscan Reader in Sustainable Consumption*. London: Earthscan.

Jacoby, J., Berning, C.K. and Dietvorst, T.F. (1977) What about disposition? *Journal of Marketing*, *41* (2): 22–8.

Jain, L., Gál, E. and Orosz, G. (2022) Nepotistic hiring and poverty from cultural, social class, and situational perspectives. *Frontiers in Psychology*, *13*: 780629.

Jones, T.M. (1991) Ethical decision making by individuals in organisations: An issue-contingent model. *Academy of Management Review*, *16*: 366–95.

Kaur, M. and Bawa, A. (2018) Disposal of used goods by consumers: An examination of the literature. *The Marketing Review*, *18* (1): 71–95.

Kristof, N.D. and WuDunn, S. (2010) *Half the Sky: How to Change the World*. Virago: First Vintage Books Edition.

Laroche, M., Bergeron, J. and Barbaro-Forleo, G. (2001) Targeting consumers who are willing to pay more for environmentally friendly products. *Journal of Consumer Marketing*, *18* (6): 503–20.

Leow, N.X. and Krishnaswamy, J. (2021) Smart cities need environmental consciousness and more social responsibilities as an outcome of COVID-19 – reflections from urban road commuters. *Foresight*, *24* (2): 276–96.

Li, Y., Yang, D., Sun, Y. and Wang, Y. (2021) Motivating recycling behavior – Which incentives work, and why? *Psychology & Marketing*, *38* (9): 1525–37.

Liebe, U., Andorfer, V.A., Gwartney, P.A. and Meyerhoff, J. (2014) Ethical consumption and social context: Experimental evidence from Germany and the United States. University of Bern Social Sciences Working Paper no. 7. www.semanticscholar.org/paper/Ethical-Consumption-and-Social-Context%3A-Evidence-Liebe-Andorfer/56b93cca21e65a76b09db0e33da26538e397111b (accessed 25 September 2015).

Littler, J. (2008) *Radical Consumption: Shopping for Change in Contemporary Culture*. Maidenhead: Open University Press.

Ma, F. (2021) 'You are first a Chinese citizen, then a consumer': Presenting and balancing identities online as Chinese international tourists. *Qualitative Sociology Review*, *17* (4): 58–81.

Mataracı, P. and Kurtuluş, S. (2020) Sustainable marketing: The effects of environmental consciousness, lifestyle and involvement degree on environmentally friendly purchasing behavior. *Journal of Global Scholars of Marketing Science*, *30* (3): 304–18.

Maycroft, N. (2009) Moving things along: Hoarding, clutter and other ambiguous matter. *Journal of Consumer Behaviour*, *8* (6): 354–64.

Mazar, N., Amir, O. and Ariely, D. (2008) The dishonesty of honest people: A theory of self-concept maintenance. *Journal of Marketing Research*, *45*: 633–44.

Modi, A.G. and Patel, J.D. (2013) Classifying consumers based upon their pro-environmental behaviour: An empirical investigation. *Asian Academy of Management Journal*, *18* (2): 85–104.

Monin, B. and Jordan, A.H. (2009) The dynamic moral self: A social psychological perspective. In D. Navarez and D. Lapsley (eds), *Personality, Identity and Character: Explorations in Moral Psychology*. New York: Cambridge University Press. pp. 341–54.

Moore, G., Quelch, J.A. and Boudreau, E. (2018) *Choice Matters: How Healthcare Consumers Make Decisions (and Why Clinicians and Managers Should Care).* Oxford: Oxford University Press.

NASA (2018) Global climate change: Vital signs of the planet. https://climate.nasa.gov/vital-signs/carbon-dioxide/ (accessed 29 December 2018).

National Consumer Council (1997) *Consumers and the Environment: Can Consumers Save the Planet?* September. London: The National Consumer Council.

Nooghabi, S.N., Burkart, S., Mahmoudi, H., Taheri, F., Damghani, A.M., Yazdanpanah, M. and Azadi, H. (2018) More food or better distribution? Reviewing food policy options in developing countries. *Food Reviews International,* 34 (6): 566–80.

NUS (National Union of Students) (2018) Here's what students think about ethical consumerism. https://sustainability.nus.org.uk/our-research/articles/here-s-what-students-think-about-ethical-consumerism (accessed 6 November 2022).

Paco, A. and Raposo, M. (2009) Green segmentation: An application to the Portuguese consumer market. *Marketing Intelligence and Planning,* 27 (3): 364–79.

Peattie, K. (2001) Golden goose or wild goose? The hunt for the green consumer. *Business Strategy and the Environment,* 10 (4): 187–99.

Peck, J. and Shu, S.B. (2018) *Psychological Ownership and Consumer Behavior.* New York: Springer.

Popovic, I., Bossink, B.A.G., van der Sijde, P.C. and Fong, C.Y.M. (2020) Why are consumers willing to pay more for liquid foods in environmentally friendly packaging? A dual attitudes perspective. *Sustainability,* 12: 2812.

Pulla, P. (2020) 'A fraud on the nation': Critics blast Indian government's promotion of traditional medicine for Covid-19. www.science.org/content/article/fraud-nation-critics-blast-indian-government-s-promotion-traditional-medicine-covid-19 (accessed 19 May 2022).

Radtke, M.L., de Almeida, S.O. and Espartel, L.B. (2022) What brought me here? Different consumer journeys for practices of sustainable disposal through takeback programmes. *Sustainability,* 14 (9): 5003.

Ranchordás, S. (2018) Citizens as consumers in the data economy: The case of smart cities. *Journal of European Consumer and Market Law,* 7 (4): 154–61.

Reczek, R.W., Irwin, J. and Zane, D. (2022) Good intentions – thoughtless buying decisions: Understanding and breaking barriers to ethical consumption. *NIM Marketing Intelligence Review,* 14 (1): 25–9.

Reddy, K.S. (2022) Private healthcare must fuse ethics with efficiency. https://indianexpress.com/article/lifestyle/health-specials/private-healthcare-must-fuse-ethics-with-efficiency-8052382/ (accessed 6 November 2022).

Reuters (2015) Corruption scandals plague India medical schools. https://gulfnews.com/lifestyle/corruption-scandals-plague-india-medical-schools-1.1537757 (accessed 19 May 2022).

Rieuwerts, J. (2015) *The Elements of Environmental Pollution.* Abingdon: Routledge.

Roper Starch Worldwide (1997) *Green Gauge Report*. New York: Roper Starch Worldwide Inc.

Roux, D. (2010) Identity and self-territory in second-hand clothing transfers. *Advances in Consumer Research*, 37: 65–6.

Sarti, S., Darnall, N. and Testa, F. (2018) Market segmentation of consumers based on their actual sustainability and health-related purchases. *Journal of Cleaner Production*, 192: 270–80.

Sego, T. (2010) Mothers' experience related to the disposal of children's clothing and gear: Keeping Mister Clatters but tossing Broken Barbie. *Journal of Consumer Behaviour*, 9 (1): 57–68.

Sharma, A.P. (2021) Consumers' purchase behaviour and green marketing: A synthesis, review and agenda. *International Journal of Consumer Studies*, 45 (6): 1217–38.

Sherry, J.F. (1990) A sociocultural analysis of a Midwestern American flea market. *Journal of Consumer Research*, 17 (June): 13–30.

Shi, T., Gu, W., Chhajed, D. and Petruzzi, N.C. (2016) Effects of remanufacturable product design on market segmentation and the environment. *Decision Sciences*, 47 (2): 298–332.

Siddiqui, S.A., Zannou, O., Karim, I., Kasmiati Awad, N.M.H.. Gołaszewski, J., Heinz, V. and Smetana, S. (2022) Avoiding food neophobia and increasing consumer acceptance of new food trends – A decade of research. *Sustainability*, 14: 10391.

Sitinjak, C., Ismail, R., Bantu, E., Fajar, R. and Samuel, K. (2022) The understanding of the social determinants factors of public acceptance towards the end of life vehicles. *Cogent Engineering*, 9 (1): 2088640.

Smith, N.C. (1990) *Morality and the Market: Consumer Pressure for Corporate Accountability*. Abingdon: Routledge.

Snow, T. (2020) Ecosystem metabolisms and functions: An eco-literacy framework and model for designers. *FormAkademisk*, 13 (4). https://doi.org/10.7577/formakademisk.3370

SOAS (School of Oriental and African Studies) (2014) *Fairtrade, Employment and Poverty Reduction in Ethiopia and Uganda*. http://ftepr.org/ (accessed 29 September 2015).

Sohn, S., Seegebarth, B. and Woisetschläger, D.M. (2022) The same only different? How a pandemic shapes consumer organic food purchasing. *Journal of Consumer Behaviour*, 21 (5): 1121–34.

Srivastava, R. (2019) Missing wombs: The health scandal enslaving families in rural India. www.reuters.com/article/india-health-slavery-idINKCN1SE078 (accessed 19 May 2022).

Starkey, D. (2015) An evening of conversation with David Starkey, 21 September, Henrietta Barnet Girls School.

Strasser, S., McGovern, C. and Judd, M. (1998) *Getting and Spending: European and American Consumer Societies in the 20th Century*. Cambridge: Cambridge University Press.

Sultana, N., Amin, S. and Islam, A. (2022) Influence of perceived environmental knowledge and environmental concern on customers' green hotel visit intention: Mediating role of green trust. *Asia-Pacific Journal of Business Administration*, *14* (2): 223–43.

Tallontire, A., Rentsendorj, E. and Blowfield, M. (2001) *Ethical Consumers and Ethical Trade: A Review of Current Literature*, Policy Series 12. Chatham: Natural Resources Centre, University of Greenwich.

Thiel, A. and Moser, C. (2018) Toward comparative institutional analysis of polycentric social-ecological systems governance. *Environmental Policy and Governance*, *28* (4): 269–83.

Trentmann, F. (2006) *The Making of the Consumer: Knowledge, Power and Identity in the Modern World*. Oxford: Berg.

Treviño, L.K., Weaver, G.R. and Reynolds, S.J. (2006) Behavioral ethics in organizations: A review. *Journal of Management*, *32*: 951–90.

United Nations (2022) UN population division data portal. https://population.un.org/dataportal/home (accessed 1 September 2022).

van Doorn, J. and Kurz, T. (2021) The warm glow of recycling can make us more wasteful. *Journal of Environmental Psychology*, *77*: 101672.

Vanderhaegen, K., Akoyi, K.T., Dekoninck, W., Jocqué, R., Muys, B., Verbist, B. and Maertens, M. (2018) Do private coffee standards 'walk the talk' in improving socio-economic and environmental sustainability? *Global Environmental Change*, *51*: 1–9.

Wan, M., Zhang, Y. and Ye, W. (2018) Consumer willingness-to-pay a price premium for eco-friendly children's furniture in Shanghai and Shenzhen, China. *Forest Products Journal*, *68* (3): 317–27.

Whan, E. (2010) *Greendex 2010: Consumer Choice and the Environment – A Worldwide Tracking Survey*. National Geographic and GlobeScan. London: GSI Publishing.

Wilson, M. and Goffnett, S. (2022) Reverse logistics: Understanding end-of-life product management. *Business Horizons*, *65* (5): 643–55.

Wu, C., Lin, Y. and Chen, T.Y. (2017) Moderating price sensitivity of low-uncertainty daily eco-friendly products: Creating benevolence trust and reducing uncertainties. *Journal of Relationship Marketing*, *16* (4): 286–301.

Xu, S., Yang, C., Huang, Z. and Failler, P. (2022) Interaction between digital economy and environmental pollution: New evidence from a spatial perspective. *International Journal of Environmental Research and Public Health*, *19* (9): 5074.

Yang, X., Tseng, Y. and Lee, B. (2021) Merging the social influence theory and the goal-framing theory to understand consumers' green purchasing behavior: Does the level of sensitivity to climate change really matter? *Frontiers in Psychology*, *12*: 766754.

Yin, J., Qian, L. and Singhapakdi, A. (2018) Sharing sustainability: How values and ethics matter in consumers' adoption of public bicycle-sharing scheme. *Journal of Business Ethics*, *149* (2): 313–32.

Zadek, S., Lingayah, S., Murphy, S. and New Economics Foundation (1998) *Purchasing Power: Civil Action for Sustainable Consumption*. London: New Economics Foundation.

Zhao, C., Carstensen, T.A., Nielsen, T.A.S. and Olafsson, A.S. (2018) Bicycle-friendly infrastructure planning in Beijing and Copenhagen – between adapting design solutions and learning local planning cultures. *Journal of Transport Geography*, 68: 149–59.

Zhu, J., Chen, J. and Dasgupta, S. (2008) Exploring the effect of a trade-in on consumers' willingness to pay for a new product. *Advances in Consumer Research*, 35: 157–8.

PART ONE CONSUMER BEHAVIOUR IN CONTEXT

Chapter 1 Understanding Consumer Behaviour
Chapter 2 Decisions, Behaviours and Interactions
Chapter 3 Consumption in B2C vs. B2B
Chapter 4 Consumer Technology and Innovation

PART TWO CONSUMERS AS INDIVIDUALS (THE PSYCHOLOGICAL ISSUES)

Chapter 5 Drive, Motivation and Hedonism
Chapter 6 The Self and Personality
Chapter 7 Perception
Chapter 8 Learning and Knowledge
Chapter 9 Attitude Formation and Change

PART THREE CONSUMERS AS SOCIAL ACTORS (THE SOCIOLOGICAL ISSUES)

Chapter 10 Reference Groups
Chapter 11 Age, Gender and Familial Roles
Chapter 12 Culture and Social Mobility
Chapter 13 Ethical Consumption
Chapter 14 Sustainable Consumption

CHAPTER 14
SUSTAINABLE CONSUMPTION

LEARNING OBJECTIVES

After reading this chapter you should be able to:

- Explain the historical perspective on how sustainable consumption has developed.
- Describe the importance of some of the principles of sustainable consumption.
- Explain the relevance of ecological modernisation to our lives in the 21st century.
- Explain the key elements of the human impact on the environment.
- Describe the approaches taken towards social sustainability.
- Provide some examples of greenwashing seen in marketing communications.
- Explain the relevance of anti-consumerism, the ecological footprint, overconsumption and simple living.
- Describe the impacts of hyperconsumption.

CHAPTER CONTENTS

Introduction

Definitions

A short look back on recent history

Principles of sustainable consumption

Consumption

Summary

Key points

How to impress your examiner

Review questions

Case study: Sea2see

Further reading

References

More online: https://study.sagepub.com/sethna5e

INTRODUCTION

Sustainable consumption is the study of resource and energy use (domestic or otherwise) and it complements analyses of production and its processes. As the term sustainability would imply, those who study sustainable consumption seek to apply the concept of 'continuance': the capacity to meet both present and future human generational needs. Thus it is about promoting resource and energy efficiency, sustainable infrastructure and providing access to basic services, green and decent jobs and a better quality of life for all. Sustainable consumption as part of sustainable development is a prerequisite in the worldwide struggle against sustainability challenges such as climate change, resource depletion, famines or environmental pollution. Its implementation helps to achieve overall development plans, reduce future economic, environmental and social costs, strengthen economic competitiveness and reduce poverty. At the current time, material consumption of natural resources is increasing (Muhammad and Khan, 2021; Schandl et al., 2018), particularly within East Asia (Abid et al., 2021). The Asia-Pacific region has now become the world's largest user of natural resources, and established systems of production and consumption have been tailored to the current high levels of resource use and emissions (Amin et al., 2022; Nakajima et al., 2018). Countries are also continuing to address challenges regarding air, water and soil pollution.

Since sustainable consumption and production aims at 'doing more and better with less', net welfare gains from economic activities can increase by reducing resource use (Ivanic and Martin, 2018; Kheirinejad et al., 2022; Shen et al., 2022), degradation and pollution along the whole life cycle, while increasing quality of life (Fuchs and Boll, 2018). There also needs to be significant focus on the operation of the entire supply chain, involving everyone from producer to final consumer. This includes educating consumers on sustainable consumption and lifestyles (Bennett and Alexandridis, 2021; Kiss et al., 2018; Uldemolins and de Magistris, 2021), providing them with adequate information through standards and labels, and engaging in sustainable public procurement (Manta et al., 2022), among others.

Should the global population reach nearly 10 billion by 2050, the equivalent of almost three planets could be required to provide the natural resources needed to sustain current lifestyles. With rises in the use of non-metallic minerals within infrastructure and construction, there has been significant improvement in the material standard of living. The per capita 'material footprint' of developing countries increased from 5 metric tons in 2000 to 9 metric tons in 2017. The material footprint is on everyone's mind as 93% of the world's 250 largest companies are now reporting on sustainability. Before we go further into particular issues, Table 14.1 highlights some facts and figures adapted from www.un.org (2022):

TABLE 14.1 Highlights of water, energy and food consumption

Water consumption	Less than 3% of the world's water is fresh (drinkable), of which 2.5% is frozen in the Antarctic, Arctic and associated glaciers. Humanity must therefore rely on 0.5% for all of its ecosystems and fresh water needs. By 2050 at least one in four people will live in a country where the lack of fresh water will be chronic or recurrent
	Humans are polluting water faster than nature can recycle and purify water in rivers and lakes
	More than 1 billion people still do not have access to fresh water and 40% of the world are affected by water scarcity
	Excessive use of water contributes to the global water stress
	Water is free from nature but the infrastructure needed to deliver it is expensive

Energy consumption	If people worldwide switched to energy-efficient lightbulbs, the world would save over 1400 million tons of CO_2 and avoid the construction of 1250 power stations
	Despite technological advances that have promoted energy efficiency gains, energy use in the global industrial sector is forecast to grow by more than 30% between 2018 and 2050 as consumption of goods increases, and by 2050, it is expected to reach around 315 quadrillion British thermal units (Btu). Commercial and residential energy use is the second most rapidly growing area of global energy use after transport
	The total global vehicle stock will increase from about 800 million in 2002 to more than 2 billion units in 2030. By this time, 56% of the world's vehicles will be owned by non-OECD countries, compared with 24% in 2002. In particular, China's vehicle stock will increase nearly 20-fold, to 390 million in 2030. This fast speed of vehicle ownership expansion implies rapid growth in oil demand
	Households consume 29% of global energy and consequently contribute to 21% of resultant CO_2 emissions
	The current global energy crisis has added new urgency to accelerate clean energy transitions and, once again, highlighted the key role of renewable energy. For renewable electricity, pre-crisis policies lead to faster growth in the UN's updated forecast. Notably, wind and solar photovoltaic systems have the potential to reduce the European Union's power sector dependence on Russia's natural gas by 2023
Food consumption	While substantial environmental impacts from food occur in the production phase (agriculture, food processing), households influence these impacts through their dietary choices and habits. This consequently affects the environment through food-related energy consumption and waste generation
	Each year, an estimated one-third of all food produced – equivalent to 1.3 billion tons worth around $1 trillion – ends up rotting in the bins of consumers and retailers, or spoiling due to poor transportation and harvesting practices
	The United States discards more food than any other country in the world: nearly 40 million tons – £80 billion every year
	Globally, 2 billion people are overweight, and of those 650 million are obese
	Land degradation, declining soil fertility, unsustainable water use, overfishing and marine environment degradation are all lessening the ability of the natural resource base to supply food
	From farm to grocery store shelf, energy and fuel are used at every step as our food moves through the supply chain, the way we grow, transport, prepare, process and package consumes around 30% of the world's available energy. Around 70% of this occurs after the farm

Source: Adapted from www.un.org.

DEFINITIONS

Sustainability is defined by the Oxford English Dictionary as avoidance of the depletion of natural resources in order to maintain an ecological balance.

The definition proposed by the 1994 Oslo Symposium on Sustainable Consumption is:

> *the use of services and related products which respond to basic needs and bring a better quality of life while minimizing the use of natural resources and toxic materials as well as emissions of waste and pollutants over the life cycle of the service or product so as not to jeopardize the needs of future generations.*

In order to achieve sustainable consumption, two developments have to take place: it requires both an increase in the efficiency of consumption as well as a change in consumption patterns and reductions in consumption levels in industrialised countries. Rich members of societies in developing countries, who have a large ecological footprint, must set the example for the increasing *middle classes* in developing countries (Meier and Lange, 2009). The first prerequisite is not sufficient on its own and can be termed weak sustainable consumption. Here, technological improvements and eco-efficiency support a necessary reduction in resource consumption. Once this aim has been met, the second development, a change in patterns and a reduction in levels of consumption, is essential. In order to achieve what can be termed strong sustainable consumption, changes in infrastructure as well as changes in the choices available to customers are required. Weak sustainable consumption has been discussed in the political arena, whereas strong sustainable consumption has been largely missing from the debate until recently (Fuchs and Boll, 2018; Green et al., 2022; Niskanen and Rohracher, 2022; Opoku et al., 2021; Willett et al., 2022).

The so-called **attitude–behaviour** or **values–action gap** describes a significant obstacle to changes in individual customer behaviour (Essiz et al., 2023). Many consumers are well aware of the importance of their consumption choices and care about environmental issues (Rahmani et al., 2021); however, most of them do not translate their concerns into their consumption patterns as the purchase decision-making process is highly complicated and relies on, for example, social, political and psychological factors. Young (2010) identified a lack of time for research, high prices, a lack of information and the cognitive effort needed as the main barriers when it came to green consumption choices. Just over 10 years on from that and we find that environmental attitudes, environmental knowledge, subjective norms, perceived behavioural control, conditional value and emotional value have a significant positive relationship with green purchase intentions (Nekmahmud et al., 2022).

Attitude–behaviour/Values–action gap
The space that occurs when the values (personal and cultural) or attitudes of an individual do not correlate with his or her actions or behaviour

BRAND EXPERIENCES: WHY BUY WHEN YOU CAN BORROW?

With an average of £500 of unworn clothes in the closets of British women and an average of 40% of clothes not being worn in closets all over Europe, it seems fairly evident that we're generally very bad shoppers. We tend to buy on impulse because something's on sale, looks good on us in the shop, or even because sales staff talk us into it.

We also tend to buy for 'one day...'; you may not have any plans to go on holiday to Morocco, but you buy an elaborate silk kaftan because maybe you'll go there one day. Or you buy a stunningly beaded gown that's appropriate for the red carpet because maybe you'll get invited to a black tie event one day.

Whether it's for a major job interview you just landed, a big date you want to impress, or a wedding you need to attend, clothing rental sites are your go-to solution for finding pricey clothes and accessories you need right now, but may not ever need again in the future.

Admittedly, there are some environmental costs to clothing rental sites: there's a lot of dry cleaning and transportation involved – but it certainly beats buying pieces for just one or two wears, then having them just sit there in your wardrobe until you discard them. In fact, there are plenty of advantages: you save money, save on wardrobe space, and in a way, you do help to save the planet, since you only rent what you need, when you need it, and allow others to 'share' the item, rather than having all interested parties buy a dress and keep it for themselves.

There are a number of service providers who have emerged recently, each with a slight differentiation.

Take Le Tote, for instance. The US-based clothing subscription service styles and curates what you receive based on your own personal needs, and you can exchange and return your stuff every month – unless you fall in love with an item, that is! In that case, you can buy it for 50% off the retail price. This is the perfect solution for people moving towns for a short time, who don't want to pack up their entire wardrobes with them. It's also great for clothing junkies who love change, but the planet, too. Brands on offer include higher end ones like House of Harlow, Kate Spade and Calvin Klein, and high street brands like Free People and FCUK.

If you want to wear Elie Saab at your best friend's wedding, Dolce & Gabbana on the beach, and Chanel to a job interview – all for around the same price that you'd pay in tax if you bought those items new, Frontrow (based in the UK) offers an array of the world's most prestigious luxury brands to rent, allowing you to feel (and look) like you're totally minted.

© Shutterstock / Cookie Studio

Style-Lend is a New York based peer-to-peer lending site which allows you to borrow or lend clothing for low prices. You can find all kinds of clothing and accessories here, and the guidelines for lenders is that their garments should be in great condition, less than 2 years old, and worth at least $250 new.

HURR Collective is an economy sharing platform (that operates similarly to Airbnb) that allows women to make money from their under-utilised wardrobes, and also rent clothes and accessories for a fraction of the retail price. Not sure what to wear? They also have complimentary personal stylists on hand to help you look your best.

(Continued)

> What if there was a way to find local clothing you can borrow – and maybe meet new people too? Darpdecade rather cheekily calls itself a *'Tinder for closets'*! Simply download the app to start swapping clothes with people near you. You'll be able to see who loves something in your virtual closet, and then the app will connect you to someone if they also have something in their wardrobe that you've got your eye on. Once the meeting is made, then you can decide to swap with that person or not. It's a great way of locating clothing you love locally and sharing with people whose taste is as good as your own. Who knows? You may even make a new friend! And the best is that it's usually 100% free, but you may need to negotiate with your swapper in case they want a damage deposit or something.
>
> Glam Corner is an Australia-based service that offers nearly 10,000 outfits you can rent. There are some great, unique features of this site: they offer a styling service, where you can consult with a stylist online, by phone or in person to know what suits you best; you can try the clothes on before you commit, and Glam Corner also makes an effort to ensure that all sizes are catered to, from tiny to curvy.
>
> If you want a bit of French girl chic in your life go online and take USA-based Armoire's quick quiz to see which clothing best suits your style and body type, and then start browsing for your perfect rental wardrobe. Armoire will have your selected pieces delivered right to your doorstep and picked up whenever you're ready to return the garments and accessories.
>
> Finally, imagine if you could go shopping in an actual store, take an outfit away, and then return it the next day? That's kind of what EKOLUV offers. This Australian clothing rental and consignment site has an actual shop in Sydney where you can try clothing on before hiring it for up to 8 days, but of course, you can also do this online. Need some extra cash? You can also sell your own high-quality (preferably eco-) designer clothing on consignment. But maybe the best part about EKOLUV is this: of all the clothing rental sites, this is definitely the most eco-friendly, thanks to their specialty in conscious-fashion brands like Yama, Kowtow, Mettle/Fairtrade and Smile. This site is so ethical, in fact, that a percentage of its profits are donated to Opportunity International Australia to help empower women.

A SHORT LOOK BACK ON RECENT HISTORY

Our Common Future (Brundtland, 1987; aka The Brundtland Report) was a report prepared for the United Nations by a World Commission on Environment and Development headed by Gro Harlem Brundtland. Interestingly, she neither coined the term sustainability nor initiated the argument that growing global human impacts on non-human environments cannot be sustained. The report, however, did proffer the notion of 'environmentally sustainable development' and triggered many subsequent meetings, global gatherings and negotiations that built on this concept. She noted that as opposed to making recommendations for national governments to merely adopt, it was decided to highlight challenges that were transnational or global in scale and that sustainability is not something that could be left for governments to sort out because it affected the future of those who currently live on our planet as well as future generations.

The Rio Earth Summit, which took place in 1992, set out the Agenda 21 proposals, which many nations adopted. Following Rio, the stage was set for the Global Convention on Biological Diversity and various other agreements on helping to protect endangered wetlands and establish rules to prevent the degradation of marine environments.

An international protocol for reducing emissions of greenhouse gases was a task for the meeting in Kyoto in 1997. However, to try to phase out the use of fossil fuels is much harder than to replace the use of the gases that thin the ozone layer. The meeting in Copenhagen in 2009 was disappointing as governments continued to prioritise short-term national economic interests, until the Paris Summit in 2015, when things started to change and to once again gain pace.

Here we should have a look at the model from which the psychologist John Elkington (1994) first developed the notion of environmentally sustainable development by introducing the 'triple bottom line' (see Figure 14.1).

The need to balance competing policy and practice agendas in the present is very much highlighted here by Elkington. The greater challenge emanating out of this is to think beyond the short-term political or policy cycles (as some governments have been doing) or even lifetimes (as some generations have been doing!) and think about the legacy we are creating for the younger generation. Mulligan (2018) calls this 'intergenerational equity'. This is not the first time this concept has been used. The Incas of Peru, who are undoubtedly one of the most admired of the South American civilisations, also believed in intergenerational equity. They felt that any societal decision should be taken with three perspectives in mind:

1. How will this affect us, here and now?
2. How will our decision affect future, yet unborn, generations?
3. How would our departed loved ones have reacted to the decisions we are about to take?

It is an interesting way to view decision-making, especially in the context of sustainable consumption.

Following on from the triple bottom line, it's worth taking a brief look at other models that are in existence currently. Figure 14.2 shows 'the nested diagram' model. The main thrust of the argument presented by Giddings et al. (2002) is that as soon as the economy, society and the environment are separated from each other, this is where the problems arise. This is why they have preferred a 'nested' version of the diagram on sustainability.

But of course, when one refers to the very broad domain of 'social' it is hard to know what is included and what is not... thus, Hawkes (2001) argued that the cultural expression that humans portray as their sense of personal and social wealth is a vitally important 'pillar' to be able to build on, and thus proffered his 'fourth pillar' model (see Figure 14.3).

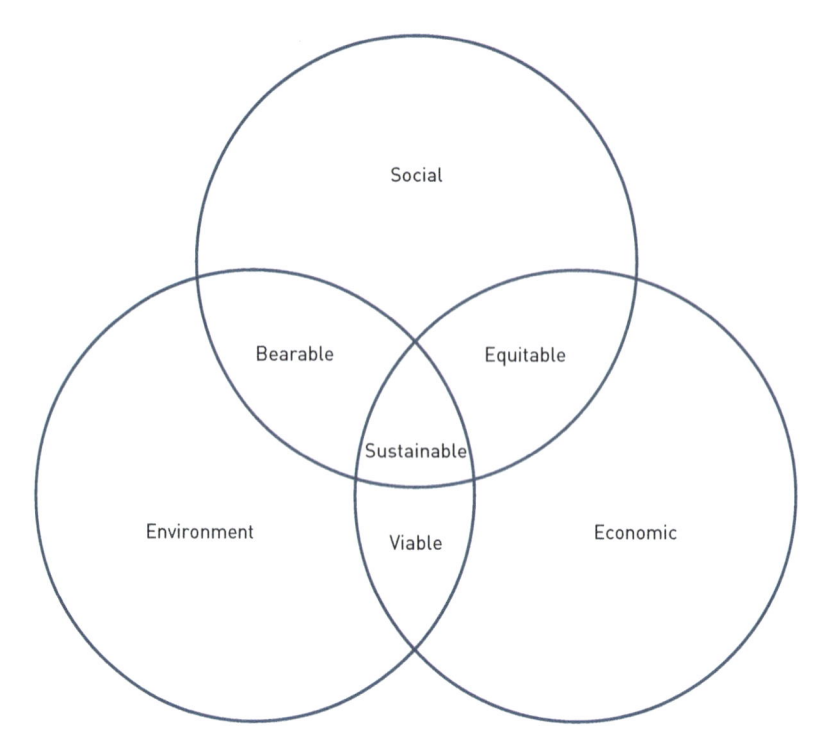

FIGURE 14.1 The 'triple bottom line' represented as three overlapping sectors

Source: Elkington (1994).

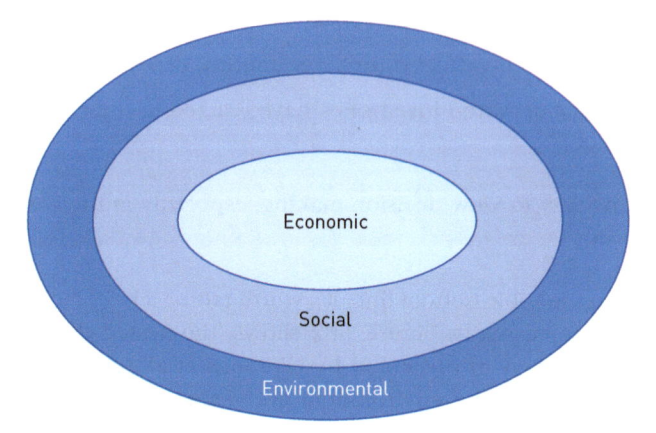

FIGURE 14.2 Nested diagram of sustainability

Source: Adapted from Giddings et al. (2002).

PRINCIPLES OF SUSTAINABLE CONSUMPTION

Arguably, there are a number of principles that form many more pillars of sustainable consumption. Here we take a brief look at some of them and leave the reader to make conclusions about the applicability of each to their consumer lives.

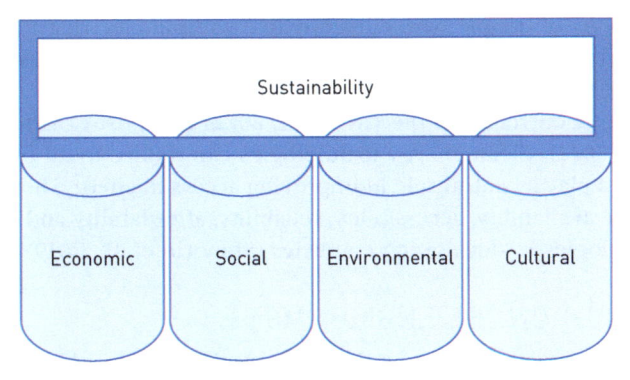

FIGURE 14.3 The fourth pillar of sustainability

Source: Representation of the work of Jon Hawkes (2001).

EARTH SYSTEM GOVERNANCE

Earth system governance is a recently developed paradigm that builds on earlier notions of environmental policy and nature conservation, but puts these into the broader context of human-induced transformations of the entire Earth system (Hofmann, 2022). It conceptualises the system of formal and informal rules, rule-making mechanisms and actor-networks at all levels of human society (from local to global) (and now artificial intelligence systems too [Bolton et al., 2021]) that are set up to steer societies towards preventing, mitigating and adapting to global and local environmental change and Earth system transformation, within the normative context of sustainable development.

ECOLOGICAL MODERNISATION

Ecological modernisation is a school of thought in the social sciences that argues that the economy benefits from moves towards environmentalism (Teelucksingh, 2018). It has gained increasing attention among scholars and policy-makers internationally (Leipold, 2021) in the last several decades. It is an analytical approach as well as a policy strategy and environmental discourse (Hajer, 1995). One basic assumption of ecological modernisation relates to environmental readaptation of economic growth and industrial development (Isik et al., 2018; Watts, 2018). On the basis of enlightened self-interest, economy and ecology (Sovacool et al., 2018) can be favourably combined: environmental productivity (Li and Zhang, 2018), that is, productive use of natural resources and environmental media (air, water, soil, ecosystems), can be a source of future growth and development in the same way as labour productivity (Lea, 2018) and capital productivity (Mamoon, 2018). This includes increases in energy and resource efficiency as well as product and process innovations such as environmental management and sustainable supply chain management (Huang and Huang, 2022; Taylor and Vachon, 2018), clean technologies (Kumar et al., 2022; Somorin et al., 2019), benign substitution of hazardous substances, and product design with the environment in mind (Al-Hamadani et al., 2021; Hassenzahl, 2018; Sroufe et al., 2000). On the point about clean technologies, it is worth noting that developing countries are faced with numerous energy challenges including the dilemma of increasing energy services to billions of people who currently live without electricity, and the need to operate low-carbon, intensive energy systems for environmental sustainability. This said, all over the world countries are battling with energy crises (Siksnelyte-Butkiene, 2022), for example currently in the UK (Wolf, 2022) in a post-Covid-19 environment (Heffron et al., 2021). Clean energy technologies can reduce fossil fuel dependency, provide jobs and play a central role in improving access to energy; however, there are questions on the availability, accessibility, reliability, affordability and appropriateness of these technologies in developing countries (Somorin et al., 2019).

HUMAN IMPACT ON THE ENVIRONMENT

Human, or anthropogenic, impact on the environment includes changes to biophysical environments and ecosystems (Slocombe, 1993), biodiversity and natural resources (Kellert et al., 2000; Taketani et al., 2022) caused directly or indirectly by humans, including global warming (Salawitch et al., 2018), environmental degradation (Kutz, 2018) (such as ocean acidification), mass extinction and biodiversity loss, ecological crises and ecological collapse (Richards, 2022). Modifying the environment to fit the needs of society is causing severe effects, which has deteriorated as the problem of human overpopulation continues (Cafaro et al., 2022). There has been some talk recently that human overpopulation may well be a contributor to epidemics and pandemics (Spernovasilis et al., 2021). As we've alluded to earlier in the chapter, some human activities that cause damage (either directly or indirectly) to the environment on a global scale include human reproduction (Goudie, 2018; Qu et al., 2022), overconsumption, overexploitation, pollution and deforestation, to name but a few. Some of the problems, including global warming and biodiversity loss, pose an existential risk to the human race, and overpopulation causes those problems. Sir David Attenborough, in a speech called 'People and Planet' at the Royal Society of Arts in 2011, described the level of human population on the planet as a multiplier of all other environmental problems. In 2013, he described humanity as 'a plague on the Earth' that needs to be controlled by limiting population growth (The Telegraph, 2013).

For nearly three decades the UN has been bringing together almost every country on Earth for global climate summits – called COPs, which stands for 'Conference of the Parties'. In that time climate change has gone from being a fringe issue to a global priority. 2021 was the 26th annual summit – giving it the name COP26. With the UK as President, COP26 took place in Glasgow. In the run up to COP26 the UK worked with every nation to reach agreement on how to tackle climate change. World leaders arrived in Scotland, alongside tens of thousands of negotiators, government representatives, businesses and citizens for 12 days of talks. Not only was it a huge task, but it was also not just yet another international summit, with most experts believing that COP26 had a unique urgency.

To understand why, it's necessary to look back to another COP.

For the first time ever, something momentous happened: every country agreed to work together to limit global warming to well below 2 degrees and aim for 1.5 degrees, to adapt to the impacts of a changing climate and to make money available to deliver on these aims. The Paris Agreement was born. The commitment to aim for 1.5 degrees is important because every fraction of a degree of warming will result in the loss of many more lives and livelihoods damaged. Under the Paris Agreement, countries committed to bring forward national plans setting out how much they would reduce their emissions – known as Nationally Determined Contributions, or 'NDCs'. They agreed that every five years they would come back with an updated plan that would reflect their highest possible ambition at that time.

CRITICAL REFLECTION

The veteran naturalist and filmmaker Sir David Attenborough told world leaders at the COP26 climate summit to 'rewrite our story', and that future generations would judge them for their success or failure at the conference, which took place over two weeks in Glasgow, Scotland.

Speaking to an audience of delegates that included US President Joe Biden, Canadian Prime Minister Justin Trudeau and German Chancellor Angela Merkel, Attenborough said the climate emergency 'comes down to a single number: the concentration of carbon in our atmosphere'.

Accompanied by footage showing the atmospheric concentration of carbon dioxide at its current level of 414 parts per million, Attenborough pointed out that CO_2 'greatly determines global temperature ... and the changes in that one number is the clearest way to chart our own story'.

'We need to rewrite our story to turn this tragedy into a triumph', he continued. 'We are after all the greatest problem-solvers to have ever existed on earth. We now understand this problem. We know how to stop the number rising and put it in reverse. We must halt carbon emissions this decade.'

Attenborough, who strode to the stage with a purpose that belied his 95 years, delivered his speech along with a film that illustrated 300,000 years of atmospheric carbon dioxide levels, along with accompanying increases and decreases in average global temperatures. Also shown were climate activists from around the world, with messages of concern and hope.

The broadcaster emphasised the fact that, little more than 10,000 years before the present day, the Earth's climate stabilised, allowing human civilisation to flourish.

'Everything we've achieved in the last 10,000 years was enabled by the stability during this time', he said, showing that the climate had not wavered by more than plus or minus one degree Celsius over the period.

But now, Attenborough stressed, conditions are changing rapidly thanks to human activity.

'Our burning of fossil fuels, our destruction of nature, our approach to industry, construction and learning are releasing carbon into the atmosphere at an unprecedented pace and scale', he said. 'We are already in trouble. The stability we all depend on is breaking.'

He went on to say: 'those who've done the least to cause this problem are being the hardest hit', pointing out that the poorest countries that have released the least CO_2 into the atmosphere are those bearing the brunt of extreme weather events made more severe by climate change.

(Continued)

> Attenborough concluded, however, with an upbeat message. 'We must use this opportunity to create a more equal world, and our motivation should not be fear, but hope', he said. To avert further instability, the international community must focus on keeping temperature change within 1.5 degrees Celsius this century, as prescribed by the UN's Intergovernmental Panel on Climate Change. To achieve that would require 'a new industrial revolution, powered by millions of sustainable innovations'.
>
> 'It comes down to this', he said. 'The people alive now [and] the generation to come will look at this conference and consider one thing: did that number [atmospheric CO_2 concentration] stop rising and start to drop as a result of commitments made here? There's every reason to believe that the answer can be yes.'
>
> *Source*: Adapted from Vetter (2021). For more data and insights see forbes.com.

Some deep ecologists, such as the radical thinker and polemicist Pentti Linkola, see human overpopulation as a threat to the entire biosphere (Kearney, 2022; van Pelt, 2018). In 2017, over 15,000 scientists around the world issued a second warning to humanity which asserted that rapid human population growth is the 'primary driver behind many ecological and even societal threats' (Independent, 2017). The years 2023–50 are crucial for the natural world: a new international agreement will be agreed to combat global biodiversity loss. The post-2020 Global Biodiversity Framework is intended to ensure that by 2050, humans are living in harmony with nature. The UN has also called for greater funding for nature conservation.

SOCIAL SUSTAINABILITY

Social life is the least defined and least understood of the different ways of approaching sustainability and sustainable development. Social sustainability has had considerably less attention in public dialogue than economic and environmental sustainability.

There are several approaches to sustainability. The first, which posits a triad of environmental sustainability, economic sustainability and social sustainability (as seen in Figure 14.1), is the most widely accepted as a model for addressing sustainability. The concept of 'social sustainability' in this approach encompasses such topics as social equity (Hamilton et al., 2018), livability (Beggs, 2018), health equity (Parkinson, 2018; Patenaude et al., 2022), community development (Pratt, 2021; Tolbert and Schindel, 2018), social capital (Adams, 2018; Giovannetti et al., 2021), social support (Erman, 2019; Parahiyanti and Nurmalita, 2022), human rights (Fabre, 2018; Nunes, 2022), labour or workers' rights (Wilson et al., 2018), placemaking (Sepulveda, 2018), social responsibility (Malecki, 2018; Turker, 2018), social justice (Morrissey and Walker, 2018), cultural competence (Alviar-Martin, 2018), community resilience (Aguiñaga et al., 2018) and human adaptation (Fox, 2018), especially after the Covid-19 pandemic (Frey et al., 2021).

A second, more recent, approach suggests that all of the domains of sustainability are social, including ecological, economic, political and cultural sustainability. These domains of social sustainability are all dependent upon the relationship between the social and the natural, with the 'ecological domain' defined as human embeddedness in the environment and the built environment (Soust-Verdaguer et al., 2022). In these terms, social sustainability encompasses all human activities. It is not just relevant to the focused intersection of economics, the environment and the social.

ENVIRONMENTALISM

Environmentalism, or environmental rights (see Carter [2018] for recent information on ideas, activism and policy), is a broad philosophy, ideology and social movement regarding concerns for environmental protection and improvement of the health of the environment, particularly as the measure for this health seeks to incorporate the impact of changes to the environment on humans, animals, plants and non-living matter (Guim and Livermore, 2021). While environmentalism focuses more on the environmental and nature-related aspects of green ideology and politics, ecologism combines the ideology of social ecology and environmentalism. 'Ecologism' is more commonly used in continental European languages, while 'environmentalism' is more commonly used in English but the words have slightly different connotations.

Environmentalism advocates the preservation, restoration and/or improvement of the natural environment, and may be referred to as a movement to control pollution or protect plant and animal diversity. For this reason, concepts such as a land ethics, environmental ethics, biodiversity, ecology and the biophilia hypothesis figure predominantly.

At its crux, environmentalism is an attempt to balance relations between humans and the various natural systems on which they depend, in such a way that all the components are accorded a proper degree of sustainability. The exact measures and outcomes of this balance are controversial and there are many different ways for environmental concerns to be expressed in practice. Environmentalism and environmental concerns are often represented by the colour green, but this association has been appropriated by the marketing industries for the tactic known as greenwashing.

Greenwashing
A compound word modelled on 'whitewash'; also called 'green sheen', greenwashing is a form of spin in which green PR or green marketing is deceptively used to promote the perception that an organisation's products, aims or policies are environmentally friendly

GREENWASHING

There are many definitions of 'greenwashing' that exist (see Table 14.2). Research shows that significant deception and misleading claims exist both in the regulated commercial sphere, as well as in the unregulated non-commercial sphere (e.g. governments, NGO partnerships, international pledges, etc.). Recently, serious concerns have been raised over rampant greenwashing, in particular with regard to rapidly emerging net zero commitments (Nemes et al., 2022).

TABLE 14.2 Definitions of greenwashing

Definition	Source
'The act of disseminating disinformation to consumers regarding the environmental practices of a company or the environmental benefits of a product or service'	Baum, L.M. (2012) It's not easy being green or is it? A content analysis of environmental claims in magazine advertisements from the United States and United Kingdom. *Environ. Commun.*, 6: 423–40.
'Greenwashing refers to the practice of falsely promoting an organisation's environmental efforts or spending more resources to promote the organisation as green than are spent to actually engage in environmentally sound practices. Thus, greenwashing is the dissemination of false or deceptive information regarding an organisation's environmental strategies, goals, motivations, and actions'	Becker-Olsen, K. and Potucek, S. (2013) Greenwashing. In S.O. Idowu, N. Capaldi, L. Zu and A. Das Gupta (eds), *Encyclopedia of Corporate Social Responsibility*. Berlin/Heidelberg: Springer. pp 1318–23.
'Disinformation disseminated by an organisation so as to present an environmentally responsible public image'	Oxford English Dictionary (2003) *Concise Oxford English Dictionary*, 10th edn, J. Pearsall (ed.). Oxford: Oxford University Press.
'Greenwashing is when a company or organisation spends more time and money on marketing themselves as environmentally friendly than on minimizing their environmental impact. It is a deceitful advertising gimmick intended to mislead consumers who prefer to buy goods and services from environmentally conscious brands'	Corcione, A. (2020) What is greenwashing? *Business News Daily*. www.businessnewsdaily.com/10946-greenwashing.html (accessed 17 February 2022).
'(1) The phenomenon of socially and environmentally destructive corporations attempting to preserve and expand their markets by posing as friends of the environment and leaders in the struggle to eradicate poverty. (2) Environmental whitewash. (3) Any attempt to brainwash consumers or policy makers into believing polluting mega-corporations are the key to environmentally sound sustainable development (4) Hogwash'	CorpWatch (2001) *Greenwash Fact Sheet*. www.corpwatch.org/article/greenwash-fact-sheet (accessed 17 February 2022).
'greenwashing is taken to mean two main things. It can be when companies – usually mega corporations and sometimes politicians – try to hide or cover up their less-than-stellar environmental records with a grand, public gesture towards green causes; the other type of greenwashing is where companies and brands use words like "green", "sustainable", "eco-friendly", or "vegan" simply as a marketing ploy, without any deep interrogation over what those terms actually mean. And crucially – without any accountability for their actions'	De Ferrer, M. (2020) What is greenwashing and why is it a problem? *Euronews*. www.euronews.com/green/2020/09/09/what-is-greenwashing-and-why-is-it-a-problem (accessed 17 February 2022).
The authors note two different major classifications of greenwashing, including 'product/service level claim greenwashing, which uses textual arguments that explicitly or implicitly refer to the ecological benefits of a product or service to create a misleading environmental claim' while 'executional greenwashing suggests nature-evoking elements such as images using colors (e.g., green, blue) or sounds (e.g., sea, birds). Backgrounds representing natural landscapes (e.g., mountains, forests, oceans), or pictures of endangered animal species (e.g., pandas, dolphins) or renewable sources of energy (e.g., wind, waterfalls) are examples of executional nature-evoking elements'	De Freitas Netto, S.V., Facao Sobrāl, M.F., Bezerra Riberio, A.R. and da Luz Soares, G.R. (2020) Concepts and forms of greenwashing: A systematic review. *Environ. Sci. Eur.*, 32: 19.
'the act of misleading consumers regarding the environmental practices of organisations (firm-level greenwashing) or the environmental benefits of a product or service (product-level greenwashing)'	Delmas, A.M. and Burbano, V.C. (2011) The drivers of greenwashing. *Calif. Manag. Rev.*, 54: 64–87.

Definition	Source
'Greenwashing is the process by which organisations spread misleading perceptions about their products or services that suggest they are more environmentally responsible than is the reality. The practice of greenwashing is used regularly by corporations, governments, and other entities to deceive the public into believing that they are doing more for the environment than they truly are in order to gain better public perception'	Ecolife (n.d.) What is greenwashing? *Ecolife Dictionary*. www.ecolife.com/define/greenwashing.html (accessed 17 February 2022).
'Greenwashing is used to describe the practice of companies launching adverts, campaigns, products, etc. under the pretence that they are environmentally beneficial, often in contradiction to their environmental and sustainability record in general'	Ethical Consumer (2020) What is greenwashing. www.ethicalconsumer.org/transport-travel/what-greenwashing (accessed 17 February 2022).
'The expressions "environmental claims" and "green claims" refer to the practice of suggesting or otherwise creating the impression (in a commercial communication, marketing or advertising) that a good or a service has a positive or no impact on the environment or is less damaging to the environment than competing goods or services. This may be due to its composition, how it has been manufactured or produced, how it can be disposed of and the reduction in energy or pollution expected from its use. When such claims are not true or cannot be verified, this practice is often called "greenwashing". "Greenwashing" can relate to all forms of business-to-consumer commercial practices concerning the environmental attributes of goods or services. According to the circumstances, this can include all types of statements, information, symbols, logos, graphics and brand names, and their interplay with colours, on packaging, labelling, advertising, in all media (including websites) and made by any organisation, if it qualifies as a "trader" and engages in commercial practices towards consumers'	European Commission (2016) *Guidance on the Implementation/Application of Directive 2005/29/EC Unfair Commercial Practices. SWD (2016) 163 Final*. https://eur-lex.europa.eu/legal-content/EN/TXT/PDF/?uri=CELEX:52016SC0163&from=FR (accessed 17 February 2022).
'Greenwashing is the process of conveying a false impression or providing misleading information about how a company's products are more environmentally sound. Greenwashing is considered an unsubstantiated claim to deceive consumers into believing that a company's products are environmentally friendly'	Kenton, W. (2021) Greenwashing. *Investopedia*. www.investopedia.com/terms/g/greenwashing.asp (accessed 17 February 2022).
'greenwash can be characterized as the selective disclosure of positive information about a company's environmental or social performance, while withholding negative information on these dimensions'	Lyon, T.P. and Maxwell, J.W. (2011) Greenwash: Corporate environmental disclosure under threat of audit. *J. Econ. Manag. Strategy, 20*: 3–41.
'the word greenwash is used to cover any communication that misleads people into adopting overly positive beliefs about an organisation's environmental performance, practices, or products; the important phenomenon of misleading environmental communication'	Lyon, T.P. and Montgomery, A.W. (2015) The means and end of greenwash. *Organ. Environ., 28*: 223–49.
'Greenwashing is the practice of promoting environmentally friendly programs to deflect attention from an organisation's environmentally unfriendly or less savoury activities'	Marquis, C. and Toffel, M.W. (2011) *The Globalization of Corporate Environmental Disclosure: Accountability or Greenwashing?* Cambridge, MA: Harvard School of Business. HBS Working Paper Number: 11–115.
Focus on 'executional greenwashing whereby nature-evoking elements in the ad execution may induce false perceptions of a brand's greenness, whether intentionally or not on the part of the advertiser'	Parguel, B., Benoit-Moreau, F. and Russell, C.A. (2015) Can evoking nature in advertising mislead consumers? The power of 'executional greenwashing'. *Int. J. Advert., 34*: 107–34.

(Continued)

TABLE 14.2 (Continued)

'Greenwashing is the unjustified appropriation of environmental virtue by a company, an industry, a government, a politician or even a non-government organisation to create a pro-environmental image, sell a product or a policy, or to try and rehabilitate their standing with the public and decision makers after being embroiled in controversy'	Sourcewatch (n.d.) Greenwashing. The Center for Media and Democracy. www.sourcewatch.org/index.php/Greenwashing (accessed 17 February 2022).
'The act of misleading consumers regarding the environmental practices of a company or the environmental benefits of a product or service'	Sustainable Furnishings Council (n.d.) Glossary. https://sustainablefurnishings.org/glossary (accessed 17 February 2022).
'Communication that misleads people (e.g., consumers and stakeholders) regarding environmental performance/benefits by disclosing negative information and disseminating positive information about an organisation, service, or product'	Tateishi, E. (2018) Craving gains and claiming 'green' by cutting greens? An exploratory analysis of greenfield housing developments in Iskandar Malaysia. *J. Urban Aff.*, *40*: 370–93.

Source: Adapted from Nemes et al. (2022).

Back in the mid-1980s, Chevron (an oil company) commissioned advertising to convince its public of its supposed exemplary environmental credentials. The campaign, titled 'People Do', showed Chevron employees protecting bears, butterflies, sea turtles and all manner of cute and cuddly animals. These were fantastically effective commercials and in 1990 they won an Effie Advertising Award, with the result that they also found their way into becoming a Harvard Business School case study. Amongst environmentalists, however, these advertisements became notorious for being the *gold standard* of greenwashing: the corporate practice of making diverting sustainability claims to cover up a questionable environmental record.

Jay Westerveld first noted the term greenwashing in 1986. These were the days when most (if not all) consumers received their news from television, radio and print media. These were the same channels that organisations regularly flooded with a wave of high-priced, slickly produced commercials and print ads. So the combination of limited public access to information and seemingly unlimited advertising enabled companies to present themselves as caring environmental stewards, even as they were engaging in environmentally unsustainable practices.

Chevron had quite a murky environmental record, which the 'People Do' campaign ignored. At the same time as the adverts were running on a plethora of media outlets, the company was also violating the Clean Air Act, the Clean Water Act and spilling oil into wildlife refuges. Of course Chevron was not the only company digging deep into the greenwashing basket of *suitable clothes*. At around the same time, DuPont (a chemical company) announced its new double-hulled oil tankers with ads featuring marine animals clapping their flippers and wings in chorus to Beethoven's 'Ode to Joy'. Friends of the Earth were quick to point out in their report 'Hold the Applause' that DuPont was the single largest corporate polluter in the USA. Other examples of corporate claims include Weyerhaeuser (a giant in the forestry sector). The company commissioned adverts claiming that it was '*serious*' about caring for fish, even as it was cutting down trees in some of its forests and destabilising salmon habitats!

Since then, consumers have become very aware of global sustainability concerns. This interest in the environment has also triggered an increased awareness of the greenwashing at play. Not surprisingly, the sustainability imperative has been driven primarily by the consumer. A few forward-thinking retailers such as Patagonia and Levi's have been pioneers in this field and should get the credit they deserve for giving conscious consumerism a bigger platform. Yet it's the consumer – specifically the Gen Z consumer – that has elevated the sustainability conversation. A recent study found that the Gen Z consumer has an outsized influence on not only their Gen X parents but even their Boomer grandparents when it comes to sustainable shopping (Petro, 2022). Over the past two years, Gen X consumers' preference to shop for sustainable brands increased by nearly 25% and their willingness to pay more for sustainable products increased by 42%. In fact, consumers across all generations – from Baby Boomers to Gen Z – are now willing to spend more for sustainable products. Just two years ago, only 58% of consumers across all generations were willing to spend more for sustainable options. Today, nearly 90% of Gen X consumers said that they would be willing to spend an extra 10% or more for sustainable products, compared to just over 34% two years ago.

Engaging customers in their sustainability efforts is top of the list for many companies – even as their core business model remains environmentally unsustainable. The Home Depot (an American home improvement supplies retailer) and Lowes (a hardware store), for example, both encourage customers to do their part by offering onsite recycling for several products, including compact fluorescent lights and plastic bags. Meanwhile, they continue to sell billions of dollars worth of environmentally damaging products per year, such as paints that are loaded with toxic ingredients and which release noxious fumes, and taun flooring which, in its production, causes devastation to indigenous land in Papua New Guinea (Global Witness, 2017).

Finally, for fans of greenwashing exposé, we now have a Greenwashing Index Score. There are five criteria upon which the score is based. When you rate an ad with the Greenwashing Index, it will generate a score based on your response to a set of statements (see Table 14.3). Your score will be included in the ad's overall score, and your comments will be added to the tally. Scoring is similar to golf: high scores are undesirable (for the advertiser).

TABLE 14.3 The Greenwashing Index Scoring Criteria

1	The ad misleads with words	Do you believe the ad misleads the viewer/reader about the company's/product's environmental impact through the things it says? Does it seem the words are trying to make you believe there is a green practice when there isn't? Focus on the words only – what do you think the ad is saying?
2	The ad misleads with visuals and/or graphics	Do you think the advertiser has used green or natural images in a way designed to make you think the product/company is more environmentally friendly than it really is?
3	The ad makes a green claim that is vague or seemingly unprovable	Does the ad claim environmental benefits without sufficiently identifying for you what they are? Has the advertiser provided a source for claims or for more information? Are the claims related to the company/product?
4	The ad overstates or exaggerates how green the product/company/service actually is	Do you believe the advertiser is overstating how green the product/company actually is? Are the green claims made by the ad believable? Do you think it's possible for the product/company to do the things depicted/stated?
5	The ad leaves out or masks important information, making the green claim sound better than it is	Do you think the ad exists to divert attention from something else the company does? Do you believe the relevant collateral consequences of the product/service are considered in the ad? Does it seem to you something is missing from the ad?

Source: Adapted from www.greenwashingindex.com (2018).

CONSUMPTION

Under the banner of consumption, we once again see a number of cornerstones that the reader needs to be aware of, so that a considered analysis of their applicability to sustainable consumption can take place based on the context of a given situation.

ANTI-CONSUMERISM

Let's start with anti-consumerism, which is a socio-political ideology that is opposed to consumerism, the continual buying and consuming of material possessions (Lekakis, 2021). Anti-consumerism is concerned with the private actions of business corporations in pursuit of financial and economic goals at the expense of the public welfare, especially in matters of environmental protection, social stratification and ethics in the governing of a society. In politics, anti-consumerism overlaps with environmental activism, anti-globalisation and animal rights activism; moreover, a conceptual variation of anti-consumerism is post-consumerism, living in a material way that transcends consumerism. Faria and Hemais (2018) have historicised this well.

Anti-consumerism arose in response to the problems caused by the long-term mistreatment of human consumers and of the animals consumed, and from the incorporation of consumer education into school curricula. Examples of anti-consumerism are the book *No Logo* (2000) by Naomi Klein, and documentary films such as *The Corporation* (2003) by Mark Achbar and Jennifer Abbott, and *Surplus: Terrorized into Being Consumers* (2003) by Erik Gandini; each made anti-corporate activism popular as an ideologically accessible form of civil and political action.

ECOLOGICAL FOOTPRINT

The ecological footprint measures human demand on nature, that is the quantity of nature it takes to support people or an economy. It tracks and regulates (Ahmed et al., 2022) this demand through an ecological accounting system. The accounts contrast the biologically productive area people use for their consumption to the biologically productive area available within a region or the world (biocapacity – the productive area that can regenerate what people demand from nature). In short, it is a measure of human impact on Earth's ecosystem and reveals the dependence of the human economy on natural capital. The ecological footprint is defined as the biologically productive area needed to provide for everything people use: fruits and vegetables, fish, wood, fibres, absorption of carbon dioxide from fossil fuel use, and space for buildings and roads.

Footprint and biocapacity can be compared on an individual, a regional, a national or a global scale. Both footprint and biocapacity change every year with number of people, per person consumption, efficiency of production and productivity of ecosystems. On a global scale, footprint assessments show how big humanity's demand is compared to what planet Earth can renew. Global Footprint Network calculates the ecological footprint from UN and other data for the world as a whole and for over 200 nations. They estimate that as of 2013, humanity has been using natural capital 1.6 times as fast as nature can renew it.

OVERCONSUMPTION

Overconsumption is a situation where resource use has outpaced the sustainable capacity of the ecosystem. A prolonged pattern of overconsumption leads to environmental degradation and the eventual loss of resource bases. Generally, the discussion of overconsumption parallels that of human overpopulation; that is, the more people, the more consumption of raw materials takes place to sustain their lives. But humanity's overall impact on the planet is affected by many factors besides the raw number of people. Their lifestyle (including overall affluence and resource utilisation) and the pollution they generate (including carbon footprint) are equally important. The developing world is a growing market of consumption. These nations are quickly gaining more purchasing power and it is expected that the Global South, which includes cities in Asia, Latin America and Africa, will account for 56% of consumption growth by 2030 (McKinsey, 2016). This means that consumption rates will plateau for the developed nations and shift more into these developing countries.

SIMPLE LIVING

Simple living encompasses a number of different voluntary practices to simplify one's lifestyle (Kraisornsuthasinee and Swierczek, 2018; Read et al., 2018). These may include, for example, reducing one's possessions, generally referred to as minimalism, or increasing self-sufficiency. Simple living may be characterised by individuals being satisfied with what they have rather than want (Freud, 2018). Although asceticism generally promotes living simply and refraining from luxury and indulgence, not all proponents of simple living are ascetics. Simple living is distinct from those living in forced poverty, as it is a voluntary lifestyle choice.

Adherents may choose simple living for a variety of personal reasons, such as spirituality, health, increase in quality time for family and friends, work–life balance, personal taste, financial sustainability, frugality, or reducing stress. Simple living can also be a reaction to materialism and conspicuous consumption. Some cite socio-political goals aligned with the environmentalist, anti-consumerist or anti-war movements, including conservation, degrowth, social justice and tax resistance.

HYPERCONSUMPTION

Having looked at simple living, it is only right to go to the other end of the spectrum with hyperconsumption. This refers to the consumption of goods for non-functional purposes and the associated significant pressure to consume those goods exerted by the modern, capitalist society, as those goods shape one's identity (Cyr and Jagos, 2019; Kazim, 2018). Lunning (2010) defines it curtly as *'a consumerism for the sake of consuming'*. Hyperconsumerism is fuelled by brands (Bosco, 2014), as people often form deep attachment to product brands, which affects people's identity, and which pressure people to buy and consume their goods. Another of the characteristics of hyperconsumerism is the constant pursuit of novelty, encouraging consumers to buy new and discard the old, seen particularly in fashion, where the product life cycle can be very short, measured sometimes in weeks only. In hyperconsumerism, goods are often status symbols, as individuals buy them not so much to use them as to display them to others, sending associated meanings (such as displaying wealth).

However, the need to consume in hyperconsumption society is driven less by competition with others than by their own hedonistic pleasure (see Chapter 5). Finally here, hyperconsumerism has also been said to have religious characteristics (Lyon, 2013), and to have been compared to a new religion that enshrines consumerism above all, with elements of religious life being replaced by consumerist life: (going to) churches replaced by (going to) shopping malls, saints replaced by celebrities, penance replaced by shopping sprees, desire for better life after death replaced by desire for better life in the present, and so on (Sayers, 2008). Sayers notes that hyperconsumerism has commercialised many religious symbols, giving an example of religious symbols worn as jewellery by non-believers.

SUSTAINABILITY MARKETING MYOPIA

Sustainability marketing myopia is a term used in sustainability marketing referring to a distortion stemming from the overlooking of socio-environmental attributes of a sustainable product or service at the expense of customer benefits and values. The idea of sustainability marketing myopia is rooted in conventional marketing myopia theory, as well as green marketing myopia.

The marketing myopia theory was originally proposed in 1960 by American economist Theodore Levitt. According to Levitt, marketers should not overlook the importance of company potential and product attributes at the expense of market needs; catering for market needs should receive first priority. A company, besides being technically sound and product-oriented, also needs to be customer-oriented in order to successfully cater for a market. Knowledge of customer needs and of innovations that can be implemented to maintain customer interest, as well as of how to adapt to the changing business market, is crucial. Marketing myopia has been highly influential in the formation of modern marketing theory, and was heeded by marketers to such an extent that some authors now speak of a 'new marketing myopia' stemming from too narrow a focus on the customer to the exclusion of other stakeholders.

Green marketing is the marketing of products that are presumed to be environmentally safe. In order to be successful, green marketing must fulfil two objectives: improved environmental quality and customer satisfaction. Misjudging either or overemphasising the former at the expense of the latter can be defined as green marketing myopia (or greenwashing, as we saw earlier). The marketing discipline has long argued that innovation must consider an intimate understanding of the customer, and a close look at green marketing practices over time reveals that green products must be positioned on a consumer value sought by targeted consumers. As such, successful green products are able to appeal to mainstream consumers or lucrative market niches and frequently command price premiums by offering 'non-green' consumer value (such as convenience and performance). When consumers are convinced of the desirable 'non-green' benefits of environmental products, they are more inclined to adopt them.

Sustainability marketing (Lloveras et al., 2022) aims at marketing sustainable products and services that 'satisfy customer needs and significantly improve the social and environmental performance along the whole life cycle', while increasing customer value and achieving the company's objectives. In turn, sustainability marketing myopia is an exaggerated focus on the socio-ecological attributes of the product over the core consumer values, a distortion of the marketing process which is likely to lead to the product failing on the market or remaining confined in a small alternative niche. Just as an excessive focus on product attributes generates marketing myopia, and just as a single-minded focus on customers results in 'new marketing myopia', in both green and sustainability marketing an unbalanced strategy neglecting one aspect (namely, product attributes) is detrimental to the effectiveness of the marketing process. However, it is important to note that sustainability marketing myopia differs from green marketing myopia in that the former follows a broader approach to the marketing myopia issue, taking into account the social attributes of a product as well as the environmental ones. At the same time, sustainability marketing myopia encompasses sustainable services and product-related services, not products alone.

CONSUMER BEHAVIOUR IN ACTION: HYDROPONICS AND AQUAPONICS

As traditional agriculture comes under scrutiny due to its recounted adverse effects on the environment – depletion of natural resources, contamination of water sources, misuse of synthetic chemical inputs – and usable land for crops declines, growers are continuously looking for alternative and safer ways to grow plants while using less space. This has led to an explosive surge in soilless production systems within both small growers and large-scale commercial productions. At the forefront of soilless systems are hydroponics and aquaponics, both providing growers with many significant benefits to growing plants while minimising potentially dangerous environmental effects.

Hydroponics is a method of growing plants, without soil, that has been utilised for thousands of years. At first, it may seem contradictory to grow plants without any soil, but hydroponics is an intricate system that works better than the traditional method of growing plants in soil. For plants to flourish they need two things: a set of plant essential nutrients and water. Due to this, if the nutrients are provided within the water and delivered to the roots, there isn't any need to have soil present in the growing system. In a hydroponic growing system, a nutrient-charged, aquatic solution is flushed through the root zone to provide the plants with the resources needed for optimal growth. There are many benefits to using hydroponic grow systems: fewer resources are consumed, arable land isn't needed, and the harvestable plants are of higher quality than when grown using traditional methods. In the last 60 or 70 years, these benefits have increased the popularity of hydroponics, and have expanded the limited possibilities of indoor and urban gardening.

Aquaponics is another innovative system of growing plants without any soil to support their root systems but is slightly different from hydroponics. Aquaponics is the combination of growing plants hydroponically and the practice of aquaculture (raising fish). Just as in hydroponics, plants in an aquaponics system are grown in a soilless environment. Instead of plants getting their nutrients from sources in the soil,

(Continued)

an aquatic solution provides the essential nutrients needed for plant growth directly to the roots, where efficient nutrient uptake can occur. However, instead of adding fertilisers to the water to provide nutrients, like what is done in hydroponics, fish are grown simultaneously in the aquatic environment to create a symbiotic relationship that results in an incredibly efficient system. In aquaponics, the fish provide a natural source of organic nutrients through their excreted waste; beneficial microbes convert the waste into usable nutrient sources for plants; the plants in turn naturally filter the water, providing a clean living environment for the fish and microbes. In aquaponics, the microbes convert the ammonia from the fish waste into nitrites and then into nitrates. Plants then take in the nitrates through their roots using them as a source for plant essential nitrogen. This combination of hydroponics and aquaculture allows aquaponics to draw upon the benefits of both systems while minimising the individual drawbacks of each.

Since aquaponics is the combining of concepts from hydroponics and aquaculture, it's clear the two systems have many similarities that make them both beneficial.

- Longer growing season than traditional gardening.
- Lessened negative environmental impacts.
- Plants grow faster.
- Higher yields.

Growing plants in soilless systems is becoming increasingly popular and provides the grower with many distinct advantages over traditional methodology. Two basic systems are popular amongst homeowners: hydroponics that solely grows plants within its contained system, and aquaponics which combines hydroponics with raising fish. Both systems have similarities and differences that must be considered before starting a project of this scale. While many believe aquaponics is the better option mostly because of its sustainability, both have distinct advantages over growing plants in a soil-based garden.

SUMMARY

In summary, readers of this chapter have been given a very small taste of some of the key issues in sustainability. This is a vast area that is continually developing, and thus trying to include everything relevant would be a futile exercise. However, we are reminded about the Sustainability Principles published by RMIT University in Australia (Mulligan, 2018), and we believe that these summarise the way forward perfectly – so much so that we've listed them here as the key points below.

KEY POINTS

- Acknowledge interconnections at all levels within the biosphere.
- Acknowledge that there are limits to growth.
- Remember that prevention is better than cure.

- Work to improve intergenerational equity.
- Face up to the challenges of intergenerational equity.
- Respect requisite diversity in both nature and culture.
- Work for relocalisation with global connectedness.
- Move from consumerism to quality-of-life goals.
- Learn how to travel hopefully in a world of uncertainty.

HOW TO IMPRESS YOUR EXAMINER

Your knowledge on ethical and sustainable consumption should be expressed using as many case examples as you can. You can exercise your very own personal consumer power to achieve better personal, social and environmental outcomes, and the examiner will be very interested in reading about these strategies!

REVIEW QUESTIONS

1. What lessons can be learnt from historic shifts in perception and attitudes towards sustainable consumption?
2. What part can consumers play in helping with climate change, resource depletion, environmental pollution, etc.?
3. What can the global society do to alleviate the struggles of 1 billion people who still do not have access to fresh water?
4. How, if at all, can food consumption be spread more equally amongst the developed and developing countries?
5. We have had the 2022 United Nations Climate Conference, more commonly referred to as COP27 – the 27th conference held in Sharm El Sheikh, Egypt, in November 2022. What happens now?
6. Would you download and use the Darpdecade app?
7. Which sustainability model is the most useful for our communities?
8. If we know that the human impact on the environment is significant, should we be prioritising what we should tackle first?
9. Social sustainability has many facets to it (as can be seen from the text earlier). Is any one facet more important than the other, and why?
10. Can you think of other examples of greenwashing from the online or offline media for any organisation of your choice?

CASE STUDY: SEA2SEE

I grew up in Africa; I'm an outdoors sort of a guy. It's sad to see the impact plastic waste has made on the environment. (Abeele, quoted in Breitnauer, 2021)

In 2015, when François van den Abeele was just starting to wear glasses, the choices were all virgin plastic. And he was following brands like O'Neill that were using recycled materials but there was nothing really in the optical industry. He felt he could do something.

After a Kickstarter campaign raised €39,000 (NZ$64,965), social and environmental entrepreneur van den Abeele was able to fund his first collection and launched Sea2see in Barcelona, Spain in 2016 with a range of 18 '*seastainable*' sunglasses. Committed to a model of sustainable innovation and social responsibility, Sea2see was the first eyewear company to champion a vertically integrated sustainable business model, creating its own infrastructure for collecting marine plastic waste and then using it as a raw material to create high-quality frames. A lot of science has gone into it, understanding which polymers can be recycled and what method to use to get the best finish.

© Shutterstock / Mohamed Abdulraheem

Their objective has been to create a global consciousness in regard to the issues of ocean plastic contamination and the unsustainable optical and fashion industry. They have pioneered a *seastainable* change in the eyewear industry proving that marine plastic waste is a great source of raw material. Where others see waste, they see raw material. They've redesigned a supply chain where waste has value in order to create a sustainable and scalable solution that reduces marine plastic and improve the lives of marginalised coastal communities living in biodiversity hotspots of developing countries. Every second, 256 kg of plastic ends up in our oceans, so surely it must be time to act?!

We don't produce glasses or watches, but a statement of change, which can be worn by anybody willing to stand for our Oceans.

Sea2see frames are made in Italy exclusively from 100% marine plastic. The waste is up-cycled into a reusable raw material in the form of pellets called UPSEA™ PLAST. The material is Cradle to Cradle™ Gold Certified, combining a quality finish with durability, lightness and fashionable, modern appeal.

Today the award-winning brand has an extensive collection of over 250 ophthalmic and sun styles for men, women and junior with a lightweight contemporary design, and a selection of looks, from fashion-oriented to timeless or sporty. The frames are stocked in leading independent optical retailers and well-known chains around the world that have committed to the promotion of their *'seastainable'* values.

Their consumers are environmentally conscious and expect ecologically friendly materials, sustainable use of resources, reduced emissions and greater social commitments from the companies they support.

Sea2see has also teamed up with the famous photographer Weston Fuller in California, in a new campaign about ocean contamination. The powerful imagery reinforces the Sea2see legacy, its environmental message and the brand's commitment to the production of high-quality eyewear and watches, made exclusively from 100% recycled marine plastic. In this new campaign with Weston Fuller, a photographer who is passionate about environmental action, they wanted to raise awareness about the devastating impact of plastic in our oceans and encourage reflection on what we can do better as consumers to protect the world in which we live. The photographs show models standing in or near water, wearing Sea2see products whilst surrounded by plastic waste. The campaign connects with consumers through direct visual reminders of contamination in the sea. It also portrays the way in which Sea2see is successfully turning recycled waste into products that are uncompromising on quality and style.

In recent years, recycling at Sea2see has picked up pace in Africa in collaboration with a growing number of fishing communities in West Africa creating a new source of income for the plastic they collect, while also being involved in an activity with an immediate positive impact on the environment. Their involvement with communities in this region has led to a new collaboration launched in 2021 with Freetheslaves.net (Ghana) – www.freetheslaves.net/where-we-work/ghana/.

Sea2see is also committed to working with non-profit conservation organisations. In 2020, the brand partnered with @searchingforchinook creating a limited edition SFC recycled sunglasses edition, to support their project to save the orcas. @searchingforchinook is a two-part documentary led by Alexandra Johnston and Maria Nangle and produced by Dolphin Project Ambassador and actress Maisie Williams.

Their watch collection launched in retail and online from March 2021 with 22 individual watch models, produced in two sizes (41 mm and 37 mm).

Five years after creating its first 'seastainable' eyewear brand, Sea2see has earned B Lab's global B Corporation certification, awarded to companies meeting strict standards of social and environmental performance.

'We are proud to say that we are a certified B Corp, which for us means being part of a movement that isn't competing to be the best in the world, it is competing to be the best for the world. This certification represents a tremendous step for us as we mark our fifth anniversary and reflect on our progress to date', said Sea2see founder and CEO François van den Abeele.

The certification process is rigorous, said van den Abeele, providing answers to 300+ detailed questions on governance, workers, communities and impact on the environment. Companies who receive the certification are also required to undergo verification every three years, by demonstrating ongoing positive impact.

Source: Adapted from www.sea2see.org.

(Continued)

CASE STUDY QUESTIONS

1. What are the benefits of nurturing a sustainable ecosystem?
2. Do you support a sustainable consumption idea, product or service, and if so what is it?
3. How do the principles of sustainable consumption (honesty, prudence and responsibility) affect your shopping behaviour?
4. How important are these three character traits as a part of your sense of self?
5. Do you need to be rich to be sustainable?

FURTHER READING

For great online content on policy and practice, head over to the Lush website and read about their amazing work on sustainable consumption: https://uk.lush.com/tag/our-policies.

For an interesting read about the values and ethics behind some people's adoption of public bicycle-sharing schemes, look at J. Yin, L. Qian and A. Singhapakdi (2018) Sharing sustainability: How values and ethics matter in consumers' adoption of public bicycle-sharing scheme, *Journal of Business Ethics, 149* (2): 313–32.

UNESCO actually provides three 'cautionary points' as regards defining sustainable consumption. More information can be found at www.unesco.org/education/tlsf/mods/theme_b/popups/mod09t06s07.html.

Finally, for a more in-depth read about the United Nations' 17 Goals to Transform Our World; go to www.un.org/sustainabledevelopment/.

MORE ONLINE

For additional materials that support this chapter and your learning, please visit:

https://study.sagepub.com/sethna5e

REFERENCES

Abid, A., Majeed, M.T. and Luni, T. (2021) Analyzing ecological footprint through the lens of globalization, financial development, natural resources, human capital and urbanization. *Pakistan Journal of Commerce & Social Sciences, 15* (4): 765–95.

Adams, T. (2018) *Social Capital: Rethinking Change: What a Theory of Social Capital Reveals about Democratic Stability.* Maastricht: University of Maastricht.

Aguiñaga, E., Henriques, I., Scheel, C. and Scheel, A. (2018) Building resilience: A self-sustainable community approach to the triple bottom line. *Journal of Cleaner Production, 173*: 186–96.

Ahmed, Z., Ahmad, M., Rjoub, H., Kalugina, O.A. and Hussain, N. (2022) Economic growth, renewable energy consumption, and ecological footprint: Exploring the role of environmental regulations and democracy in sustainable development. *Sustainable Development*, *30* (4): 595–605.

Al-Hamadani, S., Egbelakin, T., Sher, W. and Von Meding, J. (2021) Drivers of applying ecological modernization to construction waste minimization in New South Wales construction industry. *Construction Economics and Building*, *21* (3). doi: 10.5130/AJCEB.v21i3.7655

Alviar-Martin, T. (2018) Culture and citizenship. In I. Davies, L.-C. Ho, D. Kiwan, C.L. Peck, A. Peterson, E. Sant and Y. Waghid (eds), *The Palgrave Handbook of Global Citizenship and Education*. London: Palgrave Macmillan. pp. 347–61.

Amin, S., Li, C., Khan, Y.A. and Bibi, A. (2022) Fishing grounds footprint and economic freedom indexes: Evidence from Asia-Pacific. *PLoS One*, *17* (4): 1–16.

Beggs, W. (2018) Book review: *The Death and Life of the Single-Family House: Lessons from Vancouver on Building a Livable City*, by Nathanael Lauster. *Journal of Urban Affairs*, *40* (7): 1033–5.

Bennett, E.M. and Alexandridis, P. (2021) Informing the public and educating students on plastic recycling. *Recycling*, *6*: 69.

Bolton, M., Raven, R. and Mintrom, M. (2021) Can AI transform public decision-making for sustainable development? An exploration of critical earth system governance questions. *Earth System Governance*, *9*: 100116.

Bosco, J. (2014) The problem of greed in economic anthropology: Sumptuary laws and new consumerism in China. *Economic Anthropology*, *1* (1): 167–85.

Breitnauer, J. (2021) A better specs life. www.nzoptics.co.nz/articles/archive/a-better-specs-life/# (accessed 6 August 2022).

Brundtland, G.H. (1987) *Our Common Future*. www.un-documents.net/our-common-future.pdf (accessed 29 December 2018).

Cafaro, P., Hansson, P. and Götmark, F. (2022) Overpopulation is a major cause of biodiversity loss and smaller human populations are necessary to preserve what is left. *Biological Conservation*, *272*: 109646.

Carter, N. (2018) *The Politics of the Environment: Ideas, Activism, Policy*. Cambridge: Cambridge University Press.

Cyr, M.G. and Jagos, J. (2019) Hyper-consumerism and abstract landscape in Asia. *Fashion Studies*, *2* (1), 1–37.

Elkington, J. (1994) Towards the sustainable corporation: Win–win–win business strategies for sustainable development. *California Management Review*, *36* (2): 90–100.

Erman, T. (2019) From informal housing to apartment housing: Exploring the 'new social' in a gecekondu rehousing project, Turkey. *Housing Studies*, *34* (3): 519–37.

Essiz, O., Yurteri, S., Mandrik, C. and Senyuz, A. (2023) Exploring the value-action gap in green consumption: Roles of risk aversion, subjective knowledge, and gender differences. *Journal of Global Marketing*, *36* (1): 67–92.

Fabre, C. (2018) *Economic Statecraft: Human Rights, Sanctions, and Conditionality.* Cambridge, MA: Harvard University Press.

Faria, A. and Hemais, M. (2018) Historicizing the new global consumerism from the perspective of emerging worlds. In *Academy of Management Proceedings 2018.* Briarcliff Manor, NY: Academy of Management. https://doi.org/10.5465/AMBPP.2018.18564abstract

Fox, H. (2018) *Adaption and Adaptability.* MSc thesis. https://scholarworks.iupui.edu/bitstream/handle/1805/16345/HannahFox%20-%20Thesis.pdf?sequence=1 (accessed 15 August 2018).

Freud, A. (2018) Ego and id. In *The Harvard Lectures.* Abingdon: Routledge. pp. 21–35.

Frey, D.F., Macnaughton, G., Kaur, A.H. and Taborda, E.K. (2021) Crises as catalyst: A new social contract grounded in worker rights. *Health & Human Rights: An International Journal, 23* (2): 153–65.

Fuchs, D. and Boll, F. (2018) Sustainable consumption. In *Global Environmental Politics.* Abingdon: Routledge. pp. 93–112.

Giddings, B., Hopwood, B. and O'Brien, G. (2002) Environment economy and society: Fitting them into sustainable development. *Sustainable Development, 10*: 142.

Giovannetti, E., Bertolini, P. and Russo, M. (2021) Rights, commons, and social capital: The role of cooperation in an Italian agri-food supply chain. *Sustainability, 13*: 12161.

Global Witness (2017) Stained trade. www.globalwitness.org/documents/…/stained_trade_310717_lores_pages.pdf (accessed 18 May 2018).

Goudie, A.S. (2018) *Human Impact on the Natural Environment.* Chichester: John Wiley & Sons.

Green, C., Carey, G. and Joyce, A. (2022) Application of theories of the policy process in research on consumption of sustainable diets: A systematic review. *BMC Public Health, 22* (1): 1335.

Greenwashingindex.com (2018) The Greenwashing Index Scoring Criteria. www.greenwashingindex.com/about-greenwashing/ (accessed 18 June 2018).

Guim, M. and Livermore, M.A. (2021) Where nature's rights go wrong. *Virginia Law Review, 107* (7): 1347–419.

Hajer, M. (1995) *The Politics of Environmental Discourse.* Oxford: Clarendon Press.

Hamilton, E.M., Guckian, M.L. and De Young, R. (2018) Living well and living green: Participant conceptualizations of green citizenship. In W.L. Filho, R.W. Marans and J. Callewaert (eds), *Handbook of Sustainability and Social Science Research.* Cham: Springer. pp. 315–34.

Hassenzahl, M. (2018) The thing and I: Understanding the relationship between user and product. In M. Blythe and A. Monk (eds), *Funology 2, Human–Computer Interaction Series.* Cham: Springer. pp. 301–13.

Hawkes, J. (2001) *The Four Pillars of Sustainability.* Melbourne, VIC: Cultural Development Network.

Heffron, R., Connor, R., Crossley, P., Mayor, V.L.-I., Talus, K. and Tomain, J. (2021) The identification and impact of justice risks to commercial risks in the energy sector: Post

COVID-19 and for the energy transition. *Journal of Energy & Natural Resources Law*, *39* (4): 439–68.

Hofmann, B. (2022) Mainstreaming earth system governance into the UN decade of ocean science for sustainable development. *Earth System Governance*, *12*: 100139.

Huang, Y.-C. and Huang, C.-H. (2022) Examining the antecedents and consequences of sustainable green supply chain management from the perspective of ecological modernization: Evidence from Taiwan's high-tech sector. *Journal of Environmental Planning & Management*, *65* (9): 1579–610.

Independent (2017) 15,000 scientists give catastrophic warning about the fate of the world in new 'letter to humanity'. *Independent*, Indy/Life, 13 November. www.independent.co.uk/environment/letter-to-humanity-warning-climate-change-global-warming-scientists-union-concerned-a8052481.html (accessed 19 April 2018).

Isik, C., Dogru, T. and Turk, E.S. (2018) A nexus of linear and non-linear relationships between tourism demand, renewable energy consumption, and economic growth: Theory and evidence. *International Journal of Tourism Research*, *20* (1): 38–49.

Ivanic, M. and Martin, W. (2018) Sectoral productivity growth and poverty reduction: National and global impacts. *World Development*, *109*: 429–39.

Kazim, A. (2018) The emergence of hyper-consumerism in UAE society: A socio-cultural perspective. *Perspectives on Global Development & Technology*, *17* (4): 353–72.

Kearney, M. (2022) Astonishingly hyperconnected. *Issues in Science & Technology*, *38* (2): 77–80.

Kellert, S.R., Mehta, J.N., Ebbin, S.A. and Lichtenfeld, L.L. (2000) Community natural resource management: Promise, rhetoric, and reality. *Society & Natural Resources*, *13* (8): 705–15.

Kheirinejad, S., Bozorg-Haddad, O., Singh, V.P. and Loáiciga, H.A. (2022) The effect of reducing per capita water and energy uses on renewable water resources in the water, food and energy nexus. *Scientific Reports*, *12* (1): 7582.

Kiss, G., Pataki, G., Köves, A. and Király, G. (2018) Framing sustainable consumption in different ways: Policy lessons from two participatory systems mapping exercises in Hungary. *Journal of Consumer Policy*, *41* (1): 1–19.

Klein, N. (2000) *No Logo: Taking Aim at the Brand Bullies*. Toronto: Knopf Canada.

Kraisornsuthasinee, S. and Swierczek, F.W. (2018) Beyond consumption: The promising contribution of voluntary simplicity. *Social Responsibility Journal*, *14* (1): 80–95.

Kumar, P., Gacem, A., Ahmad, M.T., Yadav, V.K., Singh, S., Yadav, K.K., Alam, M.M., Dawane, V., Piplode, S., Maurya, P., Ahn, Y., Jeon, B.H. and Cabral-Pinto, M.M.S. (2022) Environmental and human health implications of metal(loid)s: Source identification, contamination, toxicity, and sustainable clean-up technologies. *Frontiers in Environmental Science*, *10*. https://doi.org/10.3389/fenvs.2022.949581

Kutz, M. (2018) *Handbook of Environmental Degradation of Materials*, 3rd edn. Oxford: William Andrew.

Lea, R. (2018) Commonwealth countries: Future growth markets for UK exports. *Perspectives* – Arbuthnot Banking Group, April. www.arbuthnotlatham.co.uk/wp-content/uploads/2018/04/9th-April-2018.pdf (accessed 25 July 2018).

Leipold, S. (2021) Transforming ecological modernization 'from within' or perpetuating it? The circular economy as EU environmental policy narrative. *Environmental Politics*, *30* (6): 1045–67.

Lekakis, E.J. (2021) Adversaries of advertising: Anti-consumerism and subvertisers' critique and practice. *Social Movement Studies*, *20* (6): 740–57.

Levitt, T. (1960) Marketing myopia. *Harvard Business Review*, July–August: 45–56.

Li, Y. and Zhang, M. (2018) Green manufacturing and environmental productivity growth. *Industrial Management & Data Systems*, *118* (6): 1303–19.

Lloveras, J., Marshall, A.P., Vandeventer, J.S. and Pansera, M. (2022) Sustainability marketing beyond sustainable development: Towards a degrowth agenda. *Journal of Marketing Management*, 1–23. https://doi.org/10.1080/0267257x.2022.2084443

Lunning, F. (2010) *Fanthropologies*. Minneapolis, MN: University of Minnesota Press.

Lyon, D. (2013) *Jesus in Disneyland: Religion in Postmodern Times*. Chichester: John Wiley & Sons.

Malecki, C. (2018) *Corporate Social Responsibility: Perspectives for Sustainable Corporate Governance*. Cheltenham: Edward Elgar.

Mamoon, D. (2018) Technology case study: Virtual lifestyles and sustainable economic development. *Journal of Economics Library*, *5* (1): 59–64.

Manta, O., Panait, M., Hysa, E., Rusu, E. and Cojocaru, M. (2022) Public procurement, a tool for achieving the goals of sustainable development. *Amfiteatru Economic*, *24* (61): 861–76.

McKinsey (2016) Urban world: The global consumers to watch. www.mckinsey.com/global-themes/urbanization/urban-world-the-global-consumers-to-watch (accessed 25 February 2018).

Meier, L. and Lange, H. (2009) *The New Middle Classes*. Dordrecht: Springer Netherlands.

Morrissey, C. and Walker, R.L. (2018) The ethics of general population preventive genomic sequencing: Rights and social justice. *Journal of Medicine and Philosophy: A Forum for Bioethics and Philosophy of Medicine*, *43* (1): 22–43.

Muhammad, B. and Khan, S. (2021) Understanding the relationship between natural resources, renewable energy consumption, economic factors, globalization and CO2 emissions in developed and developing countries. *Natural Resources Forum*, *45* (2): 138–56.

Mulligan, M. (2018) *An Introduction to Sustainability: Environmental, Social and Personal Perspectives*. Abingdon: Routledge.

Nakajima, K., Daigo, I., Nansai, K., Matsubae, K., Takayanagi, W., Tomita, M. and Matsuno, Y. (2018) Global distribution of material consumption: Nickel, copper, and iron. *Resources, Conservation and Recycling*, *133*: 369–74.

Nekmahmud, M., Ramkissoon, H. and Fekete-Farkas, M. (2022) Green purchase and sustainable consumption: A comparative study between European and non-European tourists. *Tourism Management Perspectives*, *43*: 100980.

Nemes, N., Scanlan, S.J., Smith, P., Smith, T., Aronczyk, M., Hill, S., Lewis, S.L., Montgomery, A.W., Tubiello, F.N. and Stabinsky, D. (2022) An integrated framework to assess greenwashing. *Sustainability*, *14* (8). doi: 10.3390/su14084431

Niskanen, J. and Rohracher, H. (2022) A politics of calculation: Negotiating pathways to zero-energy buildings in Sweden. *Technological Forecasting & Social Change*, *179*: 121630.

Nunes, R. (2022) *Healthcare as a Universal Human Right: Sustainability in Global Health*. Abingdon: Routledge.

Opoku, E.E.O., Kufuor, N.K. and Manu, S.A. (2021) Gender, electricity access, renewable energy consumption and energy efficiency. *Technological Forecasting & Social Change*, *173*: 121121.

Parahiyanti, C.R. and Nurmalita, R. (2022) Does marketing strategy support the sustainability of the school industry? *International Journal of Research in Business and Social Science*, *11* (5): 432–8.

Parkinson, C. (2018) Weapons of mass happiness: Social justice and health equity in the context of the arts. In *Music, Health and Wellbeing*. London: Palgrave Macmillan. pp. 269–88.

Patenaude, B., Odihi, D., Sriudomporn, S., Mak, J., Watts, E. and de Broucker, G. (2022) A standardized approach for measuring multivariate equity in vaccination coverage, cost-of-illness, and health outcomes: Evidence from the Vaccine Economics Research for Sustainability & Equity (VERSE) project. *Social Science & Medicine*, *302*: 114979.

Petro, G. (2022) Consumers demand sustainable products and shopping formats. Available at: www.forbes.com/sites/gregpetro/2022/03/11/consumers-demand-sustainable-products-and-shopping-formats/?sh=6077c1556a06 (accessed on 18 June 2022).

Pratt, N. (2021) The responsibility of community sustainability from the frontlines of climate change. *International Journal of Bahamian Studies*, *27*: 105–16.

Qu, J., Wang, Q., Sun, X. and Li, Y. (2022) The environment and female reproduction: Potential mechanism of cadmium poisoning to the growth and development of ovarian follicle. *Ecotoxicology and Environmental Safety*, *244*: 114029.

Rahmani, A.A., Wijaya, M.E. and Hirawan, F.B. (2021) Value-action gap in climate change Indonesians. *Jurnal Wilayah Dan Lingkungan*, *9* (3): 226–38.

Read, R., Alexander, S. and Garrett, J. (2018) Voluntary simplicity strongly backed by all three main normative-ethical traditions. *Ethical Perspectives*, *25* (1): 87–116.

Richards, C. (2022) *Reframing Global Warming for Better Risk Management: Climate Change, Food Insecurity and Societal Collapse*. Doctoral thesis. https://doi.org/10.17863/CAM.85343

Salawitch, R.J., Hope, A., McBride, L., Canty, T., Tribett, W. and Bennett, B. (2018) Quantification of global warming: A critical evaluation of CMIP5 GCMs and future projections using an empirical model of global climate. *EGU General Assembly Conference Abstracts*, *20*: 11274.

Sayers, M. (2008) *The Trouble with Paris: Following Jesus in a World of Plastic Promises*. Nashville, TN: Thomas Nelson.

Schandl, H., Fischer-Kowalski, M., West, J., Giljum, S., Dittrich, M., Eisenmenger, N. and Krausmann, F. (2018) Global material flows and resource productivity: Forty years of evidence. *Journal of Industrial Ecology, 22* (4): 827–38.

Sepulveda, S.N. (2018) *The Intersection of Placemaking and Planning: Examining City Placemaking Programs and Efforts*. Doctoral dissertation, The University of Texas at Austin. https://repositories.lib.utexas.edu/handle/2152/65789 (accessed 29 December 2018).

Shen, Y., Zhang, F., Gong, M. and Huang, J. (2022) The urbanization–environmental pollution nexus: An analysis based on a spatial perspective. *Emerging Markets Finance & Trade, 58* (8): 2355–67.

Siksnelyte-Butkiene, I. (2022) Combating energy poverty in the face of the COVID-19 pandemic and the global economic uncertainty. *Energies, 15* (10): 3649.

Slocombe, D.S. (1993) Environmental planning, ecosystem science, and ecosystem approaches for integrating environment and development. *Environmental Management, 17* (3): 289–303.

Somorin, T., Sowale, A., Shemfe, M., Ayodele, A.S. and Kolios, A. (2019) Clean technologies and innovation in energy. In *Energy in Africa: Policy, Management and Sustainability*. Basingstoke: Palgrave Macmillan. pp. 149–97.

Soust-Verdaguer, B., Bernardino Galeana, I., Llatas, C., Montes, M.V., Hoxha, E. and Passer, A. (2022) How to conduct consistent environmental, economic, and social assessment during the building design process. A BIM-based life cycle sustainability assessment method. *Journal of Building Engineering, 45*: 103516.

Sovacool, B.K., Tan-Mullins, M. and Abrahamse, W. (2018) Bloated bodies and broken bricks: Power, ecology, and inequality in the political economy of natural disaster recovery. *World Development, 110*: 243–55.

Spernovasilis, N., Markaki, I., Papadakis, M., Tsioutis, C. and Markaki, L. (2021) Epidemics and pandemics: Is human overpopulation the elephant in the room? *Ethics, Medicine, and Public Health, 19*: 100728.

Sroufe, R., Curkovic, S., Montabon, F. and Melnyk, S.A. (2000) The new product design process and design for environment: 'Crossing the chasm'. *International Journal of Operations & Production Management, 20* (2): 267–91.

Taketani, R.G., Dini-Andreote, F., Beier, S. and Fernandez, C. (2022) Advancements in the understanding of anthropogenic impacts on the microbial ecology and function of aquatic environments. *Frontiers in Microbiology*. https://doi.org/10.3389/fmicb.2021.820697

Taylor, K.M. and Vachon, S. (2018) Empirical research on sustainable supply chains: IJPR's contribution and research avenues. *International Journal of Production Research, 56* (1–2): 950–9.

Teelucksingh, C. (2018) Diverse environmentalism and inclusivity in Toronto's Green Economy. *Environmental Sociology, 5* (1): 47–58.

Telegraph, The (2013) David Attenborough – Humans are plague on Earth. *The Telegraph*, Earth, 22 January. www.telegraph.co.uk/news/earth/earthnews/9815862/Humans-are-plague-on-Earth-Attenborough.html (accessed 1 March 2018).

Tolbert, S. and Schindel, A. (2018) Altering the ideology of consumerism: Caring for land and people through school science. In *Sociocultural Perspectives on Youth Ethical Consumerism*. Cham: Springer. pp. 115–29.

Turker, D. (2018) Global challenges: Aligning social responsibility and sustainable development goals. In *Managing Social Responsibility*. Cham: Springer. pp. 161–76.

Uldemolins, P. and de Magistris, T. (2021) Assessing parental preferences regarding a plant-based game for educating children about more sustainable and healthier diets. *Sustainability*, *13*: 12970.

van Pelt, J.C. (2018) Climate change in context: Stress shock and the crucible of livingkind: With Karl E. Peters, 'Living with the wicked problem of climate change'; Paul H. Carr, 'What is climate change doing to us and for us?'; James Clement van Pelt, 'Climate change in context: Stress, shock, and the crucible of livingkind'; Robert S. Pickart, 'Climate change at high latitudes: An illuminating example'; Emily E. Austin, 'Soil carbon transformations'; David A. Larrabee, 'Climate change and conflicting future visions'. *Zygon: Journal of Religion and Science*, *53* (2): 462–95.

Vetter, D. (2021) Top climate experts blast rich nations for 'breakdown in trust' at COP26. www.forbes.com/sites/davidrvetter/2021/11/26/top-climate-experts-blast-rich-nations-for-breakdown-in-trust-at-cop26/?sh=cbbd268f4e98 (accessed 15 May 2022).

Watts, H.D. (2018) *The Large Industrial Enterprise: Some Spatial Perspectives*. Abingdon: Routledge.

Willett, J., Saunders, C., Hackney, F. and Hill, K. (2022) The affective economy and fast fashion: Materiality, embodied learning and developing a sensibility for sustainable clothing. *Journal of Material Culture*, *27* (3): 219–37.

Wilson, D., Lake, R.W., Kinder, K., Parks, V., Ward, K. and Doussard, M. (2018) Degraded work: The struggle at the bottom of the labor market. *The AAG Review of Books*, *6* (1): 50–8.

Wolf, M. (2022) The UK energy crisis is a burden of war. *Financial Times*, 4 September.

Young, W. (2010) Sustainable consumption: Green consumer behaviour when purchasing products. *Sustainable Development*, *18*: 20–31.

INDEX

Page numbers in *italics* refer to figures; page numbers in **bold** refer to tables.

5G mobile networks, 134

Abeele, F. van den, 564–566
Abergel, D., 328
Abergel, R., 328
abstraction, 198–199
Accenture, 135–136
accommodation to new attitudes, 362
acculturation, 478–481, **479**, *481*
achievement, 192–193, *193*
ACORN (A Classification of Residential Neighbourhoods), 486
actual state, 178–179
adaptations, 26–27
adolescence, 419, 448–450
adoption, 480
Adoption Process model, *143*, 144
advergaming, 361
advertising clutter, 316
affect, 345–346, **345**, *345*, 350, 360
affection, 274–275, *275*
affiliation, 192–193, *193*
Aflalo, T., 277
aftermarket customers, 103, 104
Against Breast Cancer, 523
age cohorts and subcultures, 418–421, 474–475
age of majority, 465
aggregator apps, 156
AIDA model, *143*, 144
Ajzen, I., 352–354, *353*
Alampay, D.A., 258
Alibaba, 261
Amazon, 42–43, 130, 141, 157, 263
ambiguity, 313–314
Amblin Productions, 94
Anarcharsis, 7
Anker, T.B., 18
anthropogenic impact on the environment, 550–552
anthropology, 23–24
anti-consumerism, 558
API (application programming interface), 157
approach–approach conflict, 194, *195*
approach–avoidance conflict, 195, *195*
apps, 6
aquaponics, 561–562
aristocracy, 482
Aristotle, 21
Arndt, J., 394
Arnould, E.J., 470
arousal theory of motivation, 185, *185*

artificial intelligence (AI), 127–129, 130–131, 132–133, 136, 157
Asch, S.E., 382, 383
aspirational groups, 385, 389, 392
assortment adjustment, 49
assortment depletion, 46
assortment extension, 49
assortment replenishment, 49
atmospherics, 267–272, *268*, *271–272*
attachment theory, 68
Attenborough, D., 551–552
attitude–behaviour gap, 544
attitude splitting, 362
attitudes
  overview of, 21, 341–344, **343**
  behaviour and, 352–355, *353–355*
  change and, 359–364, *360–362*
  dimensions of, 344–347, **345**, *345–346*
  formation of, 347–348, **348–349**, *348*
  functions of, 350–352, **351**, *351*
  as general vs. specific, 358–359
  innovation and, 148
  measurement of, 349–350, *350*
  Multiverse (case study), 367–369
  as private vs. public, 356
  vs. situation, 356–357, *357*
  toward adverts vs. brands, 357–358
  See also cognitive dissonance
ATTN, 243
attribution, 274–275, *275*
augmented reality (AR), 128, 131, 157
automatic groups (category groups), 386
automatic number plate recognition, 146–147
autonomic decision-making, 424
avoidance–avoidance conflict, 195, *195*

Baby Boomers, 419–420
backward conditioning, 303
Bain & Company, 208
Baker, J., 388
Ballmer, S., 97
Balogh, P., 329
banking, 221–222
Barrett, E., 368
Barrett, M., 142
Baumeister, R.F., 220
BBC News, 442
Beatty, C., 7
Beck, A., 7–8
Beeple, 66
behavioural segmentation, 12

beliefs, 346–348, **348–349**, 353–354, 359–360, *360*, 363. *See also* attitudes
Belk, R., 220
Bell Labs, 126
benchmarking, 154
Bendell, J., 504
Bennett, P.D., 11
Bezos, J., 263
bias, 232–233
big data, 134–135, 278
Bjerke, B., 478
Black Baccara, 440–441
Blackwell, R.D., 6
Blair, E., 367–369
Blockbuster, 94
blockchains, 135–136
blogs, 386, 403–404
Bloomberg, 260
body language, 268–269
The Body Shop, 505
Bose, J.C., 126
brain–computer interfaces, 277–278
brand associations, 322, *323*
brand communities, 387
brand knowledge, 319, 321–323, *323*
brand-loyal consumers, 274
brand switching, 358–359
brandalism, 284
brands and branding, 68–69, **69**, *69–71*, 357–359
Brandstetter, J., 383–384
Brandwatch, 286–288
Brann Consulting, 68
Bravissimo, 523
Brexit, 27, 30, 391–392, 407–408
Brown, D., 402
Browning, R., 159–160
Brundtland, G.H., 546
Bugelski, B.R., 258
Bulman, M., 7
Bulmer, M., 474
business and commercial organisations, 103–104, **103**, *105*
business-to-business (B2B) markets
 overview of, 91–92
 buyers' techniques in, 108–109, *110*
 Buygrid framework and, 110–112, **111**
 classification of, 103–108, **103**, *105–107*
 decision-making units and, 92–97, *96*
 Electric Car Scheme (case study), 117–118
 influences on buyers in, 98–103, *100*, *102*
 relationship marketing and, 14
 value analysis and, 112–115, **114–115**
business-to-consumer (B2C) markets, 14, 92
buyers, 93–94
Buygrid framework, 110–112, **111**
buying centres (decision-making units), 92–97, *96*

Calentone, R.J., 153–154
cancel culture, 468
car industry
 attitudes and, 21
 electric vehicles and, 117–118, 239
 hedonism and, 202, 203
 hygiene factors and, 191
 self-driving vehicles and, 130–131
 trading-in and, 9–10
Cashflow Board Game, 306
categorisation, 259, 264
category groups (automatic groups), 386
Cattell, R.B., 236
causal purchasing, 108–109
cautionary tale advertising, 193
CDP (consumer decision process) model, 45–46, *47*
charity, 180, 520–521
Chatterjee, P., 258
Chen, H.G., 358
Chevron, 556
childlessness, 426–427
children
 banking and, 221–222
 consumer technology and, 434–435
 learning and, 308–309
 role and influence in family of, 417–418, 426–435, *429–430*, **431**, 443–446, **446**, *447*
 self-concept of, 223
China, 260–261
choice heuristics, 199
Chung, M., 282
chunking, 259
cinemas, 24
class, 267, 482–486, **482–483**, *484*. *See also* social mobility
classical conditioning, 301–305, *302*, **304**. *See also* operant conditioning
clothing rental sites, 544–546
co-creation, 12, 113
cognition, 345–346, **345**, *345*, 360
cognitive dissonance, 149–150, *150*, 364–366, *364–365*, 399
cognitive effort, 311
cognitive innovators, 149
cognitive learning, 310–318, *310–311*, **312–314**, *317*
cognitive mapping, 259–260, 264
cognitive neuroscience, 266
cognitive structure, 311
Coleman Study (Quality of Educational Opportunity Study), 443–444
collectivism, 466, *467*
colour, 281–283, **281–282**, *283*
commercial drones, 156–157
communication, 155, 446, *447*
Communicus, 434

communities of interest, 387
compatibility, 154
compensatory decision rules, 61–62
complexity, 154
compliance, 389–392
conation, 345–346, **345**, *345*, 360
conditioned response, 302
configural model, 276, *277*
conflict resolution, 426, **427–428**
conformity, 389–392
conjunctive rule, 61
consensual parents, 446
consideration set, 43–44, *45*
consumer behaviour
　overview of, 5–13, *11*
　acculturation and, 481
　antecedents of, 18–27, *19–20, 22, 26*
　marketing mix and, 13, **13–14**
　marketing planning and, 16–18
　relationship marketing and, 13–15, **15**, *15*
　trade (case study), 27–31
　See also decision-making
consumer culture theory, 470–473
consumer-dominant logic of marketing, 48
consumer society, 205
consumer styles, 273–274
consumer technology
　overview of, 125–127
　artificial intelligence (AI) and, 127–129, 130–131, 132–133, 136, 157
　augmented reality (AR) and, 128, 131, 157
　big data and, 134–135
　blockchains and, 135–136
　children and, 434–435
　cybersecurity and, 136–137
　Internet of Things (IoT) and, 133
　jetpacks (case study), 159–160
　machine learning and, 128–129, 134
　metaverse and, 128
　mobile technologies and, 133–134
　robotics and, 129–131
　See also innovation
consumerism, 205, 470–471. *See also* ethical consumption; hedonism
consumers-to-business (C2B) markets, 18
consumption knowledge, 319, 326–328, *327*
continuous innovation, 153
conventions, 464
Cooper, R.G., 153–154
Cote, J.A., 357
Covid-19 pandemic
　attitudes and, 342, 357
　colour and, 283
　cybersecurity and, 136
　gift-giving and, 471–473
　handwashing and, 332–333
　impact on girls and women of, 76–77
　luxury brands and, 208
　masks and, 315
　psychological effects of, 383
　trade and, 30–31
　Zoom dysmorphia and, 230
Cox, L., 442
CROWN Coalition, 243
cues, 315
cultural anchoring, 142
culture shock, 481
culture(s)
　overview of, 23, 461–468, *462–463, 467*
　approaches to, 468–470, *469*
　business-to-business (B2B) markets and, 99, 102
　family and, 424–425
　Hopscotch Women's Centre (case study), 487–490
　perception and, 264–265, 281–282
　See also attitudes; beliefs; class; consumer culture theory; subcultures
customers, 6
customisation, 154–155
customs, 463–464
cybersecurity, 136–137

Danske Bank, 17
Dantec, M., 281
Darwin Pricing LLC, 131–132
Dawes, J., 71
De Forest, L., 126
de Ridder, D.T.D., 236
De Vos, G.A., 478–479
deciders, 93–94
decision-making
　overview of, 41–42
　goals and, 42–44, **44**, *44–45*
　interrupts and, 50–52, **51**, *51*
　involvement and, 63–69, *64–65*, **69**, *69–71*
　loyalty and, 70–72
　models of, 45–50, *47–48, 50*
　pre-purchase activities and, 54–62, *55, 57, 62–63*
　risk and, 52–53, *53*
　unsought goods and, 72–74, **73**, *73*
　women (case study), 75–78
decision-making units (DMUs), 92–97, *96*
decision rules, 61–62
Della Bitta, A.J., 98
DemandJump, 136
democratic decision-making (syncratic decision-making), 424
demographic fracture, 481
demographic segmentation, 12
depth interviews, 232
desired state, 178–179
deviant consumer behaviour, 6–8
Dewey, J., 45–46
Diener, E., 188–189

differentiation, 190
diffusion, 395
digital assistants, 156
digital consumer intelligence (DCI), 286
digital signage, 273
Dimitriadis, N., 145
direct marketing, 16
direct route, 362, *362*
discontinuous innovation, 153
discrimination, 304
disinhibition, 185
disposal, 9–10, 518–525, *519*
dissociative groups, 385
dissonance, 399
Dootson, P., 6–7
Dorothy Dollar, 440–441
Dove, 242–243
Doxel, 129–130
drives, 19, 178–181, *178*, 196–197, 315. *See also* motivation
drones, 129–130, 156–157
Dube, L., 382–383
Dudarev, V., 315
Dunaev, J.L., 230
dynamically continuous innovation, 153
dysmorphia, 230

e-commerce, 58–59, 260–261
early adopters, 145–146, *146*
early majority, 145–146, *146*
Earth system governance, 549
East, R., 71
eco-literacy, 508
ecological footprint, 558
ecological modernisation, 549–550
economic choice, 24
economic sustainability, 552. *See also* sustainable consumption
economics, 24–26, *26*
ego, 231–232, *232*
ego-defensive function, 350
Ehang, 130
Ehrenberg, A.S.C., 70–71
EKB model of consumer behaviour, 45–46
elaboration, 311
elaboration likelihood model, 362
elasticity of demand, 25–26, *26*
Electric Car Scheme (ECS), 117–118
electric vehicles (EVs), 117–118, 239
electricity, 126
Elkington, J., 547, *548*
emotional attachments, 63–64
emotional fracture, 481
end of life (EOL), 319
environmental sustainability, 552. *See also* sustainable consumption
environmentalism, 553
equitable performance, 149

Erichsen, C., 328
Ethereum, 66–67
ethical consumption
 overview of, 501–507
 business-to-business (B2B) markets and, 99
 categories of, 507–509, *507*, **509**
 decision-making and, 48
 disposal and, 518–525, *519*
 healthcare in India (case study), 527–531
 individuals and, 510–517, **511**, *514–515*
 the public and, 517–518
 See also sustainable consumption
ethnicity and ethnic subcultures, 470, 474–481, **476–477**, **479**, *481*
ethnocentrism, 469–470
evaluation heuristics, 199
evoked set, 43–44, *45*
evolutionary innovations, 137
expectancy, 274–275, *275*
Expectancy Theory, 192
expectations, 259
expected performance, 149
experiments, 193
extended decision-making, 50
extended family, 422
extended self, 225
extinction, 304, **304**
extroverts, 233–234

Fairtrade International, 511–513
familiarity, 313–314
family
 overview of, 22, 417–418, 422–426, *422*, *425*, **427–428**
 changing nature of, 435–438, *435*, **436–437**. *See also* gender roles
 functions of, 442–444, *443*
 Indian adolescents (case study), 448–450
 roles in consumption and, 444–446, **445–446**, *445*, *447*
 See also children
fantasy communities, 387
Farage, N., 407–408
Farnsworth, P., 126
fast-moving consumer goods (FMCG), 25, 355
Feick, L.F., 151
femininity, 466, *467*
Financial Conduct Authority (FCA), 56
Fishbein, M., 349–350, *350*, 352–353, *353*, 356–357
Fisher, R.J., 382–383
Fleming, J.A., 126
flicking, 314
flying cars, 191
focus groups, 232–233
food, 464
Forest Schools, 308–309
formal groups, 385

forward conditioning, 303
Fossil, 441
fourth pillar model, 547, *549*
Fox, J., 240
Freud, S., 231–232, *232*, 355
Freund, K., 10
Frey, T., 129
Friestad, M., 329
functional fracture, 481
Future Market Insights, 183

Gal, D., 204–205
gamification, 306, 344
gatekeepers, 93–94
Gates, B., 97
gender, 224–225, 382–383
gender roles, 426, 438–442, *440*, *441*
General Motors (GM), 9–10
generalisation, 304
generation gap, 419
Generation X, 420, 557
Generation Y (Millennials), 134, 223–224, 404, 420
Generation Z, 557
geo-targeted pricing, 131–132
geographic segmentation, 12
geographic subcultures, 474
Giddings, B., 547
gift-giving, 471–473
Gillette, 403
Global Handwashing Day, 332–333
global warming, 516
goals, 20, 42–44, **44**, *44–45*, 196–199, *197–198*
goHenry, 221–222
Goldsmith–Hofacker Innovativeness Scale, 147
Google, 141
governmental organisations, **103**, 106–107, *106*
Gravity Industries, 159–160
Great International Book Exchange, 324–325
Great Resignation, 223–224
green marketing, 560
greenwashing, 553–557, **554–557**
Greenwashing Index Score, 557, **557**
grey market, 420–421
group behaviour, 21–22
Gubar, G., 436
guided interviews, 232
guilt, 510–511, **511**
Gulzari, A., 329–330
Gupta, A., 112
Gupta, S., 71

Ha, Y., 311–312
halo effect, 363
handwashing, 332–333
Harrods, 272
Hastings, R., 94
Hawkes, J., 547, *549*

Haytko, D.L., 388
healthcare, 527–531
Heath, E., 27
hedonism, 201–205, *202*, 208–210
Hémar-Nicolas, V., 428
Henseler, J., 113
Hershey Company, 94
Herzberg, F., 190, 192
heuristics, 51, 199–201, **200–201**
Hierarchy of Effects model, *143*, 144
Hierarchy of Needs, 185–188, *186*, 235–236
high-context cultures, 468–469, *469*
higher education, 285–288, 367–369
Hoch, S.J., 311–312
Hofstede, G., 466–467, *467*
homophilous influence, 395
Hopkins, M., 7–8
Hopscotch Women's Centre, 487–490
Howard–Sheth model, 62, *63*
Hu, Y., 275
Huffman, C., 197
Hultman, C.M., 478
Human Library, 328
Humphery, K., 507
husband-dominant decision-making, 424
hydroponics, 561–562
hygiene factors, 190–192, *192*
hyper-reality, 258
hyperconsumption, 559–560

id, 231–232, *232*, 355
ideal performance, 149
impulse purchases, 49
incentives, 20
India, 448–450, 527–531
individualism, 466, *467*
inertia, 64
inferences, 275
influencers, 54
Influenster, 404–405
influentials, 93–94, 397–402
informal groups, 386
information-seekers, 274
initiators, 93–94
innovation
    overview of, 137–138, *138*
    adoption of, 142–145, **143–144**, *143*. *See also* innovation adopters
    hygiene factors and, 191
    product life cycle and, 138–142, *139–140*
    resistance to, 155–157
    See also innovative products
innovation adopters, 145–152, *146–147*, *150*, *152*
innovative products, 152–155, *153*
innovativeness, 147–152, *147*, *152*
innovators, 234–235
institutional organisations, **103**, 107, *107*

intergenerational equity, 547
International Labour Organization (ILO), 135
Internet of Things (IoT), 133
interrupts, 50–52, **51**, *51*
intrinsic self-relevance, 65–66
introverts, 233–234
involvement, 18, 63–69, *64–65*, **69**, *69–70*, 196, 316, 397–398

Jayanti, R.K., 15
jetpacks, 159–160
JICNARS (Joint Industry Committee for National Readership Surveys), 482, **482–483**
Johnson, S., 135
Johnson, S.B., 444
Johnson, T., 243
Joint Industry Committee for National Readership Surveys (JICNARS), 482, **482–483**
Jones, O., 484
Jung, C., 233
JustGiving, 180

Kahl, J., 425
Kahneman, D., 199–200
Kalmanovitz, P., 423
Kao, 513
Kapferer, J., 67–68
Kapitan, S., 100
Katragadda, G., 156
key-account management (KAM), 111–112
Key, W.B., 279
Keyes, C.L., 236
Kim, H.Y., 272
kinaesthetic processing, 262
kinesics, 268
Kirton, M.J., 148–149
Kiyosaki, R., 306
Knapper, C., 258
Knoke, D., 112
knowledge
 need for, 318–319, *318*
 sources of, 330–331
 types of, 319–330, *320*, *323–324*, *326–327*
 See also learning
Kotler, P., 48, 267–268
Kristof, N.D., 518
Krstić Randić, J., 95–96
Kyodo, J., 421
Kyoto Protocol, 547

La Rocca, A., 112
laggards, 145–146, *146*
language, 463
latchkey kids, 443–444
late majority, 145–146, *146*
latency, 57

lateral recycling, 524–525
Laurent, G., 67–68
Law of Primacy, 259, 312
laws, 99
learning
 overview of, 21, 299–301, *301*
 classical learning theory and, 301–309, *302–303*, **304**, *310*
 cognitive learning theory and, 310–318, *310–311*, **312–314**, *317*
 Global Handwashing Day (case study), 332–333
 knowledge and, 318–331, *318*, *320*, *323–324*, *326–327*
least dependent person, 428
LED light bulbs, 113
Lee, Y., 272
Leverage New Age Media, 138
Levitt, T., 560
LGBT communities, 439–442, *441*
Liebe, U., 504
Lieben, R. von, 126
life cycle assessment (LCA), 518
lifestyle studies, 238–241, **238–239**
likes, 23
Lima, Y., 383
limited decision-making, 49–50
Lindridge, A., 479
linear additive model, 275, *276*
linear averaging model, 276, *277*
Littler, J., 507
Liu, W., 204–205, 484
Lizama-Loyola, A., 425
lockdown, 30–31
long-term orientation, 466–467, *467*
Loudon, D.L., 98
Loughnan, S., 484
low-context cultures, 468–469, *469*
loyalty, 18, 70–72
loyalty schemes, 307–308
Lunning, F., 559
Lusch, R.F., 12–13, 113
Lush, 505–507
Luu, N., 15
luxury brands, 208–210, 520–521

M–R model (Mehrabian–Russell Environmental Psychology Model), 270–271, *271*
M&S, 523
machine learning, 128–129, 134
macro-environmental factors, 98, *267*, 274, 462, *462*. *See also* class; culture(s); social mobility
Madden, T.J., 281
maintaining, repairing and overhauling (MRO), 104
Marconi, G., 126
market mavens, 151–152, 227, 397–398
marketing mix, 13, **13–14**

marketing planning, 16–18
Markus, H., 346
Marmite, 157
Marriage (Same Sex Couples) Act (2013), 440
Mars Confectionery, 94
Marx, K., 483, *484*
masculinity, 225, 466, *467*
masks, 77, 315
Maslow, A.H., 185–188, *186*, 235–236
massive open online courses (MOOCs), 129, 229, 319
McCartney, T., 9
McClelland, D.C., 192–193
McFarlane, A., 421
McKinsey and Company, 76
McLeod, S.A., 188
McNulty, W.K., 188
Mehrabian, A., 270–271, *271*
memory, 311
Mental Health Foundation, 77
message intrigue, 398–399
metaverse, 128
Micic, I., 95–96
micro-environmental factors, 98, *267*, 274, 462, *462*
Microsoft, 96–97
Millennials (Generation Y), 134, 223–224, 404, 420
Milner, M., 444
mindfulness, 112–113
Mitchell, A., 189–190, *189*
mobile technologies, 133–134
modelling, 193–194, **194**, 394, *394*
Modi, A.G., *507*, 508
modified rebuy, 109, *110*
Moller, K., 112
moment of truth, 146
Moore's Law, 126
mores, 464
MOSAIC, 486
motivation
  overview of, 19–20, 177–178, 181, *181*, **182**
  challenges of, 205–206
  hygiene factors and, 190–192, *192*
  individual factors and, 192–194, *193*, **194**
  learning and, 313–315
  luxury brands (case study), 208–210
  needs and, 182–190, *185–186*, *189*
  See also drives; goals; hedonism
motivation research, 206, 232–233, 238
motivational conflict, 194–196, *195*
Mouna, A., 328
Mulligan, M., 547
multi-attribute attitude model, 348
multistage interaction model, 397, *397*
Multiverse, 367–369
Murray, H.A., 183
Musk, E., 278
Myers–Briggs Type Indicator, 235, *235*
myths, 465

Narielwalla, H., 66
National Consumer Council, 508, **509**
National Consumer League, 516
National Union of Students (NUS), 516
needs, 182–190, *185–186*, *189*. *See also* motivational conflict
Nelson, T., 238
nepotistic intentions, 512
nested diagram model, 547, *548*
Nestlé, 517
Netflix Inc., 94
neuro-linguistic programming theory, 262
neurophysiology, 266
neuroscience, 26–27, 278, 364
new task, 109, *110*
Nextiva, 183–184
NFTs (non-fungible tokens), 66–67
Nielsen Bookscan, 402
Nightingale, C.H., 482
Nightingale, K., 286
Nike, 305
non-compensatory decision rules, 61
non-fungible tokens (NFTs), 66–67, 128
normative compliance, 391
nostalgia, 418–419
novices, 320
nuclear family, 422, 436
nudges, 280
Nwankwo, S., 479

Oberg, K., 480
observability, 154
Ofcom, 432
Office for National Statistics (ONS), 30–31
Ofgem, 239
Onkvisit, S., 342
online brand communities (OBCs), 427
operant conditioning, 305–309, *310*
opinion leaders, 227
opinions, 347
optimum stimulation level (OSL), 180–181
Organisation for Economic Co-operation and Development (OECD), 99
organisational buyers. *See* business-to-business (B2B) markets
original-equipment manufacturers (OEMs), 103–104
Oslo Symposium on Sustainable Consumption, 544
overconsumption, 559

Packard, V., 279
packrats, 518–519
Palmer, G., 286
Panay, P., 96–97
paralanguage, 268
Paris Agreement, 550–551
passing off, 284

Patel, J.D., *507*, 508
Pavlov, I.P., 301–305
peer groups, 223
Pelczer, J., 100–101
perceived instrumentality, 349–350
perception
   overview of, 20–21, 255–256
   colour and, 281–283, **281–282**, *283*
   consumers' characteristics and behaviour and, 274–277, *275–277*
   culture and, 264–265
   elements of, 256–258, **256–257**, *257*
   environmental influences on, 267–272, *267, 268, 271–272*
   higher education (case study), 285–288
   information processing and, 262–263, *263–264*
   multisensory nature of, 266
   passing off and, 284
   as subliminal, 279–281, *280*
   synthetic nature of, 344
   world-view and, 258–262
peripheral route, 362, *362*
personal influence, 394–405, *396–397, 399*, **401**. *See also* word of mouth/mouse
personal protective equipment (PPE), 77, 315
personal sources, 330
personality, 20, 148, 230–237, *232–235*, **237**. *See also* psychographics; self-concept
persuasion knowledge, 319, 329
pester power, 427–435
Petrosyan, A., 145
Pfefferbaum, B., 274
Pickcel, 272
Pink Pound, 440–441
Pitcher, A., 520–521
plaster saints, 115
pluralistic parents, 446
politically correct (PC), 356
politics, 98–99
pop music, 351–352, 362–363
post-purchase dissonance, 365–366, *365*, 399
power, 192–193, *193*
power distance, 466, *467*
pre-adolescence, 419
pre-purchase activities, 54–62, *55, 57–58, 62–63*
predictive advertising, 136
preparers, 445
price, 264, 323–324, *324*, 326
price conditioning, 323–324, *324*
Price, L.L., 151
price-sensitive consumers, 274
prideworldradio.com, 440
primary groups, 384
pro bono services, 471
product(s), 6
product category knowledge, 319, 320–321

product knowledge, 319, 320–323, *323*
product life cycle, 138–142, *139–140*
product return and recycling (PRR), 522–523
Programmai, 136
Progress Pride Flags, 283
projective tests, 233, *233*
Prospect Theory, 200
protective parents, 446
proxemics, 268
psychoanalysis, 231–233, *232*
psychographics, 12, 238–241, **238–239**
psychology, 19–22, *20*
psychology of complication, 46
psychology of simplification, 46
psychophysics, 266
Public Religion Research Institute, 442
purchase knowledge, 319, 323–326, *324, 326*
purchasing agents, 423
purgers, 518–519
pyramid schemes, 325

Quality of Educational Opportunity Study (Coleman Study), 443–444
Quantum Tech, 94

radio, 126
Rai, A., 529
Rainbow Flag, 283
Ram, A., 430
Ravn, S., 385
reality TV shows, 396–397
recall test, 321
recognition test, 321
recycling, 518–525, *519*
reference groups
   overview of, 21–22, 381–382
   Brexit (case study), 407–408
   influence of, 387–392, **390**, *390–391*, **393**
   modelling and, 394, *394*
   personal influence and, 394–405, *396–397, 399*, **401**
   types and formation of, 382–387, *388*
   See also age cohorts and subcultures; family
Reijonen, H., 92
reinforcement, 316
Reisman, D., 234–235, *234*
relationship communities, 387
relationship marketing, 13–15, **15**, *15*
relative advantage, 154
religion, 463, 476–477, **476–477**
reseller organisations, **103**, 104–105
response, 315
retention, 316
revolutionary innovations, 137
Rheingold, H., 386
Rio Earth Summit (1992), 547
risk, 52–53, *53*
Risso, P., 282

rites of passage, 220, 465–466
rituals, 465
Robertson, T.S., *143*, 144
robotics, 129–131
Roddick, A., 505
Rogers, E.M., 142, *143*, 144–146, 156
role, 23
role models. *See* modelling
Ronchetto, J.R., Jr, 95
Rooney, M.C., 240
Roper Starch Worldwide, 508, **509**
Rosenberg, M.J., 349–350, *350*
routine low-priority buying, 109
Russell, J.A., 270–271, *271*

sacred consumption, 466
Safeway, 59
Saini, R., 282
Saks Off 5th, 441
salient beliefs, 347–348, **348–349**, 354, 359–360, *360*, 363
Samsioe, E., 421
Sandbrook, R., 100–101
School of Oriental and African Studies (SOAS), 511
Schubert, T.W., 220
Sea2see, 564–566
search heuristics, 199
secondary groups, 384–385
Segal, M., 479
segmentation, 12
selectivity, 259
self-actualisation, 185, *186*, 187–188, 235–236
self-concept, 20, 219–230, *221*, **226**, *227–228*, 389. *See also* personality; psychographics
self-driving vehicles, 130–131
self-enhancement, 398
self-esteem, 223, 242–243
self-image, 23
self-knowledge, 320, 329–330
self-monitoring, 228–229, *228*
selfies, 23, 240–241
Selfridges, 520–521
sensory innovators, 149
service-dominant (S-D) logic, 12–13, 113
Shah, S.K., 55
Shaw, J.J., 342
Shockley, W., 126
Shoemaker, F., 156
short-term orientation, 466–467, *467*
Silva, S.C., 92
simple living, 559
simultaneous conditioning, 303
Skinner, B.F., 193, 305
Skoda, 21
Smalls For All, 523
smart products, 141

Smith, J., 434
Smith, N.C., 514
social media, 138, *138*
social mobility, 425, 482–486, **482–483**, *484*. *See also* class
social sustainability, 552–553. *See also* sustainable consumption
social systems, 155–156
socialisation, 387–388
Socio-Economic Classification System, 483
socio-economic variables, 148
sociology, 22–23, *22*, 382
Solomon, M.R., 138
sonic logos, 266
Sosa, L., 479
Spence, C., 266
Srivastava, R., 528–529
Starbucks, 307
Starkey, D., 508
Stedman, J.M., 233
Steinmetz, K., 442
stimulus rejection, 361
store atmospherics, 267–272, *268*, *271–272*
straight rebuy, 108–109, *110*
students, 515–516
subcultures, 462, 473–481, *474*, **476–477**, *479*, *481*. *See also* age cohorts and subcultures
subjectivity, 259
subliminal perception, 279–281, *280*
subvertising, 284
Sumpradit, N., 312
supercrego, 231–232, *232*, 355
supermarkets, 6–8, 59
supplier selection problem (SSP), 111
sustainability marketing myopia, 560–561
sustainable consumption
   overview of, 541–547, **542–543**, *548*
   principles of, 548–557, **554–557**
   Sea2see (case study), 564–566
   See also ethical consumption
Sustainable Development Goals (SDGs), 42
Svahn, S., 112
sweatshops, 503
switching costs, 195
symbolic fracture, 481
symbols, 321
syncratic decision-making (democratic decision-making), 424
synthetic nature of perception, 344

Taobao, 261
Target Group Index, 238
Tata Group, 156
Tay, L., 188–189
Taylor, E., 8
technology, 98, 102. *See also* consumer technology
technophiles, 151

technophobes, 151
teenagers, 419, 448–450
television programmes, 484–485. *See also* reality TV shows
TerraCycle, 9
Thailand, 361
Thames Water, 100–101
theory of planned behaviour, 353–354, *354*
theory of reasoned action, 352–353, *353*
Thompson, C.J., 470
Tiisier-Desbordes, E., 224–225
Tinder, 399–400, 470–471
trade, 27–31
trading-in, 9–10
TrafficCloud, 136
traits, 230, 236, **237**
transactional marketing, 13–14, **15**
transgender issues, 442
transportation, 10–11
trialability, 154
trickle-down theory, 395, *396*
triple bottom line, 547, *548*
Tuten, T.L., 138
Tversky, A., 199–200
two-step flow theory, 395, *396*

Ukraine, 515
Ulrich, I., 224–225
UN Women, 77
uncertainty avoidance, 466, *467*
unconditioned response, 301–303, *303*
unconditioned stimulus, 301–303, *303*
UNICEF, 243, 449–450
United Nations (UN), 42, 422, 501, 546, 550–551
unmanned aerial vehicles (UAVs). *See* drones
unsought goods, 72–74, **73**, *73*
usage knowledge (consumption knowledge), 319, 326–328, *327*
user customers, 103, 104
users, 93–94
utilitarianism, 202–203, *202*
utopian marketplace, 204

Vaadal, K., 385
VALS (values, attitudes and lifestyles) model, 189–190, *189*, 238
value analysis, 112–115, **114–115**
value-expressive function, 350
value importance, 349–350
values–action gap, 544
van Zeeland, E., 113

Vanderhaegen, K., 512
Vargo, S.L., 12–13, 113
variety-seekers, 274
Veres, Z., 95–96, 113
Verhoef, P.C., 342–343
vicarious learning, 316–317
Vignola, M., 480
virtual communities, 386–387
virtual reality, 128
vlogs, 403–404
VoIP (voice over internet protocol), 183–184
Volkswagen Group, 21
Vroom, V.H., 192

Waithe, L., 243
Waldfogel, J., 473
Walker, B.A., 225
Walton, S., 11–12
wants, 182
Warr, P.B., 258
Weber, M., 483, *484*
Weber's Law, 264
Webster, F.E., 93
Wells, W.D., 436
Westerveld, J., 556
white lists, 516
wife-dominant decision-making, 424
Williams, D., 481
Wind, Y., 93
word of mouth/mouse, 54, 145, 394–405, *396–397*, *399*, **401**
World Association of Girl Guides and Girl Scouts (WAGGGS), 243
World Bank, 77
World Economic Forum (WEF), 76, 128, 136
World Health Organisation (WHO), 76
world-view, 258–262
Wright, P., 329
WSUP, 100–101
Wu, M.S.S., 388–389
WuDunn, S., 518

YouGov, 485
Young, W., 544

Zajonc, R.B., 346
Zaltman, G., 470
Zampini, M., 266
Zhu, Y.Q., 358
Zickfeld, J.H., 220
Zoom dysmorphia, 230
Zuckerman, M., 185, *185*